Gender Violence

Gender Violence

Interdisciplinary Perspectives
Second Edition

EDITED BY

*Laura L. O'Toole, Jessica R. Schiffman, and
Margie L. Kiter Edwards*

New York University Press

NEW YORK AND LONDON

NEW YORK UNIVERSITY PRESS
New York and London
www.nyupress.org

Library of Congress Cataloging-in-Publication Data
Gender violence : interdisciplinary perspectives / edited by Laura L.
O'Toole, Jessica R. Schiffman, and Margie L. Kiter Edwards. – 2nd ed.
p. cm.
Includes bibliographical references and index.
ISBN-13: 978-0-8147-6209-7 (cloth : alk. paper)
ISBN-10: 0-8147-6209-3 (cloth : alk. paper)
ISBN-13: 978-0-8147-6210-3 (pbk. : alk. paper)
ISBN-10: 0-8147-6210-7 (pbk. : alk. paper)
1. Women–Violence against.   2. Family violence.   3. Sex crimes.   4.
Pornography–Social aspects.   5. Women–Violence against–United States.
6. Family violence–United States.   7. Sex crimes–United States.   8.
Pornography–Social aspects–United States.   I. O'Toole, Laura L.   II.
Schiffman, Jessica R.   III. Edwards, Margie L. Kiter.
HV6250.4.W65G48 2007
362.82'92–dc22
2007001897

New York University Press books are printed on acid-free paper,
and their binding materials are chosen for strength and durability.

Manufactured in the United States of America
c 10 9 8 7 6 5 4 3 2 1
p 10 9 8 7 6 5 4 3 2 1

Contents

Preface

Conceptualizing Gender Violence

*Laura L. O'Toole, Jessica R. Schiffman, and
Margie L. Kiter Edwards*

Think about the most consuming events since the turn of the twenty-first century, those that grabbed the attention of the public through news headlines and in daily conversations. Interethnic conflicts in Sudan, Congo, and Iraq in which rival militia slaughter men and use savage serial rapes to subdue and dehumanize women. The Catholic Church hierarchy and faithful continue to grapple with the effects of dozens of years of sexual abuse of male and female children at the hands of its priests. Amish schoolgirls are murdered by a distraught man who blamed his actions on his putative past as a child sex abuser. Bullied adolescent boys execute their peers and teachers in a bloody mass murder at Columbine High School in Colorado. Thousands of female children are sold into sexual slavery by impoverished families or kidnapped for sale in lucrative, government-sanctioned sex industries around the globe. Multiple women come forward with complaints of groping and sexual harassment, yet Arnold Schwarzenegger is still elected the governor of California.

These diverse events have a common link: male perpetrators, acting alone or in groups, for whom violence and violation are rational solutions to perceived problems ranging from the need to inflate one's sexual self-esteem to denigrating rivals in war to boosting a country's GNP. They also demonstrate the real harm that women face on a daily basis in a world that views them sometimes as property, often as pawns, and usually as secondary citizens in need of control by men. These events are also similar in that they are not random. Several of these examples are deemed newsworthy on an international scale, given their political implications or the celebrity of perpetrators, but they represent only a fraction of the violence against women and children that is committed on a daily basis across the world. If you read your own community newspaper or scan local televised newscasts, you will find hundreds of similar events in any given month. These incidents, while often writ small, stand as clear testimony to the insidious problem of gender violence.

Acts of gender violence are similarly ubiquitous throughout history. Rape has been a tool of warriors for centuries. Working women experienced men's coercive sexual behaviors long before the term *sexual harassment* was coined. Gender violence often links divergent cultures as well. The incest taboo, so long identified by scholars as universal across cultures, appears to be more a taboo against speaking about incest than a successful mechanism of social control.

Violence at the beginning of the twenty-first century extends from individual relationships to the arrangement of power and authority in organizations to the relations among countries of the world. Broadly speaking, violence is a mainstay in the entertainment and news media, in national and international politics, in family dynamics, and in our social constructions of sexual desire. It simultaneously intrigues and repels us. Although most violence worldwide is male-on-male, the emergence of self-conscious women's political movements and greater global attention to universal human rights, combined with academic inquiry, begs closer scrutiny of the patterns of male violence against women and children, both in intimate relationships and in public.

As a central organizing principle among human groups, gender is the constellation of personal attributes assigned to men and women in any culture. It is a primary characteristic by which we structure intimate relationships, divide labor, assign social value, and grant privilege. In most contemporary societies, dualistic gender systems endure, with clearly demarcated boundaries between that which is considered masculine and that which is considered feminine—temperamentally, physically, sexually, and behaviorally. Gender is simultaneously a deeply embedded aspect of individual personalities and structural social arrangements; however, it is also contested social terrain. Gender relations are a complicated mix of congeniality and conflict; yet, in either case, they are almost always imbued with an asymmetrical distribution of power. They are the product of social and cultural dynamics, historical forces, political and economic structures, and interpersonal processes. In many societies and for many individuals, however, it is the *conflicted* aspects of gender relations that are the most prominent.

We understand violence as the extreme application of social control. Usually understood as the use of physical force, it can take a psychological form when manifested through direct harassment or implied terroristic threats. Violence can also be structural, as when institutional forces such as governments or medical systems impinge on individuals' rights to bodily integrity or contribute to the deprivation of basic human needs. By our definition, gender violence is any interpersonal, organizational, or politically oriented violation perpetrated against people due to their gender identity, sexual orientation, or location in the hierarchy of male-dominated social systems such as families, military organizations, or the labor force. Much of the violence in contemporary society serves to preserve asymmetrical gender systems of power. For example, compulsory aggression as a central component of masculinity serves to legitimate male-on-male violence; sexual harassment is a means of controlling the public behavior of women; assaults on gay, lesbian, and transgendered people are a way of punishing them for "gender transgressions"; and rape is a standard tool for domination in war, in prison subcultures, and in too many intimate relationships.

Clearly and consistently documented throughout human history, the forms that such violence assumes—rape, battering, child abuse, and murder—constitute some of the most pressing and enduring social problems of our times. Given the centrality of gender and the ubiquity of violence, it is no wonder that they are interwoven in our social systems. The systems in which they are embedded are complex; simplistic explanations or simple solutions will not suffice. Explicating the problem of gender violence demands a comprehensive, multifaceted framework.

This volume attempts to provide such an interdisciplinary framework. It is the outgrowth of our personal and collegial efforts to understand the phenomenon of gender violence to a fuller extent than discipline-specific analysis currently allows. We are sociologists by training and continue to see the value of our discipline in explaining the significance of context in the study of gender violence—that is, the ways in which the organization of both interpersonal interaction and social institutions such as the law, economies, and religions contribute to the social construction of gender and to gendered violence. As participants in interdisciplinary gender studies throughout our careers, we have been engaged by the important analyses of our colleagues in the social sciences and humanities that have enriched the study of gender relations, in many cases preceding sociology in uncovering significant social facts as well as the subdued and silenced voices of women. The poems and articles in this book have contributed to our own understanding of the interpersonal and structural dynamics of gender violence, as well as both the historical evolution and the contemporary manifestations of gender relations. We share that understanding here, weaving together the voices of other scholars and artists with our own thoughts on how to best interpret the vast and ever-expanding literature on gender violence. We do this while acknowledging that the literature cannot completely represent the horrifying expanse of empirical evidence and personal experiences of physical and sexual assault, harassment, and murder.

So why have we called this book *Gender Violence* rather than *Violence against Women*? Some explication of our terms is appropriate, particularly since there is not yet an approved lexicon to define the violence that we are describing, interrogating, and problematizing. Although documenting and exploring the violation of women has been the primary focus of research and activism among feminist and pro-feminist analysts, we have chosen to include a broader set of questions that spring from the study of gender and violence. In what ways are ideas about gender and sexual identity used to legitimate violence against individuals and groups, regardless of their biological sex? To what extent does the social construction of gender facilitate male-on-male violence? Can and should men, at least in some cases, be acknowledged as indirect victims of violence against women? By widening our analytical lens, we are able to incorporate important connections among violence against children, heterosexual women and men, and lesbians, gay men, and transgendered persons, and we suggest important questions about structural and interpersonal violence for future analysis.

Gender Violence is organized into three parts. Part 1 contains a sociohistorical exploration of gender violence, focusing first across cultures, then more specifically on the conditions that give rise to gender violence in the United States. Part 2 examines various forms of gendered violence. Part 3 presents the current deliberations about transforming gender relations and ending gender violence. Each section of the book includes an introduction, suggested readings, and chapters that represent important contributions to the study of gender violence from a wide spectrum of academic and activist perspectives. Although the chapters primarily address issues of gender violence in the United States, we have integrated international perspectives into the analytical framework of the book. We include research-based articles, theoretical and critical analyses, and essays.

The reader will notice that every section is prefaced by a poem. We have organized the book this way in part to set the tone for the more scholarly analysis that follows and in part to periodically break away from this analysis so as to hear women's voices unfettered by disciplinary jargon or academic theory. Understanding gender violence requires a merging of the analytical and experiential realms. Working toward a solution will ultimately require an understanding of both social dynamics and of the pain and tragedy that gender violence wreaks in the lives of women, men, and children around the world.

Among the anthologized works, the reader will note some inconsistency in terminology and capitalization in reference to racial/ethnic groups. These differences reflect the conventions and preferences of the different time periods when these chapters were originally crafted. In our introductory essays, we have chosen to capitalize all referents to racial or ethnic categories.

This volume is necessarily incomplete. There are many more insightful analyses and powerful voices than space permits. Many have yet to speak, and our search for solutions is far from complete. We hope this book will contribute to the dialogue among students, activists, and scholars concerned about understanding and eradicating gender violence. We believe such a dialogue is crucial, and we have attempted to design the book in a way that is accessible to all these constituencies.

Many people have encouraged us to take on this project and provided helpful commentary along the way. Colleagues, friends, and family who have supported and inspired us in various, often indispensable ways include Greg Adamo, Candace Archer, Andrea Bertone, Carolyn Bitzer, Suzanne Cherrin, Brandy Collier, Cindy DiMattia, Heidi Dobish, Cheryl Doerr, Tammy Kiter, Rita Maloy, Steve Maloy, Frank Newton, Kathleen O'Toole, Liz Park, Guy Rains, Cecily Sawyer-Harmon, Josh Schiffman, Judy Schneider, Angela Seguin, Monika Shafi, Margaret Stetz, Caroline Timmins, Florine Timmins, Donna Tuites, Kathleen Turkel, Emilie VanDyke, and Tara Woolfolk. Karen Gaffney, Marie Laberge, and Emma Timmins-Schiffman read chapter drafts and provided us with many helpful suggestions. Laura Levitt made a last-minute connection for us that filled an important gap in the manuscript. We offer particular thanks to Anastasia Hudgins, who produced a wonderful essay in record time and made it look easy. Emily Hayworth generously provided many hours of clerical assistance from her student workers. Liz Rooney assisted in numerous ways. Brigid Jennings provided significant clerical assistance, enabling us to complete the project in a timely fashion. We also sincerely appreciate the tenacity and courage of many current and former students at the University of Delaware, Guilford College, Roanoke College, and Shepherd University who have confronted the difficult questions we have posed about gender and violence, often bearing the weight of great personal trauma. They have taught us a lot.

Our editor, Ilene Kalish, supported our desire to revise the first edition. She particularly gave us great leeway to bring our vision to fruition. Salwa Jabado was always available to graciously answer our many questions. Finally, we thank the contributors to this volume for their vision, with special gratitude to Annie Cossins, Betsy Erbaugh, William Gay, Anastasia Hudgins, LeeAnn Iovanni, Michael Johnson, Tara Kent, Michael Kimmel, Patricia Yancey Martin, Susan Miller, Nan Stein, and Margaret Stetz.

Part I

Roots of Male Violence and Victimization of Women

The two sections in this part explore the conditions that give rise to male violence. Section 1 takes a global perspective in analyzing the widespread cultural and historical trends that are associated with patriarchal domination. In section 2, the United States is considered as a specific case to illustrate how unique sociocultural attributes can alter the terrain of gender relations and, thus, the nature and scope of gender violence. Taken together, these sections show that understanding gender violence requires broad historical and theoretical knowledge, as well as smaller-scale case-study analysis to capture the culturally specific contours that gender violence assumes. Readings in part I span the disciplines of anthropology, criminology, economics, history, political science, psychology, and sociology.

The Roots of Male Violence

The roots of gender violence run deep in human history, and this depth mak
attempts to trace them difficult. Male violence is so widespread that biological de
minism has often dominated debates about its origins. Gendered violence, as w
the term in this book, is often explained as a natural and universal consequenc
biological differences between men and women. Age-old theories posit that
strength and a variety of hormonal stimuli predispose men toward violent,
behavior. Such an amalgam of traits, juxtaposed against the purported na
ity and compliance of the weaker female, it is argued, will likely produ
men, against women, in certain situations. One form of this argument
males' innate drive to reproduce stimulates behavioral responses tha
now define as rape.

Despite the overwhelming popularity and longevity of such
compelling theories have emerged. The influence of the contem
ment on academic inquiry has led to the reframing of centra
relations. Deeply embedded intellectual traditions have be
constructionist framework that suggests that *patriarchy*
over women—is a human invention, not the inevitable
teristics. In order to denaturalize gender violence, the
roots of institutionalized male dominance and the ex
violation become valued attributes in human comm
tant implications; if patriarchy is a social constru
from it becomes more problematic and less easy
unfortunate, but taken-for-granted, aspect of t
all of its manifestations becomes a social pro
end. In order to bring about its demise, how
of uncovering its origins.

The Contributions of Marx and Engels

Although the patriarchal family is not a central concern of Karl Marx's social theory,
he did suggest that its modern form was a microcosm of the class antagonisms that
later developed on a grand scale in society (Marx 1978). In the legal, monogamous
family, women exchange sexual and domestic services for economic security, and male
sexual control of women in marriage is the equivalent of slave ownership. Applying the

3

logic of Marxian economic theory more systematically to the condition of women, Friedrich Engels linked the "world-historic defeat of the female sex" to males' desire to circumvent their wives, passing private property (originally, herds of domesticated animals) on to their children. The emergence of the concept of private property, and its appropriation by men, according to Engels (chapter 1 in this volume), are the central historical events from which the modern social order, and systematic gender violence, have emerged. In this model, women are economic dependents; eventually defined as the property of fathers or husbands, they are subject to the violence that accompanies the status of slaves.

The Marx-Engels theory was the first to attribute women's deteriorated status to a sociological, rather than biological, source. Over one hundred years of social and economic analysis have not diminished the significance of economic arrangements in ender systems of power; however, economic determinism is no more satisfactory than logical determinism in explaining the origins of patriarchal domination. Given the plexity of human social life, any singular statement of cause and effect is doomed Although economic considerations remain salient to the analysis of gender violradoxically it is Marx's general theory of human social behavior, not his brief rat ns about gender relations in the family, that has been most helpful in elabo

F nporary theories of male dominance.
human the human capacity to labor is the essential building block of history; out of ou ated all the ideas, all the technologies, all the social structures that exist ations, then periences in the material world. If all social systems are human crepreted the al hy must be included in the inventory. Both Marx and Engels intergroups were co gical record of their time to suggest that the earliest human and universal fut arian: nonhierarchical and reciprocal, with pooled resources social phenomena, t. of basic human needs. Some combination of subsequent male violence. The phy , must be responsible for the emergence of patriarchy and uisite stimuli for its inve cal potential for gender violence is presumed, but the requisite stimuli for its inve cal potential for gender violence is presumed, but the req necessarily social. Anthro and the means through which it is institutionalized, are built on this Marxian-Engels ts, sociologists, and historians studying gender have cipline contributes significant amework, though in different applications; each dis es to our project.

The Significan c Sex/Gender Systems

Anthropological research provides most the early evidence supporting a social, rather than biological, theory of gender. S ies such as those that Margaret Mead (1935) conducted among peoples of New Guin howed gendered behavior to be a relative concept: different cultures define masculin and femininity according to their own social needs; indeed, cultures may have more n two gender categories. Men are not inherently aggressive, and women not inheren passive and subordinate. The gender-based division of labor, although apparently u versal, takes many shapes and forms. Such findings have enabled social theorists to de ne sex (nature) and gender (culture) as mutually exclusive, though interrelated, pheno ena.

Studies of kinship systems in tribal social life provide a foundation for understanding early cultural definitions of gender, since all early human social life was organized through these systems. The incest taboo is a particularly significant human invention, in that it allows for the exchange of women among men of different kin groups, which in turn facilitates trade and alliances. Eventually, however, it also contributes to the ascension of men into roles of social power (Levi-Strauss 1969). Some analysts suggest that the practice of exchanging women transforms them over time into tribal resources —commodities, rather than self-determined individuals.

Gayle Rubin's classic essay "The Traffic in Women: Notes on the Political Economy of Sex" (1976) called into question many of the key assumptions about kinship and gender that had dominated anthropology prior to the modern feminist movement. Rubin uses the works of Marx, Engels, and Levi-Strauss in a fundamentally different frame of analysis: a feminist critique that reconceptualizes the essence of early kinship systems and links them to contemporary gender relations of power.

The crux of Rubin's argument is that the construction of sexual meaning, not the commodification of women per se, is the hallmark of early kinship structures. Given the elaborate differences among kinship systems historically and cross-culturally, Rubin replaces the notion of emergent patriarchy with the concept of sex/gender systems. All cultures have sex/gender systems in which a socially constructed set of relations that define and regulate sexuality, masculinity, and femininity emerge. These relations, though initially kin-centered, also serve as the framework for creating increasingly elaborate economic and political systems. In contemporary cultures, kinship exists within such a complex of institutional structures. What is crucial for feminist scholarship is this: in the earliest human groups, the exchange (and oppression) of women did not exist for its own sake. It fulfilled central functions for group survival. Contemporary sex/gender systems, still replete with oppressive sexual meaning and regulation, do not fulfill the same economic and political functions that kinship once did. Kinship has been stripped of all its early functions, save reproduction and the socialization of individuals. Following this logic, according to Rubin, the contemporary sex/gender system seems to exist only to organize and reproduce itself (1976, 199) rather than all of human activity. Contemporary sex/gender systems, therefore, serve no clear functions in reproducing oppressive and repressive gender relations.

Patriarchy and Women's Agency

Scholarly writing has traditionally viewed sex/gender systems as restrictions imposed on women by men. Whether we study the work of Marxian scholars, mid-twentieth-century anthropologists, or contemporary feminists, we find a strong tendency to portray women as passive victims of male-dominated cultures. This is not hard to understand, because academic research has derived from male-dominated social systems, in which women have had little access to political-legal, economic, or familial power. Given that patriarchy predates recorded history, however, it is difficult to trace its origins to a single causal factor, such as physical force or economic exchange. What if its *origins* were relatively benign?

Historian Gerda Lerner (1986) has proposed a theory that uses a materialist conceptualization of history (in the tradition of Marx) as a starting point for understanding the origins of patriarchy. Combining her own exhaustive study of historical artifacts from the earliest human communities and a fresh interpretation of the academic literature, Lerner builds a scenario that depends on women as cocreators of history. According to Lerner, patriarchy is initially the unintended consequence of human social organization, a process that most probably emerged out of the negotiated labor of males and females interested in mutual survival and the continuation of the species. Human biological difference does not predict or determine male dominance, but it is certainly a major factor in the elaboration of a rudimentary division of labor. Given extremely short life spans and the vulnerability of human infants, women would probably choose to engage in labor that involves less risk in order to heighten the chances that their offspring would survive. The gathering and child-rearing work that was predominantly, although not exclusively, performed by women was highly valued and central to early cultural production. It is only through the lens of modern, predominantly male interpreters that such work is devalued relative to men's hunting.

According to Lerner (1986, 53), "Sometime during the agricultural revolution, relatively egalitarian societies with a sexual division of labor based on biological necessity gave way to more highly structured societies in which both private property and the exchange of women based on incest taboos and exogamy were common." In Lerner's formulation, women may have initially viewed their procreative abilities as tribal resources independent of coercion on the part of male kin. A complex combination of ecological, climatic, and demographic changes probably intervened to produce a scarcity of women in some kin groups that eventually gave rise to the idea and practice of exchange. Although patriarchy was formally established by the beginning of recorded history, it probably took centuries for patriarchy to emerge as a concise system. By the time women became consciously aware of the emergent power relations that formed early patriarchal systems, they were hardly in a position to do much about it. Once male control was identified, Lerner's research suggests, individual women chafed under its bonds and used various forms of resistance to secure status for themselves and their children. Although women may have been active agents in the creation of cultural arrangements that eventually limited their freedom, and may even be complicit in maintaining their personal power rather than pursuing collective rights for women, there is also a long historical record of active agents in protofeminist resistance to patriarchal control.

Violence and Male Power

The use of force to maintain privilege is a significant characteristic of male behavior in patriarchal societies. It contributes to the development of elaborate systems of economic and social inequality within and across gender. A central fact acknowledged but generally underanalyzed by historians is that women were the first slaves (Lerner 1986). In the quest for women, invading clans would kill adult males on the spot and enslave women and their children. Rape and other forms of physical and psychological violence were used to control women in their new communities. It was through mastering techniques of violent coercion on female captives that men eventually learned how to dominate and control other men without simply killing them. Both violence toward women and the elaborate social structures that develop around such practices serve to appropriate key aspects of women's independence and institutionalize patriarchy. Over time, overt and covert forms of violence come to characterize "normal" gender relations, institutionally and interpersonally.

Male control of women in families, which has endured the "progress" of centuries, is certainly not the only manifestation of androcentric sex/gender systems. Just as the construction of gender differs cross-culturally, gender violence takes many cultural forms: ten centuries of foot binding in China; witch burning in sixteenth-century Europe; female genital mutilation in Africa; female castration by physicians in the late-nineteenth- and early-twentieth-century United States; and honor killings in the Middle East. Demographers suspect that female infanticide and sex-selective abortion have skewed male-to-female population ratios in many areas across the world. As these examples illustrate, gender violence is not merely a feature of micro-level interactions among intimates but is deeply embedded at the levels of community and nation-state (see table 1). So universal and widespread are the institutionalized forms of violence against women, that Caputi and Russell (1990) developed the concept of *femicide* to

TABLE 1
Locus and Manifestations of Gender Violence

Locus and Agent	The Family	The "Community"	The State
Forms of Gender Violence	Physical Aggression 　Murder (dowry/other) 　Battering 　Genital mutilation 　Foeticide 　Infanticide 　Deprivation of food 　Deprivation of medical 　　care 　Reproductive coercion/ 　　control	*Social Reference Group* (Cultural, religious, etc.) *Violence directed toward 　women within or outside 　the group. Physical Abuse* 　Battery 　Physical chastisement 　Reproductive coercion/ 　　control 　Witch burning 　Sati	Political Violence (Policies, laws, etc.) 　Illegitimate detention 　Forced sterilization 　Forced pregnancies 　Tolerating gender violence 　　by nonstate agents
	Sexual Abuse 　Rape 　Incest	Sexual Assault* 　Rape	Custodial Violence (Military/police, etc.) 　Rape 　Torture
	Emotional Abuse 　Confinement 　Forced marriage 　Threats of reprisals	*Workplace* Sexual Aggression 　Harassment 　Intimidation Commercialized Violence 　Trafficking 　Forced prostitution	
		Media 　Pornography 　Commercialization of 　　women's bodies	

SOURCE: Margaret Schuler, *Freedom from Violence: Women's Strategies from Around the World* (New York: UNIFEM, 1992), 14.

describe the systematic and global destruction of women. Although males are the primary perpetrators of violence against women, women are not only victims but are often collusive in the creation and preservation of violent traditions (such as in the case of female genital mutilation, the protection of men involved in incestuous relationships, or the perpetuation of rape myths by blaming women for their victimization). Similarly, men can also be victims of gender violence, in ways that will be more fully explored later in this volume.

The Social Reproduction of Gender Violence

Gender relations and expectations are situated in the various social structures of societies: labor markets, political systems, families, schools, health-care systems, and so on. We have thus far theorized gender as a set of social relationships, but it is also important to underscore its centrality as a deeply felt aspect of a person's identity. Our awareness of what constitutes appropriate behavior, the patterns of interaction in our families and peer groups, our selection and observation of reference groups, and the structure of opportunities available to us all contribute to our evolution as gendered beings. The extent to which violence becomes embedded in our repertoire of behaviors is, in part, related to our individual propensities to accept and internalize aspects of socially prescribed gender roles and relationships.

Connell (1987) has developed the useful concepts of *hegemonic masculinity* and *emphasized femininity* to refer to the dominant, idealized notions of sexual character that exist in a society. These idealizations are accepted as "normal" by society, although they always exist in opposition to quite a range of "real" human personalities and behaviors. For example, the hegemonic—or controlling—form of masculinity in the early-twenty-first-century United States requires the ability to be powerful, aggressive, rational, and invulnerable, to control oneself and others in a variety of social situations. This usually implies athleticism, financial success, and the heterosexual domination of women, as well as a sufficient distance from characteristics deemed feminine by the culture. The extent to which men and boys in the United States comply with this set of characteristics varies widely, but the manliness of most will be judged by their ability to measure up to this standard of masculinity.

For women, the ideal standard is clearly articulated but not as restrictive as the one prescribed for men. Emphasized femininity is constructed as a counterpoint to masculinity: emotional, nurturing, vulnerable, and dependent, sexually desirable and malleable, rather than controlling. There is a certain amount of ambivalence built into contemporary femininity, however, because these behaviors are idealized but at the same time are not highly valued by the culture. Women acting in stereotypically masculine ways have received a certain amount of social acceptance in some arenas (such as in corporate boardrooms, where the most successful women "act like men," or sporting events such as women's boxing), but the drumbeat of popular culture continually presents the traditional roles of wife, mother, and sexual ornament as of primary importance.

At various points in human history, and particularly in the present, hegemonic masculinity becomes a breeding ground for gender violence. It is reproduced generally through the early socialization of boys in families and schools, through mass-media images, and in male-dominated institutions such as the military, sports teams, politics, and science. Adherence to traditional femininity can be, quite literally, a health hazard for women, as socially prescribed acquiescence to male dominance may be an open invitation to male aggression. The roots of male dominance may be relatively simple, but the elaborate psychological and institutional systems that have evolved and sustained it over time are exceedingly complex.

We can return to the anthropological record for a glimmer of hope, however. Among its many contributions to social science is the recognition that male violence against women, although widespread, is not universal (Sanday, this volume). Understanding the conditions under which nonviolent gender relations flourish provides a springboard for continued analysis from a variety of academic disciplines and activist locations.

Contributions to This Section

The chapters in this section are examples of systematic attempts to comprehend male dominance generally, and violence against women specifically. Friedrich Engels's critical essay "The Origin of the Family, Private Property, and the State" (originally published in 1884) is included because of its centrality in most subsequent analyses of patriarchy in the social sciences. Using a Marxian framework that has since been elaborated by feminist theorists, Engels attempts to develop a conclusive argument that women's oppression is an outgrowth of the emergence of economies based on the accumulation of private property.

In "The Construction of Masculinity and the Triad of Men's Violence," Michael Kaufman continues the discussion of socially produced gender within the context of kin relationships, from a neo-Freudian psychoanalytic framework. His exploration of the embedded nature of violence in the male psyche and male behavior is strikingly different from the economic perspective elaborated by Engels, but it clearly presents a line of analysis that is central to understanding the scope of male violence.

Peggy Sanday confronts universalized notions of male violence in "The Socio-Cultural Context of Rape" by differentiating societies according to the existence and frequency of rape within them. Biological determinism does not withstand the test of cross-cultural applicability when the results of this analysis are taken into account. By distinguishing the characteristics of rape-prone and rape-free societies, we move closer to understanding some of the central problems that need to be addressed within myriad violent social systems across the globe.

SUGGESTIONS FOR FURTHER READING

R. W. Connell, *Gender and Power* (Stanford, CA: Stanford University Press, 1987).
Renate Klein and Bernard Wallner (eds.), *Conflict, Gender, and Violence* (Vienna: StudienVerlag, 2004).

Gerda Lerner, *The Creation of Patriarchy* (New York: Oxford University Press, 1986).

Carole Pateman, *The Sexual Contract* (Stanford, CA: Stanford University Press, 1988).

Alice Walker, *The Color Purple* (New York: Washington Square Press, 1982).

Women, Law and Development International, *Gender Violence: The Hidden War Crime* (self-published, 1998).

Visit from the Footbinder

Sarah Gorham

Little shoes sell quickly in shop
windows. Three-inch tracks peel
off garden sand. If too large, crop
or bandage your feet. Force heel
under instep to meet your bent
digits. Bind them like crescent
moons that peep into the night.
A mistress shouldn't stray. Slowly
she sways. She hovers and floats,
point dancer, Buddha on tiptoe.
Dab with your spirit, microscopic
drip by drip. As you walk, feel it
evaporate. Anything more is a lie.
There is no permanent I.

Chapter One

The Origin of the Family, Private Property, and the State

Friedrich Engels

The Family: Its Past, Present and Future

* * *

* * * The evolution of the family in prehistoric times consisted in the continual narrowing of the circle—originally embracing the whole tribe—within which marital community between the two sexes prevailed. By the successive exclusion, first of closer, then of ever remoter relatives; and finally even of those merely related by marriage; every kind of group marriage was ultimately rendered practically impossible; and in the end there remained only the one, for the moment still loosely united, couple, the molecule, with the dissolution of which marriage itself completely ceases. This fact alone shows how little individual sex love, in the modern sense of the word, had to do with the origin of monogamy. The practice of all peoples in this stage affords still further proof of this. Whereas under previous forms of the family men were never in want of women but, on the contrary, had a surfeit of them, women now became scarce and were sought after. Consequently with pairing marriage begins the abduction and purchase of women-widespread *symptoms,* but nothing more of a much more deeply-rooted change that had set in. * * *

The pairing family, itself too weak and unstable to make an independent household necessary, or even desirable, did not by any means dissolve the communistic household transmitted from earlier times. But the communistic household implies the supremacy of women in the house, just as the exclusive recognition of a natural mother, because of the impossibility of determining the natural father with certainty, signifies high esteem for the women, that is, for the mothers. That woman was the slave of man at the commencement of society is one of the most absurd notions that have come down to us from the period of Enlightenment of the eighteenth century. Woman occupied not only a free but also a highly respected position among all savages and all barbarians of the lower and middle stages and partly even of the upper stage. Let Arthur Wright, missionary for many years among the Seneca Iroquois, testify what her place still was in the pairing family: "As to their family system, when occupying the old long houses

[communistic households embracing several families] . . . it is probable that some one clan [gens] predominated, the women taking husbands from other clans [gentes]. . . . Usually the female portion ruled the house; the stores were in common; but woe to the luckless husband or lover who was too shiftless to do his share of the providing. No matter how many children or whatever goods he might have in the house, he might at any time be ordered to pack up his blanket and budge; and after such orders it would not be healthful for him to attempt to disobey. The house would be too hot for him; and he had to retreat to his own clan [gens]; or, as was often done, go and start a new matrimonial alliance in some other. The women were the great power among the clans [gentes], as everywhere else. They did not hesitate, when occasion required, to knock off the horns, as it was technically called, from the head of the chief and send him back to the ranks of the warriors." * * *
* * *

 * * * As wealth increased, it, on the one hand, gave the man a more important status in the family than the woman, and, on the other hand, created a stimulus to utilise this strengthened position in order to overthrow the traditional order of inheritance in favour of his children. But this was impossible as long as descent according to mother right prevailed. This had, therefore, to be overthrown, and it was overthrown; and it was not so difficult to do this as it appears to us now. For this revolution—one of the most decisive ever experienced by mankind—need not have disturbed one single living member of a gens. All the members could remain what they were previously. The simple decision sufficed that in future the descendants of the male members should remain in the gens, but that those of the females were to be excluded from the gens and transferred to that of their father. The reckoning of descent through the female line and the right of inheritance through the mother were hereby overthrown and male lineage and right of inheritance from the father instituted. We know nothing as to how and when this revolution was effected among the civilised peoples. It falls entirely within prehistoric times. That it was actually *effected* is more than proved by the abundant traces of mother right which have been collected, especially by Bachofen. How easily it is accomplished can be seen from a whole number of Indian tribes, among whom it has only recently taken place and is still proceeding, partly under the influence of increasing wealth and changed methods of life (transplantation from the forests to the prairies), and partly under the moral influence of civilisation and the missionaries. Of eight Missouri tribes, six have male and two still retain the female lineage and female inheritance line. Among the Shawnees, Miamis and Delawares it has become the custom to transfer the children to the father's gens by giving them one of the gentile names obtaining therein, in order that they may inherit from him. "Innate human causuistry to seek to change things by changing their names! And to find loopholes for breaking through tradition within tradition itself, wherever a direct interest provided a sufficient motive!" (Marx). As a consequence, hopeless confusion arose; and matters could only be straightened out, and partly were straightened out, by the transition to father right. "This appears altogether to be the most natural transition" (Marx). As for what the experts on comparative law have to tell us regarding the ways and means by which this transition was effected among the civilised peoples of the Old World—almost mere hypotheses, of course—see M. Kovalevsky, *Outline of the Origin and Evolution of the Family and Property*, Stockholm, 1890.

The overthrow of mother right was the *world-historic defeat of the female sex*. The man seized the reins in the house also, the woman was degraded, enthralled, the slave of the man's lust, a mere instrument for breeding children. This lowered position of women, especially manifest among the Greeks of the Heroic and still more of the Classical Age, has become gradually embellished and dissembled and, in part, clothed in a milder form, but by no means abolished.

The first effect of the sole rule of the men that was now established is shown in the intermediate form of the family which now emerges, the patriarchal family. Its chief attribute is not polygamy—of which more anon—but "the organisation of a number of persons, bond and free, into a family under the paternal power of the head of the family. In the Semitic form, this family chief lives in polygamy, the bondsman has a wife and children, and the purpose of the whole organisation is the care of flocks and herds over a limited area." The essential features are the incorporation of bondsmen and the paternal power; the Roman family, accordingly, constitutes the perfected type of this form of the family. The word *familia* did not originally signify the ideal of our modern Philistine, which is a compound of sentimentality and domestic discord. Among the Romans, in the beginning, it did not even refer to the married couple and their children, but to the slaves alone. *Famulus* means a household slave and *familia* signifies the totality of slaves belonging to one individual. Even in the time of Gaius the *familia, id est patrimonium* (that is, the inheritance) was bequeathed by will. The expression was invented by the Romans to describe a new social organism, the head of which had under him wife and children and a number of slaves, under Roman paternal power, with power of life and death over them all. "The term, therefore, is no older than the ironclad family system of the Latin tribes, which came in after field agriculture and after legalised servitude, as well as after the separation of the Greeks and (Aryan) Latins." To which Marx adds: "The modern family contains in embryo not only slavery (*servitus*) but serfdom also, since from the very beginning it is connected with agricultural services. It contains within itself in *miniature* all the antagonisms which later develop on a wide scale within society and its state."

Such a form of the family shows the transition of the pairing family to monogamy. In order to guarantee the fidelity of the wife, that is, the paternity of the children, the woman is placed in the man's absolute power; if he kills her, he is but exercising his right.

We are confronted with this new form of the family in all its severity among the Greeks. While, as Marx observes, the position of the goddesses in mythology represents an earlier period, when women still occupied a freer and more respected place, in the Heroic Age we already find women degraded owing to the predominance of the man and the competition of female slaves. One may read in the *Odyssey* how Telemachus cuts his mother short and enjoins silence upon her. In Homer the young female captives become the objects of the sensual lust of the victors; the military chiefs, one after the other, according to rank, choose the most beautiful ones for themselves. The whole of the *Iliad*, as we know, revolves around the quarrel between Achilles and Agamemnon over such a female slave. In connection with each Homeric hero of importance mention is made of a captive maiden with whom he shares tent and bed.

These maidens are taken back home, to the conjugal house, as was Cassandra by Agamemnon in Aeschylus. Sons born of these slaves receive a small share of their father's estate and are regarded as freemen. Teukros was such an illegitimate son of Telamon and was permitted to adopt his father's name. The wedded wife is expected to tolerate all this, but to maintain strict chastity and conjugal fidelity herself. True, in the Heroic Age the Greek wife is more respected than in the period of civilisation; for the husband, however, she is, in reality, merely the mother of his legitimate heirs, his chief housekeeper, and the superintendent of the female slaves, whom he may make, and does make his concubines at will. It is the existence of slavery side by side with monogamy, the existence of beautiful young slaves who belong to the *man* with all they have, that from the very beginning stamped on monogamy its specific character as monogamy *only for the woman*, but not for the man. And it retains this character to this day.

* * *

* * * In Euripides, the wife is described as *oikurema*, a thing for housekeeping (the word is in the neuter gender), and apart from the business of bearing children, she was nothing more to the Athenian than the chief housemaid. The husband had his gymnastic exercises, his public affairs, from which the wife was excluded; in addition, he often had female slaves at his disposal and, in the heyday of Athens, extensive prostitution, which was viewed with favour by the state, to say the least. It was precisely on the basis of this prostitution that the sole outstanding Greek women developed, who by their *esprit* and artistic taste towered as much above the general level of ancient womanhood as the Spartiate women did by virtue of their character. That one had first to become a *hetaera* in order to become a woman is the strongest indictment of the Athenian family.

In the course of time, this Athenian family became the model upon which not only the rest of the Ionians, but also all the Greeks of the mainland and of the colonies increasingly moulded their domestic relationships. But despite all seclusion and surveillance the Greek women found opportunities often enough for deceiving their husbands. The latter, who would have been ashamed to evince any love for their own wives, amused themselves with *hetaerae* in all kinds of amours. But the degradation of the women recoiled on the men themselves and degraded them too, until they sank into the perversion of boy-love, degrading both themselves and their gods by the myth of Ganymede.

This was the origin of monogamy, as far as we can trace it among the most civilized and highly-developed people of antiquity. It was not in any way the fruit of individual sex love, with which it had absolutely nothing in common, for the marriages remained marriages of convenience, as before. It was the first form of the family based not on natural but on economic conditions, namely, on the victory of private property over original, naturally developed, common ownership. The rule of the man in the family, the procreation of children who could only be his, destined to be the heirs of his wealth —these alone were frankly avowed by the Greeks as the exclusive aims of monogamy. For the rest, it was a burden, a duty to the gods, to the state and to their ancestors, which just had to be fulfilled. In Athens the law made not only marriage compulsory, but also the fulfillment by the man of a minimum of the so-called conjugal duties.

Thus, monogamy does not by any means make its appearance in history as the reconciliation of man and woman, still less as the highest form of such a reconciliation. On the contrary, it appears as the subjection of one sex by the other, as the proclamation of a conflict between the sexes entirely unknown hitherto in prehistoric times. In an old unpublished manuscript, the work of Marx and myself in 1846,[1] I find the following: "The first division of labour is that between man and woman for child breeding." And today I can add: The first class antagonism which appears in history coincides with the development of the antagonism between man and woman in monogamian marriage, and the first class oppression with that of the female sex by the male. Monogamy was a great historical advance, but at the same time it inaugurated, along with slavery and private wealth, that epoch, lasting until today, in which every advance is likewise a relative regression, in which the well-being and development of the one group are attained by the misery and repression of the other. It is the cellular form of civilised society, in which we can already study the nature of the antagonisms and contradictions which develop fully in the latter.

*** With the rise of property differentiation—that is, as far back as the upper stage of barbarism—wage labour appears sporadically alongside of slave labour; and simultaneously, as its necessary correlate, the professional prostitution of free women appears side by side with the forced surrender of the female slave. Thus, the heritage bequeathed to civilisation by group marriage is double-sided, just as everything engendered by civilisation is double-sided, double-tongued, self-contradictory and antagonistic: on the one hand, monogamy, on the other, hetaerism, including its most extreme form, prostitution. Hetaerism is as much a social institution as any other; it is a continuation of the old sexual freedom—in favour of the men. Although, in reality, it is not only tolerated but even practised with gusto, particularly by the ruling classes, it is condemned in words. In reality, however, this condemnation by no means hits the men who indulge in it, it hits only the women: they are ostracised and cast out in order to proclaim once again the absolute domination of the male over the female sex as the fundamental law of society.

A second contradiction, however, is hereby developed within monogamy itself. By the side of the husband, whose life is embellished by hetaerism, stands the neglected wife. And it is just as impossible to have one side of a contradiction without the other as it is to retain the whole of an apple in one's hand after half has been eaten. Nevertheless, the men appear to have thought differently, until their wives taught them to know better. Two permanent social figures, previously unknown, appear on the scene along with monogamy—the wife's paramour and the cuckold. The men had gained the victory over the women, but the act of crowning the victor was magnanimously undertaken by the vanquished. Adultery—proscribed, severely penalised, but irrepressible—became an unavoidable social institution alongside of monogamy and hetaerism. The assured paternity of children was now, as before, based, at best, on moral conviction; and in order to solve the insoluble contradiction, Article 312 of the *Code Napoléon* decreed: "*L'enfant conçupendant le mariage a pour père le mari,*" "a child conceived during marriage has for its father the husband." This is the final outcome of three thousand years of monogamy.

Thus, in the monogamian family, in those cases that faithfully reflect its historical origin and that clearly bring out the sharp conflict between man and woman resulting from the exclusive domination of the male, we have a picture in miniature of the very antagonisms and contradictions in which society, split up into classes since the commencement of civilisation, moves, without being able to resolve and overcome them. Naturally, I refer here only to those cases of monogamy where matrimonial life really takes its course according to the rules governing the original character of the whole institution, but where the wife rebels against the domination of the husband. That this is not the case with all marriages no one knows better than the German Philistine, who is no more capable of ruling in the home than in the state, and whose wife, therefore, with full justification, wears the breeches of which he is unworthy. But in consolation he imagines himself to be far superior to his French companion in misfortune, who, more often than he, fares far worse.

* * *

Although monogamy was the only known form of the family out of which modern sex love could develop, it does not follow that this love developed within it exclusively, or even predominantly, as the mutual love of man and wife. The whole nature of strict monogamian marriage under male domination ruled this out. Among all historically active classes, that is, among all ruling classes, matrimony remained what it had been since pairing marriage—a matter of convenience arranged by the parents. And the first form of sex love that historically emerges as a passion, and as a passion in which any person (at least of the ruling classes) has a right to indulge, as the highest form of the sexual impulse—which is precisely its specific feature—this, its first form, the chivalrous love of the Middle Ages, was by no means conjugal love. On the contrary, in its classical form, among the Provencals, it steers under full sail towards adultery, the praises of which are sung by their poets. The "*Albas*," in German *Tagelieder*, are the flower of Provençal love poetry. They describe in glowing colours how the knight lies with his love—the wife of another—while the watchman stands guard outside, calling him at the first faint streaks of dawn (*alba*) so that he may escape unobserved. The parting scene then constitutes the climax. The Northern French as well as the worthy Germans, likewise adopted this style of poetry, along with the manners of chivalrous love which corresponded to it; and on this same suggestive theme our own old Wolfram von Eschenbach has left us three exquisite Songs of the Dawn, which I prefer to his three long heroic poems.

Bourgeois marriage of our own times is of two kinds. In Catholic countries the parents, as heretofore, still provide a suitable wife for their young bourgeois son, and the consequence is naturally the fullest unfolding of the contradiction inherent in monogamy—flourishing hetaerism on the part of the husband, and flourishing adultery on the part of the wife. The Catholic Church doubtless abolished divorce only because it was convinced that for adultery, as for death, there is no cure whatsoever. In Protestant countries, on the other hand, it is the rule that the bourgeois son is allowed to seek a wife for himself from his own class, more or less freely. Consequently, marriage can be based on a certain degree of love which, for decency's sake, is always assumed, in accordance with Protestant hypocrisy. In this case, hetaerism on the part of the men is less actively pursued, and adultery on the woman's part is not so much the rule. Since, in every kind of marriage, however, people remain what they were before they married, and since the citizens of Protestant countries are mostly Philistines, this Protestant monogamy leads merely, if we take the average of the best cases, to a wedded life of leaden boredom, which is described as domestic bliss. The best mirror of these two ways of marriage is the novel; the French novel for the Catholic style, and the German novel for the Protestant. In both cases "he gets it": in the German novel the young man gets the girl; in the French, the husband gets the cuckold's horns. Which of the two is in the worse plight is not always easy to make out. For the dullness of the German novel excites the same horror in the French bourgeois as the "immorality" of the French novel excites in the German Philistine, although lately, since "Berlin is becoming a metropolis," the German novel has begun to deal a little less timidly with hetaerism and adultery, long known to exist there.

In both cases, however, marriage is determined by the class position of the participants, and to that extent always remains marriage of convenience. In both cases, this marriage of convenience often enough turns into the crassest prostitution—sometimes on both sides, but much more generally on the part of the wife, who differs from the ordinary courtesan only in that she does not hire out her body, like a wage-worker, on piecework, but sells it into slavery once for all. And Fourier's words hold good for all marriages of convenience: "Just as in grammar two negatives make a positive, so in the morals of marriage, two prostitutions make one virtue." Sex love in the relation of husband and wife is and can become the rule only among the oppressed classes, that is, at the present day, among the proletariat, no matter whether this relationship is officially sanctioned or not. But here all the foundations of classical monogamy are removed. Here, there is a complete absence of all property, for the safeguarding and inheritance of which monogamy and male domination were established. Therefore, there is no stimulus whatever here to assert male domination. What is more, the means, too, are absent; bourgeois law, which protects this domination, exists only for the propertied classes and their dealings with the proletarians. It costs money, and therefore, owing to the worker's poverty has no validity in his attitude towards his wife. Personal and social relations of quite a different sort are the decisive factors here. Moreover, since large-scale industry has transferred the woman from the house to the labour market and the factory, and makes her, often enough, the bread-winner of the family, the last remnants of male domination in the proletarian home have lost all foundation —except, perhaps, for some of that brutality towards women which became firmly rooted with the establishment of monogamy. Thus, the proletarian family is no longer monogamian in the strict sense, even in cases of the most passionate love and strictest faithfulness of the two parties, and despite all spiritual and worldly benedictions which may have been received. The two eternal adjuncts of monogamy—hetaerism and adultery—therefore, play an almost negligible role here; the woman has regained, in fact, the right of separation, and when the man and woman cannot get along they prefer to part. In short, proletarian marriage is monogamian in the etymological sense of the word, but by no means in the historical sense.

Our jurists, to be sure, hold that the progress of legislation to an increasing degree removes all cause for complaint on the part of the woman. Modern civilised systems of law are recognising more and more, first, that, in order to be effective marriage must be an agreement voluntarily entered into by both parties; and secondly, that during marriage, too, both parties must be on an equal footing in respect to rights and obligations. If, however, these two demands were consistently carried into effect, women would have all that they could ask for.

This typical lawyer's reasoning is exactly the same as that with which the radical republican bourgeois dismisses the proletarian. The labour contract is supposed to be voluntarily entered into by both parties. But it is taken to be voluntarily entered into as soon as the law has put both parties on an equal footing on paper. The power given to one party by its different class position, the pressure it exercises on the other—the real economic position of both—all this is no concern of the law. And both parties, again, are supposed to have equal rights for the duration of the labour contract, unless one or the other of the parties expressly waived them. That the concrete economic situation compels the worker to forego even the slightest semblance of equal rights—this again is something the law cannot help.

As far as marriage is concerned, even the most progressive law is fully satisfied as soon as the parties formally register their voluntary desire to get married. What happens behind the legal curtains, where real life is enacted, how this voluntary agreement is arrived at—is no concern of the law and the jurist. And yet the simplest comparison of laws should serve to show the jurist what this voluntary agreement really amounts to. In countries where the children are legally assured of an obligatory share of their parent's property and thus cannot be disinherited—in Germany, in the countries under French law, etc.—the children must obtain their parents' consent in the question of marriage. In countries under English law, where parental consent to marriage is not legally requisite, the parents have full testatory freedom over their property and can, if they so desire, cut their children off with a shilling. It is clear, therefore, that despite this, or rather just because of this, among those classes which have something to inherit, freedom to marry is not one whit greater in England and America than in France or Germany.

The position is no better with regard to the juridical equality of man and woman in marriage. The equality of the two before the law, which is a legacy of previous social conditions, is not the cause but the effect of the economic oppression of women. In the old communistic household, which embraced numerous couples and their children, the administration of the household, entrusted to the women, was just as much a public, a socially necessary industry as the providing of food by the men. This situation changed with the patriarchal family, and even more with the monogamian individual family. The administration of the household lost its public character. It was no longer the concern of society. It became a *private service*. The wife became the first domestic servant, pushed out of participation in social production. Only modern large-scale industry again threw open to her—and only to the proletarian woman at that—that avenue to social production; but in such a way that, when she fulfils her duties in the private service of her family, she remains excluded from public production and cannot earn anything; and when she wishes to take part in public industry and earn her living independently, she is not in a position to fulfil her family duties. What applies to the woman in the factory applies to her in all the professions, right up to medicine and law.

The modern individual family is based on the open or disguised domestic enslavement of the woman; and modern society is a mass composed solely of individual families as its molecules. Today, in the great majority of cases the man has to be the earner, the bread-winner of the family, at least among the propertied classes, and this gives him a dominating position which requires no special legal privileges. In the family, he is the bourgeois; the wife represents the proletariat. In the industrial world, however, the specific character of the economic oppression that weighs down the proletariat stands out in all its sharpness only after all the special legal privileges of the capitalist class have been set aside and the complete juridical equality of both classes is established. The democratic republic does not abolish the antagonism between the two classes; on the contrary, it provides the field on which it is fought out. And, similarly, the peculiar character of man's domination over woman in the modern family, and the necessity, as well as the manner, of establishing real social equality between the two, will be brought out into full relief only when both are completely equal before the law. It will then become evident that the first premise for the emancipation of women is the reintroduction of the entire female sex into public industry; and that this again demands that the quality possessed by the individual family of being the economic unit of society be abolished.

* * *

We have, then, three chief forms of marriage, which, by and large, conform to the three main stages of human development. For savagery—group marriage; for barbarism—pairing marriage; for civilisation—monogamy, supplemented by adultery and prostitution. In the upper stage of barbarism, between pairing marriage and monogamy, there is wedged in the dominion exercised by men over female slaves, and polygamy.

As our whole exposition has shown, the advance to be noted in this sequence is linked with the peculiar fact that while women are more and more deprived of the sexual freedom of group marriage, the men are not. Actually, for men, group marriage exists to this day. What for a woman is a crime entailing dire legal and social consequences, is regarded in the case of a man as being honourable or, at most, as a slight moral stain that one bears with pleasure. The more the old traditional hetaerism is changed in our day by capitalist commodity production and adapted to it, and the more it is transformed into unconcealed prostitution, the more demoralising are its effects. And it demoralises the men far more than it does the women. Among women, prostitution degrades only those unfortunates who fall into its clutches; and even these are not degraded to the degree that is generally believed. On the other hand, it degrades the character of the entire male world. Thus, in nine cases out of ten, a long engagement is practically a preparatory school for conjugal infidelity.

We are now approaching a social evolution in which the hitherto existing economic foundations of monogamy will disappear just as certainly as will those of its supplement—prostitution, Monogamy arose out of the concentration of considerable wealth in the hands of one person—and that a man—and out of the desire to bequeath this wealth to this man's children and to no one else's. For this purpose monogamy was essential on the woman's part, but not on the man's; so that this monogamy of the woman in no way hindered the overt or covert polygamy of the man. The impending social revolution, however, by transforming at least the far greater part of permanent inheritable wealth—the means of production—into social property, will reduce all this anxiety about inheritance to a minimum. Since monogamy arose from economic causes, will it disappear when these causes disappear?

One might not unjustly answer: far from disappearing, it will only begin to be completely realised. For with the conversion of the means of production into social property, wage labour, the proletariat, also disappears, and therewith, also, the necessity for a certain—statistically calculable—number of women to surrender themselves for money. Prostitution disappears; monogamy, instead of declining, finally becomes a reality—for the men as well.

At all events, the position of the men thus undergoes considerable change. But that of the women, of *all* women, also undergoes important alteration. With the passage of the means of production into common property, the individual family ceases to be the economic unit of society. Private housekeeping is transformed into a social industry. The care and education of the children becomes a public matter. Society takes care of all children equally, irrespective of whether they are born in wedlock or not. Thus, the anxiety about the "consequences," which is today the most important social factor—both moral and economic—that hinders a girl from giving herself freely to the man she loves, disappears. Will this not be cause enough for a gradual rise of more unrestrained sexual intercourse, and along with it, a more lenient public opinion regarding virginal honour and feminine shame? And finally, have we not seen that monogamy and prostitution in the modern world, although opposites, are nevertheless inseparable opposites, poles of the same social conditions? Can prostitution disappear without dragging monogamy with it into the abyss?

Here a new factor comes into operation, a factor that, at most, existed in embryo at the time when monogamy developed, namely individual sex love.

No such thing as individual sex love existed before the Middle Ages. That personal beauty, intimate association, similarity in inclinations, etc., aroused desire for sexual intercourse among people of opposite sexes, that men as well as women were not totally indifferent to the question of with whom they entered into this most intimate relation is obvious. But this is still a far cry from the sex love of our day. Throughout antiquity marriages were arranged by the parents; the parties quietly acquiesced. The little conjugal love that was known to antiquity was not in any way a subjective inclination, but an objective duty; not a reason for but a correlate of marriage. In antiquity, love affairs in the modern sense occur only outside official society. The shepherds, whose joys and sorrows in love are sung by Theocritus and Moschus, or by Longus's *Daphnis and Chloë* are mere slaves, who have no share in the state, the sphere of the free citizen. Except among the slaves, however, we find love affairs only as disintegration products of the declining ancient world; and with women who are also beyond the pale of official society, with *hetaerae,* that is, with alien or freed women; in Athens beginning with the eve of its decline, in Rome at the time of the emperors. If love affairs really occurred between free male and female citizens, it was only in the form of adultery. And sex love in our sense of the term was so immaterial to that classical love poet of antiquity old Anacreon, that even the sex of the beloved one was a matter of complete indifference to him.

Our sex love differs materially from the simple sexual desire, the *eros,* of the ancients. First, it presupposes reciprocal love on the part of the loved one; in this respect, the woman stands on a par with the man; whereas in the ancient *eros,* the woman was by no means always consulted. Secondly, sex love attains a degree of intensity and permanency where the two parties regard non-possession or separation as a great, if not the greatest, misfortune; in order to possess each other they take great hazards, even risking life itself—what in antiquity happened, at best, only in cases of adultery. And finally, a new moral standard arises for judging sexual intercourse. The question asked is not only whether such intercourse was legitimate or illicit, but also whether it arose from mutual love or not. It goes without saying that in feudal or bourgeois practice this new standard fares no better than all the other moral standards—it is simply ignored. But it fares no worse, either. It is recognized in theory, on paper, like all the rest. And more than this cannot be expected for the present.

Where antiquity broke off with its start towards sex love, the Middle Ages began, namely, with adultery. We have already described chivalrous love, which gave rise to the Songs of the Dawn. There is still a wide gulf between this kind of love, which aimed at breaking up matrimony, and the love destined to be its foundation, a gulf never completely bridged by the age of chivalry. Even when we pass from the frivolous Latins to the virtuous Germans, we find, in the *Nibelungenlied,* that Kriemhild—although secretly in love with Siegfried every whit as much as he is with her—nevertheless, in reply to Gunther's intimation that he has plighted her to a knight whom he does not name, answers simply: "You have no need to ask; as you command, so will I be forever. He whom you, my lord, choose for my husband, to him will I gladly plight my troth." It never occurs to her that her love could possibly be considered in this matter. Gunther seeks the hand of Brunhild without ever having seen her, and Etzel does the same with Kriemhild. The same occurs in the *Gudrun,* where Sigebant of Ireland seeks the hand of Ute the Norwegian, Hetel of Hegelingen that of Hilde of Ireland; and lastly, Siegfried of Morland, Hartmut of Ormany and Herwig of Seeland seek the hand of Gudrun; and here for the first time it happens that Gudrun, of her own free will, decides in favour of the last named. As a rule, the bride of a young prince is selected by his parents; if these are no longer alive, he chooses her himself with the counsel of his highest vassal chiefs, whose word carries great weight in all cases. Nor can it be otherwise. For the knight, or baron, just as for the prince himself, marriage is a political act, an opportunity for the accession of power through new alliances; the interests of the *House* and not individual inclination are the decisive factor. How can love here hope to have the last word regarding marriage?

It was the same for the guildsman of the medieval towns. The very privileges which protected him—the guild charters with their special stipulations, the artificial lines of demarcation which legally separated him from other guilds, from his own fellow guildsmen and from his journeymen and apprentices—considerably restricted the circle in which he could hope to secure a suitable spouse. And the question as to who was the most suitable was definitely decided under this complicated system, not by individual inclination, but by family interest.

Up to the end of the Middle Ages, therefore, marriage, in the overwhelming majority of cases, remained what it had been from the commencement, an affair that was not decided by the two principal parties. In the beginning one came into the world married, married to a whole group of the opposite sex. A similar relation probably existed in the later forms of group marriage, only with an ever-increasing narrowing of the group. In the pairing family it is the rule that the mothers arrange their children's marriages; and here also, considerations of new ties of relationship that are to strengthen the young couple's position in the gens and tribe are the decisive factor. And when, with the predominance of private property over common property, and with the interest in inheritance, father right and monogamy gain the ascendancy, marriage becomes more than ever dependent on economic considerations. The *form* of marriage by purchase disappears, the transaction itself is to an ever-increasing degree carried out in such a way that not only the woman but the man also is appraised, not by his personal qualities but by his possessions. The idea that the mutual inclinations of the principal parties should be the overriding reason for matrimony had been unheard of in the practice of the ruling classes from the very beginning. Such things took place, at best, in romance only, or—among the oppressed classes, which did not count.

This was the situation found by capitalist production when, following the era of geographical discoveries, it set out to conquer the world through world trade and manufacture. One would think that this mode of matrimony should have suited it exceedingly, and such was actually the case. And yet—the irony of world history is unfathomable—it was capitalist production that had to make the decisive breach in it. By transforming all things into commodities, it dissolved all ancient traditional relations, and for inherited customs and historical rights it substituted purchase and sale, "free" contract. And H. S. Maine, the English jurist, believed that he made a colossal discovery when he said that our entire progress in comparison with previous epochs consists in our having evolved from status to contract, from an inherited state of affairs to one voluntarily contracted—a statement which, in so far as it is correct, was contained long ago in the *Communist Manifesto*.

But the closing of contracts presupposes people who can freely dispose of their persons, actions and possessions, and who meet each other on equal terms. To create such "free" and "equal" people was precisely one of the chief tasks of capitalist production. Although in the beginning this took place only in a semiconscious manner, and in religious guise to boot, nevertheless, from the time of the Lutheran and Calvinistic Reformation it became a firm principle that a person was completely responsible for his actions only if he possessed full freedom of the will when performing them, and that it was an ethical duty to resist all compulsion to commit unethical acts. But how does this fit in with the previous practice of matrimony? According to bourgeois conceptions, matrimony was a contract, a legal affair, indeed the most important of all, since it disposed of the body and mind of two persons for life. True enough, formally the bargain was struck voluntarily; it was not done without the consent of the parties; but how this consent was obtained, and who really arranged the marriage was known only too well. But if real freedom to decide was demanded for all other contracts, why not for this one? Had not the two young people about to be paired the right freely to dispose of themselves, their bodies and its organs? Did not sex love become the fashion as a consequence of chivalry, and was not the love of husband and wife its correct bourgeois form, as against the adulterous love of the knights? But if it was the duty of married people to love each other, was it not just as much the duty of lovers to marry each other and nobody else? And did not the right of these lovers stand higher than that of parents, relatives and other traditional marriage brokers and matchmakers? If the right of free personal investigation unceremoniously forced its way into church and religion, how could it halt at the intolerable claim of the older generation to dispose of body and soul, the property, the happiness and unhappiness of the younger generation?

These questions were bound to arise in a period which loosened all the old social ties and which shook the foundations of all traditional conceptions. At one stroke the size of the world had increased nearly tenfold. Instead of only a quadrant of a hemisphere the whole globe was now open to the gaze of the West Europeans who hastened to take possession of the other seven quadrants. And the thousand-year-old barriers set up by the medieval prescribed mode of thought vanished in the same way as did the old, narrow barriers of the homeland. An infinitely wider horizon opened up both to man's outer and inner eye. Of what avail were the good intentions of respectability, the honoured guild privileges handed down through the generations, to the young man who was allured by India's riches, by the gold and silver mines of Mexico and Potosi? It was the knight-errant period of the bourgeoisie; it had its romance also, and its love dreams, but on a bourgeois basis and, in the last analysis, with bourgeois ends in view.

Thus it happened that the rising bourgeoisie, particularly in the Protestant countries, where the existing order was shaken up most of all, increasingly recognized freedom of contract for marriage also and carried it through in the manner described above. Marriage remained class marriage, but, within the confines of the class, the parties were accorded a certain degree of freedom of choice. And on paper, in moral theory as in poetic description, nothing was more unshakably established than that every marriage not based on mutual sex love and on the really free agreement of man and wife was immoral. In short, love marriage was proclaimed a human right; not only as man's right (*droit de l'homme*) but also, by way of exception, as woman's right (*droit de la femme*).

But in one respect this human right differed from all other so-called human rights. While, in practice, the latter remained limited to the ruling class, the bourgeoisie—the oppressed class, the proletariate, being directly or indirectly deprived of them—the irony of history asserts itself here once again. The ruling class continues to be dominated by the familiar economic influences and, therefore, only in exceptional cases can it show really voluntary marriages; whereas, as we have seen, these are the rule among the dominated class.

Thus, full freedom in marriage can become generally operative only when the abolition of capitalist production, and of the property relations created by it, has removed all those secondary economic considerations which still exert so powerful an influence on the choice of a partner. Then, no other motive remains than mutual affection.

Since sex love is by its very nature exclusive—although this exclusiveness is fully realised today only in the woman—then marriage based on sex love is by its very nature monogamy. We have seen how right Bachofen was when he regarded the advance from group marriage to individual marriage chiefly as the work of the women; only the advance from pairing marriage to monogamy can be placed to the men's account, and, historically, this consisted essentially in a worsening of the position of women and in facilitating infidelity on the part of the men. With the disappearance of the economic considerations which compelled women to tolerate the customary infidelity of the men—the anxiety about their own livelihood and even more about the future of their children—the equality of woman thus achieved will, judging from all previous experience, result far more effectively in the men becoming really monogamous than in the women becoming polyandrous.

What will most definitely disappear from monogamy, however, is all the characteristics stamped on it in consequence of its having arisen out of property relationships. These are, first, the dominance of the man, and secondly, the indissolubility of marriage. The predominance of the man in marriage is simply a consequence of his economic predominance and will vanish with it automatically. The indissolubility of marriage is partly the result of the economic conditions under which monogamy arose, and partly a tradition from the time when the connection between these economic conditions and monogamy was not yet correctly understood and was exaggerated by religion. Today it has been breached a thousandfold. If only marriages that are based on love are moral, then, also, only those are moral in which love continues. The duration of the urge of individual sex love differs very much according to the individual, particularly among men; and a definite cessation of affection, or its displacement by a new passionate love, makes separation a blessing for both parties as well as for society. People will only be spared the experience of wading through the useless mire of divorce proceedings.

Thus, what we can conjecture at present about the regulation of sex relationships after the impending effacement of capitalist production is, in the main, of a negative character, limited mostly to what will vanish. But what will be added? That will be settled after a new generation has grown up: a generation of men who never in all their lives have had occasion to purchase a woman's surrender either with money or with any other means of social power, and of women who have never been obliged to surrender to any man out of any consideration other than that of real love, or to refrain from giving themselves to their beloved for fear of the economic consequences. Once such people appear, they will not care a rap about what we today think they should do. They will establish their own practice and their own public opinion, conformable therewith, on the practice of each individual—and that's the end of it.
* * *

The Origin of the State

* * * Above we discussed separately each of the three main forms in which the state was built up on the ruins of the gentile constitution. Athens represented the purest, most classical form. Here the state sprang directly and mainly out of the class antagonisms that developed within gentile society. In Rome gentile society became an exclusive aristocracy amidst numerous plebs, standing outside of it, having no rights but only duties. The victory of the plebs burst the old gentile constitution asunder and erected on its ruins the state, in which both the gentile aristocracy and the plebs were soon wholly absorbed. Finally, among the German vanquishers of the Roman Empire, the state sprang up as a direct result of the conquest of large foreign territories, which the gentile constitution had no means of ruling. As this conquest did not necessitate either a serious struggle with the old population or a more advanced division of labour, and as conquered and conquerors were almost at the same stage of economic development and thus the economic basis of society remained the same as before, therefore, the gentile constitution could continue for many centuries in a changed, territorial form, in the shape of a Mark constitution, and even rejuvenate itself for a time in enfeebled form in the noble and patrician families of later years, and even in peasant families, as in Dithmarschen.[2]

The state is, therefore, by no means a power forced on society from without; just as little is it "the reality of the ethical idea," "the image and reality of reason," as Hegel maintains. Rather, it is a product of society at a certain stage of development; it is the admission that this society has become entangled in an insoluble contradiction with itself, that it is cleft into irreconcilable antagonisms which it is powerless to dispel. But in order that these antagonisms, classes with conflicting economic interests, might not consume themselves and society in sterile struggle, a power seemingly standing above society became necessary for the purpose of moderating the conflict, of keeping it within the bounds of "order"; and this power, arisen out of society, but placing itself above it, and increasingly alienating itself from it, is the state.

In contradistinction to the old gentile organisation, the state, first, divides its subjects according to territory. As we have seen, the old gentile associations, built upon and held together by ties of blood, became inadequate, largely because they presupposed that the members were bound to a given territory, a bond which had long ceased to exist. The territory remained, but the people had become mobile. Hence, division according to territory was taken as the point of departure, and citizens were allowed to exercise their public rights and duties wherever they settled, irrespective of gens and tribe. This organisation of citizens according to locality is a feature common to all states. That is why it seems natural to us; but we have seen what long and arduous struggles were needed before it could replace, in Athens and Rome, the old organisation according to gentes.

The second is the establishment of a public power which no longer directly coincided with the population organising itself as an armed force. This special public power is necessary, because a self-acting armed organisation of the population has become impossible since the cleavage into classes. The slaves also belonged to the population; the 90,000 citizens of Athens formed only a privileged class as against the 365,000 slaves. The people's army of the Athenian democracy was an aristocratic public power against the slaves, whom it kept in check; however, a gendarmeric also became necessary to keep the citizens in check, as we related above. This public power exists in every state; it consists not merely of armed people but also of material adjuncts, prisons and institutions of coercion of all kinds, of which gentile society knew nothing. It may be very insignificant, almost infinitesimal, in societies where class antagonisms are still undeveloped and in out-of-the-way places as was the case at certain times and in certain regions in the United States of America. It grows stronger, however, in proportion as class antagonisms within the state become more acute, and as adjacent states become larger and more populated. We have only to look at our present-day Europe, where class struggle and rivalry in conquest have screwed up the public power to such a pitch that it threatens to devour the whole of society and even the state.

In order to maintain this public power, contributions from the citizens become necessary—taxes. These were absolutely unknown in gentile society; but we know enough about them today. As civilisation advances, these taxes become inadequate; the state makes drafts on the future, contracts loans, *public debts.* Old Europe can tell a tale about these, too.

In possession of the public power and of the right to levy taxes, the officials, as organs of society, now stand *above* society. The free, voluntary respect that was accorded to the organs of the gentile constitution does not satisfy them, even if they could gain it; being the vehicles of a power that is becoming alien to society, respect for them must be enforced by means of exceptional laws by virtue of which they enjoy special sanctity and inviolability. The shabbiest police servant in the civilised state has more "authority" than all the organs of gentile society put together; but the most powerful prince and the greatest statesman, or general, of civilisation may well envy the humblest gentile chief for the uncoerced and undisputed respect that is paid to him. The one stands in the midst of society, the other is forced to attempt to represent something outside and above it.

As the state arose from the need to hold class antagonisms in check, but as it arose, at the same time, in the midst of the conflict of these classes, it is, as a rule, the state of the most powerful, economically dominant class which, through the medium of the state, becomes also the politically dominant class, and thus acquires new means of holding down and exploiting the oppressed class. Thus, the state of antiquity was above all the state of the slave owners for the purpose of holding down the slaves, as the feudal state was the organ of the nobility for holding down the peasant serfs and bondsmen, and the modern representative state is an instrument of exploitation of wage labour by capital. By way of exception, however, periods occur in which the warring classes balance each other so nearly that the state power, as ostensible mediator, acquires, for the moment, a certain degree of independence of both. Such was the absolute monarchy of the seventeenth and eighteenth centuries, which held the balance between the nobility and the class of burghers; such was the Bonapartism of the First, and still more of the Second French Empire, which played off the proletariat against the bourgeoisie and the bourgeoisie against the proletariat. The latest performance of this kind, in which ruler and ruled appear equally ridiculous, is the new German Empire of the Bismarck nation: the capitalists and workers are balanced against each other and equally cheated for the benefit of the impoverished Prussian cabbage Junkers.

In most of the historical states, the rights of citizens are, besides, apportioned according to their wealth, thus directly expressing the fact that the state is an organisation of the possessing class for its protection against the non-possessing class. It was so already in the Athenian and Roman classification according to property. It was so in the mediaeval feudal state, in which the alignment of political power was in conformity with the amount of land owned. It is seen in the electoral qualifications of the modern representative states. Yet this political recognition of property distinctions is by no means essential. On the contrary, it marks a low stage of state development. The highest form of the state, the democratic republic, which under our modern conditions of society is more and more becoming an inevitable necessity, and is the form of state in which alone the last decisive struggle between proletariat and bourgeoisie can be fought out—the democratic republic officially knows nothing any more of property distinctions. In it wealth exercises its power indirectly, but all the more surely. On the one hand, in the form of the direct corruption of officials, of which America provides the classical example; on the other hand, in the form of an alliance between government and Stock Exchange, which becomes the easier to achieve the more the public debt increases and the more joint-stock companies concentrate in their hands not only transport but also production itself, using the Stock Exchange as their centre. The latest French republic as well as the United States is a striking example of this; and good old Switzerland has contributed its share in this field. But that a democratic republic is not essential for this fraternal alliance between government and Stock Exchange is proved by England and also by the new German Empire, where one cannot tell who was elevated more by universal suffrage, Bismarck or Bleichröder. And lastly, the possessing class rules directly through the medium of universal suffrage. As long as the oppressed class, in our case, therefore, the proletariat, is not yet ripe to emancipate itself, it will in its majority regard the existing order of society as the only one possible and, politically, will form the tail of the capitalist class, its extreme Left wing. To the extent, however, that this class matures for its self-emancipation, it constitutes itself as its own party and elects its own representatives, and not those of the capitalists. Thus, universal suffrage is the gauge of the maturity of the working class. It cannot and never will be anything more in the present-day state; but that is sufficient. On the day the thermometer of universal suffrage registers boiling point among the workers, both they and the capitalists will know what to do.

The state, then, has not existed from all eternity. There have been societies that did without it, that had no conception of the state and state power. At a certain stage of economic development, which was necessarily bound up with the cleavage of society into classes, the state became a necessity owing to this cleavage. We are now rapidly approaching a stage in the development of production at which the existence of these classes not only will have ceased to be a necessity, but will become a positive hindrance to production. They will fall as inevitably as they arose at an earlier stage. Along with them the state will inevitably fall. The society that will organise production on the basis of a free and equal association of the producers will put the whole machinery of state where it will then belong: into the Museum of Antiquities, by the side of the spinning wheel and the bronze axe.

Thus, from the foregoing, civilisation is that stage of development of society at which division of labour, the resulting exchange between individuals, and commodity production, which combines the two, reach their complete unfoldment and revolutionise the whole hitherto existing society.

Production at all former stages of society was essentially collective and, likewise, consumption took place by the direct distribution of the products within larger or smaller communistic communities. This production in common was carried on within the narrowest limits, but concomitantly the producers were masters of their process of production and of their product. They knew what became of the product: they consumed it, it did not leave their hands; and as long as production was carried on on this basis, it could not grow beyond the control of the producers, and it could not raise any strange, phantom powers against them, as is the case regularly and inevitably under civilisation.

But, slowly, division of labour crept into this process of production. It undermined the collective nature of production and appropriation, it made appropriation by individuals the largely prevailing rule, and thus gave rise to exchange between individuals —how, we examined above. Gradually, the production of commodities became the dominant form.

With the production of commodities, production no longer for one's own consumption but for exchange, the products necessarily pass from hand to hand. The producer parts with his product in the course of exchange; he no longer knows what becomes of it. As soon as money, and with it the merchant, steps in as a middleman between the producers, the process of exchange becomes still more complicated, the ultimate fate of the product still more uncertain. The merchants are numerous and none of them knows what the other is doing. Commodities now pass not only from hand to hand, but also from market to market. The producers have lost control of the aggregate production of the conditions of their own life, and the merchants have not acquired it. Products and production become the playthings of chance.

But chance is only one pole of an interrelation, the other pole of which is called necessity. In nature, where chance also seems to reign, we have long ago demonstrated in each particular field the inherent necessity and regularity that asserts itself in this chance. What is true of nature holds good also for society. The more a social activity, a series of social processes, becomes too powerful for conscious human control, grows beyond human reach, the more it seems to have been left to pure chance, the more do its peculiar and innate laws assert themselves in this chance, as if by natural necessity. Such laws also control the fortuities of the production and exchange of commodities; these laws confront the individual producer and exchanger as strange and, in the beginning, even as unknown powers, the nature of which must first be laboriously investigated and ascertained. These economic laws of commodity production are modified at the different stages of development of this form of production; on the whole, however, the entire period of civilisation has been dominated by these laws. To this day, the product is master of the producer; to this day, the total production of society is regulated, not by a collectively thought-out plan, but by blind laws, which operate with elemental force, in the last resort in the storms of periodic commercial crises.

We saw above how human labour power became able, at a rather early stage of development of production, to produce considerably more than was needed for the producer's maintenance, and how this stage, in the main, coincided with that of the first appearance of the division of labour and of exchange between individuals. Now, it was not long before the great "truth" was discovered that man, too, may be a commodity; that human power may be exchanged and utilised by converting man into a slave. Men had barely started to engage in exchange when they themselves were exchanged. The active became a passive, whether man wanted it or not.

With slavery, which reached its fullest development in civilisation, came the first great cleavage of society into an exploiting and an exploited class. This cleavage has continued during the whole period of civilisation. Slavery was the first form of exploitation, peculiar to the world of antiquity; it was followed by serfdom in the Middle Ages, and by wage labour in modern times. These are the three great forms of servitude, characteristic of the three great epochs of civilisation; open, and, latterly, disguised slavery, are its steady companions.

The stage of commodity production, with which civilisation began, is marked economically by the introduction of 1) metal money and, thus, of money capital, interest and usury; 2) the merchants acting as middlemen between producers; 3) private ownership of land and mortgage; 4) slave labour as the prevailing form of production. The form of the family corresponding to civilisation and under it becoming the definitely prevailing form is monogamy, the supremacy of the man over the woman, and the individual family as the economic unit of society. The cohesive force of civilised society is the state, which in all typical periods is exclusively the state of the ruling class, and in all cases remains essentially a machine for keeping down the oppressed, exploited class. Other marks of civilisation are; on the one hand fixation of the contrast between town and country as the basis of the entire division of social labour; on the other hand, the introduction of wills, by which the property holder is able to dispose of his property even after his death. This institution, which was a direct blow at the old gentile constitution, was unknown in Athens until the time of Solon; in Rome it was introduced very early, but we do not know when.[3] Among the Germans it was introduced by the priests in order that the good honest German might without hindrance bequeath his property to the Church.

With this constitution as its foundation civilisation has accomplished things with which the old gentile society was totally unable to cope. But it accomplished them by playing on the most sordid instincts and passions of man, and by developing them at the expense of all his other faculties. Naked greed has been the moving spirit of civilisation from the first day of its existence to the present time; wealth, more wealth and wealth again; wealth, not of society, but of this shabby individual was its sole and determining aim. If, in the pursuit of this aim, the increasing development of science and repeated periods of the fullest blooming of art fell into its lap, it was only because without them the ample present-day achievements in the accumulation of wealth would have been impossible.

Since the exploitation of one class by another is the basis of civilisation, its whole development moves in a continuous contradiction. Every advance in production is at the same time a retrogression in the condition of the oppressed class, that is, of the great majority. What is a boon for the one is necessarily a bane for the other; each new emancipation of one class always means a new oppression of another class. The most striking proof of this is furnished by the introduction of machinery, the effects of which are well known today. And while among barbarians, as we have seen, hardly any distinction could be made between rights and duties, civilisation makes the difference and antithesis between these two plain even to the dullest mind by assigning to one class pretty nearly all the rights, and to the other class pretty nearly all the duties.

But this is not as it ought to be. What is good for the ruling class should be good for the whole of the society with which the ruling class identifies itself. Therefore, the more civilisation advances, the more it is compelled to cover the ills it necessarily creates with the cloak of love, to embellish them, or to deny their existence; in short, to introduce conventional hypocrisy—unknown both in previous forms of society and even in the earliest stages of civilisation—that culminates in the declaration: The exploiting class exploits the oppressed class solely and exclusively in the interest of the exploited class itself; and if the latter fails to appreciate this, and even becomes rebellious, it thereby shows the basest ingratitude to its benefactors, the exploiters.[4]

And now, in conclusion, Morgan's verdict on civilisation: "Since the advent of civilisation, the outgrowth of property has been so immense, its forms so diversified, its uses so expanding and its management so intelligent in the interests of its owners that it *has become*, on the part of the people, *an unmanageable power. The human mind stands bewildered in the presence of its own creation.* The time will come, nevertheless, when human intelligence will rise to the mastery over property, and define the relations of the state to the property it protects, as well as the obligations and the limits of the rights of its owners. The interests of society are paramount to individual interest, and the two must be brought into just and harmonious relation. A mere property career is not the final destiny of mankind, if progress is to be the law of the future as it has been of the past. The time which has passed away since civilisation began is but a fragment of the past duration of man's existence; and but a fragment of the ages yet to come. The dissolution of society bids fair to become the termination of a career of which property is the end and aim, because such a career contains the elements of self-destruction. Democracy in government, brotherhood in society, equality in rights and privileges, and universal education, foreshadow the next higher plane of society to which experience, intelligence and knowledge are steadily tending. "*It will be a revival, in a higher form, of the liberty, equality and fraternity of the ancient gentes*" (Lewis Henry Morgan, *Ancient Society*, 1877, p. 552).

NOTES

1. The reference is to *The German Ideology*.

2. The first historian who had at least an approximate idea of the nature of the gens was Niebuhr, thanks to his knowledge of the Dithmarschen families—to which, however, he also owes the errors he mechanically copied from there. [*Engels*]

3. Lassalle's *Das System der erworbenen Rechle* (*System of Acquired Rights*) turns, in its second part, mainly on the proposition that the Roman testament is as old as Rome itself, that in Roman history there was never "a time when testaments did not exist": that the testament arose rather in pre-Roman times out of the cult of the dead. As a confirmed Hegelian of the old school, Lassalle derived the provisions of the Roman law not from the social conditions of the Romans, but from the "speculative conception" of the will, and thus arrived at this totally unhistoric assertion. This is not to be wondered at in a book that from the same speculative conception draws the conclusion that the transfer of property was purely a secondary matter in Roman inheritance. Lassalle not only believes in the illusions of Roman jurists, especially of the earlier period, but he even excels them. [*Engels*]

4. I had intended at the outset to place the brilliant critique of civilisation, scattered through

the works of Fourier, by the side of Morgan's and my own. Unfortunately, I cannot spare the time. I only wish to remark that Fourier already considered monogamy and property in land as the main characteristics of civilisation, and that he described it as a war of the rich against the poor. We also find already in his work the deep appreciation of the fact that in all imperfect societies, those torn by conflicting interests, the individual families (*les families incohérentes*) are the economic units. [*Engels*]

Chapter Two

The Construction of Masculinity and the Triad of Men's Violence

Michael Kaufman

The all too familiar story: a woman raped, a wife battered, a lover abused. With a sense of immediacy and anger, the women's liberation movement has pushed the many forms of men's violence against women—from the most overt to the most subtle in form—into popular consciousness and public debate. These forms of violence are one aspect of our society's domination by men that, in outcome, if not always in design, reinforce that domination. The act of violence is many things at once. At the same instant it is the individual man acting out relations of sexual power; it is the violence of a society—a hierarchical, authoritarian, sexist, class-divided, militarist, racist, impersonal, crazy society—being focused through an individual man onto an individual woman. In the psyche of the individual man it might be his denial of social powerlessness through an act of aggression. In total these acts of violence are like a ritualized acting out of our social relations of power: the dominant and the weaker, the powerful and the power-less, the active and the passive . . . the masculine and the feminine.

For men, listening to the experience of women as the objects of men's violence is to shatter any complacency about the sex-based status quo. The power and anger of women's responses force us to rethink the things we discovered when we were very young. When I was eleven or twelve years old a friend told me the difference between fucking and raping. It was simple: with rape you tied the woman to a tree. At the time the anatomical details were still a little vague, but in either case it was something "we" supposedly did. This knowledge was just one part of an education, started years before, about the relative power and privileges of men and women. I remember laughing when my friend explained all that to me. Now I shudder. The difference in my responses is partially that, at twelve, it was part of the posturing and pretense that accompanied my passage into adolescence. Now, of course, I have a different vantage point on the issue. It is the vantage point of an adult, but more importantly my view of the world is being reconstructed by the intervention of that majority whose voice has been suppressed: the women.

This relearning of the reality of men's violence against women evokes many deep

From *Beyond Patriarchy: Essays by Men on Pleasure, Power, and Change,* Oxford University Press, 1987, pp. 1–29. Reprinted by permission.

feelings and memories for men. As memories are recalled and recast, a new connection becomes clear: violence by men against women is only one corner of a triad of men's violence. The other two corners are violence against other men and violence against oneself.

On a psychological level the pervasiveness of violence is the result of what Herbert Marcuse called the "surplus repression" of our sexual and emotional desires.[1] The substitution of violence for desire (more precisely, the transmutation of violence into a form of emotionally gratifying activity) happens unequally in men and women. The construction of masculinity involves the construction of "surplus aggressiveness." The social context of this triad of violence is the institutionalization of violence in the operation of most aspects of social, economic, and political life.

The three corners of the triad reinforce one another. The first corner—violence against women—cannot be confronted successfully without simultaneously challenging the other two corners of the triad. And all this requires a dismantling of the social feeding ground of violence: patriarchal, heterosexist, authoritarian, class societies. These three corners and the societies in which they blossom feed on each other. And together, we surmise, they will fall.

The Social and Individual Nature of Violence and Aggression

Origins of Violence

The most vexing question in the matter of men's violence is, of course, its biological roots. It would be very useful to know whether men in particular, or humans in general, are biologically (for example, genetically or hormonally) predisposed to acts of violence against other humans.

From the outset, feminism has been careful to draw a distinction between sex and gender. The strictly biological differences between the sexes form only the substrate for a society's construction of people with gender. Indeed, the appeal of feminism to many men, in addition to the desire to ally ourselves with the struggle of our sisters against oppression, has been to try to dissociate "male" from "masculine." While many of the characteristics associated with masculinity are valuable human traits—strength, daring, courage, rationality, intellect, sexual desire—the distortion of these traits in the masculine norm and the exclusion of other traits (associated with femininity) are oppressive and destructive. The process of stuffing oneself into the tight pants of masculinity is a difficult one for all men, even if it is not consciously experienced as such.

But the actual relation of sex and gender is problematic. For one thing, what might be called the "gender craft" of a society does its work on biological entities—entities whose ultimate source of pleasure and pain is their bodies.[2] What makes the relationship between sex and gender even more difficult to understand is that the production of gender is itself an incredibly complex and opaque process. As Michele Barrett and Mary McIntosh point out, although stereotypical roles do exist, each individual is not "the passive victim of a monolithically imposed system."[3]

In recent years there has been a major attempt to reclaim for biology the social behaviour of human beings. Sociobiology aims at nothing less than the reduction of human social interaction to our genetic inheritance. The study of apes, aardvarks, and tapeworms as a means of discerning the true nature of humans is almost surprising in its naivete, but at times it is socially dangerous in its conception and execution. As many critics have pointed out, it ignores what is unique about human beings: our construction of ever-changing social orders.

Indeed, humans are animals—physical creatures subject to the requirements of genes, cells, organs, and hormones of every description. Yet we do not have a comprehensive understanding of how these things shape behavior and, even if we did, behavior is just a small, fragmented moment to be understood within the larger realm of human desire and motivation. Even if we did have a more comprehensive knowledge, what is important is that humans, unlike apes or even the glorious ant, live in constantly evolving and widely differing societies. Since the era when humans came into existence, our history has been a movement *away* from an unmediated, "natural," animal existence.

Even if we could ascertain that humans in general, or men in particular, are predisposed to building neutron bombs, this does not help us answer the much more important question of how each society shapes, limits, or accentuates this tendency. To take only the question of violence, why, as societies develop, does violence seem to move from something isolated and often ritualistic in its expression to a pervasive feature of everyday life? And why are some forms of physical violence so widely accepted (corporal punishment of children, for example) while others are not (such as physical attacks on pharaohs, presidents, and pontiffs)?

That much said let us also say this: there is no psychological, biological, or social evidence to suggest that humans are not predisposed to aggression and even violence. On the other hand, a predisposition to cooperation and peacefulness is also entirely possible. It is even possible that men—for reasons of hormones—are biologically more aggressive and prone to violence than women. We do not know the answer for the simple reason that the men we examine do not exist outside societies.

But in any case, the important question is what societies do with the violence. What forms of violence are socially sanctioned or socially tolerated? What forms of violence seem built into the very structure of our societies? The process of human social development has been one of restraining, repressing, forming, informing, channeling, and transforming various biological tendencies. Could it not be that this process of repression has been a very selective one? Perhaps the repression of certain impulses and the denial of certain needs aggravate other impulses. I think of the man who feels he has no human connections in his life and who goes out and rapes a woman.

In spite of a general feminist rejection of sociobiology, this pseudoscience receives a strange form of support among some feminists. In her book, *Against Our Will: Men, Women and Rape,* Susan Brownmiller argues, not only that violent, male aggression is psychologically innate, but that it is grounded in male anatomy. And conversely, the view of female sexuality appears to be one of victimization and powerlessness. She argues, "By anatomical fiat—the inescapable construction of their genital organs—the human male was a natural predator and the human female served as his natural prey."[4] Alice Echols suggests that many cultural feminists also tend to repeat many traditional, stereotypical images of men and women.[5]

The essential question for us is not whether men are predisposed to violence, but what society does with this violence. Why has the linchpin of so many societies been the manifold expression of violence perpetrated disproportionately by men? Why are so many forms of violence sanctioned or even encouraged? Exactly what is the nature of violence? And how are patterns of violence and the quest for domination built up and reinforced?

The Social Context

For every apparently individual act of violence there is a social context. This is not to say there are no pathological acts of violence, but even in that case the "language" of the violent act, the way the violence manifests itself, can only be understood within a certain social experience. We are interested here in the manifestations of violence that are accepted as more or less normal, even if reprehensible: fighting, war, rape, assault, psychological abuse, and so forth. What is the context of men's violence in the prevalent social orders of today?

Violence has long been institutionalized as an acceptable means of solving conflicts. But now the vast apparati of policing and war making maintained by countries the world over pose a threat to the future of life itself.

"Civilized" societies have been built and shaped through the decimation, containment, and exploitation of other peoples: extermination of native populations, colonialism, and slavery. "I am talking," writes Aimé Césaire, "about societies drained of their essence, cultures trampled underfoot, institutions undermined, lands confiscated, religions smashed, magnificent artistic creations destroyed, extraordinary possibilities wiped out. . . . I am talking about millions . . . sacrificed."[6]

Our relationship with the natural environment has often been described with the metaphor of rape. An attitude of conquering nature, of mastering an environment waiting to be exploited for profit, has great consequences when we possess a technology capable of permanently disrupting an ecological balance shaped over hundreds of millions of years.

The daily work life of industrial, class societies is one of violence. Violence poses as economic rationality as some of us are turned into extensions of machines, while others become brains detached from bodies. Our industrial process becomes the modern-day rack of torture where we are stretched out of shape and ripped limb from limb. It is violence that exposes workers to the danger of chemicals, radiation, machinery, speedup, and muscle strain. It is violence that condemns the majority to work to exhaustion for forty or fifty years and then to be thrown into society's garbage bin for the old and used-up.

The racism, sexism, and heterosexism that have been institutionalized in our societies are socially regulated acts of violence.

Our cities themselves are a violation, not only of nature, but of human community and the human relationship with nature. As the architect Frank Lloyd Wright said, "To look at the plan of a great City is to look at something like the cross-section of a fibrous tumor."[7]

Our cities, our social structure, our work life, our relation with nature, our history, are more than a backdrop to the prevalence of violence. They are violence; violence in an institutionalized form encoded into physical structures and socioeconomic relations. Much of the sociological analysis of violence in our societies implies simply that violence is learned by witnessing and experiencing social violence: man kicks boy, boy kicks dog.[8] Such experiences of transmitted violence are a reality, as the analysis of wife battering indicates, for many batterers were themselves abused as children. But more essential is that our personalities and sexuality, our needs and fears, our strengths and weaknesses, our selves are created—not simply learned—through our lived reality. The violence of our social order nurtures a psychology of violence, which in turn reinforces the social, economic and political structures of violence. The ever-increasing demands of civilization and the constant building upon inherited structures of violence suggest that the development of civilization has been inseparable from a continuous increase in violence against humans and our natural environment.

It would be easy, yet ultimately not very useful, to slip into a use of the term "violence" as a metaphor for all our society's antagonisms, contradictions, and ills. For now, let us leave aside the social terrain and begin to unravel the nature of so-called individual violence.

The Triad of Men's Violence

> The longevity of the oppression of women must be based on something more than conspiracy, something more complicated than biological handicap and more durable than economic exploitation (although in differing degrees all these may feature.)
>
> —Juliet Mitchell[9]

> It seems impossible to believe that mere greed could hold men to such a steadfastness of purpose.
>
> —Joseph Conrad[10]

The field in which the triad of men's violence is situated is a society, or societies, grounded in structures of domination and control. Although at times this control is symbolized and embodied in the individual father—patriarchy, by definition—it is more important to emphasize that patriarchal structures of authority, domination, and control are diffused throughout social, economic, political, and ideological activities and in our relations to the natural environment. Perhaps more than in any previous time during the long epoch of patriarchy, authority does *not* rest with the father, at least in much of the advanced capitalist and noncapitalist world. This has led more than one author to question the applicability of the term patriarchy.[11] But I think it still remains useful as a broad, descriptive category. In this sense Jessica Benjamin speaks of the current reign of patriarchy without the father. "The form of domination peculiar to this epoch expresses itself not directly as authority but indirectly as the transformation of all relationships and activity into objective, instrumental, depersonalized forms."[12]

The structures of domination and control form not simply the background to the triad of violence, but generate, and in turn are nurtured by, this violence. These structures refer both to our social relations and to our interaction with our natural environment. The relation between these two levels is obviously extremely complex. It appears that violence against nature—that is, the impossible and disastrous drive to dominate and conquer the natural world—is integrally connected with domination among humans. Some of these connections are quite obvious. One thinks of the bull-dozing of the planet for profit in capitalist societies, societies characterized by the dominance of one class over others. But the link between the domination of nature and structures of domination of humans go beyond this. Various writers make provocative suggestions about the nature of this link.

Max Horkheimer and T. W. Adorno argue that the domination of humans by other humans creates the preconditions for the domination of nature.[13] An important sub-theme of Mary O'Brien's book *The Politics of Reproduction* is that men "have understood their separation from nature and their need to mediate this separation ever since that moment in dark prehistory when the idea of paternity took hold in the human mind. Patriarchy is the power to transcend natural realities with historical, man-made realities. This is the potency principle in its primordial form."[14] Simone de Beauvoir says that the ambivalent feelings of men toward nature are carried over onto their feelings toward women, who are seen as embodying nature. "Now ally, now enemy, she appears as the dark chaos from whence life wells up, as this life itself, and as the over yonder toward which life tends."[15] Violence against nature, like violence against women, violence against other men, and violence against oneself, is in part related to what Sidney Jourard calls the lethal aspects of masculinity.[16]

The Individual Reproduction of Male Domination

No man is born a butcher.

—Bertolt Brecht[17]

In a male-dominated society men have a number of privileges. Compared to women we are free to walk the streets at night, we have traditionally escaped domestic labor, and on average we have higher wages, better jobs, and more power. But these advantages in themselves cannot explain the individual reproduction of the relations of male domination, that is, why the individual male from a very early age embraces masculinity. The embracing of masculinity is not only a"socialization" into a certain gender role, as if there is a pre-formed human being who learns a role that he then plays for the rest of his life. Rather, through his psychological development he embraces and takes into himself a set of gender-based social relations: the person that is created through the process of maturation becomes the personal embodiment of those relations. By the time the child is five or six years old, the basis for lifelong masculinity has already been established.

Two factors, intrinsic to humans and human development, form the basis for the individual acquisition of gender. These conditions do not explain the existence of gender: they are simply preconditions for its individual acquisition.

The first factor is the malleability of human desires. For the infant all bodily activities—touch, sight, smell, sound, taste, thought—are potential sources of sexual pleasure. Or rather, they are sexual pleasure in the sense of our ability to obtain pleasure from our bodies. But this original polysexuality is limited, shaped, and repressed through the maturation process that is necessary to meet the demands of the natural and social world. Unlike other animals our sexuality is not simply instinct: it is individually and socially constructed. It is because of this, and because of the human's capacity to think and construct societies and ideologies, that gender can exist in differentiation from biological sex.

As Herbert Marcuse and, following him, Gad Horowitz have pointed out, the demands of societies of domination—of "surplus-repressive" societies—progressively narrow down sexuality into genital contact, with a heterosexual norm. (Marcuse argues that a certain "basic repression—a damming up or deflection—of human desires is necessary for any conceivable human association. But in addition to this, hierarchical and authoritarian societies require a "surplus repression" to maintain structures of domination.)[18]

This narrowing down onto genital contact is not simply a natural genital preference but is the blocking of energy from a whole range of forms of pleasure (including "mental" activities). And for reasons discussed elsewhere by Horowitz and Kaufman, the acquisition of the dominant form of masculinity is an enhancement of forms of pleasure associated with activity and the surplus repression of our ability to experience pleasure passively.

We try to compensate for this surplus repression with the pleasures and preoccupations of work, play, sports, and culture. But these are not sufficient to offset the severe limits placed on love and desire. To put this crudely, a two-day weekend cannot emotionally compensate for five days of a deadening job. And what is more, these social activities are themselves sources of struggle and tension.

The second factor that forms the basis for the individual's acquisition of gender is that the prolonged period of human childhood results in powerful attachments to parental figures. The passionate bonding of the young child to the primary parental figures obtains its particular power and salience for our personal development in societies where isolated women have the primary responsibility for nurturing infants and children, where the child's relation with the world is mediated most strongly through a small family rather than through a small community as a whole, and in which traits associated with the "opposite" sex are suppressed.

This prolonged period of human childhood is a prolonged period of powerlessness. The intense love for one or two parents is combined with intense feelings of deprivation and frustration. This natural ambivalence is greatly aggravated in societies where the attention parents are able to provide the young is limited, where social demands place additional frustrations on top of the inevitable ones experienced by a tiny person, and where one or two isolated parents relive and repeat the patterns of their own childhood. As will be seen, part of the boy's acquisition of masculinity is a response to this experience of powerlessness.

By the time children are sufficiently developed physically, emotionally, and intellectually at five or six to have clearly defined themselves separately from their parents, these parental figures have already been internalized within them. In the early years, as in later ones, we identify with (or react against) the apparent characteristics of our love objects and incorporate them into our own personalities. This is largely an unconscious process. This incorporation and internalization, or rejection, of the characteristics of our love objects is part of the process of constructing our ego, our self.

This internalization of the objects of love is a selective one, and it is a process that takes place in specific social environments. The immediate environment is the family, which is a "vigorous agency of class placement and an efficient mechanism for the creation and transmission of gender inequality."[19] Within itself, to a greater or lesser extent, the family reflects, reproduces, and re-creates the hierarchical gender system of society as a whole.[20]

As noted above, the child has ambivalent feelings toward his or her primary caring figures. Love combines with feelings of powerlessness, tension, and frustration. The child's experience of anxiety and powerlessness results not only from the prohibitions of harsh parents but also from the inability of even the most loving parents who cannot exist solely for their young, because of the demands of society, demands of natural reality, and demands of their own needs.

Both girls and boys have these ambivalent feelings and experiences of powerlessness. But the feelings toward the parents and the matter of power are almost immediately impregnated with social meaning. Years before the child can put words to it, she or he begins to understand that the mother is inferior to the father and that woman is inferior to man. That this inferiority is not natural but is socially imposed is beyond the understanding of the child and even beyond the understanding of sociobiologists, presidents, and popes. (Size itself might also feed into this perception of inferiority, or perhaps it is simply that in hierarchical, sexist society, size becomes a symbol of superiority.) In the end the biological fact of "otherness" becomes overlaced with a socially imposed otherness. The child is presented with two categories of humans: males, who embody the full grandeur and power of humanity, and females, who in Simone de Beauvoir's words, are defined as "other" in a phallocentric society.[21]

The human's answer to this powerlessness and to the desire to find pleasure is to develop an ego and a superego, that is, a distinct self and an internal mechanism of authority. An important part of the process of ego development is the identification with the objects of love. Progressively both sexes discover and are taught who the appropriate figures of identification are. But the figures of identification are not equal. Society presents the young boy with a great escape. He may feel powerless as a child, but there is hope, for as an adult male he will have privilege and (at least in the child's imagination) he will have power. A strong identification—that is, an incorporation into his own developing self—of his image of his father in particular and male figures in general is his compensation for his own sense of powerlessness and insecurity. It is his compensation for distancing himself from his first love, his mother.

In this process the boy not only claims for himself the activity represented by men and father. At the same time he steps beyond the passivity of his infantile relationship to the mother and beyond his overall sense of passivity (passivity, that is, in the sense of feeling overwhelmed by desires and a frustrating world). He embraces the project of controlling himself and controlling the world. He comes to personify activity. Masculinity is a reaction against passivity and powerlessness, and with it comes a repression of all the desires and traits that a given society defines as negatively passive or as resonant of passive experiences. The girl, on the other hand, discovers she will never possess men's power, and henceforth the most she can aspire to is to be loved by a man —that is, to actively pursue a passive aim.

Thus the achievement of what is considered the biologically normal male character (but which is really socially created masculinity) is one outcome of the splitting of human desire and human *being* into mutually exclusive spheres of activity and passivity. The monopoly of activity by males is not a timeless psychological or social necessity. Rather, the internalization of the norms of masculinity require the surplus repression of passive aims—the desire to be nurtured. The repression of passivity and the accentuation of activity constitute the development of a "surplus-aggressive" character type. Unfortunately, such a character type is the norm in patriarchal societies, although the degree of aggressiveness varies from person to person and society to society.

Part of the reason for this process is a response to the fear of rejection and of punishment. What does one fear? Loss of love and self-esteem. Why, in the child's mind, would it lose love and self-esteem? Because it does what is prohibited or degraded. In order to not do what is prohibited or degraded, during this process of identification the child internalizes the values and prohibitions of society. This is the shaping of the superego, our conscience, sense of guilt, and standards of self-worth. Through the internalization of social authority, aggressiveness is directed against oneself.[22]

This whole process of ego development is the shaping of a psychic realm that mediates between our unconscious desires, the world, and a punishing superego. But as should now be clear, the development of the ego is the development of masculine or feminine ego. In this sense, the ego is a definition of oneself formed within a given social and psychological environment and within what Gayle Rubin calls a specific sex-gender system.[23]

The boy is not simply *learning* a gender role but is becoming *part* of that gender. His whole self, to a greater or lesser extent, with greater or lesser conflict, will be masculine. Ken Kesey magnificently captured this in his description of Hank, a central character in *Sometimes a Great Notion:* "Did it take that much muscle just to walk, or was Hank showing off his manly development? Every movement constituted open aggression against the very air through which Hank passed."[24]

The Reinforcement of Masculinity

Masculinity is unconsciously rooted before the age of six, is reinforced as the child develops, and then positively explodes at adolescence. Beauvoir's comment about girls is no less true for boys: "With puberty, the future not only approaches; it takes residence in her body; it assumes the most concrete reality."[25]

It is particularly in adolescence that masculinity obtains its definitive shape for the individual. The masculine norm has its own particular nuances and traits dependent on class, nation, race, religion, and ethnicity. And within each group it has its own personal expression. Adolescence is important because it is the time when the body reawakens, when that long-awaited entrance into adulthood finally takes place, and when our culture makes the final socio-educational preparations for adult work life. In adolescence the pain and fear involved in repressing "femininity" and passivity start to become evident. For most of us, the response to this inner pain is to reinforce the bulwarks of masculinity. The emotional pain created by obsessive masculinity is stifled by reinforcing masculinity itself.

The family, school, sports, friends, church, clubs, scouts, jobs, and the media all play a role as the adolescent struggles to put the final touches on himself as a real man. The expression of male power will be radically different from class to class. For the middle-class adolescent, with a future in a profession or business, his own personal and social power will be expressed through a direct mastering of the world. Workaholism or at least a measuring of his value through status and the paycheck might well be the outcome. Fantasies of power are often expressed in terms of fame and success. For a working-class boy, the avenue of mastering the world of business, politics, the professions, and wealth is all but denied. For him male power is often defined in the form of working-class machismo. The power to dominate is expressed in a direct physical form. Domination of the factors of production or of another person is achieved through sheer bravado and muscle power. In an excellent examination of the development of white male, working-class identity in Britain, Paul Willis demonstrates that the acquisition of a positive working-class identity is coterminous with the development of a particular gender identity. Though stigmatized by society as a whole, manual labor becomes the embodiment of masculine power. "Manual labor is suffused with masculine qualities and given certain sensual overtones for 'the lads.' The toughness and awkwardness of physical work and effort . . . takes on masculine lights and depths and assumes a significance beyond itself."[26]

Adolescence is also the time of our first intense courtships. Although so much of pre- and early-adolescent sexual experience is homosexual, those experiences tend to be devalued and ignored. Relations with young women are the real thing. This interaction furthers the acquisition of masculinity for boys because they are interacting with girls who are busy acquiring the complementary femininity. Each moment of interaction reinforces the gender acquisition of each sex.

The Fragility of Masculinity

Masculinity is power. But masculinity is terrifyingly fragile because it does not really exist in the sense we are led to think it exists, that is, as a biological reality—something real that we have inside ourselves. It exists as ideology; it exists as scripted behavior; it exists within "gendered" relationships. But in the end it is just a social institution with a tenuous relationship to that with which it is supposed to be synonymous: our maleness, our biological sex. The young child does not know that sex does not equal gender. For him to be male is to be what he perceives as being masculine. The child is father to the man. Therefore, to be unmasculine is to be desexed—"castrated."

The tension between maleness and masculinity is intense because masculinity requires a suppression of a whole range of human needs, aims, feelings, and forms of expression. Masculinity is one half of the narrow, surplus-repressive shape of the adult human psyche. Even when we are intellectually aware of the difference between biological maleness and masculinity, the masculine ideal is so embedded within ourselves that it is hard to untangle the person we might want to become (more "fully human," less sexist, less surplus-repressed, and so on) from the person we actually are. But as children and adolescents (and often as adults), we are not aware of the difference between maleness and masculinity. With the exception of a tiny proportion of the population born as hermaphrodites, there can be no biological struggle to be male. The presence of a penis and testicles is all it takes. Yet boys and men harbor great insecurity about their male credentials. This insecurity exists because maleness is equated with masculinity; but the latter is a figment of our collective, patriarchal, surplus-repressive imaginations.

In a patriarchal society being male is highly valued, and men value their masculinity. But everywhere there are ambivalent feelings. That the initial internalization of masculinity is at the father's knee has lasting significance. Andrew Tolson states that "to the boy, masculinity is both mysterious and attractive (in its promise of a world of work and power), and yet, at the same time, threatening (in its strangeness, and emotional distance). . . . It works both ways; attracts and repels in dynamic contradiction. This simultaneous distance and attraction is internalized as a permanent emotional tension that the individual must, in some way, strive to overcome."[27]

Although maleness and masculinity are highly valued, men are everywhere unsure of their own masculinity and maleness, whether consciously or not. When men are encouraged to be open, as in men's support and counseling groups, it becomes apparent that there exists, often under the surface, an internal dialogue of doubt about one's male and masculine credentials.

One need think only of anxieties about the penis, that incomparable scepter, that symbol of patriarchy and male power. Even as a child the boy experiences, more or less consciously, fearful fantasies of "castration." The child observes that the people who do not have penises are also those with less power. In the mind of a four- or five-year-old child who doesn't know about the power of advertising, the state, education, interactive psychological patterns, unequal pay, sexual harassment, and rape, what else can he think bestows the rewards of masculinity than that little visible difference between men and women, boys and girls?

Of course at this early age the little penis and testicles are not much defense against the world. Nor can they measure against the impossibly huge genitals of one's father or other men. I remember standing in the shower when I was five or six years old, staring up in awe at my father. Years later I realized a full circle had turned when I was showering with my five-year-old son and saw the same crick in his neck and the same look in his eyes. This internalized image of the small, boyish self retains a nagging presence in each man's unconscious. This is so much so that, as adults, men go to war to prove themselves potent, they risk their lives to show they have balls. Expressions such as these, and the double meaning of the word *impotent,* are no accident.

Just the presence of that wonderfully sensitive bit of flesh, as highly valued as it is in patriarchal culture, is not enough to guarantee maleness and masculinity. But if there are indeed such great doubts in adolescence and beyond about one's masculine credentials, how is it that we combat these doubts? One way is by violence.

Men's Violence against Women

In spite of the inferior role which men assign to them, women are the privileged objects of their aggression.

—Simone de Beauvior[28]

Men's violence against women is the most common form of direct, personalized violence in the lives of most adults. From sexual harassment to rape, from incest to wife battering to the sight of violent pornographic images, few women escape some form of male aggression.

My purpose here is not to list and evaluate the various forms of violence against women, nor to try to assess what can be classed as violence per se.[29] It is to understand this violence as an expression of the fragility of masculinity and its place in the perpetuation of masculinity and male domination.

In the first place, men's violence against women is probably the clearest, most straightforward expression of relative male and female power. That the relative social, economic, and political power can be expressed in this manner is, to a large part, because of differences in physical strength and in a lifelong training (or lack of training) in fighting. But it is also expressed this way because of the active/passive split. Activity as aggression is part of the masculine gender definition. That is not to say this definition always includes rape or battering, but it is one of the possibilities within a definition of activity that is ultimately grounded in the body.

Rape is a good example of the acting out of these relations of power and of the outcome of fragile masculinity in a surplus-repressive society. In the testimonies of rapists one hears over and over again expressions of inferiority, powerlessness, anger. But who can these men feel superior to? Rape is a crime that not only demonstrates physical power, but that does so in the language of male-female sex-gender relations. The testimonies of convicted rapists collected by Douglas Jackson in the late 1970s are chilling and revealing.[30] Hal: "I felt very inferior to others. . . . I felt rotten about myself and by committing rape I took this out on someone I thought was weaker than me, someone I could control." Carl: "I think that I was feeling so rotten, so low, and such a creep . . ." Len: "I feel a lot of what rape is isn't so much sexual desire as a person's feelings about themselves and how that relates to sex. My fear of relating to people turned to sex because . . . it just happens to be the fullest area to let your anger out on, to let your feelings out on."

Sometimes this anger and pain are experienced in relation to women but just as often not. In either case they are addressed to women who, as the Other in a phallocentric society, are objects of mystification to men, the objects to whom men from birth have learned to express and vent their feelings, or simply objects with less social power and weaker muscles. It is the crime against women par excellence because, through it, the full weight of a sexually based differentiation among humans is played out.

This anger and pain are sometimes overlayed with the effects of a class hierarchy. John: "I didn't feel too good about women. I felt that I couldn't pick them up on my own. I took the lower-class woman and tried to make her look even lower than she really was, you know. 'Cause what I really wanted was a higher-class woman but I didn't have the finesse to actually pick these women up."

Within relationships, forms of male violence such as rape, battering, and what Meg Luxton calls the "petty tyranny" of male domination in the household[31] must be understood both "in terms of violence directed against women as women and against women as wives."[32] The family provides an arena for the expression of needs and emotions not considered legitimate elsewhere.[33] It is one of the only places where men feel safe enough to express emotions. As the dams break, the flood pours out on women and children.[34] The family also becomes the place where the violence suffered by individuals in their work lives is discharged. "At work men are powerless, so in their leisure time they want to have a feeling that they control their lives."[35]

While this violence can be discussed in terms of men's aggression, it operates within the dualism of activity and passivity, masculinity and femininity. Neither can exist without the other. This is not to blame women for being beaten, nor to excuse men who beat. It is but an indication that the various forms of men's violence against women are a dynamic affirmation of a masculinity that can only exist as distinguished from femininity. It is my argument that masculinity needs constant nurturing and affirmation. This affirmation takes many different forms. The majority of men are not rapists or batterers, although it is possible that the majority of men have used superior physical strength or physical coercion or the threat of force against a woman at least once as a teenager or an adult. But in those who harbor great personal doubts or strongly negative self-images, or who cannot cope with a daily feeling of powerlessness, violence against women can become a means of trying to affirm their personal power in the language of our sex-gender system. That these forms of violence only reconfirm the negative self-image and the feeling of powerlessness shows the fragility, artificiality, and precariousness of masculinity.

Violence against Other Men

At a behavioral level, men's violence against other men is visible throughout society. Some forms, such as fighting, the ritualized display violence of teenagers and some groups of adult men, institutionalized rape in prisons, and attacks on gays or racial minorities are very direct expressions of this violence. In many sports, violence is incorporated into exercise and entertainment. More subtle forms are the verbal putdown or, combined with economic and other factors, the competition in the business, political, or academic world. In its most frightening form, violence has long been an acceptable and even preferred method of addressing differences and conflicts among different groups and states. In the case of war, as in many other manifestations of violence, violence against other men (and civilian women) combines with autonomous economic, ideological, and political factors.

But men's violence against other men is more than the sum of various activities and types of behavior. In this form of violence a number of things are happening at once, in addition to the autonomous factors involved. Sometimes mutual, sometimes one-sided, there is a discharge of aggression and hostility. But at the same time as discharging aggression, these acts of violence and the ever-present potential for men's violence against other men reinforce the reality that relations between men, whether at the individual or state level, are relations of power.[36]

Most men feel the presence of violence in their lives. Some of us had fathers who were domineering, rough, or even brutal. Some of us had fathers who simply were not there enough; most of us had fathers who either consciously or unconsciously were repelled by our need for touch and affection once we had passed a certain age. All of us had experiences of being beaten up or picked on when we were young. We learned to fight, or we learned to run; we learned to pick on others, or we learned how to talk or joke our way out of a confrontation. But either way these early experiences of violence caused an incredible amount of anxiety and required a huge expenditure of energy to resolve. That anxiety is crystallized in an unspoken fear (particularly among heterosexual men): all other men are my potential humiliators, my enemies, my competitors.

But this mutual hostility is not always expressed. Men have formed elaborate institutions of male bonding and buddying: clubs, gangs, teams, fishing trips, card games, bars, and gyms, not to mention that great fraternity of Man. Certainly, as many feminists have pointed out, straight male clubs are a subculture of male privilege. But they are also havens where men, by common consent, can find safety and security among other men. They are safe houses where our love and affection for other men can be expressed. Freud suggested that great amounts of passivity are required for the establishment of social relations among men but also that this very passivity arouses a fear of losing one's power. (This fear takes the form, in a phallocentric, male-dominated society, of what Freud called "castration anxiety.") There is a constant tension of activity and passivity. Among their many functions and reasons for existence, male institutions mediate this tension between activity and passivity among men.

My thoughts take me back to grade six and the constant acting out of this drama. There was the challenge to fight and a punch in the stomach that knocked my wind out. There was our customary greeting with a slug in the shoulder. Before school, after school, during class change, at recess, whenever you saw another one of the boys whom you hadn't hit or been with in the past few minutes, you'd punch each other on the shoulder. I remember walking from class to class in terror of meeting Ed Skagle in the hall. Ed, a hefty young football player a grade ahead of me, would leave a big bruise with one of his friendly hellos. And this was the interesting thing about the whole business; most of the time it was friendly and affectionate. Long after the bruises have faded, I remember Ed's smile and the protective way he had of saying hello to me. But we couldn't express this affection without maintaining the active/passive equilibrium. More precisely, within the masculine psychology of surplus aggression, expressions of affection and of the need for other boys had to be balanced by an active assault.

But the traditional definition of masculinity is not only surplus aggression. It is also exclusive heterosexuality, for the maintenance of masculinity requires the repression of homosexuality.[37] Repression of homosexuality is one thing, but how do we explain the intense fear of homosexuality, the homophobia, that pervades so much male interaction? It isn't simply that many men may choose not to have sexual relations with other men; it is rather that they will find this possibility frightening or abhorrent. Freud showed that the boy's renunciation of the father—and thus men—as an object of sexual love is a renunciation of what are felt to be passive sexual desires. Our embrace of future manhood is part of an equation:

$$male = penis = power = active = masculine.$$

The other half of the equation, in the language of the unconscious in patriarchal society, is

$$female = castrated = passive = feminine.$$

These unconscious equations might be absurd, but they are part of a socially shared hallucination of our patriarchal society. For the boy to deviate from this norm is to experience severe anxiety, for what appears to be at stake is his ability to be active. Erotic attraction to other men is sacrificed because there is no model central to our society of active, erotic love for other males. The emotionally charged physical attachments of childhood with father and friends eventually breed feelings of passivity and danger and are sacrificed. Horowitz notes that the anxiety caused by the threat of losing power and activity is "the motive power behind the 'normal' boy's social learning of his sex and gender roles." Boys internalize "our culture's definition of 'normal' or 'real' man: the possessor of a penis, therefore loving only females and that actively; the possessor of a penis, therefore 'strong' and 'hard,' not 'soft,' 'weak,' 'yielding,' 'sentimental,' 'effeminate,' passive. To deviate from this definition is not to be a real man. To deviate is to arouse [what Freud called] castration anxiety."[38]

Putting this in different terms, the young boy learns of the sexual hierarchy of society. This learning process is partly conscious and partly unconscious. For a boy, being a girl is a threat because it raises anxiety by representing a loss of power. Until real power is attained, the young boy courts power in the world of the imagination (with superheroes, guns, magic, and pretending to be grown-up). But the continued pull of passive aims, the attraction to girls and to mother, the fascination with the origin of babies ensure that a tension continues to exist. In this world, the only thing that is as bad as being a girl is being a sissy, that is, being like a girl.[39] Although the boy doesn't consciously equate being a girl or sissy with homosexual genital activity, at the time of puberty these feelings, thoughts, and anxieties are transferred onto homosexuality per se.

For the majority of men, the establishment of the masculine norm and the strong social prohibitions against homosexuality are enough to bury the erotic desire for other men. The repression of our bisexuality is not adequate, however, to keep this desire at bay. Some of the energy is transformed into derivative pleasures—muscle building, male comradeship, hero worship, religious rituals, war, sports—where our enjoyment of being with other men or admiring other men can be expressed. These forms of activity are not enough to neutralize our constitutional bisexuality, our organic fusion of passivity and activity, and our love for our fathers and our friends. The great majority of men, in addition to those men whose sexual preference is clearly homosexual, have, at some time in their childhood, adolescence, or adult life, had sexual or quasi-sexual relations with other males, or have fantasized or dreamed about such relationships. Those who don't (or don't recall that they have) invest a lot of energy in repressing and denying these thoughts and feelings. And to make things worse, all those highly charged male activities in the sportsfield, the meeting room, or the locker room do not dispel eroticized relations with other men. They can only reawaken those feelings. It is, as Freud would have said, the return of the repressed.

Nowhere has this been more stunningly captured than in the wrestling scene in the perhaps mistitled book, *Women in Love,* by D. H. Lawrence. It was late at night. Birkin had just come to Gerald's house after being put off following a marriage proposal. They talked of working, of loving, and fighting, and in the end stripped off their clothes and began to wrestle in front of the burning fire. As they wrestled, "they seemed to drive their white flesh deeper and deeper against each other, as if they would break into a oneness." They entwined, they wrestled, they pressed nearer and nearer. "A tense white knot of flesh [was] gripped in silence." The thin Birkin "seemed to penetrate into Gerald's more solid, more diffuse bulk, to interfuse his body through the body of the other, as if to bring it subtly into subjection, always seizing with some rapid necromantic foreknowledge every motion of the other flesh, converting and counteracting it, playing upon the limbs and trunk of Gerald like some hard wind. . . . Now and again came a sharp gasp of breath, or a sound like a sigh, then the rapid thudding of movement on the thickly-carpeted floor, then the strange sound of flesh escaping under flesh."[40]

The very institutions of male bonding and patriarchal power force men to constantly reexperience their closeness and attraction to other men, that is, the very thing so many men are afraid of. Our very attraction to ourselves, ambivalent as it may be, can only be generalized as an attraction to men in general.

A phobia is one means by which the ego tries to cope with anxiety. Homophobia is a means of trying to cope, not simply with our unsuccessfully repressed, eroticized attraction to other men, but with our whole anxiety over the unsuccessfully repressed passive sexual aims, whether directed toward males or females. But often, Otto Fenichel writes, "individuals with phobias cannot succeed in avoiding the feared situations. Again and again they are forced to experience the very things they are afraid of. Often the conclusion is unavoidable that this is due to an unconscious arrangement of theirs. It seems that unconsciously they are striving for the very thing of which they are consciously afraid. This is understandable because the feared situations originally were instinctual aims. It is a kind of 'return of the repressed.' "[41]

In the case of homophobia, it is not merely a matter of an individual phobia, although the strength of homophobia varies from individual to individual. It is a socially constructed phobia that is essential for the imposition and maintenance of masculinity. A key expression of homophobia is the obsessive denial of homosexual attraction; this denial is expressed as violence against other men. Or to put it differently, men's violence against other men is one of the chief means through which patriarchal society simultaneously expresses and discharges the attraction of men to other men. The specific ways that homophobia and men's violence toward other men are acted out varies from man to man, society to society, and class to class. The great amount of *directly expressed* violence and violent homophobia among some groups of working-class youth would be well worth analyzing to give clues to the relation of class and gender.

This corner of the triad of men's violence interacts with and reinforces violence against women. This corner contains part of the logic of surplus aggression. Here we begin to explain the tendency of many men to use force as a means of simultaneously hiding and expressing their feelings. At the same time the fear of other men, in particular the fear of weakness and passivity in relation to other men, helps create our strong dependence on women for meeting our emotional needs and for emotional discharge. In a surplus-repressive patriarchal and class society, large amounts of anxiety and hostility are built up, ready to be discharged. But the fear of one's emotions and the fear of losing control mean that discharge only takes place in a safe situation. For many men that safety is provided by a relationship with a woman where the commitment of one's friend or lover creates the sense of security. What is more, because it is a relationship with a woman, it unconsciously resonates with that first great passive relation of the boy with his mother. But in this situation and in other acts of men's violence against women, there is also the security of interaction with someone who does not represent a psychic threat, who is less socially powerful, probably less physically powerful, and who is herself operating within a pattern of surplus passivity. And finally, given the fragility of masculine identity and the inner tension of what it means to be masculine, the ultimate acknowledgment of one's masculinity is in our power over women. This power can be expressed in many ways. Violence is one of them.

Violence against Oneself

When I speak of a man's violence against himself I am thinking of the very structure of the masculine ego. The formation of an ego on an edifice of surplus repression and surplus aggression is the building of a precarious structure of internalized violence. The continual conscious and unconscious blocking and denial of passivity and all the emotions and feelings men associate with passivity—fear, pain, sadness, embarrassment—is a denial of part of what we are. The constant psychological and behavioral vigilance against passivity and its derivatives is a perpetual act of violence against oneself. The denial and blocking of a whole range of human emotions and capacities are compounded by the blocking of avenues of discharge. The discharge of fear, hurt, and sadness, for example (through crying or trembling), is necessary because these painful emotions linger on even if they are not consciously felt. Men become pressure cookers. The failure to find safe avenues of emotional expression and discharge means that a whole range of emotions are transformed into anger and hostility. Part of the anger is directed at oneself in the form of guilt, self-hate, and various physiological and psychological symptoms. Part is directed at other men. Part of it is directed at women.

By the end of this process, our distance from ourselves is so great that the very symbol of maleness is turned into an object, a thing. Men's preoccupation with genital power and pleasure combines with a desensitization of the penis. As best he can, writes Emmanuel Reynaud, a man gives it "the coldness and the hardness of metal." It becomes his tool, his weapon, his thing. "What he loses in enjoyment he hopes to compensate for in power; but if he gains an undeniable power symbol, what pleasure can he really feel with a weapon between his legs?"[42]

Beyond Men's Violence

Throughout Gabriel García Márquez's *Autumn of the Patriarch*, the ageless dictator stalked his palace, his elephantine feet dragging forever on endless corridors that reeked of corruption. There was no escape from the world of terror, misery, and decay that he himself had created. His tragedy was that he was "condemned forever to live breathing the same air which asphyxiated him."[43] As men, are we similarly condemned, or is there a road of escape from the triad of men's violence and the precarious structures of masculinity that we ourselves re-create at our peril and that of women, children, and the world?

Prescribing a set of behavioral or legal changes to combat men's violence against women is obviously not enough. Even as more and more men are convinced there is a problem, this realization does not touch the unconscious structures of masculinity. Any man who is sympathetic to feminism is aware of the painful contradiction between his conscious views and his deeper emotions and feelings.

The analysis in this article suggests that men and women must address each corner of the triad of men's violence and the socioeconomic, psycho-sexual orders on which they stand. Or to put it more strongly, it is impossible to deal successfully with any one corner of this triad in isolation from the others.

The social context that nurtures men's violence and the relation between socioeconomic transformation and the end of patriarchy have been major themes of socialist feminist thought. This framework, though it is not without controversy and unresolved problems, is one I accept. Patriarchy and systems of authoritarianism and class domination feed on each other. Speaking of the relation of capitalism and the oppression of women, Michele Barrett says that male-female divisions

> are systematically embedded in the structure and texture of capitalist social relations . . . and they play an important part in the political and ideological stability of this society. They are constitutive of our subjectivity as well as, in part, of capitalist political and cultural hegemony. They are interwoven into a fundamental relationship between the wage-labour system and the organization of domestic life and it is impossible to imagine that they could be extracted from the relations of production and reproduction of capitalism without a massive transformation of those relations taking place.[44]

Radical socioeconomic and political change is a requirement for the end of men's violence. But organizing for macrosocial change is not enough to solve the problem of men's violence, not only because the problem is so pressing here and now, but because the continued existence of masculinity and surplus aggressiveness works against the fundamental macrosocial change we desire.

The many manifestations of violence against women have been an important focus of feminists. Women's campaigns and public education against rape, battering, sexual harassment, and more generally for control by women of their bodies are a key to challenging men's violence. Support by men, not only for the struggles waged by women, but in our own workplaces and among our friends is an important part of the struggle. There are many possible avenues for work by men among men. These include: forming counseling groups and support services for battering men (as is now happening in different cities in North America); championing the inclusion of clauses on sexual harassment in collective agreements and in the constitutions or by-laws of our trade unions, associations, schools, and political parties; raising money, campaigning for government funding, and finding other means of support for rape crisis centers and shelters for battered women; speaking out against violent and sexist pornography; building neighborhood campaigns on wife and child abuse; and personally refusing to collude with the sexism of our workmates, colleagues, and friends. The latter is perhaps the most difficult of all and requires patience, humor, and support from other men who are challenging sexism.

But because men's violence against women is inseparable from the other two corners of the triad of men's violence, solutions are very complex and difficult. Ideological changes and an awareness of problems are important but insufficient. While we can envisage changes in our child-rearing arrangements (which in turn would require radical economic changes), lasting solutions have to go far deeper. Only the development of non-surplus-repressive societies (whatever these might look like) will allow for the greater expression of human needs and, along with attacks on patriarchy per se, will reduce the split between active and passive psychological aims.[45]

The process of achieving these long-term goals contains many elements of economic, social, political, and psychological change, each of which requires a fundamental transformation of society. Such a transformation will not be created by an amalgam of changed individuals; but there is a relationship between personal change and our ability to construct organizational, political, and economic alternatives that will be able to mount a successful challenge to the status quo.

One avenue of personal struggle that is being engaged in by an increasing number of men has been the formation of men's support groups. Some groups focus on consciousness raising, but most groups stress the importance of men talking about their feelings, their relations with other men and with women, and any number of problems in their lives. At times these groups have been criticized by some antisexist men as yet another place for men to collude against women. The alternatives put forward are groups whose primary focus is either support for struggles led by women or the organization of direct, antisexist campaigns among men. These activities are very important, but so too is the development of new support structures among men. And these structures must go beyond the traditional form of consciousness raising.

Consciousness raising usually focuses on manifestations of the oppression of women and on the oppressive behavior of men. But as we have seen, masculinity is more than the sum total of oppressive forms of behavior. It is deeply and unconsciously embedded in the structure of our egos and superegos; it is what we have become. An awareness of oppressive behavior is important, but too often it only leads to guilt about being a man. Guilt is a profoundly conservative emotion and as such is not particularly useful for bringing about change. From a position of insecurity and guilt, people do not change or inspire others to change. After all, insecurity about one's male credentials played an important part in the individual acquisition of masculinity and men's violence in the first place.

There is a need to promote the personal strength and security necessary to allow men to make more fundamental personal changes and to confront sexism and heterosexism in society at large. Support groups usually allow men to talk about our feelings, how we too have been hurt growing up in a surplus-repressive society, and how we, in turn, act at times in an oppressive manner. We begin to see the connections between painful and frustrating experiences in our own lives and related forms of oppressive behavior. As Sheila Rowbotham notes, "the exploration of the internal areas of consciousness is a political necessity for us."[46]

Talking among men is a major step, but it is still operating within the acceptable limits of what men like to think of as rational behavior. Deep barriers and fears remain even when we can begin to recognize them. As well as talking, men need to encourage direct expression of emotions—grief, anger, rage, hurt, love—within these groups and the physical closeness that has been blocked by the repression of passive aims, by social prohibition, and by our own superegos and sense of what is right. This discharge of emotions has many functions and outcomes: like all forms of emotional and physical discharge it lowers the tension within the human system and reduces the likelihood of a spontaneous discharge of emotions through outer- or inner-directed violence.

But the expression of emotions is not an end in itself; in this context it is a means to an end. Stifling the emotions connected with feelings of hurt and pain acts as a sort of glue that allows the original repression to remain. Emotional discharge, in a situation of support and encouragement, helps unglue the ego structures that require us to operate in patterned, phobic, oppressive, and surplus-aggressive forms. In a sense it loosens up the repressive structures and allows us fresh insight into ourselves and our past. But if this emotional discharge happens in isolation or against an unwitting victim, it only reinforces the feelings of being powerless, out of control, or a person who must obsessively control others. Only in situations that contradict these feelings—that is, with the support, affection, encouragement, and backing of other men who experience similar feelings—does the basis for change exist.[47]

The encouragement of emotional discharge and open dialogue among men also enhances the safety we begin to feel among each other and in turn helps us to tackle obsessive, even if unconscious, fear of other men. This unconscious fear and lack of safety are the experience of most heterosexual men throughout their lives. The pattern for homosexual men differs, but growing up and living in a heterosexist, patriarchal culture implants similar fears, even if one's adult reality is different.

Receiving emotional support and attention from a group of men is a major contradiction to experiences of distance, caution, fear, and neglect from other men. This contradiction is the mechanism that allows further discharge, emotional change, and more safety. Safety among even a small group of our brothers gives us greater safety and strength among men as a whole. This gives us the confidence and sense of personal power to confront sexism and homophobia in all its various manifestations. In a sense, this allows us each to be a model of a strong, powerful man who does not need to operate in an oppressive and violent fashion in relation to women, to other men, or to himself. And that, I hope, will play some small part in the challenge to the oppressive reality of patriarchal, authoritarian, class societies. It will be changes in our own lives inseparably intertwined with changes in society as a whole that will sever the links in the triad of men's violence.

NOTES

My thanks to those who have given me comments on earlier drafts of this paper, in particular my father, Nathan Kaufman, and to Gad Horowitz. As well I extend my appreciation to the men I have worked with in various counseling situations who have helped me develop insights into the individual acquisition of violence and masculinity.

1. Herbert Marcuse, *Eros and Civilization* (Boston: Beacon Press, 1975; New York: Vintage, 1962); Gad Horowitz, *Repression* (Toronto: University of Toronto Press, 1977).

2. Part of Freud's wisdom was to recognize that, although the engendered psychology of the individual was the product of the maturation of the individual within an evolving social environment, the body was in the last analysis the subject and the object of our desires.

3. Michele Barrett and Mary McIntosh, *The Anti-Social Family* (London: Verso/New Left Books, 1982), 107.

4. Susan Brownmiller, *Against Our Will: Men, Women and Rape* (New York: Bantam Books, 1976), 6.

5. Alice Echols, "The New Feminism of Yin and Yang," in Ann Snitow *et al.*, eds., *Powers of Desire* (New York: Monthly Review Press, 1983), 439–59, and Alice Echols, "The Taming of the Id: Feminist Sexual Politics, 1968–83," in Carol Vance, ed., *Pleasure and Danger* (London: Routledge and Kegan Paul, 1984), 50–72. The two articles are essentially the same.

6. Aimé Césaire, *Discourse on Colonialism* (New York: Monthly Review Press, 1972), 21–2, first published in 1955 by Éditions Présence Africaine.

7. C. Tunnard, *The City of Man* (New York: Scribner, 1953), 43. Quoted in N. O. Brown, *Life against Death* (Middletown, Conn.: Wesleyan University Press, 1959), 283.

8. This is the approach, for example, of Suzanne Steinmetz. She says that macrolevel social and economic conditions (such as poverty, unemployment, inadequate housing, and the glorification and acceptance of violence) lead to high crime rates and a tolerance of violence that in turn leads to family aggression. See her *Cycle of Violence* (New York: Praeger, 1977), 30.

9. Juliet Mitchell, *Psychoanalysis and Feminism* (New York: Vintage, 1975), 362.

10. Joseph Conrad, *Lord Jim* (New York: Bantam Books, 1981), 146; first published 1900.

11. See for example Michele Barrett's thought-provoking book, *Women's Oppression Today* (London: Verso/New Left Books, 1980), 10–19, 250–1.

12. Jessica Benjamin, "Authority and the Family Revisited; or, A World without Fathers?" *New German Critique* (Winter 1978), 35.

13. See *ibid.,* 40, for a short discussion of Adorno and Horkheimer's *Dialectic of Enlightenment.*

14. Mary O'Brien, *The Politics of Reproduction* (London: Routledge and Kegan Paul, 1981), 54–5.

15. Simone de Beauvoir, *The Second Sex* (New York: Vintage, 1974), 162; first published 1949. Dorothy Dinnerstein pursues a similar line of argument but, in line with the thesis of her book, points to mother-raised-children as the source of these ambivalent feelings toward women. See Dorothy Dinnerstein, *The Mermaid and the Minotaur* (New York: Harper and Row, 1976), especially, 109–10.

16. Sidney Jourard, "Some Lethal Aspects of the Male Role," in Joseph H. Pleck and Jack Sawyer, eds., *Men and Masculinity* (Englewood Cliffs, N.J.: Prentice-Hall, 1974), 21–9.

17. Bertolt Brecht, *Threepenny Novel,* trans. Desmond I. Vesey (Harmondsworth, U.K.: Penguin, 1965), 282.

18. Marcuse, *op. cit.,* and Horowitz, *op. cit.*

19. Barrett and McIntosh, *op. cit.,* 29.

20. This is true not only because each socioeconomic system appears to create corresponding family forms, but because in turn, that family structure plays a large role in shaping the society's ideology. In Barrett and McIntosh's words, in our society a family perspective and family ideology have an "utterly hegemonic status" within society as a whole. And there is a dialectical interaction between family form and the organization of production and paid work (*ibid.,* 78, 130).

21. De Beauvoir, *op. cit., passim.*

22. Sigmund Freud, *Civilization and Its Discontents* (New York: W. W. Norton, 1962), 70, 72.

23. Gayle Rubin, "The Traffic in Women: Notes on the 'Political Economy' of Sex," in Rayna R. Reiter, ed., *Toward an Anthropology of Women* (New York: Monthly Review Press, 1975), 157–210.

24. Ken Kesey, *Sometimes a Great Notion* (New York: Bantam, 1965), 115. (One is eerily reminded of St. Augustine's statement, "Every breath I draw in is a sin." Quoted in Horowitz, *op cit.,* 211.)

25. De Beauvoir, *op. cit.,* 367.

26. Paul Willis, *Learning to Labor* (New York: Columbia University Press, 1981), 150. And see Stan Gray, "Sharing the Shop Floor," in M. Kaufman, ed., *Beyond Patriarchy* (Toronto: Oxford University Press, 1987).

27. Andrew Tolson, *The Limits of Masculinity* (London: Tavistock, 1977), 25.

28. Simone de Beauvoir, in the *Nouvel Observateur,* Mar. 1, 1976. Quoted in Diana E. H. Russell and Nicole Van de Ven, eds., *Crimes against Women* (Millbrae, Calif.: Les Femmes, 1976), xiv.

29. Among the sources on male violence that are useful, even if sometimes problematic, see Lenore E. Walker, *The Battered Woman* (New York: Harper Colophon, 1980); Russell and Van de Ven *op. cit.*; Judith Lewis Herman, *Father-Daughter Incest* (Cambridge, Mass.: Harvard University Press, 1981); Suzanne K. Steinmetz, *The Cycle of Violence* (New York: Praeger, 1977); Sylvia Levine and Joseph Koenig, *Why Men Rape* (Toronto: Macmillan, 1980); Susan Brownmiller, *op. cit.*; and Connie Guberman and Margie Wolfe, eds., *No Safe Place* (Toronto: Women's Press, 1985).

30. Levine and Koenig, *op. cit.,* 28, 42, 56, 72.

31. Meg Luxton, *More Than a Labour of Love* (Toronto: Women's Press, 1980), 66.

32. Margaret M. Killoran, "The Sound of Silence Breaking: Toward a Metatheory of Wife Abuse" (M.A. thesis, McMaster University, 1981), 148.

33. Barrett and Macintosh, *op. cit.,* 23.

34. Of course, household violence is not monopolized by men. In the United States roughly the same number of domestic homicides are committed by each sex. In 1975, 8.0% of homicides were committed by husbands against wives and 7.8% by wives against husbands. These figures, however, do not indicate the chain of violence, that is, the fact that most of these women were reacting to battering by their husbands. (See Steinmetz, *op. cit.,* 90.) Similarly, verbal and physical abuse of children appears to be committed by men and women equally. Only in the case of incest is there a near monopoly by men. Estimates vary greatly, but between one-fifth and one-third of all girls experience some sort of sexual contact with an adult male, in most cases with a father, stepfather, other relative, or teacher. (See Herman, *op. cit.,* 12 and *passim.*)

35. Luxton, *op, cit.,* 65.

36. This was pointed out by I. F. Stone in a 1972 article on the Vietnam war. At a briefing about the U.S. escalation of bombing in the North, the Pentagon official described U.S. strategy as two boys fighting: "If one boy gets the other in an arm lock, he can probably get his adversary to say 'uncle' if he increases the pressure in sharp, painful jolts and gives every indication of willingness to break the boy's arm" ("Machismo in Washington," reprinted in Pleck and Sawyer, *op. cit.,* 131). Although women are also among the victims of war, I include war in the category of violence against men because I am here referring to the casualty of war.

37. This is true both of masculinity as an institution and masculinity for the individual. Gay men keep certain parts of the self-oppressive masculine norm intact simply because they have grown up and live in a predominantly heterosexual, male-dominated society.

38. Horowitz, *op. cit.,* 99.

39. This formulation was first suggested to me by Charlie Kreiner at a men's counseling workshop in 1982.

40. D. H. Lawrence, *Women in Love* (Harmondsworth, U.K.: Penguin, 1960), 304–5; first published 1921.

41. Otto Fenichel, *The Psychoanalytic Theory of Neurosis* (New York: Norton, 1945), 212.

42. Emmanuel Reynaud, *Holy Virility,* trans. Ros Schwartz (London: Pluto Press, 1983), 41–2.

43. Gabriel García Márquez, *Autumn of the Patriarch,* trans. Gregory Rabassa (Harmondsworth, U.K.: Penguin, 1972), 111; first published 1967.

44. Barrett, *op. cit.,* 254–5. Willis follows a similar line of thought in his discussion of the development of the male working class. He says that patriarchy "helps to provide the real human and cultural conditions which . . . actually allow subordinate roles to be taken on 'freely' within liberal democracy" (Willis, *op. cit.,* 151). But then in turn, this reinforces the impediments to change by the maintenance of a division within the working class. As an article in the early 1970s in *Shrew* pointed out, "the tendency of male workers to think of themselves as men (i.e., powerful) rather than as workers (i.e., members of an oppressed group), promotes a false sense of privilege and power, and an identification with the world of men including the boss." Kathy McAfee and Myrna Wood, "Bread and Roses," quoted by Sheila Rowbotham, *Woman's Consciousness, Men's World* (Harmondsworth, U.K.: Penguin, 1973).

45. For a discussion of non-surplus-repressive societies, particularly in the sense of being complementary with Marx's notion of communism, see Horowitz, *op. cit.,* particularly chap. 7, and also Marcuse, *op. cit.,* especially chaps. 7, 10, and 11.

46. Rowbotham, *op. cit.,* 36.

47. As is apparent, although I have adopted a Freudian analysis of the unconscious and the mechanisms of repression, these observations on the therapeutic process—especially the importance of a supportive counseling environment, peer-counseling relations, emotional discharge, and the concept of contradiction—are those developed by forms of co-counseling, in particular, Reevaluation Counseling. But unlike the latter, I do not suppose that any of us can discharge all of our hurt, grief, and anger and uncover an essential self simply because our "self" is created through that process of frustration, hurt, and repression. Rather I feel that some reforming of the ego can take place that allows us to integrate more fully a range of needs and desires, which in turn reduces forms of behavior that are oppressive to others and destructive to ourselves. Furthermore, by giving us greater consciousness of our feelings and the means of discharge, and by freeing dammed-up sources of energy, these changes allow us to act more successfully to change the world.

Chapter Three

The Socio-Cultural Context of Rape
A Cross-Cultural Study

Peggy Reeves Sanday

In her comprehensive and important analysis of rape, Susan Brownmiller says that "when men discovered that they could rape, they proceeded to do it" and that "from prehistoric times to the present rape has played a critical function" (1975, 14–15). The critical function to which Brownmiller refers has been "to keep all women in a constant state of intimidation, forever conscious of the knowledge that the biological tool must be held in awe for it may turn to weapon with sudden swiftness borne of harmful intent" (1975, 209).

Brownmiller's attribution of violence to males and victimization to females strums a common theme in Western social commentary on the nature of human nature. Most of the popularizers of this theme present what amounts to a socio-biological view of human behavior which traces war, violence, and now rape to the violent landscape of our primitive ancestors, where, early on, the male tendency in these directions became genetically programmed in the fight for survival of the fittest. Human (viz. male) nature is conceived as an ever present struggle to overcome baser impulses bequeathed by "apish" ancestors. (For examples of this general theme, see Ardrey 1966; Lorenz 1966; Tiger 1969.)

The research described in the present paper departs from the familiar assumption that male nature is programmed for rape, and begins with another familiar, albeit less popular, assumption that human sexual behavior, though based in a biological need "is rather a sociological and cultural force than a mere bodily relation of two individuals" (Malinowski 1929, xxiii). With this assumption in mind, what follows is an examination of the socio-cultural context of sexual assault and an attempt to interpret its meaning. By understanding the meaning of rape, we can then make conjectures as to its function. Is it, as Susan Brownmiller suggests, an act that keeps all women in a constant state of intimidation, or is it an act that illuminates a larger social scenario?

This paper examines the incidence, meaning, and function of rape in tribal societies. Two general hypotheses guided the research: first, the incidence of rape varies cross-culturally; second, a high incidence of rape is embedded in a distinguishably

From the *Society for the Psychological Study of Social Issues, Journal of Social Issues* 37 (1981): 5–27 (edited). Reprinted by permission of Blackwell Publishing, Inc. Tables deleted in this volume can be found in the original.

different cultural configuration than a low incidence of rape. Using a standard cross-cultural sample of 156 tribal societies, the general objectives of the paper are:

1. to provide a descriptive profile of "rape prone" and "rape free" societies;
2. to present an analysis of the attitudes, motivations, and socio-cultural factors related to the incidence of rape.

Description of the Evidence

In most societies for which information on rape was available, rape is an act in which a male or a group of males sexually assaulted a woman. In a few cases, descriptions of women sexually assaulting a male or homosexual rape are reported. This study, however, was oriented exclusively to the analysis of rape committed by males against women.

The standard cross-cultural sample published by Murdock and White (1969) formed the basis for this research. This sample offers to scholars a representative sample of the world's known and well-described societies. The complete sample consists of 186 societies, each "pinpointed" to an identifiable sub-group of the society in question at a specific point in time. The time period for the sample societies ranges from 1750 B.C. (Babylonians) to the late 1960s. The societies included in the standard sample are distributed relatively equally among the following six major regions of the world: Sub-Saharan Africa, Circum-Mediterranean, East Eurasia, Insular Pacific, North America, South and Central America.

This analysis of rape was part of a larger study on the origins of sexual inequality (see Sanday 1981a). Due to the amount of missing information on the variables included in this larger study, thirty of the standard sample societies were excluded, reducing the final sample size to 156. Since many of the variables included in the larger study were pertinent to the analysis of the socio-cultural context of rape, the same sample was employed here.

The information for coding the variables came from codes published in the journal *Ethnology*; library materials; and the Human Relations Area Files. The data obtained from the latter two sources were coded by graduate students in anthropology at the University of Pennsylvania using codes developed by me on one-third of the standard sample societies. When the coding was completed, a random sample of societies was selected for checking. The percentage of items on which coders and checkers agreed averaged 88 percent of the twenty-one variables checked for each society. Disagreements were resolved either by myself or still another coder after rechecking the material.

There was a significant discrepancy between the number of societies for which information was obtained on rape for this study and that obtained by other authors employing the same sample. Broude and Greene (1976) were able to find information on the frequency of rape in only thirty-four of the standard sample societies, whereas for this study information was obtained for ninety-five of these societies. This discrepancy raises questions about the operational definitions of rape employed in the coding.

Although the codes used in the two studies were similar, my definition of "rape prone" included cases in which men rape enemy women, rape is a ceremonial act, and rape may be more a threat used by men to control women in certain ways than an actuality. Broude and Greene appear to have excluded such incidents from their coding and to have focused only on the intra-societal incidence of uncontrolled rape. The differences in these operational definitions are apparent from the information presented in Table 1.

A sub-sample of societies are listed in Table 1 along with the codes used in this study and the code given by Broude and Greene (1976). Broude and Greene report no information in nine societies where information on the incidence of rape was recorded in this study. The two codes agree in seven out of the remaining nine and disagree in two cases. Broude and Greene report that among the Azande rape is a rare occurrence, while in this study the Azande were classified as rape prone due to the practice of raiding for wives. Broude and Greene report that rape is absent among the Omaha, whereas I found evidence from several sources that rape is present. The ethnographic descriptions which led to my rape codes for the eighteen societies listed in Table 1 can be found in the following sections profiling "rape prone" and "rape free" societies.

Broude and Greene (1976) find that rape is absent or rare in 59 percent of the thirty-four societies for which they found information on the frequency of rape (see Table 2). They say that rape is "common, not atypical" in the remaining 41 percent. In this study, 47 percent of the societies were classified as "rape free"; 35 percent were classified in an intermediate category; and 18 percent were classified as "rape prone" (see Table 2). Thus

TABLE 1
Comparison of Two Codes for Rape

| Society No.[a] | Society Name | Sanday Code[b] | | Broude & Greene Code[b] |
		Rape Code	Type of Rape[c]	
11	Kikuyu	3	Ceremonial rape	No information
19	Ashanti	1	Rape is rare or absent	No information
13	Mbuti	1	Rape is rare or absent	Agrees with Sanday Code
14	Mongo	1	Rape is rare or absent	Agrees with Sanday Code
28	Azande	3	Rape of enemy women Rape cases reported	Disagrees (Rape rare)
41	Tuareg	1	Rape is rare or absent	No information
60	Gond	1	Rape is rare or absent	No information
66	Mongols	1	Rape is rare or absent	No information
70	Lakher	1	Rape is rare or absent	Agrees with Sanday Code
91	Arunta	3	Ceremonial rape	No information
108	Marshallese	3	Gang rape is accepted	Agrees with Sanday Code
127	Saulteaux	3	Rape used as threat	No information
143	Omaha	3	Rape used as punishment	Disagrees (Rape absent)
158	Cuna	1	Rape is rare or absent	Agrees with Sanday Code
163	Yanomamo	3	Rape of enemy women	Agrees with Sanday Code
166	Mundurucu	3	Rape used as punishment	Agrees with Sanday Code
169	Jivaro	1	Rape is rare or absent	No information
179	Shavante	3	Rape used as punishment	No information

[a]Refers to standard sample number listed by Murdock and White (1969).
[b]See Table 2 for the two rape codes.
[c]For each of the societies listed, the ethnographic descriptions of the incidence of rape are presented later in this paper.

TABLE 2
Cross-Cultural Incidence of Rape

Sanday Code	No. and % of Societies		Broude & Greene (1976:417) Code	No. and % of Societies	
Incidence of Rape (RA4)—	N	%	Frequency of Rape	N	%
1. *Rape Free*. Rape is reported as rare or absent.	45	47%	1. Absent	8	24%
2. Rape is reported as present, no report of frequency, or suggestion that rape is not atypical.	33	35%	2. Rare: isolated cases	12	35%
3. *Rape Prone*. Rape is accepted practice used to punish women, as part of a ceremony, or is *clearly* an act of moderate to high frequency carried out against own women or women of other societies.	17	18%	3. Common: not atypical	14	41%
Total	95	100%		34	100%

both studies support the first general hypothesis of this study: sexual assault is not a universal characteristic of tribal societies. The incidence of rape varies cross-culturally.

Profiles of "Rape Prone" Societies

In this study a "rape prone" society was defined as one in which the incidence of rape is high, rape is a ceremonial act, or rape is an act by which men punish or threaten women.

An example of a "rape prone" society is offered by Robert LeVine's (1959) description of sexual offenses among the Gusii of southwestern Kenya. In the European legal system which administers justice in the District where the Gusii live, a heterosexual assault is classified as rape when a medical examination indicates that the hymen of the alleged victim was recently penetrated by the use of painful force. When medical evidence is unobtainable, the case is classified as "indecent assault." Most cases are of the latter kind. The Gusii do not distinguish between rape and indecent assault. They use the following expressions to refer to heterosexual assault: "to fight" (a girl or woman); "to stamp on" (a girl or woman); "to spoil" (a girl or woman); "to engage in illicit intercourse." All of these acts are considered illicit by the Gusii. LeVine uses the term rape "to mean the culturally disvalued use of coercion by a male to achieve the submission of a female to sexual intercourse" (1959, 965).

Based on court records for 1955 and 1956 LeVine estimates that the annual rate of rape is 47.2 per 100,000 population. LeVine believes that this figure grossly underestimates the Gusii rape rate. During the same period the annual rape rate in urban areas of the United States was 13.85 per 100,000 (13.1 for rural areas). Thus, the rate of Gusii rape is extraordinarily high.

Normal heterosexual intercourse between Gusii males and females is conceived as an act in which a man overcomes the resistance of a woman and causes her pain. When a bride is unable to walk after her wedding night, the groom is considered by his friends "a real man" and he is able to boast of his exploits, particularly if he has been able to make her cry. Older women contribute to the groom's desire to hurt his new wife. These women insult the groom, saying:

> "You are not strong, you can't do anything to our daughter. When you slept with her you didn't do it like a man. You have a small penis which can do nothing. You should grab our daughter and she should be hurt and scream—then you're a man." (LeVine 1959, 969)

The groom answers boastfully:

> "I am a man! If you were to see my penis you would run away. When I grabbed her she screamed. I am not a man to be joked with. Didn't she tell you? She cried—ask her!" (LeVine 1959, 969)

Thus, as LeVine says (1959, 971), "legitimate heterosexual encounters among the Gusii are aggressive contests, involving force and pain-inflicting behavior." Under circumstances that are not legitimate, heterosexual encounters are classified as rape when the girl chooses to report the act.

LeVine estimates that the typical Gusii rape is committed by an unmarried young man on an unmarried female of a different clan. He distinguishes between three types of rape: rape resulting from seduction, premeditated sexual assault, and abduction (1959).

Given the hostile nature of Gusii sexuality, seduction classifies as rape when a Gusii female chooses to bring the act to the attention of the public. Premarital sex is forbidden, but this does not stop Gusii boys from trying to entice girls to intercourse. The standard pose of the Gusii girl is reluctance, which means that it is difficult for the boy to interpret her attitude as being either willing or unwilling. Misunderstandings between girl and boy can be due to the eagerness of the boy and his inability to perceive the girl's cues of genuine rejection, or to the girl's failure to make the signs of refusal in unequivocal fashion. The boy may discover the girl's unwillingness only after he has forced himself on her.

Fear of discovery may turn a willing girl into one who cries rape. If a couple engaging in intercourse out of doors is discovered, the girl may decide to save her reputation by crying out that she was being raped. Rape may also occur in cases when a girl has encouraged a young man to present her with gifts, but then denies him sexual intercourse. If the girl happens to be married, she rejects the boy's advances because she is afraid of supernatural sanctions against adultery. Out of frustration, the boy (who may not know that the girl is married) may resort to rape, and she reports the deed. In some cases one or more boys may attack a single girl in premeditated sexual assault. The boys may beat the girl badly and tear her clothing. Sometimes the girl is dragged off to the hut of one of them and forced into coitus. After being held for a couple of days the girl is freed. In these cases rupture of the hymen and other signs of attack are usually present.

The third type of rape occurs in the context of wife abduction. When a Gusii man is unable to present the bridewealth necessary for a normal marriage and cannot persuade a girl to elope, he may abduct a girl from a different clan. The man's friends will be enlisted to carry out the abduction. The young men are frequently rough on the girl, beating her and tearing her clothes. When she arrives at the home of the would-be lover, he attempts to persuade her to remain with him until bridewealth can be raised. Her refusal is ignored and the wedding-night sexual contest is performed with the clansmen helping in overcoming her resistance.

Of these three types of rape, the first and third are unlawful versions of legitimate patterns. Seduction is accepted when kept within the bounds of discretion. Abduction is an imitation of traditional wedding procedures. Abduction lacks only the legitimizing bridewealth and the consent of the bride and her parents. In both of these cases LeVine says, "there is a close parallel between the criminal act and the law-abiding culture pattern to which it is related." Seduction and abduction classify as rape when the girl chooses to report the incident.

Data collected from the standard cross-cultural sample allows us to place the hostility characterizing Gusii heterosexual behavior in cross-cultural perspective. Broude and Greene (1976), who published codes for twenty sexual practices, find that male sexual advances are occasionally or typically hostile in one-quarter (26 percent) of the societies for which information was available. They found that males were typically forward in verbal (not physical) sexual overtures in 40 percent of the societies, that females solicited or desired physical aggression in male sexual overtures in 11 percent of the societies, and that males did not make sexual overtures or were diffident or shy in 23 percent of the societies.

Examination of a variety of "rape prone" societies shows that the Gusii pattern of rape is found elsewhere but that it is by no means the only pattern which can be observed. For example, in several societies the act of rape occurs to signal readiness for marriage and is a ceremonial act. Since this act signifies male domination of female genitals, its occurrence was treated as a diagnostic criterion for classification as "rape prone."

Among the Kikuyu of East Africa it is reported that in former times, as part of initiation, every boy was expected to perform the act of ceremonial rape called *Kuihaka muunya* (to smear oneself with salt earth) in order to prove his manhood. It was thought that until a boy had performed the act of rape he could not have lawful intercourse with a Kikuyu woman and hence could not marry. During the initiation period boys would wander the countryside in bands of up to one hundred in number. The object of each band was to find a woman on whom to commit the rape. The ideal woman was one from an enemy tribe who was married. In practice it appears that the ceremonial rape consisted of nothing more than masturbatory ejaculation on the woman's body or in her presence. Immediately after the act the boy was able to throw away the paraphernalia which marked him with the status of neophite (Lambert 1956).

Rape marks a girl as marriageable among the Arunta of Australia. At age fourteen or fifteen the Arunta girl is taken out into the bush by a group of men for the vulva-cutting ceremony. A designated man cuts the girl's vulva, after which she is gang raped by a group of men which does not include her future husband. When the ceremony is concluded the girl is taken to her husband and from then on no one else has the right of access to her (Spencer and Gillen 1927).

In other rape-prone societies, rape is explicitly linked to the control of women and to male dominance. Among the Northern Saulteaux the assumption of male dominance is clearly expressed in the expectation that a man's potential sexual rights over the woman he chooses must be respected. A woman who turns a man down too abruptly insults him and invites aggression. There is a Northern Saulteaux tale about a girl who was considered too proud because she refused to marry. Accordingly, a group of medicine men lured her out into the bush, where she was raped by each in turn (Hallowell 1955). Such tales provide women with a fairly good idea of how they should behave in relation to men.

The attitude that women are "open" for sexual assault is frequently found in the societies of the Insular Pacific. For example, in the Marshall Islands one finds the belief that "every woman is like a passage." Just as every canoe is permitted to sail from the open sea into the lagoon through the passage, so every man is permitted to have intercourse with every woman (except those who are excluded on account of blood kinship). A trader, well acquainted with the language and customs of one group of Marshall Islanders, reported the following incident. One day while standing at the trading post he saw twenty young men enter the bushes, one after another. Following the same path, he discovered a young girl stretched out on the ground, rigid and unconscious. When he accused the young men of cruel treatment they replied: "It is customary here for every young man to have intercourse with every girl" (Erdland 1914, 98–99).

In tropical-forest societies of South America and in Highland New Guinea it is fairly frequent to find the threat of rape used to keep women from the men's houses or from viewing male sacred objects. For example, Shavante women were strictly forbidden to observe male sacred ceremonies. Women caught peeking are threatened with manhandling, rape, and disfigurement (Maybury-Lewis 1967).

Perhaps the best known example of rape used to keep women away from male ritual objects is found in the description of the Mundurucu, a society well known to anthropologists due to the work of Robert and Yolanda Murphy. The Mundurucu believe that there was a time when women ruled and sex roles were reversed, with the exception that women could not hunt. During that time, it is said, women were the sexual aggressors and men were sexually submissive and did women's work. Women controlled the "sacred trumpets" (the symbols of power) and the men's houses. The trumpets are believed to contain the spirits of the ancestors, who demand ritual offering of meat. Since women did not hunt and could not make these offerings, men were able to take the trumpets from them, thereby establishing male dominance. The trumpets are secured in special chambers within the men's houses, and no woman can see them under penalty of gang rape. Such a threat is necessary because men believe that women will attempt to seize from the men the power they once had. Gang rape is also the means by which men punish sexually "wanton" women (Murphy and Murphy 1974).

Another expression of male sexual aggressiveness, which is classified as rape in this study, is the practice of sexually assaulting enemy women during warfare. The Yanomamo, described by Napoleon Chagnon and Marvin Harris, are infamous for their brutality toward women. The Yanomamo, according to Harris (1977), "practice an especially brutal form of male supremacy involving polygyny, frequent wife beating, and gang rape of captured enemy women." The Yanomamo, Harris says, "regard fights over women as the primary causes of their wars" (1977, 69). Groups raid each other for wives in an area where marriageable women are in short supply due to the practice of female infanticide. The number of marriageable women is also affected by the desire on the part of successful warriors to have several wives to mark their superior status as "fierce men." A shortage of women for wives also motivates Azande (Africa) warfare. Enemy women were taken by Azande soldiers as wives. Evans-Pritchard calls these women "slaves of war" and says that they were "not regarded very differently from ordinary wives, their main disability being that they had no family or close kin to turn to in times of trouble" (1971, 251). The absence of close kin, of course, made these women more subservient and dependent on their husbands.

Another source on the Azande discusses how the act of rape when committed against an Azande woman is treated. If the woman is not married, this source reports, the act is not treated as seriously. If the woman is married, the rapist can be put to death by the husband. If the rapist is allowed to live, he may be judged guilty of adultery and asked to pay the chief twenty knives (the commonly used currency in marriage exchanges) and deliver a wife to the wronged husband. This source indicates that the rape of a woman is not permitted but the punishments are established, suggesting that rape is a frequent occurrence (Lagae 1926).

Among some American Indian buffalo hunters, it is not uncommon to read that rape is used as a means to punish adultery. There is a practice among the Cheyenne of the Great Plains known as "to put a woman on the prairie." This means that the outraged husband of an adulterous woman invites all the unmarried members of his military society to feast on the prairie where they each rape the woman (Hoebel 1960). Among the Omaha, a woman with no immediate kin who commits adultery may be gang raped and abandoned by her husband (Dorsey 1884). Mead reports that the Omaha considered a "bad woman" fair game for any man. No discipline, no set of standards, other than to be cautious of an avenging father or brother and to observe the rule of exogamy, Mead says, kept young men from regarding rape as a great adventure. Young Omaha men, members of the Antler society, would prey upon divorced women or women considered loose (Mead 1932).

Summarizing, a rape-prone society, as defined here, is one in which sexual assault by men of women is either culturally allowable or largely overlooked. Several themes interlink the above descriptions. In all, men are posed as a social group against women. Entry into the adult male or female group is marked in some cases by rituals that include rape. In other cases, rape preserves the ceremonial integrity of the male group and signifies its status vis-à-vis women. The theme of women as property is suggested when the aggrieved husband is compensated for the rape of his wife by another man, or when an adulterous woman is gang raped by her husband and his unmarried compatriots. In these latter cases, the theme of the dominant male group is joined with a system of economic exchange in which men act as exchange agents and women comprise the medium of exchange. This is not to say that rape exists in all societies in which there is ceremonial induction into manhood, male secret societies, or compensation for adultery. For further illumination of the socio-cultural context of rape we can turn to an examination of rape-free societies.

Profiles of "Rape Free" Societies

Rape-free societies are defined as those where the act of rape is either infrequent or does not occur. Forty-seven percent of the societies for which information on the incidence or presence of rape was available (see Table 2) were classified in the rape-free category. Societies were classified in this category on the basis of the following kinds of statements found in the sources used for the sample societies.

Among the Taureg of the Sahara, for example, it is said that "rape does not exist, and when a woman refuses a man, he never insists nor will he show himself jealous of a more successful comrade" (Blanguernon 1955, 134). Among the Pygmies of the Ituri forest in Africa, while a boy may rip off a girl's outer bark cloth, if he can catch her, he may never have intercourse with her without her permission. Turnbull (1965), an anthropologist who lived for some time among the Pygmies and became closely identified with them, reports that he knew of no cases of rape. Among the Jivaro of South America rape is not recognized as such, and informants could recall no case of a woman violently resisting sexual intercourse. They say that a man would never commit such an act if the woman resisted, because she would tell her family and they would punish him. Among the Nkundo Mongo of Africa it is said that rape in the true sense of the word—that is, the abuse of a woman by the use of violence—is most unusual. If a woman does not consent, the angry seducer leaves her, often insulting her to the best of his ability. Rape is also unheard of among the Lakhers, and in several villages the anthropologist was told that there had never been a case of rape.

Other examples of statements leading to the classification of rape free are listed as follows:

> Cuna (South America), "Homosexuality is rare, as is rape. Both . . . are regarded as sins, punishable by God." (Stout 1947, 39)

> Khalka Mongols (Outer Mongolia), "I put this question to several well-informed Mongols: —what punishment is here imposed for rape? . . . one well-educated lama said frankly: "We have no crimes of this nature here. Our women never resist." (Maiskii 1921, 98)

> Gond (India), "It is considered very wrong to force a girl to act against her will. Such cases of ghotul-rape are not common . . . If then a boy forces a girl against her will, and the others hear of it, he is fined." (Elwin 1947, 656)

The above quotes may obscure the actual incidence of rape. Such quotes, leading to the classification of societies as "rape free," achieve greater validity when placed within the context of other information describing heterosexual interaction.

There is considerable difference in the character of heterosexual interaction in societies classified as "rape prone" when compared with those classified as "rape free." In "rape free" societies women are treated with considerable respect, and prestige is attached to female reproductive and productive roles. Interpersonal violence is minimized, and a people's attitude regarding the natural environment is one of reverence rather than one of exploitation. Turnbull's description of the Mbuti Pygmies, of the Ituri forest in Africa, provides a prototypical profile of a "rape free" society (1965).

Violence between the sexes, or between anybody, is virtually absent among the net-hunting Mbuti Pygmies when they are in their forest environment. The Mbuti attitude toward the forest is reflective of their attitude toward each other. The forest is addressed as "father," "mother," "lover," and "friend." The Mbuti say that the forest is everything — the provider of food, shelter, warmth, clothing, and affection. Each person and animal is endowed with some spiritual power which "derives from a single source whose physical manifestation is the forest itself." The ease of the Mbuti relationship to their environment is reflected in the relationship between the sexes. There is little division of labor by sex. The hunt is frequently a joint effort. A man is not ashamed to pick mushrooms and nuts if he finds them, or to wash and clean a baby. In general, leadership is minimal and there is no attempt to control, or to dominate, either the geographical or human environment. Decision making is by common consent; men and women have equal say because hunting and gathering are both important to the economy. The forest is the only recognized authority of last resort. In decision making, diversity of opinion may be expressed, but prolonged disagreement is considered to be "noise" and offensive to the forest. If husband and wife disagree, the whole camp may act to mute their antagonism, lest the disagreement become too disruptive to the social unit (see Turnbull 1965).

The essential details of Turnbull's idyllic description of the Mbuti are repeated in other "rape free" societies. The one outstanding feature of these societies is the ceremonial importance of women and the respect accorded the contribution women make to social continuity, a respect which places men and women in relatively balanced power spheres. This respect is clearly present among the Mbuti and in more complex "rape free" societies.

In the West African kingdom of Ashanti, for example, it is believed that only women can contribute to future generations. Ashanti women say:

> I am the mother of the man. . . . I alone can transmit the blood to a king. . . . If my sex die in the clan then that very clan becomes extinct, for be there one, or one thousand male members left, not one can transmit the blood, and the life of the clan becomes measured on this earth by the span of a man's life. (Rattray 1923, 79)

The importance of the feminine attributes of growth and reproduction are found in Ashanti religion and ritual. Priestesses participate with priests in all major rituals. The Ashanti creation story emphasizes the complementarity and inseparability of male and female. The main female deity, the Earth Goddess, is believed to be the receptacle of past and future generations as well as the source of food and water (Rattray 1923, 1927). The sacred linkage of earth-female-blood makes the act of rape incongruous in Ashanti culture. Only one incident of rape is reported by the main ethnographer of the Ashanti. In this case the man involved was condemned to death (Rattray 1927, 211).

In sum, rape-free societies are characterized by sexual equality and the notion that the sexes are complementary. Though the sexes may not perform the same duties or have the same rights or privileges, each is indispensable to the activities of the other (see Sanday 1981a for examples of sexual equality). The key to understanding the relative absence of rape in rape-free as opposed to rape-prone societies is the importance, which in some cases is sacred, attached to the contribution women make to social continuity. As might be expected, and as will be demonstrated below, interpersonal violence is uncommon in rape-free societies. It is not that men are necessarily prone to rape; rather, where interpersonal violence is a way of life, violence frequently achieves sexual expression.

Approaches to the Etiology of Rape

Three general approaches characterize studies of the etiology of rape. One approach focuses on the broader socio-cultural milieu; another turns to individual characteristics. The first looks at how rapists act out the broader social script; the second emphasizes variables like the character of parent-child interaction. A third approach, which may focus on either individual or social factors, is distinguishable by the assumption that male sexual repression will inevitably erupt in the form of sexual violence. These approaches, reviewed briefly in this section, guided the empirical analysis of the socio-cultural context of rape in tribal societies.

Based on his study of the Gusii, LeVine (1959) hypothesizes that four factors will be associated with the incidence of rape cross-culturally:

1. severe formal restrictions on the nonmarital sexual relations of females;
2. moderately strong sexual inhibitions on the part of females;
3. economic or other barriers to marriage that prolong the bachelorhood of some males into their late twenties;
4. the absence of physical segregation of the sexes.

The implicit assumption here is that males who are denied sexual access to women will obtain access by force unless men are separated from women. Such an assumption depicts men as creatures who cannot control their sexual impulses, and women as the unfortunate victims.

LeVine's profile of the Gusii suggests that broader social characteristics are related to the incidence of rape. For example, there is the fact that marriage among the Gusii occurs almost always between feuding clans. The Gusii have a proverb which states, "Those whom we marry are those whom we fight" (1959, 966). The close correspondence between the Gusii heterosexual relationship and intergroup hostilities suggests the hypothesis that the nature of intergroup relations is correlated with the nature of the heterosexual relationship and the incidence of rape.

The broader approach to the etiology of rape is contained in Susan Brownmiller's contention that rape is the means by which men keep women in a state of fear. This contention is certainly justified in societies where men use rape as a threat to keep women from viewing their sacred objects (the symbol of power) or rape is used to punish women. In societies like the Mudurucu, the ideology of male dominance is upheld by threatening women with rape. Just as the quality of intergroup relations among the Gusii is reflected in heterosexual relations, one could suggest that the quality of interpersonal relations is reflected in the incidence of rape. In societies where males are trained to be dominant and interpersonal relations are marked by outbreaks of violence, one can predict that females may become the victims in the playing out of the male ideology of power and control.

A broader socio-cultural approach is also found in the work of Wolfgang and Ferracuti (1967) and Amir (1971). Wolfgang and Ferracuti present the concept of the subculture of violence which is formed of those from the lower classes and the disenfranchised. The prime value is the use of physical aggression as a demonstration of masculinity and toughness. In his study of rape, Amir placed the rapist "squarely within the subculture of violence" (Brownmiller 1975, 181). Rape statistics in Philadelphia showed that in 43 percent of the cases examined, rapists operated in pairs or groups. The rapists tended to be in the 15–19 age bracket, the majority were not married, and 90 percent belonged to the lower socio-economic class and lived in inner-city neighborhoods where there was also a high degree of crime against the person. In addition, 71 percent of the rapes were planned. In general, the profile presented by Amir is reminiscent of the pattern of rape found among the Kikuyu, where a band of boys belonging to a guild roamed the countryside in search of a woman to gang rape as a means of proving their manhood and as a prelude to marriage. Brownmiller (1975, 181) summarizes Amir's study with the following observations:

> Like assault, rape is an act of physical damage to another person, and like robbery it is also an act of acquiring property: the intent is to "have" the female body in the acquisitory meaning of the term. A woman is perceived by the rapist both as hated person and desired property. Hostility against her and possession of her may be simultaneous motivations, and the hatred for her is expressed in the same act that is the attempt to "take" her against her will. In one violent crime, rape is an act against person and property.

The importance of the work of Wolfgang and Ferracuti, Amir, and Brownmiller's observations lies in demonstrating that rape is linked with an overall pattern of violence and that part of this pattern includes the concept of woman as property. From the short descriptions of rape in some of the societies presented above, it is clear rape is likely to occur in what I would call, to borrow from Wolfgang, cultures of violence. Rape-prone societies, as noted, are likely to include payment to the wronged husband, indicating that the concept of women as property also exists. This concept is not new to anthropology. It has been heavily stressed in the work of Levi-Strauss, who perceives tribal women as objects in an elaborate exchange system between men.

The second type of approach to the understanding of rape focuses on the socialization process and psychoanalytic variables. This approach is reflected in the following quote from the conclusions of David Abrahamsen, who conducted a Rorschach study on the wives of eight convicted rapists in 1954. Abrahamsen (1960, 165) says:

> The conclusions reached were that the wives of the sex offenders on the surface behaved toward men in a submissive and masochistic way but latently denied their femininity and showed an aggressive masculine orientation; they unconsciously invited sexual aggression, only to respond to it with coolness and rejection. They stimulated their husbands into attempts to prove themselves, attempts which necessarily ended in frustration and increased their husbands' own doubts about their masculinity. In doing so, the wives

unknowingly continued the type of relationship the offender had had with his mother. There can be no doubt that the sexual frustration which the wives caused is one of the factors motivating rape, which might be tentatively described as a displaced attempt to force a seductive but rejecting mother into submission.

Brownmiller (1975, 179) includes this quote in her analysis of police-blotter rapists, and her reaction to it is rather interesting. She rejects Abrahamsen's conclusions because they place the burden of guilt not on the rapist but on his mother and wife. The fact of the matter is that dominance cannot exist without passivity, as sadism cannot exist without masochism. What makes men sadistic and women masochistic, or men dominant and women passive, must be studied as part of an overall syndrome. Abrahamsen's conclusions certainly apply to Gusii males and females. With respect to the way in which Gusii wives invite sexual aggression from their husbands consider the following description of various aspects of Gusii nuptials:

> . . . the groom in his finery returns to the bride's family where he is stopped by a crowd of women who deprecate his physical appearance. Once he is in the house of the bride's mother and a sacrifice has been performed by the marriage priest, the women begin again, accusing the groom of impotence on the wedding night and claiming that his penis is too small to be effective. . . . When the reluctant bride arrives at the groom's house, the matter of first importance is the wedding night sexual performance. . . . The bride is determined to put her new husband's sexual competence to the most severe test possible. She may take magical measures which are believed to result in his failure in intercourse. . . . The bride usually refuses to get onto the bed: if she did not resist the groom's advances she would be thought sexually promiscuous. At this point some of the young men may forcibly disrobe her and put her on the bed. . . . As he proceeds toward sexual intercourse she continues to resist and he must force her into position. Ordinarily she performs the practice known as *ogotega*, allowing him between her thighs but keeping the vaginal muscles so tense that penetration is impossible. . . . Brides are said to take pride in the length of time they can hold off their mates. (LeVine 1959, 967–969)

The relations between parents and children among the Gusii also fit Abrahamsen's conclusions concerning the etiology of rape. The son has a close and dependent relationship with his mother. The father is aloof from all his children, but especially his daughters. The father's main function is to punish, which means that for the Gusii girl, her early connection with men is one of avoidance and fear. On the other hand, the relationship of the Gusii boy with his mother is characterized by dependence and seduction.

Studies of the etiology of rape suggest several hypotheses that can be tested cross-culturally. These hypotheses are not opposed; they are stated at different explanatory levels. One set phrases the explanation in socio-cultural terms, the other in psycho-cultural terms. Still another, only touched on above, suggests that male sexuality is inherently explosive unless it achieves heterosexual outlet. This latter assumption, implicit in LeVine's hypotheses mentioned above, also draws on the notion, most recently expressed in the work of Stoller (1979), that sexual excitement is generated by the desire, overt or hidden, to harm another. If the latter were the case, we would be led to believe that rape would exist in all societies. The argument presented here, however, suggests that rape is an enactment not of human nature, but of socio-cultural forces.

Thus, the prevalence of rape should be associated with the expressions of these forces. Some of these expressions and their correlation with the incidence of rape are examined in the next section.

Socio-Cultural Correlates of Rape

Four general hypotheses are suggested by the work of LeVine, Brownmiller, Abrahamsen, Wolfgang, and Amir. These hypotheses are:

1. sexual repression is related to the incidence of rape;
2. intergroup and interpersonal violence is enacted in male sexual violence;
3. the character of parent-child relations is enacted in male sexual violence;
4. rape is an expression of a social ideology of male dominance.

These hypotheses were tested by collecting data on: variables relating to child rearing; behavior indicating sexual repression; interpersonal and intergroup violence; sexual separation; glorification of the male role and an undervaluation of the female role.

All but the first of the general hypotheses listed above were supported. There is no significant correlation between variables measuring sexual repression and the incidence of rape. Admittedly, however, sexual repression is very difficult to measure. The variables may not, in fact, be related to sexual abstinence. These variables are: length of the post-partum sex taboo (a variable which indicates how long the mother abstains from sexual intercourse after the birth of a child); attitude toward premarital sex (a variable which ranges between the disapproval and approval of premarital sex); age at marriage for males; and the number of taboos reflecting male avoidance of female sexuality.

The correlations support the hypothesis that intergroup and interpersonal violence is enacted in sexual violence against females. Raiding other groups for wives is significantly associated with the incidence of rape. The intensity of interpersonal violence in a society is also positively correlated with the incidence of rape, as is the presence of an ideology which encourages men to be tough and aggressive. Finally, when warfare is reported as being frequent or endemic (as opposed to absent or occasional) rape is more likely to be present.

The character of relations between parents and children is not strongly associated with the incidence of rape. When the character of the father-daughter relationship is primarily indifferent, aloof, cold, and stern, rape is more likely to be present. The same is true when fathers are distant from the care of infants. However, there is no relationship between the nature of the mother-son tie (as measured in this study) and the incidence of rape.

There is considerable evidence supporting the notion that rape is an expression of a social ideology of male dominance. Female power and authority is lower in rape-prone societies. Women do not participate in public decision making in these societies, and males express contempt for women as decision makers. In addition, there is greater sexual separation in rape-prone societies, as indicated by the presence of structures or places where the sexes congregate in single-sex groups.

The correlates of rape strongly suggest that rape is the playing out of a socio-cultural script in which the expression of personhood for males is directed by, among other things, interpersonal violence and an ideology of toughness. If we see the sexual act as the ultimate emotional expression of the self, then it comes as no surprise that male sexuality is phrased in physically aggressive terms when other expressions of self are phrased in these terms. This explanation does not rule out the importance of the relationship between parents and children, husbands and wives. Raising a violent son requires certain behavior patterns in parents, behaviors that husbands may subsequently act out as adult males. Sexual repression does not explain the correlations. Rape is not an instinct triggered by celibacy, enforced for whatever reason. Contrary to what some social scientists assume, men are not animals whose sexual behavior is programmed by instinct. Men are human beings whose sexuality is biologically based and culturally encoded.

Conclusion

Rape in tribal societies is part of a cultural configuration that includes interpersonal violence, male dominance, and sexual separation. In such societies, as the Murphys (1974, 197) say about the Mundurucu: "men . . . use the penis to dominate their women." The question remains as to what motivates the rape-prone cultural configuration. Considerable evidence (see Sanday 1981a) suggests that this configuration evolves in societies faced with depleting food resources, migration, or other factors contributing to a dependence on male destructive capacities as opposed to female fertility.

In tribal societies women are often equated with fertility and growth, men with aggression and destruction. More often than not, the characteristics associated with maleness and femaleness are equally valued. When people perceive an imbalance between the food supply and population needs, or when populations are in competition for diminishing resources, the male role is accorded greater prestige. Females are perceived as objects to be controlled as men struggle to retain or to gain control of their environment. Behaviors and attitudes prevail that separate the sexes and force men into a posture of proving their manhood. Sexual violence is one of the ways in which men remind themselves that they are superior. As such, rape is part of a broader struggle for control in the face of difficult circumstances. Where men are in harmony with their environment, rape is usually absent.

The insights garnered from the cross-cultural study of rape in tribal societies bear on the understanding and treatment of rape in our own. Ours is a heterogeneous society in which more men than we like to think feel that they do not have mastery over their destiny and who learn from the script provided by nightly television that violence is a way of achieving the material rewards that all Americans expect. It is important to understand that violence is socially and not biologically programmed. Rape is not an integral part of male nature, but the means by which men programmed for violence express their sexual selves. Men who are conditioned to respect the female virtues of growth and the sacredness of life do not violate women. It is significant that in societies where nature is held sacred, rape occurs only rarely. The incidence of rape in our society will be reduced to the extent that boys grow to respect women and the qualities so often associated with femaleness in other societies—namely, nurturance, growth, and nature. Women can contribute to the socialization of boys by making these respected qualities in their struggle for equal rights.

Gender Violence in the United States

As in any society, social relations in the United States have been influenced by the cultural, political, and economic conditions within which they have emerged. Gender, as a central organizing principle in societies, has mediated the distribution of power and the division of labor throughout the nation's history. In the early colonial period, for example, households and communities were the primary institutions operating in the lives of European settlers. The political sphere was governed from afar, and politics, in general, were less directly experienced by Americans than is the case today. In European American families, gender relations were determined in part by traditional relations in their countries of origin, as well as by the specific experiences of being bound together in an economy in which households were the central producing and consuming units. In some communities, families were also affected by collective acceptance or abhorrence of the sex/gender systems of native tribes with whom settlers came into contact. For example, in Free Love and other utopian experiments of the early colonial period, European colonists experimented with radical sexual and familial practices such as interracial marriages, multiple-partner unions, and nonsexual companionable communities (D'Emilio and Freedman 1988), based in some cases as much on their observations of native groups as on their collective sense that these alternative patterns were liberating for males and females.

By and large, however, gender was organized around the division of labor in what was an agricultural-based subsistence economy, although mediating relationships such as those formed in churches and communities provided significant contributions. Monogamous, heterosexual families were prescribed and blessed by Christian churches, and communities regulated sanctions regarding the use of force and violence in the context of daily relationships. There is evidence that women had more decision-making power, relative to men, in the household-based economy of the colonial period than in any other period in American history. Historical documents also suggest that women were seen as autonomous sexual beings in their own right, rather than merely the object possessions of men. Nevertheless, domestic violence, rape, incest, and various other forms of sexual coercion are documented in the personal and public records that have been preserved from the early colonial period (D'Emilio and Freedman 1988).

Large-scale economic change in any social system has profound repercussions in the various other institutions that compose the system. In the nineteenth-century United States, the gradual evolution from a predominantly agrarian subsistence economy to an industrial capitalist structure had profound concomitant effects on the social organization of gender in families, in the political sphere, and in the cultural meanings and artifacts of the society. One major change was that wage-earning replaced home-manufacture as the driving force in a family's acquisition of durable goods, and wage-earners became increasingly central in the household. Between the late 1700s and the close of the nineteenth century, men became increasingly associated with wage labor in the industrial economy (Pleck and Pleck 1980). Women, although they continued to labor in and out of the industrial economy, were increasingly associated with a supposedly nonproductive family sphere, and this association contributed to a decline in their economic and social power relative to men. It is during this time period that womanhood became associated with frailty, domestic subservience, and romantic love, and men's familial and emotional attachments to women became increasingly invisible as they were increasingly defined by their work outside the home (Cancian 1988).

Changes in the organization of family alter not only social definitions of masculinity and femininity but also the regulation of sexuality. In the early industrial period, the transition of the family from a system of production to primarily one of consumption was accompanied by an overall shift in functions for the family as a social unit. Family became associated with intimacy and privacy, juxtaposed against an ever-expanding public sphere of formal organizations. Sexuality became increasingly less public as it is situated in the ideal, self-contained nuclear family unit. Neighbors and extended family members lost power over the regulation of community behavior. Culturally, the nineteenth century is often depicted as a time of repressed sexuality; indeed, the privatization of family, and the situation of sexuality within its boundaries, contributed to the lessening of public discourse about, and public displays of, sexuality.

As suggested in the preceding section, the exploitation of women by men in both intimate relationships and institutional contexts often exists simultaneously with economic systems that are exploitative and hierarchically organized. As the United States industrialized, conditions emerged within which violating women was more easily rationalized, given their perceived status as weak, intellectually inferior, and less central to the productive sphere of society. Contributing to women's vulnerability is the invisibility of this exploitation in the privatized family. This is the case in the United States, even though family is culturally defined as a haven of nurturing and love.

The sexual and feminist revolutions of the 1960s profoundly challenged the ideal depictions of masculinity, femininity, family, and sexuality in ways that affect both private and public activity. Sexuality increasingly has been cast as a public issue, sparking heated debates about nature, morality, and cultural values. Changes in sexual practice have been evolving simultaneously with changes in family organization, work roles, and the very structure of the U.S. economy. As the industrial labor market has been replaced by a primarily service-oriented economy, more women have entered the paid work force, usually in jobs earmarked specifically for them. The current postindustrial service economy is still organized around a dual labor market in which "women's work" is devalued and, overall, women are compensated less than men.

The convergence of deindustrialization, an expanding female labor market, and increasing cultural preoccupation with sexuality alter the prevailing social conditions and, hence, gender relations. One result of this convergence is that much of women's work is sexualized—that is, women's sexuality is a crucial part of the actual labor process. Sexual meanings are often scripted into the provision and marketing of goods and services that are presumably nonsexual (Tancred-Sheriff 1989), from the expectations for behavior in "women's occupations" such as receptionists and nurses to the automobile and power-tool advertisements that feature women in semierotic poses. Even though many women have benefited economically and professionally from challenges to these images by the contemporary women's movement and the incremental changes in women's legal rights, the majority still labor in low-paid, sex-typed jobs and are made more vulnerable still by their limited access to political power.

Innovations in communications and information technology promote the increasing interdependence of nations around the world in the development of a global economy wherein wealthy nations that provide services, information, and finances partner with developing nations as manufacturing sites and the sources of raw materials. Rooted in a long history of colonialism, the Western world's exploitation of developing nations in Latin America, for example, exacerbates gender inequality within these newly industrializing nations. Acosta-Belen and Bose (2001, 60) suggest that women are "a last colony" in the new global economy, noting that "women and colonies are both low-wage and nonwage producers, share structural subordination and dependency, and are overwhelmingly poor." Within this "world gender order . . . there is a patriarchal dividend for men arising from unequal wages, unequal labor force participation, and a highly unequal structure of ownership, as well as cultural and sexual privileging" (Connell 2001, 167).

Citizenship, Masculinity, and Violence

Although gender violence is personally experienced first and foremost in the context of intimate relationships, it would be inaccurate to present the family as the central locus and agent of violence. Indeed, violence in intimate contexts can only exist in communities that condone it. Community acquiescence to gender violence certainly varies; in some settings the support is more overt than in others. Yet analysts continue to show the ways in which larger cultural contexts shape and reproduce the meanings and practices that hold sway in the most basic relationships we form.

It is crucial to bear in mind that much of the world's violence—including gender violence—is institutional (Connell 1987). For example, the military and similar institutions of formal control, such as the police, play a substantial role in both shaping violent masculinity and socializing male members to distance themselves from femininity. Attempts by organizations to maintain internal continuity, as well as the legitimacy of their socialization rituals, often result in institutional tolerance for the violent behavior of members; thus, gay bashing, sexual harassment of female co-workers, and rape in the context of war are often tolerated, and even rewarded. Programs for male athletes provide a general training ground for social and political leadership in the United States; they figure prominently in recruitment for, and daily routines within, military-style organizations. Sports events are replete with militaristic metaphor and pageantry. Woven together as primary contexts for the formation of male identity, militarism and sports form a well-integrated system for shaping men for life in civil society. They are simultaneously shaping the behavior patterns and worldview that men take into their intimate relationships with women, other men, and children.

In the United States, the social construction of citizenship has included a double standard of strong gender-related assumptions. Historically, the right to own property, vote, attend institutions of higher education, and participate in the occupation of one's choice, as well as the responsibility to join the armed services of the country and the ability to engage in combat, have all been regulated by the government in ways that have included gender restrictions. In the United States, where violence has long been "an American norm and a behavioral theme" (Barak 2003, 26), the nation's system of adversarial internal politics and a penchant for involvement in global conflicts have contributed to the male-centeredness of political and military institutions. The ever-increasing significance of these related institutions in everyday life contribute to a civic culture that not only tolerates but also teaches violence as a skill (Ewing 1982). This is particularly true for men, for whom the civic advocacy of violence is strong.

Connell (1987) theorizes that the hegemonic masculine ideal incorporates key aspects of militarism and notes that in many cultures, war is the true test of masculinity. Given the targeting of males for team sports and war toys, and with media role models, internalization of militaristic tendencies is most strongly associated with masculinity, rather than femininity, in the United States. The negative consequences of such a dichotomous conceptualization of gender are further exacerbated by the philosophy of conquest deeply embedded in the United States. Both popular cultural forms and official government policy reflect the ways in which the United States accepts and celebrates attempts to conquer that which belongs to the living world, both in the physical environment and among human and other animal communities. Finally, all of us, male and female, participate in the cultural and linguistic idealization of war. For example, we celebrate military personnel's sacrifices and unconsciously use military metaphors in our communications with each other—we attack a problem, are under the gun to find a solution, and frequently beat an idea to death (Ewing 1982).

Sex, Markets, and "Normal" Violence in the United States

A great deal of gender violence takes place in the context of sexual relationships; thus, it is important to understand the social construction of dominant sexual practices. Infusing sexual relationships with violence is not by any means limited to the United States. Edwin Schur (1988) suggests, however, that globally, sex has been increasingly "Americanized," assuming distinct cultural forms as sexual meanings emerge in conjunction with gender and economic inequality, exaggerated consumerism, and the larger American culture of violence.

Schur's ideas are consistent with those of others who see clear correlations between economic stratification and gender inequality. Connell notes, "To the extent that particular institutions become dominant in world society, the patterns of masculinity embedded in them may become global standards" (2001, 166). From this perspective, contemporary capitalist market economies provide the context for an increasingly complex commodification of sexuality. In a culture that promotes the belief that basic human needs can be met by purchasing the right products, it is no surprise that a huge sex entertainment industry emerges. The buying and selling of sex through prostitution, "gentlemen's clubs," telephone sex services, chat rooms, and explicit videos are logical outgrowths of a profit-oriented market economy in a society that is preoccupied with sex. Perhaps the most blatant example of the commodification of sex in today's capitalist world market is sex tourism, in which men vacation in places such as Thailand and the Philippines, often in conjunction with official business trips.

Treating sex as a commodity, in conjunction with the system of gendered behaviors and expectations that constitute our ideals of masculinity and femininity, produces a distinct brand of sexuality in the United States. Sexuality has come to be a desired product, in and of itself, rather than a component of committed relationships. Mass-media depictions of sexuality frequently "eroticize dominance" (Schur 1988), and given the massive exportation of U. S. media products, Americanized sex is heavily marketed worldwide by the entertainment industry. Sex and violence are both dominant components of American cultural experience; fused together in the same film, television, advertising, and literary packages, they are easily marketed domestically and globally.

The more sexual needs can be fulfilled by using products, rather than relating to people in affection-based relationships, the more depersonalized sexuality becomes. The more depersonalized and isolated our notions of sexuality become, the less we value partners as individuals; and the more women are seen as objects—toys, tools, machines, or disembodied anatomical parts—the easier it is to violate them. The regular degradation of women and portrayal of coerced sexuality in explicitly pornographic materials, as well as in mainstream movies, television shows, music videos, and computer games, provides a backdrop for rationalizing gender violence in everyday interactions.

Other Dimensions of Power and Stratification

Power, financial success, and physical strength define ideal manhood in the United States, yet these valued resources are not distributed evenly among the male population. Because status attributions exist within the category *men*, "men construct their masculinities in accord with their position in social structures, and therefore, their access to personal and social resources" (Messerschmidt 1997, 92). For both sexes, race, class, age, and sexual orientation are among the most significant stratifying characteristics. Given the competitive and consumption-oriented nature of American society, both economic and social mobility are desirable, and the route to success may include physical force and coercion—taking power when it is not offered for the sake of personal gain.

Social psychologists use the concept of *relative deprivation* to partially explain class conflict or racial unrest. When social and economic affluence are characteristic of a society, but such affluence is unevenly distributed in visible ways, social conflict is likely to emerge. This is particularly true in societies like the United States where equality based on merit is often professed as a social ideal. We can apply the concept of relative deprivation to the study of gender violence as well. When ideal masculinity involves possession of certain characteristics that are unequally distributed—money, physical attractiveness, or athleticism, for example—men who are deficient in some central areas may become frustrated and angry. One way that men who experience relative deprivation may compensate for such real or perceived deficiencies is through the use of physical strength to gain power. Such a route to power may be more easily taken in a society where economic resources are shrinking and Whiteness is overvalued. This by no means suggests that gender violence is confined to lower-income men or men of color, but relative deprivation may help us understand some of the motivations to violence among these groups. Indeed, despite their access to considerable economic and political resources, wealthy and high-status men may also feel relative deprivation when gauging their physical competence or communicative abilities against the masculine ideal, resulting in the use of domestic violence to compensate for perceived deficiency in their relationships with women. Adolescent and young adult males who feel humiliated when they are unable to attract and successfully court women may engage in gay-bashing to manage their feelings of sexual inadequacy. Measuring up to the ideal standard is difficult in a performance-oriented, market-driven, and highly stratified culture. In such a context, men seek and use power over women and other men to access rewards in social institutions (J. Pleck 1980).

Taking power in this context often involves the use of violence as a substitute for eliciting power from socially legitimate means. Male domination is further maintained by creating a culture of fear that renders women continuously self-conscious and anxious in contemporary U.S. society. Together, a combination of "sledgehammer" forms of violence (such as rape) and "dripping tap" forms of violence (such as obscene phone calls) (Wise and Stanley 1987) produce an overall climate that supports men's ability to control women through the mere *threat* of violence. For example, Ester Madriz (1997) reveals that women not only experience a pervasive fear of violation but that they also expend considerable energy trying to minimize the likelihood of victimization by being "good girls." In other words, they voluntarily comply with an elaborate set of social rules that restrict women's behavior by altering their appearance, limiting their mobility, and invoking male sponsors (in the form of answering-machine voices, for example), to hide the fact that they are women alone.

Contributions to This Section

We have briefly outlined the sociohistorical foundations of the contemporary American sex/gender system. The United States is only one of the case studies we could select to illustrate the fluidity of cultural definitions about gender and sexuality; indeed, culturally specific social conditions provide the basis for the great variation that still exists in gender relations worldwide. Economy, state, and media are central institutions that construct and enforce gender relations. One way to situate our understanding of both gender and violence is to analyze the social evolution of these institutions in the United States. By contextualizing sexual violence within a particular ideological belief system and set of sociohistorical conditions, the sociological perspective presented in the articles in this section makes a significant contribution to a macro-level analysis that is so often lost in public discussions of gender violence.

We have already discussed some of Edwin Schur's general propositions regarding the social construction of sex in contemporary American society. Included here is a portion of his larger work that focuses specifically on the institutionalization of sexual coercion in the United States. Schur encourages us to conceptualize gender violence as emanating from a pathological society; thus, large-scale social change is necessary if we are to eliminate gender violence.

Michael Kimmel considers not only how gender structures violence but also how violence contributes to the social construction of gender, more specifically, violent masculinity. He uses examples of recent events, such as the September 11 terrorist attacks, to challenge the notion that perpetrators of violence are simply deviant individuals in a just society.

Carol J. Sheffield's classic article "Sexual Terrorism" extends our conceptualization of both gender violence and terrorism. Sheffield reminds us that violation takes many forms and that fear of violence is, itself, both a violation and a powerful mechanism of social control in the lives of women.

SUGGESTIONS FOR FURTHER READING

Margaret Atwood, *The Handmaid's Tale* (New York: Ballantine Books, 1985).

John D'Emilio and Estelle B. Freedman, *Intimate Matters: A History of Sexuality in America* (New York: Harper and Row, 1988).

Ester Madriz, *Nothing Bad Happens to Good Girls: Fear of Crime in Women's Lives* (Berkeley: University of California Press, 1997).

James Messerschmidt, *Masculinity and Crime: Critique and Reconceptualization of Theory* (Lanham, MD: Rowman and Littlefield, 1993).

Michael A. Messner, *Power at Play: Sports and the Problem of Masculinity* (Boston: Beacon Press, 1992).

Andrea Smith, *Conquest: Sexual Violence and American Indian Genocide* (Cambridge, MA: South End Press, 2005).

Need

A Chorale for Black Woman Voices

Audre Lorde

For Patricia Cowan[1] and Bobbie Jean Graham[2] and the hundreds of other mangled Black Women whose nightmares inform these words.

> *tattle tale tit.*
> *your tongue will be slit*
> *and every little boy in town*
> *shall have a little bit.*
>
> —nursery rhyme

I

(Poet)
This woman is Black
so her blood is shed into silence
this woman is Black
so her blood falls to earth
like the droppings of birds
to be washed away with silence and rain.

(Pat)
For a long time after the baby came
I didn't go out at all
and it got to be pretty lonely.
Then Bubba started asking about his father
made me feel
like connecting to the blood again
maybe I'd meet someone
we could move on together
help make the dream real.

An ad in the paper said
   "Black actress needed
   to audition in a play by Black Playwright."
I was anxious to get back to work
and this was a good place to start
so Monday afternoon
on the way home from school with Bubba
I answered the ad.

In the middle of the second act
he put a hammer through my head.

(Bobbie)
If you're hit in the middle of Broadway
by a ten-ton truck
your caved-in chest bears the mark of a tire
and your liver pops like a rubber ball.
If you're knocked down by a boulder
from a poorly graded hill
your dying is stamped with the print of rock.

But when your boyfriend methodically
beats you to death
in the alley behind your apartment
while your neighbors pull down their window shades
because they don't want to get involved
the police call it a crime of "passion"
not a crime of hatred.

Yet I still died
of a lacerated liver
and a man's heelprint
upon my chest.

II

(Poet)
Dead Black women haunt the black maled streets
paying our cities' secret and familiar tithe of blood
burn blood beat blood cut blood
seven-year-old-child rape-victim blood
of a sodomized grandmother blood
on the hands of my brother
as women we were meant to bleed
but not this useless blood
each month a memorial
to my unspoken sisters fallen
red drops upon asphalt.

(All)
We were not meant to bleed
a symbol for no one's redemption
Is it our blood
that keeps these cities fertile?

(Poet)
I do not even know all their names.
Black women's deaths are not noteworthy
not threatening or glamorous enough
to decorate the evening news
not important enough to be fossilized
between right-to-life pickets
and a march against gun-control
we are refuse in this city's war
with no medals   no exchange of prisoners
no packages from home   no time off
for good behavior
no victories. No victors.

(Bobbie)
How can I build a nation
afraid to walk out into moonlight
lest I lose my power
afraid to speak out
lest my tongue be slit
my ribs kicked in
by a brawny acquaintance
my liver bleeding life onto the stone.

(All)
How many other deaths
do we live through daily
pretending
we are alive?

III

(Pat)
What terror embroidered my face
onto your hatred
what unchallenged enemy
took on my sweet brown flesh
within your eyes
came armed against you
with only my laughter   my hopeful art
my hair catching the late sunlight
my small son eager to see his mama work?

On this front page
My blood stiffens in the cracks of your fingers
raised to wipe a half-smile from your lips.
Beside you a white policeman
bends over my bleeding son
decaying into my brother
who stalked me with a singing hammer.

I need you. For what?
Was there no better place
to dig for your manhood
except in my woman's bone?

(Bobbie)
And what do you need me for, brother,
to move for you   feel for you   die for you?
We have a grave need for each other
but your eyes are thirsty
for vengeance
dressed in the easiest blood
and I am closest.

(Pat)
When you opened my head with your hammer
did the boogie stop in your brain
the beat go on
did terror run out of you like curdled fury
a half-smile upon your lips?
And did your manhood lay in my skull
like a netted fish
or did it spill out like milk or blood
or impotent fury off the tips of your fingers
as your sledgehammer clove my bone
to let the light out
did you touch it as it flew away?

(Bobbie)
Borrowed hymns veil a misplaced hatred
saying you need me   you need me   you need me
a broken drum
calling me   Black goddess   Black hope   Black
strength   Black mother
yet you touch me
and I die in the alleys of Boston
my stomach stomped through the small of my back
my hammered-in skull in Detroit
a ceremonial knife
through my grandmother's used vagina

the burned body hacked to convenience
in a vacant lot
I lie in midnight blood like a rebel city
bombed into submission
while our enemies still sit in power
and judgment
over us all.

(*Bobbie & Pat*)
Do you *need* me submitting to terror   at nightfall
to chop into bits and stuff warm into plastic bags
near the neck of the Harlem River
they found me   eight months swollen
with your need
do you need me to rape in my seventh year
bloody semen in the corners of my childish mouth
as you accuse me of being seductive.

(*All*)
Do you need me imprinting upon our children
the destruction our enemies print upon you
like a Mack truck or an avalanche
destroying us both
carrying their hatred back home
you relearn my value
in an enemy coin.

IV

(*Poet*)
I am wary of need that tastes like destruction.

(*All*)
I am wary of need
that tastes like destruction.

(*Poet*)
Who learns to love me
from the mouth of my enemies
walks the edge of my world
a phantom in a crimson cloak
and the dreambooks speak of money
but my eyes say death.

The simplest part of this poem
is the truth in each one of us
to which it is speaking.

How much of this truth can I bear
to see
and still live
unblinded?
How much of this pain can I use?

"We cannot live without our lives."

(All)
"We cannot live
without our lives."[3]
(1979, 1989)

NOTES

1. Patricia Cowan, 21, bludgeoned to death in Detroit, 1978.

2. Bobbie Jean Graham, 34, beaten to death in Boston, 1979. One of twelve Black women murdered within a three-month period in that city.

3. "We cannot live without our lives." From a poem by Barbara Deming.

Chapter Four

Sexual Coercion in American Life

Edwin Schur

An Epidemic of Forced Sex

Appraisers of the current sexual "scene" rarely discuss sexual victimization. Yet intimidation, coercion, and violence are key features of sexual life in America today. We may profess to view coercive sexuality as deviant. But, actually, it is in many respects the norm.[1] To be sure, we are not all rapists, sexual harassers, or child abusers. However, these behaviors are extremely widespread and may well be increasing. They are not isolated departures from some benign patterning of our sexual activities. On the contrary, they constitute important indicators of where our current value priorities and socioeconomic structures are leading us sexually.

We do not know, and indeed cannot know, precisely how much sexual coercion there is. But the estimates are daunting. In recent years, the Federal Bureau of Investigation has been reporting close to eighty thousand rapes a year and estimating that one forcible rape occurs somewhere in the United States every seven minutes. It is widely recognized that even these figures greatly understate the problem. Rape is known to be one of the most underreported crimes. Victimization surveys, in which sampled members of the general population are queried about all crimes committed against them (including those they did not report to the police), show rates of rape four times as high as the official ones.[2]

Sexual abuse of children—we are just beginning to realize—is also extremely widespread, and may be growing. In the Russell study, 16 percent of the women reported at least one incident of incestuous abuse before the age of eighteen (12 percent before age fourteen), and 31 percent reported some sexual abuse by a nonrelative before they had reached eighteen (20 percent before age fourteen). Combining the two categories of abuse (when actual physical contact of some kind was involved) produced overall figures of 38 percent (before age eighteen) and 28 percent (before fourteen). When noncontact experiences (exhibitionism, advances not acted upon) were added the totals were, respectively, 54 percent and 48 percent. Only 2 percent of incest cases and 6 percent of other cases had ever been reported to the police. Rate comparisons for different time periods and between age cohorts, furthermore, convinced Russell that both incest and sexual abuse of children outside the family may have "quadrupled since the early 1900s."[3]

Sexual harassment of working women is another highly prevalent yet officially "invisible" pattern in present-day American life. Here again, the proportion of incidents that is reported and acted upon is extremely low. But surveys among the general female population, and also in particular work settings or occupational categories, have disclosed very high rates of sexual intimidation and exploitation by male employers, supervisors, and fellow workers. For example, in a 1976 *Redbook* magazine survey, 88 percent of the nine thousand readers who responded reported having experienced some form of sexual harassment at work, and 92 percent considered the problem serious. Surveys of workers at the United Nations, middle-management workers in large corporations, and students at major universities have likewise produced evidence of extensive sexual intimidation and exploitation.[4]

The behaviors I have mentioned so far are not, of course, the only types of sexual coercion that Americans experience. Relatively few prostitutes or other sex workers sell their sexuality by free choice. Even where they have not been directly coerced into such work, we might well conclude that some degree of indirect and broadly social coercion has shaped their decision. Nor are noncommercial sexual relations necessarily free of coercion. I discuss below the (far from infrequent) occurrence of wife rape. But short of such outright assault, a subtle coercion exists whenever an individual feels pressured into undesired sexual activity.

It is true that virtually all social relations display a certain amount of coercion in this very broad sense. Yet we do not have to apply the term that expansively to see that coercive sexuality is an alarming presence in our society. The major types of direct and severe coercion that I have noted constitute, in themselves, a national disgrace. Nor is it the case that all modern societies exhibit similar patterns. At least with respect to rape, it continues to be true that "the United States shows a significantly higher rate than most, if not all, European jurisdictions."[5] Such conclusions are based on the necessarily limited—and, as between countries, not always fully comparable—official statistics. Nonetheless, the differences have tended to be too great (American rates running from five to thirty times those of various other Western countries) to be accounted for on that basis alone.

Given the sketchy character of available evidence, similar cross-national comparisons regarding child abuse and sexual harassment would have to be even more tentative. Yet one suspects that America—in these as in so many sexual matters—might again be in the lead. In any case, whether we top other countries in these respects or not, the figures we do have for our own society give cause for great concern. There are, admittedly, no scientific criteria by which to prove what constitutes a high rate of sexual coercion. But the statistics I have cited should speak for themselves. The magnitude of coercive sexuality in America today greatly exceeds what one should expect to find in a humane and liberated society.

Feminists sometimes assert that rape is not really "sexual" behavior. In arguing that its essence is violence and hostility, they seek to underscore the coerciveness of rape to depict it as being totally unlike lovemaking. However, they usually do go on to point up the links between rape and certain approved outlooks on sex. We should not assume it is only by chance that male hostility and aggression often take this particular form. Rape not only tells us something about male attitudes toward women. It also tells us something about men's ideas about sexuality.

A common defense against charges of sexual harassment (at least in its milder forms) emphasizes the sexual aspect but denies the coercion. The supposedly offending behaviors, it is claimed, merely reflect normal sexual interaction in the workplace. We should see this argument not as a defense of harassment, but rather as an indictment of normal outlooks. However, even if it provides no excuse for sexually offensive acts, the very making of this argument does usefully highlight the systemic aspect of sexual coercion. As in the case of rape as well, this particular form of coercive sexuality bears a close connection to approved scenarios of male-female interaction. I am going to discuss these links extensively throughout this chapter. In such instances, the combination of sexuality and coercion constitutes both the offense and the "normality." As regards sexual abuse of children, the influence of approved interaction scenarios may be less evident. But with the growing sexualization of children in our society, the line between normative behavior and sexual offense may, in this case too, be growing hazier.

How successful have feminists and other activists been in alerting us to these problems of sexual victimization? There have been, during the past two decades, efforts to kindle public concern on each of them. First the cause for greatest alarm was rape, then worker harassment; now the "hot issue" is child abuse. Yet one has the impression that, despite these successive eruptions of activist effort and media attention, the public's understanding of coercive sexuality remains shallow.

The very fact that these issues seem to come and go suggests that people approach them piecemeal. In addition, the individualizing tendency I mentioned earlier interferes with thinking systematically about sexual coercion. And it is characteristic of moral crusades to focus on specific categories of individual offenders. Thus, much of the public alarm has been directed toward "rapists," "child molesters," and sexist employers. In terms of short-run policy measures, this may not be too bad. Yet it distracts us from the full dimensions and sociocultural groundings of the problems.

Perhaps only in the current attention to pornography is there any focus on coercive sexuality as a key feature of modern American life. And even there, the inferences about connections may be misguided. Pornography, for example, is taken to be the cause of rape, without regard for the attitudinal and structural factors that may underlie both rape and pornography. Then too, except on this one matter, the New Right (with its heavy concentration on such issues as abortion, homosexuality, and sex education) has most likely diverted attention away from the overall relation between sexuality and coercion.

One suspects, indeed, that many Americans continue to view acts of sexual coercion as pathological violations of our society's norms. Some probably believe that the frequency of these behaviors has been exaggerated. Others may become concerned about one type of sexual offense, without ever placing it as part of a more general pattern. From the standpoint of systematically reducing sexual coercion in American life, these views are not very helpful. The offenses are not, in fact, unrelated to each other. And we cannot simply attribute them to individual wrongdoers. In fact, we cannot appreciate them apart from the normal workings of our sexual system or our social system. To a considerable extent they are integral to those systems, rather than departures from them.

The Context of Coercion

Sexuality and Indifference

There are, indeed, many good reasons for expecting to find a close link between sex and coercion in modern American society. Coercive sexuality is a predictable corollary of American outlooks on sex. In particular, sexist attitudes and habits, a misguidedly mechanistic approach to the question of what sex is, and the commercializing instinct encouraged under modern capitalism combine to shape our sexual thinking and sexual goals. All these tendencies (and the general cultural values that they reflect) push us in the direction of sexual indifference and insensibility. When one adds the pervasive socioeconomic inequality that depresses and diminishes the lives of so many Americans, the stage is well set for sexual coercion to be widespread.

Under the general conditions of modern life, Toffler and other critics warned, people become disposable. Our distorted thinking about sexuality and the tenacious hold on us of sexist outlooks only serve to exacerbate this broad tendency. Virtually all the aspects of social and sexual relations are conducive to sexual intimidation and victimization. In an era of secondary relations (to recall Kingsley Davis's term), the other person tends to be seen as a means of achieving our own purposes. He or she is not valued intrinsically. Even in the context of supposedly intimate relationships, using the other person may become the actual norm. The prospect of that happening in other situations, then, must be extremely high.

How is this general tendency affected by our more specific ideas regarding sex? The modernization of sex has contributed to an objectified and scientized conception of sexual acts. Sex came to be seen largely as the production of orgasms and the satisfaction of biological needs. It was studied primarily as a matter of physiological capacity and measurable results. From that standpoint, the way in which sexual needs were satisfied was not deemed terribly important. Nor was there much emphasis, really (despite the usual humanistic call for it), on mutuality in sexual relations. Rather, the focus was on sex as something the individual got, or gave. In addition, the positive valuation of sexuality as natural led the biologically oriented sexual modernizers to develop a quantitative theme. They seemed to imply that as regards sexuality (and as Americans tended to assert in so many areas), more is better. High total sexual outlet, it seemed, was good, and low total outlet bad.

When applied in a context of mutual "pleasuring," and as an antidote to longstanding sexual repression, these new ideas had considerable value. But as I have already suggested, they produced distortion as well. There has been relatively little discussion of their possible bearing on sexual coercion and violence. It seems clear, however, that thinking of sex in this way—particularly when social relations of all kinds tend to be depersonalized anyway—might facilitate sexual abuse. The individual is encouraged to view sex not only as a need that must be satisfied but also as a "thing" that should be sought and obtained. If it cannot be gotten in more acceptable ways, then perhaps it should be taken—by force, if necessary.

Such a conception of one's sexuality meshes well with the contemporary decline in ability to really see the other person. This ability is impaired by the widespread dissemination of unreal sexual imagery, as well as by the general depersonalization in American life. When such imagery triggers abstracted sexual response, there is a sense in which the actual person on the receiving end of that response isn't really there at all. In addition, the fact that many people in our society are routinely selling their sexual services must also contribute to a dulling of sexual sensitivity. When sexuality can be bought and sold so readily, and treated as a mere service, how much attention must be paid to the person with whom one "has" sex?

That these types of response may make it easier to abuse people sexually should be obvious. A psychological distancing from the other person enables the abuser to disregard the latter's wishes and feelings. (The same basic point has been made regarding the relative ease of killing people through high-altitude bombing and other even more detached techniques of modern warfare.) Such distanced others are more readily conceived of as being there to be used. They can do things for us, or we can with seeming impunity do things to them.

Let me reiterate that, while coerced sex is totally unlike lovemaking, the abuser may nonetheless think that what he (or she) is "getting" is "sex." (Indeed, it is the modernized conception of sexuality just commented on that makes such a belief possible. Only with an orgasm-preoccupied view of sex could coerced sex acts be held to produce "satisfaction.") Based on their interviews with over a hundred convicted rapists, two researchers insist on "the part that sex plays in the crime. The data clearly indicate that from the rapists' point of view rape is in part sexually motivated." They go on to describe rape as "a means of sexual access," and to comment that "when a woman is unwilling or seems unavailable for sex, the rapist can seize what isn't volunteered."[6] In a similar vein, another writer—who interviewed a general sampling of men regarding their attitudes toward rape—states: "In the conception of sex as a commodity, sex is something a man can buy, sell, get for free, or steal (rape)."[7]

Disposable Women

Sexual indifference within our society provides a general impetus for the use of coercion. Distribution of the results, however, is highly skewed. At least with respect to adults (and it might also be true of child abuse, though at present we cannot be sure) most sexual victimizers are male and most of the victims are female. This is not just due to average disparities in physical strength. As writers on rape and sexual harassment—and on the situation of women more generally—have frequently noted, it reflects the overall social dominance of males and subordination of females. The power that is involved in this patterning of coercion is not just physical. It is social, psychological, economic, and—in the broadest sense—political.

Sexual objectification exhibits this skewed distribution. In our society, it is primarily women who are presented as sex objects. They are presented in that way for—and (the idea lingers) they exist for—the sexual pleasure of men. (In that not-yet-dispelled conception, they also exist to service men in other ways—primarily as housekeepers and childrearers.) When the general status of females is limited (in large measure) to their sexuality, men are likely to see every specific woman primarily as a potential source of sexual satisfaction. The object-like status of women, furthermore, is closely tied up with ideas of sexual property.

Equating women with their sexuality (the process Firestone called "sex privatization") and restricting them in other spheres are two sides of the same (sexist) coin. This extreme sexualization implies limiting women's access to, and not taking them seriously in, nonsexual roles. If they are to be kept in their place, women's freedom of choice must be restricted and their economic dependence on men preserved. Social stigmatization of women, whenever and wherever they step out of line, helps to sustain these limitations.[8]

Much like the alleged pedestal, which in fact helps keep women down, thinking of women as "the sex" helps to ensure their control by men. In this conception their primary use is sexual, and they are all too easily seen as being sexually usable. Presumably, one can conceive of a situation in which men were socially and economically dominant and yet not sexually coercive. However, the trivialization and sexualization of women are highly conducive to such coercion—at least in a society such as ours in which a general pattern of sexual indifference prevails. Furthermore, forced sex is in a way the ultimate indicator, and preserver, of male dominance. Its occurrence and even the perception that it may at any time occur reassure males of their power and help to keep women subordinate.

These conceptions of their dominance, and of woman's secondary (and largely sexual) status, are—as feminists have been insisting—heavily built into the basic socialization of males in our society. Men have learned to respond to women—at least initially, and sometimes more lastingly—not as individuals but in category terms. And, to a large extent, it is a woman's sexual presence that overwhelms other bases for response. In addition, the socialization of most males has strongly endorsed the idea that it is normal for males to be sexually aggressive. This fact lay behind Susan Griffin's claim, in an already-classic discussion of "Rape: The All-American Crime," that "in our society, it is rape itself that is learned."[9]

It should be emphasized here how very closely male conceptions of sexual satisfaction have been tied to images of conquest. Most American men, it is reasonable to believe, still tend to think in terms of "making out" and "scoring." Add the counterpart term for anticipated female acquiescence, "putting out," and one has a capsule summary of culturally approved male outlooks on sex. The crucial point, of course, is that men are *supposed* to try to coerce women into sexual activity.

To the extent this scenario embodied the traditional double standard, "good" women were supposed to say no (however much they desired sexual relations) and to put up resistance by fending off advances. In general, the socialization counterpart of male sexual aggression was female sexual passivity. Citing this theme, feminists depicted women as having been socialized to be victims. In some ways, both sexes were learning their roles in the rape scenario. And this basic learning, we can be fairly certain, continues to be reinforced through pornographic depictions of rape—in which, characteristically, both persons are portrayed as (eventually) enjoying the action.

The most insidious aspect of these learned conceptions is that they are so closely linked to our general ideas concerning masculinity and femininity. As Diana Russell has aptly suggested, a "virility mystique" inclines men to associate sex with coercion and violence. Real men are supposed "to be able to separate their sexual responsiveness from their needs for love, respect, and affection." They are expected to respond, not to specific female persons, but to the presence or depiction of any sexy woman. They are supposed to be able to perform sexually in each and every such instance. Russell concludes, I think sensibly, that "if men were not taught to separate sexual feelings from feelings of warmth and caring, rape would be unthinkable, and fewer men would impose their sexuality on unwilling women in other less extreme ways too."[10]

The other side of this equation has been the female's induced submissiveness and absorption in fantasies of romance. Germaine Greer argued, in *The Female Eunuch*, that the masculine-feminine distinction in modern society rests on a "castration" of women: "Men have commandeered all the energy and streamlined it into an aggressive conquistadorial power, reducing all heterosexual contact to a sadomasochistic pattern."[11] Sexual autonomy and assertiveness are not, in this pattern, open to women. As a recent analysis of mass-marketed romances brought out, these popular depictions reinforce the belief that "pleasure for women is men."[12] Attracting them, arousing their lust, and perhaps being overwhelmed by them is what women are for.

By no means do I wish to imply that giving women equal opportunity with respect to sexual coercion would be a good thing. Free choice to formulate one's own sexual desires, and the ability to pursue them actively, ought to be maximized. But this must be done without encouraging victimization. The equalizing of a sexual distortion cannot be viewed as a social gain. My comments here are intended only to underscore the key role our prevailing gender system plays in perpetuating and shaping coercive sexuality. There is little doubt that that role is substantial. The individual (male as well as female) becomes "disposable" under conditions of social modernity. But for women this situation has long obtained—not just as a vague threat, but as a recurring feature of their daily lives.

Inequality and Violence

Modern American society is characterized by high levels of socioeconomic inequality and interpersonal violence. These conditions, separately and in combination, help to determine present-day patterns of sexual victimization. The reference to combined (or additive) effects is important, for most experts are agreed that a great deal of the violence in our society is due to the inequality. One of the major theories about the occurrence of large-scale violence attributes it to "relative deprivation." As the term *relative deprivation* indicates, you don't have to be in absolutely dire straits to feel deprived

—and, as a consequence, frustrated, resentful, and hostile. This helps to explain how there can be such high levels of violence in a society that many think of as being extremely affluent.

Actually, as economists and sociologists frequently point out, that affluence has been much exaggerated. One recent textbook summary cites 1984 Census figures in noting that "many Americans can barely make ends meet or are living in poverty. Over 15 percent of all American families have incomes below the official poverty level, and over half have incomes below $25,000." The same writers go on to comment that "although America's poor people seldom die of starvation and generally have more than the hopelessly poor of the third world, they lead lives of serious deprivation compared not only with the wealthy but with the middle class as well. This relative deprivation profoundly affects the style and quality of their lives."[13]

In our media-saturated society, the constant depiction of affluent lifestyles—to which almost all Americans are exposed—can only increase a poor person's feelings of frustration and resentment. Author Charles Silberman has aptly noted that "the poor may be invisible to the rest of us, but we are not invisible to them; their television sets thrust them inside our homes every day of the week. For members of the lower class, consequently, life is a desperate struggle to maintain a sense of self in a world that offers little to nourish, and much to destroy, it."[14] To the extent feelings of relative deprivation lie behind some acts of sexual coercion, these media presentations may have special significance.

The playboy mentality, much routine advertising, and perhaps even the basic conception of women as objects to be appropriated and displayed convey the message that sexuality is linked to affluence. As I mentioned earlier, the poor person therefore feels doubly deprived. Among males, there must be a nagging realization that one is not going to be able to get either the affluence or the women who are depicted as most desirable. (And, though its influence on sexual coercion is not as great, poor women must have a sense that achieving the pinnacle of sexual desirability is probably beyond them.)

For the man especially—given our culture's definition of masculinity—taking sex through force or violence may be one kind of response. It may represent an eruption of general and pent-up frustration and hostility. Yet it may also sometimes be seen as a "solution" of sorts to the perceived sexual deprivation. (In this regard, I would stress once more that our mechanistic conception of sexuality allows the belief that what one is getting through such acts is "sex.") We know, of course, that not all poor people commit acts of sexual coercion. And, if we had complete information about those incidents of coercive sexuality that are not currently recorded, we might well find that middle-class rates exceed those of the lower classes.

However, that is no reason to doubt that poverty and the attitudes it engenders help to determine the extent of sexual coercion in our society. Researchers often want to test formal theories quantitatively, to determine the main cause of rape, or child abuse, or harassment. Given our tendency to individualize, especially, it is understandable that "cause" might be thought of in terms of supposed differences between offenders and nonoffenders. The question "Why do some persons do this, while others do not?" is certainly a legitimate one to pursue. On the other hand, when a behavior pattern becomes endemic to the entire society, the very issue of widespread prevalence becomes at least as important as that of individual differentiation.

From that standpoint, statistical comparison studies of individuals tend to be inadequate. A less rigorous but more far-reaching examination of multiple factors that may contribute to the overall situation may be appropriate. I think that is true in this case. Some instances of sexual coercion may be traceable primarily to poverty and its frustrations, others primarily to the depersonalizing and sexist outlooks that affect all of us. Often, some combination of these influences may be involved. Statistical tabulations and correlations are not going to enable us to isolate a single primary cause of a pattern that is this pervasive. Depersonalization, sexism, and inequality all help to shape it.

So too does the violence that suffuses American life. Since the 1960s, several national commission reports (on crime, civil disorders, and violence) have documented and publicized the prevalence of interpersonal violence in our society. It has come to be recognized that violence has had a central place in our history,[15] and hence cannot be viewed as some contemporary aberration. Criminologists frequently note that violent crimes comprise only a small proportion of all criminal offenses. Yet it is generally agreed that the United States exhibits extremely high rates of crimes of violence. A recent summary of data available in the early 1980s, for example, showed that if one combined cases (for 1981) of homicide, forcible rape, robbery, and aggravated assault, one found a recorded total of 1,321,910 such offenses. If one considered instead "personal victimizations" (which included rape, robbery, assault, and theft) reported in a national victimization survey (for 1980) one came up with a total of 21,642,000 offenses.[16]

Crime rates do fluctuate over time, for a number of reasons. For example, the age structure of the population (proportion in the most crime-prone categories), the extent to which people are concentrated in urban settings, and (as regards officially recorded statistics) the level of police resources and activity can all affect crime rates. However, nobody disputes that there is a great deal of violent crime in America today, nor that fear of being a victim of such violence is widespread.[17] Even though, statistically, the probability of such victimization is lower than that of being killed or injured accidentally, such fear is understandable and its personal impact all too real.

If Americans are highly fearful of violence, they may nonetheless become inured to it. The greatest danger from television depictions of violence, I believe, comes through an indirect and long-term impact of that sort. There is much less likelihood of specific crimes being caused by direct imitation of fictional enactments of violence than of the audience developing a general sense that violent behavior is now routine. If and when such a feeling does develop, then people—in all kinds of situations—may be more likely to resort to violence than they would have been otherwise. The daily litany of local killings reported on the evening news may, in that sense, be at least as consequential as more lurid, but fictional, portrayals of crime and violence.

For our purposes here, media (and pornographic) depictions of sexuality are, obviously, of special relevance. Wide exposure to depictions that link sex and violence can —again, more probably through subtle attitudinal change than by direct example— lead people increasingly to associate the two. As I mentioned earlier, the likelihood is not great that an individual will immediately go out and commit a rape following a specific exposure to pornography. But if Americans are fed a steady diet of such depictions, it could, more generally, erode those sensibilities that should help to deter sexual coercion. Extensive use of sadomasochistic imagery in the highly popular rock music videos is one sign that this diet is growing. Violent pornography readily and inexpensively available on videocassettes is another.

If we go beyond sheer physical violence to consider the more general question of coercion, we again find ample supporting "tradition" in our culture. Americans place a high value on results, and have not always been too scrupulous regarding the means used to achieve them. Notwithstanding our alleged disposition to support the underdog, we are quick to exploit personal advantage. Our culture's approval, or at the very least acceptance, of "cutthroat competition"—whether in business, athletics, or elsewhere—enables Americans to disregard the costs to others of their efforts to get ahead. And, similarly, pressuring other people to do things they might not want to do is in the vaunted tradition of American salesmanship.

I have suggested four general factors that may contribute to the prevalence of sexual coercion: depersonalization, leading to sexual indifference; the persisting devaluation (and sexualization) of women; pervasive socioeconomic inequality; and culturally induced habituation to force and violence. My emphasis, in these comments, has been on features of our culture and social system that are conducive to people's committing acts of sexual victimization. But the same sociocultural factors produce victims as well as offenders. Inequality, especially, contributes to both sides of the victimization process, but in an interestingly unbalanced way.

Given the current feminization of poverty (in which females represent a large proportion of those below the official poverty line),[18] we would expect many women, too, to develop feelings of relative deprivation that could lead to violent behavior. Presumably some instances of maternal child abuse reflect such a situation. Generally speaking, however, felt deprivation does not drive women into becoming sexual victimizers. Here we see the combination of inequality and basic socialization coming into play. It is men whose status has rested on demonstrating (along with financial success) their aggressiveness through sexual conquest and control. Women have been socialized to be relatively passive, and to play the sexual object role. Sexual aggressiveness, at least until very recently, has been deemed inappropriate—indeed unfeminine—behavior.

When women have experienced feelings of sexual deprivation, they have tended to internalize them rather than to try by aggressive means to assuage them. And by the same token the frustrations of economic deprivation have pushed women in different directions from those characteristically taken by men. The latter are much more likely to become sexually coercive in such situations. And when they adopt illicit means of alleviating their financial plight, men will tend toward methods we define as masculine —for example, armed robbery, which women as well would be perfectly capable of in physical terms. Women will deal with the situation in ways more consistent with approved female roles. Thus, their major cash-producing deviance will involve selling their sexuality. (Among men, but on a considerably smaller scale, homosexual prostitution represents a similar adaptation to economic insufficiency.)

The Balance of Power

As regards situations of direct sexual coercion, economic dependency may, again, contribute to women's victimization. Power, we must remind ourselves, is central to the entire phenomenon of coercive sexuality. Equality and coercion are mutually exclusive concepts; one can only be coerced by someone who has greater power. This power is not only physical, though physical power may indeed sometimes be involved. (Thus, depending on their strength relative to that of a male attacker, some women may be at a physical disadvantage when assaulted sexually. Weak and unaggressive males in prison may be especially vulnerable to "homosexual" rape—usually carried out, in fact, by heterosexuals. The vulnerability to abuse by adults of young children of either sex also is, in part, physical.)

But more significant, overall, are disparities in social (perhaps also psychological) and economic power. The widespread subjection of women to sexual victimization is part and parcel of their general subordination and devaluation in our society. That women's claims of victimization are not often enough taken seriously, nor the offenders severely punished, are further indicators of women's relatively low social power. This general condition is regularly seen in the high vulnerability to coercion of specific women—especially in certain key situations.

Marriage is one of these, and employment another. (A third area—less significant because of its more limited social class distribution and because the woman's financial independence is likely to be greater—is psychotherapy. Recent disclosures of sexual abuse of female patients by male therapists have highlighted the power disparity and authority-dependency aspects of this relationship.)[19] In both of these crucial life situations, financial and social dependency frequently mean that a woman has extremely limited freedom of action. She cannot easily walk away from the situation, if equally secure alternatives are not available to her. This helps to explain the high vulnerability of women to abuse by their husbands. It also highlights the predicament of women workers who are being subjected to sexual harassment.

Reducing Sexual Coercion

America did not invent sexual coercion. But its current cultural priorities and system of social stratification certainly encourage its prevalence. No doubt some amount of forced sex has existed in most societies. Yet ours seems unusually coercion-prone. It is important to recognize this as a general state of affairs. We are not going to alter the situation very much by doing something to (or "for") individual rapists, harassers, and child abusers. For coercion to be significantly reduced, our cultural priorities and approved behavior patterns—as well as the distribution of income and opportunity— are going to have to change.

Actually, in this area more than on other sexual issues, law enforcement does have a role to play. These situations are very different from the victimless crime ones. As regards some potential rapists, for example—especially the more affluent ones (who have more to lose by being caught and punished)—stringent laws may have some real deterrent effect. Then, too, these offenses are so horrendous that a strong symbolic statement (through law) condemning them seems warranted. Even so, and however just we may find it to punish the violators, we need to recognize that the effects of such measures can only be limited ones.

Ultimately, the root conditions themselves will have to be confronted. This means an all-out attack on sexism and depersonalization. But it also means that we must reduce the inequities and priorities that our form of capitalism sustains. Based in part on data drawn from anthropology, Julia and Herman Schwendinger assert that a society's "mode of production" is the most basic determinant of the prevalence of rape. They state further that "the exploitative modes of production that have culminated in the formation of class societies have either produced or intensified sexual inequality and violence."[20]

The problem in applying this to modern societies is that virtually all of them (socialist societies included) are class societies of some sort. Modern capitalism has no monopoly on exploitation or violence, nor on sexism. On the other hand, our particular no-holds-barred version of capitalism does seem to provide special encouragement of coercion. Whether uniquely or not, it does I believe promote the "amoral individualism" and "callous and instrumental indifference to suffering"[21] that the Schwendingers cite as major factors in our rape situation. Whatever one thinks, overall, about the relative merits of socialism and capitalism, the fact remains that rape (and other sexual coercion) will not be significantly reduced if the present systematic inequality is allowed to persist. As the Schwendingers note, such a reduction requires addressing the economic underpinnings of violence and violent crime in general.[22] On this point, at the very least, their argument seems unassailable.

NOTES

1. For a discussion of this matter, see Edwin M. Schur, *Labeling Women Deviant* (New York: Random House, 1984), especially chap. 4, "Victimization of Women: Deviance or Conformity?"

2. An overview and analysis of the different kinds of rape statistics can be found in Diana E. H. Russell, *Sexual Exploitation* (Beverly Hills, CA: Sage, 1984), 29–65.

3. Diana E. H. Russell, *The Secret Trauma: Incest in the Lives of Girls and Women* (New York: Basic Books, 1986), 60–62, 84, 78.

4. See Alliance Against Sexual Coercion, *Fighting Sexual Harassment* (Boston: Alyson, 1981); Lin Farley, *Sexual Shakedown* (New York: Warner Books, 1978); Eliza G. C. Collins and Timothy B. Blodgett, "Sexual Harassment: Some See It, Some Won't," *Harvard Business Review* (March-April 1981): 77–95; Donna J. Benson and Gregg E. Thomson, "Sexual Harassment on a University Campus," *Social Problems* 29 (February 1982): 236–51; and Bernice Lott, Mary Ellen Reilly, and Dale R. Howard, "Sexual Assault and Harassment: A Campus Community Case Study," *Signs* 8 (winter 1982): 296–319.

5. Gilbert Geis, "Forcible Rape: An Introduction," in Duncan Chapell, Robley Geis, and Gilbert Geis (eds.), *Forcible Rape* (New York: Columbia University Press, 1977), 31; see also Russell, *Sexual Exploitation*, 30–31.

6. Diana Scully and Joseph Marolla, "Riding the Bull at Gilley's: Convicted Rapists Describe the Rewards of Rape," *Social Problems* 32 (February 1985): 257.

7. Timothy Beneke, *Men on Rape* (New York: St. Martin's Press, 1982), 26.

8. See Schur, *Labeling Women Deviant,* on the reproduction of gender in everyday interaction. See also Nancy Henley and Jo Freeman, "The Sexual Politics of Interpersonal Behavior," in Jo Freeman (ed.), *Women: A Feminist Perspective,* 2d ed. (Palo Alto, CA: Mayfield, 1979).

9. Susan Griffin, "Rape: The All-American Crime," *Ramparts* (September 1971), as reprinted in Chappell, Geis, and Geis (eds.), *Forcible Rape,* 50.

10. Diana E. H. Russell, *The Politics of Rape* (New York: Stein and Day, 1975), 263–64.

11. Germaine Greer, *The Female Eunuch* (New York: Bantam, 1972), 7.

12. Ann Barr Snitow, "Mass Market Romance: Pornography for Women Is Different," in Ann Snitow, Christine Stansell, and Sharon Thompson (eds.), *Powers of Desire* (New York: Monthly Review Press, 1983), 253.

13. Joseph Julian and William Kornblum, *Social Problems,* 5th ed. (Englewood Cliffs, NJ: Prentice-Hall, 1986), 201–2.

14. Charles E. Silberman, *Criminal Violence, Criminal Justice* (New York: Random House, 1978), 110.

15. Hugh Davis Graham and Ted Robert Gurr, *The History of Violence in America* (New York: Bantam, 1969).

16. As summarized in Joseph F. Sheley, *America's "Crime Problem"* (Belmont, CA: Wadsworth, 1985), 90.

17. See the discussion in Silberman, *Criminal Violence, Criminal Justice,* 3–20; see also John E. Conklin, *The Impact of Crime* (New York: Macmillan, 1975).

18. For a concise discussion, see Barbara Ehrenreich, *The Hearts of Men* (Garden City, NY: Doubleday Anchor Books, 1983), 172–82.

19. See Joanna Bunker Rohrbaugh, *Women: Psychology's Puzzle* (New York: Basic Books, 1979), 393–95; and Phyllis Chesler, *Women and Madness* (New York: Avon, 1972).

20. Julia R. Schwendinger and Herman Schwendinger, *Rape and Inequality* (Beverly Hills, CA: Sage, 1983), 179.

21. Ibid., 204.

22. Ibid., 220.

Chapter Five

Contextualizing Men's Violence
The Personal Meets the Political

Michael Kimmel

I

I'd like to begin with two different images of men and their relationship to violence. First, I'd like you to close your eyes and picture the following scenes, scenes which will no doubt be familiar from newspapers or television news. What gender comes into your mind when I mention the sneering, arrogant guards at border crossings in Chechnya, the caravans of jeeps and trucks following their warlords in the Congo, Somalia, or the Sudan, the cheering throngs that hear of yet another terrorist bombing or attack in Israel, the youths slinging their automatic weapons as they swagger down the streets of bombed-out Baghdad?

Now, what gender comes to your mind when I invoke the following significant social problems that today haunt the United States, Europe, and other advanced metropolitan countries: teen violence, urban violence, gang violence, drug-related violence, school shootings?

Chances are you've imagined men. And not just any men, but younger men, men in their teens and twenties, and men of a specific social class—poor, working class, or lower middle class.

Think again about the ways in which we understand those social and political movements, those violent outbursts of ethnic nationalist hatred. Do the commentators ever even mention that these are phalanxes of young men? Now, imagine that these were all women—would that not be *the* story, the issue to be explained? Would not a gender analysis be the center of every single story? The fact that these are men seems so obvious as to raise no questions, generate no analysis.

I want to make that visible. But first, listen to the voice of another young man, this one a twenty-three-year-old stock boy named Jay in a San Francisco corporation, who was asked by author Tim Beneke to think about under what circumstances he might commit rape. He has never committed rape, mind you. He's simply an average guy,

A much earlier version of this chapter was prepared for a conference on "Male Roles and Masculinities in the Perspective of a Culture of Peace" sponsored by UNESCO, Oslo, Norway, 24–28 September 1997. I have benefited from comments from Amy Aronson, Oystein Holter, Michael Kaufman, Jorgen Lorentzen, and Laura O'Toole.

considering the circumstances under which he would commit an act of violence against a woman. Here's what Jay says:

> Let's say I see a woman and she looks really pretty and really clean and sexy and she's giving off very feminine, sexy vibes. I think, wow I would love to make love to her, but I know she's not interested. It's a tease. A lot of times a woman knows that she's looking really good and she'll use that and flaunt it and it makes me feel like she's laughing at me and I feel degraded. . . . If I were actually desperate enough to rape somebody it would be from wanting that person, but also it would be a very spiteful thing, just being able to say "I have power over you and I can do anything I want with you" because really I feel that they have power over me just by their presence. Just the fact that they can come up to me and just melt me makes me feel like a dummy, makes me want revenge. They have power over me so I want power over them. (Beneke, 1982: 43–4)

Notice how the stock boy speaks not with the voice of someone in power, of someone in control over his life, but rather with the voice of powerlessness, of helplessness. For him, violence is a form of revenge, a form of retaliation, of getting even, a compensation for the power that he feels women have over him.

Let's stay with Jay for a moment. His words are the words of someone who does not see himself as powerful, but as powerless. And I think that perspective has been left out of our analyses of men's violence, both at the interpersonal, micro level of individual acts of men's violence against women—rape and battery, for example—and the aggregate, social and political analysis of violence expressed at the level of the nation-state, the social movement, or the military institution.

How do we typically see men's violence? We see it as the expression of men's power, of men's drive for power, for domination, for control. Now this makes a certain sense, because most of the theorizing about men's violence has been done by feminist women. It was feminist women who first noticed that men's violence was a social problem, not simply some expression of some innate biological drive. And feminist women have understood men's propensity for violence from the perspective of those against whom that violence has so often been directed. So men's violence—whether against women or against national enemies—has been theorized as an expression of men's drive for domination, a senseless need for power. Even mass rape in Bosnia in the early 1990s was theorized as an expression of men's desperate need to control their enemies by humiliation. Gang warfare was seen as an expression of men needing to dominate their territory, as was violence against women in the military, and in its academies, in firehouses, and harassment in offices and on campuses.

So we have often come to understand masculinity as the drive for power, domination, and control. Some years ago, I would give a lecture in which that was a dominant theme. I would argue that men have all the power and that we have to "give up" that power to make the world equal for women. But what do you think was the reaction when I said that? Typically, the women would sit and nod appreciatively, in agreement. The men immediately raised their hands. "What are you talking about?" they'd ask. "I have no power at all! My wife bosses me around! My kids boss me around! My boss bosses me around! I'm completely powerless!"

In their eyes, the feminist definition of masculinity as a drive for power and domination is theorized *from women's perspective*. It's how women experience masculinity. And, in that sense, it's right. But it's not how men experience their masculinity. Men do not feel as though we are in power. Individual men *feel* powerless.

I think that is the reason that some antifeminist groups have gained such popularity in the United States and elsewhere. Men's rights groups argue that those feelings of powerlessness are true and that women, these days, have all the power. "Let's get it back!" they shout. Have you listened to those "men's" shows on AM radio lately? The sense of defensive anger on the part of men who feel so powerless is startling.

I think the voices of the men tell us something important. Their sense of powerlessness is *real*, as in they experience it; but it may not be *true*—that is, an accurate analysis of their situation. Men, as a group, may be in power; individually, men don't feel so powerful. This exposes the theoretical inadequacy of simply focusing on whether or not men have the power, and whether or not men feel powerful. Of course men are *in* power, both as a group over women, and some men—by virtue of class, race, sexuality, or any other dynamic of difference—over other men.

Masculinity is not, however, the experience of power; it is the experience of *entitlement* to power. (Michael Kaufman makes the same point in his "Triad of Men's Violence" chapter in this volume.) Let me illustrate this with an anecdote from my life. Not long ago, I appeared on a television talk show opposite three "angry white males"— that is, three men who felt that they had been the victims of workplace discrimination. The men described how they were the new "victims" of reverse discrimination, and that they had been qualified for jobs or promotions and had not gotten them. And they were angry!

The show's title, no doubt to entice a large potential audience, was "A Black Woman Took My Job." In my comments to these men, I invited them to consider what the word "my" meant in that title. What made them think that the job was "theirs"? Why wasn't the title "A Black Woman Got *The* Job" or "A Black Woman Got *A* Job"?

That title exposed men's sense of entitlement. They felt those jobs were theirs, by natural right, divine right, birth right—some "right" that conveyed things to them, simply for being white men. From their perspective, some other person—black and female—got "their" job. White men have been the beneficiaries of the single greatest affirmative-action program in world history—in fact, it is world history!

In this light, we can consider the story of *Iron John*, made so famous by Robert Bly in the mid 1990s (Bly, 1991). In the legend, there are four male characters, a little boy and three kings—the boy's father, the father of his chosen bride, and, of course, Iron John himself, who turns out to be a great king as well. At every mythopoetic gathering, discussion group, retreat, or conference where the work was discussed, virtually all the middle-aged men present—most who are themselves fathers—identify with the young boy. And it's obvious that the author does as well, punctuating his narration with occasional recollections of his own father. No one identifies with the father, the king, but with the son, the little prince.

What are we to make of this? Well, who is the prince? He is the man who is entitled to be in power but who is not yet in power. He is entitled to power but feels powerless.

It is from this place—shall we call it the "Inner Prince"—that I believe men speak, a place of gnawing anxiety, a place of entitlement unfulfilled. No wonder men are defensive when we present feminism to them—it feels like they will be forced to give up this sense of entitlement (as well as, of course, the rewards that are promised to follow directly upon its achievement). Feminism, to men, feels like loss, a loss of the possibility to claim their birthright of power. And violence may be more about getting the power to which you feel you're entitled than an expression of the power you already think you have.

This model of violence as the result of a breakdown of patriarchy, of entitlement thwarted, has become one of the foundations of the field of masculinity studies as it has developed over the past two decades. It is also the bedrock of therapeutic work with violent men. Again and again, what the research on rape and domestic violence finds is that men initiate violence when they feel a loss of power to which they felt entitled. Thus, he hits her when she fails to have the dinner ready, when she refuses to meet his sexual demands, that is, when his power over her has broken down—not when she has dinner ready or is willing to have sex, which are, after all, expressions of his power and its legitimacy.

II

And just as men become violent individually when they experience the breakdown of patriarchal power, when they feel the loss of their entitlement, so too do men become violent collectively, in social movements of men. In particular, they become violent in the atavistic expressions of ethnicity, racism, nativism, xenophobia, and nationalism that today tear the global community apart. If what I've been exploring is what we might call the social psychology of gendered violence, let me now try and speculate about the political economy and moral economy of men's violence expressed at a national or local political level. Let's explore the links between ethnic nationalist violence, terrorism, and urban gang violence on the one hand and this social psychology of entitlement on the other.

Let's begin with the demographics. Who exactly are these young men who form the columns of ethnic nationalist soldiers? Who are the terrorists of 9/11, the suicide bombers? Who are the legions of neo-Nazis, white supremacists, and other Aryan warriors that have been springing up all over the world?

They're not just terrorists or bombers or freedom fighters; they're men. And not just any men—they are young men, mostly in their twenties. And they are fairly well educated young men, mostly the sons of the lower middle class. Their fathers are the artisans, small shopkeepers, and craftsmen who populate the urban marketplaces, who set up shop as independent producers, the petite bourgeoisie. They are independent tradesmen, skilled independent workers (plumbers, electricians, carpenters). They own a small store, a small family farm. They're very highly skilled workers in large industries like steel or automobile manufacturing.

That is, they *were.* They've been downsized, laid off, or outsourced. They've closed the small mom-and-pop store when Wal-Mart moved in down the road. They fore-closed on the family farm.

Once, these fathers felt free, independent, and in control of their own economic destiny. They experienced the camaraderie of political community in the workplace and unquestioned domestic patriarchal control at home. But they left only a bitter legacy to their sons, who expected that the words "and son" would one day swing over the door of their father's shop—the sons who expected to experience the same eco-nomic autonomy as independent producers as their fathers, who felt *entitled* to it. And who felt *entitled* to be the kings of their own castle.

Perhaps the most significant result of economic globalization has been the world-wide squeezing of this lower middle class, its proletarianization. These young men face an uncertain economic future, a future in which, *if they are lucky,* they will obtain jobs in their own home cities—but in factories, not in shops of their own. Ethnic national-ism gives voice to the inchoate economic fears of lower-middle-class men as they face the proletarianization that accompanies incorporation into the global economy. The fathers are incapable of shielding their sons from this; fathers' control is weakened as they capitulate to the state. The disintegration of material resources of domestic patri-archy leads to the rebellion of the sons. As Barrington Moore (1966) argued four decades ago, the real revolutionaries are not drawn from those social groups on the rise but, rather, represent the cry of those over whom history is about to roll.

I am suggesting that ethnic nationalist violence is the expression of a gendered protest against proletarianization by lower-middle-class younger men. Thus, it would follow empirically that ethnic nationalist violence is likely to erupt in regions where traditions of local and regional autonomy were abridged by centripetal political machines emanating from centralizing states, as well as where traditions of local craft autonomy have been subsumed within larger patterns of global economic develop-ment. Participants have been those economic actors who had enjoyed historical tradi-tions of autonomy—the lower middle classes of artisans, skilled workers, and trades-men who dominate urban craft production and the entrepreneurs and small shopkeepers who dominate local urban trade. In Iran, for example, the backbone of the revolutionary movement was the lower-middle-class shopkeepers, the *bazaaris*, as well as students. This was also the case among the Taliban in Afghanistan. The Basque movement included shopkeepers and small-scale businessmen and skilled workers. Members of the ETA were virtually all young men (mean age at induction was twenty-four), educated (over 40 percent had some university training), who were the sons of artisans and lower-middle-class shopkeepers whose upward mobility was blocked by the region's economic dependence (see, for example, Kriesberg, 1989).

In American cities, ethnic and racial violence is almost invariably the work of young men whose economic mobility is thwarted and who often articulate a gendered politi-cal discourse of that projected downward mobility, even as the media continues to observe their behavior in racial terms. The extreme Right in the United States are almost all younger lower-middle-class men, in their early twenties, educated at least through high school and often beyond. They are the sons of skilled workers in indus-tries like textiles and tobacco, the sons of the owners of small farms, shops, and grocery stores. Buffeted by global political and economic forces, the sons have inherited little of their fathers' legacies. The family farms have been lost to foreclosure; the small shops squeezed out by Wal-Marts and malls. These young men face a spiral of downward mobility and economic uncertainty. They complain that they are squeezed between the omnivorous jaws of global capital concentration and a federal bureaucracy which is, at best, indifferent to their plight and, at worst, complicit in their demise.

It appears that everywhere nationalist movements set up shop it is these frustrated young men who are the shopkeepers. Couple this with the ways in which the history of the nation state in the West has been the progressive appropriation of the means of violence by the state, and the result is particularly explosive. This process has always left a cadre of young males resentful, especially when the traditional avenues of expressing their manhood—economic autonomy, control over their own labor, a sense of secure place in a local political and social community—were eroded by state centralization and proletarianization. This resentment can turn to rage against that centralizing state. "Once," they will say, "we were kings. But now they have made us pawns."

What better way to channel that energy than to cast state policies as authoritarian paternalism, its policies emasculating and "feminizing," and thus brandish weapons as a way to assert a claim to "righteous" manhood? Ethnic nationalism is the rebellion of the sons against the regime of the father, who is depicted as either emasculated by dependence on the superpowers or as emasculating of his sons, who therefore carry the hope and future of the traditionally glorious and now-suppressed nation.

If globalization is "gendered" in that the primary losers are these downwardly mobile sons of the lower middle class, then it is also gendered on the other side as well. Think of the gender of immigrants, especially those young male workers from developing countries who daily stream into the advanced industrial nations of Western Europe and the United States. The in-migration of disproportionate numbers of younger male migrants, clustered in ethnic enclaves in major industrial cities, heightens political and economic tensions experienced by both the new migrants and older, more established lower-middle-class males, who see increased economic competition in an already tightening labor market. It is young males who huddle in migrant labor camps or who live twelve to a room in America's suburbs.

Of course, you will point out, rightly, that these violent ethnic nationalists and white supremacists receive significant support from women. But the gender composition of ethnic nationalist violence is only a small part of the story. (On the other hand, had these movements been composed entirely of women, gender would be virtually the *only* story, and everyone would be commenting on it.) Far more significant is the gender *ideology*, the meanings of manhood that are being played out through ethnic, racial, and nationalist violence. To ignore this would be to fail to listen to the voices of the participants themselves. They frequently use a gendered language that speaks about how "they" would not let "us" be men—to take care of our families, have the jobs we were raised to expect, experience the control, power, and authority that we wanted and that we were assured was our destiny. How such a language is corrupted into the rapacious nihilism of warlordism, the systematic terror of ethnic cleansing, or the coldly rational mind of terrorism is one of the more profound political and moral questions of our time.

III

Let me offer two examples of these issues that can better illustrate the sorts of arguments I am making here. First, consider the writer of a letter to the editor of a small upstate New York newspaper written in 1993 by an American GI, after his return from service in the Gulf War. He complains that the legacy of the American middle class has been stolen, handed over by an indifferent government to a bunch of ungrateful immigrants and welfare cheats. "The American dream," he writes (cited in Dyer, 1997: 63), "has all but disappeared, substituted with people struggling just to buy next week's groceries."

That letter writer was Timothy McVeigh from Lockport, New York. Two years later, McVeigh blew up the federal building in Oklahoma City in what is now the second worst act of terrorism ever committed on American soil.

McVeigh was representative of the small legion of white supremacists—from older organizations like the John Birch Society, the Ku Klux Klan, and the American Nazi Party to neo-Nazis, racist skinheads, and White Power groups like Posse Comitatus and the White Aryan Resistance to the radical militias. They feel bewildered and buffeted by economic forces beyond their control, forces that deprive them of their entitlement. As one issue of *The Truth at Last*, a White Supremacist magazine, put it,

> Immigrants are flooding into our nation willing to work for the minimum wage (or less). Super-rich corporate executives are flying all over the world in search of cheaper and cheaper labor so that they can "lay off" their American employees. . . . Many young White families have no future! They are not going to receive any appreciable wage increases due to job competition from immigrants. (Cited in Dobratz and Shanks Meile, 2001: 115)

What they want, says one member, is to "take back what is rightfully ours" (cited in Dobratz and Shanks Meile, 2001: 10).

Their anger often fixes on the "others"—minorities, immigrants—in part because these are the people with whom they compete for entry-level, minimum-wage jobs or those, like women and gays and lesbians, to whom they perceive the government kowtows. Above them all, enjoying the view, hovers the purported international Jewish conspiracy.

What holds these "paranoid politics"—antigovernment, anti-global-capital, but pro-small-capitalist, racist, sexist, anti-Semitic, homophobic—together is a rhetoric of masculinity. These men feel emasculated by big money and big government—they call the government "the Nanny State"—and they claim that "others" have been handed the birthright of native-born white men.

In the eyes of such downwardly mobile white men, most white American men collude in their emasculation. They've grown soft, feminized, weak. White supremacist websites abound with complaints about the "whimpering collapse of the blond male"; in *The Turner Diaries,* a canonical touchstone text for American white supremacists, the narrator rails against "legions of sissies and weaklings, of flabby, limp-wristed, non-aggressive, non-physical, indecisive, slack-jawed, fearful males who, while still heterosexual in theory and practice, have not even a vestige of the old macho spirit" (cited in Hamm, 2002: 286).

American white supremacists thus offer American men the restoration of their masculinity—a manhood in which individual white men control the fruits of their own labor and are not subject to the emasculation of Jewish-owned finance capital, a black- and feminist-controlled welfare state. Theirs is the militarized manhood of the heroic John Rambo—a manhood that celebrates their God-sanctioned right to band together in armed militias if anyone, or any governmental agency, tries to take it away from them. If the state and capital emasculate them, and if the masculinity of the "others" is problematic, then only "real" white men can rescue this American Eden from a feminized, multicultural, androgynous melting pot.

Sound familiar? For the most part, the terrorists of 9/11 come from the same class and recite the same complaints as American white supremacists. Virtually all were under twenty-five, educated, lower middle class or middle class, downwardly mobile. Journalist Nasra Hassan (2001: 38) interviewed families of Middle Eastern suicide bombers (as well as some failed bombers themselves) and found "none of them were uneducated, desperately poor, simple minded or depressed," the standard motivations ascribed to those who commit suicide.

Although several of the leaders of Al Qaeda were wealthy—Osama bin Laden is a multimillionaire, and Ayman al-Zawahiri, the fifty-year-old doctor thought to be bin Laden's closest adviser, is from a fashionable suburb of Cairo—many of the hijackers were engineering students, for whom job opportunities had been dwindling dramatically. One-fourth of the hijackers had studied engineering. Kamel Daoudi studied computer science at a university in Paris; Zacarias Moussaoui, who did not hijack one of the planes but is the first man to be formally charged with a crime in the United States for the events of September 11, took a degree at London's South Bank University. Marwan al-Shehhi, a chubby, bespectacled twenty-three-year-old from the United Arab Emirates, was an engineering student, and Ziad Jarrah, a twenty-six-year-old Lebanese, had studied aircraft design (Rothstein, 2001; Maas, 2001: 51; Elliott, 2001: 66).

Politically, these terrorists opposed globalization and the spread of Western values; they opposed what they perceived as corrupt regimes in several Arab states (notably Saudi Arabia and Egypt), which they claimed were merely puppets of U.S. domination. "The resulting anger is naturally directed first against their rulers," writes the historian of Islam Bernard Lewis (2001: 57), "and then against those whom they see as keeping those rulers in power for selfish reasons."

Central to their political ideology is the recovery of manhood from the devastatingly emasculating politics of globalization. The Taliban saw the Soviet invasion and Westernization as humiliations. Osama bin Ladin's 7 October, 2001 videotape describes the "humiliation and disgrace" that Islam has suffered for "more than eighty years." And over and over, Nasra Hassan writes (2001: 38), she heard the refrain, "The Israelis humiliate us. They occupy our land, and deny our history."

Terrorism is fueled by a fatal brew of antiglobalization politics, convoluted Islamic theology, and virulent misogyny. According to Barbara Ehrenreich (2001: M1), while these formerly employed or self-employed males "have lost their traditional status as farmers and breadwinners, women have been entering the market economy and gaining the marginal independence conferred even by a paltry wage." As a result, "the man who can no longer make a living, who has to depend on his wife's earnings, can watch Hollywood sexpots on pirated videos and begin to think the world has been turned upside down."

The Taliban's policies thus had two purposes: to remasculinize men and to refeminize women. Another journalist, Peter Marsden (2002: 99), has observed that those policies "could be seen as a desperate attempt to keep out that other world, and to protect Afghan women from influences that could weaken the society from within." The Taliban prohibited women from appearing in public unescorted by men, from revealing any part of their body, or from going to school or holding a job. Men were required to grow their beards, in accordance with religious images of Mohammed, yes, but also, perhaps, because wearing beards has always been associated with men's response to women's increased equality in the public sphere, since beards symbolically reaffirm biological natural differences between women and men, while gender equality tends to blur those differences.

The Taliban's policies removed women as competitors and also shored up masculinity, since they enabled men to triumph over the humiliations of globalization as well as to triumph over their own savage, predatory, and violently sexual urges that would be unleashed in the presence of uncovered women.

All these issues converge in the life of Mohammed Atta, about whom the most has been written and conjectured. (My portrait is drawn largely from Yardley, 2001). Atta was slim, sweet-faced, neat, meticulous, a snazzy dresser. The youngest child of an ambitious lawyer father and pampering mother, Atta grew up shy and polite, a mama's boy. "He was so gentle," his father said. "I used to tell him 'Toughen up, boy!'"

Both Atta and McVeigh failed at their chosen professions. McVeigh, a business college dropout, found his "calling" in the military during the Gulf War, where his exemplary service earned him commendations; but he washed out of Green Beret training—his dream job—after only two days (Dyer, 1997: 215–6). And Atta's two sisters were both doctors, one a physician and one a university professor. His father constantly reminded him that he wanted "to hear the word 'doctor' in front of his name. We told him your sisters are doctors and their husbands are doctors and you are the man of the family" (Yardley, 2001: B9).

Atta decided to become an engineer, but his "degree meant little in a country where thousands of college graduates were unable to find good jobs." After he failed to find employment in Egypt, he went to Hamburg, Germany, to study to become an architect. He was "meticulous, disciplined and highly intelligent," an "ordinary student, a quiet friendly guy who was totally focused on his studies," according to another student in Hamburg.

But his ambitions were constantly undone. His only hope for a good job in Egypt was to be hired by an international firm. He applied and was constantly rejected. He found work as a draftsman—highly humiliating for someone with engineering and architectural credentials and an imperious and demanding father—for a German firm involved with razing lower-income Cairo neighborhoods to provide more scenic vistas for luxury tourist hotels.

Defeated, humiliated, emasculated, a disappointment to his father, and a failed rival to his sisters, Atta retreated into increasingly militant Islamic theology. By the time he assumed controls of American Airlines Flight 11, he evinced a hysteria about women. In the message he left in his abandoned rental car, he made clear what mattered to him in the end. "I don't want pregnant women or a person who is not clean to come and say good-bye to me," he wrote. "I don't want women to go to my funeral or later to my grave." Of course, Atta's body was instantly incinerated, and no burial would be likely (CNN report, October 2, 2001).

The terrors of emasculation experienced by the lower middle classes all over the world will no doubt continue, as they struggle to make a place for themselves in shrinking economies and shifting cultures. They may continue to feel a seething resentment against women, whom they perceive as stealing their rightful place at the head of the table, and the governments that displace them. Globalization feels like a game of musical chairs, in which, when the music stops, all the seats are handed to others by nursemaid governments.

The events of September 11—as well as the tragic events of April 19, 1995—resulted from an increasingly common combination of factors—the massive male displacement that accompanies globalization, the spread of American consumerism, and the perceived corruption of local political elites—that fused with a masculine sense of entitlement, their rightful legacy, to produce this volatile mix. Somebody else—some "other"—had to be held responsible for their downward mobility, their failures, and the failures of their fathers to deliver their promised inheritance. The terrorists didn't just get mad. They got even.

Such themes were not lost on the disparate bands of young white supremacists. American Aryans admired the terrorists' courage as they chastised their own compatriots. "It's a disgrace that in a population of at least 150 million White/Aryan Americans, we provide so few that are willing to do the same [as the terrorists]," bemoaned Rocky Suhayda, Nazi Party chairman from Eastpointe, Michigan (cited in Ridgeway, 2001: 41). "A bunch of towel head/sand niggers put our great White Movement to shame."

IV

Finally let me offer an alternative way to frame these questions. Instead of focusing on what we are doing wrong, perhaps it also makes sense to discuss what other societies are doing right. Can it be otherwise? Why do some societies *not* experience this same violence of the entitled younger men? What do they do differently?

Twenty-five years ago, anthropologist Peggy Reeves Sanday (see this volume) proposed a continuum of propensity to commit rape on which all societies could be plotted—from rape prone to rape free. (For the curious, by the way, the United States was ranked as a highly rape-prone society and Norway as a rape-free society.) Sanday found that the single best predictors of rape-proneness were (1) whether the woman continued to own property in her own name after marriage, a measure of women's autonomy, and (2) father's involvement in child-rearing, a measure of how valued parenting is and how valued women's work is.

A decade later, the Norwegian social anthropologists Signe Howell and Roy Willis

(1990) posed the obverse question: what can we learn from peaceful societies? In their fascinating collection *Societies at Peace*, they suggested several fruitful themes. For one thing, they found that the definition of masculinity had a significant impact on the propensity toward violence. In those societies in which men were permitted to acknowledge fear, levels of violence were low. In those societies, however, where masculine bravado, the repression and denial of fear, was a defining feature of masculinity, violence was likely to be high. It turns out that those societies in which such bravado is prescribed for men are also those in which the definitions of masculinity and femininity are very highly differentiated.

Thus, for example, in *Societies at Peace*, Joanna Overing tells us that in the Amazon jungle, the extremely violent Shavante define manhood as "sexual bellicosity," a state both superior and opposed to femininity, whereas their peaceful neighboring Piaroas define manhood *and womanhood* as the ability to cooperate tranquilly with others in daily life.

In sum, these are a few of the themes that anthropologists have isolated as leading toward both interpersonal violence and intersocietal violence:

1. the ideal for manhood is the fierce and handsome warrior;
2. public leadership is associated with male dominance, both of men over other men and of men over women;
3. women are prohibited from public and political participation;
4. most public interaction is between men, not between men and women or among women;
5. boys and girls are systematically separated from an early age;
6. initiation of boys is focused on lengthy constraint of boys, during which time the boys are separated from women, taught male solidarity, bellicosity, and endurance, and trained to accept the dominance of older groups of men;
7. emotional displays of male virility, ferocity, and sexuality are highly elaborated;
8. the ritual celebration of fertility focuses on male generative ability, not female ones.
9. male economic activities and the products of male labor are prized over female.

Taken together, these works (Sanday, Howell and Wills, and Overing's chapter in Howell and Wills) provide a series of possible policy-oriented goals toward which we might look if we are to reduce the amount of gendered violence in society. First, it seems clear that the less gender differentiation between women and men, the less likely will be gendered violence. This means that the more "like women" men can be seen (nurturing, caring, frightened) and the more "like men" women can be seen (capable, rational, competent in the public sphere), the more likely that aggression will take other routes besides gendered violence.

Men's violence toward women is the result of entitlement thwarted; men's violence toward other men often derives from the same thwarted sense of entitlement. I would propose a curvilinear relationship between male-to-male violence and male violence against women and the entitlement to patriarchal power. To find peaceful societies one should look for those cultures in which entitlement to power is either not thwarted or not present. Thus, societies with the least male-male gendered violence would be those in which patriarchy is either intact and unquestioned or those in which it is hardly present at all and hasn't been for some time.

To diminish men's violence against women, and to reduce the violent confrontations that take place in the name of such mythic entities as nation, people, religion, or tribe, we must confront the separation of symbolic and structural spheres. Women's involvement in public life is equally important as men's involvement as parents. And the definition of masculinity must be able to acknowledge a far wider range of emotions, including fear, without having that identity as a man threatened. And we must develop mechanisms to dislodge men's sense of identity from that false sense of entitlement.

The value of anthropological comparisons is that they provide documentation that it need not be this way, that it can be otherwise. They give empirical solidity to our hopes, a nonutopian concreteness to our vision. Making it otherwise, however, will require dramatic transformations, in the ideal definition of what it means to be a man and in the cultural prescriptions that govern the relationships among men and between women and men.

Over 250 years ago, the British moral philosopher David Hume ([1748] 1999) wrote the following in his *Enquiry Concerning Human Understanding*:

> Should a traveler, returning from a far country, bring us an account of men wholly different from any with whom we were ever acquainted; men who were entirely divested of vice, ambition, or revenge; who knew no pleasure but friendship, generosity, and public spirit; we should immediately, from these circumstances, detect the falsehood, and prove him a liar, with the same certainty as if he had stuffed his narration with stories of centaurs and dragons, miracles and prodigies.

Hume's remarks remind us of the cynicism with which critiques of prevailing ideologies are likely to be met. But he also suggests the possibility that such a world might yet be within our grasp.

Chapter Six

Sexual Terrorism

Carole J. Sheffield

*No two of us think alike about it, and yet it is clear to me,
that question underlies the whole movement, and our little
skirmishing for better laws, and the right to vote, will yet be
swallowed up in the real question, viz: Has a woman a right
to herself? It is very little to me to have the right to vote, to
own property, etc., if I may not keep my body, and its uses,
in my absolute right. Not one wife in a thousand can do
that now.*

—Lucy Stone, in a letter to Antoinette
Brown, July 11, 1855

The right of men to control the female body is a cornerstone of patriarchy. It is
expressed by their efforts to control pregnancy and childbirth and to define female
health care in general. Male opposition to abortion is rooted in opposition to female
autonomy. Violence and the threat of violence against females represent the need of
patriarchy to deny that a woman's body is her own property and that no one should
have access to it without her consent. Violence and its corollary, fear, serve to terrorize
females and to maintain the patriarchal definition of woman's place.

The word *terrorism* invokes images of furtive organizations of the far right or left,
whose members blow up buildings and cars, hijack airplanes, and murder innocent
people in some country other than ours. But there is a different kind of terrorism, one
that so pervades our culture that we have learned to live with it as though it were the
natural order of things. Its target is females—of all ages, races, and classes. It is the
common characteristic of rape, wife battery, incest, pornography, harassment, and all
forms of sexual violence. I call it *sexual terrorism* because it is a system by which males
frighten and, by frightening, control and dominate females.

The concept of terrorism captured my attention in an "ordinary" event. One afternoon I collected my laundry and went to a nearby laundromat. The place is located in a
small shopping center on a very busy highway. After I had loaded and started the

From Jo Freeman (ed.), *Women: A Feminist Perspective*, 5th ed. (Mountain View, CA: Mayfield Press, 1994).
Reprinted by permission of author.

machines, I became acutely aware of my environment. It was just after 6:00 P.M. and dark, the other stores were closed, the laundromat was brightly lit, and my car was the only one in the lot. Anyone passing by could readily see that I was alone and isolated. Knowing that rape is often a crime of opportunity, I became terrified. I wanted to leave and find a laundromat that was busier, but my clothes were well into the wash cycle, and, besides, I felt I was being "silly," "paranoid." The feeling of terror persisted, so I sat in my car, windows up and doors locked. When the wash was completed, I dashed in, threw the clothes into the dryer, and ran back out to my car. When the clothes were dry, I tossed them recklessly into the basket and hurriedly drove away to fold them in the security of my home.

Although I was not victimized in a direct, physical way or by objective or measurable standards, I felt victimized. It was, for me, a terrifying experience. I felt controlled by an invisible force. I was angry that something as commonplace as doing laundry after a day's work jeopardized my well-being. Mostly I was angry at being unfree: a hostage of a culture that, for the most part, encourages violence against females, instructs men in the methodology of sexual violence, and provides them with ready justification for their violence. I was angry that I could be victimized by being "in the wrong place at the wrong time." The essence of terrorism is that one never knows when is the wrong time and where is the wrong place.

Following my experience at the laundromat, I talked with my students about terrorization. Women students began to open up and reveal terrors that they had kept secret because of embarrassment: fears of jogging alone, shopping alone, going to the movies alone. One woman recalled feelings of terror in her adolescence when she did child care for extra money. Nothing had ever happened, and she had not been afraid of anyone in particular, but she had felt a vague terror when being driven home late at night by the man of the house.

The male students listened incredulously and then demanded equal time. The harder they tried, the more they realized how very different—qualitatively, quantitatively, and contextually—their fears were. All agreed that, while they experienced fear in a violent society, they did not experience terror, nor did they experience fear of rape or sexual mutilation. They felt more in control, either from a psychophysical sense of security that they could defend themselves or from a confidence in being able to determine wrong places and times. All the women admitted feeling fear and anxiety when walking to their cars on the campus, especially after an evening class or activity. None of the men experienced fear on campus at any time. The men could be rather specific in describing where they were afraid: in Harlem, for example, or in certain parts of downtown Newark, New Jersey—places that have a reputation for violence. But either they could avoid these places or they felt capable of self-protective action. Above all, male students said that they *never* feared being attacked simply because they were male. They *never* feared going to a movie or to a mall alone. Their daily activities were not characterized by a concern for their physical integrity.

The differences between men's and women's experiences of fear underscore the meaning of sexual terrorism: that women's lives are bounded by both the reality of pervasive sexual danger and the fear that reality engenders. In her study of rape, Susan Brownmiller argues that rape is "nothing more or less than a conscious process of intimidation by which all men keep all women in a state of fear."[1] In their study *The Female Fear*, Margaret T. Gordon and Stephanie Riger found that one-third of women said they worry at least once a month about being raped. Many said they worry daily about the possibility of being raped. When they think about rape, they feel terrified and somewhat paralyzed. A third of women indicated that the fear of rape is "part of the background" of their lives and "one of those things that's always there." Another third claimed they never worried about rape but reported taking precautions, "sometimes elaborate ones," to try to avoid being raped.[2] Indeed, women's attempts to avoid sexual intrusion take many forms. To varying degrees, women change and restrict their behavior, life-styles, and physical appearances. They will pay higher costs for housing and transportation and even make educational and career choices to attempt to minimize sexual victimization.

Sexual terrorism includes nonviolent sexual intimidation and the threat of violence as well as overt sexual violence. For example, although an act of rape, an unnecessary hysterectomy, and the publishing of *Playboy* magazine appear to be quite different, they are in fact more similar than dissimilar. Each is based on fear, hostility, and a need to dominate women. Rape is an act of aggression and possession. Unnecessary hysterectomies are extraordinary abuses of power rooted in men's concept of women as primarily reproductive beings and in their need to assert power over that reproduction. *Playboy*, like all forms of pornography, attempts to control women through the power of definition. Male pornographers define women's sexuality for their male customers. The basis of pornography is men's fantasies about women's sexuality.

Components of Sexual Terrorism

The literature on terrorism does not provide a precise definition.[3] Mine is taken from Hacker, who says that "terrorism aims to frighten, and by frightening, to dominate and control."[4] Writers agree more readily on the characteristics and functions of terrorism than on a definition. This analysis will focus on five components to illuminate the similarities and distinctions between sexual terrorism and political terrorism. The five components are ideology, propaganda, indiscriminate and amoral violence, voluntary compliance, and society's perception of the terrorist and the terrorized.

An *ideology* is an integrated set of beliefs about the world that explains the way things are and provides a vision of how they ought to be. Patriarchy, meaning the "rule of the fathers," is the ideological foundation of sexism in our society. It asserts the superiority of males and the inferiority of females. It also provides the rationale for sexual terrorism. The taproot of patriarchy is the masculine/warrior ideal. Masculinity must include not only a proclivity for violence but also all those characteristics claimed by warriors: aggression, control, emotional reserve, rationality, sexual potency, etc. Marc Feigen Fasteau, in *The Male Machine*, argues that "men are brought up with the idea that there ought to be some part of them, under control until released by necessity, that thrives on violence. This capacity, even affinity, for violence, lurking beneath the surface of every real man, is supposed to represent the primal untamed base of masculinity."[5]

Propaganda is the methodical dissemination of information for the purpose of promoting a particular ideology. Propaganda, by definition, is biased or even false information. Its purpose is to present one point of view on a subject and to discredit opposing points of view. Propaganda is essential to the conduct of terrorism. According to Francis Watson, in *Political Terrorism: The Threat and the Response*, "Terrorism must not be defined only in terms of violence, but also in terms of propaganda. The two are in operation together. Violence of terrorism is a coercive means for attempting to influence the thinking and actions of people. Propaganda is a persuasive means for doing the same thing."[6] The propaganda of sexual terrorism is found in all expressions of the popular culture: films, television, music, literature, advertising, pornography. The propaganda of sexual terrorism is also found in the ideas of patriarchy expressed in science, medicine, and psychology.

The third component, which is common to all forms of political terrorism, consists of "indiscriminateness, unpredictability, arbitrariness, ruthless destructiveness and amorality."[7] Indiscriminate violence and amorality are also at the heart of sexual terrorism. Every female is a potential target of violence—at any age, at any time, in any place. Further, as we shall see, amorality pervades sexual violence. Child molesters, incestuous fathers, wife beaters, and rapists often do not understand that they have done anything wrong. Their views are routinely shared by police officers, lawyers, and judges, and crimes of sexual violence are rarely punished in American society.

The fourth component of the theory of terrorism is voluntary compliance. The institutionalization of a system of terror requires the development of mechanisms other than sustained violence to achieve its goals. Violence must be employed to maintain terrorism, but sustained violence can be costly and debilitating. Therefore, strategies for ensuring a significant degree of voluntary compliance must be developed. Sexual terrorism is maintained to a great extent by an elaborate system of sex-role socialization that in effect instructs men to be terrorists in the name of masculinity and women to be victims in the name of femininity.

Sexual and political terrorism differ in the final component, perceptions of the terrorist and the victim. In political terrorism we know who is the terrorist and who is the victim. We may condemn or condone the terrorist, depending on our political views, but we sympathize with the victim. In sexual terrorism, however, we blame the victim and excuse the offender. We believe that the offender either is "sick" and therefore in need of our compassion or is acting out normal male impulses.

Types of Sexual Terrorism

While the discussion that follows focuses on four types of sexual terrorism—rape, wife abuse, sexual abuse of children, and sexual harassment—recent feminist research has documented other forms of sexual terrorism, including threats of violence, flashing, street hassling, obscene phone calls, stalking, coercive sex, pornography, prostitution, sexual slavery, and femicide. What women experience as sexually intrusive and violent is not necessarily reflected in our legal codes, and those acts that are recognized as criminal are often not understood specifically as crimes against women—as acts of sexual violence.

Acts of sexual terrorism include many forms of intrusion that society accepts as common and are therefore trivialized. For example, a recent study of women's experiences of obscene phone calls found that women respondents overwhelmingly found these calls to be a form of sexual intimidation and harassment.[8] While obscene phone calls are illegal, only in rare cases do women report them and the police take them seriously. In contrast, some forms of sexual terrorism are so extraordinary that they are regarded not only as aberrant but also as incomprehensible. The execution of fourteen women students at the University of Montreal on December 6, 1989, is one example of this. Separating the men from the women in a classroom and shouting, "You're all fucking feminists," twenty-five-year-old Marc Lepine systematically murdered fourteen women. In his suicide letter, claiming that "the feminists have always enraged me," Lepine recognized his crime as a political act.[9] For many women, this one act of sexual terrorism galvanized attention to the phenomenon of the murder of women because they are women. "Femicide," according to Jane Caputi and Diane E. H. Russell, describes "the murders of women by men motivated by hatred, contempt, pleasure, or a sense of ownership of women."[10] Most femicide, unlike the Montreal massacre, is committed by a male acquaintance, friend, or relative. In *Surviving Sexual Violence*, Liz Kelly argues that sexual violence must be understood as a continuum—that is, "a continuous series of events that pass into one another" united by a "basic common character."[11] Viewing sexual violence in this way furthers an understanding of both the "ordinary" and "extraordinary" forms of sexual terrorism and the range of abuse that women experience in their lifetimes.

Many types of sexual terrorism are crimes, yet when we look at the history of these acts, we see that they came to be considered criminal not so much to protect women as to adjust power relationships among men. Rape was originally a violation of a father's or husband's property rights; consequently, a husband by definition could not rape his wife. Wife beating was condoned by the law and still is condemned in name only. Although proscriptions against incest exist, society assumes a more serious posture toward men who sexually abuse other men's daughters. Sexual harassment is not a crime, and only recently has it been declared an actionable civil offense. Crimes of sexual violence are characterized by ambiguity and diversity in definition and interpretation. Because each state and territory has a separate system of law in addition to the federal system, crimes and punishments are assessed differently throughout the country.

Rape

Rape statutes have been reformed in the past decade, largely to remove the exemption for wife rape and to use gender-neutral language. The essence of the definition of rape, however, remains the same: sexual penetration (typically defined as penile-vaginal, but may include oral and anal sodomy or penetration by fingers or other objects) of a female by force or threat of force, against her will and without her consent.[12]

Traditional views of rape are shaped by male views of sexuality and by men's fear of being unjustly accused. Deborah Rhode argues, in *Justice and Gender,* that this reflects a "sexual schizophrenia." That is, forced sexual intercourse by a stranger against a chaste woman is unquestionably regarded as a heinous crime, whereas coercive sex that does not fit this model is largely denied.[13] Since most women are raped by men they know, this construction excludes many forms of rape.

Because rape is considered a sexual act, evidence of force and resistance is often necessary to establish the nonconsent needed to convict rapists. Such proof is not demanded of a victim of any other crime. If females do not resist rape as much as possible, "consent" is assumed.

By 1990, forty-two states had adopted laws criminalizing rape in marriage: sixteen states recognize that wife rape is a crime and provide no exemptions; twenty-six states penalize wife rape but allow for some exemptions under which husbands cannot be prosecuted for raping their wives. Eight states do not recognize wife rape as a crime.[14] In spite of statutory reform, wife rape remains a greatly misunderstood phenomenon, and the magnitude of sexual abuse by husbands is not known. In Diana E. H. Russell's pioneering study on rape in marriage, 14 percent of the female respondents reported having been raped by their husbands.[15] The prevalence of wife rape, however, is believed to be much higher; approximately 40 percent of women in battered women's shelters also report having been raped by their husbands.[16] Victims of wife rape, according to one study, are at a greater risk of being murdered by their husbands, or of murdering them, than women who are physically but not sexually assaulted.[17]

Wife Abuse

For centuries it has been assumed that a husband had the right to punish or discipline his wife with physical force. The popular expression "rule of thumb" originated from English common law, which allowed a husband to beat his wife with a whip or stick no bigger in diameter than his thumb. The husband's prerogative was incorporated into American law. Several states once had statutes that essentially allowed a man to beat his wife without interference from the courts.[18]

In 1871, in the landmark case of *Fulgham v. State*, an Alabama court ruled that "the privilege, ancient though it be, to beat her with a stick, to pull her hair, choke her, spit in her face or kick her about the floor or to inflict upon her other like indignities, is not now acknowledged by our law."[19] The law, however, has been ambiguous and often contradictory on the issue of wife abuse. While the courts established that a man had no right to beat his wife, it also held that a woman could not press charges against her abusive husband. In 1910, the U.S. Supreme Court ruled that a wife could not charge her husband with assault and battery because it "would open the doors of the court to accusations of all sorts of one spouse against the other and bring into public notice complaints for assaults, slander and libel."[20] The courts virtually condoned violence for the purpose of maintaining peace.

Laws and public attitudes about the illegality of wife abuse and the rights of the victim have been slowly evolving. During the 1980s, there was a proliferation of new laws designed to address the needs of victims of domestic violence and to reform police and judicial responses to wife abuse. These measures include temporary or permanent protection orders, state-funded or state-assisted shelters, state-mandated data collection, and proarrest or mandatory arrest policies.[21] Most states, however, continue to define domestic violence as a misdemeanor crime, carrying jail sentences of less than one year. Felony crimes are punishable by more than one year in jail, and police officers tend to arrest more often for felony offenses. The distinction between misdemeanor and felony crimes is also based on the use of weapons and the infliction of serious injuries.[22] While wife abuse is still considered a misdemeanor crime, a National Crime Survey revealed that at least 50 percent of the domestic "simple assaults" involved bodily injury as serious as or more serious than 90 percent of all rapes, robberies, and aggravated assaults.[23]

Sexual Abuse of Children

Defining sexual abuse of children is very difficult. The laws are complex and often contradictory. Generally, sexual abuse of children includes statutory rape, molestation, carnal knowledge, indecent liberties, impairing the morals of a minor, child abuse, child neglect, and incest. Each of these is defined, interpreted, and punished differently in each state.

The philosophy underlying statutory-rape laws is that a child below a certain age— arbitrarily fixed by law—is not able to give meaningful consent. Therefore, sexual intercourse with a female below a certain age, even with consent, is rape. Punishment for statutory rape, although rarely imposed, can be as high as life imprisonment. Coexistent with laws on statutory rape are laws on criminal incest. Incest is generally interpreted as sexual activity, most often intercourse, with a blood relative. The difference, then, between statutory rape and incest is the relation of the offender to the child. Statutory rape is committed by someone outside the family; incest, by a member of the family. The penalty for incest, also rarely imposed, is usually no more than ten years in prison. This contrast suggests that sexual abuse of children is tolerated when it occurs within the family and that unqualified protection of children from sexual assault is not the intent of the law.

Sexual Harassment

Sexual harassment is a new term for an old phenomenon. The research on sexual harassment, as well as the legal interpretation, centers on acts of sexual coercion or intimidation on the job and at school. Lin Farley, in *Sexual Shakedown: The Sexual Harassment of Women on the Job,* describes sexual harassment as "unsolicited nonreciprocal male behavior that asserts a woman's sex role over her function as a worker. It can be any or all of the following: staring at, commenting upon, or touching a woman's body; requests for acquiescence in sexual behavior; repeated nonreciprocated propositions for dates; demands for sexual intercourse; and rape."[24]

In 1980 the Equal Employment Opportunity Commission issued federal guidelines that defined sexual harassment as any behavior that "has the purpose or effect of unreasonably interfering with an individual's work performance or creating an intimidating or hostile or offensive environment." Such behavior can include "unwelcome sexual advances, requests for sexual favors, and other verbal or physical conduct of a sexual nature."[25] It was not until six years later, however, that the Supreme Court, in *Meritor Savings Bank FSB v. Vinson,* ruled that sexual harassment was a form of sex discrimination under Title VII of the Civil Rights Act of 1964.[26]

In October 1991 national attention was focused on the issue of sexual harassment as a result of allegations made against Supreme Court Justice nominee Clarence Thomas by Professor Anita Hill. (Thomas was subsequently confirmed as a Supreme Court Justice by a vote of fifty-two to forty-eight.) While there was a blizzard of media attention about sexual harassment, what emerged most clearly from the confirmation hearings was that the chasm between women's experiences of sexual harassment and an understanding of the phenomenon by society in general had not been bridged. Perhaps most misunderstood was the fact that Professor Hill's experience and her reaction to it were typical of sexually harassed women.[27]

Characteristics of Sexual Terrorism

Those forms of sexual terrorism that are crimes share several common characteristics. Each will be addressed separately, but in the real world these characteristics are linked together and form a vicious circle, which functions to mask the reality of sexual terrorism and thus to perpetuate the system of oppression of females. Crimes of violence against females (1) cut across socioeconomic lines; (2) are the crimes least likely to be reported; (3) when reported, are the crimes least likely to be brought to trial or to result in conviction; (4) are often blamed on the victim; (5) are generally not taken seriously; and (6) fuse dominance and sexuality.

Violence against Females Cuts across Socioeconomic Lines

The question "Who is the typical rapist, wife beater, incest offender, etc?" is raised constantly. The answer is simple: men. Female sexual offenders are exceedingly rare. The men who commit acts of sexual terrorism are of all ages, races, and religions; they come from all communities, income levels, and educational levels; they are married, single, separated, and divorced. The "typical" sexually abusive male does not exist.

One of the most common assumptions about sexual violence is that it occurs primarily among the poor, uneducated, and predominately nonwhite populations. Actually, violence committed by the poor and nonwhite is simply more visible because of their lack of resources to secure the privacy that the middle and upper classes can purchase. Most rapes, indeed, most incidents of sexual assault, are not reported, and therefore the picture drawn from police records must be viewed as very sketchy.

The data on sexual harassment in work situations indicates that it occurs among all job categories and pay ranges. Sexual harassment is committed by academic men, who are among the most highly educated members of society. In a 1991 *New York Times* poll, five out of ten men said they had said or done something that "could have been construed by a female colleague as harassment."[28]

All the studies on wife abuse testify to the fact that wife beating crosses socioeconomic lines. Wife beaters include high government officials, members of the armed forces, businessmen, policemen, physicians, lawyers, clergy, blue-collar workers, and the unemployed.[29] According to Maria Roy, founder and director of New York's Abused Women's Aid in Crisis, "We see abuse of women on all levels of income, age, occupation, and social standing. I've had four women come in recently whose husbands are Ph.D.s—two of them professors at top universities. Another abused woman is married to a very prominent attorney. We counseled battered wives whose husbands are doctors, psychiatrists, even clergymen."[30]

Similarly, in Vincent De Francis's classic study of 250 cases of sexual crimes committed against children, a major finding was that incidents of sexual assault against children cut across class lines.[31] Since sexual violence is not "nice," we prefer to believe that nice men do not commit these acts and that nice girls and women are not victims. Our refusal to accept the fact that violence against females is widespread throughout society strongly inhibits our ability to develop meaningful strategies to eliminate it. Moreover, because of underreporting, it is difficult to ascertain exactly how widespread it is.

Crimes of Sexual Violence Are the Least Likely to Be Reported

Underreporting is common for all crimes against females. There are two national sources for data on crime in the United States: the annual Uniform Crime Reports (UCR) of the Federal Bureau of Investigation, which collects information from police departments, and the National Crime Survey (NCS), conducted by the U.S. Department of Justice, which collects data on personal and household criminal victimizations from a nationally representative sample of households.

The FBI recognizes that rape is seriously underreported by as much as 80 to 90 percent. According to FBI data for 1990, 102,555 rapes were reported.[32] The FBI Uniform Crime Report for 1990 estimates that a forcible rape occurs every five minutes.[33] This estimate is based on reported rapes; accounting for the high rate of underreporting, the FBI estimates that a rape occurs every two minutes. The number of forcible rapes reported to the police has been increasing every year. Since 1986, the rape rate has risen 10 percent.[34]

The National Crime Survey (renamed in 1991 as the National Crime Victimization Survey) data for 1990 reports 130,260 rapes.[35] This data is only slightly higher than FBI data; researchers argue that NCS data has serious drawbacks as well.[36] Just as victims are reluctant to report a rape to the police, many are also reluctant to reveal their victimization to an NCS interviewer. In fact, the NCS does not ask directly about rape (although it will in the future). A respondent may volunteer the information when asked questions about bodily harm. The NCS also excludes children under twelve, thus providing no data on childhood sexual assault.

In April 1992 the National Victim Center and the Crime Victims Research and Treatment Center released a report entitled "Rape in America," which summarized two nationwide studies: the National Women's Study, a three-year longitudinal survey of a national probability sample of 4,008 adult women, and the State of Services for Victims of Rape, which surveyed 370 agencies that provide rape crisis assistance.[37] The National Women's Study sought information about the incidence of rape and information about a number of health issues related to rape, including depression, posttraumatic stress disorder, suicide attempts, and alcohol- and drug-related problems.

The results of the National Women's Study confirm a belief held by many experts that the UCR and NCS data seriously underrepresents the occurrence of rape. According to the National Women's Study, 683,000 adult women were raped during a twelve-month period from the fall of 1989 to the fall of 1990.[38] This data is significantly higher than UCR and NCS data for approximately the same period. Moreover, since rapes of female children and adolescents under the age of eighteen and rapes of boys or men were not included in the study, the 683,000 rapes of adult women do not reflect an accurate picture of all rapes that occurred during that period. The data in this study also confirms the claim that acquaintance rape is far more pervasive than stranger rape. While 22 percent of victims were raped by someone unknown to them, 36 percent were raped by family members: 9 percent by husbands or ex-husbands, 11 percent by fathers or stepfathers, 16 percent by other relatives. Ten percent were raped by a boyfriend or ex-boyfriend and 29 percent by nonrelatives such as friends or neighbors (3 percent were not sure or refused to answer).[39]

Perhaps the most significant finding of the National Women's Study is that rape in the United States is "a tragedy of youth."[40] The study found that 29 percent of rapes occurred to female victims under the age of eleven, 32 percent occurred to females between the ages of eleven and seventeen, and 22 percent occurred to females between the ages of eighteen and twenty-four.[41] Other research suggests that one in four women will be the victim of rape or an attempted rape by the time they are in their midtwenties, and at least three-quarters of those assaults will be committed by men known to the victims.[42] Lifetime probability for rape victimization is as high as 50 percent; that is, one out of two women will be sexually assaulted at least once in her lifetime.[43]

The FBI's Uniform Crime Report indexes 10 million reported crimes a year but does not collect statistics on wife abuse. Since statutes in most states do not identify wife beating as a distinct crime, incidents of wife abuse are usually classified under "assault and battery" and "disputes." Estimates that 50 percent of American wives are battered every year are not uncommon in the literature.[44] Recent evidence shows that violence against wives becomes greatest at and after separation.[45] Divorced and separated women account for 75 percent of all battered women and report being battered fourteen times as often as women still living with their partners.[46] These women are also at the highest risk of being murdered by their former husbands. Thirty-three percent of all women murdered in the United States between 1976 and 1987 were murdered by their husbands.[47]

"The problem of sexual abuse of children is of unknown national dimensions," according to Vincent De Francis, "but findings strongly point to the probability of an enormous national incidence many times larger than the reported incidence of the physical abuse of children."[48] He discussed the existence of a wide gap between the reported incidence and the actual occurrence of sexual assaults against children and suggested that "the reported incidence represents the top edge of the moon as it rises over the mountain."[49] Research definitions as to what constitutes sexual abuse and research methodologies vary widely, resulting in reported rates ranging from 6 percent to 62 percent for female children and 3 percent to 31 percent for male children.[50] David Finkelhor suggests that the lowest figures support the claim that child sexual abuse is far from a rare occurrence and that the higher reported rates suggest a "problem of epidemic proportions."[51]

In a study of 126 African-American women and 122 white women in Los Angeles County, 62 percent reported at least one experience of sexual abuse before the age of eighteen.[52] The same men who beat their wives often abuse their children. Researchers have found that "the worse the wife-beating, the worse the child abuse."[53] It is estimated that fathers may sexually abuse children in 25 percent to 33 percent of all domestic abuse cases. There is also a strong correlation between child abuse and the frequency of marital rape, particularly where weapons are involved.[54]

Incest, according to author and researcher Florence Rush, is the "best kept secret."[55] The estimates, however speculative, are frightening. In a representative sample of 930 women in San Francisco, Diana E. H. Russell found that 16 percent of the women had been sexually abused by a relative before the age of eighteen and 4.5 percent had been sexually abused by their fathers (also before the age of eighteen).[56] Extrapolating to the general population, this research suggests that 160,000 women per million may have been sexually abused before the age of eighteen, and 45,000 women per million may have been sexually abused by their fathers.[57]

Accurate data on the incidence of sexual harassment is impossible to obtain. Women have traditionally accepted sexual innuendo as a fact of life and only recently have begun to report and analyze the dimensions of sexual coercion in the workplace. Research indicates that sexual harassment is pervasive. In 1978 Lin Farley found that accounts of sexual harassment within the federal government, the country's largest single employer, were extensive.[58] In 1988 the U.S. Merit Systems Protection Board released an updated study that showed that 85 percent of working women experience harassing behavior at some point in their lives.[59]

In 1976 over nine thousand women responded to a survey on sexual harassment conducted by *Redbook* magazine. More than 92 percent reported sexual harassment as a problem, a majority of the respondents described it as serious, and nine out of ten reported that they had personally experienced one or more forms of unwanted sexual attentions on the job.[60] The Ad Hoc Group on Equal Rights for Women attempted to gather data on sexual harassment at the United Nations. Their questionnaire was confiscated by UN officials, but 875 staff members had already responded; 73 percent were women, and more than half of them said that they had personally experienced or were aware of incidents of sexual harassment at the UN.[61] In May 1975, the Women's Section of the Human Affairs Program at Cornell University in Ithaca, New York, distributed the first questionnaire on sexual harassment. Of the 155 respondents, 92 percent identified sexual harassment as a serious problem, 70 percent had personally experienced some form of sexual harassment, and 56 percent reported incidents of physical harassment.[62] A 1991 *New York Times*/CBS poll found that four out of ten women experienced sexual harassment at work, yet only 4 percent reported it.[63]

In *The Lecherous Professor*, Billie Wright Dziech and Linda Weiner note that the low reportage of sexual harassment in higher education is due to the victims' deliberate avoidance of institutional processes and remedies.[64] A pilot study conducted by the National Advisory Council on Women's Educational Programs on Sexual Harassment in Academia concluded:

> The sexual harassment of postsecondary students is an increasingly visible problem of great, but as yet unascertained, dimensions. Once regarded as an isolated, purely personal problem, it has gained civil rights credibility as its scale and consequences have become known, and is correctly viewed as a form of illegal sex-based discrimination.[65]

Crimes of Violence against Females Have the Lowest Conviction Rates

The common denominator in the underreporting of all sexual assaults is fear. Females have been well trained in silence and passivity. Early and sustained sex-role socialization teaches that women are responsible for the sexual behavior of men and that women cannot be trusted. These beliefs operate together. They function to keep women silent about their victimization and to keep other people from believing women when they do come forward. The victim's fear that she will not be believed and, as a consequence, that the offender will not be punished is not unrealistic. Sex offenders are rarely punished in our society.

Rape has the lowest conviction rate of all violent crimes. The likelihood of a rape complaint ending in conviction is 2 to 5 percent.[66] While the intent of rape reform legislation was to shift the emphasis from the victim's experiences to the perpetrator's acts,[67] prosecutions are less likely to be pursued if the victim and perpetrator are acquainted, and juries are less likely to return a conviction in cases where the victim's behavior or *alleged behavior* (emphasis mine) departed from traditional sex-role expectations.[68]

Data on prosecution and conviction of wife beaters is practically nonexistent. This is despite the fact that battery is, according to the U.S. Surgeon General, the "single largest cause of injury to women in the U.S." and accounts for one-fifth of all emergency room visits by women.[69] Police departments have generally tried to conciliate rather than arrest. Guided by the "stitch rule," arrests were made only when the victim's injuries required stitches. Police routinely instructed the parties to "break it up" or "talk it out" or asked the abuser to "take a walk and cool off." Male police officers, often identifying with the male abuser, routinely failed to advise women of their rights to file a complaint.[70]

As a result of sustained political activism on behalf of abused women, many states have revised their police training and have instituted pro- or even mandatory arrest policies. In 1984 the Attorney General's Task Force on Family Violence argued that the legal response to such violence be predicated on the abusive act and not on the relationship between the victim and the abuser.[71] A key issue, however, is the implementation of such reform. The record shows that the criminal justice system has responded inconsistently.[72]

Studies in the late 1970s and 1980s showed that batterers receive minimal fines and suspended sentences. In one study of 350 abused wives, none of the husbands served time in jail.[73] And while the result of pro- and mandatory arrest policies is a larger number of domestic violence cases entering the judicial system,[74] "there is considerable evidence that judges have yet to abandon the historical view of wife abuse."[75] In 1981, a Kansas judge suspended the fine of a convicted assailant on the condition that he buy his wife a box of candy.[76] In 1984 a Colorado judge sentenced a man to two years on work release for fatally shooting his wife five times in the face. Although the sentence was less than the minimum required by law, the judge found that the wife had "provoked" her husband by leaving him.[77] Recent task force reports on gender bias in the courts reveal a pattern of nonenforcement of protective orders, trivialization of complaints, and disbelief of females when there is no visible evidence of severe injuries.[78] In 1987 a Massachusetts trial judge scolded a battered women for wasting his time with her request for a protective order. If she and her husband wanted to "gnaw" on each other, "fine," but they "shouldn't do it at taxpayers' expense." The husband later killed his wife, and taxpayers paid for a murder trial.[79]

The lack of support and protection from the criminal justice system intensifies the double bind of battered women. Leaving the batterer significantly increases the risk of serious injury or death, while staying significantly increases the psychological terrorism and frequency of abuse. According to former Detroit Police Commander James Bannon, "You can readily understand why the women ultimately take the law into their own hands or despair of finding relief at all. Or *why the male feels protected by the system in his use of violence*" (emphasis mine).[80]

In his study of child sexual abuse, Vincent De Francis found that plea bargaining and dismissal of cases were the norm. The study sample consisted of 173 cases brought to prosecution. Of these, 44 percent (seventy-six cases) were dismissed, 22 percent (thirty-eight cases) voluntarily accepted a lesser plea, 11 percent (six cases) were found guilty of a lesser charge, and 2 percent (four cases) were found guilty as charged. Of the remaining thirty-five cases, they were either pending (fifteen) or terminated because the offender was committed to a mental institution (five) or because the offender absconded (seven), or no information was available (eight). Of the fifty-three offenders who were convicted or pleaded guilty, thirty offenders escaped a jail sentence. Twenty-one received suspended sentences and were placed on probation, seven received suspended sentences without probation, and two were fined a sum of money. The other 45 percent (twenty-three offenders) received prison terms from under six months to three years; five were given indeterminate sentences—that is, a minimum term of one year and a maximum term subject to the discretion of the state board of parole.[81]

In Diana E. H. Russell's study of 930 women, 648 cases of child sexual abuse were disclosed. Thirty cases—5 percent—were reported to the police; four were cases of incestuous abuse, and twenty-six were extrafamilial child sexual abuse. Only seven cases resulted in conviction.[82]

Most of the victims of sexual harassment in the Cornell University study were unwilling to use available procedures, such as grievances, to remedy their complaints, because they believed that nothing would be done. Their perception is based on reality; of the 12 percent who did complain, over half found that nothing was done in their cases.[83] The low adjudication and punishment rates of sexual-harassment cases are particularly revealing in light of the fact that the offender is known and identifiable and that there is no fear of "mistaken identity," as there is in rape cases. While offenders accused of familial violence—incest and wife abuse—are also known, concern with keeping the family intact affects prosecution rates.

Blaming the Victim of Sexual Violence Is Pervasive

The data on conviction rates of men who have committed acts of violence against females must be understood in the context of attitudes about women. Our male-dominated society evokes powerful myths to justify male violence against females and to ensure that these acts will rarely be punished. Victims of sexual violence are almost always suspect. We have developed an intricate network of beliefs and attitudes that perpetuate the idea that "victims of sex crimes have a hidden psychological need to be victimized."[84] We tend to believe either that the female willingly participated in her victimization or that she outright lied about it. Either way, we blame the victim and excuse or condone the offender.

Consider, for example, the operative myths about rape, wife battery, incest, and sexual harassment.

Rape

All women want to be raped.

No woman can be raped if she doesn't want it (you-can't-thread-a-moving-needle argument).

She asked for it.

She changed her mind afterward.

When she says no, she means yes.

If you are going to be raped, you might as well relax and enjoy it.

Wife Abuse

Some women need to be beaten.

A good kick in the ass will straighten her out.

She needs a punch in the mouth every so often to keep her in line.

She must have done something to provoke him.

Incest

The child was the seducer.

The child imagined it.

Sexual Harassment

She was seductive.

She misunderstood. I was just being friendly.

Underlying all the myths about victims of sexual violence is the belief that the victim causes and is responsible for her own victimization. In the National Women's Study, 69 percent of the rape victims were afraid that they would be blamed for their rape, 71 percent did not want their family to know they had been sexually abused, and 68 percent did not want people outside of their family knowing of their victimization.[85] Diana Scully studied convicted rapists and found that these men both believed in the rape myths and used them to justify their own behavior.[86] Underlying the attitudes about the male offender is the belief that he could not help himself: that is, he was ruled by his biology and/or he was seduced. The victim becomes the offender, and the offender becomes the victim. These two processes, blaming the victim and absolving the offender, protect the patriarchal view of the world by rationalizing sexual violence. Sexual violence by a normal male against an innocent female is unthinkable; therefore, she must have done something wrong or it would not have happened. This view was expressed by a Wisconsin judge who sentenced a twenty-four-year-old man to ninety days of work release for sexually assaulting a five-year-old girl. The judge, claiming that the child was an "unusually promiscuous young lady," stated that "no way do I believe that [the defendant] initiated sexual contact."[87] Making a victim believe she is at fault erases not only the individual offender's culpability but also the responsibility of the society as a whole. Sexual violence remains an individual problem, not a sociopolitical one.

One need only read the testimony of victims of sexual violence to see the powerful effects of blaming the victim. From the National Advisory Council on Women's Educational Programs Report on Sexual Harassment of Students:

I was ashamed, thought it was my fault, and was worried that the school would take action against me (for "unearned" grades) if they found out about it.

This happened seventeen years ago, and you are the first person I've been able to discuss it with in all that time. He's still at —— —, and probably still doing it.

I'm afraid to tell anyone here about it, and I'm just hoping to get through the year so I can leave.[88]

From *Wife-Beating: The Silent Crisis,* Judge Stewart Oneglia comments,

Many women find it shameful to admit they don't have a good marriage. The battered wife wraps her bloody head in a towel, goes to the hospital, and explains to the doctor she fell down the stairs. After a few years of the husband telling her he beats her because she is ugly, stupid, or incompetent, she is so psychologically destroyed that she believes it. (Langley and Levy 1977, 151)

A battered woman from Boston relates,

I actually thought if I only learned to cook better or keep a cleaner house, everything would be okay. I put up with the beating for five years before I got desperate enough to get help.[89]

Another battered woman said,

When I came to, I wanted to die, the guilt and depression were so bad. Your whole sense of worth is tied up with being a successful wife and having a happy marriage. If your husband beats you, then your marriage is a failure, and you're a failure. It's so horribly the opposite of how it is supposed to be.[90]

Katherine Brady shared her experience as an incest survivor in *Father's Days: A True Story of Incest.* She concluded her story with the following:

I've learned a great deal by telling my story. I hope other incest victims may experience a similar journey of discovery by reading it. If nothing else, I would wish them to hear in this tale the two things I needed most, but had to wait years to hear: "You are not alone and you are not to blame."[91]

Sexual Violence Is Not Taken Seriously

Another characteristic of sexual violence is that these crimes are not taken seriously. Society manifests this attitude by simply denying the existence of sexual violence, denying the gravity of these acts, joking about them, and attempting to legitimate them.

Many offenders echo the societal norm by expressing genuine surprise when they are confronted by authorities. This seems to be particularly true in cases of sexual abuse of children, wife beating, and sexual harassment. In her study of incest, Florence Rush found that child molesters very often do not understand that they have done anything wrong. Many men still believe that they have an inalienable right to rule "their women." Batterers, for example, often cite their right to discipline their wives; incestuous fathers cite their right to instruct their daughters in sexuality. These men are acting on the belief that women are the property of men.

The concept of females as the property of men extends beyond the family unit, as the evidence on sexual harassment indicates. "Are you telling me that this kind of horsing around may constitute an actionable offense?" queried a character on a television special on sexual harassment.[92] This represents the typical response of a man accused of sexual harassment. Men have been taught that they are the hunters, and women—all women—are fair game. The mythology about the workaday world abounds with sexual innuendo. Concepts of "sleazy" (i.e., sexually accessible) nurses and dumb, big-breasted, blond secretaries are standard fare for comedy routines. When the existence of sexual violence can no longer be denied, a common response is to joke about it in order to belittle it. "If you are going to be raped, you might as well enjoy it" clearly belittles the violence of rape. The public still laughs when Ralph threatens Alice with "One of these days, POW—right in the kisser." Recently, a television talk-show host remarked that "incest is a game the whole family can play." The audience laughed uproariously.

Sexual Violence Is about Violence, Power, and Sex

The final characteristic common to all forms of violence against females is perhaps the most difficult to comprehend. During the past decade, many researchers argued (as I did in earlier versions of this article) that sexual violence is not about sex but about violence. I now believe, however, that the "either-or" dichotomy—either sexual violence is about sex or it's about violence—is false and misleading. Male supremacy identifies females as having a basic "flaw"—a trait that distinguishes males and females and legitimates women's inferior status. This "flaw" is female sexuality: it is tempting and seductive and therefore disruptive, capable of reproducing life itself and therefore powerful.[93] Through sexual terrorism men seek to bring this force under control. The site of the struggle is the female body and female sexuality.

Timothy Beneke, in *Men on Rape,* argues that "not every man is a rapist but every man who grows up in America and learns American English learns all too much to think like a rapist" and that "for a man, rape has plenty to do with sex."[94] Twenty years of research and activism have documented that women largely experience rape, battery, incest, and sexual harassment as violence. That women and men often have vastly different experiences is not surprising. Under patriarchy men are entitled to sex; it is a primary vehicle by which they establish and signal their masculinity. From the male perspective, female sexuality is a commodity, something they must take, dominate, or own. Our popular culture routinely celebrates this particular notion of masculinity. Women are permitted to have sex, but only in marriage (the patriarchal ideal), or at least in love relationships. Women earn their femininity by managing their sexuality and keeping it in trust for a potential husband. The double standard of sexuality leads inevitably to coercion and sexual violence.

Many believe that re-visioning rape as violence not only accurately reflects many women's experiences but also is a more productive strategy for reforming legislation and transforming public attitudes. While arguing that "theoretically and strategically" the "rape as violence" position is the better one, attorney and author Susan Estrich points out that such an approach obscures the reality that the majority of rapes are coerced or forced but unaccompanied by conventional violence.[95] In fact, one consequence of this approach is that it precludes protest from women who experience sexual intrusions in ways not typically seen as violent.

It is argued that in sexual harassment the motive is power, not sex. There is a wide consensus that sexual harassment is intended to "keep women in their place." Yet, the means by which this is attempted or accomplished are sexual: rude comments about sex or about a woman's body, pornographic gestures or posters, demands for sexual favors, rape, etc. Clearly, to the harassers, a woman's place is a largely sexual one; her very presence in the workplace sexualizes it. In the accounts of women's experiences with sexual harassment in *Sexual Harassment: Women Speak Out,*[96] themes of sexual power and sexual humiliation resonate in each essay.

In wife battery the acts of violence are intended to inflict harm on the woman and ultimately to control her, but the message of the violence is explicitly sexual. For example, the most common parts of a woman's body attacked during battering are her face and her breasts—both symbols of her sexuality and her attractiveness to men. During pregnancy, the focus of the attack often shifts to the abdomen—a symbol of her reproductive power. In addressing the "either-or" debate in the sexual abuse of children, David Finkelhor points out, "sex is always in the service of other needs. Just because it is infused with nonsexual motives does not make child sexual abuse different from other kinds of behavior that we readily call 'sexual.'"[97]

Conclusion

The dynamic that underscores all manifestations of sexual terrorism is misogyny—the hatred of women. Violence against women is power expressed sexually. It is violence eroticized. Diana E. H. Russell argues that "we are socialized to sexualize power, intimacy, and affection, and sometimes hatred and contempt as well."[98] For women in the United States, sexual violence and its threat are central issues in their daily lives. Both violence and fear are functional. Without the power to intimidate and punish women sexually, the domination of women in all spheres of society—political, social, and economic—could not exist.

NOTES

1. Brownmiller 1975: 5.
2. Gordon and Riger 1989: 22.
3. Yonah Alexander, "Terrorism and the Mass Media: Some Considerations," in Yonah Alexander, David Carlton, and Paul Wilkinson (eds.), *Terrorism: Theory and Practice* (Boulder, CO: Westview Press, 1979), 159; Ernest Evans, *Calling a Truce to Terrorism: The American Response to International Terrorism* (Westport, CT: Greenwood Press, 1979), 3; Charmers Johnson, "Perspectives on Terrorism," in Walter Laqueur (ed.), *The Terrorism Reader* (Philadelphia: Temple University Press, 1978), 273; Thomas P. Thornton, "Terror as a Weapon of Political Agitation," in Harry Eckstein (ed.), *The Internal War* (New York: Free Press, 1964), 73; Eugene Walter, *Terror and Resistance* (New York: Oxford University Press, 1969), 6; Francis M. Watson, *Political Terrorism: The Threat and the Response* (Washington, DC: R. B. Luce Co., 1976), 15; Paul Wilkinson, *Political Terrorism* (New York: John Wiley and Sons, 1974), 11.
4. Frederick F. Hacker, *Crusaders, Criminals and Crazies: Terrorism in Our Time* (New York: W. W. Norton and Co., 1976), xi.
5. Marc Feigen Fasteau, *The Male Machine* (New York: McGraw-Hill Book Co., 1974), 144.
6. Watson, 15.
7. Wilkinson, 17.
8. Sheffield 1989: 487.
9. Malette and Chalouh 1991: 100.
10. Caputi and Russell 1990: 34.
11. Kelly 1988: 76.
12. Estrich 1987: 8; USDOJ 1991: 43; Koss and Harvey 1991: 4.

13. Rhode 1989: 245.

14. Russell 1982: 21–22.

15. Ibid., xxii.

16. Ibid., xxvi.

17. J. Campbell 1989: 340.

18. *Bradley v. State,* 1 Miss. (7 Walker) 150 (1824); *State v. Block,* 60 N.C. (Win.) 266 (1864).

19. *Fulgham v. State,* 46 Ala. 143 (1871).

20. *Thompson v. Thompson,* 218 U.S. 611 (1910).

21. Schweber and Feinman 1985: 30.

22. *Arrest in Domestic Violence Cases: A State by State Summary* (New York: National Center on Women and Family Law, Inc., 1987), 1.

23. Langan and Innes 1986: 1.

24. Lin Farley, *Sexual Shakedown: The Sexual Harassment of Women on the Job* (New York: McGraw-Hill Book Co., 1978), 1415.

25. U.S. House of Representatives 1980: 8.

26. *Mentor Savings Bank FSB v. Vinson,* 477 U.S. 57 (1986).

27. Lewin 1991: A22; *Sexual Harassment: Research and Resources: A Report in Progress* (New York: National Council for Research on Women, 1991), 10–13.

28. Kolbert 1991: 1.

29. Roger Langley and Richard C. Levy, *Wife-Beating: The Silent Crisis* (New York: E. P. Dutton, 1977), 43.

30. Ibid., 44.

31. Vincent De Francis, *Protecting the Child Victim of Sex Crimes Committed by Adults* (Denver: American Humane Society, 1969), vii.

32. USDOJ 1991: 16.

33. Ibid., 7.

34. Ibid., 16.

35. UDOJ 1992: 5.

36. Koss and Harvey 1991: 11–17.

37. National Victim Center 1992: 1.

38. Ibid., 2.

39. Ibid., 4.

40. Ibid., 3.

41. Ibid.

42. Parrot and Bechofer 1991: ix.

43. Crites 1987: 36.

44. Langley and Levy, 3.

45. Zorza 1991: 423.

46. Harlow 1991: 5.

47. Caputi and Russell 1990: 35.

48. De Francis, vii.

49. Ibid.

50. Finkelhor 1986: 19.

51. Ibid.

52. Russell 1986: 69.

53. Bowker et al. 1988: 164.

54. Ibid.

55. Rush 1980: 5.

56. Russell 1986: 10.

57. Ibid.

58. Farley, 31.

59. Rhode 1989: 232.

60. Ibid., 20.

61. Ibid., 21.

62. Ibid., 20.

63. Kolbert 1991: A17.

64. Dziech and Weiner 1990: xxi.

65. Till 1980: 3.

66. Rhode 1989: 246.

67. Koss and Harvey 1991: 5.

68. LaFree 1989: 240.

69. Zorza 1991: 243.

70. Rhode 1989: 239.

71. Attorney General's Task Force 1984: 4.

72. Ibid.

73. Rhode 1989: 241.

74. Goolkasian 1986: 3.

75. Crites 1987: 41.

76. Ibid., 45.

77. Ibid.

78. Schafran 1987: 280, 283–84.

79. Goodman 1987: 13.

80. James Bannon, quoted in Del Martin, *Battered Wives* (New York: Pocket Books, 1977), 115.

81. De Francis, 190–91.

82. Russell 1986: 85.

83. Farley, 22.

84. Georgia Dullea, "Child Prostitution: Causes Are Sought," *New York Times,* September 4, 1979, p. C11.

85. National Victim Center 1992: 4.

86. Scully 1990: 58.

87. Stanko 1985: 95.

88. Till 1980: 28.

89. Ibid., 115.

90. Ibid., 116.

91. Katherine Brady, *Father's Days: A True Story of Incest* (New York: Dell, 1981), 253.

92. Till 1980: 4.

93. Sheffield 1987: 172.

94. Beneke 1982: 16.

95. Estrich 1987: 83.

96. Sumrall and Taylor 1992.

97. Finkelhor 1984: 34.

98. Russell 1986: 393.

Part II

Forms of Sexual Coercion and Violence

Part 2 consists of five sections, each of which explores a specific form of gender violence. Every section includes a historical sketch of the phenomenon studied, as well as a discussion of suggested remedies for addressing the violence. We examine multiple causes and consequences of various forms of gender violence and draw attention to the similarities that exist among them. Section 1 presents sexual harassment as a widely experienced form of gender violence that is often trivialized in public discourse. In section 2, we explore rape in multiple cultural contexts. Section 3 offers theoretical and policy analyses of intimate partner abuse. The effects of gendered violence on children, as both victims and observers, forms the subject in section 4. In section 5, we consider pornography and prostitution as contested social problems. In addition to articles that represent history and the social sciences, part 2 includes literary analysis and personal narrative.

Sexual Harassment

By now we are all familiar with stories of sexual harassment in and outside of organizations: the woman who quits her job to escape unwanted sexual advances from her boss; the jogger who faces catcalls from men on her morning run; the sexualized hazing rituals that young men—and increasingly women—are forced to endure when pledging Greek organizations or joining athletic teams; the young boy teased relentlessly by classmates for "acting like a girl." Until recently, few people linked sexual harassment to the larger issues of gender construction and related power inequities in societies; many still do not.

The hearing in which Supreme Court Justice Clarence Thomas's alleged harassment of Professor Anita Hill surfaced and the allegations of sexual harassment and impropriety that undermined the moral legitimacy of the Clinton administration thrust the subject of sexual harassment into the public consciousness as never before. These cases are only the tip of the iceberg; yet, they forced an international awakening to a problem that had been previously thought of as normal (hetero)sexual banter, inconsequential for either perpetrators or victims. In 1998, the U.S. Supreme Court expanded previous conceptualizations of sexual harassment with a landmark finding that federal workplace laws also apply to harassment between persons of the same sex (*Oncale v. Sundowner Offshore Services, Inc.*, 96-568, 1998).

Estimates suggest that between 50 and 90 percent of women experience sexual harassment during their work lives (Schneider, Swan, and Fitzgerald 1997; Welsh 1999). In 2005 alone, the Equal Employment Opportunity Commission (EEOC) reported receiving 12,679 charges of sexual harassment, of which over 14 percent were filed by males (EEOC 2006). Still, many women and men whose experiences meet the legal definitions of sexual harassment do not define their situations as such. Research suggests that there are gender differences in perceptions of sexual harassment; women perceive a wider range of behaviors as harassment and are more likely to report than men (Rotundo, Nguyen, and Sackett 2001; Russell and Trigg 2004). Many victims do not file charges if they lack social support networks or fear reprisal.

The fact that sexual harassment was not legally defined until 1980 made gathering "official data" on the problem difficult prior to the last decades of the twentieth century. That sexual harassment was only so recently defined is also very likely the consequence of two significant sociological phenomena: the social construction of sexuality and the organization of human activities into public and private spheres. The emergence of sex/gender systems has been accompanied by sexual definition and regulation, and the realization that in a predominance of cultures, sexuality is "normal" when it is exercised in heterosexual relationships featuring male dominance and female passivity.

Widespread acceptance of polarized gender roles, subsumed in the rhetoric of biological determinism, has allowed behaviors now legally defined as harassment to be explained uncritically as nature taking its course. While human "progress" is ultimately defined as our ability to transcend the natural, purportedly innate sexual urges have consistently been viewed as some of the more difficult impulses to control—particularly in men.

The organization of human activities into public and privates spheres has its roots in the sexual division of labor, but it is a fairly modern phenomenon. Modern societies dichotomize public and private and conceptualize sexuality as a personal and private domain; yet the fact remains that a great deal of what we understand about sexuality is constructed in the public sphere, and a good deal of sexual interaction occurs in public places (Hearn and Parkin 1987). Our intellectual frame of reference, until quite recently, assumed that sexuality was safely tucked away in the private arena, or at least significantly neutralized in workplaces and schools, thus veiling the extent to which sexuality pervades our activities in the public sphere.

Contemporary feminism provided a context within which sexual harassment *could* be named. By questioning biological determinism and, indeed, the very social structures within which gender relations take shape, scholars and activists could begin to theorize sexual harassment as a condition shaped by the distribution and mobilization of social power. Claiming the personal as political, women at the forefront of second-wave feminism threw conventional sexual regulations and definitions into the boiling cauldron of dissent. Once sexuality resurfaced in public discourse and was increasingly exposed as both a social construction and locus of power relations, the "discovery" of sexual harassment was inevitable.

Identifying Sexual Harassment

The second-class status of women was identified simultaneously by contemporary feminists sharing experiences in informal consciousness-raising groups and those involved in the work of more formal inquiries, such as that conducted by the presidential Commission on the Status of Women in the United States in the early 1960s (Freeman 1984). Sexual harassment was one of the common threads of experience that women began to weave into an analysis of male power in patriarchal societies. Women shared experiences of intimidation, unwanted sexual advances, intrusive touching, and sexually charged innuendo—a seemingly endless litany of offensive and controlling behaviors that pervaded the public sphere and often shattered the privacy that women expected in the home. Women were harassed by strangers in the street, superiors in the workplace, professors in their college classrooms, and faceless voices over the telephone. The earliest research on sexual harassment focused on the experiences of women at work. In the 1970s, work had been conceptualized as the primary route to financial independence and self-worth for women. That the organizations within which women labored were potentially fraught with intimidation was of immense concern to feminist activists and scholars. One of the first large-scale surveys of working women found that 70 percent of respondents had experienced some form of harassment at work (Farley

1978). MacKinnon (1979) stretched the definitional boundaries of harassment by introducing the notion of a sexualized environment—a workplace in which the "white noise" is focused on sexual innuendo, causing many women significant anxiety and discomfort that ultimately affects their capacity to work.

In 1980, the U.S. government specified sexual harassment in the *Code of Federal Regulations* (No. 1604.11, 925) under provision of Title VII of the Civil Rights Act of 1964, adopting a broad-ranging definition that included quid pro quo forms of harassment (requests for sexual favors where submission is linked to conditions of employment), unwanted sexual advances, and the existence of hostile working conditions. Both gender studies and legal decisions have, over the past several decades, further expanded the range of contexts and experiences that constitute the phenomenon of sexual harassment. Especially significant have been the recognition of same-sex harassment, the existence of racialized harassment in the lives of women and men of color, and the hostility of heterosexualized environments toward many gay, lesbian, and transgendered individuals.

Explaining Harassment at Work

Given its predominance, initial explanations for sexual harassment at work were focused on the sexual harassment of women by men. Conventional wisdom favors the natural/biological model that explains sexual harassment as an outgrowth of the natural attraction between men and women being played out in public contexts. Those who subscribe to the biological model generally accept the corollary that the naturally aggressive sexuality of men contributes to the phenomenon but that only "sick" men escalate from normal sexual banter to sexual harassment (Tangri, Burt, and Johnson 1982).

Early feminist theory generally rejected the premises of the biological model. In adopting a more structural approach that focused on the distribution of power and the division of labor in organizations, feminists stressed the hierarchical nature of modern organizations and developed frameworks that problematized women's location in organizational structures relative to men (Kanter 1977), the nature of women's work (Gutek and Morasch 1982) and eventually the social construction of gender in organizational contexts (Acker 1990). These organizational perspectives derived strength from the gender demography of modern organizations in which the vast majority of women workers are segregated into low-wage, sex-typed jobs with less access to organizational power than men. Indeed, a significant number of women who experience harassment are victimized by superiors or other powerful men in their schools or workplaces.

While useful in explaining the harassment experiences of many women, organizational power is not the only dynamic operating to facilitate harassment in organizations. Enough research established the existence of contra-power harassment by working peers and subordinates to suggest that the work roles and occupations of women were significant per se, regardless of the distribution of organizational power (Gutek and Morasch 1982; Tangri, Burt and Johnson 1982; Gutek 1985). "Sex-role spillover" occurs when women at work are expected to be nurturers, mediators, and/or sexually available in accordance with the "natural" roles that they are expected to fill in the home (Gutek and Morasch 1982). This scenario is most likely to be experienced by women in traditionally female occupations, such as clerical work, where the association of job to gender is strong. The combination of sex-role spillover, and the sheer numbers of women in sex-typed occupations, produces high victimization rates among women.

Although this model added a significant dimension to the organizational model of harassment, women in nontraditional occupations also experience sexual harassment. In fact, research suggests that women in male-dominated professions and/or male-dominated institutions suffer higher rates of victimization than women in more socially sanctioned female occupations (Padavic and Reskin 1990; Mansfield et al. 1991). Women who step beyond the boundaries of women's work into male-dominated institutions such as policing, military, and athletic organizations also face hostility, intimidation, and harassment (Gregory and Lees 1999; Hearn and Parkin 2001). Women of color in both the trades and professional occupations face racial and sexual harassment in their jobs (Buchanan and Ormerod 2002). Women's intrusion into the formerly homosocial worlds of these institutions may threaten both male solidarity and male social privilege (Yoder 1991).

Research on organizational cultures has facilitated our understanding of how organizations become sexualized. Organizations are now recognized as social systems with their own cultures that shape both organizational goals and interpersonal relations at work. In addition to company guidelines that enforce sexual regulations (such as no dating between employees), there are value systems, communicative processes, and customs that tell employees how they may behave as sexual beings at work. Some organizations have explicit sexual goals and concomitant sexualized cultures (Hearn and Parkin 1987), such as pornographic book stores, "gentlemen's clubs," and stores that specialize in intimate apparel and sex toys. Most organizations, however, have ostensibly suppressed sexuality; their goals are explicitly nonsexual. Though sexuality may appear suppressed, however, many of these organizations may tacitly encourage oppressive male sexuality among employees through exploitative ad campaigns, company events such as employee picnics and holiday parties, or through the frequent use of sexual metaphor in communicative processes. The experience of female employees at the Mitsubishi automobile factory in Normal, Illinois, provides a case in point. In 1998, the company settled a class-action lawsuit brought by female employees claiming a hostile work environment in which they were subjected to a daily barrage of demeaning, sexually degrading, and often physically intrusive behaviors from male employees. The $34 million that was distributed to more than four hundred women is, at this writing, the largest sexual harassment settlement in the history of Title VII (http://www.eeoc.gov/press/5-23-01.html).

Traditional organizational cultures are often sexually charged, specifically toward heterosexuality. This frequently contributes to the harassment and intimidation of lesbians and gay men. Research on lesbians in the workplace has shown patterns of harassment similar to those experienced by heterosexual women (Schneider 1982; Taylor 1986). Heterosexist work environments are also settings where hegemonic masculinity must be proved by men on the shop floor (Collinson and Collinson 1989;

Messerschmidt 1993). Miller, Forest, and Jurick (2003) studied the complex process of negotiation that gay and lesbian officers undertake to survive in the homophobic and often hostile environment of policing. Straight men who abhor the exploitation of women and the marginalization of gays and lesbians are also affected negatively by aggressively (hetero)sexist environments. Taken together, research shows that organizational structures, cultures, and work roles are not mutually exclusive; thus, harassment is a pervasive and multifaceted organizational problem for women, as well as for some men.

Sexual harassment is not peculiar to organizations or their structures, however, but a manifestation of the continued male dominance and heteronormativity of the larger sociocultural system. For example, gender scholars have theorized that male sexual aggression is not a natural attribute but part of a social script that boys and men are socialized to accept and that girls and women are taught to expect. Men are socially rewarded for enacting sexual and occupational dominance, which serves both collective and self-interests.

Harassment outside the Workplace

Although the predominance of harassment research has focused on work and occupations, sociocultural theories provide an important link between sexual harassment at work and that which occurs in other public and private contexts. Studies of the phenomenon of street harassment (Bernard and Schlaffer 1983; Gardner 1995) show that harassment is not only a vehicle through which individual men exercise power over women, but that it often functions as a ritual of male bonding for participants. Bernard and Schlaffer's (1983) early research among street harassers found that few men engaged in solitary harassment—catcalls, whistles, and groping behaviors were viewed as group activities.

Public harassments are simultaneously expressions of male solidarity and bravado, and mechanisms for the social control and intimidation of females. Robinson's (2005) research on the relationships between masculinity and the harassment of girls in secondary schools supports the thesis of group bonding to exercise male power that is "constituted within broader cultural values and power relationships, especially those operating around gender and sexuality and their intersections with other sites of difference, such as 'race' and class" (2005, 20). Her research shows how male students perform hegemonic masculinity through both sexist and sexual harassment of girls. In the case of harassment of children by their peers, efforts to effectively deal with the problem are often muddied by the fact that teachers and parents tacitly accept behaviors that are frequently antecedent to harassment: teasing and bullying (Stein 1995).

Gays and lesbians are frequently targeted in public places. The anti-gay-and-lesbian violence that is often meted out based on the mere "appearance" of being gay—a perception of "gender betrayal" that threatens homophobic individuals and groups—can ultimately affect not only gays and lesbians but also "heterosexuals unwilling to be bound by their assigned gender identity" (Vazsquez 1992, 161).

The maintenance of institutionalized male privilege that is emphasized in sociocultural explanations of harassment is equally applicable to harassment that occurs in the private sphere, whether the perpetrator is a stranger or an intimate. Obscene or threatening phone calls function both to fill a psychological need of the male caller and the collective social need of men to keep women self-conscious and in their proper place (Smith and Morra 1994). As technology becomes ever more sophisticated, so do the methods of perpetrating sexist and sexual harassment. The Internet, by virtue of its capabilities to facilitate both in-time conversations and invasive communications, is now recognized as a locus of sexual harassment as well.

The Politics of Sexual Harassment

Because feminists in the United States were the first to name the problem of sexual harassment, there is a longer history of sexual harassment politics here than in other parts of the world. Countries in the European Union have more recently adopted nation-based and collective policies as a result of high-profile harassment claims in the United States and their own societies. Comparative research, however, shows distinctly different conceptualizations, reflecting variations in culture, political institutions, and transnational politics (Saguy 2003; Zippel 2006).

Zippel suggests that in the United States, there is a *politics of fear* wherein male employees are instructed to fear women's lawsuits, whereas in Germany, there is a *politics as usual* that allows men to ignore harassment and the laws that regulate it (2006, 5). Saguy suggests that France has a generally more laissez-faire attitude toward workplace sexuality, where touching and sexual banter are still common. Many French consider U.S workplaces to be intolerant; yet more extreme forms of harassment are socially constructed as violence against women in the French cultural context (2003, 4–5). During the 1990s in the European Union, in keeping with a long tradition of protecting worker and human rights, all forms of harassment came to be conceptualized as violations of worker dignity (Zippel 2006).

The primary differences in the trajectories and approaches in the United States and Europe are fairly striking. In the United States, sexual harassment policy has primarily evolved since the 1970s through the legal-regulatory process of using the courts to shape law. Having been originally regulated under the Civil Rights Act of 1964 as a form of workplace *discrimination*, the primary effect has been to penalize the differential treatment of women (and eventually men) based on their sex. In Europe, sexual harassment regulations have been handled through creating laws in parliaments. Here all forms of harassment tend to be treated legally as *violence* against a person, and primary focus is on the experience of harm rather than discrimination (Saguy 2003; Zippel 2006). Nevertheless, in both the United States and the countries of the European Union, there is consensus that women should not be coerced to exchange sex for any work-related benefit (Zippel 2006). The continuing transnational debate is focused on what sorts of behavior, in what contexts, should be considered sexual harassment. Responses are deeply rooted in cultural differences in the construction of policy and sexuality norms.

Hearn and Parkin identify a contradictory process at work in contemporary societies that is most certainly related to the politics of sexual harassment: there is a constant tension between the growing recognition and the persistent lack of recognition of harassment as a social problem (2001, 50). Clearly, it is still a highly contested phenomenon. Recent research suggests that both men and women who hold sexist beliefs about women are more tolerant of sexual harassment than either nonsexist women or men (Russell and Trigg 2004). Thus, gender is a less significant predictor of how sexual harassment will be defined and confronted than are attitudes about women. Although research on the effect of sexual harassment training in workplaces is limited, there is some evidence that it is associated with increasing men's capacity to define a broad range of unwanted sexual remarks, touching, and other behaviors as sexual harassment (Antecol and Cobb-Clark 2003, 827). Such training, however, is by no means universal in organizations or accessible to men outside them.

Contradictions notwithstanding, sexual harassment in all its forms has been found to have deleterious effects on its victims. Some victims of sexual harassment have described their experiences as psychological rape, and indeed the literature suggests that the physical, psychological, and economic consequences of sexual harassment are similar to those experienced by victims of other forms of trauma. Recognizing that rape and sexual harassment are closely situated on the continuum of sexual exploitation, for example, Quina (1990) makes a strong case for more serious consideration of sexual harassment as a social problem and for the development of more comprehensive healing strategies for victims. Victims are affected economically, socially, and psychologically, given the ubiquity of sexual harassment and its aftereffects.

There is still much cultural labor to do to achieve the political goals of feminists to realize equality *and* to eliminate violence against women. Legal and political changes will continue to evolve within the context of recognizing more fully the gendered nature of institutions and efforts toward changing the heteronormative and masculinist cultures in which they are embedded. Sexual harassment has been metaphorically described as the "dripping tap" of sexual violence and exploitation (Wise and Stanley 1987), a constant and vivid reminder of the status of women and sexual minorities in contemporary cultures.

Contributions to This Section

The articles in this section attempt to both contextualize and explain a range of sexual harassment experiences.

In "Changed Women and Changed Organizations," Barbara Gutek and Mary Koss review research on the sexual harassment of women at work from an organizational perspective. Moving beyond the consequences of sexual harassment for individual victims, the authors discuss the ways in which sexual harassment should be problematized from the standpoint of organizational effectiveness.

Centralizing the significance of context, Christine Williams explores the experiences of women in sexualized environments in "Sexual Harassment in Organizations: A Critique of Current Research and Policy" and focuses on the extent to which demeaning and degrading situations may come to be accepted as job requirements rather than harassment. She asks us to reframe the notion of *perpetrator* to include organizations and not just individuals.

In "The Confluence of Race and Gender in Women's Sexual Harassment Experiences," Tara Kent reviews theories of sexual harassment that have traditionally erased the experiences of women of color. She also shows how the legal system has traditionally forced women to choose between race and gender in filing harassment charges, even though their experiences attest to the ways in which perpetrators use gender and race simultaneously to create hostile work situations for them.

Finally, in "Sexual Harassment on the Internet," Azy Barak shows how the Internet is increasingly used to harass and intimidate women, discussing the implications of this phenomenon for research and policy considerations.

SUGGESTIONS FOR FURTHER READING

Jeff Hearn and Wendy Parkin, *Gender, Sexuality, and Violence in Organizations* (London: Sage, 2001).

Anita Faye Hill and Emma Coleman Jordan (eds.), *Race, Gender, and Power in America: The Legacy of the Hill-Thomas Hearing* (New York: Oxford University Press, 1995).

Catharine A. MacKinnon and Reva B. Siegel (eds.), *Directions in Sexual Harassment Law* (New Haven, CT: Yale University Press, 2004).

Abigail C. Saguy, *What Is Sexual Harassment? From Capitol Hill to the Sorbonne* (Berkeley: University of California Press, 2003).

Katherine S. Zippel, *The Politics of Sexual Harassment: A Comparative Study of the United States, the European Union, and Germany* (Cambridge: Cambridge University Press, 2006).

Anatomy Lesson

Cherríe Moraga

A black woman and a small beige one talk about their bodies.
About putting a piece of their anatomy in their pockets
upon entering any given room.

When entering a room full of soldiers who fear hearts,
you put your heart in your back pocket,
the black woman explains. It is important, not to intimidate.
The soldiers wear guns, *not* in their back pockets.

You let the heart fester there. You let the heart seethe.
You let the impatience of the heart build and build
until the power of the heart hidden begins to be felt in the room.
Until the absence of the heart begins to take on the shape
of a presence.
Until the soldiers look at you and begin to beg you
to open up your heart to them, so anxious are they to see
what it is they fear they fear.

Do not be seduced.

Do not forget for a minute that the soldiers wear guns.
Hang onto your heart.
Ask them first what they'll give up to see it.
Tell them that they can begin with their arms.

Only then will *you* begin to negotiate.

From *Loving in the War Years*, South End Press, 1983, p. 68. Reprinted by permission.

Chapter Seven

Changed Women and Changed Organizations
Consequences of and Coping with Sexual Harassment

Barbara A. Gutek and Mary P. Koss

In the 1944 film *Gaslight* starring Ingrid Bergman and Charles Boyer, the husband slowly drives his wife toward insanity by causing the gaslights to flicker, all the while claiming that the lights are perfectly fine (Hamilton and Dolkart 1991). The metaphor of gaslighting communicates the psychological torture inherent in sexual harassment. A woman who is harassed may be unsure at first if what she is experiencing really is harassment, may be unsure what to do about it, and may not receive support from others when she enlists assistance in stopping the harassment. Consider the following scenario.

When Jane Doe took a job with a major hotel chain, her new boss promised that the job had "unlimited potential" for a bright, ambitious person. Jane, an ambitious young woman, liked almost everything about her job except the frequent sexist joking and sexual innuendos that pervaded the work place. Others went along with the jokes, but Jane complained. In response, her boss pressed her for details of her private life, dating behavior, and sexual preferences. He told her that in the "family atmosphere" of the organization, this was normal and expected. When she complained to her boss's boss, she was assured that she did not need to disclose any personal information. Yet nothing changed in her department. Her increasing discomfort led her to talk to her boyfriend about the behavior that she now labeled sexual harassment. Her boyfriend asked her what she did to encourage her boss to make these comments and urged her to behave in a more professional manner. Jane then went to the human resources department with the intention of lodging a sexual harassment complaint against her boss. The HR specialist told her that she was responsible for handling her boss, and that the organization did not have a sexual harassment policy because it never needed one. In the meantime, her boss's comments took on an increasingly hostile tone, and on her next performance appraisal, Jane received a rating of poor for "attitude." Devastated, she decided to seek help from a therapist, who gave her a battery of tests, informed her that she was suffering from a mild case of depression, and was unduly obsessed about her work. He suggested she come in twice a week in order to learn to deal with her feelings about work in a "constructive and empowering way." Still there was no change at work except the frequency and hostility of the comments, which were increasingly directed specifically at Jane. She also felt a new sense of isolation. Some workers who formerly were friendly began to treat Jane in a hostile manner. Jane began thinking about quitting her job, but she didn't have another job lined up and the therapy was expensive. She felt depressed about being diagnosed as mildly depressed, a label she had never previously used to describe herself. Her boyfriend complained that she wasn't much fun anymore. Shortly thereafter, in casual conversation with a woman who worked in the same building, Jane discovered the woman had formerly worked for Jane's boss. Her experiences with Jane's boss were amazingly parallel to Jane's own experiences with him. She told Jane she eventually quit the organization. A few days later, when her boss made an unusually crude comment, Jane turned to him and slapped him across the face. He walked out of the room, came back with his supervisor, and together they told Jane she was fired for unprofessional behavior. As a last resort, Jane went to see an attorney who advertised in the newspaper that he would help people who had been wrongfully terminated. When she told him her story, he told her she probably could not win a sexual harassment case in court: she had hit her boss, and she wasn't sure that witnesses would corroborate her story. He did, however, suggest that she might be able to get her job back if they argued that she hit her boss because she was suffering from PMS.

This report, a composite of real experiences encountered by one of the authors in cases brought to court, represents a worst case scenario of the unfolding of a sexual harassment case and shows how sexual harassment can confront a victim with perceptions that are often invalidated by those around her. The more she seeks validation for her view, the more hostile and rejecting her world becomes, until she feels she is failing in her most important life roles. How different this scenario would be if Jane worked in an organization that was sensitive to sexual harassment, valued its female employees, had a sexual harassment policy and procedures, and enforced them. How different too the scenario might be if Jane's boyfriend and therapist offered constructive suggestions for altering the situation rather than blaming her.

This article focuses on some consequences of sexual harassment of women. How does sexual harassment affect a female victim and the organization for which she works? How does she attempt to cope with harassment when she is confronted with it? These topics are interconnected because the responses of victims will be influenced by the amount of support and understanding received from significant others and employers. Likewise, the extent of emotional, physical, and psychological damage a woman experiences from harassment also depends on the responsiveness of other people and the organization for which she works.

Sexual harassment has been conceptualized as part of a spectrum of gender-based abuses that all involve exploitation and physical or sexualized violence (Hamilton, Alagna, King, and Lloyd 1987; Russell 1984), and the sexual victimization literature has served as a model for responses to harassment (Koss 1990; Quina and Carlson 1989). The parallels between sexual harassment and childhood sexual abuse, particularly incest, are many (Hamilton et al. 1987; Salisbury, Ginorio, Remick, and Stringer 1986). Like the victim of incest, the sexually harassed woman is economically if not emotionally dependent on the aggressor. The abuse is humiliating, so there is motivation to keep it a secret. It often continues for a long time and is experienced as an abuse of power and a betrayal of trust. Finally, retraumatization by the legal system is likely if redress from responsible authorities is sought. Sexual harassment differs from other forms of sexual victimization primarily in its direct impact on economic status and career well-being, which are only affected indirectly by other forms of victimization (Salisbury et al. 1986).

Empirical documentation of the psychological impact of harassment is difficult to obtain because the symptomatology is multiply determined. In addition to the impact of the sexual harassment itself, the aftereffects are influenced by disappointment in the way others react; the stress of harassment-induced life changes such as moves, loss of income, and disrupted work history; the triggering of unresolved issues from previous victimizations sustained by the woman; and finally, the trauma of litigation. Measuring the impact of harassment involves outcomes within three domains, which include somatic health, psychological health, and work variables including attendance, morale, performance, and impact on career track. In short, there is no single impact of sexual harassment. Instead, there are many different impacts depending on the domain examined and point in the process where the assessments are made.

It is unfortunate that there is a catch-22 quality inherent in research on the psychological and somatic reactions to sexual harassment. To show that harassment is harmful to the victim requires the demonstration that it has caused physical and emotional distress. Yet evidence of breakdown in the victim undermines her credibility and competence as a person and as an employee (Gutek 1993b; Hamilton and Dolkart 1991; Jensvold 1991). Clinicians who evaluate victims of sexual harassment need to be aware that they are evaluating someone undergoing multiple abnormal stressors (Brown 1991). They must also be mindful of the ways in which mental health practitioners become tools of the harasser or institution including forced psychotherapy and illegal forced fitness-for-duty examinations (Jensvold 1991).

Effects on the Harassed Woman

Carefully controlled studies of effects of harassment have not been done. Information about impacts comes primarily from self-reported effects included in prevalence studies, convenience samples, specialized populations such as victims who have filed complaints or visited a counseling center, and anecdotal accounts of harassment. Thus, a review of outcomes yields a list of possible effects but does not allow conclusions about their prevalence or the conditions under which any particular effect will occur.

Work Outcomes

Nearly one in ten women reported that they left their jobs as a result of sexual harassment in the original U.S. Merit Systems Protection Board (1981) study and in three separate studies of employed people in Los Angeles (Gutek, Nakamura, Gahart, Handschumacher, and Russell 1980; Gutek 1985). During a recent two-year period, over thirty-six thousand federal employees quit their jobs, were transferred or reassigned, or were fired because of sexual harassment (U.S. Merit Systems Protection Board 1987). Among eighty-eight cases filed with the California Department of Fair Employment and Housing, almost half had been fired, and another quarter had quit out of fear or frustration (Coles 1986). Some of the women who are fired or quit their jobs are unable to find or unwilling to take another job in the same field or occupation. Thus, sexual harassment can derail a career or lead or force a woman into an occupation which pays less well and/or offers fewer opportunities for advancement.

Among other negative work-related outcomes that have been reported is deterioration of interpersonal relationships at work (Bandy 1989; Culbertson, Rosenfeld, Booth-Kewley, and Magnusson 1992; DiTomaso 1989; Gutek 1985). Harassment can constrain the potential for forming friendships or work alliances with male co-workers (Schneider 1982). As a result of harassment university students report that they dropped courses and changed majors, academic departments and programs, and career intentions (Adams, Kottke, and Padgitt 1983; Benson and Thomson 1982; Fitzgerald, Shullman, Bailey, Richards, Swecker, Gold, Ormerod, and Weitzman 1988; Lott, Reilly, and Howard 1982). Lowered self-esteem and decreased feelings of competence may follow the realization that rewards may have been based on sexual attraction rather than ability (McCormack 1985).

Sexual harassment also affects women's satisfaction with the job and commitment to the organization (Culbertson et al. 1992). Among women who were harassed in Los Angeles County, 38% said the harassment affected the way they thought about their jobs (Gutek 1985). O'Farrell and Harlan (1982) reported that harassment had a strong negative impact on a woman's satisfaction with co-workers and supervisors in their study of women in blue-collar jobs. It was less strongly related to satisfaction with promotions and satisfaction with work content. Negative affect such as anger or disgust at being harassed has been associated with loss of motivation, distraction, and dreading work (Jensen and Gutek 1982). General hostility toward women, which seems especially prevalent in some blue-collar jobs, is often expressed in a sexually harassing manner (Carothers and Crull 1984; DiTomaso 1989; Wolshok 1981).

The impact of sexual harassment on women's job performance is less clear. According to Martin (1978; 1980), the exclusion of policewomen from informal social interaction networks which results from sexual harassment denies them the feedback that is necessary for successful job performance. But Gruber and Bjorn (1982) found that women autoworkers reported that sexual harassment had relatively little effect on their work behavior or sense of competence. Sexual harassment may not affect the diligence or effort a woman puts into her work, but lack of access to information and support from others in the work environment may well have an indirect effect on her work performance (see DiTomaso 1989; Collinson and Collinson 1989).

Sexual harassment and sex discrimination appear to go together. Women who report a lot of sexual harassment in their organization also tend to believe the organization is discriminatory in its treatment of women (DiTomaso 1989; Ragins and Scandura 1992). A study in Finland (Högbacka, Kandolin, Haavio-Mannila, and Kauppinen-Toropainen 1987) also showed that women who had encountered sexual harassment in their work group were more likely than other women to experience sex discrimination. Harassment and discrimination were not related for men.

Psychological and Somatic Outcomes

Beyond work outcomes, sexual harassment has been associated with a variety of negative effects on the victim. For example, Gruber and Bjorn (1982) found that in their sample of 138 women in mostly unskilled jobs in the auto industry, sexual harassment negatively affected self-esteem and life satisfaction. It was unrelated to family/home satisfaction, political efficacy, or personal control. Benson and Thomson (1982) found that sexual harassment was associated with a low sense of self-confidence, and Gutek (1985) found that sexual harassment sometimes affected the woman's relationship with other men.

Depending on the severity of the abuse, between 21% and 82% of women indicated that their emotional or physical condition worsened as a result of harassment (U.S. Merit Systems Protection Board 1981). In a sample of ninety-two women who had requested assistance for sexual harassment, virtually all reported debilitating stress reactions affecting work performance and attitudes, psychological health, and physical health (Crull 1982). The physical symptoms frequently reported by victims include gastrointestinal disturbances, jaw tightness and teeth grinding, nervousness, binge-eating, headaches, inability to sleep, tiredness, nausea, loss of appetite, weight loss, and crying spells (Crull 1982; Gutek 1985; Lindsey 1977; Loy and Stewart 1984; Safran 1976; Salisbury et al. 1986). Among the emotional reactions reported by victims of sexual harassment were anger, fear, depression, anxiety, irritability, loss of self-esteem, feelings of humiliation and alienation, and a sense of helplessness and vulnerability (Gutek 1985; Safran 1976; Silverman 1976–77; Tong 1984; Working Women's Institute 1979).

Many writers have speculated that gender-based abuse is related to the high rates of depression among women compared to men (Hamilton et al. 1987; McGrath, Keita, Strickland, and Russo 1990). More recently similarities have been noted between the symptoms seen in the aftermath of sexual harassment and the symptoms characteristic of post-traumatic stress disorder (PTSD) as defined in the American Psychiatric Association's (1987) *Diagnostic and Statistical Manual* (Hamilton and Dolkart 1991; Jensvold 1991; Koss 1990). The PTSD diagnosis conceptualizes the symptoms seen in the aftermath of severe stressors as normal responses to abnormal conditions (APA 1987). Considerable evidence suggests that PTSD can and does develop in persons with no history of psychopathology prior to the stressor.

Four criteria are required to qualify for the PTSD diagnosis: exposure to a stressor outside the realm of normal human experience, reexperiencing of the trauma, heightened arousal, and avoidance of people and interests that remind the victim of the trauma. The hallmark of PTSD is intrusive reexperiencing of the trauma, which may not occur until months or years following the trauma when recollections are triggered by some actual or symbolic reminder of the trauma. Recollections are in the form of daytime memories or nightmares and are accompanied by intense psychological distress. One victim of sexual harassment described her reexperiences as follows. "Memories of my intimate experiences with him continued to plague me. At unexpected moments, particularly when I was alone in my car, I would suddenly feel him there with me. His fingertips would draw my face toward his, and I would again feel his kiss, catching me unaware and sending a jolt of anxiety through my body" (Anonymous 1991, 506). As this excerpt illustrates, reexperiencing is more than a visual phenomenon; physical reactions associated with the trauma reoccur as well. To reduce the distress of reexperiencing, trauma victims often go to great lengths to avoid reminders of the trauma.

A recent survey of 3,020 women provides prevalence data for sexual harassment in a nationally representative sample of women of whom 2,720 had been employed at some point in their lives (Kilpatrick 1992). Data were collected by a random-digit-dial telephone survey. Measurement included standard questions to assess both major depression and PTSD as defined by the DSM-III-R. The findings are provocative and are presented here to apprise readers of the most recent research. However, the study has not yet been published, and the material that follows is taken from brief oral testimony before Congress that precluded examination of methodology and data analysis (Kilpatrick 1992) and a conference presentation (Saunders 1992).

Women suffering from PTSD and depression were more likely to have been sexually harassed than women who have never experienced PTSD or depression, suggesting that sexual harassment may contribute to depression and PTSD. Women who were diagnosed as having PTSD or depression reported more of each of seven types of harassment than did employed women in general. For example, 37% of women suffering from PTSD and 31% of women currently suffering from depression reported that they had been told sex stories by a supervisor, compared to 17% of the whole sample of employed women; 16% and 14% of women suffering from PTSD and depression, respectively, compared to 7% of women in general, said they were touched sexually by a supervisor; and 17% and 15% of PTSD and depressed women, respectively, compared to 6% of employed women in general, reported that they were kissed or fondled by a supervisor. Among women who reported that they felt sexually harassed, women suffering from PTSD or depression appeared to have more negative beliefs about the effects of sexual harassment than other women who reported that they felt sexually harassed. For example, among the 488 women in the survey who felt sexually harassed, 57% of women in general but 62% of women suffering from PTSD and 65% of women suffering depression thought their career would be hurt if they complained about the harassment. In addition, although 35% of the harassed women said the harassment interfered with their job, 43% of women with PTSD and 45% of depressed women said that sexual harassment interferes with their job. In general, the harassed women suffering from PTSD and depression were as likely as women in general to tell their boss to stop the offensive behavior: 74% of women in general and 77% and 69% of women diagnosed as having PTSD and depression, respectively, said they told their bosses to stop the offensive behavior. Women suffering from PTSD were less likely, however, than other harassed women to file a formal complaint: 6% of women with PTSD, 13% of depressed women, and 12% of employed women who were harassed filed a formal complaint about the harassment. More definitive consideration of these results must await publication of a comprehensive report of the project. If the initial results hold, they suggest researchers might pay more attention to the role of sexual harassment in a variety of psychological and somatic problems encountered by women. Sexual harassment might well contribute to both PTSD and depression in women.

Effects on the Organization

Although relatively little research has addressed the effects of harassment on women victims, even less has focused on the effects on the organization. In general, the scant literature available is highly speculative and anecdotal. According to one form of logic, sexual harassment has no effects on the organization, at least no negative effects. If it were counterproductive or hurt the organization's effectiveness, it would have been sanctioned a long time ago. One perspective that views sexual harassment as relatively benign is the natural/biological view, in which sexual harassment is seen as an expression of natural, biological attraction between men and women (Tangri, Burt, and Johnson 1982). In fact, many managers and workers think the seriousness and frequency of sexual harassment is overrated. For example, among readers of *Harvard Business Review* responding to a questionnaire about sexual harassment (Collins and Blodgett 1981), two-thirds of the men and about half of the women agreed or partly agreed with the statement, "The amount of sexual harassment at work is greatly exaggerated." In a systematic sample of employed people in Los Angeles County, less than 5% of either sex said sexual harassment was a major problem at their workplace (Gutek 1985). Other studies yield much higher figures. A recent study involving a stratified random sample of Navy enlisted personnel and officers found that over 60% of women and over 30% of men said sexual harassment is a problem in the Navy (Culbertson et al. 1992). Among a random sample of adults in Connecticut, 56% of men and 72% of women indicated that sexual harassment was either a "serious" or "very serious" problem (Loy and Stewart 1984).

Rather than being benign, sexual harassment has no doubt had negative effects on organizations all along, but these effects were invisible because sexual harassment itself was invisible, unnamed, and unreported. In its assessment of the magnitude of sexual harassment in the federal workforce, the U.S. Merit Systems Protection Board (1981) sought to assign a dollar figure to sexual harassment, estimating the cost of absenteeism, medical costs, and turnover attributable to harassment. Since, as noted above, about 10% of women have quit a job because of sexual harassment, turnover costs alone are substantial. The direct costs in absenteeism, medical expenses and indirect costs in the form of loss of motivation, distraction at work, and loss of commitment to the organization are also likely to be substantial, given the magnitude of harassment. Unfortunately, solid research on these effects is lacking. Today, most large corporations do have sexual harassment policies and procedures for dealing with allegations of harassment. According to a recent report (Bureau of National Affairs 1987), 97% of the companies in their study had sexual harassment policies, but the majority of these policies were established well after 1980, the year the EEOC published guidelines on sexual harassment. Indeed when the *Harvard Business Review* conducted its survey in 1981 (Collins and Blodgett 1981), only 29% of respondents said they worked in companies where top executives had issued statements to employees disapproving of sexual conduct. Even where policies are in place today, the procedures which support the policies leave much to be desired, e.g., they advise victims to seek help from a supervisor when the supervisor is the harasser in up to half of incidents of harassment (Gutek 1985). Research on the effectiveness of various types of procedures for handling sexual harassment is yet to be conducted (but see Rowe 1981).

Another area where there is very little evidence is in the response of organizations to charges of harassment. The temptation to ignore the complaint or put it off until later is great (Biaggio, Watts, and Brownell 1990; Gutek 1985). Many managers and administrators are uncomfortable dealing with sensitive issues like harassment, and even well-meaning ones may handle the situation badly. Finally, finding instances of sexual harassment in the organization is disconcerting and embarrassing. "It must be recognized that harassment charges are embarrassing to institutions, and administrators may wish to suppress reports even though such suppression potentially places institutions in greater legal jeopardy than a direct response to complaints" (Biaggio, Watts, and Brownell 1990, 216).

Workers who allege harassment are whistleblowers (Miceli and Near 1988; Near and Miceli 1987) and, as the carrier of bad news, may be blamed for "causing trouble." The effects on any workplace caught in the throes of an investigation into an allegation of sexual harassment or divided by a court case of harassment may be more visible to management than the effects of harassment itself. This is especially likely if harassment victims do not report the harassment. While there are anecdotal reports of managers' resentment at having to deal with sexual harassment allegations and male employees' fears that they will be unjustly accused, the topic has not been addressed in research.

Victims' Responses to Sexual Harassment

When a sample of employees is surveyed about what they would do if they were harassed, most say they would tell the person to stop (Dunwoody-Miller and Gutek 1985). In a Finnish study, 53% of both sexes said they would "have a talk" with the harasser (Högbacka et al. 1987). In addition, many men and women believe women should be able to handle sexual harassment themselves (Benson and Thomson 1982; Collins and Blodgett 1981; Gutek 1985, chap. 4; Sheppard 1989). In a random-sample survey of Los Angeles County workers, 79% of the women who had received at least one sexual overture from a man at work reported that they were confident they could handle future overtures (Gutek 1985). Thus, the majority of people apparently believe that sexual harassment is something that can and should be handled individually, i.e., by the person who is harassed.

A review of the literature on responses to harassment suggests that they fit into a two-by-two table: One axis consists of individual attempts to cope with harassment and coping responses involving another party such as a supervisor, therapist, physician, spouse, co-worker, or an outside agency or institution, e.g., the Equal Employment Opportunity Commission, a law firm, or a state agency. The second axis consists of indirect (e.g., ignoring, avoiding, evading) versus direct (e.g., confronting) responses. As will be noted below, individual, indirect coping responses (e.g., ignore the incident, avoid the perpetrator) are more common than responses that fit into the other three quadrants.

Individual Responses to Harassment

Real victims do not usually tell the harasser to stop. Their initial attempts to manage the initiator are rarely direct: typically, harassers are more powerful, physically and organizationally, than the victims, and sometimes the perpetrator's intentions are unclear. The first or the first several harassing events are often ignored (Benson and Thomson 1982; Dunwoody-Miller and Gutek 1985; Lindsey 1977; Loy and Stewart 1984; MacKinnon 1979). In their study of women automobile assembly workers, Gruber and Bjorn (1982) found that 23% of women said they ignored the harassment, and 22% responded "mildly" (by telling the man, "I've heard all that before" or "I'm not your type" [p. 286]). A woman may be especially likely to ignore the behavior or respond mildly if she can ascribe the man's behavior to some extenuating circumstance (e.g., "It had to do with the pair of pants I was wearing. He thought they were nice" [Gutek 1985, 791]. "At the time he had been feeling lonely. He had left his wife" [Gutek 1985, 86]). She may also interpret or reinterpret the situation so that the incident is not defined as sexual harassment (Rabinowitz 1990). Interpreting the situation as "horse-play" or "laughing it off" is common (e.g., Gutek 1985; Ragins and Scandura 1992). "There were a lot of men where I worked. A lot of horseplaying." "It was not really serious. He is a very young man and I think he was just joking or playing around" (Gutek 1985, 83). Gruber and Bjorn (1982) also found that making light of the harassment was a fairly common response (reported by 10% of the women autoworkers they studied).

Sometimes the woman tries to avoid the man, an indirect strategy reported by 51% of women officers and 68% of enlisted women in a recent U.S. Navy study (Culbertson et al. 1992; see also Loy and Stewart 1984, Table 3). Benson and Thomson (1982) found that female students try to avoid taking classes from male professors known to harass students. Given the differential in power (Zalk 1990), it certainly seems easier for students to avoid a potential harasser than to confront him. The ultimate step in avoiding the harasser is to quit the job, a common response of women who confront serious harassment (Loy and Stewart 1984).

Direct strategies (confronting the harasser) are less often used but are reported to be effective. Rowe (1981), for example, found the following direct response to be quite effective: Write a letter to the harasser, describing explicitly what is objectionable and outline a proper working relationship. Hand deliver the letter to the harasser and wait while he reads it. A letter has several advantages over a verbal request that the harassment cease. A written response shows that the victim felt strongly enough about the matter to write the letter and allows the woman to deliberate in choice of words. Perhaps most importantly, the letter serves as a record that the victim confronted the perpetrator, copies of which can be sent to various administrators in the organization and can be shown in a court of law, should the harassment continue or should the perpetrator retaliate.

Other forms of direct response include hitting or insulting the harasser, tactics that are not commonly tried. In their study of automobile workers, Gruber and Bjorn (1982) found that 15% of women autoworkers verbally "attacked" the harasser and 7% physically attacked or stopped the harasser.

Coping Responses Involving Others

Individual responses to harassment are considerably more common than responses involving a third party or another institution, perhaps because most of the options involving other people are also direct (i.e., confrontational). When they could not avoid the harasser, Benson and Thomson (1982) found that students reported the following kind of indirect strategy involving others: bringing a friend along whenever they were forced to interact with the harasser. Direct responses involving others are used by a minority of women victims, and the more formal forms of protest (filing a grievance or lawsuit) are less common than simply reporting the harassment to someone in authority (Grauerholz 1989). In a survey of workers in Finland, only 20% of women (and 5% of men) said they would report harassment to a supervisor if they were harassed. In the random-sample survey of workers in Los Angeles, 18% of women who were harassed actually did report the harassment to someone in authority (Gutek 1985). Comparable figures for a random sample of Navy personnel were 24% for enlisted women and 12% for women officers (Culbertson et al. 1992). Gruber and Bjorn (1982) found that 7% of the harassed automobile workers they studied reported the matter to someone in authority (see also Loy and Stewart 1984, Table 3).

Only 5% of women victims responding to the 1987 U.S. Merit Systems Protection Board study either filed a formal complaint or requested an investigation. In the 1989 Navy study, among those women who were harassed, 12% of enlisted women and 5% of female officers filed a grievance. The Women's Legal Defense Fund (1991) concluded that in the civilian workforce between 1% and 7% of women who are harassed file a formal complaint or seek legal help. Available evidence suggests that less than half are decided in favor of the woman alleging harassment (Terpstra and Baker 1988; 1992). According to the first U.S. Merit Systems Protection Board study of the federal workforce (1981), only 2% of the people harassed took official action; half that number won their cases. The court cases discussed in the media constitute a very small percentage of cases of sexual harassment.

In general, harassment victims do not make official complaints either to their organization or to another agency for several reasons: they feel that making a complaint will not accomplish anything, they are concerned about retaliation for complaining (Culbertson et al. 1992; Gutek 1985), and often they do not want to hurt the harasser and they fear that complaining might negatively affect his job and/or family (Gutek 1985). Women who blame themselves for the harassment are especially concerned about protecting "the person who bothered" her (Jensen and Gutek 1982). Some women also report that they were too embarrassed or afraid to report the harassment (Culbertson et al. 1992). In the U.S. Navy study, the most common negative reaction reported by women who did complain about harassment was "I was humiliated in front of others" (reported by 33% of enlisted women and 34% of officers).

The Effectiveness of Different Coping Strategies

The available research suggests that the indirect strategies of coping with harassment by reinterpreting, ignoring, and avoiding are very common but not particularly effective. Quitting a job or leaving school may be effective in stopping the immediate harassment of that person, but it has other consequences for the person who leaves, and it is unlikely to stop the harasser from harassing other women (Rabinowitz 1990). If they are not particularly effective, why then are the indirect responses so commonly tried? Gruber and Bjorn (1982) suggested three reasons why individual, indirect methods may be so common. First, indirect methods such as reinterpreting the situation or avoiding the harasser may allow a woman to "manage" the situation without disrupting the work setting or her relationship with other people at work (Benson and Thomson 1982; Collins and Blodgett 1981; Gutek 1985; Sheppard 1989).

Second, women may perceive the direct methods as riskier and less certain in their outcomes than the indirect methods. Avoiding the perpetrator may seem safer than confronting him or filing a complaint against him. Although there is some evidence that fear of retaliation is a realistic fear (Coles 1986), there is no evidence that direct methods of coping with harassment are necessarily riskier than indirect methods, particularly if riskiness is equated with effectiveness of stopping the harassment. While they appear to be more effective in stopping the harassment than indirect methods of coping with sexual harassment, it is possible to make a case that direct attempts at dealing with harassment may be problematic for women as a group. By forcing the perpetrator and/or the organization to deal with the issue, the woman making the complaint may be viewed as disrupting the workplace, and she may well engender hostile reactions (Biaggio, Watts, and Brownell 1990; DiTomaso 1989). Unfortunately, the topic of riskiness of various types of responses to harassment has not been studied.

Third, Gruber and Bjorn (1982) suggested that some harassment is ambiguous because it combines a degree of sexual interest with offensive behavior. "This ambiguity may reduce a woman's ability to respond in an assertive or direct manner" (p. 276; see also Gutek 1985, chap. 4). Along similar lines, in a scenario study, Williams and Cyr (1992) found that male (but not female) students rated the perpetrator's behavior as less harassing if the woman target had made a prior commitment to a friendly relationship with the harasser.

Contingencies in Response to Harassment

Although the individual, indirect responses to sexual harassment are common, it makes sense to ask whether some women or some situations encourage women to respond directly or to involve other people or institutions. For example, a victim of harassment might more readily employ a direct response to harassment if she has a supportive supervisor and works in an organization having a sexual harassment counselor or prominently displayed posters forbidding sexual harassment. Unfortunately, few of the circumstances under which women victims use different kinds of coping responses are known, and data suggest only one tentative conclusion. Women who were more severely harassed tended to respond in a more assertive and direct manner than those who were not severely harassed (Gruber and Bjorn 1982; Loy and Stewart 1984). Victims are more likely to ignore the harassment, joke about it, or evade the harasser when the harassment is mild. A recent scenario study showed that student respondents thought the victim would be more likely to report the incident if she had not previously been friendly toward the perpetrator (Williams and Cyr 1992), but, as noted above, existing research of inexperienced raters shows that their reactions are not always consistent with the behaviors of real victims.

Characteristics of the woman victim might also affect how she responds to harassment. Gruber and Bjorn (1986) tested three hypotheses about coping with sexual harassment. They found support for the hypothesis that women with less organizational power would respond less actively and directly than women with some organizational power. (They defined power as having high job skills, having high job status, and/or not being at a lower organizational level than the harasser.) They also found some support for a second hypothesis, namely that women with fewer personal resources (i.e., those having low self-esteem, low personal control, strong sense of being trapped in their job) would respond in an indirect manner more often than women with more personal resources. Similar findings were reported by Jensen and Gutek (1982), who found that women who tended to exhibit behavioral self-blame (i.e., felt their own behavior contributed to the harassment) were less likely than other women victims to discuss the harassment with others or report it to others. They also found that women who had traditional sex-role attitudes were less likely than other women to report the harassment to someone. Finally, Gruber and Bjorn (1986) found no support for their third hypothesis that black women, representing people who have low "sociocultural power," would respond less assertively than white women (see also Culbertson et al. 1992 for consistent findings).

It should be noted that both Gruber and Bjorn's (1986) and Jensen and Gutek's (1982) studies were cross-sectional, and, thus, it is not possible to draw definitive causal relationships from the data. Although it is appealing to assume that failing to report the harassment led to lower self-esteem and/or behavioral self-blame, it is also possible that low self-esteem and/or self-blame prevented victims from directly dealing with the harassment in some manner.

Stages of Response to Harassment

Another approach to the study of responses to harassment, illustrated by the scenario described at the beginning of this chapter, is a stage model. Most harassment is not a one-time occurrence but unfolds over time. How a woman responds probably depends on the progression of the harassment. Has she already tried ignoring, evading, or joking? Is the harassment continuing, escalating, becoming more hostile or threatening? The progressive reactions to harassment observed among women in psychotherapy document a sequence of changes in the victim's central beliefs about herself, her coworkers, and the work world (Salisbury et al. 1986). Four stages of response can be identified.

(1) Confusion/Self-Blame. The sexual harassment was a series of events. After each incident, the victim believed that the harassment was going to level off or eventually stop. When the harasser's behavior escalated, which it did in virtually all of the cases studied, the victim felt out of control and helpless.

(2) Fear/Anxiety. Subsequent to the harasser's continuing behavior, the victim felt trapped and became "paranoid." She feared potential retaliation at work, the future of her career, and potential financial ruin. Outside of work, she feared being called on the phone in the early morning, having her home watched, or being followed in a car. Concentration, motivation, work performance, and attendance were adversely affected, and self-esteem declined.

(3) Depression/Anger. Once the woman recognized that she was a legitimate victim who was not to blame for her harassment, anxiety often shifted to anger. Often this shift occurred when she decided to leave her job or was fired. This anger about being treated unfairly was a prime motive to file charges. While filing charges may have represented a positive step by the victim to take control of her destiny, it often led to a decided deterioration in the work situation.

(4) Disillusionment. The organizational response to sexual harassment was often hurtful and disappointing. By speaking up, the woman encountered a whole new set of institutional abuses. Often, the woman eventually realized that she had been naïve about getting help in the system. She then questioned her expectations about fairness, loyalty, and justice. These ingenuous beliefs gradually become replaced by the insight that justice doesn't always prevail.

Discussion

This review of the clinical and empirical literature on the outcomes of sexual harassment shows that the topic has received very little attention, especially in comparison to the abundance of research that has been devoted to the definition of harassment and to the frequency of its occurrence (Gutek and Dunwoody 1988). What is available tends to be anecdotal, case studies, or nonrepresentative self-reports. Relatively little has made its way into journals but has been confined to conference presentations, books, and book chapters. Furthermore, the body of studies fails to do justice to the complexity of the outcome questions. Thus, the literature allows us to list categories of outcomes but does not allow us to draw conclusions about the frequency of different outcomes or the conditions leading to the various outcomes. The review suggests that sexual harassment is hardly benign—either for the individual or the organization. It raises three questions: why is there so little research, what kind of research is needed, and what are the pros and cons of researching outcomes?

Why So Little Research on Outcomes and Reactions?

In general, this review reveals an appalling lack of empirical data on outcomes, especially in comparison to research on other forms of gender-based sexual exploitation. There are several possible explanations for the lack of data on the impact of harassment. The primary one is that the topic is embraced by none of the major funding agencies. It is illegal but is not viewed as a serious crime by justice authorities, and it is a victimization but viewed as a minor one in terms of psychological adjustment by mental health agencies. As a consequence, much more is known about the impacts of rape or child sexual abuse than is known about sexual harassment. Almost all the research on sexual harassment has been done without funding and it suffers for it. Much of the research is opportunistic, uses students, and focuses on issues easy to study without funding (e.g., how students respond to various sexual harassment scenarios). The data reviewed here suggest that sexual harassment may be a far more significant contributor to women's distress than has been acknowledged; funds for in-depth, controlled studies should be made available.

What Kinds of Research Are Needed?

The widespread prevalence of sexual harassment demands that future research include studies in which victims are followed prospectively in time from the point of victimization and administered standardized measurements across the three domains of outcome: psychological distress, somatic effects, and work-related changes. Also important are the development of measures of responses to harassment, as exemplified by recent work by Fitzgerald and Brock (1992), and studies of the variables that mediate or moderate the impact of harassment. These should include *person variables* (e.g., age, demographic characteristics, preexisting personality functioning, perception of the meaning of the trauma, and qualities assigned to the self and others postharassment), *event variables* (e.g., severity, duration, frequency of abuse, degree of personal violation, and whether victimization was shared with others or suffered alone), *organization variables* (e.g., policies in place, response to the harassment, quality and availability of resources to assist victims, and degree of physical and emotional safety ensured posttrauma), and *environment variables* (e.g., immediate response of significant others, quality and continuity of social support, and community and company attitudes and values about harassment, corporate climate).

Samples of women from general populations (e.g., college students, employed women) as well as specific populations (e.g., victims who have filed law suits, victims who have sought help from counseling centers) should be followed over time to gain a better understanding of the development of work outcomes as well as somatic and psychological outcomes. The inclusion of the mediating and moderator variables discussed above will elucidate the conditions under which sexual harassment leads to the various outcomes that have been identified in this review. In doing so, the research may suggest strategies for minimizing negative outcomes for victims of harassment. While minimizing negative outcomes is less desirable than eliminating sexual harassment altogether, it helps.

Finally, an understanding of the true costs of sexual harassment borne by organizations and their employees, as well as the more visible costs of dealing with charges of harassment, investigations, and lawsuits, may encourage organizations to provide a more supportive environment for female employees who encounter harassment.

The Pros and Cons of Focusing on Outcomes

A focus on outcomes suggests a linear sequence in which some stimulus (sexual harassment in this case) necessarily leads to one or more outcomes. Undoubtedly there are women who are sexually harassed by a legal or standardly accepted lay definition of harassment but who may experience few or none of the outcomes discussed in this chapter. Does the failure to exhibit outcomes negate the person's experience of harassment, i.e., will the presence of outcomes be taken as a necessary condition for the existence of harassment? Will a woman be able to successfully allege harassment if she keeps her job, receives a positive performance evaluation, or gets a raise? Will she be able to successfully charge harassment if she does not need a therapist, has no physical symptoms, and sleeps and eats well? Will it be necessary to show adverse impacts including somatic and psychological effects in order to have one's charge of harassment taken seriously? In the formal complaint process, a reliance on the existence of negative outcomes as proof of the allegation of harassment has contributed to the retraumatization of harassment victims. Women who allege harassment may be required by their own attorneys or counselors in their companies to undergo fitness-for-duty examinations or psychotherapy (Jensvold 1991). One problem with a reliance on negative effects as an indicator of harassment is that they contribute to a common stereotype of women, namely, the "sick woman" syndrome. Sexual harassment made her sick.

Unfortunately, the charge that the woman has been psychically or physically damaged by the harassment leaves open an alternate interpretation of her "sickness," namely that she has always been emotionally or physically fragile or damaged. Thus, by coming forth and complaining about harassment or filing a sexual harassment lawsuit, a woman runs the risk of being portrayed either as a person made sick by harassment or, worse, a person who has always had physical and/or psychological problems (Gutek 1993a). Prospective studies and archival research may be possible in settings such as the military to allow comparison of pre- and post-trauma psychological status and health care utilization. Sustained research on the conditions under which any particular effect occurs should provide valuable information in court cases and alleviate the double bind now faced by many women who take their cases to court.

Chapter Eight

Sexual Harassment in Organizations
A Critique of Current Research and Policy

Christine L. Williams

Introduction

In 1979, my sister and I were hired by a catering firm to wait tables at the grand opening of a ballroom dance hall in Oklahoma City. When we arrived at the hall, we were told to put on uniforms consisting of a tight red leotard with spaghetti straps and matching clingy skirt. I was outraged by this sexual objectification; my sister didn't mind. I decided to take the job anyway. As a struggling college student I wanted the money to buy Christmas presents, but I didn't feel right about it. Halfway through the evening I put on a cardigan because I grew cold, thus provoking a fight with the caterer. He let me wear the sweater (although he moved me to the "coat check" station), and he vowed never to hire me again.

Was I sexually harassed? Was my sister? Granted, this took place before the 1986 Supreme Court ruling that declared sexual harassment an illegal form of workplace gender discrimination. According to the Supreme Court, sexual harassment occurs when submission to or rejection of sexual advances is a term of employment, used as a basis for making employment decisions, or if the advances create a hostile or offensive working environment. In 1988, the Equal Employment Opportunity Commission issued the following guidelines to clarify the legal definition of sexual harassment:

> Unwelcome sexual advances, requests for sexual favors and other verbal or physical conduct of a sexual nature constitute sexual harassment when: submission to such conduct is made either explicitly or implicitly a term or condition of an individual's employment; submission to or rejection of such conduct . . . is used as a basis for employment decisions . . . ; or such conduct has the purpose or effect of unreasonably interfering with an individual's work performance or creating an intimidating, hostile or offensive working environment. (Tamminen, 1994, p. 44)

At the ballroom dance hall, my sister and I were explicitly required to wear a sexual outfit that I considered to be degrading and offensive, and I lost out on future

From *Sexuality and Culture* 1 (1998): 19–43. Copyright © 1998 by Transaction Publishers. Reprinted by permission of the publisher.

employment because I resisted this rule. Thus, my experience seems to fit the legal definition of sexual harassment. Nevertheless, it is not obvious to me that either of us would
have labeled our experiences sexual harassment, even if this law had been in place in
1979. Many people today work in jobs in which they are routinely subjected to deliberate
or repeated sexual behavior that is unwelcome, as well as other sex-related behaviors that
they consider hostile, offensive, or degrading. They rarely label their experiences sexual
harassment, however, because they are institutionalized as part of their jobs.

In this essay, I discuss several ways that sexual harassment can be institutionalized in
work organizations. Drawing on recent studies of organizational sexuality, I argue that
organizations can be perpetrators of sexual harassment. I describe several ways in
which organizations subject workers to unwanted sexual advances, use sexuality as the
basis for making employment decisions, and create and/or tolerate a hostile or offensive working environment. I contend that, unless the organizational forms of sexual
harassment are recognized and understood, there is little possibility of eradicating
sexual harassment from the workplace.

This essay is organized around a critique of current sexual harassment research. The
prevailing research and policy focus—on discrete acts perpetrated by individual men
against individual women—obscures the many ways in which organizations routinely
and intentionally exploit the sexuality of workers. I identify three problems with this
research: (1) most studies use objective behaviors as the primary indicator of sexual
harassment, not the subjective interpretation of those behaviors; (2) researchers typically define sexual harassment as an individual behavior problem; and (3) most studies
focus exclusively on the sexual harassment of women by men. Finally, I criticize the
policy recommendations that typically accompany research on sexual harassment.
Each of the problems I identify with sexual harassment studies is linked to the general
failure to examine organizational context. The ultimate goal of this essay is to encourage researchers to develop a broader research definition of sexual harassment that can
address both individual and organizational forms of sexual harassment.

Objective Behaviors and Subjective Meanings

Many social science researchers have found the legal definition of sexual harassment
vague and difficult to operationalize in part because it focuses on the subjective experience of hostility and offensiveness, and not objective behaviors (Folgero and Fjeldstad,
1995). Consequently, many social scientists interested in ascertaining the frequency of
sexual harassment have devised lists of what they consider proscribed behaviors.
According to Arvey and Cavanaugh's (1995) review of this research of the past five
years, these lists of behaviors vary considerably among researchers. They cite one 1994
study that asked respondents to report on how frequently they were stared at, and
referred to as a "girl, hunk, doll, babe or honey," and another that only included acts of
intercourse or genital stimulation in its definition of sexual harassment.

Not surprisingly, this method of ascertaining the frequency of sexual harassment
produces incomparable and inconsistent results (Arvey and Cavanaugh, 1995). Estimates of the percentage of women who have experienced sexual harassment range

between 42 percent and 90 percent (Terpstra and Baker, 1989). A far smaller percentage of women actually call what happens to them sexual harassment, however. In a recent Defense Department survey, for example, 78 percent of the women soldiers surveyed said they had experienced some type of offensive sexual behavior in the previous year, but one-third of these respondents did not consider the incidents sexual harassment (*San Francisco Chronicle*, 15 June 1996, A7). Paludi and Barickman write that "the great majority of women who are abused by behavior that fits legal definitions of sexual harassment—and who are traumatized by the experience—do not label what has happened to them sexual harassment" (Paludi and Barickman, 1991, p. 68).

At least part of the discrepancy between researchers' estimates and employees' self-reports of sexual harassment can be attributed to organizational context. Some of the behaviors that researchers define as constituting sexual harassment are in fact *requirements* of some jobs. A great many jobs in the service and entertainment industries require that employees submit to hostile or degrading sexual stares, language, and even occasional touching. Obviously, this is the case in the "sex trades," including prostitution, phone sex, and strip bars. In these jobs, submission to such behaviors is a virtual condition of employment (Allison, 1994). But recent studies of restaurant work (Giuffre and Williams, 1994), the hotel and tourism trade (Adkins, 1995), and hospital work (Foner, 1994) suggest that these sexual behaviors are widespread and normative throughout the labor market.

In some cases, organizations actually mandate the sexualized treatment of employees. For example, many waitresses work in a highly sexually charged atmosphere where sexual expectations are embedded in their jobs. Giuffre and Williams (1994) cite the example of one waitress, who claimed that customers often "talk dirty" to her:

> I remember one day, about four or five years ago when I was working as a cocktail waitress, this guy asked me for a Slow Comfortable Screw [the name of a drink]. I didn't know what it was. I didn't know if he was making a move or something. I just looked at him. He said, "You know what it is, right?" I said, "I bet the bartender knows!" (laughs) . . . There's another one, "Sex on the Beach." And there's another one called a "Screaming Orgasm." Do you believe that? (Giuffre and Williams, 1994, p. 387)

This waitress works for an organization that subjects all employees to sexual comments as a condition of employment. Although she personally finds sexy drink names offensive, she neither complains about it nor labels it sexual harassment: once it becomes clear that a "Slow Comfortable Screw" is a "legitimate" and recognized restaurant demand, she accepts it (albeit reluctantly) as part of her job description. The fact that the offensive behavior is institutionalized makes it beyond reproach in her eyes.

This problem of labeling behaviors as sexual harassment is not eliminated by specifying in questionnaires that respondents report only "unwanted" sexual behaviors. This term is paradoxical for many workers. By agreeing to work in a specific job or industry, many people understand that they will be subjected to sexual innuendo, bantering, ogling, and other sexual behaviors as part of their jobs. In some highly sexualized organizations, employees actually are required to sign consent forms promising that they will not sue their employers for sexual harassment. "Consenting" to this treatment does not necessarily make the specific behaviors any less hostile or degrading to the individual, but it does make the process of identifying sexual harassment more complex because they are endorsed or at least tolerated by organizations. The current definition of sexual harassment in research and in policy requires employees to distinguish between sexual behaviors that are organizationally sanctioned and those that are not, a process fraught with ambiguity.

In another example, Adkins found that women hired for several different jobs in the British tourism industry were required to engage in sexualized interactions with customers and co-workers (see also Gherardi, 1995, p. 43). A catering manager describes the work of her female assistants:

> She "expected" women workers to be able to cope with sexual behaviour and attention from men customers as "part of the job." She said that if "the women catering assistants complain, or say things like they can't cope, I tell them it happens all the time and not to worry about it. . . . It's part of the job. . . . If they can't handle it then they're not up to working here." (Adkins, 1995, p. 130)

While some women may enjoy and even profit from sexualized interactions at work, resisting these behaviors may be impossible. For instance, in this particular case, reporting sexually offensive behavior to the catering manager would not result in a complaint of sexual harassment; more likely, it would result in the loss of a job. In many service jobs, customers or clients have carte blanche to treat workers in sexually degrading ways, and workers are required to flirt with them. These organizationally sanctioned behaviors are codified in two maxims of successful marketing: "The customer is always right," and "Sex sells." (For analyses of employer liability for sexual harassment by customers, see Deadrick, Kezman, and McAfee, 1996; Garvey, 1996.)

In some service jobs, sexualized behavior is not mandated, but it is tolerated, as is the case in medical and nursing work. According to Nancy Foner, aides who work in nursing homes are frequently subjected to "sexual overtures and fondling" from the residents:

> Aides tend to laugh off such actions from confused residents, but they are often hostile if the resident is alert. "I can't stand that man," said one aide, referring to a patient deemed to be "90 percent all there." "He put his hands all over you. Now Welch, he massages your thighs when you wash him, but he don't know what he's doing." Another aide said she was initially horrified when after washing a resident known to be a lesbian, the woman loudly proclaimed, "You fucked me, now you want me to fuck you?" "I ran to tell the nurse," the aide explained. "I said I have something to tell you. And she said, Oh, yeah, she does that all the time." (Foner, 1994, p. 37)

Supervisors were well aware of this treatment of aides by the residents but did nothing to stop it or prevent it from recurring.

The growing popularity of so-called "Gentlemen's Clubs" among salesmen is another example of organizational tolerance of an offensive sexual behavior. There are now over a hundred high-end clubs in twenty-two U.S. cities that cater to businessmen (Katz, 1995, p. A16). According to a recent survey by *Sales and Marketing Magazine*, nearly half of the salesmen responding admitted to entertaining clients at a topless bar (Zeiger, 1995). In the following account, Zeiger describes going to a bar in Detroit with two businessmen (a salesman and his boss) who were entertaining a client (a representative from a trucking company):

> We hand the waitress credit cards and ask for a cash advance of $600. She brings us 60 ten-dollar bills, which we hand over to [the company salesman]. [The salesman] makes a big show of riffling through the plank-thick stack of cash, stands, and begins hollering, "Hey, we got the money! Where are the girls?" ... A petite cheerful young woman [appears] at our table. The salesman and his boss grin at each other in satisfaction, then motion the woman over towards the trucking rep. ... The woman yanks at [the trucking rep's] shirt, baring his chest, and begins grinding against the rep in time to a Van Halen song, pushing her tongue into his ear, pressing her naked breasts into his face. Her attire, at this moment, consists of a G-string and high heels. ... As the woman lowers to her knees on the floor, licking her way delicately down to the rep's stomach ... , the boss whispers to me ... "I like to think of this as cementing the business relationship." (Zeiger, 1995, p. 48)

Taking clients to strip-tease bars is offensive to some saleswomen (and salesmen) and may informally bar women from participating in some sales occupations, but to date, there have been no suits filed with the EEOC citing these bars as the cause of sexual harassment (MacKinnon, 1995). Workers do not and perhaps cannot label this practice sexual harassment because it is endorsed by their work organizations.

The focus on specific behaviors in definitions of sexual harassment also ignores the possibility of ambiguity and ambivalence that workers experience in interpreting interactions (Fiske and Glick, 1995; Hollway and Jefferson, 1996). Sexual behaviors rarely have unambiguous meanings, and they typically evoke ambivalent responses. Women who are eager to fit in and be accepted by co-workers may interpret offensive acts as initiation rituals or similar tests of their dedication to the group. In an underground coal mine studied by Vaught and Smith (1980), the women who were new to the work group were stripped from the waist down and "greased" by their male co-workers, which involved tying down the novice in a spread-eagle position and applying coal grease to the genitals. When one of the women filed a suit against the company, she was met with open hostility from the work group. According to one woman's account,

> Us older women don't have anything to do with her except to tell her to drop the whole idea and not get our brothers in trouble. She was crying in the bath house the other day about how we treated her, and Babs slapped her and told her to drop her damned suit and behave herself and everything would be all right. Today in the union meeting [she] arose and tearfully apologized to her brothers and sisters for the hard feelings she had caused, and announced that she was dropping her lawsuit against the company and the men of Number Six Unit. (Vaught and Smith, 1980, p. 180)

From the standpoint of an outside observer, this "greasing" may appear to constitute a sexually hostile and offensive behavior. But, within the organizational context, even this egregious act is legitimized and excused by some employees as "part of the job," and hence outside the definition of sexual harassment.

Researchers who focus on behaviors—without taking into account the institutional and cultural context of the behavior—thus gain an incomplete picture of sexual harassment in the workplace. As Sylvia Gherardi notes,

> Organizational sexuality is a social practice which lays down explicit and culturally elaborated rules of behaviour with local validity. Behaviour that scandalizes and may constitute sexual harassment in one occupational community may be entirely acceptable a few floors up or down in the same building. (Gherardi, 1995, p. 187)

The ubiquity of sexually degrading aspects of jobs may actually neutralize them in the eyes of both workers and employers. Once sexual harassment becomes normalized in an organization, individual workers may not define their experiences as sexual harassment, even if they feel sexually degraded by them.

Researchers may find it difficult to include context in their studies of sexual harassment due to their overreliance on survey research methods. Surveys, by their very nature, strip context from respondents' reports of their experiences and feelings (Feagin, Orum, and Sjoberg, 1991). It is no coincidence that many of the studies reported here are based on qualitative methods, which are better able than surveys to record ambivalence and social context. Survey researchers themselves are urging more emphasis on field studies and other open-ended methods to solve their validity problems (e.g., Arvey and Cavanaugh, 1995; Fitzgerald, 1993).

Individual Acts and Organizational Norms

Objectivist methods also contribute to the second problem with research on sexual harassment: a majority of studies frame the problem as one facing individual women confronted by the unwanted sexual demands of individual men. Most sexual harassment research has been conducted by psychologists who focus on individuals as their units of analysis. Indeed, much of what we know about sexual harassment is based on analogue studies administered to college undergraduates (Fitzgerald, 1993; Frazier, Cochran, and Olson, 1995). Here is an example of such methods, taken from a recent study of gender differences in the perception of sexual harassment using a sample of 197 college students:

> The response measure was a 60-item questionnaire consisting of 20 different interactions between a man and a woman, each occurring in three situations. The three situations were: (a) the work place involving a married supervisor and an unmarried subordinate, (b) a college campus involving an unmarried professor and one of his/her unmarried students, and (c) two college students who dated before and meet at a party. . . . Each interaction was described separately (e.g., "John puts his arm around Kathy's waist and tells her she looks nice," "John sneaks up behind Kathy and tickles her on the ribs"), after which the participants indicated the extent to which they perceived it as sexually harassing for each of the three situations. The same interactions were presented in all three situations. The content for the 20 interactions was based on allegations made in an actual sexual harass-

ment case that was known to one of the authors and settled out of court. Some items were added to increase the severity or obviousness of the harassing acts (e.g., "John fondles Kathy's breasts," "John says to Kathy, 'If you don't make love to me, I'll make it difficult for you'"). All items were rated on a 7-point Likert scale, with endpoints of (1) "definitely is not sexual harassment" and (7) "definitely is sexual harassment." A rating of (4) was defined as "unsure." The average rating across the 20 interactions in each situation was the measure of perceived sexual harassment. (Katz, Hannon, and Whitten, 1996)

Studies such as this one may be useful in providing evidence that men and women college students on average define sexual harassment differently. However, because these scenarios lack any information on the organizational context of the sexual behaviors, this method can only assess respondents' abstract principles, a problem which is exacerbated by the fact that many college students have very limited experience in the labor force. Using hypothetical examples of harassment (even if based on real or exaggerated court cases) gives little insight into how employed men and women actually decide when their personal experiences fit the definition of sexual harassment (Fitzgerald and Shullman, 1993; Gutek and Koss, 1993).

Even more troublesome, this study, like many others, focuses exclusively on individuals as the source of sexual harassment. Note that "John" is the perpetrator in all cases. This style of research is therefore limited because it ignores how organizations routinely exploit workers' sexuality (see also Vaux, 1993). In the previous section I argued that many work organizations mandate or tolerate the sexual harassment of employees by clients, customers, or co-workers. Here I argue that organizations routinely control and exploit the sexual expression of workers. This constitutes sexual harassment, I argue, because those who do not or cannot conform to organizational control of their sexuality face discrimination in the labor market.

Employers sometimes choose to hire employees whom they consider sexually attractive and alluring, or whom they think their customers would find attractive. Although not every assessment of attractiveness made by employers has a sexual component (e.g., attractiveness may be assessed using the criteria of neatness and cleanliness), several jobs in the economy do select and reward workers who display an explicitly sexual appearance. This practice is most conspicuous in some predominantly female service occupations: airline attendants and secretaries, for example, are often subjected to explicit appearance rules that emphasize heterosexual attractiveness (Hochschild, 1983; Pringle, 1988). In the British tourism industry studied by Lisa Adkins (1995), being sexually attractive was an *explicit* requirement for all occupations in which women were clustered. In many of these jobs, women were required to wear uniforms that emphasized their sexual availability (e.g., skirts, high heels, blouses worn off-the-shoulder).

The assessment of sexual attractiveness is racialized. In the amusement park and hotel that Adkins studied, all the women employees were white, suggesting that nonwhites may not conform to employers' assessment of sexual attractiveness. Different assumptions are made about workers' sexuality depending on whether they are white, black, Asian, or Hispanic, contributing to the race and gender segregation of the labor force. Describing his image of the ideal "Hooters Girl"—the official name for the scantily clad waitresses at the Hooters restaurant chain—an executive of the organization was quoted: "Our image of the Hooters Girl is the all-American, cheerleader, surfer girl next door. . . . We hire girls that best fit that description" (Soriano, 1994, p. B1). This is an image that black women do not "fit." Given the stereotype of black women as "fallen" women, Duncan Kennedy writes, "a provocative costume is more likely to be interpreted as a uniform indicating actual employment as a prostitute, or at least as slutty rather than sexy if worn by a black woman than it is if worn by a white woman" (Kennedy, 1993, p. 164). Consequently, black women may be at a disadvantage compared to white women in obtaining service jobs which involve a high degree of sexual exploitation. In fact, in some of the jobs where black women are overrepresented, they are not in the public view (e.g., telephone operators), or they may be required to actively mute their sexual attractiveness, a situation Judith Rollins discovered when she applied for a job as a house cleaner (Rollins, 1985; see also Glenn, 1992).

This sorting out of employees based on racial/ethnic stereotypes about sexuality and sexual attractiveness results in limits on job opportunities and contributes to income inequality among women. These limitations also affect men, although the economic impact may be less severe because jobs that employ only "sexually attractive" women may not be as well paying as those in which men are more commonly clustered. However, in a currently pending case, men have charged the Hooters restaurant chain with employment discrimination for refusing to hire them as "Hooters Girls" (*San Francisco Chronicle,* 16 November 1995, A8).

There is some evidence of employers refusing to hire women for fear that women will bring sexuality with them into the workplace and, in worst-case scenarios, charge their innocent co-workers with sexual harassment. This fear was inscribed in the military's previous exclusion of women from serving aboard combat ships and in Titan missile silos (Stiehm, 1989). Fear of women's sexuality motivates informal discriminatory practices as well: Epstein writes that some established executive and professional men refuse to take on women protégés "because they fear accusations of sexual intimacy" (Epstein, 1981, p. 288). In fact, sexual rumors and innuendo are not uncommon strategies for undermining professional careers, as recent well-publicized cases attest (e.g., Burrough and Helyar, 1990; Cunningham and Schumer, 1984).

This widespread practice of evaluating employees in terms of their sexual attractiveness raises important questions about the definition of sexual harassment. Is it sexual harassment for individuals to be chosen for jobs because the employer finds them physically attractive? Is it sexual harassment for an employer to reject a job candidate because his/her body does not fit the employer's notion of what the job requires? Is it sexual harassment for an employer to refuse to hire a person because they fear their own sexual desire will be aroused by that person, or because that person might provoke uncontrollable sexual desire in their co-workers? In each of these cases, workers are judged on the basis of their sexual attributes, and those who do not conform to expectations suffer job discrimination. These behaviors thus seem to fit the legal definition of sexual harassment, yet they are ignored in most research on sexual harassment.

In addition to sexual attractiveness, candidates for jobs are frequently evaluated in terms of their sexual orientation and marital status. The division of labor by gender, which places women in jobs where they are subservient to men, is linked to employers' stereotypical views of women's traditional roles as wife and mother in families (Kwolek-Folland, 1994). The fact that so-called "women's jobs" pay less than comparable male jobs is a legacy of the long-standing belief that women need less money than men because they are economic dependents within families (Kessler-Harris, 1990). Some employers deliberately seek out a predominantly female, married labor force, on the assumption that these employees demand less pay and fewer benefits (Nelson, 1986). Of course, compensating women at lower salaries than men perpetuates women's dependence on a male wage, thus bolstering heterosexual marriage.

These widespread practices all seem to fit the legal definition of sexual harassment. In the case of an organization that only hires married women, conduct of a sexual nature (i.e., heterosexuality) is a term of employment and is used for making employment decisions. Yet such organizational practices are rarely considered sexual harassment by researchers.

In their failure to regard these organizational practices that exploit workers' sexuality as sexual harassment, researchers are following the lead of recent court decisions. According to Sarah Burns, employers are liable for sexually harassing conduct only in certain circumstances:

> The prevailing rule is that an employer is liable for the acts of its agents when they were acting within the scope of their authority; accordingly, where a supervisor uses his supervisory power to make a sexual demand on someone under his authority, the employer is liable. Where the conduct did not directly involve the abuse of authority, the employer may be liable for the acts of its employees (supervisory and nonsupervisory), and perhaps others as well, where the employer knew or should have known of the conduct and failed to take prompt and effective remedial action. (Burns, 1995, pp. 203–204)

Note that organizational policies per se are not mentioned, only the specific "conduct" or "acts" of individuals. Moreover, according to Burns, the current Supreme Court guidelines for assessing the harm caused by any instance of sexual harassment depends on what a "reasonable person would find hostile or abusive—and the victim must subjectively perceive the environment to be abusive otherwise the conduct has not actually altered the conditions of the victim's employment" (Burns, 1995, p. 201).

Jobs in which sexual exploitation is a required and routine feature of the work are not likely to fit this legal test for the "reasonable person" standard. As Folgero and Fjeldstad (1995, p. 311) point out, "in a cultural setting where sexual harassment is generally accepted as part of the job, feelings of harassment may be suppressed to a degree where the victim actively denies that the problem exists." Although their general point is valid, "victim" is an inaccurate word to use here, as those workers who deny that any problem exists probably do not feel victimized by sexual harassment. In fact, those who deny the existence of sexual harassment may "victimize" those who do define their experiences as sexual harassment: in the service jobs they studied, Folgero and Fjeldstad found that those who did actively complain of sexual harassment were admonished by their co-workers to either "take it—or leave it." Thus, many workers believe that any "reasonable" person would tolerate the sexual demands of the job. In these contexts, only exceptional acts perpetrated by individuals acting outside of their job requirements are defined as sexual harassment; organizational sexual harassment encoded in job descriptions is not even acknowledged.

Men Harass Women

A third problem with sexual harassment research is that the vast majority of studies focus exclusively on the experiences of women workers (Tinsley and Stockdale, 1993; Vaux, 1993). Although sexual harassment clearly disadvantages more women than men (Gutek, 1985), this approach treats men and women as monolithic categories, ignoring the alternative and competing interests that separate and divide different groups of men and women on the issue of sexual harassment.

The nearly exclusive focus on the sexual harassment of women by men is in part a legacy of how sexual harassment law developed. In 1979, Catharine MacKinnon successfully argued that sexual harassment should be considered a form of employment sex discrimination, which had been outlawed in 1964 as part of the Civil Rights Act. In arguing this, she was able to establish its illegality without waging a contentious and lengthy battle to introduce new legislation (Gutek, 1993b). Although there is no question that sexual harassment is a major factor contributing to gender discrimination in employment, this focus on gender highlights antagonisms between men and women and elides other sexualized power dynamics in the workplace. (For a legal analysis of this issue, see Grose, 1995.)

For example, researchers rarely discuss the harassment of gays and lesbians in the workplace as forms of sexual harassment (an exception is Kitzinger, 1994). Gays and lesbians face enormous pressure to conceal their sexual identity at work: Many employers outright refuse to hire them and fire those whose sexual orientation becomes known to them. Even successful concealment of sexual orientation does not protect gays and lesbians from significant unequal treatment: typically they are not eligible for the benefits that heterosexual married people receive for their family members (Rubinstein, 1993, p. 243).

In *The Corporate Closet*, Woods and Lucas (1993) explore the subtle and not-so-subtle forms of discrimination and harassment faced by gay professional men. The men in their study often confronted homophobic attitudes among their bosses and co-workers, mostly in the form of off-color jokes and disparaging remarks about gay men. One Wall Street broker described a "locker room mentality on the trading floor" that included "tons of antigay jokes and AIDS jokes"; an emergency room surgeon said that some of his colleagues refused to operate on patients who appeared to be gay because they assumed that all gays were HIV-positive (Woods and Lucas, 1993, pp. 16–17). Kitzinger (1994) argues that lesbians attempting to pass as heterosexual may feel especially vulnerable to sexual harassment because many fear that any resistance to unwanted (hetero)sexual attention would be interpreted as evidence of their true sexual orientation (see also Hall, 1989; Schneider, 1993).

Some exclusionary practices are more unintended in their consequences: for example, heterosexual co-workers typically wear wedding rings, display photos of their family members, and bring their spouses or dates to company functions. Engagements and weddings are frequent lunch-time topics that spill over into discussion during work hours; in some organizations, engagement parties and baby showers may even be held during work breaks. Many of the men in the Woods and Lucas study were constantly quizzed about their marital status; they described fending off well-meaning colleagues who constantly tried to arrange dates for them. Gay men and lesbians may feel excluded from such socially affirming heterosexual mating rituals. For some, the pressures to "fit in" are so great that they fabricate a counterfeit identity—either inventing heterosexual partners or convincing their co-workers that they are celibate. While these experiences are not overt instances of sexual harassment, they can constitute a hostile working environment for people forced to conceal their sexual identity and can contribute to stress disorders (Gonsiorek, 1993).

Some professional gay men who are closeted at work are of the opinion that their public and private lives should be kept separate because their sexuality has nothing to do with their work. They thereby promote what Woods and Lucas call the "asexual imperative":

> Like their straight peers, [gay men] often believe that sexuality has no place at work; unlike them, however, they use the imperative to protect themselves, to rationalize their own [in]visibility. Recognizing the penalties they might pay for being openly gay at work —fearing they cannot be candid about their sexuality—they embrace the idea that they should not be, that it would be unprofessional, rude, disruptive, or tacky. (Woods and Lucas, 1993, p. 36)

However, insisting that sexuality is irrelevant to work does not make it so. Instead, those who do not disclose any information about their sexual orientation are typically assumed to be heterosexual. The "don't ask, don't tell" policy barring openly gay and lesbian individuals from serving in the military finesses the heterosexual privileges underlying the "asexual imperative" (Britton and Williams, 1995). While it is entirely legal for soldiers to admit their heterosexual proclivities by displaying photos of their husbands or wives, leaving their survivor benefits to them, or living with them in subsidized housing, gay men and lesbians are prohibited from doing the same. Only gays and lesbians are required to meet the "asexual imperative"; heterosexuality remains unchallenged as the institutionalized norm.

The heterosexual norm also lies behind the prevailing assumption in both research and policy that single-sex work groups are immune from the problem of sexual harassment (Grose, 1995). Few studies consider the possibility of gay-gay and lesbian-lesbian sexual harassment. Moreover, the exclusive focus on male-female sexual harassment deflects attention from the ways in which heterosexual men are sexually harassed by other men. One study of restaurant workers found that some heterosexual men felt threatened by the sexual bantering of gay men—even though similar behaviors from heterosexual men or women did not upset them (Giuffre and Williams, 1994). Some have argued that the military ban on gays and lesbians is based on heterosexual men's fears of suffering sexual harassment from gay men (Britton and Williams, 1995; Enloe, 1994). As these examples suggest, some heterosexual men may deploy double standards in their definition of sexual harassment. Understanding these double standards is crucial for obtaining a more complete picture of sexual power dynamics in the workplace: since heterosexual men occupy most positions of power in work organizations they are, therefore, in positions to set organizational policies that affect all workers.

Perhaps more common than the sexual harassment of heterosexual men by gay men, however, is the sexual harassment of heterosexual men by other heterosexual men. The language of power and hierarchy is infused with sexual metaphors (Acker, 1990). In corporate high finance, for example, successful businessmen are sometimes referred to as "big swinging dicks" (Lewis, 1989). Men often malign each other's sexual potency to establish their dominance or to mark the boundaries of the "in group" (Collinson, 1988; Roy, 1960). Often male sexual joking takes the form of ritual humiliation, as in the coal mine studied by Vaught and Smith (1980). Lewis (1989) describes the horrific treatment of newcomers among the stock and bond traders at Salomon Brothers. In this example, the head of mortgage trading, Lewie Ranieri, initiates Andy, a new member of his department:

> [Ranieri] had this big smile on his face. He was standing real close to Andy and asking him how a deal was going. Andy was saying how he hoped to sell some bonds in Japan and London, and Lewie just stood there nodding with this weird smile. Andy said something else, and all Lewie did was stand there and smile. Then Andy felt the joke. Lewie was holding a Bic lighter right under Andy's balls. His pants were about to catch fire. Andy hit the roof. (Lewis, 1989, p. 122)

Although surviving this sexual harassment and learning to participate in it coveys insider status to neophyte men, it is often experienced as degrading, embarrassing, and hurtful (Collinson, 1988).

This sexualized language and behavior is also racialized. In predominately white organizations, black men cannot participate in the sexual banter and one-up-manship of the organization without appearing to be a viable threat to the power relations of the organization. Consequently, black corporate executives may have to play down their sexuality and any intimation about their sexual prowess, since it is threatening to white supremacy (Thomas, 1989).

The sole focus on male-female sexual harassment thus ignores a great deal of sexually degrading and hostile behaviors that can occur in the workplace. Jane Gallop (1995) decries this research and policy focus as heterosexist, because it conflates sexual behavior with heterosexual behavior and because it assumes that all male-female interactions (and only male-female interactions) are potentially sexual. Gallop offers the following advice to researchers:

> We must resist the heterosexist understanding of sexual harassment, not merely for the liberal reason that it unwittingly contributes to the invisibility of people and practices that are not heterosexual. Rather [because we] are unintentionally reinforcing the mindset that produces sexual harassment. What causes someone to assume his relation to the opposite sex is sexual is in fact not merely sexism but heterosexism. (Gallop, 1995, pp. 10–11)

Recognizing that not all sexuality is heterosexual makes identifying sexual harassment extremely complex. But women are not the only targets of sexual exploitation and degradation, nor are all women innocent of sexually harassing others. Interlocking matrices of power in work organizations provide the occasion for sexual exploitation of a number of groups—including gays, lesbians, racial/ethnic minority group members, and relatively powerless heterosexual men. Research should reflect this complexity, not obscure it by focusing exclusively on male-female sexual harassment (see also Vaux, 1993).

In sum, current social science understanding of the extent and nature of sexual harassment in the workplace is limited due to researchers' failure to examine organizational context. Research that identifies only discrete acts perpetrated by individual men against individual women ignores and obscures a great deal of unwanted, degrading, and hostile uses of sexuality in the workplace. Researchers should expand their focus to include both individual and organizational forms of sexual harassment.

Conclusion

Sexual harassment researchers often endorse specific policies and procedures to deal with the problem of sexual harassment. Typically, these recommendations encourage victims of sexual harassment to report their experiences to their supervisors or to other powerful members of their organizations (Gutek, 1997). For example, in the working-class jobs studied by Gherardi, the women tried to defend themselves from the men who sexually harassed them "by seeking the protection of a paternal/marital figure, for instance a supervisor, a shop steward, an older man or a foreman" (Gherardi, 1995, p. 55). But she notes that this strategy unwittingly bolstered the worldview of the harassers, who viewed men as the natural predators—and protectors—of female sexuality.

Of course, appealing to company officials for redress is useless when organizations themselves foster and promote the sexual exploitation and degradation of employees. An individual complaining about the company dress code, customer abuse, or co-worker discrimination on the basis of sexual orientation might be dismissed—which is what happened to me in 1979. Moreover, simply instituting a process for handling complaints through a chain of command does not guarantee that individuals are able to use it. But, once legal and paralegal redress is available, it becomes the individual's failure— and not the institution's—if they do not use it (Brant and Too, 1994).

Relying on individuals to identify sexual harassment and complain about it is a very problematic strategy for a second reason. As I have argued, there may be both structural and social-psychological reasons preventing victims of harassment from identifying it as such. Systematic, organizational forms of harassment may be difficult to define as harassment precisely because they are normalized throughout the workplace. If sexual harassment is embedded in the job, individuals are not likely to label such practices sexual harassment. Furthermore, many people may have an interest in denying that sexual harassment exists in their workplaces.

Why must researchers and policymakers rely on workers' definitions of the situation to prove that sexual harassment exists and provide remedies for it? To prove that gender discrimination in the workplace exists, sociologists do not generally survey women on whether they have personally experienced a selected list of sexist behaviors. Few researchers use hypothetical vignettes to describe sexist encounters and then ask respondents their opinions on whether these encounters constitute gender discrimination. Findings of systematic differences in the treatment of men and women are taken as adequate proof that organizations are "gendered" in ways that benefit men — regardless of men's or women's definitions of the situation (e.g., Acker, 1990; Reskin and Padavic, 1994). A similar approach should be taken in research on sexual harassment. Unless we problematize organizations' differential treatment of workers on the basis of sexuality, sexual harassment will continue to be the normative experience of women (and many men) in the workplace.

Another policy response to sexual harassment is the institution of sensitivity and awareness training programs (Fitzgerald and Shullman, 1993). There is no evidence that these programs are effective, but they are growing in popularity in part because they protect companies from sexual harassment lawsuits by demonstrating a commitment to addressing the problem (Gutek, 1997). However, if organizations themselves are implicated in sexual harassment, then training and rehabilitation programs for individual employees cannot provide an adequate solution to the problem.

Training and rehabilitation programs are also entirely ineffective in addressing client or customer sexual harassment of workers. Ethics departments at major corporations have devoted a great deal of attention to regulating relationships between employees and their clients who work in other organizations, in order to eliminate conflicts of interest in business dealings. In some organizations, for example, it is against company policy for suppliers, clients, or potential clients to give gifts to any employee. Yet few corporations have taken comparable steps to prohibit clients from sexually harassing employees. There are a growing number of exceptions, however; for instance, the sexual harassment policy of a large resort reads in part, "As an employee of the resort, you can assist us by reporting to the management any harassment by either an employee or guest" (Deadrick, Kezman, and McAfee, 1996, p. 111). Unions of flight attendants and other service workers have also achieved some success in instituting policies to protect workers from abusive server-customer relationships (Cobble, 1996).

Some researchers have suggested that the only solution to the problem of sexual harassment in the workplace is to ban sexual expression altogether. Lobel (1993) reviews several key perspectives in organization research which fully proscribe sexuality from the workplace. Included in these perspectives are the voices of some feminist researchers who view (hetero) sexuality as necessarily male-dominated and oppressive to women and thus seek to banish it from the workplace (see also Pringle, 1989).

It is probably impossible to eliminate sexuality entirely from the workplace. Many workers actually enjoy the sexual dimension of their jobs, including flirtatious interactions with their co-workers (Cockburn, 1991, Pringle, 1989). As previously discussed, efforts to eliminate sexuality may ultimately and unintentionally reaffirm heterosexuality because it is the normative standard in most organizations.

Eliminating sexuality is a questionable goal at any rate since the problem with sexual harassment is not that it is *sexual*; the problem is that sexual harassment is a form of workplace discrimination (Gallop, 1995). But developing a set of guidelines to eliminate sexual harassment is a daunting task. We need a sexual harassment policy that recognizes the full scope of the problem: sexual harassment is not only perpetrated by individuals, but it is also institutionalized in organizations and in workplace culture. Co-workers are not the only source of sexual harassment; clients and customers can and often do sexually harass employees. Heterosexual women are not the only victims of sexual harassment; lesbians and men also confront unwanted sexual demands and hostility. And organizational sexual harassment is often racialized. Because sexual harassment is an organizational behavior—and not only an individual problem—a great deal of work on the part of organizations will be needed to eliminate it.

NOTE

This article was presented at the 1997 meetings of the American Sociological Association in Toronto, Canada, I would like to thank the following people for their helpful suggestions and criticisms: Dana Britton, Martin Button, Barry Dank, Minette Drumwright, Patti Giuffre, Ricardo Gonzalez, Hallie Kintner, Chandra Muller, Roberto Refinetti, Gretchen Ritter, Debra Umberson, and anonymous reviewers. This article is based on research undertaken at the Center for Advanced Study in the Behavioral Sciences, where I was supported by NSF Grant #SES-9022192.

Chapter Nine

The Confluence of Race and Gender in Women's Sexual Harassment Experiences

Tara E. Kent

Models of workplace sexual harassment vary by field, and conceptualizations can be found in the feminist, legal, psychological, and sociological literatures. Although current theories of harassment vary widely, sexual harassment is most generally understood to constitute unwanted and unwelcome sexual and sexist attention, advances, and requests for sexual favors experienced by people at work.[1] The term *sexual harassment* is commonly (and legally) applied to conduct that creates an intimidating, hostile, or offensive work environment or has the effect of interfering with an individual's work performance.

This chapter will review several of the dominant conceptualizations of harassment, including legal definitions and judicial applications, and feminist theoretical approaches to gender violence and sexual harassment. Although feminist scholars have provided a wealth of literature and theoretical understandings of sexual harassment, I argue that the current conceptualizations remain limited for several reasons. A central complication in current understandings of sexual harassment (and in many conceptualizations of gender violence) is grounded in a limited understanding of gender. That is, dominant discourses on sexual harassment still rely on a type of "gender essentialism" to describe and explain harassment.

A second, and related, limitation in the current understandings of harassment stems from the fact that few perspectives of harassment are derived from women's lived experiences. Both limitations extend into legal definitions and the application of law on harassment as well. In this chapter, I offer a way of making sense of why such limitations persist in the literature and suggest we work toward the development of a more holistic account of workplace harassment.

Catharine MacKinnon's (1979) work on sexual harassment was one of the earliest comprehensive studies of workplace harassment, and her theoretical approach is still widely used today to understand the power differentials between women and men in the sphere of work. She conceptualizes harassment as the unwanted imposition of sexual requirements in the context of relationships of unequal power. In this view, sexual harassment is a pattern of interpersonal behavior that functions to reinforce and perpetuate the subordination of women. According to MacKinnon, sexual harassment is a manifestation of the differences in power between the sexes and is a form of discrimination through which inequality at the institutional level is maintained. MacKinnon's view of workplace harassment is premised on the idea that a gender dichotomy guides all social relations and that women experience systematic and organized domination by men. MacKinnon's perspective is widely shared by scholars of gender violence, and the canon of literature on the subject reflects this basic thesis.

As described by MacKinnon and several other theorists, institutionalization of the subordination of women (which leads to sexual harassment and other forms of gender violence) occurs as a result of masculinist ideology and sexist stereotyping in our culture. These perspectives contend that dominant ideological notions of masculinity and femininity create normative constraints on our social roles. Numerous scholars argue that ideological beliefs surrounding the notion that men should dominate women are methodically disseminated in popular culture, the academy, and in legal and health institutions (Bart 1989; Kelly 1988; MacKinnon 1979; Rich 1993; Sheffield 1984), and such beliefs become internalized through gender-role socialization. For instance, Adrienne Rich (1993) argues that everyday gender/sexual socialization nurtures power, dominance, and control in boys, while girls are taught to be passive and meek. Borrowing MacKinnon's phraseology, Rich contends that this daily "eroticizing of women's subordination" (235) is rooted within a heterosexual paradigm and offers some explanation of the wide-scale incidents of rape, sexual harassment, and domestic violence in the United States. Rich asserts that such forms of sexual terrorism remain pervasive due to acceptance of the social arrangements between women and men as normal, natural, and inevitable. Embedded in her notion of compulsory heterosexuality is the ideology of heterosexual romance. This ideology, as taught through movies and fairy tales, indoctrinates many young girls into believing in the primacy and uncontrollability of the male sexual drive.

Liz Kelly (1988) utilizes a similar framework to explain sexual victimization of women. She conceptualizes a continuum of heterosexual behaviors that involve the daily objectification of women on one end and overt forms of sexual violence against women on the other end. This continuum connects typical male-dominant heterosexual sexual encounters to abhorrent male behavior. MacKinnon's view of sexual harassment applies this same perspective on sex roles, and she argues that each element of the female gender stereotype, created by masculinist discourse, renders women sexual victims. MacKinnon identifies female stereotypic traits and acknowledges the sexually submissive implication each trait holds:

> Vulnerability means the appearance/reality of easy sexual access; passivity means receptivity and disables resistance, enforced by trained physical weakness; softness means pregnability by something hard. Incompetence seeks help as vulnerability seeks shelter, inviting the embrace that becomes the invasion, trading exclusive access for protection . . . from the same access. . . . Women's infantilization evokes pedophilia; fixation on dismembered body parts evokes fetishism; idolization of vapidity, necrophilia. (1982: 530)

Accordingly, women are sexualized and objectified according to male desire. MacKinnon argues that female identity is defined according to women's sexual attractiveness to men, a power that men hold and possess over women.

These perspectives emphasize a link between ideology and socialization that operates to sustain a system in which women are routinely victimized, and they show how such victimization may become normalized. More specific models for explaining harassment developed out of the sex-role dichotomy hypothesis, such as the sex-role spillover model (Gutek 1985). This model posits that sexual harassment is a result of sex roles being asserted over work roles. In this way, the sexual expectations of women and men are extended into the workplace, and women become sexually victimized by men within the sphere of work. Extending from this perspective, incidents of "contrapower harassment" (Rospenda, Richman, and Nawyn 1998) provide insight into ways that sociocultural power operates to sustain patriarchal culture in the workplace. In contrapower harassment encounters, both interpersonal and individually based modes of power enable individuals to harass people who hold higher organizational power positions. For instance, Grauerholz (1989) found that women faculty are frequently harassed by male students. The growing body of research on contrapower harassment reveals that power can be fluid and specific to the interpersonal relationship between the parties; hence, sexual harassment encounters may entail nuances not previously accounted for by the earlier approaches to sexual harassment.

Perspectives that rely on the sex-role dichotomy to explain sexual harassment, and gender violence in general, share an assumption that *all women* are in a unified position, situated subordinately to men. For instance, according to MacKinnon, all women, regardless of race, class, age, sexual identity, ethnicity, or nationality, share the common experience of domination by men and thus have more in common with one another than they do with any man. These theories offer a great deal of explanatory power in terms of a hegemonic hold over beliefs about women's and men's sexual roles. Only limited notions of women and men are extended through our institutions, and this perspective of "reality" becomes dominant, ever present and widely learned. However, these models do not necessarily consider the confluence of gender, race, and class in sexual harassment encounters. Although much of this work offers strong understanding of sexual harassment, these perspectives are limited because such analyses give primacy to gender while obscuring other components of social location.

These conceptualizations of sexual harassment may be critiqued for following a type of gender essentialism. Gender essentialism is the notion that a unitary, essential woman's experience can be isolated and described independently of race, class, sexual orientation, and other realities of experience (Harris 1991). This is the notion that a universal or true essence of gender purportedly exists beneath the veneer of race and class distinctions. Gender essentialism pervaded the earliest theoretical movements in feminist thinking and continues to guide some perspectives on gender violence. Women of color, lesbian feminists, and postmodern theorists advanced critiques of the hegemony of such false gender universals and critiqued feminist thought for sustaining an inherent Eurocentrism that defined womanhood according to white middle-class standards. Such conceptions are limited in providing a framework for understanding sexual harassment (and gender violence in general), and the notion that all women share a unified position as victims to men ignores the complexities of power and obscures the relativity of gendered power relations as they operate in conjunction with race and social class.

Theoretical approaches that rely on sex-role dichotomies to understand power differentials are limited by the gender essentialism that pervades our perception of female sexuality. The problem of gender essentialism applies to the current understanding of sexual harassment. Dominant theories emphasize differences between women and men and thereby subordinate differences among women. As outlined above, these perspectives place the perceptions of, and behaviors of, all women in the same category, regardless of race or class or sexual identity. Female stereotypes posed by these theorists, including vulnerability, passivity, and softness, are most directly applied to white women of privilege. Therefore, such analyses of sexual harassment and the sexualizing of women are exclusive to middle-class, white, heterosexual women, and these perspectives ignore the differences in the way men perceive different groups of women.

A body of work in feminist theory has recently proliferated that attempts to grapple with and explain the means by which race and class mediate gender experiences and how these constructs work in concert. As Sandra Harding asserts, "there are no gender relations *per se*, but only gender relations as constructed by and between classes, races and cultures" (1991: 179). This approach, which is sometimes referred to as "multiracial feminism" (Zinn and Dill 1996) contends that a range of interlocking inequalities constructs gender. As conceptualized by Collins (1991), one may conceive of the social relations of domination by placing the "axes" of race, class, and gender into a matrix, emphasizing the way the different axes operate in conjunction with one another. Casting aside mathematical metaphors for an ethnomethodological approach, West and Fenstermaker (1995) similarly construct a notion of gender that considers gender, race, and class as an ongoing "interactional accomplishment" of daily lived activity that reveals how power is exercised and inequality reproduced. These frameworks (Collins 1991; West and Fenstermaker 1995; Zinn and Dill 1996) imply that all women's experiences are mediated by race, class, and gender significations, a perspective guided by the idea that race, class, and gender operate simultaneously to shape women's experiences and identities.

The multiracial feminist approach provides context for making sense of the variations in stereotypical belief systems about different groups of women. Belief systems about women's sexuality are specifically conceived of according to social/historical circumstances of different race and class groups. Specifically, belief systems about the frailty and passivity of women, called the "cult of true womanhood," proliferated during the era of American industrial development, whereby white families of means employed servants to do the domestic labor. Hence, the development of the "frail woman" or "lady of the house" ideology was reliant and dependent on less-privileged women carrying the burden of domestic labor. In the same way that class-privileged white women have been stereotyped as passive and vulnerable, the dominant ideology of the slave era fostered the creation of interrelated, socially constructed controlling images of Black womanhood (Collins 1991; hooks 1984). Therefore, the dominant group perceives Black women's sexuality very differently from white women's sexuality. Specifically, Black women are stereotyped as matriarchs (aggressive and assertive), mammies (obedient and asexual), welfare mothers (lazy with many children), and Jezebels (many sexual partners and encounters) (Collins 1991; hooks 1984). Additional examples of belief systems about women of color are offered by Defour (1990): Hispanic women have been described as hot-blooded, ill-tempered, religious, overweight, lazy, always pregnant, loudmouthed, and deferent to men. Native American women are perceived as poor, sad, uneducated, isolated, and devoted to male elders. Asian women have been described as small, docile, and submissive; however, they are also viewed by some as the exotic sexpot who will cater to the whims of every man (Defour 1990: 49).

Popular images and perceptions of women of color may dictate the way that they are perceived and sexualized in contrast to white women. Ideological notions surrounding perceptions of women of color may indicate that the nature of sexual harassment is likely to be very different when experienced by women of color, and Defour (1990) argues that such images may in fact make these women *more* vulnerable to sexual harassment than white women.

Empirical research challenges the assertion that all women share common experiences with sexual harassment. Differences among diverse groups of women include frequency of harassment (Gruber and Bjorn 1982, 1986; Kalof et al. 2001; Schneider 1982; Segura 1992), type of harassment (Berrill 1990; Mecca and Rubin 1999), and severity of harassment (Gruber and Bjorn 1982, 1986). These studies suggest that differences in harassing experiences may be due to social characteristics including race (Defour 1990; Gruber and Bjorn 1986; hooks 1984; Kalof et al. 2001; Karsten 1994; Murrell 1996; Scarville et al. 1999), age (Martin 1980; McIlwee 1980; Riemer and Bridwell, 1982), marital status (Benson and Thomson 1982), sexual identity (Schneider 1982), and social class (Murell 1996). This growing body of literature that explores diversities in harassment experiences points to a need to revise the widely used view of sexual harassment, and to consider the multiracial feminist approach.

Empirical research conducted on the topic of sexual harassment of women of color supports the thesis that women of color experience harassment differently than white women do. Gruber and Bjorn (1982, 1986) found, in two studies, that not only are black women more likely to be sexually harassed than whites, but Black women are also harassed *more severely* than white women. Research on Chicanas found similar results: women of Mexican descent reported higher rates of sexual harassment than white women did (Segura 1992). Furthermore, several theorists argue that women of color are more likely to be victims of sexual harassment for numerous reasons (Defour 1990; Karsten 1994; Mecca and Rubin 1999; Murrell 1996). Specifically, women of color may be more vulnerable to sexual harassment due to economic factors and popular images and stereotypes of women of color.

Such sexual stereotyping, based on race, may result in harassing behaviors targeted at women of color that include elements of *both* sexual and racial stereotypes. For instance, situations of sexual imposition may also contain racist overtones (Mecca and Rubin 1999). One such incident is described by Defour (1990: 47): "A full professor sexually assaults his undergraduate research assistant. The professor does not view this attack as rape because he believes that Hispanic women always desire sex." A university professor describes a similar incident, stating that she commonly hears jokes by her male students that contain elements of racism and sexism. She gives the example, "a man isn't a man until he has had sex with a [B]lack or Hispanic woman" (Demby 1990: 189). Buchanan and Ormerod (2002) refer to this type of harassment as racialized sexual harassment, as they found in their study that African American women could not easily separate issues of race and gender in their accounts of victimization in the workplace. Similarly, Janice Yoder and Patricia Aniakudo (1997) conclude from their work on discriminatory practices against African American women in a profession dominated by men that "gender cannot be enacted separately from race and class" (325), as "race and gender are omnirelevant, inseparable, and intertwined" (337).

To explore the experiences of women of color with sexual harassment, I reviewed public records of court cases obtained through Lexis Nexis. Several of these cases involved race-specific sexual innuendo, with specific mention of the perceived sexualized attributes of women *based on their racial/ethnic identity*. This indicates that women of color view their sexual harassment experiences as tied to their race. For instance, in the case of *Nikki Chatman v. Gentle Dental Center of Waltham* (1997), Chatman alleged that her supervisors subjected her to "sexual harassment and discrimination based on sex and race" (230). Chatman specified in her deposition that one supervisor allegedly spoke of the unique sexual traits and physical features of Black women (and men), including what he described as fullness of lips and buttocks and enlarged genitalia (230). In *Elba Colon Hernandez v. Patrick Wangen* (1996), Hernandez alleged to be subject to ongoing, unwanted sexual imposition, touching, and sexual and racial innuendo. In her deposition she described a pattern of banter that focused on the supposed unique physical and sexual characteristics of Puerto Rican women. Further evidence of race and gender conflation is apparent in the case of *Judy Carroll v. Village of Shelton, Nebraska* (1996). Carroll, a Native American, was allegedly subject to a combination of racial slurs and unwanted sexual advances (901). Her supervisor allegedly made comments that connected her physical attributes to her ethnicity, and she reported that she was often called names such as "Pocahontas." In *Nancy Wanchik v. Great Lakes Health Plan, Inc.* (2001), Wanchik argued that her working environment was "infected not only by sexism but by routine racial and ethnic aspersions" (33). The record indicates that "Wanchik alleges that she heard [several supervisors] tell numerous dirty jokes degrading towards women and minorities. She recalled a few illustrations of their offensive content: specifically that men in supervisory positions told ethnic jokes that mocked and impersonated minorities and . . . several supervisors joked about what [they] 'liked to do with Asian women,' and another manager described his group sexual fantasies" (25). These examples provide further evidence that the nature of sexual harassment varies greatly among diverse groups of women and that sexual stereotypes vary by race and ethnicity.

The specific sexual beliefs about women of color may further render them at greater risk for sexual harassment. For example, if women are perceived as sexually aggressive or "hot-blooded" or always desirous of sex, women of color face serious struggles to be taken seriously in the professional realm. Ideological perceptions of women of color may further exacerbate their victimization; Murrell (1996) found that individuals may be less likely to perceive women of color as victims of harassment, and Foley (1995) found that participants viewed a forced sexual encounter as less serious when the victim was a Black woman than when she was a white woman. This growing body of research indicates not only that the experiences of women of color are qualitatively different from those of white women but that women of color may experience more frequent and more severe forms of sex/race harassment. Ideology may also contribute to differences in the extent to which women of color possess adequate recourse against sexual harassment, and legal scholars contend that many of these complications extend into the legal application of sexual harassment policy.

Gender Essentialism and Legal Policy

Several legal theorists argue that similar problems of gender essentialism, as outlined in the above conceptualizations of sexual harassment, extend into legal definitions and applications of sexual harassment policy. Specifically, women's experiences with workplace harassment vary widely and involve many factors not included in legal policy (Crenshaw 1991a; Fitzgerald, Shullman, et al. 1988; Winston 1991). Feminist legal theorists consider antidiscrimination law (from which sexual harassment law is derived) limited because of the inadequacy of these policies to address effectively the diversity of women's experiences. Legal scholars use a similar critique of gender essentialism to ground these arguments, and these scholars contend that conceptions of antidiscrimination law rely on notions of a unified woman's experience, based on the concerns of white women. According to Collins (1991: 224), African American women continue to be inadequately protected by Title VII of the Civil Rights Act of 1964 (Scarborough 1989, as cited by Collins). The primary purpose of the statute is to eradicate all aspects of discrimination. But judicial treatment of Black women's employment-discrimination claims has encouraged Black women to identify race *or* sex as the so-called primary discrimination.

Kimberlé Crenshaw (1991a) elaborates on this point in her analysis of antidiscrimination policy. She argues that such policies utilize a single-axis analysis of discrimination that does not include the multidimensionality of the experiences of women of color. Crenshaw states that subordination and disadvantage are not experienced as either racist or sexist but that women of color experience a distinct form of discrimination, which includes overt elements of both sexism and racism. She argues that the unidimensional understanding distorts race and sex legal analysis because the operative conceptions of race and sex become grounded in experiences that actually represent only a subset of a much more complex phenomenon. The entire legal framework that has translated the "racial minority experience" and the "woman's experience" into concrete policy, she argues, must be rethought to include the multidimensionality of the experiences of women of color.

In order to reveal the inability of unidimensional frameworks to address the concerns of women of color, Crenshaw utilizes court rulings that apply such policies. For instance, Crenshaw (1991a: 58–59) reviews the case of *DeGraffenreid v. General Motors* and describes how the plaintiffs charged that they had been illegally discriminated against because they are Black women. The courts concluded that "Black women" are not a special class protected under discrimination laws and that plaintiffs cannot "combine statutory remedies." Instead, the court ruled that under discrimination law, plaintiffs may "state a cause of action for race discrimination, sex discrimination, or alternatively either, but not a combination of both" (as cited in Crenshaw 1991a: 59). Crenshaw further argues that such an essential notion of womanhood prevents women of color from full protection of the law, because their experiences are so far removed from those of white women (60). Crenshaw concludes that this reveals the inability of the law, as interpreted by the court, to embrace intersectionality, as well as the centrality of white female experiences in the conceptualization of gender discrimination.

Judith Winston (1991) extends the concerns about the unidimensionality of antidiscrimination law by assessing recovery of compensatory and punitive damages to women of color who are victims of intentional acts of employment discrimination. Winston argues that current policies do not adequately address the issue of discrimination at the intersection of race and gender and therefore deny women of color full compensation of punitive damages.

Similar to the concerns raised about legal theory and antidiscrimination law, sexual harassment policy does not allow for the specificity of harassment among women who occupy multiple oppressions. Because sexual harassment was declared a form of gender discrimination under Title VII of the Civil Rights Act of 1964, the application of the law follows from the same dilemma of exclusion as antidiscrimination law. Should a woman of color experience racialized, sexist harassment, she must choose between the two. These policies hence assume that all women experience harassment and discrimination the same way. In this way, under harassment and discrimination law, "woman" becomes one essentialized category, a category that does not necessarily reflect the experience of any woman. Therefore, policy that attempts to address the experiences of women needs to incorporate the multiplicity and diversities of women.

Future Directions

Documentation of wide-scale sexual harassment has necessitated that sociologists and feminist scholars develop varied approaches to understanding why women are at risk in their working environments. The sense-making offered by numerous scholars tends to include accounts of ideological beliefs in male sexual aggression and sexual objectification of women, normative gender-role socialization, and the structure of the gendered labor force. When taken together, these positions offer some understanding of sexual harassment of women; however, none offers a full account of the complexities of power and harassment that take place at the intersection of race, class, and gender. As several scholars argue, sexual harassment is believed to be a ubiquitous phenomenon that cuts across age, race, marital status, class, and occupational distinctions. But this framework for understanding sexual harassment does not include implicit or explicit definitions of the unique harassing experiences of women of color, despite empirical research that supports the supposition that harassment experiences are widely diverse.

Differences among diverse groups of women include frequency of harassment, type of harassment, and severity of harassment. Studies suggest that differences in harassing experiences may be due to social characteristics including race, age, marital status, sexual identity, and social class. Current scholarly and legal understandings of sexual harassment remain limited due to the inability to account for such differences. Research that points to variation in sexual harassment encounters reveals the necessity of developing a new understanding of sexual harassment that encompasses such differences.

Current conceptualizations of sexual harassment could be further expanded to include the findings of such research.

Multiple factors, such as the racialized construction of women's sexuality and economic status, reveal the likelihood that women of color in the workplace experience harassing behaviors that include elements of *both* sexual and racial stereotypes. Murrell (1996: 57) notes that for women of color "sexual harassment should be defined as a form of both sex discrimination and race discrimination because they are historically and experientially tied to one another." Furthermore, empirical research indicates that women of color identify harassing behavior as intertwined with racial and sexual elements (Segura 1992).

Scholarly definitions of sexual harassment (and gender violence in general) do not account for qualitative differences among women of diverse ethnicities. The multifaceted nature of harassment, as outlined in this chapter, provides evidence of the limitations of current conceptualizations of harassment that exclude explicit mention of the diverse ways women are sexualized. Legal theorists argue that similar problems of gender essentialism extend into legal definitions and applications of sexual harassment policy and that currently social policy does not adequately address the compounding impact of multiple oppressions. I propose that definitions of sexual harassment are most effective in encompassing the complexities of harassing treatment when grounded in the direct experiences of women. Multiracial experiences must inform theories of sexual harassment to account for the way gender relations work in concert with race and class relations. For sexual harassment policy to adequately address the experience of women, policy must incorporate the multiplicity and diversities of women.

N O T E

1. Although both men and women experience sexual harassment in the work force, the scope of this chapter is limited to women's experiences with sexual harassment.

Chapter Ten

Sexual Harassment on the Internet

Azy Barak

Sexual harassment (SH) is a well-known social problem that affects people at work, school, military installations, and social gatherings (for a comprehensive review, see Paludi and Paludi, 2003; Sbraga and O'Donohue, 2000). A worldwide phenomenon (Barak, 1997), it has been thoroughly investigated in recent decades in terms of prevalence, correlates, individual and organizational outcomes, and prevention; the range of studies provides an interdisciplinary perspective covering psychological, sociological, medical, legal, and educational aspects of the phenomenon. SH potentially relates to any human being; however, in fact, most victims are women (Gruber, 1997; Paludi and Paludi, 2003); other target populations—men, homosexuals, and children—are sexually harassed, too, although to a lesser degree. Similarly, most victims of SH on the Internet are women, though other populations have been targeted as well (Barnes, 2001). The purpose of the current article is to review the limited existing professional literature that refers to SH in cyberspace, to propose a typology—equivalent to that offline—of types of SH on the Internet, to analyze the dynamics of online SH, to review what is known about the effects of SH on the Internet, and to propose a comprehensive approach for preventing SH on the Internet.

The Internet provides an environment in which healthy and pathological behaviors may be pursued (Suler, 1999). Indeed, the Internet is known to possess the two contradictory aspects, as it is exploited for good or for evil purposes (Barak and King, 2000). Joinson (2003), in a thoughtful review, explored how new technological tools have constructive, positive aspects for people's advancement and joy, as well as destructive, negative aspects that humiliate, terrorize, and block social progress. Similarly, specifically in the context of women using the Internet, Morahan-Martin (2000) noted the "promise and perils" facing female Net users. SH and offense on the Internet is considered a major obstacle to the free, legitimate, functional, and joyful use of the Net, as these acts drive away Net users as well as cause significant emotional harm and actual damage to those who remain users, whether by choice or by duty. The objective of this article is to act as a catalyst for needed research and absent theoretical analysis (cf. Adam, 2002) in this important area and to provide a framework for prevention so that, eventually, the positive face of the Internet will prevail.

Offline Sexual Harassment

SH is a prevalent phenomenon in face-to-face, social environments (Gutek and Done, 2001; Paludi and Paludi, 2003; Sbraga and O'Donohue, 2000). It is widespread at work (e.g., Petrocelli and Repa, 1998; Richman et al., 1999), schools of all levels (Matchen and DeSouza, 2000; McMaster, Connolly, Pepler, and Craig, 2002; Timmerman, 2003), and the military (Fitzgerald, Drasgow, and Magley, 1999; Fitzgerald, Magley, Drasgow, and Waldo, 1999). SH is not a local phenomenon but exists in all countries and cultures, although its perceptions and judgment, and consequently definitions, significantly differ from one culture to another (Barak, 1997). Originally, Till (1980) classified SH behaviors into five categories, which were used for intensive assessment and research attempts to describe the behaviors and understand their causes, correlates, impact on victims, personal coping with occurrences, and more. Later, following a series of studies, suggestion was made to change the classification of types of SH into three distinct categories: gender harassment, unwanted sexual attention, and sexual coercion (Fitzgerald, Gelfand, and Drasgow, 1995).

Gender harassment involves unwelcome verbal and visual comments and remarks that insult individuals because of their gender or that use stimuli known or intended to provoke negative emotions. These include behaviors such as posting pornographic pictures in public or in places where they deliberately insult, telling chauvinistic jokes, and making gender-related degrading remarks. *Unwanted sexual attention* refers to uninvited behaviors that explicitly communicate sexual desires or intensions toward another individual. This category includes overt behaviors and comments, such as staring at a woman's breasts or making verbal statements that explicitly or implicitly propose or insinuate sexual activities. *Sexual coercion* involves putting physical or psychological pressure on a person to elicit sexual cooperation. This category includes actual, undesired physical touching, offers of a bribe for sexual favors, or making threats to receive sexual cooperation. Empirical research has found the three types of sexually harassing behaviors to be distinctive from one another, to be reliably and validly measurable in terms of perceptions and ratings of actual behaviors, and to correlate with various relevant personal, situational, and social factors (cf. Fitzgerald Gelfand, and Drasgow 1995; Paludi and Paludi, 2003).

Sexual Harassment in Cyberspace

All three types of SH that exist offline also exist on the Internet. However, because of the virtual nature of cyberspace, most expressions of SH that prevail on the Net appear in the form of gender harassment and unwanted sexual attention. Nevertheless, as sexual coercion is the type that occurs the least often offline, too, it is impossible to conclude whether its relatively low prevalence in cyberspace is a result of the medium or its very nature. In terms of virtual imposition and assault, sexual coercion does exist nonetheless on the Net, though without, of course, the physical contact.

Gender harassment in cyberspace is very common. It is portrayed in several typical forms that Internet users encounter very often, whether communicated in verbal or in graphical formats and through either active or passive manners of online delivery. *Active verbal SH* mainly appears in the form of offensive sexual messages, actively initiated by a harasser toward a victim. These include gender-humiliating comments (e.g., "Leave the forum! Go to your natural place, the kitchen"), sexual remarks (e.g., "Nipples make this chat room more interesting"), so-called dirty jokes, and the like. All these are considered harassing and offending when they are neither invited or consented to nor welcomed by the recipient. This type of gender harassment is usually practiced in chat rooms and forums: however, it may also appear in private online communication channels, such as the commercial distribution through e-mail (a kind of spamming) of pornographic sites, sex-shop accessories, sex-related medical matters (such as drugs such as Viagra and operations similar to penis enlargement). Mitchell, Finkelhor, and Wolak (2003) reported that 62 percent of the adolescents in their survey received unwanted sex-related e-mails to their personal address, 92 percent from unknown senders. Of the 73 percent of respondents who unintentionally entered sex sites, most did so as a result of automatic linking, pop-up windows, and unintended results while using a search engine.

Passive verbal SH, on the other hand, is less intrusive, as it does not refer to one user communicating messages to another. In this category, the harasser does not target harassing messages directly to a particular person or persons but, rather, to potential receivers. For instance, this type of harassment refers to nicknames and terms attached to a user's online identification or to personal details that are clearly considered offensive (e.g., CockSucker, WetPussy, XLargeTool, or GreatFuck for nicknames; "want a fuck?" in Internet relay chat (IRC) user's details, for offensive message). This category also includes explicit sex messages attached to one's personal details in communication software (e.g., "The best clit licker in Germany" in a personal info section of an ICQ User Details) or on a personal Web page. Scott, Semmens, and Willoughby (2001) pointed out how flaming—a common, online, aggressive verbal behavior that typically and frequently appears in online communities—particularly creates a hostile environment for women. Although flaming is not necessarily aimed at women, it is considered, in many instances, to be a form of gender harassment because flaming is frequently, typically, and almost exclusively initiated by men. The common result of flaming in online communities is that women depart from that environment or depart the Internet in general—what has been termed *flamed out*. "Flamed out highlights the fact that the use of male violence to victimize women and children, to control women's behaviour, or to exclude women from public spaces entirely, can be extended into the new public spaces of the Internet" (ibid., p. 11). A constructive solution has been the design of women-only sanctuaries that offer communities where flaming is rare and obviously not identified with men.

Similar to verbal gender harassment, graphic-based harassment can be active and passive, too. *Active graphic gender harassment* mainly involves the intentional sending of erotic and pornographic still pictures or digital videos through individual online communication channels, such as e-mail, or posting them in an online environment. Pictures (and videos) might be judged as less or more offensive as a result of personal sensitivities, on one hand, and the explicitness and nature of their content, on the other. For instance, it could be expected that the picture of an innocent nude will be perceived as less offensive than the close-up picture of a vagina or the animation of a penis when ejaculating. *Passive graphic gender harassment* mainly includes pictures and movies published on web sites (Carnes, 2003; Gossett and Byrne, 2002). Contrary to materials published in designated pornography sites or online sex shops, where surfers usually deliberately choose to enter and know what materials to expect, SH comes into effect when Web users do not know in advance and have no prior clue concerning what might later prove offensive to them. The massive use of forced pop-up windows and redirected links to porno sites makes this type of gender harassment highly prevalent.

The degree to which each of the four possibilities of gender harassment actually becomes subjectively experienced personal harassment is dependent on two major factors, one objective and one subjective: (a) the nature of the verbal or graphic stimulus in terms of explicitness, blatancy, or clamorousness, in addition to its continuity and repetition and (b) the personal attitudes, sensitivities, and preferences of the recipient. The combination of these factors determines the degree of subjective experience of offense.

Unwanted sexual attention in cyberspace usually necessitates direct personal verbal communication between a harasser and a victim. This may appear in personal communication, with messages directly relating to sex and sexuality. In this category are messages that refer to or ask about a victim's sex organs ("how large are your boobs?"), sex life ("when did you fuck last time?"), or intimate subjects ("do you have your period now?"); invite, insinuate, or offer sex-related activities ("I'd like to show you my super tool"); or impose sex-related sounds or images on a message. In contrast to gender harassment, unwanted sexual attention is specifically intended to solicit sexual cooperation of some sort, either virtual or in face-to-face contact. Obviously, for sexual attention or invitation to become harassing, it must be uninvited and unwelcome on the part of the victim. Therefore, a person who deliberately enters a chat room that clearly exists for the sake of finding partners, all the more so sex partners, is implicitly consenting, even inviting, sexual suggestions; hence, a message of sexual attention cannot be regularly considered harassing in this context. Unwanted sexual attention on the Internet may take place in public forums or chat rooms as well as in private communications. It may be communicated through synchronous or asynchronous channels. It may be verbal or nonverbal (i.e., via images and/or sounds) in nature. It may be explicit and direct or implicit and indirect. It may be as aggressive as suggesting sexual acts or more moderate in offering a massage or in asking a sex-related intruding question. Perpetrators of these types of behavior look for sex contact; however, their basic motive might be to cause emotional harm and to abuse victims, not necessarily to gain sexual cooperation.

Sexual coercion on the Internet is essentially different from gender harassment and unwanted sexual attention. Online sexual coercion entails the use of various means, available or possible online, to elicit sexual cooperation by putting some kind of pressure on a victim. Although the use of physical force is impossible online, victims might perceive threats to use physical force realistic on the Internet as in face-to-face situations. Likewise, explicit threats of some kind of harm to an Internet user or to his or her relatives or friends or threats of damage to a users' property might be a source of great anxiety. Even following a person's virtual tracks—by trailing his or her visits in chat rooms and forums—might cause panic. Thus, online stalking (also termed *cyber-stalking*), if it involves sexual insinuations and hints, should be considered a form of psychological pressure to achieve sexual gains—that is, a form of sexual coercion (Adam, 2001; Deirmenjian, 1999; Griffiths, Rogers, and Sparrow, 1998; Spitzberg and Hoobler, 2002).

However, online sexual coercion might be manifested by activities that more closely parallel offline situations. Experienced perpetrators, for example, might use their technical knowledge to break into a victim's personal computer and cause damage or threaten to do so. Sending frightening e-mails, sending viruses, and flooding an e-mail inbox are just a few examples of actual—as opposed to virtual—online sexual coercion (e.g., Dibbell, 1998).

Online sexual coercion might also be expressed in the form of bribes and seductions to achieve sexual gains. The online environment not only is an easy and convenient way to convey these types of messages, and perhaps especially effective for those perpetrators who have high writing skills, but also readily allows impersonation and cheating of innocent people. Thus, the use of incentives—baits—to encourage sexual cooperation is rather common. In this regard, one should note the well-documented phenomenon of pedophiles who operate online and seduce young children through the effective use of luring correspondence and the offer of various attractive baits (Durkin, 1997; Durkin and Bryant, 1999; Fontana-Rosa, 2001; Fulda, 2002; Quayle, Holland, Linehan, and Taylor, 2000; Quayle and Taylor, 2002, 2003). Likewise, the illegal practice of child pornography—in exploiting nude pictures of innocent children—makes use of baits and pressures to achieve children's cooperation to satisfy the needs of Internet-based pedophiles (Jenkins, 2001).

Cases and Prevalence of SH on the Internet

Various authors refer to SH in cyberspace and describe it as prevalent and risky. Unfortunately, no empirical survey on the extent and prevalence of SH in cyberspace has been carried out to date; thus, writers refer to general impressions and sporadic reports. For instance, Cooper, McLoughlin, Reich, and Kent-Ferraro (2002) referred to SH by e-mail as a common abuse of women in workplaces. Leiblum and Döring (2002) argued that the Internet provides a convenient vehicle, commonly used, to force sexuality on women through nonsocial (logging into Web pages) and social (interpersonal communication) uses of the Net. McCormick and Leonard (1996) contended that because of the Net's so-called boys club atmosphere (apparently more relevant up to the mid-1990s than today), this environment is typically characterized by antiwomen attitudes and behaviors, including SH. Employing the same conception, Döring (2000) stated that men's created sexualized online atmosphere, mainly through pornographic materials, make unwanted sexual advances more likely. Adam (2001) argued that the phenomenon of SH on the Internet downplays the positive process of empowerment that women gain from egalitarian use of the Internet. McGarth and Casey (2002) saw cyberspace as an ideal environment for sex offenders to commit SH and imposition because of its unique characteristics (see below). Cooper, Golden, and Kent-Ferraro (2002) described the case of a man with a paraphilia-related disorder who obsessively used chat and e-mails to communicate his sexual thoughts to women. Cunneen and Stubbs (2000) reported a phenomenon in which Australian men solicited sex among Filipino women through the Internet in return for economic privileges. Barak and Fisher (2002) even predicted—in regard to the Internet's special characteristics—that the scope of sex offenses on the Internet would grow in the future. Several specific and restricted research studies provide some indication of the scope of SH behavior on the Internet. Griffiths (2000) reported the finding of a British survey that 41 percent of regular Internet female users had been sent unsolicited pornographic materials or been harassed or stalked on the Internet. Mitchell, Finkelhor, and Wolak, (2001), in a survey of American teenagers, found that 19 percent of these youths—mostly older girls—had experienced at least one sexual solicitation while online in the past year (3 percent had received so-called aggressive solicitations). Goodson, McCormick, and Evans (2001) found that 24 percent of the female and 8 percent of the male college students who accessed online sexually explicit materials had experienced SH.

The Dynamics of SH on the Internet

A leading model pertaining to the causes and dynamics of SH was conceptualized by Pryor and colleagues (Pryor, Giedd, and Williams, 1995; Pryor, La Vite, and Stoller, 1993; Pryor and Whalen, 1997); it argues that SH behavior is determined by the interaction of a person's and a situation's characteristics. Consistent evidence supports this general equation (e.g., O'Hare and O'Donohue, 1998). There is no reason to believe that this process is different in the online environment: quite the contrary, because of the special characteristics informing online communication and online behavior. Specifically, it may be argued that the online disinhibition effect (Joinson, 1998, 1999, 2001; Suler, 2004) that promotes exposure of the so-called true self (McKenna and Seidman, 2005), on one hand, and the special features of computer-mediated communication, on the other, produce human behaviors that more closely reflect authentic inner personal needs and desires. In reference to the personal factor in the equation, it has been well established that SH is not about sex but about power (Barak, Pitterman, and Yitzhaki, 1995: Bargh, Raymond, Pryor, and Strack, 1995; Hoffspiegel, 2002; Wayne, 2000; Zurbriggen, 2000); that is, contrary to what seems to be an obvious reason for imposed sexual or sexually related activities—satisfaction of a perpetrator's sex drive—it has repeatedly been argued, and empirically supported, that sex is only a means of satisfying the perpetrator's need for power and domination. In cyberspace, the online disinhibition effect causes Internet users to behave less defensively and more naturally; that is, powerful factors that exist in and are typical of cyberspace, such as anonymity, invisibility, lack of eye contact, easy escape, and neutralizing of status, influence people to remove facade and masks when online to employ much fewer games and tricks and to reduce the use of existing social (or specific environmental) norms and behavioral standards in determining their behavior. Rather, when affected by the online disinhibition effect, users behave more consistently with their basic personality characteristics. At the same time, Internet communication in general is heavily affected by what has been termed "the Penta-A Engine" (Barak and Fisher, 2002), composed of anonymity, availability, affordability, acceptability, and aloneness. This engine is powerful enough to influence surfers' behaviors in a way that they become more daring, open, and ready to take risks in getting involved with sex-related activities than would otherwise be the case, or certainly to a much lesser extent, in the offline environment (Cooper, McLoughlin, and Campbell, 2000; Cooper, Scherer, Boies, and Gordon, 1999; Cooper and Sportolari, 1997).

Associating these factors—online disinhibition, together with elevated openness, venture, and bravado—with an atmosphere characterized by typical masculine attitudes (e.g., Kendall, 2000; Scott, Semmens, and Willoughby, 2001) produces a high probability of SH behaviors, especially by men against women. In masculine-dominated environments, the users' personal needs, values, desires, habits, and expectations become more transparent and blatant. Moreover, these personal proclivities apparently are accelerated by the effects of increased salience of social identities in online environments (e.g., Douglas and McGarty, 2001, 2002; Postmes, Spears, and Lea, 2002; Spears, Postmes, Lea, and Wolbert, 2002). According to this viewpoint (commonly referred to as SIDE, or Social Identity explanation of Deindividuation Effects), people in cyberspace may incline under certain circumstances to follow group standards of behavior rather than using their own standards; in other words, a social or a group identity (and expressed norms of behavior) may replace an individual identity (Reicher, 1987). These two explanatory models of the nature of online behavior, which imply that it is affected by disinhibition, by SIDE, or their combination, lay the grounds for the dynamic of online SH. The effects of online disinhibition might reinforce exposure of a person's true self or inner self (Barak, 2004; Bargh, McKenna, and Fitzsimons, 2002; McKenna and Seidman, 2005); thus, people who possess personality traits engendering a proclivity to sexually harass (Barak and Kaplan, 1996; Pryor, La Vite, and Stoller, 1993; Pryor and Stoller, 1994; Sheskin and Barak, 1997) might tend to behave according to their inner urge while online. Similarly, people who are affected by the SIDE process while in cyberspace might follow typical male-dominating, power-based, masculine attitudes and behaviors toward women.

The situational component of the equation is highly significant in cyberspace. Several of the unique characteristics of this environment not only encourage and reinforce harassment behaviors but also actually elicit them by providing an atmosphere in which harassers receive reinforcement to behave consistently with their SH proclivities. First, there are technical and practical features of the Internet that make antisocial behaviors more common. Thus, a harasser can take advantage of being unidentifiable, anonymous, and invisible, in addition to having immediate, easy-to-execute, almost untraceable escape-route mechanisms (Postmes, Spears, Sakhel, and De Groot, 2001; Sassenberg and Kreutz, 2002; Suler and Phillips, 2000). In addition, the highly interactive nature of cyberspace allows reinforcement contingency, which apparently contributes to the maintenance and escalation of behaviors (cf. Rafaeli and Sudweeks, 1997). By the same token, one should keep in mind that the virtual environment enables people to provide themselves with relative protection from SH and other aggressions.

Ben-Ze'ev (2003, 2004) has thoroughly discussed and analyzed the effects of emotional closeness and openness in cyberspace as a function of the relative privacy and the individually selective exposure experienced in this environment. Because surfers can increase their privacy (for instance, by using nicknames), in his view the potential harm from SH in cyberspace is reduced relative to offline encounters.

Second, the problematic legal status of the Internet, in addition to serious difficulties in enforcing laws and regulations pertaining to it, creates an environment in which breaking a law is common (e.g., Hiller and Cohen, 2002; Lessig, 1999). The (near) lack of clear legal boundaries, the absence of visible authorities and enforcement vehicles, and the absence of significant sanctions encourage people with criminal intentions to do what they would have been restrained from doing in offline situations. Related to this is the fact that the Internet has provided availability and easy access to public records, which include a great amount of private information that can be (and are) abused by cyberharassers and cyberstalkers (Tavani and Grodzinsky, 2002). The third and perhaps most critical ingredient that causes the online environment to be risky, particularly in regard to being victimized by SH, pertains to its culture and social norms. Cyberspace is a culture that is characterized by dominant masculine values and aggressive communications, one that perhaps also delivers a message that antiminority behaviors are welcome and even praised. Specifically in regard to women, quite a few online environments—practiced in chat rooms or in forums—are characterized by an antiwomen spirit, the attitude communicated by verbal messages, by providing links to selective sites, and by displaying obscene pictures. Research of offline environments has consistently shown the relationship between social norms and the phenomenon of SH, so that the degree of tolerance positively correlates with the extent and severity of harassment (e.g., Ellis, Barak, and Pinto, 1991; Folgero and Fjeldstad, 1995; Pryor, Giedd, and Williams, 1995; Williams, Fitzgerald, and Drasgow, 1999).

The interaction between a proclivity to sexually harass by people who possess problematic attitudes and are searching for an opportunity to execute behaviors to satisfy their needs and desires, which are magnified in cyberspace, and an environment that enables and often reinforces such behaviors clearly produces the dynamics of SH on the Internet; that is, a person who tends to sexually harass would not have behaved this way without the situational opportunities provided by the Net; SH would not be taking place in cyberspace without people whose needs and intentions are to sexually offend. The combination of an environment in which SH is invited by virtue of its special characteristics and people who possess a particular pattern of personality characteristics makes online SH almost inevitable. For this reason, as argued by Finn and Banach (2000), women who innocently use the Net for legitimate causes, such as seeking health information, may encounter dangerous situations. Similarly, women who seek online friendly connections often encounter harassment and "virtual rape" (Döring, 2000). Power-driven men express their attitudes on the Internet—even when gender differences are supposedly minimized (Sussman and Tyson, 2000). Women find it difficult to hide—their writings can be validly identified in most cases, despite invisibility, anonymity, and even the lack of personal handwriting (Koppel, Argamon, and Shimoni, 2002). Furthermore, gender inequality, as expressed by gender-stereotypic behaviors, has been found not to be reduced by online anonymity (Postmes and

Spears, 2002). Apparently, different populations behave differently online, according to their culture and indigenous social norms—toward children (Calvert, 1999; Griffiths, 1997), women (Boneva and Kraut, 2002; Morahan-Martin, 1998), or ethnic groups (Back, 2002; Matei and Ball-Rokeach, 2002)—a fact that might trigger stereotypic, sometimes hostile, behaviors by other groups. In analyzing Web pages and the self-expressions of men and women on the Net through their Web presence, Miller and Arnold (2001) came to the conclusion that "Internet provides new ways of being in the World, but not in a way which is intrinsically mysterious or different from other aspects of being. . . . The frames for action in cyberspace are not necessarily less (or more) problematical than in real life—because they are part of real life" (p. 92).

It is important to note, however, that perceptions of SH behaviors might be reinforced or, in contrast, lessened online. This was found by Biber, Doverspike, Baznik, Cober, and Ritter (2002), who compared in-person and online communication discourse media. They revealed that misogynist comments, nicknames, and comments about dress (all considered gender harassment) were rated more harassing when they appeared online than offline. Ben-Ze'ev (2003) explained the difference in judgmental standards by the difference between text-based and face-to-face communication. Requests for company, considered unwanted sexual attention, however, were rated more harassing offline than online. For this reason—perhaps consistent with the online disinhibition effect—it might be advisable to refer to hard evidence and professional judgment (though not perfect either) in regard to evidence of SH in cases in which a lawsuit is threatened (McGarth and Casey, 2002).

Effects of SH on the Internet

Offline SH has a severe impact on its victims. Dansky and Kilpatrick (1997) reviewed a variety of empirical studies on the effects of SH and pointed to severe work-related and school-related effects (reduced performance and satisfaction, decreased motivation and morale, lower productivity, and the like), as well as psychological effects, reflected in psychological disorders, negative emotions, and related behavioral consequences. Similarly, O'Donohue, Downs, and Yeater (1998), in a broad review of the literature, found consistent negative psychological, occupational, and economic consequences for victims. In the same vein, Schneider, Swan, and Fitzgerald (1997) and Glomb et al. (1997) found a series of psychological and job-related negative effects of SH of working women in several different types of organizations. Munson, Hulin, and Drasgow (2000) found that experiences of SH by university employees yielded severe outcomes, independent of dispositional influences or response biases. Van Roosmalen and McDaniel (1998) found that SH had direct effects on women's physical (e.g., nausea, sleeplessness) and mental health (e.g., loss of self-esteem, feelings of helplessness and isolation, depression). Furthermore, Harned and Fitzgerald (2002) found a link in three independent samples between SH and eating disorders, psychological distress, self-esteem, and self-blame—for women but not for men. Wonderlich et al. (2001), too, found a significant link between sexual assault and severe eating behaviors, sometimes many years after the abuse had taken place. Krakow et al. (2000) found sleeping disorders that consequently affected depression and suicidal proclivities. Pathe and Mullen (1997) reported that severe emotional (e.g., increased anxiety) and behavioral (nightmares, appetite disturbances) effects characterized most female victims of stalking. Stein and Barrett-Connor (2000) found significant effects of sexual assault on victims' health. Redfearn and Laner (2000) showed that women who were victims of sexual abuse had problematic effects in regard to their sexual attitudes and behaviors. Avina and O'Donohue (2002) reviewed the relevant literature and showed that the effects of SH on victims consistently met the criteria of post-traumatic stress disorder (PTSD). Davis, Coker, and Sanderson (2002) and McGuire and Wraith (2000), who reviewed the effects of stalking on victims, described the immense disruption to their lives, as well as increased physical injuries, health problems, PTSD, substance abuse, and contemplation of suicide.

In contrast to the above review, little is as yet empirically known about the effects of SH that is experienced on the Internet. In 1998, Morahan-Martin noted the domination of the Internet by male users, its aggressive language, and limited attention to ethics and netiquette, on one hand, and the avoidance by women of the free use of the Internet, on the other. Although much has changed in terms of women's presence on the Internet (Pew Internet Project, 2003; UCLA Center for Communication Policy, 2003), it seems that the social norms in relation to the status of women versus men, as well as of other minority groups (e.g., homosexuals, children), have a spillover effect, and they penetrate the Internet. Therefore, it is common to find reports, usually based on impressions and informal complaints, about the negative impact of SH of women on the Net (e.g., Döring, 2000; Finn and Banach, 2000). More specifically, Gáti, Tényi, Túry, and Wildmann (2002) reported a case describing a causal connection between the online SH of a sixteen-year-old girl and her developing of anorexia nervosa. Although a clear-cut, causal connection between traumatic life events and the development of eating disorders has not been established, this case clearly resembles descriptions reported by Harned and Fitzgerald (2002) in regard to offline SH effects.

Prevention of SH on the Internet

Generally, three parallel ways of preventing offline SH have been advised and executed: legislation and law enforcement, changing of the organizational-social culture, and education and training of potential victims as well as of potential harassers (cf. Paludi and Paludi, 2003; Sbraga and O'Donohue, 2000).

Legislation seems to be necessary to erect strict, well-defined boundaries for interpersonal sex-related behaviors and to define the sanctions attached to unlawful conduct (Gutek, 1997; Riger, 1991). Legislation also plays an important social role in communicating the social context of what is accepted and what is not in a given society and, thus, serves as a clear sign of values and morals. Law enforcement is necessary for implementing laws, so that they do not just remain theoretical declarations. Although legislation and law enforcement are of top priority offline and take place in all societies, their usefulness in cyberspace is only partial for a number of well-known reasons. For example, the owner of a computer server, the owner of a Web site, and different Web surfers might be located in different locations, including different countries, and therefore subject to different legal systems. In addition, there is the physical location of the server itself. Thus, a server may physically be located in Aruba and owned by a Brazilian who happens to reside in Morocco; a Web site accessed by that server offers a chat room hosted by an Israeli who resides in France; in the chat room, an Australian man sexually harasses, by means of unwanted verbal sexual attention, a Danish female surfer who entered the site. In addition, because of anonymity, high-level privacy, invisibility, and the often lack of individual traces that characterize the Internet environment, the efficiency of enforcing the law is at best very partial.

As noted above, legal guidelines and procedures are desirable and highly important but only secondary in combating SH. As Barak (1992) argued and as has been consistently found in places where prevention attempts were implemented and followed up (e.g., Bell, Quick, and Cycyota, 2002; O'Hare-Grundmann, O'Donohue, and Peterson, 1997), effective means of combating SH should include two major aspects: changing the culture and norms in which SH might take place and educating potential victims and harassers. By focusing on these two independent factors—referring as they do to the situation and to the person components of the SH equation reviewed above—the behavioral product, it is believed, will be changed (Pryor, Giedd, and Williams, 1995; Pryor, La Vite, and Stoller, 1993). In a way, this approach parallels Joinson's (2003), which employs the strategic and motivated user and expected and emergent effects (SMEE); he argued that a surfer's behavioral and psychological outcomes are a function of the effects of the media (i.e., situation) and of user aspects (i.e., person).

Attempts at changing the culture in regard to SH should include the delivery of clear, consistent messages of zero tolerance for SH and the rejection of any leniency, in addition to stances that are antimisogyny, proegalitarian, advocating interpersonal sensitivity and acceptance, respecting minorities, and the like (Bell, Quick, and Cycyota, 2002: Fitzgerald, Drasgow, and Magley, 1999: Glomb et al., 1997). Educational interventions may include awareness and training workshops for potential victims (e.g., Barak, 1994; Paludi and Barickman, 1998) as well as for potential harassers (e.g., Paludi and Barickman, 1998; Robb and Doverspike, 2001).

Although the targeting of specific populations offline, especially in local organizations, is doable and desirable, it is impractical in cyberspace; that is, it is practically impossible to change the culture of the Internet because of its limitless space and multicultural users. However, much can be done in local online communities through the exercise of responsible, dedicated leadership endorsing a firm anti-SH policy. Such an approach can be implemented through continuous messages, verbal messages and attractive banners, as well as by transparent sanctioning against any deviation from these standards. Obviously, this step will not prevent SH on the Internet as a whole; however, it will create safe havens for surfers who want to take advantage of online communities while avoiding ridicule and emotional harm. In Ben-Ze'ev's (2003) terms, this means that two unique personal values of online communication—privacy and openness—should be overtly and explicitly negotiated and settled between users to avoid unwanted, unwelcome behaviors.

In regard to educating potential victims and harassers, this can be carried out in various forms. For instance, the subject of SH on the Internet can be taught in schools in the framework of programs devoted to smart and safe Internet use (Dombrowski, LeMasney, Ahia, and Dickson, 2004; Oravec, 2000; Teicher, 1999). Such an educational intervention—offered to children, as well as to any vulnerable population—may review standards of netiquette behavior, together with tips on identifying hostile and malicious communications and impingement of privacy and boundaries (Plaut, 1997). Furthermore, online guides that contain explanations, recommendations, tips, and instructions can be posted on numerous sites to complement previous training and to highlight important issues. It is apparent that educational attempts will not prevent people with high proclivities to sexually harass resulting from their personal needs and dispositions; however, these will perhaps make them aware of possible negative outcomes, to themselves and to victims. It is hoped that for some of these people, educational intervention might change perceptions, attitudes, and values. At the very least, make them aware of considerations new to them and, thus, contribute to changing their potential problematic behaviors.

Conclusion

The Internet has a great potential to empower minorities and people who feel oppressed, weak, disadvantaged, or discriminated against. The empowerment process refers to a variety of groups, among them women (e.g., Döring, 2000; Harcourt, 1999, 2000), children (e.g., D'Alessandro and Dosa, 2001) the old (e.g., McMellon and Schiffman, 2002), ethnic minorities (Matei and Ball-Rokeach, 2002), and people who are disabled (Bowker and Tuffin, 2002). At the same time, however, cyberspace might be a dangerous, even degrading environment for these very same populations, thus functioning in an opposite direction from empowerment—namely, further weakening, humiliation, and alienation. SH exists on the Internet as much as it exists off the Internet; indeed, SH behaviors parallel those offline. The special characteristics of the Internet, such as anonymity, make this medium more prone to provide the means needed for unlawful and unethical behaviors, despite the ability of surfers to mask their identifying features as well as their ability to abruptly disconnect contact at will.

Although implementation of legal procedures and their enforcement on the Internet are practically impossible, steps could be taken to reduce the prevalence of SH on the Net. Attempts should be made at changing the violent, threatening, dominant, domineering, hostile, and malicious facets of the Internet culture by a consistent, comprehensive, and determined delivery of messages, as well as by setting leadership examples, using every means of communication available in cyberspace. Changing social norms and behavioral standards regarding the acceptance of and lenient attitudes toward SH will eventually influence many users and, consequently, affect the scope of SH.

Concomitant with attempts at modifying Internet culture, at least in indigenous communities, and notwithstanding the expected difficulties in executing this change, much effort should be made in designing and implementing educational interventions.

These programs should focus on developing awareness and influencing values and attitude sets toward specific populations and on modifying specific, relevant target behaviors. The initiative to develop and operate such programs could be by governmental or public offices and interested associations. The social benefit and, consequently, the free effective use of the Net make such initiatives worthwhile, to say the least.

Rape

We live in a culture in which sexual assaults are common. Although there is general agreement that rape, the most extreme form of sexual violence, is horrific, validating the voices of those who claim to have been sexually assaulted is complicated by our expectations about sexual behavior and our beliefs about gender. The difficulty of coming to widespread agreement on events so steeped in conflicting values and beliefs illustrates the polarities inherent in our social understandings of sex, power, autonomy, and the body.

Despite over thirty years of extensive research on rape that has produced massive policy changes in fields such as criminal justice, social work, psychology, and education the problem persists. Overwhelming evidence indicates that rape and coercive sexual experiences occur frequently and are a common experience for women. The National Violence Against Women Survey found that "almost 18 million women and almost 3 million men in the United States have been raped" (Tjaden and Thoennes 2006, iii). Among female college students, between one-fifth and one-quarter were found to have experienced rape or attempted rape over their college years (Fisher, Cullen, and Turner 2000). Despite the variance in research methods, populations studied, and findings, the picture that emerges from these and many other studies is that rape is a frequent occurrence, although we must be careful not to universalize this claim to all cultures (Helliwell 2000).

During the past decade, there has been both a marked *increase* in rapes reported to police (Butterfield 2003) and a definitive *decline* in rapes reported in a national crime survey in which individuals are asked about their experiences with crime (RAINN 2005). In the United States, increasing reports of rapes make it the fastest growing violent crime. European countries are also experiencing increased reporting, although conviction rates have not kept pace (United Nations Division for the Advancement of Women 2005). The drop in rapes reported in crime surveys may reflect the general decline in violent crime, tougher sentences for those convicted, and more intensive supervision of sex offenders (Gilligan and Talbot 2000), though more investigation of these issues is necessary to fully understand the phenomenon.

There are two widely accepted explanations for the dramatic increase in reported rapes. The first suggests that more women are raped due to a backlash against the advances in women's rights over the past several decades. There is some evidence to support this thesis; available historical records indicate that rape may have been relatively rare in the pre-industrial era (Porter 1986), and a crime-data study found that there is a temporary rise in rape rates when women's status increases relative to men's (Whaley 2001). Accordingly, rape may be on the increase as gender relations are destabilized in response to the gains of the women's movement. Since the early 1970s, when virtually no services were available for victims of rape, rape crisis centers and hotlines have opened up in most U.S. communities and various locales around the world. It is now common for police departments and court personnel in a variety of regions to receive specific training in assisting rape victims. Elements of both explanations have most likely contributed to the tremendous increase in reported rapes in those places where such data is collected.

Theorizing Rape

Early feminist theorists of rape forged an understanding of sexual assault that started from women's experiences and attempted to counter the prevailing perception that rape was rare, and usually the fault of the woman. Susan Brownmiller (1975), in one of the first feminist texts to address a theory of rape, posits rape as inevitable and rooted in the physical capacities of the body; men rape, and women are raped. This leads to the claim that, in Brownmiller's view, marriage grew out of the need for women to find protection from other men. This claim suggests that although the body shapes society, social forces do not shape rape. Andrea Dworkin (1993) theorized that rape is an expression of male supremacy, whereby men rape because they can. Her perspective implicates social structures that privilege men rather than the physiological capacity of the male body.

More recently, some feminists have complicated the discussion by stating that we have obscured true rape by defining the term too broadly. They reject a too-extensive focus on women as victims, which results in a mistaken belief that women require protection from men. For example, Katie Roiphe (1994) asserts that women are being convinced (by feminists) to define sexual experience as sexual abuse. In her view, the incidence of rape is much overstated.

Others, who have developed a more nuanced understanding of rape, point out that such arguments position women "between victimhood and agency . . . as a matter of choice" and ignore that "[a]s intersubjective, embodied beings, [women] are simultaneously subject to and implicated in the social structures that surround us" (Cahill 2001, 136). Contemporary theorists such as Cahill and Mardorossian (2002) attempt to clarify the multilayered experiences of women as physical and social beings who are all harmed by rape but who perceive each occurrence of rape according to their embodied experiences as female, raced, sexed, classed, and aged beings. Cahill believes that

> rape needs to be rethought as a pervasive, sustained, and repetitive, but not ultimately defining, element of the development of women's experience; as something that is taken up and experienced differently by different women but also holds some common aspects; as a factor that marks women as different from men; as an experience that perhaps begins with the body but whose significance does not end there. (2001, 4–5)

Mardorossian (2002) cautions us that rape is viewed differently in the West, "where sex has come to be defined as key to one's identity [as opposed to some Eastern cultures where] . . . rape is marked as the defiling of the family's and village's honor rather than the victims' right to self-determination" (763).

Building and expanding on Sanday's (this volume) earlier work, Helliwell (2000) alerts us to the danger of assuming that rape is universal. She posits that, in the West, rape reproduces and marks a sexual polarity that is not shared by all cultures. Her study in Indonesia found that, to the Gerai people, rape is unthinkable. In that culture, sex and reproduction are shaped by a belief in the bodily sameness of men and women and an identity *between* men and women as opposed to the construct of *difference* that we assume in the West. She cautions us not to universally apply notions of a sexed body as understood to be the same everywhere. She asks us to consider

> relinquish[ing] some of our most ingrained presumptions concerning difference between men and women and, particularly, concerning men's genitalia and sexuality as inherently brutalizing and penetrative and women's genitalia and sexuality as inherently vulnerable and subject to brutalization. Instead, we must begin to explore the ways rape itself *produces* such experiences of masculinity and femininity and so inscribes sexual difference onto our bodies. (812)

Mardorossian's work contributes a corrective to the tendency to develop a "homogeneous standpoint among rape victims" (2002, 750). She cautions us that women's experiences of rape are "steeped in historically and culturally contingent constructions [that] require that we attend to the signifying practices (including feminist ones) through which they are given meaning" (750).

These new theories hold promise for developing an understanding of rape that encompasses both what is held common in the experience and what is experienced differently among those affected by it. It is possible that "we will be able to understand rape only ever in a purely localized sense, in the context of the local discourses and practices that are both constitutive of and constituted by it" (Helliwell 2000, 798).

Rape and the Law

Punishment for rape has historically had little to do with acknowledgment of the harm to the raped person. Instead, the most severe punishment has been meted out in response to a perception of damage to male property. Ancient Judaic law, for example, specified punitive fees to be paid to fathers or husbands for the loss of virginity or exclusive sexual access to a raped woman (Porter 1986). Punishment for rape has often been a reflection of gender, class, and/or race bias. During the time of slavery, the racial double standard ensured that the sexual abuse of enslaved African women was not legally classified as rape. Among the most heinous examples of socially stratified responses were the numerous death sentences and lynchings of African American men who were accused of raping White women from Reconstruction through the early half of the twentieth century in the American South (Davis 1983; Pleck 1990). There is convincing evidence that many of the rape charges leveled against African American men were politically motivated (Pleck 1990). During the same time period, White men who raped African American women never received severe punishment if they received any at all (Edwards n.d.). More recently, Benedict (1992) claims that the press "prefers [rapes] against White victims while ignoring those against Blacks" (251). The relative value of sexual property to those in positions of power motivates them to use accusations of rape or rape itself for purposes of social control.

Even today, women who bring rape charges can be executed as "adulterers" for permitting the violation to occur. In Pakistan, for example, vendetta rapes are carried out against women as retribution for actions of their male relatives. "No distinction is made between rape . . . and extra-marital intercourse [with punishment for the latter ranging up to] stoning to death for married persons and 100 lashes for unmarried persons" (Shaheed 1994, 216—217; also see Bucha 2005). It is only recently and sporadically that the focus, at least in some parts of the world, has shifted away from concerns about damage to male property and the threat to the male-dominated social order and turned instead toward a discourse of power and politics played out in gender relations. For example, though rape was nominally considered a war crime when used as a method of warfare, it had rarely been prosecuted under the jurisdiction of international tribunals set up to adjudicate war crimes. Recent conflicts in Rwanda and the former Yugoslavia, however, have led to specific "gender-conscious prosecution of rape as a crime of war" (Wood 2004, 283).

For women, particularly in traditional societies, changes in how rape is perceived will take on very different shape. As more Eastern countries move away from Western forms of democracy and recommit to indigenous and traditional forms of law, in which women's voices are often silenced or subsumed under their male relatives', redress for rape will look very different than it does in the United States.

One of the most tangible effects of the feminist movement's attention to rape in the West has been an unprecedented rewriting of rape laws. The intention of the reforms has been to remove the barriers to "legal protection to female victims who failed to adhere to conventional standards of propriety, for disregarding women's experience of sexual violation, and for inflicting emotional distress on rape victims who report and prosecute rape charges" (Goldberg-Ambrose 1992, 173). Some reforms have focused on altering the legal definition of who can make a legitimate claim as a victim. In Mexico, for instance, prior to 1991, "the law stated that women had to be 'chaste and honest' to qualify as rape victims" (de la Luz Lima 1992, 19). Efforts to enable married women to bring rape charges against abusive husbands have been another focus of reform in both the United States (Russell 1990) and England (Hall, James, and Kertesz 1984). In South Africa specialized rape courts with trained prosecutors, judges, and counselors have eased the process for victims (Itano 2003). Gender-neutral laws, widely adopted in the United States, have redefined rape so that the sex of the victim and offender are immaterial. Although these changes have enabled male victims of male rape to come forward, few have, due in part to social stigma about being perceived as homosexual or feminized if they were raped by men. Female perpetrators of rape are still rare.

Other reforms have attempted to change rules of evidence in order to reflect new attitudes about rape. One such effort has been the institution of "rape shield" laws, which prohibit the introduction of a victim's past sexual history in court except under specific conditions. Currently, lawmakers are targeting "date-rape drugs," such as

Rohypnol, Ketamine, and GHB, used to incapacitate potential victims (Saum, Mott, and Dietz 2001). Increased use of DNA evidence in rape cases has circumvented the traditional "he said–she said" character of some rape trials. For some victims, the reopening of decades-old cases, made possible through DNA matches, has brought both a sense of closure and a reexperience of the violation (Preston 2005). Men convicted of rape years ago have likewise been exonerated (Dewan 2005).

Although efforts to change laws have been, for the most part, well-intentioned, results have been imperfect. Gender-neutral laws, for example, focus on a "universal, hence necessarily non-bodily, understanding of rape" (Cahill 2001, 118). Feminists see the changes as necessary to erase the different values socially ascribed to the experiences of men and women. However, the outcome of treating women as not sexed "invokes an illusory generic that is implicitly sexed male [so that] the meanings that are specific to women's lives are rendered invisible" (ibid., 123). "[A] strategy which explicitly seeks a universal and all-encompassing definition of rape . . . should inspire suspicion as to its ability to describe a phenomenon that is so profoundly gendered as well as raced" (ibid., 112).

These concerns about the law are immaterial for rape victims in parts of the world overwhelmed by conflict. In many of those cases, rape is one more horrifying facet of a life circumscribed and diminished by generalized violence. The rule of law is a distant hope (see Lefort 2003 and UNIFEM 2004 for examples). In fact, victims' continued lack of power is still evidenced by the difficulty of obtaining justice in cases of rape. In a study of U.S. lawyers and judges, Martin, Reynolds, and Keith found that "gender bias is an aspect of social interaction in legal contexts" (2002, 689) that appears to have implications for how they perceive rape. Studies from England, Scotland, Australia, Canada, and Scandinavia report mishandling of rape victims by the criminal justice system (Temkin 1986), and contemporary news reports from Pakistan (Bucha 2005; Kristof 2005) and Africa (International Society for Human Rights n.d.) indicate how difficult it is for women in many parts of the world to socially, and even physically, survive bringing rape charges. Despite reforms, the police, the courts, and the public in general often blame victims for their victimization, an attitude even more pronounced for male victims.

Reports of rape, however, continue to be discounted by police and prosecutors, and convictions are rare. Of those rape trials that do result in the conviction of an offender for rape, almost all represent approximations of the stereotypical heterosexual stranger rape (Estrich 1987). If the victim and offender are acquainted, others are less likely to judge the event to be a legitimate rape (Bourque 1989). Studies have found that most rape or attempted rape victims know their attackers (Littel and Matson 2000). A plausible correlation can be drawn between the degree of acquaintance, public perception of the legitimacy of a rape charge, and the response of the criminal justice system. At one end of the continuum, marital rape is associated with lack of public recognition and laws defined in such a way that few cases can be prosecuted. In practice, married women and prostitutes have abridged rights to sexual self-determination. Likewise, in what appears to be an almost universal silence on the issue, male rape victims rarely make reports (Pelka 1997). Public awareness is limited to a casual acceptance of the brutality of prison rape, while rape of men by other men outside of prisons is barely acknowledged. In fact, despite gender-neutral laws, male rape may be neither regulated nor prohibited in practice.

Most rapes are still not reported to law enforcement officials. Surveys in England and New Zealand have found low rates of reporting (Temkin 1986), and it is estimated that fewer than half of rape victims define the experience as rape (Fisher, Daigle, Cullen, and Turner 2003). The frequency of rape among intimates is astounding. Compared to women of all ages, those between the ages of sixteen and twenty-four are victims of rape at much higher rates (Humphrey and Kahn 2000), no doubt connected to the onset of dating relationships. Among sexually victimized college women, fully nine out of ten knew their assailants (Fisher, Cullen, and Turner 2000). One recent study conducted among women who experienced other forms of partner violence concluded that 14 percent to 20 percent were also raped, and only 6 percent of them reported it to police, even though not reporting doubled their risk of reassault (McFarlane and Malecha 2005). Victims' failure to report rape—or even to comprehend that rape is a crime—deserves further exploration.

Effects of Sexual Aggression

For women, sexually coercive experiences are associated with high levels of anxiety, guilt about sexual activity, and poor social and familial adjustment (Rogers 1984); depression and hostility (Check, Elias, and Barton 1988); alienation (Williams 1984); suicide attempts (Weis and Borges 1973; Warshaw 1988; McFarlane and Malecha 2005); feelings of diminished self-worth, depressed expectations for the future, eating disorders, lack of concentration, and sleep disorders (Warshaw 1988); phobias and delayed traumatic response (Burgess and Holmstrom 1974); increased use of alcohol and illicit drugs (McFarlane and Malecha 2005); and circumscribed activity (thereby affecting educational and work opportunities) (Association of American Colleges 1978; Hall 1985). In addition, women who have been sexually assaulted by acquaintances may suffer more complicated effects (Hall 1985) and show a slower degree of recovery than women who are raped by strangers (Warshaw 1988). The looming threat of contracting AIDS and other sexually transmitted diseases as the result of rape has increased the psychological trauma as well as the very real physical risk for victims (Carillo 1992; McFarlane and Malecha 2005). Rape appears to be a life-altering event in which "the embodied being of the victim is going to be deeply, even fundamentally affected" (Cahill 2001, 9).

Information on how rape affects male victims is sparse. The tremendous stigma attached to the victim of male-on-male rape, redolent of homophobia, has contributed to an apparent absence of knowledge about the effects of rape victimization. The little information available indicates that, whether victimized in prison or out, male victims of rape experience a diminishment of manhood—a reduction to the status of women. What consequences ensue for the victim remain to be discovered.

Living in a culture where the threat of sexual attack is pervasive shapes and constrains the lives even of those women who have not directly experienced sexual assault (see Sheffield, this volume). Although the threat of rape poisons the atmosphere in which women live, it is also becoming apparent that public attention to the issue may plant fears and therefore contribute to a sense of threat that is both real and cautionary. It is urgent that we find a balance between adequate information about the threat of rape to aid in both self-protection and identification of abusers as well as to identify the power women hold to experience their strength and autonomy.

Contributions to This Section

In the excerpt from Mary White Stewart's work, "Real Victims, Reasonableness, and Rape," the author acknowledges the ambiguity of acquaintance rape. Our responses to claims of rape between people who know each other reflect how embedded our pre-conceptions are about men, women, and sex. Stewart illustrates the complexity of the interaction itself and how it alternates between the routine sexualized play that is a feature of male-female interaction, and violence and violation. It is the muddy character of the interaction that inspires the foundation for the author's proposal of a new legal concept, the situated reasonable woman standard.

In "Subcultural Theory of Rape Revisited," Laura L. O'Toole draws on theories of masculinity and empirical studies of rape among fraternity members and athletes to explore masculinist subcultures where rape is acceptable behavior. The author concedes that although not all rapes take place within an identifiable male group, the large number of rapes that do occur within such contexts requires that we give attention to subcultures of violent heterosexual masculinity.

Margaret Stetz points to the great personal cost for women who have spoken publicly about sexual violation in war. Though we can see the concrete results of these women's testimony in the commitment of the international community to envision wartime rape as a crime against humanity, Stetz finds that, for the most part, governments and the military have not heeded their message. She cautions us not to callously discard their legacy but rather to use it to resist a tradition of the misuse of women's bodies by the military.

In "Undeclared War: African-American Women Writers Explicating Rape," Opal Palmer Adisa explores the writings of African American women and finds a common thread. According to Adisa, rape is conceptualized by these authors as a battle, with women's bodies as the contested territory, thus creating a revolutionary body of work that attempts to reclaim the power to define experience and simultaneously provide inspiration for resistance and change.

SUGGESTIONS FOR FURTHER READING

Jeff Benedict, *Out of Bounds: Inside the NBA's Culture of Rape, Violence, and Crime* (New York: HarperCollins, 2004).

Maria Bevacqua, *Rape on the Public Agenda: Feminism and the Politics of Sexual Assault* (Boston: Northeastern University Press, 2000).

Ann Cahill, *Rethinking Rape* (Ithaca, NY: Cornell University Press, 2001).

Nancy Venable Raine, *After Silence: Rape and My Journey Back* (New York: Crown, 1998).

Peggy Reeves Sanday, *Fraternity Gang Rape: Sex, Brotherhood, and Privilege on Campus,* 2nd ed. (New York: NYU Press, 2007).

Alice Siebold, *Lucky: A Memoir* (Farmington Hills, MI: Scribner, 1999).

Patricia Tjaden and Nancy Thoennes, "Extent, Nature, and Consequences of Rape Victimization: Findings from the National Violence Against Women Survey" (Washington, DC: National Institute of Justice, 2006).

The Rape

Jeanne Murray Walker

So I can never forget, I've kept one small glove.
My husband, Wilfred, had the most delicate hands.
In Pittsburgh during that winter
the wind raged like a criminal
come to finish us off. I sang hymns,
"Leaning On The Everlasting Arms,"
and lay all night awake in Wilfred's embrace.
To stay warm enough to live—that became our religion.
One morning on the doorstep of our apartment house
we saw a frozen baby, a plucked chicken, blue as steel.
The next week Wilfred found work stoking the furnace
in a garment factory—twenty-seven men applied.
I thought they'd chosen Wilfred
because love conquers all,
and I was right. Oh, I was right.
The boss gave Wilfred leather gloves
and sent him every night back home
from their hot furnace, florid as a rose.
I could smell the boss in Wilfred's hair.
When we lay down on our narrow bed,
the boss smiled at me out of Wilfred's eyes.

In what part of me did I understand?
I knew it in my arms. I could feel
that man's hot shadow shouldering up
at night when I held Wilfred,
but my tongue had turned to stone.

One Saturday afternoon when I was asleep alone,
the boss's boots hammered up our stairs.
He wanted me, it turns out. Wilfred
was a corridor between us. Wilfred
is an opening in both directions,

From the *Midwest Quarterly,* 1980, pp. 316–17. Reprinted by permission.

I thought, as I heard the man unlock the door
with Wilfred's key. He was wearing
a double breasted suit and Wilfred's gloves.
He laid the gloves on the radiator. He said, "Sing."

Slowly I started the old music
he never had a right to hear:
   Take my hand and let it move
   At the impulse of thy love,
   At the impulse of thy love.
That afternoon I thought I hated all of them.
I thought I hated Jesus.

Chapter Eleven

Real Victims, Reasonableness, and Rape

Mary White Stewart

The Complexity of Acquaintance Rape

In the not-too-distant past, girls in the United States learned that their sexuality was a gift to bestow on the man who chose them—a gift they would give once and for all and that would solidify their identity. Historian Anne Swidler writes about this in an analysis of the relationship between love and adulthood in a changing culture.[1] She suggests that if women are to marry once, and only once, and if divorce is viewed as a failure, they are likely to "save themselves" for marriage, which is the culmination of their preparation for adulthood and the opportunity for the solidification of self. However, if women have more than one chance to seek a partner over a lifetime, divorce being a growth experience rather than an indication of failure, they are likely not to guard their virginity as a gift to bestow on some lucky partner. Women are likely to be more sexually free and to view their sexuality as theirs rather than as being held in safekeeping for someone else. (Of course, women in many other cultures are not in any position to choose to have a number of sexual partners, to express themselves sexually as they wish. Virginity until marriage is imposed on them with a penalty of death for its violation.)

The changes in the participation of women in the sexual arena that have come about as a result of the sexual liberation movement in the United States and other Western countries, as well as the achievement of significant educational and economic gains, have led to an environment in which women may be more vulnerable to acquaintance rape than they were in the past. Of course, the definition of rape has changed as well, and the consequences of pregnancy have changed, so these must be taken into account in an understanding of the change in rape rates and the characteristics of rape over time. Going back a few decades, the consequences of pregnancy were sure and immediate for most young women. Legal abortions were almost completely unavailable during the early years of the sexual liberation movement, and women had a great deal to lose by obtaining one, just as they did for having a baby without being married. Middle-class women who were in high school or college were likely to have to quit, at least for a year, and virtually go into hiding until they had the baby and put him or her up for adoption. Another choice open to these girls was to get married, and as Friedan points out, over one-quarter of the brides walked down the aisle pregnant during the 1950s. The specter of pregnancy hung over both boys and girls, and the knowledge of the consequences of sex likely stopped many boys from forcing themselves on their girlfriends or dates. With the freedom achieved through the ready availability of birth control, the consequence of sex did not have to be pregnancy, and if one did become pregnant, the availability of legal abortion, achieved in 1973 with *Roe v. Wade*, meant that marriage was not a forgone conclusion. Coupled with and related to this physical freedom from fear, the sexual revolution removed women's legitimate justifications for "saving themselves." Now women who were cool, modern, and "with it" were women who owned their own bodies and did what they pleased with them. Women who refused sex were viewed as backward, stuck, regressed in some way, limiting themselves in an unnatural and unhealthy way. Perhaps because the stakes are not so high as they once were, men felt that forcing sex was not such a major problem; she was not going to be ruined if she had sex with him, and he probably would not have to marry her—or even tell her he loved her. So the barrier was lower, and her "loss" was less from his point of view, as well as that of others who might accuse her of overreacting or of ruining his life for a minor infraction if she claimed to have been forced to have sex. Hence, if he forced her to have sex, she might feel less legitimate than previously in reporting him or defining it as rape. She was contradicting her definition of self as free and equal and sexual and was on the border of seeing herself and being seen as being vindictive or blaming him for something they both wanted.

One would never suggest that acquaintance rape and date rape did not occur in the 1950s. Indeed, some of those marriages based on the girl's pregnancy were probably the result of date rape. But the sexual barriers between males and females were much higher. The consequences of breaking them were lifelong and severe. By the 1970s, young women in the middle class at least had few readily acceptable reasons for not having sex with their dates, and sex was certainly not viewed as a prelude to marriage. For many girls, the question was, "Why not?" The motto, "If it feels good, do it," applied to sex as well as drugs. Exploration in both of these areas was applauded. Male and female sexuality was defined differently as well, with females generally learning not to reveal their sexual desires openly but to succumb to the sexual needs of the man, his needs being viewed as irrepressible and not fully within his control. While sex may have been forced on women, their protestations unheeded, this may well have reflected the girl's inability to assert her sexual wants under the circumstances as much as his unwillingness to "take no for an answer."

Girls in the lower class were in a somewhat different position. First, abortion was relatively expensive and therefore unavailable for many of them. Cultural norms supported marriage in the case of pregnancy rather than abortion or adoption, and religious values were likely to define sex before marriage (for girls) as taboo. Lillian Rubin writes about the disastrous sexual dance between lower-class boys and girls.[2] These young people, who dreamed of a life different from that of their parents, removed from the drudgery and limitations of low education and low income, found themselves repeating the pattern their parents had followed. Girls who dreamed of sun-kissed cottages filled with sun-kissed babies, and boys who dreamed of adventure and power rather than the dreary, repetitious, often dirty work of their fathers, found themselves right back in their parents' tracks when the girl became pregnant. The class and religious condemnation of birth control and abortion, together with the attraction of taboo sexual relations, resulted in these couples getting married when the girl became pregnant, becoming parents before they even got to know each other, and living with the constrictions of limited educational and occupational preparation.

There was, however, at least in the middle class, a difficult relationship between current and past expectations. In fact, the girls who were supposed to feel so free and open and in charge of their own sexuality are the same girls who only a few years earlier were worried about limiting their sexual activity to "petting above the waist" to prevent their boyfriend from becoming too aroused and finding themselves "in trouble." They had grown up clearly aware of the distinction between the good girls and the bad girls, and although the bad girls might have had more fun (smoking, dying their hair, and "going all the way"), the good girls had a future married to someone and being cared for and loved. That was worth waiting for. In addition, these boys who were now happily acclaiming the wonders of female sexual freedom were the same boys who divided girls into the "bad" but fun ones and the "good girls" they would eventually introduce to their parents. They had not forgotten the distinction; they were just celebrating the sudden availability of so many more girls who were willing to be bad.

Acquaintance rape is such a troublesome concept in part because the questionable behavior (forced sex) takes place within a context that is often extremely confusing. This very confusion—stemming from knowing the other person, if only slightly, the socialization messages of both men and women, and the complexity of the moment— creates difficulties not just in interpretation but in the impact of the rape. When women know a man from seeing him in the elevator, the lobby, or around campus, this acquaintance lends an air of familiarity and safety to their encounters. If she then has a drink with him or he takes her home after work, his sexual pressure or sexual advances reflect a very different context than if he were a stranger who pushed himself on her. When she is familiar with him, she is likely to see the sexual advance as part of an ongoing relationship and to respond very differently than she would to a total stranger. There are subtle yet powerful definitions of the situation that operate in this instance in which he is neither a stranger nor a friend or date. These are situations in which the cues and the anticipated consequences are very different than they would be in a stranger rape. Here the woman is responding to a familiar yet unknown person, one with whom she has some past and can anticipate some future, and her responses are likely to be ones that maintain the status quo as much as possible. Women learn early on that they are responsible for the social and emotional environment, that they are to do the emotional work in a situation or a relationship, and they are likely to consider the impact of their reaction on the ongoing situation at work or at school. Women who have been raped by men they know consider not only how others will see their behavior in the situation but also the long-term impact of their reaction in the specific situation on others in their social world.

Sociologist Erving Goffman points out that in our everyday interactions, we are likely to avoid talking or behaving in such as way as to ruin the interaction; we try to maintain a semblance of normalcy.[3] Women particularly learn to take care of others and to take care of the relationship, so they are likely to make an effort to not "overreact" or "misinterpret," and at the same time they learn not to trust their own feelings or perceptions and so may respond more slowly or weakly than would be effective. This caretaking tendency can be counterproductive for women because they may be viewed as not adequately resisting sexual advances. And indeed, given that they may be required to prove physical resistance, they may be viewed as complying. The fact that acquaintance rape is more complex and multifaceted than the relatively rare stranger rape by no means implies that we cannot differentiate acquaintance rape from consensual sex. Rape or sexual assault is forced intercourse or other penetration. It is the refusal of the man to heed the woman's *no*. Whether she is incapacitated by drugs and alcohol and cannot resist or assert her will, or whether she does and is overpowered by fear or physical force, she is the victim of rape. The person who is raped has had her power destroyed by someone she knows. She has been violated as a person with a separate and identifiable self, a person with integrity, by someone with whom she has a relationship. This violation is not a simple reconstruction "the morning after" and cannot be reduced to a misunderstanding.

The difficulty we have as a society dealing with commonplace, ordinary types of violence against women reveals the depth of our stereotypes about masculinity and femininity and about sexual relationships, and it demands that we become willing to reconceptualize rape. It is essential to take into account the characteristics of the situation in which the sexual interaction takes place. One cannot apply the rules and expectations that clarify stranger rape to acquaintance rape. These are not simply acts at different ends of a continuum; they are essentially different and are in many ways unrelated. Although both reflect the view that male sexual demands, whether tied to consensual sex or forced sex, must be met, this does not distinguish them from ordinary sex or from one another. Further, both types of rape, similarly to consensual sex, reflect a view of male sexuality as dominant and aggressive and female sexuality as subordinate and passive. They are distinguished because the lines between sex and aggression are blurred in acquaintance rape, whereas they are not in stranger rape. Although men who rape strangers may draw on cultural constructions of woman's sexuality or character that allow them to justify their behavior, it is quite clear that these rapes are attacks. Acquaintance rape, on the other hand, dances between friendliness, flirtation, normal and everyday sexual advances and responses, and the shift to extraordinary pressure, force, confusion, and perhaps compliance. There is a point in acquaintance rape when the consensual interaction is transformed into one of resistance and conflict, but the interaction is a complex tangle of ongoing acts that are contextually based. The meaning of the interaction is fluid, preventing the easy separation of choice from force. This process is complicated by the familiarity of the sexual interaction in a consensual setting. The recognition on the part of the woman that it is moving from consent to force comes creeping into her awareness rather than arriving full blown and recognizable.

Just as it is important to distinguish the relatively uncommon stranger assault from the more common acquaintance or date rape, it is also important to recognize that although acquaintance rapes have common elements, they too are very different. It may be possible to place date rape on a continuum. At one end would be the situation in which a woman meets a man at a bar or some other public place, and he takes her home and forces sex on her while in the car. Clearly this is very close to stranger rape; in fact, as one detective I interviewed said about this kind of rape, the rape began when he saw her in the bar, not when he tried to penetrate her. These people did not know each other, their interaction was brief, and the assault was not co-mingled with the intimacy that characterizes an ongoing knowledge of or relationship with a co-worker or fellow student. At another end of this continuum, we would place the woman who has had a sexual relationship with a man but who in this instance does not want to have sex with him. If her resistance, her refusal, and her *no* are ignored, this too is rape.

Reasonable Man or Reasonable Woman: What's the Difference?

Many legal scholars and feminist scholars have suggested that the issues that are so difficult in rape cases would be better resolved through the use of a legal standard that takes into account the realities women experience. The myths and stereotypes about rape and women who are raped would be tempered were the point of view of women rather than of men to be incorporated into legal judgments. Adoption of a "reasonable woman standard" could have a dramatic impact on the process that victims experience and would allow for the woman's perspective of her own experience to be validated. Such a standard could be expected to diminish the strength of rape myths and stereotypes and to increase both reporting and conviction in rape cases.

The principle of reasonableness dates back at least 140 years and has today gained a prominent position in almost every area of American law.[4] The principle provides a range of allowable departures from a standard of absolute conformity to a social norm. It balances individual freedom with community security, reflecting the nature of the social contract in which individuals agree to conform to community standards.[5] This standard was initially embodied in the now archaic "reasonable man" standard. Historically, the legal status "man" referred specifically to males, since women were legally property or chattel.[6] "Man" reflected a male society in which male values were the standard, women being perceived as both intellectually and emotionally inferior and childlike. For almost two hundred years the legal landscape remained fundamentally male dominated, reflecting a society in which no woman was man's equal and married women were legal nonentities.

During the past several decades, it has become generally accepted that the long-held reasonable man standard excludes women's reality from the courtroom. Against the backdrop of the feminist movement and the Supreme Court assertion of equal protection, the courts began to reassess the male-dominated standards that had pervaded American jurisprudence.[7] As a consequence, many courts began to use a formally gender-neutral reasonable person standard, incorporating social norms and the values of both man and woman in its definition.[8]

However, critics suggest that the reasonable person standard, rather than being objective, is fundamentally flawed, reflecting its deep roots in the reasonable man standard and providing only a cosmetic change rather than a substantive one. In fact, the apparent neutralizing of the reasonableness standard may make it too easy for the courts to overlook woman's experiences and the meaning of these experiences by creating a false impression that these are already included within the general test of reasonableness.[9] That is, the reasonable person standard keeps alive the *illusion* of a universal and unitary subject of the law. The dissatisfaction with the reasonable person standard became the catalyst for a movement to develop a standard of reasonableness that would, in effect, force the courts to recognize the female point of view.[10] The obvious question, "Is there a female point of view?" emerges and is certainly worth considering; however, one might ask the same question about the reasonable man standard, which has heretofore escaped such scrutiny. Although there can be no singular women's perspective, given class, race, and other differences, surely one could say the same about a male point of view. I would argue that there is no "female" point of view, but women's perceptions of certain phenomena such as rape or battery probably have more in common than do men's and women's views on these. The research on jury decision making and attribution of blame and responsibility suggests that men and women do evaluate behavior in rape cases quite differently.[11]

Some have suggested that in cases specifically and predominantly involving women, such as rape cases or a battered woman accused of killing her batterer, a reasonable woman standard should be applied. This suggests that in particular situations involving relationships, and women's and men's definition of sexuality, women's views are underrepresented, or not represented, and need to be. This also assumes, however, that in other areas, men and women have parallel or compatible perspectives, which is doubtful.

Although courts have been slow to apply the standard, within the past fifteen years the reasonable woman standard has gained a measure of legal force through hostile-work-environment cases and cases in which women have killed their abusive spouses. A number of recent hostile-workplace harassment cases illustrate the application of a reasonable woman standard, concluding that a woman and man might differ in their perception of objectionable conduct.[12] In sharp contrast to battered-women cases or those involving women who kill, the reasonable woman standard has proven problematic in rape cases. Some researchers suggest that it might be counterproductive because the standard incorporates assumptions about the "due care" a woman should have exercised. That is, a "reasonable woman" could be expected to know the culture in which she lives and to understand how men will interpret her statements or behavior and should therefore not reasonably place herself in dangerous situations.[13] In this way, the reasonable woman standard in rape cases may perpetuate or reinforce rape myths and stereotypes rather than challenge them, supporting the view that a woman who hitchhikes, has drinks with a man, or invites a man to her home is indeed "asking for it."

The intuitive appeal of a reasonable woman standard is not completely synchronous with the practical concerns that shape its application. It has been criticized as both too broad and too narrow—too broad in implying sameness among women on the basis of sex while ignoring differences in race, class, or ethnicity; too narrow in its depiction of femininity, reflecting cultural images of femininity that cast women in the role of the passive victim. For example, in *Radtke*, the Michigan Supreme Court concluded, "Courts utilizing the reasonable woman standard pour into the standard stereotypic assumptions of women which infer women are sensitive, fragile, and in need of a more protective standard. Such paternalism degrades women and is repugnant to the very ideals of equality that the act is intended to protect."[14] The claim is that the adoption of the reasonable woman standard undermines the effort to establish the moral irrelevance of gender codifying gender inequality. However, it seems more reasonable to assert that a standard acknowledging a woman's reality does not ipso facto diminish her. We disagree that it is the goal of the justice system to make gender morally irrelevant. Rather, gender is undeniably a dominant social identity, reflecting structural and social characteristics that provide context to social interaction. Gender is one of the most powerful definers of the self, and its relevance cannot be ignored. Nor can wishing it to be so make it so, even in a court of law.[15]

Two alternatives to the reasonable woman standard have been suggested by legal scholars. One is the "modified reasonable person standard," which would take into account the relevant central characteristics and significant group associations of the individuals in question.[16] Another calls for a "contextualized reasonable woman standard," which focuses on the victim's actual reactions and the actual circumstances surrounding the victim's behavior, thereby allowing for each woman's experience to be viewed from her perspective and allowing for the multiplicity of images and voices that exist among women to be expressed and acknowledged.[17]

In recent work, my colleagues and I suggest a "situated reasonable woman" standard that requires the reasonableness of both actors' behavior to be assessed within the parameters of the dynamic interaction and its social context.[18] This standard would allow courts to acknowledge the reality of everyday interactions and that people's perceptions shape their behavior in process. The focus on interaction highlights the characteristics that are salient at the moment, including gender, race, age, physical attributes, status, power, and history of the relationship. The "situated reasonable person standard" acknowledges and incorporates the notion that what constitutes normal behavior is dependent on the situation, the interactants, and the social world in which they are embedded.

On a Personal Level

Most states have revised their rape laws to include several levels of sexual assault with a broader range of penalties. A perpetrator may be charged with first-, second-, or third-degree rape, each with a different maximum sentence. First-degree rape is defined as forced sexual assault with aggravating circumstances. Second-degree rape is forced sexual intercourse, and third-degree rape is nonconsensual intercourse or intercourse with threat to self or property. This calibrated system of rape has increased reporting and probably convictions as well. Another significant change that has occurred as a result of feminist activism has been the inclusion of the man's force or threat of force in determining whether the sex was consensual rather than simply addressing the woman's consent or level of resistance. These changes are important ones and incorporate into the legal system the reality of the rape experience. Still, since most rapes fall into the third category, nonconsensual intercourse, women are still reluctant to report. The process of reporting and prosecuting a case demands an enormous amount of strength and a complete sense of confidence. It also requires an ability to withstand condemnation and criticism. It may be that only if the damage the woman suffers is extreme, or if she has "nothing to lose," will she risk the humiliation and public scrutiny required to pursue a charge of rape.

If the reader will place herself in the shoes of the victim for a moment, she will see how difficult the situation is. In my case, for example, as a person known in the community and the university, with relatively high-profile siblings and other family in the community, reporting an acquaintance rape would be unthinkable. Whereas I would not find it terribly difficult (I imagine) to report a stranger rape because I would construct it as an attack, an assault, an obvious crime, I would be very hesitant to suffer the humiliation and the enormous familial and personal strain that would come with accusing a colleague or acquaintance with rape if indeed that were the case. I would no doubt respond just as most rape victims do: try to ignore it, avoid it, forget about it, deal with it on my own without involving others.[19] I would anticipate little support from colleagues and an inconsistent response from family and friends. I would anticipate being told, and telling myself, that I was an adult and certainly old enough to be responsible for my own behavior. I would convince myself that I probably misinterpreted his behavior or that I led him to misinterpret mine. I might convince myself that it was not really rape at all. And I would be fearful and embarrassed, knowing that others would pull out all the rape myths and stereotypes I know so well and impose them on me. It would simply not be worth it. Women I interviewed who were raped by acquaintances told me time and again that they did not report for these very same reasons: they would not be believed; it would ruin their lives; it just was not worth it.

Giving careful thought to the way one would respond to rape by an acquaintance or lover and to the impact it would have on one's familial, friendship, and work relationships reveals some of the complexities faced by women who experience rape. More important, such a thoughtful consideration almost inevitably leads to the conclusion that rape, like battery or harassment, is far more than a legal issue; it is a deeply painful and deeply destructive personal assault.

NOTES

1. Swidler, A., 1980, "Love and Adulthood in American Culture," in N. Smelser and E. Erikson (eds.), *Themes of Work and Love in Adulthood*, Cambridge, MA: Harvard University Press.

2. Rubin, Lillian, 1976, *Worlds of Pain: Life in the Working Class Family*, New York: Basic Books.

3. Goffman, E., 1959, *The Presentation of Self in Everyday Life*, New York: Doubleday.

4. Unikel, R., 1992, " 'Reasonable' Doubts: A Critique of the Reasonable Woman Standard in American Jurisprudence," *Northwestern University Law Review* 87: 326–375.

5. Gluckman, M., 1967, "Judicial Process among Barotse," In D. Lloyd and M. D. A. Freeman (eds.), *Lloyds Introduction to Jurisprudence* (5th ed.), London: Sweet and Maxwell, pp. 904–910.

6. Dobash, R. E., and R. Dobash, *Violence against Wives: A Case against the Patriarchy*, New York: Free Press. See also Brownmiller, Susan, 1975, *Against Our Will: Men, Women, and Rape*, New York: Simon and Schuster; Estrich, Susan, 1987, *Real Rape*, Cambridge, MA: Harvard Uni-

versity Press; and Daly, Mary, 1978, *Gyn/Ecology: The Metaethics of Radical Feminism*, Boston: Beacon Press.

7. Unikel, " 'Reasonable' Doubts." See also Cahn, N. R., 1992, "The Looseness of Legal Language: The Reasonable Woman Standard in Theory and Practice," *Cornell Law Review* 77: 1398–1446; Estrich, *Real Rape*; Bender, L., 1988, "A Lawyer's Primer on Feminist Theory and Tort," *Journal of Legal Education* 38: 20–21; and Meads, M. A., 1993, "Applying the Reasonable Woman Standard in Evaluating Sexual Harassment Claims: Is It Justified?" *Law and Psychology Review* 17: 208–223 (for a discussion of the history of and challenges to the "reasonable man" standard).

8. Adler, R. S., and E. R. Pierce, 1993, "The Legal, Ethical, and Social Implications of the 'Reasonable Woman' Standard in Sexual Harassment Cases," *Fordham Law Review* 61: 773 (for a discussion of the gender-neutral standard, the "reasonable person" standard, and the "reasonable woman" standard).

9. Abrams, K., 1989, "Gender Discrimination and the Transformation of Workplace Norms," *Vanderbilt Law Review* 42: 1183–1203. See also Dobbin, S., S. Gatowski, M, Stewart, and J. Ross, 1986, "Reasonableness and Gender in the Law: Moving beyond the Reasonable Person and Reasonable Woman Standards," paper presented at the Annual Meetings of the International Sociology of Law Research Council, July 10–13, Glasgow, Scotland.

10. Allen, H., 1988, "One Law for All Reasonable Persons?" *International Journal of the Sociology of Law* 16: 419–432. See also Unikel, " 'Reasonable' Doubts"; and Meads, "Applying the Reasonable Woman Standard."

11. Ward., C., 1995, *Attitudes toward Rape: Feminist and Social Psychological Perspectives*, Thousand Oaks, CA: Sage.

12. Meads, "Applying the Reasonable Woman Standard."

13. Cahn, "The Looseness of Legal Language." For a good discussion of this ironic impact of applying a "reasonable woman" standard in rape cases, see Estrich, *Real Rape*.

14. *Radtke v. Everett*, 1991, 47 N. W. 2d. 660 (Michigan Court of Appeals).

15. Unikel, " 'Reasonable' Doubts"; Dobbin, Gatowski, Stewart, and Ross, "Reasonableness and Gender in the Law."

16. Unikel, " 'Reasonable' Doubts."

17. Cahn, "The Looseness of Legal Language."

18. Stewart, M., S. Dobbin, and S. Gatowski, 2000, "The Reasonableness of the Reasonable Woman Standard," unpublished manuscript.

19. Oden, Mary, and Jody Clay-Warner, 1998, *Confronting Rape and Sexual Assault*, Wilmington, DE: Scholarly Research Books.

Chapter Twelve

Subcultural Theory of Rape Revisited

Laura L. O'Toole

Identifying the conditions and causes of rape has been a major project of feminist scholars and criminologists across social science disciplines for the last twenty years. This project continues to command attention, as both total numbers of reported rapes and rape rates continue to skyrocket during the 1990s in the United States. In 1990, the number of reported rapes in the United States exceeded 100,000 for the first time, after a decade of steady increase. The U.S. rape rate rose from 33.6 per 100,000 persons in 1982 to 42.8 in 1992 (Federal Bureau of Investigation 1993); and there still is every indication that these numbers reflect but a small proportion of actual rapes.

Sociology has contributed to a number of important theoretical perspectives in the study of rape. Conceptualized until quite recently as a crime committed by psychologically impaired individuals, rape has been redefined as a crime that is most frequently committed by "everyman" (Russell 1984). Sociological research has been crucial in bringing about this redefinition. For example, surveys investigating the sexual behavior and attitudes of young men in college and university populations find that anywhere from one quarter to more than half of respondents report that they have forced women to engage in sex against their will (Kanin 1967, 1985; Kanin and Parcell 1977; Koss, Gidicz, and Wisniewski 1987; Muehlenhard and Linton 1987; Warshaw 1988).

Two theoretical explanations for the epidemic of rape are most frequently validated in the literature. *Gender role socialization* theory focuses on the ways the dominant culture indoctrinates males to be sexual aggressors (Griffin 1971; Sanday 1981b; Beneke 1982), to expect sex on demand (Scully and Marolla 1985), to believe aggression is a normative component of heterosexual relationships (Berger and Searles 1985; Hennenberger and Marriott 1993), and to embrace victim-blaming myths about rape (Griffin 1971; Check and Malamuth 1983; Margolin, Miller, and Moran 1989; Feltey, Ainslie, and Geib 1991). This perspective is supported by a plethora of research that identifies the sources through which this information is communicated to males throughout the life cycle. These agents include the media, with particular emphasis on pornography (Longino 1980; MacKinnon 1984), R-rated Hollywood films (Donnerstein and Linz 1986), music videos (Schur 1988) and "gangsta rap" (hooks 1994a), peers (Ageton 1983; Kanin 1985), and even religious dogma that supports female submissiveness and male control of female sexuality (Brownmiller 1975).

Political-economic theories of rape were developed based on women's historical powerlessness and their legal definition as the property of men (Russell 1982; Schwendinger and Schwendinger 1983). Indeed, rape was originally considered a property crime against the father or husband of the victim. More recently, this perspective has analyzed the commodification of women's sexuality in advertising and the multibillion-dollar sex industry as a central aspect of rape. This commodification of sexuality, combined with the eroticization of dominance exemplified in many media portrayals of sexuality, contributes to escalating sexual violence (Schur 1988). The dehumanizing effects of commodification provide legitimacy for violence against categories of people defined as things or property. Thus, sexual violence results from both the dehumanization of women defined as sexual property and the social definition of this violence as a source of erotic pleasure (Schur 1988).

Recently, attempts have been made to integrate aspects of these two dominant theoretical models with classical models of deviant behavior or biological sexuality. For example, in their analysis of rape and structural variables across the United States, Larry Baron and Murray A. Straus (1989) find relationships between rape rates and variables such as circulation rates of pornographic magazines and the legal status of women. They also implicate general conditions of social disorganization and the culturally legitimated use of violence in gender relationships in the escalation of rape. Lee Ellis (1989) employs an evolutionary model of human sexuality to suggest that natural selection has predisposed human males toward sexual aggression, which is manifested through operant conditioning and is perhaps indirectly influenced by the social learning process, including the use of pornographic materials. Of these two, the evolutionary model requires close scrutiny given its foundation in biological determinism. That, however, is not the intent of this chapter. Rather, it is to look more closely at another perspective developed in the 1970s, then critiqued and abandoned in the 1980s. This theory, based upon classic criminological evidence suggesting the existence of violent subcultures (Wolfgang and Ferracuti 1967), has received primarily unfavorable treatment by scholars in the field.

Application of the violent subculture perspective to rape behavior has focused upon explaining higher rates of rape in lower-class and racial-ethnic communities. The main tenet of this perspective is that certain communities, with firmly established boundaries, adopt norms and lifestyle preferences that differ from those of the larger culture. In the case of rape, it has been suggested that norms and values that condone, and in some cases glorify, sexual violence are institutionalized in the subculture and subsequently passed on through the intergenerational transmission of knowledge. Menachem Amir's (1971) study of rape and rapists in Philadelphia was the first empirical application of this theory, and his work was used extensively by Susan Brownmiller, who further legitimated the rape subculture perspective in her classic feminist tome *Against Our Will: Men, Women and Rape* (1975).

Rape Subculture Theory: Controversy and Critique

Major critiques of the subcultural perspective revolve around its race and class bias. The literature that explores the prevalence of rape in various social categories finds that this crime cuts across race and class boundaries. This becomes particularly clear when the phenomena of acquaintance rape and rape in marriage are taken into account. Evidence from victimization studies supports a model of violent criminality in which race is significant; however, "conduct" variables such as previous criminal record account for more variance than "status" variables such as race (Hindelang 1981, 461). Although economic and social stressors contribute to the victimization process, sociologists have argued that the disproportionately higher rates of reported rapes in lower-class and racial-ethnic communities more likely indicate oversurveillance by criminal-justice authorities, as well as underreporting among the middle and upper classes (Hindelang 1981). Moreover, by focusing on communities traditionally labeled deviant by dominant institutions, we obscure the levels of sexual violence in the larger society (Andersen 1993). This focus also serves to deemphasize the significance of societally produced male gender role socialization and the societal commodification of female sexuality as major precipitators of rape. Thus, subculture of violence theories have been dismissed as insufficient at best, and biased at worst, in their capacity to explain the phenomenon of rape. Indeed, the only scenario in which the term *subculture* is used unabashedly to explain rape behavior is the prison world of male-on-male rape.

The controversial nature of the subcultural theory of rape has contributed to its inadequate scrutiny (Baron, Straus, and Jaffe 1988). Baron and Straus suggest that use of the term *subculture* is problematic both for measurement reasons and because the norms that legitimate violence are widely diffused (1989, 149). Although they suggest that certain groups may institutionalize cultural support for violence more than others, their efforts are applied toward a state-level, rather than micro-level, analysis.

Bringing Gender In

I would agree that we have not sufficiently tested rape subculture theory. I would argue, however, that we have cast it aside without realizing the major problem with its application to the study of rape. The problem is that we have taken a predominantly gender-neutral frame of reference and applied it unaltered to a gendered phenomenon. Classic deviant subculture theory has focused primarily on lower-class, urban, and often racial-ethnic males; yet, in applying this theory to rape, it is the class and ethnicity—not the maleness—of the perpetrators that have been most accountable for the behavior. The rape behavior itself is but one item on a laundry list of other criminal activities that characterize these groups.

It may be time to revisit rape subculture theory using the vehicle of gender analysis. Bombarded by images of women as toys and violence as erotic, "everyman" may indeed have the capacity to rape; but every man does not rape. Indeed, a spate of recent contextualized studies of rape suggest that there may be clusters of individuals whose in-group identification and ritual behaviors may fit the sociological definition of subculture, although the literature stops short of defining them as such. These are masculinist subcultures, which may cut across race and class but share the signatory characteristics of hypermasculinity and the glorification of coercive sexuality. Nestled within the sex/gender system of the larger culture and specific patriarchal institutions, masculinist subcultures appear to flourish, even as the feminist movement, the U.S. Congress, local crime units, and college campuses focus increasingly on creating strategies to prevent rape.

Masculinity and Violence in Theory and Practice

Social scientists have long identified dichotomous sets of behavioral characteristics associated with masculinity and femininity that operate in instrumental and relational contexts. Shaped by conscious and unconscious learning processes, as well as the structure of institutions, traditional Western masculinity is constructed with heavy emphasis on rationality, competition, athleticism, financial success, aggression, control over emotion, and heterosexuality. Michael Kaufman (this volume) suggests that the requirements of masculinity reproduce and reinforce a "triad" of men's violence: against women, other men, and self.

Observable as these traits may be, however, there has been a problematic tendency to conceptualize masculinity as a rigid monolith. R. W. Connell's (1987) theory of masculinity is particularly useful for understanding both the social processes through which variant forms of masculinity are constructed and the ways in which violence becomes both an ideological and practical component of many—but not all—men's lives.

Connell suggests that at any given historical moment there exists at a societal level an ordering of masculinity and femininity that produces controlling conceptualizations for public consumption (1987, 183). This ordering is rooted in the structural dominance of men over women. The dominant, "stylized" prescriptions, while generally inconsistent with the observable variety of existent behaviors and beliefs, nonetheless serve as the ideological basis for social relations. The socially constructed ideal for men, *hegemonic masculinity,* is more rigid and controlling than what he refers to as *emphasized femininity,* which has a variety of acceptable forms. The various nonconformist and subordinated masculinities that exist are greatly devalued; thus, men in our culture, more so than women, have a stake in conformity to the dominant masculine ideal: to be perceived as less than a "real man" places one in the position of being equated with the globally subordinate female.

Peer pressure is a strong influence in the acquisition and display of masculinity. It is already operating in the sex talk and dirty play of preadolescent little-leaguers studied by Gary Alan Fine (1986) and the marauding school boys invading girls' turf in the schoolyards observed by Barrie Thorne (1993). Such youngsters are acting on their perceptions of the gender order; but as children, they lack many of the resources necessary to fully emulate the dominant model. Given that physical strength and prowess can be called upon to claim masculinity, however, violence is learned early and often retrieved from the tool kit of masculinity to prove manhood when social power or financial resources are inaccessible.

What the research literature on masculinity has yet to uncover are the events that may occur in the transition from exploratory peer group to full-blown masculinist subculture, and why some boys and men circumvent such groups in their selectively internalized construction of masculinity. Traditional deviant subculture theory has asked all the wrong questions about gender (Messerschmidt 1993), and rape subculture theory so far has asked too few.

Identifying Male Rape Subcultures

Over the years, studies of rape perpetrators have focused primarily on likelihood of raping, belief in rape myths, sexual history, attitudes toward women, motivation, race, and means of forcing sex (Bourque 1989). Associating peer-group pressure with coercive sexuality among males is not new, but until quite recently it has been underanalyzed. S. S. Ageton's (1983) three-year analysis of data from the National Youth Survey found that rapists in the sample were more likely than nonoffenders to be involved with delinquent peers. Offenders also differed from their nonoffending counterparts in their attitudes that legitimated rape and sexual assault. The extent to which the attitudes and behaviors associated with peer-group affiliation may be directly related to rape behavior cannot be gauged. Eugene J. Kanin's (1985) analysis of date rapists shows that 41 percent of self-identified rapists participated in gang rapes and 85 percent reported considerable or great pressure from peers to be heterosexually active; yet contextualized analysis that might dovetail with these findings in the development of a subcultural explanation for the proliferation of date and gang rapes in contemporary U.S. society has not emerged.

J. W. Messerschmidt (1993), in a groundbreaking profeminist analysis of masculinity and crime, has developed the first systematic criminological theory to extensively integrate an analysis of masculinity. He suggests that "because men situationally accomplish masculinity in response to their socially constructed circumstances, various forms of crime can serve as suitable resources for doing masculinity within the specific social contexts of the street, the workplace, and the family" (1993, 119). In looking at incidents such as the gang rape of a jogger in Central Park in 1989, Messerschmidt, using Connell's framework as a basis for his analysis, suggests that gang rapes are "simply resources for demonstrating essential 'male nature' when more conventional means are unavailable" (1993, 115). Although Messerschmidt provides significant insight by identifying the functions of group rape in solidifying alliances and facilitating intragroup masculinity contests, his examples focus primarily on the lower and working classes; thus, while he contends that such events are not race and class specific, his important work suffers due to the invisibility of privileged offenders in the sociological casebook. In addition, we still understand little about the peer-group affiliations of single-offender rapists through this analysis.

Recent social scientific studies and media accounts of sexual aggression in college fraternities and among members of male sports teams provide the first significant empirical examples from which we can begin to develop a gender-based, rather than class-based, subculture of rape theory. These studies identify groups with clear and defining boundary characteristics that have institutionalized normative systems and rituals prescribing sexual coercion as central aspects of subcultural identity and existence. Indeed, adherence to the norms and participation in the rituals are often qualifications for group initiation and ongoing membership.

The Fraternity Subculture

Colleges and universities are the settings for an increasing number of sexual assaults: rapes by members of the campus community, rapes by strangers, date rapes, and gang or "party" rapes (Bohmer and Parrot 1993). While the likelihood of committing sexual assault increases among residents of various all-male housing units, research on assailants suggests that it is fraternity pledges who are most likely to rape on campus (Koss, cited in Bohmer and Parrot 1993, 21–22). Two in-depth studies of fraternity involvement in ritual gang-rape behavior provide context for understanding this finding. Patricia Yancey Martin and Robert A. Hummer (1989) formulate an organizational perspective for understanding rape in fraternities, within which the social construction of brotherhood involves value for traditional masculinity and a normative structure that promotes loyalty, secrecy, and group protection. During the pledge process, fraternities require recruits to participate in a variety of ritual practices, not unlike those used in military boot camps, that identify athletic masculinity and require subordination of self to the group. Pledges are also evaluated on their social ability with women, and sexual access to women is an advertised benefit of group membership in the recruitment process (1989, 468).

Once accepted into the brotherhood, a complex system of norms and rituals influences the behavior of members. Martin and Hummer suggest that secret rituals, handshakes, and mottoes function to maintain group boundaries and exemplify the expectation of loyalty among brothers (1989, 464). Norms defining women as servers and sexual prey become translated into sexual aggression when fused with those prescribing the use of alcohol, violent behavior, and competition.

Peggy Reeves Sanday's (1990) research characterizes the group rape as a ritual bonding activity of men in fraternities. The purpose of the activity is less to achieve sexual gratification than it is to affirm the shared masculinity and brotherhood of members. Men in Sanday's study considered "pulling train" or the "express," in which brothers line up to take their turn having sex with a (usually) intoxicated woman, a routine aspect of their "little sister" program (1990, 7).

Sanday describes the gang rape as a collective phenomenon, made possible by the loss of individual identity during initiation ritual. In citing the example of one male informant, she suggests, "The experiences [he] endured provide powerful evidence for the suggestion that personhood, in this case defined in terms of the brotherhood, is socially constructed" (1990, 137). Pledges are routinely ridiculed as sexually inadequate until admitted as members. They are treated as "despised women" and referred to in terms demeaning them as homosexuals. Many initiation rituals are designed to cleanse these inadequacies; thus, Sanday argues that the successful pledge is stamped with two collective images: the purified body accepted into brotherhood and the despised and dirty feminine (1990, 155–56).

Both of these studies provide evidence of strong boundary maintenance, including hostility toward out-group members, secret rituals, "groupthink," and shared normative systems that are overtly and overwhelmingly preoccupied with hypermasculinity. Although the gang rape is conceptualized in these analyses as a logical outcome of the fraternity culture, Robin Warshaw (1988) emphasizes that more one-on-one rapes occur in fraternity houses than gang rapes. We can nonetheless hypothesize that the subcultural norms regarding masculinity and femininity in conjunction with the promise of secrecy and protection by brothers contribute to date rapes as well.

The Sport Subculture

With respect to campus rapes, the second most implicated category of assailants is college athletes (Bohmer and Parrot 1993). A recent report suggested that NCAA basketball and football players were reported to the police for committing sexual assaults 38 percent more than males in the general college population, averaging one report of an athlete for sexual assault every eighteen days between 1983 and 1986 (Hoffman 1986). In a study of locker-room discourse among members of two "big time" college sport teams, Curry (1991) identifies a pattern of fraternal bonding not unlike that characterizing the fraternities described above. A similar preoccupation with masculinity, defined rigidly through physical prowess and heterosexual performance, results in locker-room talk that dehumanizes women and promotes rape. Warshaw (1988, 112) similarly finds athletic teams to be "breeding grounds" for rape: "They are organizations which pride themselves on the physical aggressiveness of their members and which demand group loyalty and reinforce it through promoting the superiority of their members over outsiders." As with fraternities, the gang rape among athletes is conceptualized by Warshaw as "group sex," in effect a homoerotic bonding of members to each other where the woman involved is no more than an instrument through which the ritual activity is enabled.

Colleges are not the only contexts within which male sport subcultures can emerge. Examples abound from high school through the professional sports. The recent case of the "Spur Posse" in Lakewood, California, a predominantly White suburban area, exemplifies the ways in which sexual performance becomes a membership criterion for participants. The posse is a group of twenty to thirty Lakewood High School athletes, nine of whom were accused of raping and molesting girls as young as ten years old (Gross 1993). Although the gang had been involved in other delinquent behaviors, it came into the national spotlight when it was revealed that the sexual assaults were linked to an ongoing masculinity contest wherein each act of sexual intercourse—consensual or forced—resulted in a point in the tally (Mydans 1993). The self-proclaimed high-scorer of the group had accumulated sixty-six points by the time of the arrests (Gross 1993).

Fraternities and sports teams provide a starting point from which other male institutions can be explored. Each of the above examples provides insight into male groups with distinct boundaries, as well as value systems, ritual activities, and discourses that promote sexual aggression as a qualification of initiation and ongoing membership.

Such characteristics are routinely analyzed in conjunction with subcultural affiliation in the sociological literature.

Another potential arena for applying a subcultural perspective is the U.S. military, which has received increasing public and governmental scrutiny since media exposure of the 1991 Tailhook assault of female Naval officers by their peers and superordinates. The extent to which such events are stimulated by the peer-group affiliation of assailants would be an interesting case to explore. The emergence of information about ritual sexual abuse in pseudoreligious contexts, for example, could also be analyzed from a subcultural perspective. Thus far, the academic discourse has been primarily restricted to the heated debates of psychotherapists over the reality of this phenomenon.

Other subcultures detached from such institutional frameworks, but equally dangerous, might be identified and analyzed. In her foreword to Sanday's *Fraternity Gang Rape,* Judge Lois G. Forer describes patterns across a number of multiple-offender rape cases that have come before her: all the participants could be said to be members of "gangs," all were operating on their own "turf," consumed large quantities of alcohol, and had sex with their victims in the presence of the group (1990, xiv). The gangs described ranged from unemployed inner-city youths to married buddies whose weekly "night out" was a ritual of rape in the park with a young woman picked up by a member for a date.

The increase of information about such cases strengthens the potential value of a subcultural perspective to inform future research on rape. Further support comes from the existence of "good guys." Martin and Hummer (1989) tell us that some fraternity pledges withdraw from fraternity recruitment drives by choice; not all team athletes become involved in subcultural bonding and ritual activities. Many other men show no preference for either activity. Presumably some of these men may become involved in coercive sexuality; some will not. It is the extent to which peers—and centrally, peers in close-knit, primary group contexts—develop a subcultural existence that highlights heterosexual and violent masculinity that needs to be further explored.

Methodological Implications of a Masculinist Rape Subculture Model

Sociological understanding of the subcultural groups specified, as well as the identification of other groups as subcultural entities, requires theoretical attention to the merits of subcultural theory when fused with the other existing and legitimated theories of rape. In addition, empirical testing of hypotheses about the correlation of male subcultures with the widespread proliferation of sexual violence requires important considerations with respect to research design and data analysis. The methodological implications of such a theoretical perspective, for example, beg us to question the usefulness of crime statistics, including demographic and geographical characteristics, in explaining rape. These statistics provide only surface information and are insufficient without being integrated with more micro-level contextual analyses. Baron and Straus (1989) suggest that a major failing of rape research has been the search for a single cause. A multicausal explanation might benefit strongly from inclusion of a masculinist subculture perspective with the dominant models of gender socialization and political-economic theory.

The plausibility of a gender-based subcultural analysis, teamed with the necessity of facilitating social change, requires more context-specific analysis of rape and the formulation of research questions about group affiliation and pressure. What conditions facilitate the emergence of rape subcultures and provide them with members? Why do some men resist such group affiliation? What normative patterns, rituals activities and discourses, boundary-maintenance mechanisms, and other group characteristics set these subcultures apart from conventional male friendship groups? How many rapes — stranger or acquaintance, single assailant or multiple offender — can we begin to attribute to the group affiliation of perpetrators? Where and under what conditions do such rapes occur? These questions conceivably can be integrated into survey research among victims and self-reported perpetrators, as well as in more qualitative analyses involving fieldwork; but they are questions that need to be asked and in a more systematic manner than we have asked them thus far.

Rape subculture theory deserves another round of exploratory research. Stripped from the controversial grip of race and class bias, we may come to learn important information about sexual violence that not only will enhance our sociological understanding of rape but will be central in finding solutions to this escalating social problem.

Chapter Thirteen

What the West Failed to Learn about War from the "Comfort Women"

Margaret D. Stetz

After nearly fifty years of bearing their psychic and physical scars in secret, the survivors of Japan's system of World War II military sexual slavery began to testify publicly about the war crimes that were committed against them. Starting in 1991 with Kim Hak Sun, a so-called "comfort woman" from the Republic of Korea, these courageous women recounted their histories from a half-century earlier: stories of forced confinement in brothels after abduction or coercion and of countless daily rapes, over periods of months and sometimes years, by soldiers of the Japanese Imperial Army. Ever since they came forward—from the Philippines, Indonesia, Taiwan, China, Burma, Malaysia, and especially from Korea, the home country of the largest number of victims—the world has heard in explicit detail about their sexual abuse. This egregious sexual violence was authorized by governmental policies that reflected not only racism but also misogyny and contempt for members of the powerless socioeconomic classes from which many of the women came.

In light of the decade and a half in which details about the experiences of these former military sex slaves have circulated around the globe, we can see quite clearly the effect that their testimony has had in some areas, as well as the absence of effect in others. The positive results of their having come forward are obvious. These include the narrow and specific—the identification of several surviving Japanese officials responsible for instituting and/or overseeing the "comfort system" and thus the December 1996 ban by the Department of Justice under President Bill Clinton on allowing these war criminals entry into the United States (Lee 2001, 152–53). But the farther-reaching consequences include the momentous step taken for the first time in June 1996 by the International Criminal Tribunal of the Hague to prosecute wartime rape as a crime against humanity (Stetz 2001, 95). Without the "comfort women's" insistence on the need for a new view of the heinous nature of organized sexual violence during war, the stories of more-recent rape victims happening in 2005–6 in Sudan might not have been treated as seriously by the international community.

At the same time, however, we must also reflect on the widespread failure of governments in general and military institutions in particular to learn the lessons that the survivors have communicated so bravely, at such cost to themselves. These lessons include the need for governments to be accountable for the actions of their agents in authorizing, condoning, or committing rape and then to articulate and demonstrate their accountability to future generations. Perhaps most appalling has been the refusal of Japan to accept full legal responsibility and so to issue official governmental apologies (as opposed to personal apologies by various prime ministers), as well as to offer government-sponsored reparations (as opposed to charity from privately collected funds) to the survivors. Many of us know about the repeated dismissals of the "comfort women's" lawsuits in a variety of Japanese courts (Stetz 2002, 28). Most of us are aware, too, of the continuing struggles to write into all Japanese students' textbooks more complete and accurate accounts of the victimization of Asian women by the emperor's forces before and during World War II, and we have heard of the opposition by Japanese nationalists to this truth telling. In April 2005, the nationalists' effort to prevent full historical disclosure in textbooks, along with the Japanese prime minister's continuing visits to the Yasukuni shrine, which houses the ashes of war criminals, unleashed passionate and sometimes violent protests in Korea and especially in China that threatened diplomatic relations across Asia (Cody 2005, A12).

I would like, however, to focus on the failures of countries other than Japan to learn from the "comfort women's" stories. Rather than blaming Japan alone, we should turn our attention to nations in a different region, one that has been every bit as guilty of choosing not to render justice to the survivors and of ignoring the implications of their testimony about war, militarism, sexual abuse, and exploitation. I refer to the West. I am speaking not merely of the denials of claims filed by the survivors in Western courts, especially in the United States, or of the opposition to those lawsuits by the U.S. State Department under President George W. Bush (Stetz 2002, 26–28). I mean instead to point a finger at the ways in which institutions such as the U.S. military, both at home and abroad, have failed to learn—indeed, have rarely even tried to learn—the important lessons taught by the "comfort women's" experiences. This is not a Western problem alone, for, at the same time, international entities, such as the United Nations' peacekeeping forces, have also shown a shameful disregard of the truths evident from the "comfort women's" stories and have instead reenacted the patterns of sexual assault, exploitation, and trafficking of women in combat areas.

Why, we might ask first, have so many governmental and nongovernmental bodies alike felt free to shut their ears to the "comfort women's" teachings? It is not as though the survivors of World War II sexual slavery have been invisible since Kim Hak Sun came forward. On the contrary, they have been the subject of innumerable journalistic profiles in newspapers and magazines, memoirs and oral histories published in books, television and cinematic documentaries, academic studies, stage plays, novels, photographic exhibitions, and even art installations.[1] To pay no heed to the significance of the stories the former "comfort women" have repeated again and again has required a conscious effort. Fueling that effort, however, have been two potent ideologies: sexism and racism. In all parts of the world, women's voices, women's complaints, and women's sufferings matter less than those of men, especially when it comes to the making of policy. In the West, moreover, the concept of listening to Asian women (let alone poor and relatively uneducated Asian women) as sources of information, wisdom, and advice about military matters is utterly unknown. Most of what the former "comfort women" have had to say about what happens during wartime when men are given limitless power over women's bodies and the authorization, whether explicit or tacit, to commit rape has gone unheeded.

If any single survivor's voice, however, did have the potential to break through Western indifference, it was that of Jan Ruff-O'Herne. Almost uniquely among the perhaps two hundred thousand women in Asia who were kidnapped, coerced, or recruited through trickery and imprisoned in Japanese military brothels, Jan Ruff-O'Herne was white, educated, from a privileged background, and an English speaker. As a woman of Dutch extraction who grew up in what later became Indonesia and who lived after World War II in both England and Australia, she has been a figure with great appeal to Western audiences. A strong believer in colonialism, she has spoken in idyllic terms of life in Java before Indonesian independence and has lent support to conservative currents of nostalgia for white Western rule. At the same time, however, her history as a former "comfort woman" has given her a unique sense of solidarity with Asian women that makes her views appealing to progressive, antiracist readers, too. Her 1994 memoir, *50 Years of Silence*, was published in Sydney, Amsterdam, and New York and, therefore, reached audiences on three continents. A documentary of the same name, based on her autobiography, enjoyed wide release and even played repeatedly across the United States on television stations owned by the Corporation for Public Broadcasting.

There were certainly important lessons for those in positions of power to absorb from the account of her experiences in the 1940s, had political or military officials in the West cared to receive them. Chief among them involved the reports of what happened to Ruff-O'Herne after her Japanese military captors suddenly released her and several other white women from the Semarang military brothel, where she was raped daily for three months, and sent her, along with the others, to a regular prison camp. The war was nearing an end, and it was clear that the Japanese high command was concerned about the possibility of an Allied victory and thus with the consequences of Allied troops finding white women being subjected to rape. What occurred next is of tremendous significance to the understanding of issues involving wartime sexual violence. As Ruff-O'Herne tells her readers,

> One of the Japanese guards entered the house of one of the women at night. At first he made out that he had come for a chat and to do some trading. Then, suddenly, he turned on her and tried to rape her. Obviously he knew where we had come from and must have thought we were an easy target. There followed a lot of screaming and shouting and uproar and the soldier disappeared into the night.
>
> The incident of this attempted rape was immediately reported to the camp commandant. At morning roll call, one of the Japanese guards was called and ordered to stand in the centre of the compound. The commandant marched up to him and dressed him down severely in a language we could not understand.
>
> The guard stood there, terrified. The commandant then took out his revolver and handed it to the guard. The poor man was then forced to shoot himself through the mouth. (Ruff-O'Herne 1994, 113–14)

Ruff-O'Herne's account offers clear proof, first, that whether or not soldiers rape women and otherwise abuse prisoners during wartime is not merely a matter of individual desire, volition, or impulse; it is instead a reflection of military policy. So-called sex acts are, like all acts performed by soldiers who live under a chain of command, reflections of decisions made at a higher level. As Ruff-O'Herne notes in commenting on this incident, "A short while ago we had been raped by at least ten Japanese a day, with the approval of the Japanese Emperor, Hirohito, the Kempeitai [Japanese military police], and the highest military authorities. Now this man was forced to shoot himself for trying to do exactly the same thing" (114). In other words, the sexual assault of women occurred when—and only when—it suited the purposes of the military authorities and of the government that backed those authorities. The story that Ruff-O'Herne tells also gives the lie to the defense often used by those who attempt to rationalize or excuse the existence of forced prostitution or rape as a necessary "outlet" for soldiers in times of combat. Having access to women's bodies, even though this may be against the will of the women themselves, is (as the misogynist argument goes) a morale booster; therefore, military authorities set up brothels, allow brothels to be established near bases, or turn a blind eye to instances of rape in general, because they supposedly are concerned above all with the morale of their troops.

It is clear, however, that nothing could be more demoralizing for his comrades than to witness a soldier being forced to execute himself. In Ruff-O'Herne's anecdote, the commander of the prison camp was not in the least interested in protecting the other soldiers' morale; he was interested only in reminding them that, in the face of an impending Allied invasion and possible Japanese surrender, raping white women was against orders, and the price of disobeying any order was death. Matters of sexuality did not occupy a space apart from ordinary questions of discipline, obedience, and military or governmental policy. On the contrary, they were as much under scrutiny and control as any other questions of conduct.

The Imperial Japanese Army did indeed regulate rape. Apart from exceptional moments, such as the one that Ruff-O'Herne records, when military authorities prohibited a specific rape, they created the conditions under which sexual abuse was permitted, encouraged, and even required. They also determined who the victims would be, for the "comfort system," as it was called, was integrally tied to racist notions of the inferiority of all Asian populations other than the Japanese and thus of the suitability of non-Japanese women for sexual exploitation. Most of the roughly two hundred thousand Asian women believed to have been used as military sex slaves belonged, therefore, to nations and ethnic groups that Japanese racial ideology defined as "lower." As Bonnie B. C. Oh explains, "racial hierarchy . . . was determined by the skin color and by the geographical proximity of their native land to Japan." Korean women ranked below Okinawans, "Then came the Taiwanese, Chinese, the Filipinas, and so on" (Oh 2001, 10).

In her classic feminist polemic *Bananas, Beaches and Bases,* Cynthia Enloe reminded readers that, more often than not, what "passes for inevitable, inherent, 'traditional' or biological has in fact been *made*" (Enloe 1990, 3; emphasis in original). This is certainly true of military sexual violence. When armed forces commit rape, there is nothing "natural" or biologically necessary about it. Military rape of women not only becomes inevitable; it is deliberately *made* inevitable, when the following conditions are in place: (1) when male soldiers feel that they have limitless power over women (whether civilian women or even women in the military); (2) when they believe themselves racially, ethnically, religiously, or otherwise distinct from and superior to women under their control and/or believe that gender alone constitutes a hierarchical difference sufficient to excuse their abuse of the subordinate party; and (3) when they are convinced that they are acting with the approval of those higher up (whether in the military itself or within the government), even while they are violating international law. To allow these conditions to exist is not merely to invite sexual violence but to promote it.

These are some of the lessons that the West could have learned—indeed, should have learned—from the testimony offered, at great price, by the elderly and often infirm women who have come forward since the early 1990s. They have spoken out at hearings, unofficial tribunals, press conferences, marches, protest rallies, and other gatherings, all of which have been covered by a variety of media. Conclusions based on their experiences have also circulated in a report issued to the United Nations Commission on Human Rights in 1996 by Radhika Coomaraswamy, the UN's Special Rapporteur on Violence against Women (Lee 2001, 156–57). Because officials around the globe, especially military officials, have refused to pay attention, we have seen new and increasingly horrific episodes of sexual victimization arising out of every combat situation in the past two decades. Whether we look to recent or current wars in the Middle East and in Africa, each time another example of war-related sexual violence or sexual exploitation by military forces is exposed to public view, authorities throw up their hands and feign surprise, instead of admitting that they could have predicted and prevented these occurrences, given the understanding of history that the "comfort women's" stories provide.

The United Nations and the United States alike have in practical terms turned their backs on the situation in Darfur, where, from 2003 through 2006, there has been mass rape of Black Sudanese women committed by non-Black Sudanese militia (known as the "Janjawid") with government backing. According to Lisa Alvy, writing for the *National NOW Times*, using information supplied by Amnesty International, the crimes against women in Darfur have included being "forced into sexual slavery" (Alvy 2004/2005, 13). In this new setting, the old sufferings of the "comfort women" of World War II repeat themselves.

Meanwhile, in the war that raged throughout Congo for a decade from the mid-1990s onward, "Congolese women have been victims of rape on a scale never seen before," as each of the "dozens of armed groups in this war has used rape" (Nolen 2005, 56). Perhaps more appalling, though quite predictable, have been the developments in Congo following the implementation of a UN-backed peace accord among the warring factions. As revealed by the *Washington Post* in November 2004, "Sexual exploitation of women and girls by U.N. peacekeepers and bureaucrats in the U.N. mission in Congo 'appears to be significant, wide-spread and ongoing,' according to a confidential U.N. report that documents cases of pedophilia, prostitution and rape" (Lynch 2004, A27). In Congo, the very soldiers who were put in place to bring a bloody conflict to a halt have used their mission as an opportunity to abuse the civilian population in numerous ways, including sexually. Although the UN code of conduct forbids such conduct, it does not enforce its own rules; the home countries from which the soldiers come "are responsible for punishing any of their military personnel who violate the code while taking part in a United Nations peacekeeping mission" (Lacey 2004, A8). Given unlimited power over destitute Black African women (as well as children) and an absence of oversight or accountability for their actions, the international peacekeeping forces in Congo, who come from fifty nations, have felt free to commit rape with impunity.

Allegations of rape involving those charged with establishing order have not been confined to the African continent. In the war in Iraq, civilian Iraqi women have accused U.S. soldiers on a variety of occasions of sexual assault. Quoting reports published in the *Guardian* newspaper in Britain, the feminist journal *Off Our Backs* has cited transcripts of U.S. Army investigations into thirteen alleged rapes by American servicemen, none of which, however, has resulted in any action being taken against those accused ("News: Iraq" 2005, 7–8).

The picture is scarcely better for American servicewomen in Kuwait, Afghanistan, and Iraq, a number of whom have been targets of rape by their male colleagues. As Ann Scott Tyson wrote in May 2005 in the *Washington Post*, "Reported sexual assaults have risen in the Central Command region, which includes the Middle East and Central Asia, from 24 in 2002 and 94 in 2003 to 123 in 2004, according to figures the Miles Foundation obtained from the Pentagon's Joint Task Force on Sexual Assault Prevention and Response" (Tyson 2005, A3). Although these figures include assaults by men on other men, women make up the majority of rape victims.

If the news from the American theater of action seems bleak, it is equally grim for servicewomen still in the United States during a time of war. In August 2003, the *New York Times* revealed that the rate of rape reported through a survey at the U.S. Air Force Academy alone was put at 12 percent of all women cadets—"a problem of sexual assault that they [women cadets who spoke out] described as widespread and the product of a culture hostile toward women. The women said victims of rape who came forward were routinely punished for minor infractions while their attackers escaped judgment, prompting most victims to remain silent." At the same time, "nearly 70 percent" of the 579 women who responded to the survey "said they had been the victims of sexual harassment" (Schemo 2003, A11).

To ignore the stories of such women is to leave all women in warfare—indeed, all women everywhere—less secure. Sexual violence is not confined to the Air Force Academy, for a follow-up study in spring 2004 brought to public attention the grave danger to women enrolled in the army and naval academies, as well. Thus, Daniel De Vise stated in the *Washington Post*, "One female student in seven attending the nation's military academies last spring said she had been sexually assaulted since becoming a cadet or midshipman, according to a report on the first survey of sexual misconduct on the three campuses released yesterday by the Defense Department" (De Vise 2005, A1). In the U.S. military, gender itself is still a difference that equals inferiority of status. As the "comfort women's" stories suggest to any observer willing to learn from them, wherever women are perceived as inferior to and of less worth than military men, the conditions are in place for sexual violence. Being at war, moreover, increases the likelihood of male military violence against women, including the abuse of women married to soldiers, as Cynthia Enloe has suggested in her examination of U.S. Defense Department records of domestic violence in military households (Enloe 2000, 189). The distressing realities of harassment and rape uncovered by the recent surveys of U.S. military institutions were easy to anticipate.

Through their bravery and selflessness in bringing to light the terrible war crimes committed against them during World War II, the aged survivors of Japan's "comfort system" have achieved immense success. Because of them, wartime rape and forced prostitution are now subjects reported regularly in the world press, as well as documented and protested by large numbers of human rights organizations and feminist groups. Unfortunately, though, despite their best efforts, the former "comfort women" continue to have little or no effect on military culture in the West, which remains unaltered in its view of women's bodies (those of both civilian and military women) and of sexual access to those bodies as rightfully under the control of military men.

Against all odds, the Asian women who have testified publicly since the early 1990s have tried to create an important legacy of information and knowledge and thus to prevent future abuses. Given their advanced age, with many of them now in their eighties, they soon will be unable to continue speaking out and passing on their wisdom. That they already have been marginalized and swept aside by the military and governmental institutions that most need to learn from their words is more than merely a matter for regret; it is an incalculable loss for women's human rights and a threat to human security in general.

NOTE

1. A brief list of these would include special issues of academic journals, such as the 1997 issue of *Positions: East Asia Cultural Critique*; volumes of historical studies, such as George Hicks's *The Comfort Women* (1994) and Yuki Tanaka's *Japan's Comfort Women* (2002); volumes of survivors' testimonies, such as Keith Howard's *True Stories of the Korean Comfort Women* (1995), the edited collection produced by the Washington Coalition for Comfort Women Issues, Inc., called *Comfort Women Speak* (2000), and Maria Rosa Henson's autobiography, *Comfort Woman* (1999); films and documentaries, such as Christine Choy and Nancy Tong's *In the Name of the Emperor* (1995) and Dai Sil Kim-Gibson's *Silence Broken* (1999); novels, such as Nora Okja Keller's *Comfort Woman* (1997) and Therese Park's *A Gift of the Emperor* (1997); Chungmi Kim's drama *Comfort Women*, which was performed at the Urban Stages Theatre in New York City (2004); visual works and installations by artists such as Taeko Tomiyama, Yoshiko Shimada, Miran Kim, and Mona Higuchi; displays of photographs, such as those exhibited in Washington, D.C., at Georgetown University's Leavey Center in 1996 and at the Cannon Office Building of the U.S. House of Representatives in 1998.

Chapter Fourteen

Undeclared War
African-American Women Writers Explicating Rape

Opal Palmer Adisa

Preamble

Slavery was a war, and the bodies of Africans were the battlefield. African women, men, and children were held captive in the holds of ships when brought to these shores. Stripped, poked, fondled, and teeth-counted, they were sold on auction blocks. They worked from sunrise to sunset in the cotton and cane fields of the Americas, were tied to stakes, and had designs beaten into their bodies. African people were lynched for plotting to escape, for insubordination, for asserting their humanity.

The war waged against African women under slavery was particularly insidious because, in addition to other forms of physical abuse, rape was used as the major means of control. This manifestation of white men's misogynistic attitude towards slave women resulted in miscegenation. In addition, slave women, although clearly the victims of this abuse, were labeled promiscuous and salacious. However, contrary to what scholars like Eugene D. Genovese (1974) have suggested about the great love affair between masters and their slave women, there is little tangible evidence to support such a claim. Angela Davis (1983) notes how some scholars have ignored the testimonies of slave women.

> Despite the testimonies of slaves about the high incidence of rape and sexual coercion, the issue of sexual abuse has been all but glossed over in the traditional literature on slavery. It is sometimes even assumed that slave women welcomed and encouraged the sexual attention of white men. What happened between them, therefore, was not sexual exploitation, but rather "miscegenation." (Davis 1983, 25)

What power did a slave woman have to voice her abuse? Who would have listened to her? What laws were there to protect her? Slave women were muted by their debased social status.

> The two freest people in America are the white man and the black woman. (Anonymous)

From *Women's Studies International Forum* 15, no. 3 (1992): 363–74. Elsevier Science Ltd., Pergamon Imprint, Oxford, UK. Reprinted by permission.

The above statement represents an attempt to obfuscate and demean the suffering that African-American women have had and continue to experience as second-class citizens of the United States. Freedom was never something for which a slave woman could barter, for even when she was granted a modicum of mobility, she was still subjected to the sexual will of any white man. The Black woman's "freer" status is based on a myth which we must reject in order to understand more fully the true circumstances in which she lives. From the moment a woman was captured on the coast of West Africa, her body became a battlefield that she constantly tried to wrest from the master's control.

One need only read *Incidents in the Life of a Slave Girl* (1973 [1861]), the autobiography of Linda Brent, to understand the precarious fate of most female slaves. Brent writes, "But I now entered on my fifteenth year—a sad epoch in the life of a slave girl. My master began to whisper foul words in my ear. Young as I was, I could not remain ignorant of their import" (26). The fact that Brent was only fifteen, and her master, an established medical doctor with a wife, did not prevent him from wielding his power over her, stalking her, and making it clear to her how completely powerless she was: "My master met me at every turn, reminding me that I belonged to him, and swearing by heaven and earth that he would compel me to submit to him" (27). Brent's experience illustrates how the majority of African-American women were thrust into battle with few weapons. They not only relied upon resilience and cunning to avoid their masters for as long as possible, but also to stay clear of jealous mistresses who took every opportunity to vent their anger and frustration on hapless slaves.

Given the context of slavery, a war in which the targeted group was forcibly removed from its home, thrust into a foreign environment, forced to learn a new language, and forbidden to use arms in its defense, rape was, as Angela Davis puts it, "an unveiled element of counter-insurgency" (1971, 12). For slaves, to organize openly was tantamount to signing one's death warrant. By raping the Black woman, not only did the white master violate her in the most devastating way, he also revealed the impotency of the entire slave community. "Rape is the act of the conqueror," Susan Brownmiller (1975, 35) asserts. But the significance of the act extends past sheer aggression because it was intended not only to assert control over Black women but also to dehumanize and reduce them to the level of animals.

Realizing that it would be cheaper and more convenient to "breed" one's own slave rather than rely on the dying slave trade, plantation owners further reduced slave women to the status of breeders. Brownmiller (1975) reviews the historical context:

> Since it was the slaveholding class that created the language and wrote the laws pertaining to slavery, it was not surprising that legally the concept of raping a slave simply did not exist. One cannot rape one's own property. The rape of one man's slave by another white man was considered a mere "trespass" in the eyes of the plantation law. The rape of one man's slave by another slave had no official recognition in law at all. (162–163)

After two hundred years of continuous abuse, African-American women became adept at spotting a rapist. Although they could not always circumvent being raped, they devised ways to endure it, and they hemmed alertness into their skirts.

As with the slave woman, rape remained one of life's hazards for the emancipated African-American woman. The short-lived political and economic gains of

Reconstruction were countered by the tyranny of the Ku Klux Klan that burned homes, lynched men, and raped women of the African-American community. Testimonies gathered from African-American men and women after the Memphis Riots, 1865, dramatically reveal the inextricable linking of lynching, home burning, and raping of women. Frances Thompson, testifying in 1865 before the chairman appointed to investigate the damage done to the community after the riots, reports thus:

> They drew their pistols and said they would shoot us and fire the house if we did not let them have their way with us. All seven of the men violated us two. Four of them had to do with me, and the rest with Lucy. (Thompson 1973, 174)

Earlier in her testimony to the chairman, Frances Thompson testified that two of the seven men were police; she saw their stars. Even after slavery, African-American people had little or no protection under the law and were subject to the most debasing kinds of abuse. Past and present analysis shows that rape is not a crime of uncontrollable sexual passion, but one used to vent misogyny and to exert physical, political, and economic control.

FBI statistics indicate that one out of three women will be raped in her lifetime, one out of four before the age of eighteen. Shocking as these figures are, African-American women are more likely to be raped than any other women, are least likely to be believed, and must often watch their rapists treated with impunity or mild punishment. Brownmiller (1975) cites from a study of rape convictions conducted in the city of Baltimore in 1967, which highlights this phenomenon:

> Of the four categories of rapist and victim in a racial mix, blacks [men] received the stiffest sentences for raping white women and the mildest sentence for raping black women. Of the 26 blacks convicted in Baltimore of raping white women, only one got less than five-to-ten years. Of the five white men convicted in Baltimore of raping black women, one received a sentence of from 15 to 20 years, three received less than five years, and one received a suspended sentence. (216)

Statistics such as these prove that Black women's bodies have historically provided the battlefield, as well as the reward for victory, in a continuing war on the African-American community.

From this historical context, a body of work has emerged which, I believe, is an attempt by African-American women to heal their wounds and garner strength. The preponderance of works by African-American writers in which rape is the direct subject or is used as a metaphor, a figurative way of talking about the abuses that African-American women have and continue to suffer, is by no means surprising. Some of the poets draw from their own experiences as survivors of rape. Others draw upon cultural paradigms that promote the subjugation of women and vindicate the acts of abusive men. Whatever their inspiration, these poets all realize that every woman is vulnerable in a society that allows, and sometimes even encourages, their physical abuse. African-American poets illustrate how rape has been, and remains, the most lethal weapon used to oppress, suppress, and dehumanize Black women in order to subvert their struggles to lead independent lives.

From Ann Petry's *The Street* (1946), Dorothy West's *The Living Is Easy* (1982), Pauline Hopkins' *Contending Forces* (1978), Margaret Walker's *Jubilee* (1967), to Toni

Morrison's *The Bluest Eye* (1970), Alice Walker's *The Color Purple* (1982), and Gayle Jones' *Corregidora* (1975), the brutal rape of Black women is recounted in painful detail. But it is in the works of poetry—from that of Frances E. W. Harper (1969), to Jayne Cortez (1983), Sonia Sanchez (1981), Ntozake Shange (1979)—that the bestiality of such an act is rendered raw by metaphor and imagery, and the terror that it produces is most graphically recounted. Rape stalks African-American women's lives, and the poets, in particular, have turned their most potent weapon, their pen, to their defense.

From the very beginning, African-Americans writing about slavery and the postslavery years have described the plight of the Black woman in an attempt to solicit the pathos of the wider community. Their artistic endeavors were limited, however, since their primary goal was to assert the humanity of the slave woman and to establish her virtue. Francis Harper, the nineteenth-century African-American poet, abolitionist, and antilynching crusader, euphemized the horrors of rape for moral reasons. She writes in the sixth stanza of "Bury Me in a Free Land,"

> If I saw young girls from their mothers' arms
> Bartered and sold for their youthful charms,
> My eye would flash with a mournful flame,
> My death-paled cheek grow red with shame. (Harper 1969, 36)

Harper, undoubtedly aware of the commonly held perception of slave women as immoral, refrains from using the word "rape," yet her meaning is clear. Harper relies on words like "charm," "mournful flame," and "shame," to convey the crime, her revolt, and the dishonor which she shares with her less fortunate sisters. The poem ends triumphantly, and the priority is clear: the zeal for freedom and dignity.

> I ask no monument, proud and high,
> To arrest the gaze of the passers-by;
> All that my yearning spirit craves,
> Is bury me not in a land of slaves. (Harper 1969, 37)

In their efforts to garner sympathy for slave women, writers like Harper faced a major difficulty in attempting to impugn the patriarchal structure of society with its double code for women. Paternalistic conceptions of women are rooted in Judeo-Christian ethics which espouse the idea that woman, Eve, is the temptress who causes man's fall and eviction from paradise. Hazel Carby (1987) examines the implications of this notion:

> The institutionalized rape of black women has never been as powerful a symbol of black oppression as the spectacle of lynching. Rape has always involved patriarchal notions of women being, at best, not entirely unwilling accomplices, if not outwardly inviting a sexual attack. (39)

Thus, the rape of slave women, and later the freed African-American woman, was indirectly condoned by society. Most recently, however, contemporary African-American poets have fought back without hesitating to name the crime, point to the accuser, and take up arms in defense of their bodies and personage.

Present in the work of many African-American poets is the historical antecedent— the unacknowledged suffering of their foremothers. Their poetry forges the link between the exploitation in their and their ancestors' lives, simultaneously commenting on the precarious position that African-American women still occupy in this society. Amina Baraka's "Soweto Song" (1983) is particularly effective because its subject, speaking in the first person, becomes all African women who were taken as slaves, and all women reading this poem become the warrior preparing for battle. Moreover, Soweto, the physical place, is viewed as an extension of the southern United States. The poet suggests that the same war which began in slavery is continuing:

> i come from the womb of Africa
> to praise my black diamond
> to shine my black gold
> to fight my people enemies
> to stand on my ancestors shoulders
> to dance in the hurricane of revolution
>   Soweto, Soweto, Soweto,
> i come with my hammer & sickle
> i come with bullets for my gun
> to fire on my enemies
> to stab the savages that sucked my breast
> to kill the beast that raped my belly
> i come painted red in my peoples blood
> to dance on the wind of the storm
> to help sing freedom songs
>   Soweto, Soweto, Soweto, (70)

A striking feature of this poem is that Baraka uses the lower-case form of the character "i." Since capitalization is used throughout the remainder of the poem in a conventional manner, we are left to surmise the significance of the lower-case "i." While the "i" in the poem admits to the singularity of the persona's struggle, the poet also infuses the subject with a great deal of power. After a while the "i" no longer reads as first-person singular but rather as the collective "we." Moreover, the poem's tone seems to declare: I'm prepared; I know this is a war; therefore I am armed and ready to do battle. The simple, repetitive refrain, "i come/to" functions as an evocation, a war chant to boost the spirit and inspire the warriors.

The poem's structure forces us to pause at the lines "To stab the savages that sucked my breast / to kill the beast that raped my belly." Baraka turns the tables upside down by taking the terms historically used to refer to African-Americans and hurling them at the former masters. The racist epithets "savage" and "beast" become accusations exposing the rapist aggressor's true nature.

Although the momentum of the poem remains active until the end, the focus shifts, the tone is softened, and the emphasis is on rebuilding and moving forward. The repetitive structure and the deliberate slowness of the language are done to highlight the determined move toward freedom.

> i come to carve monuments in the image of my people
> i come to help hold the flag of freedom
> i come to bring my tears to wash your wounds

> i come to avenge slavery
> i come to claim by blood ties
> i come to help free my people
> Soweto, Soweto, Soweto, (70)

Connected with the freedom of the people is the need to "avenge slavery." Slavery is the war that must be acknowledged; due compensation must be paid.

The works of African-American female poets are like a broken record trapped in the groove on the issues of rape and slavery. The poems can be interpreted as ritual baths performed to cleanse them, rid them of this desecration. The proliferation of female body imagery and the control and restrictions imposed on African-American women's reproductive rights are evident in the poems. Akua Lezli Hope's "Lament" (1983) makes vivid this point.

> my contraceptive history
> pregnant with pain
> the breech birth of clashing cultures
>
> forced cervical dilation
> snake steel rods
> insidious constraint and rape
>
> sometimes i bear mulattoes
> strangers to my skin
> strongwilled aliens
> strangers to my heart (141)

Hope introduces a sentiment not often, in fact seldom, expressed by African-American women writers. The poem's persona, through abortion, rejects those offspring forced on her as a result of being raped. The clear distancing between the mother and her children, expressed in the third stanza, represents the woman's protest against her rape, her refusal to accept the product of her violation. Her mulatto children remain aliens, "strangers to my heart," perhaps because it is easier to kill an intruder, or stranger.

In the next stanza of "Lament," Hope makes no attempt to justify the act of infanticide; it is not done out of love, but rather rejection. Although the decision causes anguish, there is no indication that the persona feels remorse, nor does she oscillate because she has no other alternative.

> i remove rods
> to early brand or slay them
> each choice conceives anguish
> capitulation harkens suffering
> rebellion beckons despair
> upon my womb
> upon my womb (141)

Since a woman's body is the battlefield, she must make it the source of her resistance: "upon my womb / i swear silent oaths / razor-toothed and lockjawed" (141). The passion and force embedded in these three lines is unquestionable. The womb, considered a sacred part of a woman's femininity, becomes her armor.

Wars, no matter how long they last, change over a period of time. Poets Abbey Lincoln and June Jordan transport us to the present and demonstrate how rape continues to be ubiquitous as well as intimate. More African-American women are being raped by their "brothers," often a male disguised as their "friend." The war has spread, and there are no clear demarcations to distinguish battlefield or safe zone. Even though slaves were granted freedom, the African-American woman is still not free, not even in her home that she works to secure. The fact is that no place is safe; all are suspect.

Abbey Lincoln's "On Being High" (1983) explores date rape under the rubric of the African-American female as a bitch, a woman who is open to all sexual advances. The poem's theme is that African-American women's pursuit of love is thwarted.

> On a date, I thought, with somebody I thought I knew,
> bursting with blooming love songs,
> I was raped . . . While terror ran rampant in a tearful face, the lawful sheriff,
> investigating, questioned him first . . .
> Then, securing me alone to talk, leered and said
> I oughta drop the case.
> Unsure of my rights, I sent my head on higher
> and dropped the case. (187)

Lincoln makes it blatantly evident that the law offers no protection for African-American women, an injustice heightened by the fact that many African-American women are unsure of their rights. It is not because they are ignorant. They know instinctively that the books are stacked against them, and they have little to no recourse. So the phrase "I sent my head higher" is perplexing because while it could suggest pride, or refusal to be defeated, the act is merely a gesture in the face of the reality: her rapist is exonerated. She remains as defenseless as her slave sister, whose only weapon was her guile.

June Jordan, the poet/activist who has been raped on two occasions, divides "Rape Is Not a Poem" (1980a) into four sections. The first section serves as a prelude, a metaphorical analogy to the rape that comes later. Her matter-of-fact tone heightens the anger, the utter contempt and betrayal that she feels.

> One day she saw them coming into the garden
> where the flowers live.
> They
> found the colors beautiful and
> they discovered the sweet smell
> that the flowers held
> so
> they stamped upon and tore apart
> the garden
> just because (they said)
> those flowers?
> They were asking for it. (79)

While it can be argued that the reference to a woman's sexual anatomy as a flower is cliché, the comparison nonetheless illustrates the destruction of an organic thing by those who plunder simply to make a point. Moreover, the men's entrance into the garden is clearly an invasion. The act of rape that they commit is to assuage their fear, their feeling of impotence. Rape confirms their power to dominate what is "discovered," to seize what is "held," to destroy by right of conquest.

The poem then moves from the metaphorical into the realm of reality. The setting is clear, the people are tangible, the dialogue appears civil, bordering on mundane. Before the dialogue collapses into triteness, however, there appears dissonance, conflict, a suppressed war.

> I let him into the house to say hello.
> "Hello," he said.
> "Hello," I said.
> "How are you?" he asked me.
> "Not bad," I told him.
> "You look great," he smiled.
> "Thanks; I've been busy: I am busy."
> "Well, I guess I'll be heading out, again," he said.
> "Okay," I answered and, "Take care," I said.
> "I'm gonna do just that," he said.
> "NO!" I said: "No! Please don't. Please leave me alone. Now. No.
>   Please!" I said.
> "I'm leaving," he laughed: "I'm leaving you alone; I'm going now!"
> "NO!" I cried: "No. Please don't do this to me!" But he was not
>   talking anymore and there was nothing else that I could say to
>   make him listen to me. (79–80)

Surprisingly, the persona does not identify the act, does not cry rape. Instead she begs, "Please don't do this to me!" Why the restraint? Does the persona acquiesce because she knows ultimately that she must yield to the stronger, brutal force? Dialogue is aborted. Even the tone of the third section, while it names her anger, is intellectual, an attempt to place the act within a larger historical context.

> And considering your contempt
> And considering my hatred consequent to that
> And considering the history
> that leads us to this dismal place where
> (your arm
> raised
> and my eyes
> lowered)
> there is nothing left but the drippings
> of power and
> a consummate wreck of tenderness/I
> want to know:
> Is this what you call
> Only Natural? (80)

In the last two lines the question the persona poses, "Is this what you call / Only Natural?" is sardonic, but her disillusionment is apparent. In section four of this poem, Jordan flings the adage "Men are dogs" out the window. She describes her dog in a gentle manner, then ends the poem, "You should let him teach you how / to come down" (81). The implication is clear: a dog is or can be more appropriate than the man who violated her, and can in fact teach her persecutor restraint.

In yet another poem, "The Rationale, or She Drove Me Crazy" (1980b), Jordan assumes the voice of a rapist who goes before the judge and in his defense pleads, "Then I lost control; I couldn't resist. / What did she expect? . . ." (11). The rapist is portrayed as a man driven out of control by an apparently sexy woman walking on the streets alone. As in the other poem, the irony of the situation, and the innate contradiction of society with its blatant disregard for women is revealed in a tag that Jordan saves for the end: "third time apprehended / for the theft of a Porsche" (12). Once again the rapist is not punished for his assault of a woman but rather for his theft of a car officially deemed more valuable than women.

With the invention of the pill and the widespread advocacy of other forms of birth control, women have supposedly been liberated, at least sexually. The idea that women own their own bodies because they are allowed to make decisions about conception, along with the notion that men's deeply ingrained prejudices against women have changed, if not false, is overly optimistic. The reality does not substantiate this propaganda. The truth is that incidents of rape continue to escalate, while undisguised misogyny is a constant and reoccurring blitz in all forms of media.

A close look at social dynamics reveals that as a result of women being granted apparent sexual "freedom," people appear to be less sensitive to incidents of rape. Sexual liberation allows for different classifications of rape and, implicitly, different levels of abuse—some violations may appear less horrendous than others. Both of these facts combine to make it just as difficult now as in the past for women to prove rape, much less receive justice.

Yet another damaging effect of women's sexual "freedom" is the fact that women often buy into this advocacy of sexual promiscuity and so dismiss, or downplay, being raped. bell hooks (1989), the African-American feminist, examines this trend as it is depicted in the movie *She's Gotta Have It*, produced and directed by an independent African-American male filmmaker, Spike Lee. Lee says his intention for the movie is "to portray a radical new image of black female sexuality." However, hooks asserts that the portrayal of Nola Darling in *She's Gotta Have It* reinforces and perpetuates old norms overall" (hooks 1989, 141). In her essay " 'whose pussy is this': a feminist comment," hooks demonstrates how the movie makes rape palatable and "is perfectly compatible with sexist pornographic fantasies about rape to show a woman enjoying violation" (139). In the scene where the rape occurs (the scene is not identified as such), Nola Darling, the sexually liberated protagonist, invites one of her beaus, her rapist, over. The implication is that Nola complied with the actions of the rapist, that she was "ravished." She is reduced to not even owning her most private part. As her "lover"/assailant is ramming her from the rear, as if she is a bitch in heat, he demands of her, "Whose pussy is this?" She submits, "Yours." And as hooks rightly notes, "It is difficult for anyone who has fallen for the image of her as sexually liberated to not feel let down, disappointed both in her character and in the film" (139).

What has contributed to the all too frequent portrayal of rape in the electronic media as an act enjoyed by women? How has this image contributed to women's confusion over their own rights, and over the ability to differentiate between rape versus pleasure? How has this portrayal contributed to making women believe that they are accomplices in their own violation and are responsible for men's actions toward them? hooks postulates that the scene in *She's Gotta Have It*

> impresses on the consciousness of black males, and all males, the sexist assumption that rape is an effective means of patriarchal social control, that it restores and maintains male power over women. It simultaneously suggests to black females, and all females, that being sexually assertive will lead to rejection and punishment. (1989, 139)

This indicates that the war, which began for African-American women in slavery, continues just as dangerously as before. Now, however, not only do we have to be vigilant before the known rapist but before those pretending to be friends who would use our professed sexual liberation as a weapon to disarm and silence us like Nola Darling in *She's Gotta Have It*.

Ntozake Shange (1979) demonstrates in a prose/poem the extent to which rape is intended to implant in a woman's mind the idea that she is defenseless. If she fails to conform to patriarchal dictates, her actions will be viewed as subversive, and violence may be used to force her to submit. Shange points out the pervasiveness of rape and how it affects females all over the world.

> I'm so saddened that being born a girl makes it dangerous to attend midnight mass unescorted. Some places if we're born girls & some one else who's very sick & weak & cruel/attack us & break our hymen/we have to be killed/sent away from our families/forbidden to touch our children. These strange people who wound little girls are known as attackers, molesters, & rapists. They are known all over the world & are proliferating at a rapid rate. To be born a girl who will always have to worry not only about the molesters, the attackers & the rapist/but also about their peculiarities/does he stab too/or shoot/does he carry an ax/does he spit on you/does he know if he doesn't drop sperm we can't prove we've been violated/those subtleties make being a girl too complex/for some of us & we go crazy/or never go anyplace. (28)

This prose/poem successfully conveys the message that rape is international and that in some societies, rape victims are not only blamed for their victimization but are further punished by being killed, ostracized, and/or banished. However, Shange does not conclude that the threatened female must withdraw inward, resort to madness or reclusiveness, for safety. She, like Jordan, knows that there is no safe place, not even in one's home.

> some of us have never had an open window or a walk alone/but sometimes our homes are not safe for us either/rapist attackers & molesters are not strangers to everyone/they are related to somebody/& some of them like raping & molesting their family members better than a girl-child they don't know yet/ (28)

Shange offers no resolution to the problem, but she does assert, that as women "we owe no one anything/not our labia, not our clitoris, not our lives." In a triumphant note, with a voice that shoves away the hand that would silence our voices, Shange demands that we have "our lives/to live" (29).

In another prose/poem, "otherwise i would think it odd to have rape prevention month," Shange seems to adopt a snide posture toward rape prevention month. She is suggesting that rape is so pervasive and has become so much a part of patriarchal domination that to set aside only a month to deal with this cancerous disease is to fail to comprehend truly the enormity of the situation or appreciate the plight of women. Shange offers nine alternatives, in which she points out the ludicrousness and futility of the program. In Alternative No. 8, she seems to suggest a means for women to empower themselves:

> unless the streets are made safe for us/we shall call a general strike/in factories/at home/at school. We shall say we cannot come to work/it is not safe. (30)

Shange apparently forgets her message, conveyed in her other poem: home is not safe; no place is. Nonetheless, she focuses in this poem on the need for women to organize and demand that their collective voices be heard.

The poet who is most unflinching on the subject of rape, who dramatizes it and renders it in explicit war terminology, is Jayne Cortez (1983). In her poem "Rape," Cortez uses graphic language to shock out of its complacency a society that habitually victimizes women. Cortez's outrage over injustice is vociferous, and her alliance with her sisters is uncompromising. Just as significant as her dedication to this alliance is her willingness to name the rapists for what they are: vicious, ruthless, fascist, and racist. The rapist is not made a figurative beast or a misdirected man out of control. She portrays a rapist who is unquestionably human, rational, and culpable for the terror that he engenders in women.

Cortez writes about women who seem to recognize and accept the fact that they are at war with a society that allows men to assert their dominance by subjugating and demoralizing women's bodies. "Rape" got its impetus from two much-publicized cases that occurred in the mid-1970s: the cases of Inez Garcia, a Native American woman, and Joanne Little, an African-American woman. These women's stories are significant because they both refused to submit, play dead, pick themselves up after the ordeal, and continue on with their lives as if they had not been abused. Inez Garcia and Joanne Little encouraged all women not to submit, to fight back. Both cases generated support from women's groups around the country, and after much networking, letter writing, protesting, both women were acquitted of their rapists' deaths. Cortez writes:

> What was Inez supposed to do for
> the man who declared war on her body
> the man who carved a combat zone between her breasts
> was she supposed to lick crabs from his hairy ass
> kiss every pimple on his butt
> blow hot breath on his big toe
> draw back the corners of her vagina and
> hee haw like a Calif. burro

> This being war time for Inez
> she stood facing the knife
> the insults and
> her own smell drying on the penis of
> the man who raped her
>
> She stood with a rifle in her hand
> doing what a defense department will do in times of war
> And when the man started grunting and panting and
>   wobbling forward like
> a giant hog
> She pumped lead into his three hundred pounds of
>   shaking flesh
> Sent it flying to the virgin of Guadeloupe
> then celebrated day of the dead rapist punk
> and just what the fuck else was she suppose to do? (89)

Cortez establishes the war motif from the beginning. She makes it clear that the man instigates the violence and emphasizes the logical necessity of the woman's response to his threat. Thus, Inez is likened to a defense department that has but two options under fire. Her shooting the rapist empowers all women who have been made to feel responsible for their violation.

In the second half of the poem, which is dedicated to Joanne Little's victory, Cortez repeats the war imagery and poses the same rhetorical question. By explicitly describing the details that took place during the events leading up to both women's retaliation, Cortez forces the reader to experience their violation vicariously. We, faced with the graphic reality of the violence and humiliation perpetrated on Garcia and Little, understand how a woman can be provoked enough to take up the rifle or the ice pick in her defense.

> And what was Joanne supposed to do for
> the man who declared war on her life
> Was she supposed to tongue his encrusted toilet stool
>   lips
> suck the numbers off his tin badge
> choke on his clap trap balls
> squeeze on his nub of rotten maggots and
> sing god bless america thank you for fucking my life
>   away
>
> This being wartime for Joanne
> she did what a defense department will do in times of war
> and when the piss drinking shift sniffing guard said
> I'm gonna make you wish you were dead black bitch come
>   here
> Joanne came down with an ice pick in
> the swat freak mother fucker's chest
> yes in the fat neck of the racist policeman

> Joanne did the dance of the ice pick and once again
> from coast to coast
> house to house
> we celebrate day of the dead rapist punk
> and just what the fuck else were we supposed to do (89–90)

The poet does not distinguish the persona from the general pool of women. Her affinity is clear. She understands that in another place and time she could be either Inez or Joanne; in fact any female could. That is why we, all women, celebrate the "day of the dead rapist punk." While the focus of the poem is on the women, and recounting the ordeals that led to their victory, Cortez reminds us of the larger political context under which we live. Her indictment is clear in the line "sing god bless america thank you for fucking my life away." She reminds us that the fate of these women is implicitly condoned by the white, racist, misogynist system that regards females as commodities, garbage dumps on which to heap its waste.

The historical and political context inserted in many of these poets' works demonstrates their commitment to making a tangible contribution to the African-American community. In choosing to write about the issue of rape, they automatically participate in both the fictional and real worlds. Furthermore, writers like Jayne Cortez use factual events to heighten the poignancy and sense of urgency in their work and to emphasize the seriousness of their artistic mission. By uncovering and dismantling the social paradigms that work to oppress women, they hope to present a model and a means with which women can fight back.

Alice Walker uses the same techniques as Cortez—the use of factual evidence—to shed light on the system of abuse used to put down Black women who have increasingly refused to be passive victims, have taken courage from their other sisters, and are fighting back with all they have. In an essay entitled "Trying to See My Sister" (1989), Walker discusses how this African-American woman's refusal to be raped resulted in unreasonable and excessive punishment. She uses the case of Dessie Woods, which generated much protest in the 1970s (1975), but with a less successful outcome than those of Inez Garcia and Joanne Little. Walker notes, "The woman who saved her life, and saved them both from rape, was given twenty-two years, later reduced to twelve." Dessie Woods served six years before being released from jail on July 9, 1981. Walker recounts how all her attempts to see Woods were met with stumbling blocks. She also records that Woods was kept in solitary confinement for extended periods of time and regularly given Prolixin.

The incidents leading up to the conviction of Dessie Woods are not particularly unusual given the historical abuse of Black women. Woods had accompanied another African-American woman to visit the friend's brother in prison in Lyons, Georgia. After the visit they discovered that there was no bus to get back home to Atlanta, so they hitchhiked a ride from a white man in a police uniform. The man bought them lunch in a restaurant before driving them into the woods under the pretense of taking them to the bus station. He said he intended to have sex with both of them, and they protested, but to no avail. When he stopped the car, Woods' friend jumped out and ran. In her essay, Walker recounts the events that led Woods to kill her attempted rapist.

The man drew his gun and pointed it after her. The other woman (Dessie) threw her five feet two inches against the five-foot-nine, 215 pound man and struggled to take his gun. In the process of that struggle, the gun went off twice. The man was killed by two bullet shots to the head.

Woods' friend was given a five-year sentence, with three and a half years on probation, but for "slaying the dragon," as Walker puts it, Woods was given twenty-two years. What does this incident teach us? That the woman who defends herself and/or another woman from rape will be punished; her mobility will be restricted; she will be isolated lest she evoke others to be like her; and she will be experimented on with drugs in an attempt to squash her spirit and/or make her dysfunctional. Dessie Woods' case teaches us the painful lesson that to defend oneself in this war that women face daily is to take on the most brutal battalion. Current events seem to point towards the more pessimistic possibility in Jordan's declaration in "Against the Wall": "if you undertake to terrorize and to subjugate and to stifle even one moment more of these, our only lives, we will take yours, or die trying" (Jordan 1978, 149). While Dessie Woods ultimately did not die as a result of defending her life, society punished this "insignificant" African-American woman for daring to refuse the sexual advances of a law-enforcing, southern white man. As Walker concludes, "It is obvious that Black women do not have the right to self-defense against racist and sexist attacks by white men. I realize I am in prison as well" (1989, 23–24). All women are in prisons as long as society continues its overt and covert racist and chauvinistic practices.

Cortez, Walker, and Jordan are among those who understand the political implications of rape. They show that the subjugation of Black women results from their, and their community's, systematic disempowerment. In her essay "Against the Wall" (1978), June Jordan makes this comparison clear. Jordan begins with the personal, the individual woman, to emphasize the historical antecedents—slavery and the perilous role of slave women—which still informs the assault to which African-American women continue to be prey. Jordan writes of the African-American woman's need to assert her right to be, to go where she pleases when she pleases, and declares that no man has the right to attack her because she insists on her autonomy.

> The writer is a woman, and Black, besides. Consequently the act of taking a walk means that she, this writer, will be perceived as a provocative/irresponsible/loose/insubordinate creature on the streets, by herself, moving along as though she had a natural right to wander around, after dark. (147)

Notice the restrictions imposed on her mobility; women's place has been defined, and even the time of the day when women can occupy this place has been stipulated. Obedience is demanded in exchange for "protection." Independence results in castigation and the burden of shouldering the responsibility for her own victimization.

> If she's raped, if guys on the corners molest her innate sovereignty by making obscene remarks and noises as she passes by, if a bunch of punks decide to mug and mutilate her person, people will say: But why was she there? And I will answer: Why in the world should she be anywhere else? . . . Of course, rape is not new. In a way, that is the meaning

of my identity: I have been raped. Somebody stronger than I am will attempt, yet again, and again, to maim and to desecrate my inalienable right to self-determination . . . Or he will claim that he had to invade and conquer my home because I was friendly with Cubans or other kinds of problematic types who were misleading my infantile mentality. (148–149)

In this passage, Jordan draws a link between the rape of a woman and the rape of a nation because they are both part of the same phenomenon. Both originate within the same paradigm: colonialism equals oppression. Embedded in this matrix is the general notion that women and developing nations are childlike, infants who need the tyranni-cal guidance of men—the patriarchal syndrome at work. Jordan condemns the system that allows for the exploitation of women and developing countries to be so easily jus-tified. Her appeal is not only to women but to all conscious humans to stop and evalu-ate their actions. The rape of a woman—or a country—cannot be dismissed and explained away.

Jordan and Ntozake Shange are representative of poets who introduce the interna-tional perspective and demonstrate the commonality of women's struggle. These writers assert that the liberation of women is inextricably connected to the sovereignty of developing nations throughout the world. The rape of their individual bodies paral-lels the rape of their communities and, in a wider political context, exemplifies the same power game at work in the rape of so-called Third World countries by the West. The intention is the same: to make women/developing countries feel small, inferior, afraid to act on their own behalf, withdraw inside themselves, accept the abuse, and nod thanks.

> Because all of us who are comparatively powerless, because we have decided that if you interfere, if you seek to intrude, if you undertake to terrorize and to subjugate and to stifle even one moment more of these, our only lives, we will take yours, or die trying. (Jordan 1978, 149)

Statements such as this voice an otherwise silent pain. These poets' works allow women to throw off the guilt of perceiving themselves as accomplices in their own oppression; they inform women that we are not alone in facing the same daily bom-bardment of life in a combat zone. They insist that women can and must fight back, must refuse to surrender our lives to oppression. As June Jordan advises those who rape the lives of women and nations, "We will take yours, or die trying" (1978, 70).

For African-American women, rape continues as an ever-present threat to their par-ticular bodies. It is as June Jordan says, "the meaning of her identity." To be an African-American woman in this society is to be subject to rape. As such, rape is not a trope in the works of African-American women writers and poets; it is a lived experience that has left many scars, and it is still the source of much suffering. Thanks to the heroic efforts of women such as Inez Garcia, Joanne Little, and Dessie Woods, and the careful articulation of women poets and writers, most women can now identify the war and name the battle. As a result, women have taken up arms in their own defense and will not be disarmed, except by death. While society refuses to acknowledge that women are at war for the right to be independent humans in charge of our own bodies, we no longer need to wait for society to acknowledge this fact and grant us the right to bear arms. We are beyond the point where we need to have our reality defined for us. We will not turn back. We will not shut up. We will not be shoved in some corner. And we will not submit to rape.

Battering in Intimate Relationships

The gendered system that values the violent and controlling behavior of men while devaluing its victims permeates our lives. Controlled violence is endemic in sports, and the worlds of business and politics are rife with examples of extreme power and authority. These characteristics, admired in one circumstance, spill over into the routine interactions of men and women in the realm of their private lives. This spillover affects the high incidence of male-on-male violence, as well as the abuse of women by men. The violence that occurs between intimates seems to contradict what we believe should constitute such relationships; yet our response as a society is ambivalent. Although we claim to abhor the violence, we rationalize it and often overlook it.

A Legacy of Abuse

Although domestic violence is horrific, public concern and official response have been muted for much of human history. During the Middle Ages in Europe, church law exerted a strong influence on behavior. Women were subject to the authority of men, who had the explicit support of the church to correct women's behavior through punishment. The legacy of medieval law, which permitted the authorized abuse of women, continued through the eighteenth-century Napoleonic Code, which in turn influenced the law in much of Europe. Such laws assured that men had absolute family power, including the use of violence against family members up to the point of murder (Davidson 1978).

Efforts to protect women from the abuse of male intimates have had limited success. In the mid-1600s in colonial Massachusetts, the Puritans "enacted the first laws anywhere in the world against wife beating" (Pleck 1989, 20), based on the belief that family violence was a sin. Neighbors were expected to be watchful of each other's behavior and to interfere when necessary. There were, of course, limits to the Puritans' vigilance, and records from that era include numerous cases of severe violence against wives (Pleck 1987; Eldridge 1997).

Urbanization and its attendant close living quarters made acts of violence against wives widely visible in nineteenth-century England. Police records from that era indicate that wife abuse was very common, with insubordinate and nonsubmissive behavior frequently cited as cause by the abusers (Tomes 1978). In his 1869 essay "The Subjection of Women," John Stuart Mill addressed the plight of battered women in England. His concern for wives "against whom [a husband] can commit any atrocity except killing her, and, if tolerably cautious, can do that without much danger of the legal penalty" (Mill 1988, 57) helped to mobilize efforts to rewrite English law.

In the mid-1800s in the United States, the "ideal of an anger-free family" developed in close association with industrialization (Stearns and Stearns 1986, 11). The new standards for family behavior focused on the family and home as a refuge from the outer world of work and strife. During the late 1800s, efforts to address wife abuse were initiated as part of larger concerns about cruelty to children (Pleck 1989). By that time it appears that wife beaters may have been "more restrained in their violence" (Pleck 1989, 100) and that fewer men beat their wives. Perhaps this resulted from changing views of the paternalistic responsibilities of men toward women. Conversely, the blurring of gender lines and dependency patterns as more women work for wages and control their own finances may contribute to apparent increases in abuse today (Peterson 1992).

A Movement for Change

Motivated by the second wave of the women's movement, the first refuge for battered women, Chiswick Women's Aid, opened in England in 1972. Provided with an alternative to staying at home with a violent spouse, local women overwhelmed the facility. The first shelter for battered women in the United States opened in Minnesota in 1974 (Dobash and Dobash 1992). Today such shelters exist in most communities in the United States, and they are increasing worldwide.

Advocates working with victims of domestic violence soon realized that lasting change in social conditions would not occur without increased public education and legislative action. Beginning in the mid-1970s, legislation in Great Britain and the United States provided legal remedies and program funding for battered women (Dobash and Dobash 1987). Although battered women have no doubt benefited from the increase in resources provided by such legislation, one troubling result of relying on governmental institutions for financial and legal resources is "the state's role in reproducing relations of dominance and subordination" (Shepard and Pence 1999, 8). These are the very same institutions that form the underpinnings of intimate violence and that maintain the social inequities that support abuse (Shepard and Pence 1999, 10).

By the beginning of the twenty-first century, activists and scholars recognized that not all women experience intimate violence the same way. Initial claims that battering occurs among all demographic groups were intended to avoid harmful categorization of some people as naturally violent and others as passive victims. What "began as an attempt to avoid stereotyping and stigma" (Richie 2005, 53) has led to a "false sense of unity" (52) that masks the raced and classed nature of gender violence as experienced by women of color and poor women. As we continue to grapple with the "complex association between demographic and cultural factors" (West 2005, 170) that contribute to intimate violence, we must "remain self-conscious" so as not to collude in silencing the voices of battered women of color (Knadler 2004, 2). Spurred on primarily by activism and writing produced by women in marginalized positions, scholars of domestic violence have begun to understand that "every culture has tenets that disenfranchise women, as well as empower them" (Dasgupta 2005, 67). Ignoring the particularities of marginalized battered women's stories prevents our understanding of "marginalized men as simultaneously being victimized by the state AND victimizing women" (Lawrence 1996, 25, original emphasis).

Addressing the Problem of Battering

Legal reform has focused primarily on increasing the criminalization of domestic violence (Pleck 1989; Zimring 1989). Because family privacy serves as a rationale to avoid criminalizing battering, the effort to expand criminal law to include responses to wife abuse is an uphill struggle against a history of a narrow jurisprudence that proposes to intervene only in cases of "the taking of life, parental incest, and the imminent threat to the life or health of a minor child" (Zimring 1989, 552).

Worldwide reports reveal that alone, legal responses to domestic violence are ineffective. Herzberger and Channels (1991) found that suspects in violent offenses are treated more leniently by the court if they are related to their victims. In the United States, police continue to be reluctant to respond appropriately to domestic-violence calls (Caputo 1991; Belknap and Hartman 2000), and the characteristics of abusers play a more central role than the level of abuse in deciding police intervention (Dutton 1988; Gondolf 1988). Albert Roberts (1984) documents police insensitivity to victims and lack of awareness of the dangers of domestic violence. Furthermore, as recently as 2005, "the United States Supreme Court ruled in a 7 to 2 decision that police officers are exempt from legal action, even if their refusal to enforce a valid restraining order results in death" (Delaware NOW 2005).

The response of the police and courts in other countries is similar. In Scotland, for example, domestic-violence cases are treated much less seriously by the courts than are comparable non-domestic-violence cases (Wasoff 1982). In Egypt, the criminal code continues to "misuse . . . Qur'anic text to dismiss the abuse of women in the family sphere" (Ammar 2000, 35).

Efforts to change police and court procedures undertaken in locales around the world have met with some success. Due to the tremendous mobilization of the Brazilian women's movement, for example, separate police stations staffed by women are dedicated to addressing crimes of violence against women (Thomas 1994). In 1991, Brazil's highest court of appeal overturned a lower court's acceptance of the traditional "honor defense," which permitted a man to murder his wife if she had committed adultery. In Egypt, pro-womanist groups successfully lobbied for changes in interpretations of Shari'a to permit women to work in the criminal justice system (Ammar 2000).

According to Edwards (1987), civil and criminal court systems process cases of violence against wives and live-in partners in accordance with a number of factors that influence police investigation, prosecution, and sentencing, including

> the physical severity and visibility of the injuries; . . . the degree to which women conform to or deviate from appropriate female roles of wife, mother, homemaker; . . . the degree to

which women are seen as responsible; . . . the degree to which women are thought to have provoked their own demise either by: a) being sexually inappropriate [by having relationships with other men or being lesbian] b) being inappropriate in terms of gender, that is, bad mothers, bad cooks, bad housewives c) challenging either the gender assumptions of their expected roles or challenging male domination. (158)

Although three approaches have emerged to address violence within intimate relationships—legal, therapeutic, and restorative justice (see Miller and Iovanni, this volume)—it is the legal system that predominates. Given the focus on the criminal justice approach, and its inherent problems, efforts to evaluate how it is used to address intimate violence must be a priority. As Stubbs (2002) points out, "social and cultural dimensions . . . give meaning to the violence" (44), and the criminal justice system provides an imperfect method for assessing that meaning and addressing it.

Intersectionality and Domestic Violence

According to feminist analysts, patriarchal power relations produce gender ideologies and cultural conditions that create and sustain domestic violence. Combined with the cultural advocacy of violence as an effective and desirable interpersonal dynamic, these power structures produce what Ewing (1982) refers to as the "civic advocacy of [male] violence" (5). Stubbs asserts that "domestic violence . . . arises through strategies that attempt to implement gender ideologies" (2002, 43, citing Ptacek 1999).

The abuse of female intimates is made possible by the structural support of systems that maintain and reproduce male dominance and female submission (Radford 1987). According to this theory, the state, through its treatment of victims, is complicit in reinforcing passive acquiescence and conformity to narrow gender roles (Edwards 1987). Beliefs in the sanctity of the idealized family, which protect it from public scrutiny, serve to permit the abuses of women by men to whom they are tied by familial relationships. Anderson and Umberson (2001) note that batterers "construct masculine identities through the practice of violence" and that "the practice of domestic violence helps men to accomplish gender" (359–360).

The social institutions to which women turn for assistance have often been insensitive, resistant, and hostile. For members of minority communities in the United States, the responses of helping agencies are complicated by racism; thus, for abused women of color, the criminal approach to domestic violence presents a dilemma. Because police have not historically been perceived as the allies of minority communities, it is difficult for many women of color to depend on them for assistance (Miller 1993). Although Weis (2001) finds them more likely than white women to be critical of abusers, some African American women believe that abusive African American men are reacting to the deprivation they experience from racism.

In American Indian communities, extreme poverty, joblessness, rural isolation, and alcohol abuse may contribute to high rates of intimate violence, especially when understood within the frame of cultural decimation (Bachman 1992). Like African American men, violent American Indian men may have internalized the "qualities ascribed to them for centuries by the society around them" (Gunn Allen 1986). In this context, domestic violence is due to colonization and the replacement of the egalitarian social structure that existed in some tribes with the patriarchal hierarchy promoted by missionary colonists.

Asian women in the United States, particularly recent immigrants, face tremendous barriers to legal remedies for domestic violence. Traditional values of family loyalty and honor combined with beliefs that women's status is secondary to men's may promote interpersonal violence and prevent women from seeking help. Problems of reporting to official institutions include language barriers, isolation, fear of deportation (compounded for those with illegal immigrant status), and the cultural insensitivity of some service providers (Lai 1986).

Latina and Hispanic women represent a diverse group that encompasses a variety of ancestral lands, skin colors, religious beliefs, and socioeconomic classes. Valid statistical information on domestic violence in the Hispanic and Latina/o communities is sparse due in large part to cultural barriers that prevent access to services. For example, sharing explicit information and the intrusive questioning of police and counselors may be experienced as highly inappropriate. Emphasis on modesty and indirect communication may prevent women from sharing their concerns even within the family (Ginorio and Reno 1986). All of these issues are complicated by a dearth of services for those who are not fully comfortable communicating in English and who fear accessing services because they are immigrants who do not have full legal status (see Hass, Dutton, and Orloff 2000).

Battered lesbians and gay men also face issues of prejudice and a lack of appropriate services. Shelter programs are often inhospitable to lesbians (Geraci 1986) and virtually nonexistent for gay men. Homophobia is so pervasive that many lesbians and gay men never attempt to bring their cases to the criminal justice system.

Emerging Global Issues in Domestic Violence

In 2006 the World Health Organization (WHO) released data from a comprehensive survey of intimate partner violence conducted in ten countries. Researchers "found that rates of partner violence ranged from a low of 15 percent in Yokohama, Japan, to a high of 71 percent in rural Ethiopia" (Rosenthal 2006, A5). As the most wide-ranging international study to date, the WHO results confirm that violence from intimate partners is a significant problem in every country studied.

International research also reveals that the forms domestic violence takes may be culture and society specific (Davies 1994). For example, in Papua New Guinea, men's violence "prevents or limits women's participation in development" (Bradley 1994, 16). Such programs, which are seen as threats to male authority, may expose women to more violence and may undermine traditional systems that have offered women some protection in the past. Lane's (2003) study of Bangladesh links the likelihood of marital violence to the relative conservatism of communities. In more conservative areas violence was associated with women's increased autonomy, but there is reduced risk for

autonomous women in less conservative areas. Unlike the West, where domestic violence is hidden due to the silence of victims and the complicity of social institutions, in
other parts of the world it is seen as inevitable (Ammar 2000) or "normal and therefore
not a problem" (Bradley 1994, 20).

These findings serve as cautionary examples. The imbalance of global and economic
power between developed and developing nations mirrors and, perhaps, enhances the
disparity of power between intimate partners (see Erez and Laster 2000, 8–9).
Although the "economic content in violent behavior" is often overlooked, it comes into
sharp focus in cases of dowry violence in India where "wife abuse [is] a means of
extracting transfers" of money from the wife's family to the husband's (Bloch and Rao
2002, 1029). In this era of massive human migration, we must also be aware that "the
intersection of race, gender and international relations situates the immigrant . . .
woman in such a way that she has limited prospects for resistance" (Erez and Laster
2000, 10; see Shalhoub-Kevorkian 2000). Although domestic violence is widespread,
responses must acknowledge the specific concerns of the culture in which they take
place. It is important to recognize that in all societies "social values are dynamic and
challenged by the direct and indirect activism of individual women" at the local level
(Ammar 2000, 40).

Effects of Domestic Violence

Popular culture provides inaccurate and often humorous portrayals of domestic violence (e.g., the ubiquitous wife chasing her husband with a rolling pin). Dolan's (2003)
study of films depicting spousal abuse revealed that women characters frequently killed
their husbands and were supported in doing so by the criminal justice system. The
reality is much different.

Current understanding of the range of behaviors that constitute domestic violence
includes slapping, biting, kicking, punching, throwing objects, confining, denying care
(food or medication), abuse of pets and property destruction, sexual abuse, stabbing,
shooting, choking, threatening, insulting, and degrading. According to Leonard (2002),
men most often make use of their hands, fists, and feet, and beating to death and stran-
gulation are specifically male methods of killing intimate partners. The "most dominant form [of intimate assault] is man to woman within a partnership or former partnership" (Stanko 2000, 229), though it can comprise any relationship between
intimates or family members. The killing of one spouse by the other accounts for
approximately 25 percent of homicides in the United States, about 50 percent in
Canada, and 66 percent in Denmark. Another study indicates that though there is a
decrease in lethal violence between married couples, there is a corresponding rise in
murder rates in unmarried couples (Browne and Williams 1993). A woman is most at
risk to kill or be killed when she attempts to report the abuse or leave an abusive relationship (Browne 1987), and risk of harm to her children increases with separation
(Bancroft and Silverman 2002). In some cases, battering may increase during preg-

nancy (Gelles 1975), which contributes to the incidence of low birthweight (U.S. Senate Committee on the Judiciary 1990) and birth defects (Chiles 1988). Pregnant victims of domestic violence suffer significantly higher medical complications than pregnant women who are not abused (Parker, McFarlane and Soeken 1996). Staying "for the children's sake" is simply not a valid option in most cases.

Women aged sixteen to twenty-four experience partner violence at higher rates than any other age group (Hart and Rennison 2003). Subject to tremendous pressure to conform, young women often feel that involvement in a dating relationship is necessary to fit in. Lack of experience negotiating affection and sexual behavior, along with typical adolescent rejection of adult assistance, further complicate the dynamics of abusive dating relationships (see Levy 1991). Adolescents who experience partner abuse are at increased risk for "depression and premature exits from adolescence to adulthood" (Hagan and Foster 2001). For lesbian and gay adolescents, fear of familial and social rejection may further enhance the dangerous effects of battering in intimate relationships.

Contributions to This Section

The selections that follow address historical, societal, and personal aspects of domestic violence. Read together, these works provide a foundation for comprehending the contemporary intransigence of domestic violence and facilitate a wider understanding of the problem.

Michael Johnson looks back over three decades of research in "Domestic Violence: The Intersection of Gender and Control" to question assumptions about domestic violence as explicable by a single concept. He develops a three-pronged typology to explain the distinctions among types of intimate partner violence and then clarifies what has appeared to be contradictory data.

bell hooks problematizes the term *battered woman* in "Violence in Intimate Relationships: A Feminist Perspective." In hooks's view, the term emphasizes an extreme aspect of male violence against women and thus eclipses the mild physical abuse that is normalized in intimate relationships. The term *battered woman* implies an ongoing dynamic of abuse that may not apply to the less severe and isolated incidents many women experience, and it may be rejected by women thus labeled.

Terri Whittaker's "Violence, Gender, and Elder Abuse: Toward a Feminist Analysis and Practice" addresses the abuse of elderly women by elderly men. Whittaker finds that the current orthodoxy, in which overgeneralized explanations of elder abuse contribute to victim blaming, masks the gendered nature of most elder abuse.

Susan Miller and LeeAnn Iovanni ask us to consider recent U.S. developments to address domestic violence. They point to several important innovations in the areas of policy, the criminal justice system, and restorative justice and highlight the daunting gaps that remain if we are to effectively assist battered women and work toward ending domestic violence.

SUGGESTIONS FOR FURTHER READING

Edna Erez and Kathy Laster (eds.), *Domestic Violence: Global Responses* (Bicester, UK: A B Academic, 2000).

Bonita Lawrence, *Voix Feministes/Feminist Voices* (Ottawa, Ontario: Canadian Research Institute for the Advancement of Women, 1996).

Elizabeth Leonard, *Convicted Survivors: The Imprisonment of Battered Women Who Kill* (Albany: State University of New York Press, 2002).

Susan Miller, *Victims as Offenders: The Paradox of Women's Violence in Relationships* (New Brunswick, NJ: Rutgers University Press, 2005).

Elizabeth Pleck, *Domestic Tyranny: The Making of American Social Policy against Family Violence from Colonial Times to the Present* (New York: Oxford University Press, 1987).

Anna Quindlen, *Black and Blue* (New York: Dell, 1998).

Natalie Sokoloff (ed.), *Domestic Violence at the Margins: Readings on Race, Class, Gender, and Culture* (New Brunswick, NJ: Rutgers University Press, 2005).

To Judge Faolain, Dead Long Enough
A Summons

Linda McCarriston

Your Honor, when my mother stood
before you, with her routine
domestic plea, after weeks
of waiting for speech to return
to her body, with her homemade
forties hairdo, her face purple still
under pancake, her jaw off just a little,
her *holy of holies* healing,
her breasts wrung, her heart
the bursting heart of someone
snagged among rocks deep
in a sharkpool—no, not "someone,"

but a woman there, snagged
with her babies, *by* them,
in one of hope's pedestrian
brutal turns—when, in the tones
of parlors overlooking the harbor,
you admonished that, for the sake
of the family, the wife
must take the husband back to her bed,
what you willed not to see before you
was a woman risen clean to the surface,
a woman who, with one arm flailing,
held up with the other her actual

burdens of flesh. When you clamped
to her leg the chain of *justice,*
you ferried us back down to *the law,*
the black ice eye, the maw, the mako
that circles the kitchen table nightly.
What did you make of the words

she told you, not to have heard her,
not to have seen her there? Almost-
forgiveable ignorance, you were not
the fist, the boot, or the blade,
but the jaded, corrective ear and eye
at the limits of her world. Now

I will you to see her as she was, to ride
your own words back into light: I call
your spirit home again, divesting you
of robe and bench, the fine white hand
and half-lit Irish eye. Tonight, put on
a body in the trailer down the road
where your father, when he can't
get it up, makes love to your mother
with a rifle. Let your name be
Eva-Mary. Let your hour of birth
be dawn. Let your life be long
and common, and your flesh endure.

Chapter Fifteen

Domestic Violence
The Intersection of Gender and Control

Michael P. Johnson

Does a chapter on domestic violence even belong in a book on gender violence? After all, for over thirty years there have been reputable social scientists who have been willing to argue that women are as violent in intimate relationships as are men and that domestic violence has nothing to do with gender. Suzanne Steinmetz's controversial paper on "the battered husband syndrome" started this line of argument with the following conclusion: "An examination of empirical data [from a 1975 general survey] on wives' use of physical violence on their husbands suggests that husband-beating constitutes a sizable proportion of marital violence" (Steinmetz 1977–78, 501). A paper published in December 2005 provides a contemporary example (among many) of the same argument: "[Our] considerations suggest the need for a broadening of perspective in the field of domestic violence away from the view that domestic violence is usually a gender issue involving male perpetrators and female victims" (Fergusson, Horwood, and Ridder 2005, 1116).

Actually, despite thirty years of sometimes acrimonious debate, the research evidence does clearly indicate that what we typically think of as domestic violence is primarily male-perpetrated and most definitely a gender issue. However, this conclusion is clear only if one breaks out of the standard assumption that intimate partner violence is a unitary phenomenon. Once one makes some basic distinctions among types of intimate partner violence, the confusion that characterizes this literature melts away (Johnson 2005).

The first section of this chapter will demonstrate how attention to distinctions among types of intimate partner violence makes sense of ostensibly contradictory data regarding men's and women's violence in intimate relationships. The second section describes the basic structure of the types of intimate partner violence that most people associate with the term *domestic violence,* violence that is associated with coercive control, that is, one partner's attempt to take general control over the other. The third section presents a theory of domestic violence that is focused on the relationship between gender and coercive control. The fourth section addresses the role of gender in the type of intimate partner violence that does not involve an attempt to take general control over one's partner. The final section of the chapter deals with some of the intervention and policy implications of what we know about these types of intimate partner violence and their relationship to gender.

Gender and the Perpetration of Different Types of Intimate Partner Violence

How is it that thirty years of social science research on domestic violence has not produced a definitive answer to the question of whether or not men and women are equally involved in intimate partner violence? The reason is that the field has been caught up in a debate about *the* nature of intimate partner violence—as if it were a unitary phenomenon. Those who had reason to believe that intimate partner violence was perpetrated equally by both men and women cited evidence from large-scale survey research that showed rough gender symmetry in intimate partner violence. Those who believed that intimate partner violence was perpetrated almost entirely by men against their female partners cited contrary evidence from studies carried out in hospital emergency rooms, police agencies, divorce courts, and women's shelters. And each group argued that the other's evidence was biased. However, *both* groups can be right if (a) there are multiple forms of intimate partner violence, (b) some of the types are gender-symmetric and some are not, and (c) general surveys are biased in favor of the gender-symmetric types and agency studies are biased in favor of the asymmetric types. There is considerable evidence that this is in fact the case. There are three major types of intimate partner violence, they are not equally represented in the different types of samples studied by social scientists, and they differ dramatically in terms of gender asymmetry.

The most important distinctions among types of intimate partner violence have to do with the role of coercive control as a context for violence. Two of the three major types of intimate partner violence involve general power and control issues. *Intimate terrorism* is an attempt to take general control over one's partner; *violent resistance* is the use of violence in response to such an attempt. *Situational couple violence*, the third type of intimate partner violence, does not involve an attempt to take general control on the part of either partner.[1]

Although there were always clues to be found in the domestic violence literature of the 1970s and 1980s that there was more than one type of intimate partner violence (Johnson 1995), researchers have only recently begun to do research specifically focused on these distinctions. In order to make these distinctions, researchers ask questions not only about the violence itself but also about nonviolent control tactics. They then use the answers to those questions to distinguish between violence that is embedded in a general pattern of power and control (intimate terrorism and violent resistance) and violence that is not (situational couple violence). The specific measures used have varied from study to study, but the findings have been quite consistent.

Studies in both the United States and England have shown that the intimate partner violence in general surveys is heavily biased in favor of situational couple violence, whereas the intimate partner violence in agency samples is biased in favor of male intimate terrorism and female violent resistance (Graham-Kevan and Archer 2003a, 2003b; Johnson 2001). For example, using data from a 1970s Pittsburgh survey, Johnson

(2001) found that situational couple violence constituted 89 percent of the male violence in the general survey sample, 29 percent in a court sample, and only 19 percent in the shelter sample. Why is this? The bias in general surveys comes from two sources: (a) the reality that situational couple violence is much more common than intimate terrorism and violent resistance, and (b) the biasing effect of the fact that as many as 40 percent of individuals approached in general surveys refuse to participate (Johnson 1995). Potential respondents who are terrorizing their partners are unlikely to agree to participate in a survey about family life for fear they will be exposed. Their violently resisting partners are unlikely to agree out of fear of being "punished" by their intimate terrorist partner for participating in such a survey. Thus, general surveys include very little intimate terrorism or violent resistance. In contrast with general surveys, agency samples are biased because intimate terrorism is more likely than situational couple violence to involve the sort of frequent and severe violence that comes to the attention of shelters, hospitals, the courts, and the police. Thus, agency samples include mostly cases of intimate terrorism and violent resistance.

Data from these studies also clearly demonstrate a strong relationship between gender and the different types of intimate partner violence. For example, in the Pittsburgh study intimate terrorism is almost entirely male-perpetrated (97%), and violent resistance is therefore female-perpetrated (96%), whereas situational couple violence is roughly gender-symmetric (56% male, 44% female).

When one puts together these findings regarding gender, type of intimate partner violence, and sample biases, the history of dissension regarding the gender symmetry of intimate partner violence is explained. Family-violence theorists who have argued that domestic violence is gender-symmetric have relied largely on general surveys, which are biased heavily in favor of situational couple violence, and they have found rough gender symmetry in their research, leading them to the false conclusion that domestic violence is not about gender. Feminist researchers, in contrast, have relied largely on agency samples that are heavily biased in favor of intimate terrorism (and violent resistance), showing a heavily gendered pattern, with men as the primary perpetrators of intimate terrorism and women sometimes resisting with violence. I would argue that intimate terrorism is what most people mean when they use the term "domestic violence," and it is indeed primarily perpetrated by men against their female partners.

Domestic Violence (Intimate Terrorism) as Gendered Violence

In intimate terrorism, violence is one control tactic in an array of tactics that are deployed in an attempt to take general control over one's partner. The control sought in intimate terrorism is general and long-term. Although each particular act of intimate violence may appear to have any number of short-term, specific goals, it is embedded in a larger pattern of power and control that permeates the relationship. It is this type of intimate partner violence that comes to mind for most people when they hear the term "domestic violence," and it is this type that receives the most media attention, in movies

Figure 1. Domestic violence/intimate terrorism (adapted from Pence and Paymar 1993).

such as *Sleeping with the Enemy* and *Enough,* in television talk shows and documentaries that deal with intimate partner violence, and in newspaper and magazine articles that address the problem of domestic violence.

Figure 1 is a widely used graphical representation of such partner violence deployed in the service of general control (Pence and Paymar 1993). A brief tour of the wheel, starting with economic abuse and moving through the other forms of control, might help capture what Catherine Kirkwood calls a "web" of abuse (Kirkwood 1993).

It is not unusual for an intimate terrorist to deprive his[2] partner of control over economic resources. He controls all the money. She is allowed neither a bank account nor credit cards. If she works for wages, she has to turn over her paychecks to him. He keeps all the cash, and she has to ask him for money when she needs to buy groceries or clothes for herself or their children. He may require a precise accounting of every penny, demanding to see the grocery bill and making sure she returns every bit of the change.

This economic abuse may be justified through the next form of control, male privilege: "I am the man of the house, the head of the household, the king in my castle." Of course, this use of male privilege can cover everything. As the man of the house, his word is law. He doesn't have to explain. She is to do his bidding without question. And don't talk back. All of this holds even more rigidly in public, where he is not to be humiliated by back-talk from "his woman."

How does he use the children to support his control? First of all, they too know he is the boss. He makes it clear that he controls not only them but their mother as well. He may use them to back him up, to make her humiliation more complete by forcing them into the room to assist him as he confronts her, demanding their verbal support and generally requiring their collaboration with his actions. He may even have convinced them that he should be in charge, that he does know what is best (father knows best), and that she is incompetent, lazy, or immoral. In addition, he may use her attachment to the children as a means of control, by threatening to take them away from her or hurt them if she isn't a "good wife and mother." Of course, being a good wife and mother means doing as he says.

Then there is isolation. He keeps her away from everyone else. He makes himself her only source of information, of affection, of money, of everything. In a rural setting he might be able to literally isolate her, moving to a house trailer in the woods, with one car that he controls, no phone, keeping her there alone. In an urban setting, or if he needs her to go out to work, he can isolate her less literally, by driving away her friends and relatives and intimidating the people at work, so that she has no one to talk to about what's happening to her.

When she's completely isolated, and what he tells her about herself is all she ever hears about herself, he can tell her over and over again that she's worthless—humiliating her, demeaning her, emotionally abusing her. She's ugly, stupid, a slut, a lousy wife, an incompetent mother. She only manages to survive because he takes care of her. She'd be helpless without him. And who else is there to tell her otherwise? Maybe he can even convince her that she can't live without him.

If she resists, he can intimidate her. Show her what might happen if she doesn't behave. Scream at her. Swear at her. Let her see his rage. Smash things. Or maybe a little cold viciousness will make his point. Kick her cat. Hang her dog. That ought to make her think twice before she decides not to do as he says. Or threaten her. Threaten to hit her or to beat her or to pull her hair out or to burn her. Or tell her he'll kill her, and maybe the kids too.

Pull all these means of control together, or even a few of them, and the abuser entraps and enslaves his partner in a web of control. If she manages to thwart one means of control, there are others at his disposal. Wherever she turns, there is another way he can control her. She is ensnared by multiple strands. She can't seem to escape— she is trapped. But with the addition of physical violence there is more to power and control than entrapment. There is terror.

For this reason the diagram does not include the violence as just another means of control, another spoke in the wheel. The violence is depicted, rather, as the rim of the wheel, holding all the spokes together. When violence is added to such a pattern of power and control, the abuse becomes much more than the sum of its parts. The ostensibly nonviolent tactics that accompany that violence take on a new, powerful, and frightening meaning—controlling the victim not only through their own specific constraints but also through their association with the knowledge that her partner will do anything to maintain control of the relationship, even attack her physically. Most obviously, the threats and intimidation are clearly more than idle threats if he has beaten her before. But even his "request" to see the grocery receipts becomes a "warning" if he has put her into the hospital this year. His calling her a stupid slut may feel like the beginning of a vicious physical attack. As battered women often report, "All he had to do was look at me that way, and I'd jump." What is for most of us the safest place in our world—home—is for her a place of constant fear.

Violent resistance. What is a woman to do when she finds herself terrorized in her own home? At some point, most women in such relationships do fight back physically. For some, this is an instinctive reaction to being attacked, and it happens at the first blow—almost without thought. For others, it doesn't happen until it seems he is going to continue to assault her repeatedly if she doesn't do something to stop him. For most women, the size difference between them and their male partner ensures that violent resistance won't help, and may make things worse, so they turn to other means of coping. For a few, eventually it seems that the only way out is to kill their partner.

Violence in the face of intimate terrorism may arise from any of a variety of motives. She may (at least at first) believe that she can defend herself, that her violent resistance will keep him from attacking her further. That may mean that she thinks she can stop him right now, in the midst of an attack, or it may mean that she thinks that if she fights back often enough he will eventually decide to stop attacking her physically. Even if she doesn't think she can stop him, she may feel that he shouldn't be allowed to attack her without being hurt himself. This desire to hurt him in return even if it won't stop him can be a form of communication ("What you're doing isn't right, and I'm going to fight back as hard as I can"), or it may be a form of retaliation or payback, along the lines of "He's not going to do that without paying some price for it." In a few cases, she may be after serious retaliation, attacking him when he is least expecting it and doing her best to do serious damage, even killing him. But there is sometimes another motive for such premeditated attacks—escape. Sometimes, after years of abuse and entrapment, a victim of intimate terrorism may feel that the only way she can escape from this horror is to kill her tormenter (Walker 1989).

It is clear that most women who are faced with intimate terrorism do escape from it. For example, Campbell's research finds that within two and a half years, two-thirds of women facing intimate terrorism are no longer in violent relationships (J. Campbell et al. 1998). The evidence also indicates, however, that escaping safely from such relationships can take time. Intimate terrorists entrap their partners using the same tactics they use to control them. If a woman has been so psychologically abused that she believes that her partner really can take her children away from her, how can she leave and abandon them to him? If a woman has no access to money or a job, how can she feed and clothe herself and her children when they escape? If she is monitored relentlessly and isolated from others, how can she get away and where can she go? If her partner has threatened to kill her and the children if she tries to leave, how can she leave safely?

What women in such situations typically do is gradually gather the resources they need to escape safely, sometimes doing this on their own, more often seeking help from others. They hide away small amounts of money until they have enough to get a small start, and they start working or going to school to develop a viable source of income, and they make plans with friends or a shelter to hide them during the period immediately after their escape, and they involve the police and courts for protection, and they join support groups to help them with their transition to independence and the emotional trauma produced by the psychological abuse, and on and on. The process is not a simple one. Catherine Kirkwood (1993) describes it as a "spiral" in which women leave multiple times, only to return, but each time garnering information and resources that will eventually allow them to leave for good. The process is complicated not only by the intimate terrorist's commitment to keeping her but also by the gender structure of institutions that may make it more difficult to leave than it would be in a more equitable society.

A Gender Theory of Domestic Violence (Intimate Terrorism)

Let me begin with a reminder that the foregoing discussion indicates that in heterosexual relationships the strongest correlate of type of intimate partner violence is gender. In heterosexual relationships intimate terrorism is perpetrated almost entirely by men and, of course, the violent resistance to it is from their female partners. The gendering of situational couple violence is less clear and will be addressed in the next section.

To a sociologist, the tremendous gender imbalance in the perpetration of intimate terrorism suggests important social structural causes that go beyond simple differences between men and women. For over two decades now, feminist sociologists have argued that gender must be understood as an institution, not merely an individual characteristic. Although some gender theorists have couched this argument in terms of rejecting gender as an individual characteristic in favor of focusing at the situational or institutional level of analysis (e.g., Ferree 1990), I prefer a version of gender theory that incorporates gender at all levels of social organization, from the individual level of sex differences in identities and attitudes, and even physical differences, through the situational enforcement of gender in social interaction to the gender structure of organizational and societal contexts (Ferree, Lorber, and Hess 2000; Risman 2004). The application of gender theory to intimate terrorism that follows will start with individual sex differences and work up to the gender structure of the economy, the family, and the criminal justice system.

Why is intimate terrorism in heterosexual relationships (and violent resistance to it) so clearly a matter of men abusing women? First, gender affects the use of violence to control one's partner in heterosexual relationships simply because of average sex differences in size and strength. The use of violence as one tactic in an attempt to exercise general control over one's partner requires more than the willingness to do violence. It requires a credible threat of a damaging violent response to noncompliance. Such a threat is, of course, more credible coming from a man than a woman simply because of the size difference in most heterosexual couples. Furthermore, still at the level of individual differences but focusing on gender socialization rather than physical differences, individual attitudes toward violence and experience with violence make such threats more likely and more credible from a man than from a woman. Put simply, the exercise

264 MICHAEL P. JOHNSON

of violence is more likely to be a part of boys' and men's experience than girls' and women's—in sports, fantasy play, and real-life conflict.

Second, individual misogyny and gender traditionalism are clearly implicated in intimate terrorism. Although critics of feminist theory often claim that there is no relationship between attitudes toward women and domestic violence (Felson 2002, 106), the research that has addressed this question in fact clearly supports the position that individual men's attitudes toward women affect the likelihood that they will be involved in intimate terrorism. One example is Holtzworth-Munroe's work, which shows that both of her two groups of intimate terrorists are more hostile toward women than are either nonviolent men or men involved in situational couple violence (e.g., Holtzworth-Munroe et al. 2000). More generally, Sugarman and Frankel (1996) conducted a thorough review of the research on this question, using a statistical technique that allowed them to combine the findings of all the studies that had been published up to that time. Whereas Holtzworth-Munroe demonstrated an effect of *hostility* toward women, Sugarman and Frankel focused on the effects of men's attitudes toward the role of women in social life and found that traditional men were more likely to be involved in attacks on their partners than were nontraditional men. The details of the Sugarman and Frankel review provide further support for the important role of attitudes toward women in intimate terrorism. They found that men's attitudes toward women were much more strongly related to violence in studies using samples that were dominated by intimate terrorism than in studies that were dominated by situational couple violence. Of course, this is exactly what a feminist theory of domestic violence would predict. It is intimate terrorism that involves the attempt to control one's partner, an undertaking supported by traditional or hostile attitudes toward women.

Third, at the level of social interaction rather than individual attitudes, our cultures of masculinity and femininity ensure that whatever the level of violence, its meaning will differ greatly depending on the gender of the perpetrator (Straus 1999). When a woman slaps her husband in the heat of an argument, it is unlikely to be interpreted by him as a serious attempt to do him physical harm. In fact, it is likely to be seen as a quaint form of feminine communication. Women's violence is taken less seriously, is less likely to produce fear, and is therefore less likely either to be intended as a control tactic or to be successful as one (Swan and Snow 2002).

Fourth, general social norms regarding intimate heterosexual partnerships, although certainly in the midst of considerable historical change, are heavily gendered and rooted in a patriarchal heterosexual model that validates men's power (Dobash and Dobash 1979, 1992; Yllö and Bograd 1988). These norms affect the internal functioning of all relationships, regardless of the individual attitudes of the partners, because couples' social networks are often involved in shaping the internal workings of personal relationships (Klein and Milardo 2000). When those networks support a male-dominant style of marriage or a view of marriage as a commitment "for better or worse," they can contribute to the entrapment of women in abusive relationships.

Finally, the gendering of the broader social context within which the relationship is embedded affects the resources the partners can draw on to shape the relationship and to cope with or escape from the violence. For example, the gender gap in wages can create an economic dependency that enhances men's control over women and contributes to women's entrapment in abusive relationships. The societal assignment of caregiving responsibilities primarily to women further contributes to this economic dependency, placing women in a subordinate position within the family and creating a context in which institutions such as the church that could be a source of support for abused women instead encourage them to stay in abusive relationships—for the sake of the children or for the sake of the marriage. Then there is the criminal justice system, heavily dominated by men and involving a culture of masculinity that has not always been responsive to the problems of women experiencing intimate terrorism, which was often treated as if it were situational couple violence (Buzawa 2003). On a more positive note, there have been major changes in all of these systems as a result of the women's movement in general and the battered women's movement in particular (Dobash and Dobash 1992). These changes are probably a major source of the recent dramatic decline in nonfatal intimate partner violence against women and fatal intimate partner violence against men in the United States (Rennison 2003).[3]

What about Situational Couple Violence?

It is not surprising that the institution of gender, in which male domination is a central element, is implicated in the structure of intimate terrorism, which is about coercive control. In contrast, situational couple violence, which is the most common type of partner violence, does not involve an attempt on the part of one partner to gain general control over the other, and by some criteria it appears to be more gender-symmetric. The violence is situationally provoked, as the tensions or emotions of a particular encounter lead one or both of the partners to resort to violence. Intimate relationships inevitably involve conflicts, and in some relationships one or more of those conflicts turns into an argument that escalates into violence. The violence may be minor and singular, with one encounter at some point in the relationship escalating to the level that someone pushes or slaps the other, is immediately remorseful, apologizes, and never does it again. Or the violence could be a chronic problem, with one or both partners frequently resorting to violence, minor or severe, even homicidal. In general, there is considerable variability in the nature of situational couple violence, a variability that has not yet been explored adequately enough to allow us to make confident statements about its causes.

Nevertheless, some researchers *have* made confident statements about one aspect of situational couple violence—its gender symmetry, a symmetry that in my view is mythical. The myth of gender symmetry in situational couple violence has been supported by the widespread use of a particularly meaningless measure of symmetry—incidence. Respondents in a survey are presented with a list of violent behaviors ranging from a push or a slap to an attack with a weapon. They are then asked to report how often they have committed each violent act against their partner (or their partner against them) in the previous twelve months. "Incidence of partner violence" is then defined as the percentage of a group (e.g., men or women) who have committed the act (or some set of the acts, often identified as mild or severe violent acts) at least once in the previous twelve months. The much-touted gender symmetry of situational couple violence is gender symmetry only in this narrow sense. For example, in the 1975 National Survey of Family Violence that initiated the gender-symmetry debate, 13 percent of women and 11 percent of men had committed at least one of the acts listed in the Conflict Tactics Scales (Steinmetz 1977–78). However, by any sensible measure of the nature of the violence, such as the specific acts engaged in, the injuries produced, the frequency of the violence, or the production of fear in one's partner, intimate partner violence (even situational couple violence) is not gender-symmetric (Archer 2000; Brush 1990; Hamberger and Guse 2002; Johnson 1999; Morse 1995; Tjaden and Thoennes 2000).

Thus, although situational couple violence may not be as gendered as intimate terrorism and violent resistance, many of the gender factors discussed earlier are implicated in the patterning of situational couple violence. For example, in situational couple violence the likelihood of injury or fear is influenced by size differences. A slap from a woman is still perceived as an entirely different act than is one from a man. Most important, our cultures of masculinity and femininity contribute to the couple communication problems that are often associated with situational couple violence (Johnson 2006).

Policy and Intervention

Different problems require different solutions. The fact that there is more than one type of intimate partner violence means that to some extent we must tailor our policies and intervention strategies to the specific characteristics of each of the types. Although situational couple violence is much more common than intimate terrorism—surveys indicate that one out of every eight married couples in the United States experiences some form of situational couple violence each year—most of our policies and interventions are designed to address intimate terrorism rather than situational couple violence. This focus on intimate terrorism has developed for a number of reasons: (a) the women's movement has been extremely effective in educating both the public and the criminal justice system about the nature of intimate terrorism, (b) intimate terrorism is more likely to come to the attention of agencies because it so often involves chronic and/or severe violence and because victims of intimate terrorism are more likely than victims of situational couple violence to need help in order to cope with the violence or to escape from it, and (c) the significant percentage of partner homicides that are a product of intimate terrorism emphasize the need for effective intervention in such situations.

Although conservative men's groups have decried this dominant focus on intimate terrorism because it ignores the violence of women (which they do not acknowledge is almost always either violent resistance or situational couple violence), the safest approach to intervention is to start with the assumption that every case of intimate partner violence involves intimate terrorism. The reason for this is that interventions for situational couple violence (such as couples counseling) are likely to put a victim of intimate terrorism at considerable risk. If we were to do as one recent article suggested and recommend counseling that would help couples to "work together to harmonize their relationships" (Fergusson, Horwood, and Ridder 2005), we would be asking women who are terrorized by their partners to go into a counseling situation that calls for honesty, encouraging victims to tell the truth to a partner who in many cases has beaten them severely in response to criticism and who might well murder them in response to their attempt to "harmonize" (Johnson 2005).

Thus, our understanding of the differences among these types of intimate partner violence suggests that the best strategy in individual cases is to assume intimate terrorism and to work closely with the victim only (not the couple) until it is absolutely clear that the violence is situational couple violence. In the shelter movement, which for the most part works on a feminist empowerment model, this means working with the victim on coping with the violence within the relationship, providing safe temporary shelter, involving the courts through arrest or protection from abuse orders, developing a safety plan for the immediate future, and—if the victim so wishes—developing the strategies and resources needed to escape from the relationship safely.

How can we as a society work to reduce the incidence of intimate partner violence? First, we need to send the message that violence against intimate partners will not be tolerated. Arrest and prosecution would send that message both to the general public and to the individuals who are arrested. Second, the educational programs about relationship violence that have been developed in the battered women's movement and presented in many school districts around the country could become a regular part of our school curricula, teaching children and adolescents about equality and respect in our personal relationships. Finally, we can work to increase support for programs in hospitals, shelters, and the courts that screen for intimate partner violence and help its victims either to stop the violence or to escape from it safely.

NOTES

1. There is a fourth type, *mutual violent control*, that involves two intimate terrorists vying for control of their relationship. This type appears in very small numbers in some samples and there is some debate about whether it is a true type or an artifact of the constraints of imperfect operationalization.

2. I am going to use gendered pronouns here because the vast majority of intimate terrorists are men terrorizing female partners. That does not mean that women are *never* intimate terrorists. There are a small number of women who do terrorize their male partners (Steinmetz 1977–78), and there are also women in same-sex relationships who terrorize their female partners (Renzetti and Miley 1996).

3. It is important to note that this discussion of gender is relevant only to heterosexual relationships. In same-sex relationships, some aspects of gender may still be important (e.g., gender differences in attitudes toward and experience with violence might produce more violence in gay men's relationships than in lesbian relationships), others will be largely irrelevant (e.g., gay and lesbian relationship norms are more egalitarian, and sex differences in size and strength will be less likely to be significant), and some will play themselves out in quite different ways (e.g.,

reactions of the criminal justice system may be affected by officers' attitudes toward gay men and lesbians). Although we know considerably less about same-sex relationships than we do about heterosexual relationships, there is a growing literature that is important not only in its own right but also because it sheds light on some of the inadequacies of theories rooted in research on heterosexual relationships (Renzetti 1992, 2002; Renzetti and Miley 1996).

Chapter Sixteen

Violence in Intimate Relationships
A Feminist Perspective

bell hooks

We were on the freeway, going home from San Francisco. He was driving. We were arguing. He had told me repeatedly to shut up. I kept talking. He took his hand from the steering wheel and threw it back, hitting my mouth—my open mouth, blood gushed, and I felt an intense pain. I was no longer able to say any words, only to make whimpering, sobbing sounds as the blood dripped on my hands, on the handkerchief I held too tightly. He did not stop the car. He drove home. I watched him pack his suitcase. It was a holiday. He was going away to have fun. When he left I washed my mouth. My jaw was swollen and it was difficult for me to open it.

I called the dentist the next day and made an appointment. When the female voice asked what I needed to see the doctor about, I told her I had been hit in the mouth. Conscious of race, sex, and class issues, I wondered how I would be treated in this white doctor's office. My face was no longer swollen so there was nothing to identify me as a woman who had been hit, as a black woman with a bruised and swollen jaw. When the dentist asked me what had happened to my mouth, I described it calmly and succinctly. He made little jokes about how "we can't have someone doing this to us now, can we?" I said nothing. The damage was repaired. Through it all, he talked to me as if I were a child, someone he had to handle gingerly or otherwise I might become hysterical.

This is one way women who are hit by men and seek medical care are seen. People within patriarchal society imagine that women are hit because we are hysterical, because we are beyond reason. It is most often the person who is hitting that is beyond reason, who is hysterical, who has lost complete control over responses and actions.

Growing up, I had always thought that I would never allow any man to hit me and live. I would kill him. I had seen my father hit my mother once and I wanted to kill him. My mother said to me then, "You are too young to know, too young to understand." Being a mother in a culture that supports and promotes domination, a patriarchal, white-supremacist culture, she did not discuss how she felt or what she meant. Perhaps it would have been too difficult for her to speak about the confusion of being hit by someone you are intimate with, someone you love. In my case, I was hit by my companion at a time in life when a number of forces in the world outside our home had

From *Talking Back: Thinking Feminist*, Thinking Black, South End Press, 1989, pp. 84–91. Reprinted by permission.

already "hit" me, so to speak, made me painfully aware of my powerlessness, my marginality. It seemed then that I was confronting being black and female and without money in the worst possible ways. My world was spinning. I had already lost a sense of grounding and security. The memory of this experience has stayed with me as I have grown as a feminist, as I have thought deeply and read much on male violence against women, on adult violence against children.

In this essay, I do not intend to concentrate attention solely on male physical abuse of females. It is crucial that feminists call attention to physical abuse in all its forms. In particular, I want to discuss being physically abused in singular incidents by someone you love. Few people who are hit once by someone they love respond in the way they might to a singular physical assault by a stranger. Many children raised in households where hitting has been a normal response by primary caretakers react ambivalently to physical assaults as adults, especially if they are being hit by someone who cares for them and whom they care for. Often female parents use physical abuse as a means of control. There is continued need for feminist research that examines such violence. Alice Miller has done insightful work on the impact of hitting even though she is at times antifeminist in her perspective. (Often in her work, mothers are blamed, as if their responsibility in parenting is greater than that of fathers.) Feminist discussions of violence against women should be expanded to include a recognition of the ways in which women use abusive physical force toward children not only to challenge the assumptions that women are likely to be nonviolent, but also to add to our understanding of why children who were hit growing up are often hit as adults or hit others.

Recently, I began a conversation with a group of black adults about hitting children. They all agreed that hitting was sometimes necessary. A professional black male in a southern family setting with two children commented on the way he punished his daughters. Sitting them down, he would first interrogate them about the situation or circumstance for which they were being punished. He said with great pride, "I want them to be able to understand fully why they are being punished." I responded by saying that "they will likely become women whom a lover will attack using the same procedure you who have loved them so well used and they will not know how to respond." He resisted the idea that his behavior would have any impact on their responses to violence as adult women. I pointed to case after case of women in intimate relationships with men (and sometimes women) who are subjected to the same form of interrogation and punishment they experienced as children, who accept their lover assuming an abusive, authoritarian role. Children who are the victims of physical abuse—whether one beating or repeated beatings, one violent push or several—whose wounds are inflicted by a loved one, experience an extreme sense of dislocation. The world one has most intimately known, in which one felt relatively safe and secure, has collapsed. Another world has come into being, one filled with terrors, where it is difficult to distinguish between a safe situation and a dangerous one, a gesture of love and a violent, uncaring gesture. There is a feeling of vulnerability, exposure, that never goes away, that lurks beneath the surface. I know. I was one of those children. Adults hit by loved ones usually experience similar sensations of dislocation, of loss, of new-found terrors.

Many children who are hit have never known what it feels like to be cared for, loved without physical aggression or abusive pain. Hitting is such a widespread practice that any of us are lucky if we can go through life without having this experience. One undiscussed aspect of the reality of children who are hit finding themselves as adults in similar circumstances is that we often share with friends and lovers the framework of our childhood pains, and this may determine how they respond to us in difficult situations. We share the ways we are wounded and expose vulnerable areas. Often, these revelations provide a detailed model for anyone who wishes to wound or hurt us. While the literature about physical abuse often points to the fact that children who are abused are likely to become abusers or be abused, there is no attention given to sharing woundedness in such a way that we let intimate others know exactly what can be done to hurt us, to make us feel as though we are caught in the destructive patterns we have struggled to break. When partners create scenarios of abuse similar, if not exactly the same, to those we have experienced in childhood, the wounded person is hurt not only by the physical pain but by the feeling of calculated betrayal. Betrayal. When we are physically hurt by loved ones, we feel betrayed. We can no longer trust that care can be sustained. We are wounded, damaged—hurt to our hearts.

Feminist work calling attention to male violence against women has helped create a climate where the issues of physical abuse by loved ones can be freely addressed, especially sexual abuse within families. Exploration of male violence against women by feminists and nonfeminists shows a connection between childhood experience of being hit by loved ones and the later occurrence of violence in adult relationships. While there is much material available discussing physical abuse of women by men, usually extreme physical abuse, there is not much discussion of the impact that one incident of hitting may have on a person in an intimate relationship, or how the person who is hit recovers from that experience. Increasingly, in discussion with women about physical abuse in relationships, irrespective of sexual preference, I find that most of us have had the experience of being violently hit at least once. There is little discussion of how we are damaged by such experiences (especially if we have been hit as children), of the ways we cope and recover from this wounding. This is an important area for feminist research precisely because many cases of extreme physical abuse begin with an isolated incident of hitting. Attention must be given to understanding and stopping these isolated incidents if we are to eliminate the possibility that women will be at risk in intimate relationships.

Critically thinking about issues of physical abuse has led me to question the way our culture, the way we as feminist advocates, focus on the issue of violence and physical abuse by loved ones. The focus has been on male violence against women and, in particular, male sexual abuse of children. Given the nature of patriarchy, it has been necessary for feminists to focus on extreme cases to make people confront the issue, and acknowledge it to be serious and relevant. Unfortunately, an exclusive focus on extreme cases can and does lead us to ignore the more frequent, more common, yet less extreme case of occasional hitting. Women are also less likely to acknowledge occasional hitting for fear that they will then be seen as someone who is in a bad relationship or someone whose life is out of control. Currently, the literature about male violence against women identifies the physically abused woman as a "battered woman." While it has been important to have an accessible terminology to draw attention to the issue of male violence against women, the terms used reflect biases because they call attention to only one type of violence in intimate relationships. The term "battered woman" is problematical. It is not a term that emerged from feminist work on male violence against women; it was already used by psychologists and sociologists in the literature on domestic violence. This label "battered woman" places primary emphasis on physical assaults that are continuous, repeated, and unrelenting. The focus is on extreme violence, with little effort to link these cases with the everyday acceptance within intimate relationships of physical abuse that is not extreme, that may not be repeated. Yet these lesser forms of physical abuse damage individuals psychologically and, if not properly addressed and recovered from, can set the stage for more extreme incidents.

Most importantly, the term "battered woman" is used as though it constitutes a separate and unique category of womanness, as though it is an identity, a mark that sets one apart rather than being simply a descriptive term. It is as though the experience of being repeatedly violently hit is the sole defining characteristic of a woman's identity and all other aspects of who she is and what her experience has been are submerged. When I was hit, I too used the popular phrases "batterer," "battered woman," "battering" even though I did not feel that these words adequately described being hit once. However, these were the terms that people would listen to, would see as important, significant (as if it is not really significant for an individual, and more importantly for a woman, to be hit once). My partner was angry to be labeled a batterer by me. He was reluctant to talk about the experience of hitting me precisely because he did not want to be labeled a batterer. I had hit him once (not as badly as he had hit me), and I did not think of myself as a batterer. For both of us, these terms were inadequate. Rather than enabling us to cope effectively and positively with a negative situation, they were part of all the mechanisms of denial; they made us want to avoid confronting what had happened. This is the case for many people who are hit and those who hit.

Women who are hit once by men in their lives and women who are hit repeatedly do not want to be placed in the category of "battered woman" because it is a label that appears to strip us of dignity, to deny that there has been any integrity in the relationships we are in. A person physically assaulted by a stranger or a casual friend with whom they are not intimate may be hit once or repeatedly, but they do not have to be placed into a category before doctors, lawyers, family, counselors, etc., take their problem seriously. Again, it must be stated that establishing categories and terminology has been part of the effort to draw public attention to the seriousness of male violence against women in intimate relationships. Even though the use of convenient labels and categories has made it easier to identify problems of physical abuse, it does not mean the terminology should not be critiqued from a feminist perspective and changed if necessary.

Recently, I had an experience assisting a woman who had been brutally attacked by her husband (she never commented on whether this was the first incident or not), which caused me to reflect anew on the use of the term "battered woman." This young woman was not engaged in feminist thinking or aware that "battered woman" was a category. Her husband had tried to choke her to death. She managed to escape from him with only the clothes she was wearing. After she recovered from the trauma, she considered going back to this relationship. As a church-going woman, she believed that her marriage vows were sacred and that she should try to make the relationship work. In an effort to share my feeling that this could place her at great risk, I brought her Lenore Walker's *The Battered Woman* because it seemed to me that there was much that she was not revealing, that she felt alone, and that the experiences she would read about in the book would give her a sense that other women had experienced what she was going through. I hoped reading the book would give her the courage to confront the reality of her situation. Yet I found it difficult to share because I could see that her self-esteem had already been greatly attacked, that she had lost a sense of her worth and value, and that possibly this categorizing of her identity would add to the feeling that she should just forget, be silent (and certainly returning to a situation where one is likely to be abused is one way to mask the severity of the problem). Still I had to try. When I first gave her the book, it disappeared. An unidentified family member had thrown it away. They felt that she would be making a serious mistake if she began to see herself as an absolute victim, which they felt the label "battered woman" implied. I stressed that she should ignore the labels and read the content. I believed the experience shared in this book helped give her the courage to be critical of her situation, to take constructive action.

Her response to the label "battered woman," as well as the responses of other women who have been victims of violence in intimate relationships, compelled me to critically explore further the use of this term. In conversation with many women, I found that it was seen as a stigmatizing label, one which victimized women seeking help felt themselves in no condition to critique. As in, "who cares what anybody is calling it—I just want to stop this pain." Within patriarchal society, women who are victimized by male violence have had to pay a price for breaking the silence and naming the problem. They have had to be seen as fallen women, who have failed in their "feminine" role to sensitize and civilize the beast in the man. A category like "battered woman" risks reinforcing this notion that the hurt woman, not only the rape victim, becomes a social pariah, set apart, marked forever by this experience.

A distinction must be made between having a terminology that enables women, and all victims of violent acts, to name the problem and categories of labeling that may inhibit that naming. When individuals are wounded, we are indeed often scarred, often damaged in ways that do set us apart from those who have not experienced a similar wounding, but an essential aspect of the recovery process is the healing of the wound, the removal of the scar. This is an empowering process that should not be diminished by labels that imply this wounding experience is the most significant aspect of identity.

As I have already stated, overemphasis on extreme cases of violent abuse may lead us to ignore the problem of occasional hitting, and it may make it difficult for women to talk about this problem. A critical issue that is not fully examined and written about in great detail by researchers who study and work with victims is the recovery process. There is a dearth of material discussing the recovery process of individuals who have been physically abused. In those cases where an individual is hit only once in an intimate relationship, however violently, there may be no recognition at all of the negative impact of this experience. There may be no conscious attempt by the victimized person to work at restoring her or his well-being, even if the person seeks therapeutic help, because the one incident may not be seen as serious or damaging. Alone and in isolation, the person who has been hit must struggle to regain broken trust—to forge some strategy of recovery. Individuals are often able to process an experience of being hit mentally that may not be processed emotionally. Many women I talked with felt that even after the incident was long forgotten, their bodies remain troubled. Instinctively, the person who has been hit may respond fearfully to any body movement on the part of a loved one that is similar to the posture used when pain was inflicted.

Being hit once by a partner can forever diminish sexual relationships if there has been no recovery process. Again there is little written about ways folks recover physically in their sexualities as loved ones who continue to be sexual with those who have hurt them. In most cases, sexual relationships are dramatically altered when hitting has occurred. The sexual realm may be the one space where the person who has been hit experiences again the sense of vulnerability, which may also arouse fear. This can lead either to an attempt to avoid sex or to unacknowledged sexual withdrawal wherein the person participates but is passive. I talked with women who had been hit by lovers who described sex as an ordeal, the one space where they confront their inability to trust a partner who has broken trust. One woman emphasized that to her, being hit was a "violation of her body space" and that she felt from then on she had to protect that space. This response, though a survival strategy, does not lead to healthy recovery.

Often, women who are hit in intimate relationships with male or female lovers feel as though we have lost an innocence that cannot be regained. Yet this very notion of innocence is connected to passive acceptance of concepts of romantic love under patriarchy which have served to mask problematic realities in relationships. The process of recovery must include a critique of this notion of innocence which is often linked to an unrealistic and fantastic vision of love and romance. It is only in letting go of the perfect, no-work, happily-ever-after union idea that we can rid our psyches of the sense that we have failed in some way by not having such relationships. Those of us who never focused on the negative impact of being hit as children find it necessary to reexamine the past in a therapeutic manner as part of our recovery process. Strategies that helped us survive as children may be detrimental for us to use in adult relationships.

Talking about being hit by loved ones with other women, both as children and as adults, I found that many of us had never really thought very much about our own relationship to violence. Many of us took pride in never feeling violent, never hitting. We had not thought deeply about our relationship to inflicting physical pain. Some of us expressed terror and awe when confronted with physical strength on the part of others. For us, the healing process included the need to learn how to use physical force constructively, to remove the terror—the dread. Despite the research that suggests children who are hit may become adults who hit—women hitting children, men hitting women and children—most of the women I talked with not only did not hit but were compulsive about not using physical force.

Overall the process by which women recover from the experience of being hit by loved ones is a complicated and multifaceted one, an area where there must be much more feminist study and research. To many of us, feminists' calling attention to the reality of violence in intimate relationships has not in and of itself compelled most people to take the issue seriously, and such violence seems to be daily on the increase. In this essay, I have raised issues that are not commonly talked about, even among folks who are particularly concerned about violence against women. I hope it will serve as a catalyst for further thought, that it will strengthen our efforts as feminist activists to create a world where domination and coercive abuse are never aspects of intimate relationships.

Chapter Seventeen

Violence, Gender, and Elder Abuse
Toward a Feminist Analysis and Practice

Terri Whittaker

Introduction

The last twenty-five years have witnessed a mass of research and intervention targeted at child abuse and domestic violence. However, it is only fairly recently, in the context of rapid demographic change and growing anxiety about the family, that policy makers and academics have shown an interest in elder abuse (Phillipson 1993). Specifically, there has been an upswing in research emanating in the main from the USA which has focused on the modern phenomenon of elder abuse (Sengstock and Liang 1982; Phillips 1986; Godkin et al. 1989; Pillemer and Wolf 1986; Quinn and Tomita 1986; Eastman 1984; Pritchard 1992; Bennett and Kingston 1993; Decalmer and Glendenning 1993).

This new momentum in research interest has been dominated by professionals and "experts" from the field of "family violence" and by a health/welfare model of elder abuse. This approach locates causation within individuals or families and seeks to develop typologies or "profiles" of abusers/abused within various models of family violence in an attempt to make predictions about those most at risk of harm (Parton 1985). This selective claiming and framing of elder abuse as a product of interpersonal dynamics and/or of various forms of family violence is linked to significant theoretical, definitional, and methodological problems which have led to wide-ranging and contradictory findings (McCreadie 1991; Decalmer and Glendenning 1993). Nonetheless this "orthodoxy" looks set fair to achieve the status of "common sense" amongst those working in the area of elder abuse. Within the literature on elder abuse there is a curious lack of discussion about why it occurs and little reference to the complex social and political problems inherent in the construction and resolution of social problems.

One of the few consistent findings from the research literature on elder abuse is that the majority of "victims" of elder abuse are old women (McCreadie 1991, 21). This is especially so in relation to physical and/or sexual abuse (Pillemer and Wolf 1986; Holt 1993). However, there has been no systematic attempt to develop a feminist analysis of elder abuse, which appears to have been screened out of the debate on the grounds that women have been found to abuse their elders too (Godkin et al. 1989; Pillemer and Wolf 1986; Pillemer and Suitor 1988). This paper represents an attempt to acquire and trans-

From *Journal of Gender Studies* 4, no. 1 (1995): 35–46. Reprinted by permission of Taylor and Francis Ltd.

form "orthodox" knowledge in an effort to illustrate the gendered nature of elder abuse and chart the beginnings of a feminist analysis. The need for more adequate theorizing about causation is identified particularly at the social structural level and in relation to the social and political construction of the "family," old age, and masculinity.

Elder Abuse: Definitions, Prevalence, and Incidence

Definitions

The first stage in developing any adequate form of policy or practice amongst those involved in elder abuse necessitates reaching agreement on what it is, how common it is, why it happens, and how best to respond to it.

McCreadie's (1991) review of available USA and UK research reveals that the process of reaching agreement about elder abuse is fraught with difficulties. It appears that professionals and academics have been heavily involved in debates about definitions, incidence, and prevalence at the expense of adequate theorizing. The main problems seem to centre around which criteria to include or exclude in various definitions of abuse and around whether or not elder abuse is different from other forms of "family violence."

These difficulties have been attributed to differences in emphasis and perspective amongst investigators and a tendency to distinguish between typologies and conceptualizations of elder abuse and neglect. This "definitional disarray" and failure to reach consensus is a major thread throughout the published literature. There appears to be no attempt to include the victim's subjective experience of abuse as part of the definitional debate, and virtually no attention is paid to issues of inequalities of power between victim and perpetrator other than to stress that old people are not children and that dependency exists as a two-way process within relationships between them and their abusers (Ogg and Bennett 1992).

Prevalence and Incidence of Elder Abuse

The concern with numbers of old people who are abused appears to be another false trail. As yet we cannot say exactly how common elder abuse is. There has been no major study of the prevalence or incidence of elder abuse in Britain. Evidence from the USA indicates that 10 percent of elders supported by family members are at risk (Eastman and Sutton 1982, 12). In Britain, Ogg and Bennett (1992, 63) have translated American figures to arrive at an estimate of "eight elderly people who are subjected to abuse or inadequate care within a patient register of 200." Other investigators have commented upon the methodological problems pertaining to much of the American research relating to prevalence/incidence (Decalmer and Glendenning 1993, 12), while others point to difficulties inherent in the fact that much elder abuse is hidden and unreported (McPherson 1990, 360).

Hairsplitting discussions about what is elder abuse and how common it is obscure the evidence that a significant number of old women are exposed to unacceptable forms of violence from adult men in particular and detracts from thinking about why it happens. Much more important than establishing an agreed definition or a prevalence rate is agreeing on a set of rules about what is permissible or not and ensuring that old people are protected as and when necessary and/or appropriate.

Victims and Perpetrators

Until recently, most research attention has been focused on the characteristics of the "victims" of elder abuse and on the production of a stereotypical picture of the nature of old age. The "classic" victim of elder abuse has been painted by various British, Canadian, and American researchers (Horrocks 1988; Tomlin 1989; Bennett 1990) as

1. Female aged over 75.
2. Living at home with adult carer/s.
3. Physically and/or mentally impaired.
4. Roleless. Lost previous roles as wife/mother/caregiver.
5. Isolated, fearful.

This profile of the "victim" of abuse has run parallel with liberal explanations of elder abuse concentrated on depicting a straight correlation between biological aging and dependency (Phillips 1986, 198). The situational or "carer stress" model in which elder abuse is persistently explained in these terms has had huge appeal for professionals who, while not condoning abuse as such, have been able to empathize with this picture of old age and the strain of caring. In so doing, there has been a tendency to downplay the gender significance of elder abuse and to look for victim-related sources of stress, thereby falling into the "victim blaming" trap and colluding with various forms of institutionalized ageism and sexism (Traynor and Hasnip 1984).

Recently, a more complex picture of victims and perpetrators has begun to emerge which indicates that old men are also victims of elder abuse while women are also perpetrators. Though there is consistent agreement that the overwhelming majority of abusers are men and the majority of victims are old women, research does demonstrate that frail, vulnerable old men are also victims of abuse and that some of their abusers are women (Godkin et al. 1989; Pillemer and Wolf 1986; Pillemer and Suitor 1988).

Within newer research there is a suggestion of gender-specific differences in the forms and types of abuse which occur (Homer and Gilleard 1990; Holt 1993). Miller and Dodder (1989) separated physical abuse from neglect and discovered a statistically different sex bias in that men were more likely to physically abuse while women were more likely to neglect the old person in their care. They point to the high rates of reported neglect by women and stress that this may create the appearance of large numbers of female abusers when in fact the nature and extent of physical or sexual elder abuse by men is as yet unknown and there is much more resistance to disclosure of abuse of this type. Holt (1993), investigating ninety cases of elder abuse, discovered a female-to-male victim ratio of 6:1 and that all but two abusers were male. Holt hypothesized that the common denominator between male and female victims of abuse was physical and mental frailty and their consequent vulnerability to abuse by those in positions of power and authority.

Orthodox research, underpinned by liberal notions of old age as dependency and a concern with preserving the "family," has generally failed to adequately examine the significance of gender as a centrally important feature of elder abuse. This may account for the shift in research focus away from the characteristics of predominantly female victims towards the characteristics and circumstances of perpetrators and a concern with the "dynamics" of their interpersonal relationships. In this context, the resistance to the idea that elder abuse is predominantly a male problem has been manifested in various forms including a focus on an increasing number of female abusers and the claim that women are also perpetrators of elder abuse. In this way, "experts" justify refusing to engage with feminist analysis and fail to recognise or acknowledge men's power in the world and in the family.

Women are of course quite capable of abusing power and trust or of exploiting old people to fulfil their own emotional and material needs. However, it seems they rarely resort to physical and/or sexual abuse. This does not imply that women are morally superior but suggests that if we refuse to consider gender-specific behaviours, we may lose important clues as to why elder abuse occurs.

The Perpetrators and Their Characteristics and Circumstances

In recent years, the focus of attention in elder abuse has shifted from "granny battering." New research has drawn on theories of family pathology to challenge the ideas of a close association between abuse and the physical and/or mental state of the "victim," suggesting that the characteristics and circumstances of the perpetrators may be more important risk indicators (Pillemer and Wolf 1986; Homer and Gilleard 1990). The notion of "inadequate care," which is underpinned by a model of a stressed and/or pathological abuser, has been introduced to facilitate this shift (Fulmer and O'Malley 1987). Various attempts have been made to identify the predisposing factors leading to abuse, and researchers have emphasized the dependency of "carers" on victims and on drugs or alcohol as significant factors.

As a result, earlier ways of seeing and thinking about elder abuse as a form of "granny battering" have been dismissed. What is called "the initial stereotyped plot" (Bennett and Kingston 1993) is set aside in favour of a new orthodoxy in which it is held that elder abuse is much more complex, consisting of a varied set of characteristics and relationships which occur within the context of the relationship between the victim and the carer (Homer and Gilleard 1990).

From a feminist perspective there is some irony in the continued use of the word "carer" and the deliberate misuse of gender-neutral language to mask gender-specific behaviour. Language such as "carers," victims, perpetrators, abusers, and abused all serve to obscure the gender significance of data. This, together with information relating to the inadequate personality types of the "carers," forms the basis for "compassion" as opposed to "control" philosophies of assessment and intervention (Bennett and

Kingston 1993). In this context, notions of family autonomy and support for "carers" dominate policy and practice formulations, while legal and punitive modes of intervention are considered unhelpful (Newberger and Bourne 1977).

The Relationship between Elder Abuse and "Family" Violence

Recently, there has been a growing interest and concern among researchers in the nature and extent of the relationship between elder abuse and other forms of family violence. Elder abuse is said to occur in a context of family relations, and therefore it is argued, more attention needs to be paid to the literature relating to child and spouse abuse (Pillemer and Suitor 1988). Some writers have argued that elder abuse should be seen as a part of the spectrum of domestic abuse which affects all ages (Department of Health Social Service Inspectorate 1992), while others have sought to establish a special category for elder abuse and associated programmes of assessment and intervention (Finkelhor and Pillemer 1988).

The growing interest in domestic violence in general and child abuse and spouse abuse in particular looks set to dominate the discourse on elder abuse. However, as with early research and debates on child abuse the interest is confined to certain liberal and conservative theories of family violence which are often not made explicit. In this context, the growing interest in the "family" is not about making the gender significance of research data more explicit or about exposing the problems of sexual politics inherent in elder abuse. Instead, the research reflects a growing anxiety about the nature of the "family" and a concern to enshrine and safeguard "normal" family relationships.

Five major explanations rooted in theories of family violence are examined at various points in the research (Pillemer 1986). They are:

1. Pathology of abuser: intra-individual dynamics.
2. Cycle of violence: violence transmitted between generations.
3. Dependency: of abused and/or abuser.
4. Isolation: limited social networks/denial of access.
5. External stress: unemployment, bereavement, inadequate community care, low income, poor housing.

Pillemer and Suitor (1988, 49), reviewing the literature associated with these themes, argue:

> These factors may directly precipitate domestic violence against the elderly. That is *families* that have one of these characteristics may be at greater risk of elder abuse. (my italics)

What is crucial here is the focus on the "family" rather than particular individuals who may have abused or been abused. Indeed the literature is now beginning to be peppered with references to "abusive families" (Godkin et al. 1989) as "systems" or sets of interrelationships which are not functioning properly. Thus, elder abuse becomes a *symptom* of what is wrong within the *family,* and the personality traits and behaviour of both victims and abusers become fair game, however widely they vary. Discussion of the complex gender issues and sexual politics inherent in the relationship between them is completely avoided, and there is no attempt to explain why it is mostly men who abuse. Instead, we are prompted towards compassionate responses as we learn that "carers" have histories of psychosocial disorder, are addicted to drugs or alcohol, and/or are dependent upon the predominantly frail and vulnerable old women they are "caring" for:

> Elders *(mostly women)* mistreated by spouses *(mostly male)* were more apt to suffer from physical abuse, to be in poorer emotional health and to be more dependent on them for companionship, financial resources, management and maintenance of property. The perpetrators were more likely to have both recent and long term medical complaints and to have experienced a recent decline in physical health. . . . They were also more likely to have a history of mental illness and alcoholism. (Wolf and Bergman 1989, 163; my italics)

Another twist to the tale of the "problem relative" (Pillemer and Finkelhor 1989) lies in the notion of the "cycle of violence." Here, some commentators argue that elder abuse is directly related to the fact that perpetrators were themselves products of domestic violence which had become learned behaviour and normative for them (Fulmer and O'Malley 1987). The child-abuse literature has shown how dangerous these ideas are and pointed to the way they feed myths about "pathological" families and fuel class and race stereotypes to the point where abusers have been known to tell their victims that abuse is quite normal (Nelson 1987, 48).

The idea that "perpetrators" abuse because they were themselves abused says nothing about the number of perpetrators who were abused in childhood who do not go on to abuse young or old women or about the number of women who were abused in childhood but have not married or had relationships with men who abused them at any point in their lifespan. There has been no attempt to describe or confirm a causal link between childhood or family abuse and adults who abuse old people, yet it is important not to underestimate the strength of these ideas. Not only do they have a spurious liberal appeal by saying that individual men are not to blame, but they are also internalized by all of us and their effect is to prompt compassionate and therapeutic responses and to absolve the abuser of responsibility by inferring that he is a victim too!

From Anger to Analysis: Toward a Feminist Analysis of Elder Abuse

There is scope for growing anger as one reads the annals of academic enquiry into elder abuse. However, if we are to move from the suspicion of conspiracy toward a better understanding of why elder abuse occurs and to an adequate examination of the complex gender, social, and political issues therein, we must move beyond rage and "problem families."

Ageing society is primarily a female society. It is well known that women generally outlive men and that ageism and sexism combine to produce a socially constructed dependency in old age in which the feminization of poverty is a key feature (Taylor and Ford 1983; Walker 1990; Glendenning 1987). These social processes are so pervasive that it is but a small step from here to accept as inevitable the discrimination and disadvantage which old women experience and to render them and their experiences invisible. MacDonald and Rich (1984) note that for older women, invisibility is symbolic of the process and politics of aging and point to the way this extends to the feminist movement, which until recently has given very little thought to the position of older women in the family. Any adequate analysis of elder abuse must take account of the social structural position of old women in our society and how this relates to their position within the family and the resources they have at their disposal to resist abusive behaviours.

In this context, it is perhaps not so extraordinary that the high levels of severe physical abuse experienced by old women who rely on their "carers" for financial, practical, and emotional support are explained by reference to demographics, longevity, and variations in reporting elder abuse (Johnson et al. 1985; Pillemer and Wolf 1986). The sexual, social, and economic politics which underpin their relationships with men within the "family" are not explored. Does this mean, as Schecter (1982) suggests, that we are indifferent to the pain and danger in old women's lives or that we prefer to hide behind principles of family autonomy and self-determination rather than get involved? Feminist analysis starts with gender. In looking at why elders get abused we are not looking at some psychopathological abuser or dependent, provoking, or controlling old woman who "initiates" abuse (Penhale 1993). Nor are we looking at problems of "inadequate caregiving" or even at "dysfunctional families." A feminist analysis will consider problematic sexual and adult-child politics and take account of the marginalization of old people in general and old women in particular within our society. In this context, elder abuse is not the product of a pathological family but of a patriarchal family in which men have access to and power over those less powerful and more vulnerable than themselves and regard them as their property. In so doing they are protected by societal norms which uphold the sanctity and privacy of "home" despite it being the prime site of women's oppression.

From this perspective, the references in the literature to the provoking and controlling characteristics and behaviours of "noncompliant" dependent victims (Steinmetz 1988; Homer and Gilleard 1990)—"the caregiver is seen as being driven to a sense of helplessness, rage and frustration" (Decalmer and Glendenning 1993, 15)—can be seen as attempts by old women to struggle against and resist the power and control of men and women in their lives. However these behaviours are more commonly seen as indicators of carer stress and used to explain and justify abusive behaviours and prompt compassionate responses which absolve the abuser from responsibility. Instead of problematizing the biology of old age and associated vulnerability and dependency, feminists consider the socially constructed aspects of dependency which women young and old experience (albeit differently) and look for answers to abuse in the cultural representation of masculinity, femininity, and sexuality.

As yet the voices of "survivors" of elder abuse have not been heard above those of "experts" in the field, so we know very little about the strategies or tactics employed by victims to resist or cope with abuse. The difficulties inherent in helping victims to talk and tell due to fear of stigma, institutionalization, or physical and mental frailty can be overcome by validating the feelings and experiences of old women. Feil (1993) has developed techniques for communicating with vulnerable old people which may prove useful in this respect. However, there is an urgent need for feminists to test the transferability of knowledge and expertise relating to "disclosure" processes to the area of elder abuse (Kelly 1988). There is a need to build up a body of knowledge based on old women's experiences of abuse and to learn about what is helpful from this. Feminist policies for tackling abuse must therefore be concerned with advocacy and empowerment and with increasing the resources old women have available to them to empower themselves and help them resist male violence.

Feminist theory holds that abuse of women is just one part of a spectrum of male violence and that it is a mistake to separate off any particular manifestation or to see it as a special case. This is not to argue against the complexity of elder abuse or to suggest that feminist theory, with its focus on gender, is the only dimension for analysis and theorizing about the phenomenon. It is, however, an argument against those who insist that elder abuse deserves a special category because of the dependency or vulnerability of victims or because of the difficulties inherent in locating responsibility due to the fact that old women are legally autonomous beings.

The argument about legal autonomy is a spurious one. Everything we know about male violence to women tells us that their legal status as adults offers little in the way of the protection women say they want from the men who abuse them (Kelly 1987). Equally, the argument for special categories and programmes due to the dependency and vulnerability of old people is at best misguided paternalism, and at worst another example of resistance to feminist analysis. While the orthodox insistence on separation of elder abuse from the spectrum of other forms of male violence remains unchallenged, thinking and theorizing about elder abuse will continue to be powerfully constrained and woefully inadequate. One of the lessons learned from child-abuse work which is transferable is that the answer as to why the majority of abusers are male will not be found in studying their victims or in gender-blind studies of their personal inadequacies or those of their families (Dobash and Dobash 1992).

From Analysis to Practice

A feminist challenge to orthodox practice with elder abuse will tackle notions of old women as burdensome, controlling, and provoking individuals who initiate their own abuse by stressed-out carers within dysfunctional families, or as legally autonomous adults who cannot be protected because of their rights to say "no." No matter how scientifically and academically respectable orthodox thinking on elder abuse is, the first aim of feminist practice must be to develop and argue an alternative theory which recognizes abuse for what it is—a crime against the person. It is well known that the "family" is filled with many different forms of male violence and oppression and that violence is perpetrated on old and young alike (Dobash and Dobash 1992). Feminists must develop analyses of elder abuse which acknowledge the social and cultural construction of abuse and locate causation outside of the personality traits and characteristics of either abuser or abused. There is an urgent need for feminists to grasp the nettle with regard to elder abuse. The fact that they have yet to do so is a reflection not only of the powerfully constraining effects of orthodox thinking and the resistance to feminist analysis, but also of deeply entrenched ageism within the movement.

From a different analysis and meaning arise different policies and practice. It is apparent that the ideological and methodological debates within elder abuse are mirroring those which occurred in the child-protection area and that elder abuse has been claimed by "experts" in family violence (Penhale 1993). It is thus not surprising that many agencies attempting to deal with elder abuse have looked for guidance to the experiences of the child-abuse orthodoxy, which unlike elder abuse has been successfully challenged by feminist thinking and practice. However, child-abuse procedures based on normative versions of the "family" are not, as various writers have noted, transferable wholesale to the area of elder abuse (Decalmer and Glendenning 1993; Penhale 1993). There is a need for much more research, debate, and discussion before an adequate theory, policy, or practice of elder abuse is articulated or implemented.

There is an urgent need, therefore, for feminists to contest the hold by family-violence "experts" on elder-abuse terrain. Elder abuse has to be located within a feminist analysis of the "family," and dominant ideologies about old women and "dependency" within the family have to be challenged. Feminists have to press for changes at the policy level which will place more resources at the disposal of old women to enable them to resist various forms of abuse by "families" in old age. Some feminists have pointed to the feminization of poverty in old age and recognized economic independence as a crucial form of self care and empowerment for old women. This is certainly a crucial element in any successful preventative strategy (Groves 1983; Groves and Finch 1983).

Research has indicated that most "victims" of elder abuse want to remain in their own homes and families (Department of Health Social Service Inspectorate 1992), so moves to enable the exclusion of abusive men and to find alternative forms of "care" in the community would be important elements in a feminist policy/practice framework, as would the development of "safe places" for old women who need respite from abuse and do not want to be placed in a residential home. This is particularly challenging in the context of changes in community care legislation and policy which are forcing more and more old people to rely on already overstretched and underresourced systems of "family" or "informal" care. This can only increase the risk of abuse especially for the very old and frail, who are predominantly women.

Various writers have pointed to the inadequate legal framework which exists in terms of elder abuse and to the need for balance between protection and intrusion upon adult status and autonomy (Griffiths et al. 1992). Feminists will be concerned with finding such a balance and ensuring that old women are not infantilized but do get the protection from abuse they need. This means working with a range of agencies to improve collaboration and coordination and arguing for forms of intervention which locate responsibility where it belongs and acknowledge the risks of abuse which old women are exposed to. The growing professionalization and medicalization of old age in general and elder abuse in particular should be treated with caution. A decade ago Parton (1985) pointed to how the health/welfare model of child abuse dominated research, policy, and practice. This orientation locates the causes of elder abuse within "burnt out" or pathological "carers" and/or within dependent, controlling elders. It assumes that abuse occurs mainly in dysfunctional families and seeks to identify the "type" of individual that would harm their elders and/or the characteristics of the victim which may put them at greater risk. This focus on inadequate personality types or "profiles" of abused/abuser as risk indicators is highly problematic if a feminist analysis of elder abuse leads to the conclusion that it is a product of the social, political, and cultural construction of the "family," old age, masculinity, and sexuality.

The child-abuse literature demonstrates the fact that therapeutic or compassionate philosophies of assessment of intervention which obscure the complex gender and power issues around abuse have done very little to reduce risk (Parton 1985). Feminists will be aware of the need to work for changes in theory, policy, and practice in relation to elder abuse and to press for changes in the law which are appropriate. This means contesting orthodox notions of the "family" and the tendency to reduce domestic violence to "system" faults. The family is clearly not a monolithic structure which serves everyone's needs equally. The inequalities of power and the conflicts of interest and struggle for scarce resources within families have to be acknowledged. This is not an argument for no intervention but for wider and more adequate theorizing about causation.

What Is to Be Done about Abusers?

The literature on elder abuse has virtually nothing to say about abusers beyond the production of their psychosocial profiles as risk indicators. Whether the abuser is mentally ill, dependent on drugs or alcohol, prone to violence, or isolated and unemployed, there is no discussion of the links between the abuse and wider social and political systems. In Britain at any rate, there is little or no real debate about the criminal aspects of elder abuse. Attempts by some lawyers to guide practitioners on how the law can be used to pursue criminal proceedings (Griffiths et al. 1992) appear to be widely ignored, and there is an almost unspoken assumption, fuelled by compassionate philosophies of assessment and intervention, that the criminalization of elder abuse is inappropriate.

A feminist analysis and practice relating to elder abuse will have to question whether or not criminal proceedings are the most appropriate way of dealing with offences. Arguments against criminalization come from those who believe that abuse is a "family" matter, from those who believe it punishes and blames the victim still further, from those who argue that labels such as "abuse" and associated proceedings prevent disclosure, and from those who believe that prosecution and prison will not change the man, whereas therapy might. Feminists will argue that the decriminalization of elder abuse and the reluctance to consider "control" forms of assessment/intervention are misguided because it is giving a very clear message to society at large and men in particular that there is nothing very serious or wrong about abusing old women. It is also a way of supporting the idea that abusers are overstressed, pathetic, dependent, or disturbed characters and certainly not responsible for their actions.

Elder abuse, like other forms of abuse, must be seen as a crime against the person. Anything else is unjust. While it is clear that prison is not successful at reforming anyone, to abandon it as a possibility is to collude with those who want to see elder abuse as a separate category of behaviour and abusers as not responsible for it. As long as the orthodoxy perpetuates the ideology of abusers being "driven" to it by provoking, controlling, noncompliant, burdensome old women, abusers will internalize it for themselves and statutory workers will concur. The argument that involving the police only increases victims' feelings of self-blame is an important one, but experience of working with other survivors indicates that victims are ambivalent about their feelings and that one way of helping is for society to say quite clearly, "He is responsible" (Kelly 1987). What is clear is that arguments about what should be done should not come from denial and an inability to face up to and accept the reality and seriousness of elder abuse.

Until and unless the complex gender issues inherent in elder abuse are addressed as a product of dominant ideologies about the "family," about old age, masculinity, and sexuality, there can be no adequate theory or practice. Attempting to begin the difficult task of posing an alternative explanation of elder abuse and thereby giving it a different meaning is an essential part of the wider political struggle towards real prevention and change. Feminists have a wealth of experience and knowledge to bring to the task at hand. Their expertise and commitment is needed urgently.

Chapter Eighteen

Domestic Violence Policy in the United States
Contemporary Issues

Susan L. Miller and LeeAnn Iovanni

Introduction

In the past twenty-five years, we have witnessed an explosion of interest, activism, criminal justice reforms, and lawmaking in the area of violence against women, albeit with some backlash.[1] Concomitantly, there is a greater awareness of how poverty and race cut across social problems such as woman battering and how victims both are embedded in social networks that can empower or impede them and also face structural constraints in seeking safety and violent-free lives. Economic justice, in both the labor and housing realms, has received increased attention in recent years. Though not exhaustive, this chapter explores many of the key issues that involve and affect battered victims/survivors. We group the major issues into these areas: policy (particularly economic justice), the criminal justice system, and restorative justice. We hope to inspire new thinking and research directions.

Policy

Violence Against Women Act (VAWA)

One of the huge successes attributed to the battered women's movement is the federally funded Violence Against Women Act (VAWA). Its importance is twofold: First, it recognizes nationally the scope and pervasiveness of the problem and the commitment to work toward eradicating domestic violence and better protecting victims. Second, its very presence introduces an agent of social change. Congress renewed the ten-year-old federal Violence Against Women Act in September 2005. This far-reaching and popular legislation established new federal crimes for domestic violence, sexual assault, and stalking. The original law created the National Domestic Violence Hotline (1-800-799-SAFE), which has received one million phone calls since 1996 (www.ndvh.org/about.html). With funds of $795 million a year, the VAWA supports battered women's shelters and law-enforcement training and focuses on crucial aspects of violence against women, such as treating children affected by violence, enhancing health care for rape victims, holding repeat offenders and stalkers (including high-tech stalkers) accountable, and easing housing issues for battered women.

In addition, VAWA targets underserved populations and rural victims; increases resources for police, prosecutors, and victim service providers; and improves legal protections for battered immigrant women and children. A recent cost-benefit analysis study found that VAWA is an efficient social program, noting that VAWA saved $12.6 billion in averted victimization costs (Clark, Biddle, and Martin 2002). The VAWA has been instrumental in changing the nation's perception of violence against women. Federal recognition and financial support have set new expectations for responding to the problem and have resulted in improved law enforcement and other professional services across the country. For the VAWA to serve as a vehicle for social change, it will mean an actual change in the attitudes of those charged with implementing new laws and policies.

Battering and Welfare Reform

Hailed as a way to reduce poverty through the elimination of entitlements combined with mandatory employment, the 1996 Personal Responsibility Work Opportunity and Reconciliation Act (PRWORA) ushered in a host of government programs to facilitate the transition from welfare to work.[2] There is a well-documented relationship between welfare recipients and battering, with battered women on welfare reporting significantly higher rates of violence vis-à-vis women in the general population as well as in comparable national samples of low-income women both on and off welfare (Tolman and Raphael 2000). In fact, women living in poverty face greater risk of violence than other women and have fewer resources to draw on for assistance (Schram 2002). Although poverty does not cause the violence, it does exacerbate battered women's vulnerability, increase the difficulty of finding work and childcare, and contribute to job absenteeism and job loss (Moe and Bell 2004). Poor battered women endure a host of problems, including a greater likelihood of periodic unemployment and physical and mental health problems (Lloyd and Taluc 1999).

Recent scholarship on the poverty–welfare–domestic-violence nexus includes not only prevalence studies but also research on the effects of domestic violence on women's ability to comply with welfare reforms; the connections between poverty and abuse over the life course; and social service practices, policy implementation, and implications (Brush, Raphael, and Tolman 2003). What seems clear is that employment may be the key to escaping abuse (and conversely, the elimination of domestic violence will help lift women out of poverty), but the means of escape are often just out of the grasp of many battered women. Moreover, welfare-reform policies may not take into account the unique nature of abuse that many recipients face, suggesting that more comprehensive reforms are necessary. Public-health scholars believe that mothers who are the caregivers for children with health problems or who have health problems of their own are harmed by welfare reform as well (Romero et al. 2003). Prior research demonstrates that domestic violence is strongly correlated with physical and mental health issues. Low-income women who already face barriers to employment due to these problems are required to increase work outside the home as a result of welfare reform (Ahluwalia et al. 2001; Raphael 2000). In addition to their greater physical and mental health needs, counseling and medical needs are further compromised for battered women without health insurance.

In recognition of the obstacles to employment that many battered women face, the PRWORA includes a Family Violence Option (FVO) that provides a temporary waiver of time limits in finding employment and of work requirements so that battered women will not be penalized; at least thirty states implement this option (Raphael and Haennicke 1999). However, many women are reluctant to disclose their abuse (Tolman and Raphael 2000) or are not informed about the FVO waiver. For instance, in Maryland, caseworkers lacked training on how to identify and respond to issues related to battering; in New York City, less than half of the individuals who self-identified as battering victims were referred to special domestic violence caseworkers, and only about one-third who were referred were granted FVO waivers (NOW 2003). In Wisconsin, about 75 percent of battered women who were welfare recipients were not told of available services such as counseling, housing, or the possibility of using work time to seek help (NOW 2003). Only one in four battered immigrant women in California received any information about the domestic violence waivers for which they were eligible (NOW 2003).

Bell's research (2003) demonstrates how the cyclical nature of violent relationships and lack of childcare affect women's ability to work to meet the requirements for Temporary Assistance to Needy Families (TANF). Very few women desired or were able to sever ties with their batterers because of their greater need for financial support and childcare assistance. They were often in low-wage employment that consists of erratic hours (mostly nights and weekends) and does not allow time off to care for sick children or attend mandatory visits to welfare agencies, thus increasing their dependency on their abusive partners or ex-partners (Bell 2003; Scott, London, and Myers 2002). In fact, participants in Bell's research were likely to use the threat of seeking formal child support as a way to ensure compliance from their ex-partner. They valued the informal childcare arrangements and financial assistance from their abuser, despite the fact that child support was used as a mechanism of control by abusers or to facilitate relationship reconciliation. Thus, to meet the work requirements of TANF, battered women experienced an increased dependence on abusive partners and their good will; when the support was withdrawn, women cycled back onto TANF. This issue is increasingly problematic because the new welfare act requires that the paternity of the recipient's children be established and that child support be sought from the children's father. The paternity requirement is particularly harmful to a battered woman because public assistance is often the only way she can afford to leave an abusive relationship and support herself and her children. Ordering her to interact with her children's father, as well as forcing him to pay child support, could jeopardize both her safety and her children's.

When women join the workforce, a number of additional concerns confront them, such as abusers' harassment at the workplace by making numerous phone calls or by interference such as sabotaging alarm clocks, destroying professional clothing, disabling the family car, and causing bruises that harm appearance and undermine self-confidence, all of which limit women's ability to maintain employment (Moffit 2002; Raphael 1996). Prior research findings on the direct effects of employment on domestic violence have been equivocal, with some studies finding no effect of work on abuse, some finding that work increases violence but only if the abuser is unemployed, and still other studies finding that work decreases violence (see Brush 2003; Gennetian 2003). Domestic violence can also affect employment indirectly by causing mental health problems that are negatively correlated with employment (Moore and Selkowe 1999). It is likely that abusers implicitly know that women with their own economic resources would have the financial means to leave (Tolman and Raphael 2000: 667). Clearly, there is a need to combat hardships faced by low-income women who experience violence, to provide competent childcare, time off to seek health care or counseling, and emotional support and practical assistance to leave an abusive situation (Romero et al. 2003). There is also a need to better protect women in the workplace and train/place them in jobs that do not require contact with the public (as most service occupations do), subsidize childcare, and provide transportation services that are necessary for all low-income women, but especially for battered women (Bell 2003).

Battering and Housing

Domestic violence is ranked as the primary cause of homelessness in 44 percent of cities surveyed (U.S. Conference of Mayors 2003) because victims who leave their abusers often have nowhere to go. In addition, abusers typically control the household finances as one method of manipulating victims into powerless positions, leaving battered women who flee with no means to secure first and last month's rent or security deposits. Isolation from friends and family members is a common abuser ploy as well, so when victims are alienated and estranged from people who could help them—or when friends and family are also threatened by the abuser's violence—victims have nowhere to turn. Public housing options cannot meet the demand. For instance, Philadelphia, San Antonio, and Washington, DC, have only met 24, 10, and 31 percent, respectively, of their residents' housing needs (Hirst 2003: 136). The national average waiting time is one to five months (U.S. Conference of Mayors 2003). There is an extensive application process for acquiring federally subsidized housing, and many applicants are rejected based on their credit or criminal histories. For battered women, abusers' controlling economic tactics may jeopardize possession of a good credit report. Victims might have criminal records, reflecting activities where they participated in crime under duress or coercion by their abusers.

As a consequence of new mandatory and pro-arrest laws, battered women could be subjected to a domestic violence arrest resulting from a situation in which the police did not identify the primary aggressor action or self-defensive action and arrested both the victim and offender, even though she may have acted in self-defense. An additional hurdle in some public housing jurisdictions is that applicants must submit a letter of recommendation from respected community members: "[F]or victims of domestic violence, these tasks may take an enormous effort. Victims may be cut off from the community, may have a deflated sense of self-worth, and may be unprepared to speak in their own defense" (Hirst 2003: 137). Lastly, almost all public housing authorities do not offer priority housing for battering victims, despite the fact that their lives and those of their children may be in danger.

Battered women in public housing may also find themselves amid the fallout of the "war on crime." Following the nation's general get-tough policies, law-enforcement and prosecution agencies use "three strikes" or "one strike" laws, instituted by state legislatures, to better combat repeat offenders (Danner 1998). These draconian laws were designed to end perceptions of "softness" in sentencing and to deter potential criminals by advertising the severe consequences of committing crime. As part of the effort to crack down on government assistance to citizens deemed undeserving, "one strike" laws are used against criminals residing in or visiting public housing, creating a new group of victims by permitting evictions of any resident or visitor engaged in criminal activity. Of the more than five million people living in public housing in the United States, most are minorities and most are female-headed households. In 2002, the U.S. Supreme Court upheld a federal housing law, the Anti-Drug Abuse Act of 1988 (revised 1994), designed to evict public housing tenants for any resident or guest arrested for drug-related or violent crimes (Schram 2002). This law unintentionally puts battered women at risk of losing their homes if they call police to report violence, essentially holding battered women responsible for their partners' abuse. Ironically, they could remain in public housing but risk more beatings if they do not report the violence (see Hornstein, Kaye, and Atkins 2002).

These policies pose a danger for battered women who are tenants in public housing, entrapped in an abusive household with few options and no control over a violent partner or ex-partner. If a battered woman's partner is also a drug user, the law assumes equal responsibility on her part. In a recent U.S. Supreme Court opinion, *HUD v. Rucker* (2002), the Court held that the public housing agency's actions were consistent with regulations and that "no matter the level of culpability, tenants who cannot control the criminal activities of household members or guests do not deserve to live in public housing" (Hirst 2003: 140). This seems paradoxical, given that the goal of public housing is to create safe and affordable housing for low-income citizens, not to punish families in which one member or guest engages in criminal activity, such as battering (Hirst 2003: 141).

Many states are moving toward creating legislation that will better protect battered women from eviction. For instance, in Delaware, changes to landlord-tenant codes are being introduced in legislation to protect battered women from public housing eviction because of domestic violence or for calling the police too many times (personal communication from Delaware Community Legal Aid Society, November 11, 2005). This issue was challenged recently in the Oregon courts, where a battered woman's wrongful eviction was overturned through the use of a "disparate impact" claim. The judge accepted the disparate-impact reasoning that the One Strike Law produced a disproportionately negative effect on women because women constitute the majority of domestic violence victims. The judge also agreed, however, that domestic violence does not contribute to an unsafe housing environment. Although not a binding precedent for future cases, the example of a disparate-impact claim in Oregon can guide other battering victims in wrongful-eviction cases.

Criminal Justice System Issues

Arrest Policies

One of the biggest changes in the criminal justice system's response to domestic violence has been the legal and procedural changes of the 1980s and 1990s that mandate police to arrest perpetrators. Prior to this, police viewed arrest as the least desirable outcome and were trained instead to offer crisis intervention at the scene or simply separate the couple. In response to pressure from victim-advocacy groups, as well as successful civil suits launched against police departments that failed to respond adequately to domestic violence, most jurisdictions have modified their antiquated law-enforcement practices to favor arrest.

These mandatory, pro-arrest policies, which were designed to protect victims by treating domestic violence as seriously as police would treat assaults committed by strangers, have often resulted in unintended negative consequences (see Iovanni and Miller 2001). One serious consequence of these policy changes is that more and more women who fight back are arrested on domestic violence charges, despite many women's long histories of victimization and the compelling reasons why they resorted to using violence. Most women appear to use violence in self-defense or to protect their children's safety (Miller 2005), yet some states treat women who use defensive violence the same as batterers, who typically use violence to control, intimidate, or cause fear in their partner. Increasingly, female victims arrested for domestic violence are mandated to batterer treatment programs intended for male abusers.

This practice raises concerns about an overreliance on the criminal justice system as a solution to battering by making uniform arrests without consideration for the gendered context of the violence. Because victims' use of force is typically qualitatively different from that of their abusers (in terms of motivations, injury, consequences, ability to change behavior or cause fear), a gender-neutral arrest policy that fails to distinguish between primary aggressor action versus self-defensive action is inherently unjust. The confusing message of a dual arrest also serves both to reinforce the offender's belief that he is not responsible and to contravene victim empowerment.

Civil Protection Orders

Civil restraining orders, or orders of protection, were developed in response to the reluctance of the criminal justice system to effectively address the criminal nature of domestic violence (see Iovanni and Miller 2001). Restraining orders can provide various types of relief, including financial arrangements, restrictions on custody, and establishing limits to abusers' access to victims such as limits on access to residence, place of employment, children, and children's schools. Restraining orders also serve as an alternative form of victim protection if the level of evidence does not meet the standard of a criminal proceeding or if the victim would be a weak prosecution witness due to drug or alcohol abuse, for example. Because violation of a protective order is a criminal offense that can result in arrest, civil restraining orders expand police power and increase officers' ability to monitor repeat offenders (Finn and Colson 1990). The effectiveness of civil orders ultimately rests on law enforcement's response, and it can be enhanced with serious prosecutorial and judicial actions and meaningful punishment for offenders (Gelb 1994). The limitations of a protection order were never more striking as in the recent *Castle Rock v. Gonzales* ruling. The case began in 1999 when Jessica Gonzales's estranged husband kidnapped the couple's three daughters from her front yard and killed them; many people believed these murders could have been prevented if the Castle Rock, Colorado, police department had not repeatedly refused to act on her protective order. In June 2005, the U.S. Supreme Court ruled against Gonzales's claim that the Castle Rock police were negligent, conveying the message that restraining orders are ineffectual. Not only are battered women inadequately served by the imperfect response of the criminal justice system, they are now endangered by weakened civil relief for their immediate safety concerns.

Restorative Justice

An alternative to the traditional criminal justice system's emphasis on punishing offenders, restorative justice focuses on the reparation of harm. Various practices fall under the general rubric of restorative justice, but family group/community conferencing that accords a central role to community is the hallmark of restorative practice. Victims have the opportunity to participate in the process and a chance to speak and to receive an apology. Interventions and reparation agreements are reached through purportedly consensual decision making. In the language of restorative justice, "community" is broadly interpreted to mean family, friends, or neighbors, as well as representatives in various contexts such as spiritual, criminal justice, social service, or business (Frederick and Lizdas 2003: 18). The essential premise is that neither can the victim heal nor the offender change without receiving community support and addressing any social norms that tacitly tolerate violence against women (Presser and Gaarder 2004). Community involvement can also address diverse racial, ethnic, religious, or cultural diversity issues that may be misinterpreted or misunderstood by police and court officials. Conferences can further serve as reintegrative shaming ceremonies, as opposed to stigmatization experiences, and facilitate the offender's remorse and his desire to change (Braithwaite and Daly 1994).

The potential for victim orientation and empowerment, the language of restoration and reparation, and involvement of the community in holding offenders accountable and regulating their behavior have certainly resonated with battered women's advocates. Scholars have also embraced the promise of restorative justice for battered women (see Umbreit 2000 and Presser and Gaarder 2004). But although restorative practices have been implemented in the juvenile offending arena with some success, questions can be raised about their applicability for battered women. Stubbs (2002) contends that restorative justice may not effectively address the harms of gendered violence or truly give voice to victims. Battering relationships are characterized by instrumental use of a range of abusive tactics in an established pattern of domination and control, where the batterer often sees himself as the victim of his partner's nagging and disobedience. He has offered many empty apologies in the past, a controlling tactic itself. Moreover, battered women have grown accustomed to hiding because of fear and stigma, and silence and accommodation to the abuser have become survival strategies. Battered women's agency can be further constrained by the fact that they share children with their abuser, a source of manipulation and intimidation. Any optimism that such an offender can be expected to assume responsibility for the harm and make amends, or that a victim will be able to face her batterer on equal footing and assert her interests, needs to be tempered. There is also no guarantee that a woman will not be revictimized by further emotional abuse in the face-to-face meeting. Gendered power imbalances and women's relational concerns can thus result in agreements that are not fully consensual or equitable (Stubbs 2002).

Finally, it cannot be assumed that any "community" assembled for a restorative process has adequate knowledge about battering, shares a condemnation of it, or has the resources to monitor it (Stubbs 2002). As it stands now, it is questionable whether current restorative justice practices can ensure the safety of victims and their children, restore victim autonomy, or promote changes in community norms that tolerate violence against women (Frederick and Lizdas 2003). Still, others hope that victim safety can be ensured with facilitators who are specially trained in the dynamics of battering and in assessing the dangerousness of perpetrators, and with lay and professional participants who are adequately prepared for their roles (Busch 2002). The victim's supporters, for instance, must be prepared to stand up for her against her abuser (Busch 2002). Outcome plans must be carefully monitored over the long term, and resorting to the formal justice process should always be an option (Busch 2002; Braithwaite and Daly 1994).

Future Directions

The battered women's movement has succeeded in exposing the private nature of violence and bringing it into the national spotlight, creating battered women's shelters and challenging criminal justice practices. Laudable advances in the way society responds to violence against women and challenges to traditional thinking about battering have achieved the goals of a more inclusive movement and of increasing awareness about economic justice in housing and employment. These achievements, however, have come at the cost of true social transformation. Feminist philosophy has been compromised, and feminist practitioners and scholars have had to align themselves with the state, transforming their grassroots activism into a more state-controlled enterprise in order to secure federal legislation and dollars. These concessions have shifted the discourse and action away from challenging the root causes of battering—including issues related to power and privilege—and away from prevention efforts. Proactive programs within the public health arena, such as recent programs funded by the Centers for Disease Control and Prevention, focus more on prevention efforts that target young adolescents, raise public awareness through media campaigns, and emphasize the economic cost to society. Other programs that rely on a more layered approach, or coordinated community response, show more promise for meeting the profound need for proactive strategies that can be conducted collaboratively within social and institutional networks in school, religious, health, therapeutic, and peer communities.

Greater research and policy efforts must also be directed toward an expansion of victim understandings. For instance, although it is commonly known in academic circles that battering occurs in all relationships, whether heterosexual or gay/ lesbian/bisexual/transgendered (GLBT), it is only in recent years that state and local coalitions against domestic violence have made a more concerted effort to identify and respond with resources to all groups. Studies have revealed that 46 percent of lesbians and gay men have used physical aggression in their relationships (Kelly and Warshafsky 1987) and that one in five urban gay men is battered by his partner (Savin-Williams 2002). However, despite the indications that the prevalence of same-sex violence equals or exceeds that of heterosexual couples, most feminist theories of battering typically focus on heterosexual couples and exclude gay/lesbians (Renzetti 1999). But the roots and impact of same-sex violence can be viewed as similar to heterosexual violence because "the routine and intentional use of intimidation tactics in relationships is not a gender issue but a power one" (Elliott 1996, cited in Perilla et al. 2003, 20). The research on violence in GLBT relationships shows us how "any behavior can be used as power and control, how any behavior can be used as a survival tactic, and the fact that victims may well identify as abusers" (Worcester 2002: 1401). Better research on these hidden groups is needed given that samples are typically small and collected from clinical settings or gay bars or events and that studies oversample white and middle-class women. The invisibility of lesbians as a whole and their having to explicitly identify themselves and disclose their sexual orientation to be included in a study (Burke and Follingstad 1999; Giorgio 2002; Perilla et al. 2003; Turrell 2000)—something they may be reluctant to reveal due to children, housing, or work concerns—presents unique challenges regarding confidentiality safeguards. Moreover, the self-acknowledgment of being GLBT and the disclosure risks associated with family, employment, and other social situations make it difficult for victims to seek help. Thus, it is necessary to examine a host of factors, both personal and societal, to understand the use, motivation, and consequence of violence, as well as to scrutinize shelter and legal resources to ensure that they are inclusive of all kinds of victims.

It is also important to point out that, notwithstanding its successes, the battered women's movement has been criticized for being launched by white, middle-class women. Historically it has ignored the fact that women's differential experiences with violence occur within complicated dynamics that include access to resources, credibility with the criminal justice system, and perceptions of, and experiences with, service providers and law enforcement. Today, however, there is much greater attention given to the different ways that violence affects victims from marginalized communities whose life experiences are shaped by race, socioeconomic class, ethnicity, and immigration status. This notion of "intersectionality" attempts to acknowledge that victims of relationship battering simultaneously experience victimizations and oppressions outside their relationships, including racism, heterosexism, and class oppression (Crenshaw 1994). These interlocking sites of oppression and inequality, which reflect histories of conquest, immigration, and slavery, account for the different ways that victims experience battering and take us beyond an exclusive focus on male dominance and misogyny (Russo 2001b). For instance, given the legacy of racism and distrust between people of color and the police, battered black or Latina women may be reluctant to seek police assistance, believing that this would be disloyal to their race or offer police further opportunities to harass their communities. Similarly, stereotypes of the "passive" victim have also been challenged as applying to a white, middle-class model that sets up victims who fight back as aggressive and dangerous or less deserving of help. Research reveals that compared to white women, black women are more likely to fight back due to a "long history of physical abuse and oppression, both within their homes and in the larger society, [so] they had to be prepared to defend themselves" (West and Rose 2000: 488).

In addition to the unique problems of battered women in various racial, ethnic minority, and immigrant groups (e.g., Mexican, Latina, South and Southeast Asian, Korean, Haitian, African American; see Sokoloff 2005), women in these groups often share a lack of familiarity with, as well as a fear of, service and criminal justice systems, social isolation due to friends and family remaining in their countries of origin, poor English skills, and denial of services due to lack of required documentation. These are in addition to the more typical hardships faced by most battered women, such as transportation, housing and childcare issues, and economic dependency on their abusers.

Today it has become clear that no single response will work to help all women to live free from violence. Thus, it is critical that cultural context and the unique barriers this creates for battered women are an integral part of any contemporary analysis of battering dynamics and system responses. Furthermore, although victims continue to need access to housing, reliable transportation, job training, employment, affordable childcare, and ways to escape their abusers' control, intervention strategies must be balanced with prevention efforts that will ultimately eradicate battering.

NOTES

1. Abusers have always tried to manipulate circumstances and deny or minimize their violent behavior, but recent research documents that men have become even more savvy about domestic violence case processing and manipulate women with threats, particularly over children and custody issues, and even self-inflict wounds (Miller 2005). Backlash groups created by men, and often joined by their second wives, are growing on Internet sites and are making more public proclamations about the need for shelters for male victims and harsher penalties for violent women.

2. PRWORA eliminates AFDC (Aid to Families with Dependent Children), an open-ended entitlement program, with its replacement, TANF (Temporary Assistance for Needy Families).

Children and Gender Violence

Big happiness, small happiness. In China, these colloquialisms signify the birth of a son and of a daughter, respectively. Although China is not the only country where a cultural preference for males persists, it has attracted international attention because it has the world's worst case of "missing" girls. In most nations, the average sex ratio at birth is about 105 boys for every 100 girls; in China, the sex ratio was 111 to 100 in 1990, and by 2005, it had grown to 119 to 100 (Riley 1996; Yardley 2005). This disturbing trend is rooted in more than patriarchal cultural ideology, however. In societies where males are more highly rewarded for their labor than are women, and adult daughters are expected to leave their families but sons are responsible for caring for elderly parents, sons are a good investment, whereas daughters are a liability (Renzetti, Edleson, and Bergen 2001). This situation is exacerbated in China, where an aggressive population control policy that imposes heavy economic penalties on families that have more than one child has been in place since 1979. Although this strategy has enabled China to address overpopulation, it has inadvertently promoted female infanticide, both through outright murder and through fatal neglect in the form of starvation and abandonment. The widespread availability of ultrasound technology has facilitated the systematic removal of girls from the population through sex-selective abortion, despite laws against using the technology for prenatal sex determination. The killing of girl children is not only tragic for the individuals affected; it will have serious social repercussions, in terms of marriage patterns, family structure, and the labor force, for years to come.

Children are linked to a gendered system of power through their historical social position as the personal property of fathers, as well as their location in sex-stratified political states. Their rights to self-determination about work, bodily integrity, basic care, and life itself have been contested over time. By the early 1950s, the notion of children's rights emerged as an international policy issue worthy of serious attention. The United Nations approved the Declaration on the Rights of the Child in 1959, establishing as fundamental the right to access health care, housing, and education, as well as to be free from abuse, neglect, and exploitation. Thirty years later, the United Nations adopted the Convention on the Rights of the Child, expanding protections to prohibit involvement in armed conflict, prostitution, and pornography. Notably, the United States is one of only two countries (the other being Somalia) that refuses to sign the 1989 pact.

The preceding three sections have focused on how sexual assault, harassment, and domestic violence are experienced by adults. In this section, we examine how children encounter various forms of gendered violence in their homes and communities.

Children's Exposure to Violence

The typical child in the United States watches twenty-eight hours of television per week and plays video games about fifty minutes per day (Mooney, Knox, and Schacht 2007). Given that these media are replete with violent images—much of them gendered in nature—concern about the effects of mass media on youth is warranted, particularly because it is through the mass media that "the social constructions of violence and social control emerge for popular consumption and legitimation" (G. Barak 2003, 200). Although most research suggests that viewing these images has no significant direct effect on engaging in violent behavior, exposure to media violence seems to promote higher levels of aggression when combined with other influencing factors, including experiencing violence at home (Jaffe, Wolfe, and Wilson 1997) and having a peer group that supports sexually aggressive behavior (Malamuth 1989). Also cause for concern is that video games have become increasingly interactive and incredibly realistic. When a child plays a "first-shooter" game, for example, he not only witnesses graphic violence, he *becomes* the perpetrator. As one retired military officer reports in the film *Game Over*, some of these games are so effective in teaching people how to kill that the army uses them to train soldiers.

Another way in which children are exposed to violence is through witnessing attacks that occur in their homes and communities. Around the world, thousands of children live through war-related violence, and in the United States, children of color who live in impoverished urban neighborhoods are disproportionately exposed to community violence. It is within their own families, however, that children are most likely to witness violent assaults; and research suggests that exposure to domestic violence appears to produce the most trauma for children (Groves and Zuckerman 1997).

Estimates of the number of children who witness parental assaults vary widely depending on how data are collected. Using retrospective accounts from adults, Carlson (1984a) estimated that about 3.3 million young children are exposed to "serious violence" (likely to cause injury) each year. Based on national survey results in which adults admitted that their children had witnessed violent marital incidents, Straus and Gelles (1992) conclude that at least one-third of America's children have witnessed parental violence, usually on repeated occasions. Whether children see it or hear it or witness only the aftermath, domestic violence is a terrifying experience that profoundly affects the way they understand their world. Girls tend to suffer from lowered self-esteem, and boys exhibit greater levels of hostility and aggression (Edleson 1999). Both boys and girls who witness violence exhibit symptoms associated with post-traumatic stress disorder (anxiety, depression, sleep disturbances, and somatic complaints), and these problems often persist in adulthood (McNeal and Amato 1998).

Physical Abuse

Although there is no consensus on whether children who witness the abuse of their mothers should themselves be considered victims of neglect or emotional abuse, it is clear that some incidents of child abuse directly emanate from intimate partner violence. For example, batterers may intentionally abuse, abduct, or even murder their children as strategies for controlling and punishing their wives (Greif and Hegar 1993; also see Johnson, this volume). In addition, some children are injured by combative adults when they intervene in a violent episode in an attempt to protect their mothers.

Even in those families not characterized by domestic violence, children are regularly subject to physical assault. National survey results reveal that nearly 75 percent of parents admit to having used violence against their children. Most of these assaults involve "minor" acts—slapping, spanking, and pushing—that a majority of parents view as acceptable disciplinary practices (Gelles and Straus 1988; see also Straus 1994).

Because corporal punishment has long been considered culturally appropriate in the United States, the debate over what constitutes child abuse continues. Current legal definitions focus on two standards: harm and endangerment. Thus, children are considered victims of physical abuse if they sustain observable injuries that last at least forty-eight hours, or, in the absence of such injuries, if they are at substantial risk for such injury (U.S. DHHS 1988, 1996). Using this conservative definition of abuse, child protection agencies receive approximately three million reports of child maltreatment (including neglect and physical, sexual, and psychological abuse) each year. Of those reports, about 903,000 are substantiated; thus, at least 12 out of 1,000 children are abused in the United States, and about 800 of those children die as a result of abuse (U.S. DHHS 2003). Obviously, the taken-for-granted ideal of a protected childhood and the child-centeredness of the contemporary middle class, which are relatively new concepts historically (Vinovskis 2001), are neither universally accepted nor consistently integrated into family life.

For all other forms of physical violence, men are the majority of perpetrators, but research indicates that women physically abuse and neglect children at an equal or somewhat higher rate than do men. However, a more complete understanding of the relational context and social conditions in which that abuse occurs requires us to carefully consider its gendered nature. When the relative amount of time that women and men spend with children is taken into consideration, it becomes apparent that men account for the majority of child physical abuse per hour of exposure. Furthermore, men's physical violence toward children is more likely to cause serious injuries and death (Alfaro 1987; Hegar, Zuravin, and Orme 1991).

The most predominant explanation for child physical abuse and neglect in the United States is that it results from caregivers experiencing unusually high stress and/or having a lack of knowledge and parenting skills. Similar to elder abuse, child abuse is often viewed as a consequence of being "driven over the edge" by the burden of caregiving (see Whittaker, this volume). Specific acts of child abuse, especially those that result in death, are sometimes portrayed as the unanticipated consequence of otherwise culturally acceptable disciplinary practices that "got out of hand" because the caregiver was enraged, exhausted, and/or not consciously aware of what constituted excessive force against a child. The most well-known example of this is shaken-baby syndrome, in which a crying infant is shaken so severely that the act results in brain damage or death.

Children not only experience abuse at the hands of their adult caregivers but are also victimized by siblings. In fact, some scholars consider sibling abuse the most common form of family violence (Finkelhor and Dziuba-Leatherman 1994). Sibling abuse has only recently received serious attention because altercations between siblings are usually dismissed as "sibling rivalry" (Wiehe 1997). However, sibling abuse can be distinguished from nonabusive, conflictual sibling interactions using criteria similar to those that characterize other abusive relationships: severity of injury, frequency and duration of the interactions, the degree of power disparity between the siblings, and the extent to which the interactions involve an element of secrecy or coercive pressure (Barnett, Miller-Perrin, and Perrin 2005, 197—198). Moreover, sibling violence is a gendered phenomenon—boys use more severe forms of violence, and engage in violent behavior more often, than do girls, against both their sisters and their brothers (Hoffman, Kiecolt, and Edwards 2005). In critically questioning the degree to which violence between siblings is "normal," it seems fruitful to look more closely at this behavior in the context of research on bullying among peers (see Stein, this volume).

There has been a tendency to ignore or minimize both parental and sibling abuse because they occur within the family, a social institution characterized by privacy and personal choice in the contemporary United States. However, when families use violence, they send a strong message to children "that it is legitimate to use physical force to accomplish your goals under at least some circumstances" (Carlson 1984b, 573). This is especially pertinent considering that both youth and adults who perpetrate all other forms of violence "are, more often than not, victims themselves" (G. Barak 2003, 315).

Sexual Abuse

Child sexual abuse has been recognized as a social problem since the late 1970s, when women began to speak out about sexual assaults they had suffered as children, often at the hands of family members or trusted members of their communities. These personal testimonies sparked scholars to take a new look at an issue that had been relegated to silence. With the publication of *The Best Kept Secret*, Florence Rush became one of the first people to place contemporary child sexual abuse in a historical and cultural context. Finding that the sexual use of children was supported by early religious law, she asserted that "the sexual abuse of children by adults has never been established as an irrefutable legal and moral violation and to this day remains a debatable polemic" (1980, 73).

In the United States and around the world, children are still sexually exploited in a variety of ways, including pornography, prostitution, sexual molestation, and rape by both family members and unrelated persons. It is very difficult to develop comprehensive statistics on the sexual victimization of children given the multiple forms, locations, and causes of the abuse. This difficulty in gathering reliable information is compounded by the nature of such abuse—children are not generally prepared to discuss sexual matters inside or outside the family, and children may be threatened with dire consequences if they divulge the secret. Other children do not seek assistance because they feel complicit in their victimization, especially when the abuser is a family member whom they love.

Legal definitions of sexual abuse in the contemporary United States emphasize the notion of consent. Most states consider incest illegal in all circumstances, and every state has laws identifying the age at which a person is considered capable of consenting to sexual activity with an unrelated person (ranging from fourteen to eighteen). Government data reveal that children are sexually abused in 10 percent of documented child-maltreatment cases (U.S. DHSS 2003), and self-report surveys indicate that at least 20 percent of women and 5 percent of men were sexually victimized as children (Finkelhor 1994). Girls are more likely to be abused within the family than outside it, and most incestuous abuse is committed by fathers and stepfathers against daughters (Finkelhor, Hotaling, Lewis, and Smith 1990; U.S. DHSS 2003). However, reports of boys being sexually abused, especially by male coaches and religious leaders, have been increasing (Kimmel 2005).

Child sexual assault is correlated with myriad emotional, cognitive, physical, psychological, and behavioral effects, most of which are mediated by the victim's age or developmental level and the relationship of the perpetrator to the victim. The most frequently identified problems in this population, across age groups, are symptoms of post-traumatic stress disorder (PTSD). For adolescent girls, sexual victimization is also correlated with sexual acting out and running away, both of which place girls at high risk for revictimization, unplanned pregnancy, and sexually transmitted diseases (Barnett, Miller-Perrin, and Perrin 2005; Baynard, Williams, Siegel, and West 2002).

Many child advocates recognize pornography and prostitution as mutually supporting activities that serve to sexualize and commodify children. As the global economy has spurred free trade and extensive travel, increased attention to the commercial exploitation of children through the international sex-tourism industry is a growing concern. The availability of the Internet exacerbates the problem by giving men detailed information about how to participate in these activities with little risk of detection or punishment (Klain 1999).

Violence in Schools and Communities

In the wake of the Columbine and San Diego school shootings, there has been considerable media attention to, and public concern about, peer homicide in schools. Although these events are terrifying and tragic, the chance of a child being killed at school is remote (NCJRS 2003). Because of its frequency, the numbers of people affected by it, and the widespread and damaging outcomes for victims, sexual harassment is arguably the most virulent form of gender violence experienced by children.

Children may be introduced to sexual harassment as early as kindergarten, when girls are subjected to a barrage of verbal attacks on their abilities, their options, and their bodies, all intended to remind them that they are expected to limit their aspirations (Sadker and Sadker 1994). Not only does the harassment make girls feel like second-class citizens, but it also has a chilling effect on their willingness to call attention to themselves by participating in class, which ultimately may cause their school performance to suffer. When gendered power roles are enacted in classrooms and on school playgrounds, there are detrimental consequences for boys as well (Thorne 1993). Boys who do not meet standards of athleticism are insulted as "girls" or "sissies," subjected to humiliating practices such as being spit on or disrobed, and assaulted both physically and sexually.

Even children who do not directly experience such assaults are affected by the excessive pressure to meet cultural ideals of masculinity and femininity. Youth who internalize rigid gender expectations may cope with feelings of anxiety, inferiority, and powerlessness by engaging in self-destructive behavior such as alcohol and drug use, early involvement in sexual activity, participation in high-risk ventures, and self-inflicted violence. Suicide is now the third leading killer of youth in the United States, and gay male youth have unusually high rates of attempted suicide (Garland and Zigler 1993; Remafedi 1994). Whatever the specific nature of the abuse, and regardless of whether it is self-inflicted or imposed by a family member, friend, or stranger, the widespread victimization of children is an indictment of a society that professes great concern for children but fails to adequately protect them. Children will continue to be victimized as long as adults, who hold the power in relation to children, can rely on the authority of the state to uphold patriarchal traditions.

Contributions to This Section

The readings in this section urge us to reconsider commonly held beliefs about why, how, and by whom children are victimized. These articles challenge assumptions about children and gender violence by arguing for a more complex, nuanced understanding of the problems associated with children and gender violence.

In "Family Violence, Feminism, and Social Control," Linda Gordon uses child protection agency records to explore the tensions and contradictions between the needs and desires of clients and the interpretations and actions of social-welfare workers during the early 1900s. Her portrayal encourages us to look beyond the simple dichotomy of dominating abuser and helpless victim.

In "Locating a Secret Problem: Sexual Violence in Elementary and Secondary Schools," Nan Stein reports that her review of recent cases of peer-perpetrated sexual harassment reveals two particularly disturbing trends: sexual harassment is becoming more prevalent at younger ages, and this form of gendered violence is becoming increasingly dangerous and sexualized.

In "Men, Masculinity, and Child Abuse: A Sex and Gender Question," Annie Cossins develops a theoretical perspective on child sexual abuse that locates this form of victimization within the construction of normal male sexuality. She examines the social context in which adult men come to view children as sexually appealing and available.

In "Child Sexual Abuse and the Regulation of Women: Variations on a Theme," Carol-Ann Hooper also considers how child sexual abuse stems from the social construction of masculinity. Her article reveals how the feminist perspective on this problem has been marginalized in official policies designed to address it.

In "Who Stole Incest?" Louise Armstrong challenges us to frame incest as a social issue that demands political solutions. Armstrong, who was one of the first people to assert a feminist position on the sexual abuse of children (see *Kiss Daddy Goodnight*, 1978), critiques the dominant cultural discourse that frames incest as an illness rather than a crime of violence against children.

SUGGESTIONS FOR FURTHER READING

Dorothy Allison, *Bastard Out of Carolina* (New York: Dutton, 1992).
Annie Cossins, *Masculinities, Sexualities, and Child Sexual Abuse* (New York: Springer, 2000).
Connie May Fowler, *Before Women Had Wings* (New York: Ballantine Books, 1996).
James Garbarino, *Raising Children in a Toxic Environment* (San Francisco: Jossey-Bass, 1995).

The Second Photograph

Margaret Randall

I have found another portrait.
You have me on your lap
flanked by my two grandmothers
both looking congenitally worried
as well they should.

You, on the other hand, seem vaguely crazed
as you certainly were,
your lips and eyes focused on different planes.

I have looked long and hard
at the hands in this picture.
Both women hide theirs, differently.
Yours, Grandpa, are loosely circled
about my three-year-old body.
Your right covers my left, your left
comes round my party-dressed buttocks,
your fingers strangely held as if in secret sign.

I am reading this into the image.
I am reading it because now, half a century later,
I understand why my eyes in the picture
take the camera head on, demanding answers.

Albuquerque, Spring 1986

From Margaret Randall's *Memory Says Yes* (Curbstone Press, 1988). Reprinted with permission of Curbstone Press. Distributed by Consortium.

Chapter Nineteen

Family Violence, Feminism, and Social Control

Linda Gordon

In studying the history of family violence, I found myself also confronting the issue of social control, incarnated in the charitable "friendly visitors" and later professional child protection workers who composed the case records I was reading. At first I experienced these social control agents as intruding themselves unwanted into my research. My study was based on the records of Boston "child-saving" agencies, in which the oppressions of class, culture, and gender were immediately evident. The "clients" were mainly poor, Catholic, female immigrants. (It was not that women were responsible for most of the family violence but that they were more often involved with agencies for reasons we shall see below.) The social workers were exclusively well educated and male and overwhelmingly White Anglo-Saxon Protestant (WASP). These workers, authors of case records, were often disdainful, ignorant, and obtuse—at best, paternalistic—toward their clients.

Yet, ironically, these very biases created a useful discipline, showing that it was impossible to study family violence as an objective problem. Attempts at social control were part of the original definition and construction of family violence as a social issue. The very concept of family violence is a product of conflict and negotiation between people troubled by domestic violence and social control agents attempting to change their supposedly unruly and deviant behavior.

In this essay I want to argue not a defense of social control but a critique of its critiques and some thoughts about a better, feminist, framework. I would like to make my argument as it came to me, through studying child abuse and neglect. Nine years ago when I began to study the history of family violence, I assumed I would be focusing largely on wifebeating because that was the target of the contemporary feminist activism which had drawn my attention to the problem. I was surprised, however, to find that violence against children represented a more complex challenge to the task of envisioning feminist family policy and a feminist theory of social control.

Linda Gordon, "Family Violence, Feminism, and Social Control," was originally published in *Feminist Studies* 12, no. 3 (fall 1986): 453–78. Reprinted by permission of the publisher, Feminist Studies, Inc.

Social Control

Many historians of women and the family have inherited a critical view of social control, as an aspect of domination and the source of decline in family and individual autonomy. In situating ourselves with respect to this tradition, it may be useful to trace very briefly the history of the concept. "Social control" is a phrase usually attributed to the sociologist E. A. Ross. He used the phrase as the title of a collection of his essays in 1901, referring to the widest range of influence and regulation societies imposed upon individuals.[1] Building on a Hobbesian view of human individuals as naturally in conflict, Ross saw "social control" as inevitable. Moving beyond liberal individualism, however, he argued for social control in a more specific, American Progressive sense. Ross advocated the active, deliberate, expert guidance of human life not only as the source of human progress but also as the best replacement for older, familial, and communitarian forms of control, which he believed were disappearing in modern society.

Agencies attempting to control family violence are preeminent examples of the kind of expert social control institutions that were endorsed by Ross and other Progressive reformers. These agencies—the most typical were the Societies for the Prevention of Cruelty to Children (SPCCs)—were established in the 1870s in a decade of acute international alarm about child abuse. They began as punitive and moralistic "charitable" endeavors, characteristic of nineteenth-century elite moral purity reforms. These societies blamed the problem of family violence on the depravity, immorality, and drunkenness of individuals, which they often traced to the innate inferiority of the immigrants who constituted the great bulk of their targets. By the early twentieth century, the SPCCs took on a more ambitious task, hoping not merely to cure family pathology but also to reform family life and childraising. Describing the change slightly differently, in the nineteenth century, child protection agents saw themselves as paralegal, punishing specific offenses, protecting children from specific dangers; in the early twentieth century, they tried to supervise and direct the family lives of those considered deviant.

The view that intervention into the family has increased, and has become a characteristic feature of modern society, is now often associated with Talcott Parsons's writings of the late 1940s and 1950s. Parsons proposed the "transfer of functions" thesis, the notion that professionals had taken over many family functions (for example, education, childcare, therapy, and medical care). Parsons's was a liberal, optimistic view; he thought this professionalization a step forward, leaving the family free to devote more of its time and energy to affective relations. There was already a contrasting, far more pessimistic, interpretation, emanating from the Frankfurt school of German Marxists, who condemned the decline of family autonomy and even attributed to it, in part, the horrors of totalitarianism.

The latter tradition, critical of social control, has conditioned most of the historical writing about social control agencies and influences. Much of the earlier work in this mid-twentieth-century revival of women's history adopted this perspective on social control, substituting gender for class or national categories in the analysis of women's subordination. In the field of child saving in particular, the most influential historical work has adopted this perspective.[2] These critiques usually distinguished an "us" and a "them," oppressed and oppressor, in a dichotomous relation. They were usually functionalist: they tended to assume or argue that the social control practices in question served (were functional for) the material interests of a dominant group and hindered (were dysfunctional to) the interests of the subordinate. More recently, some women's historians have integrated class and gender into this model, arguing that the growth of the state in the last 150 years has increased individual rights for prosperous women but has only subjected poor women to ever greater control.[3] Alternatively, women's historians represent social control as half of a bargain in which material benefits—welfare benefits, for example—are given to those controlled in exchange for the surrender of power or autonomy.[4]

The development of women's history in the last decade has begun to correct some of the oversimplifications of this "anti-social-control" school of analysis. A revival of what might be called the Beardian tradition (after Mary Beard) recognizes women's activity —in this case, in constructing modern forms of social control.[5] Historians of social work or other social control institutions, however, have not participated in the rethinking of the paradigm of elite domination and plebeian victimization.[6]

The critique of the domination exercised by social work and human services bureaucracies and professionals is not wrong, but its incompleteness allows for some serious distortion. My own views derive from a study of the history of family violence and its social control in Boston from 1880 to 1960, using both the quantitative and qualitative analysis of case records from three leading child-saving agencies.[7] Looking at these records from the perspective of children and their primary caretakers (and abusers), women, reveals the impoverishment of the anti-social-control perspective sketched above and its inadequacy to the task of conceptualizing who is controlled and who is controlling in these family conflicts. A case history may suggest some of the complexities that have influenced my thinking.

In 1910 a Syrian family in Boston's South End, here called the Kashys, came to the attention of the Massachusetts Society for the Prevention of Cruelty to Children (MSPCC) because of the abuse of the mother's thirteen-year-old girl.[8] Mr. Kashy had just died of appendicitis. The family, like so many immigrants, had moved back and forth between Syria and the United States several times; two other children had been left in Syria with their paternal grandparents. In this country, in addition to the central "victim," whom I shall call Fatima, there was a six-year-old boy and a three-year-old girl, and Mrs. Kashy was pregnant. The complainant was the father's sister, and indeed all the paternal relatives were hostile to Mrs. Kashy. The MSPCC investigation substantiated their allegations: Mrs. Kashy hit Fatima with a stick and with chairs, bit her ear, kept her from school, and overworked her, expecting her to do all the housework and to care for the younger children. When Fatima fell ill, her mother refused to let her go to the hospital. The hostility of the paternal relatives, however, focused not only on the mother's treatment of Fatima but mainly on her custody rights. It was their position that custody should have fallen to them after Mr. Kashy's death, arguing that "in Syria a woman's rights to the care of her chn [abbreviations in original] or the control of property is not recognized." In Syrian tradition, the paternal grandfather had rights to the children, and he had delegated this control to his son, the children's paternal uncle.

The paternal kin, then, had expected Mrs. Kashy to bow to their rights; certainly her difficult economic and social situation would make it understandable if she had. The complainant, the father's sister, was Mrs. Kashy's landlady and was thus in a position to make her life very difficult. Mrs. Kashy lived with her three children in one attic room without water; she had to go to the ground level and carry water up to her apartment. The relatives offered her no help after her bereavement, and Mrs. Kashy was desperate; she was trying to earn a living by continuing her husband's peddling. She needed Fatima to keep the house and care for the children.

When Mrs. Kashy resisted their custody claims, the paternal relatives called in as a mediator a Syrian community leader, publisher of the *New Syria*, a Boston Arabic-language newspaper. Ultimately the case went to court, however, and here the relatives lost as their custody traditions conflicted with the new preference in the United States for women's custody. Fatima's wishes were of no help to the agency in sorting out this conflict, because throughout the struggle she was ambivalent: sometimes she begged to be kept away from her mother, yet when away, she begged to be returned to her mother. Ultimately, Mrs. Kashy won custody but no maternal help in supporting her children by herself. As in so many child abuse cases, it was the victim who was punished: Fatima was sent to the Gwynne Home, where—at least so her relatives believed—she was treated abusively.

If the story had stopped there one might be tempted to see Mrs. Kashy as relatively blameless, driven perhaps to episodes of harshness and temper by her difficult lot. But thirteen years later, in 1923, a "school visitor" brought the second daughter, now sixteen, to the MSPCC to complain of abuse by her mother and by her older, now married, sister Fatima. In the elapsed years, this second daughter had been sent back to Syria; perhaps Mrs. Kashy had had to give up her efforts to support her children. Returning to the United States eighteen months previously, the girl had arrived to find that her mother intended to marry her involuntarily to a boarder. The daughter displayed blood on her shirt which she said came from her mother's beatings. Interviewed by an MSPCC agent, Mrs. Kashy was now openly hostile and defiant, saying that she would beat her daughter as she liked.

In its very complexity, the Kashy case exemplifies certain generalizations central to my argument. One is that it is often difficult to identify a unique victim. It should not be surprising that the oppressed Mrs. Kashy was angry and violent, but feminist rhetoric about family violence has often avoided this complexity. Mrs. Kashy was the victim of her isolation, widowhood, single motherhood, and patriarchal, hostile in-laws; she also exploited and abused her daughter. Indeed, Mrs. Kashy's attitude to Fatima was patriarchal: she believed that children should serve parents and not vice versa. This aspect of patriarchal tradition served Mrs. Kashy. But, in other respects, the general interests of the oppressed group—here the Syrian immigrants—as expressed by its male, *petit-bourgeois* leadership, were more inimical to Mrs. Kashy's (and other women's) aspirations and "rights" than those of the elite agency, the MSPCC. Furthermore, one can reasonably surmise that the daughters were also actors in this drama, resisting their mother's expectations as well as those of the male-dominated community, as New World ideas of children's rights coincided with aspirations entirely their own. None of the existing social control critiques can adequately conceptualize the complex struggles in the Kashy family, nor can they propose nonoppressive ways for Fatima's "rights" to be protected.

Feminism and Child Abuse

Feminist theory in general and women's history in particular have moved only slowly beyond the "victimization" paradigm that dominated the rebirth of feminist scholarship. The obstacles to perceiving and describing women's own power have been particularly great in issues relating to social policy and to family violence, because of the legacy of victim blaming. Defending women against male violence is so urgent that we fear women's loss of status as deserving, political "victims" if we acknowledge women's own aggressions. These complexities are at their greatest in the situation of mothers because they are simultaneously victims and victimizers, dependent and depended on, weak and powerful.

If feminist theory needs a new view of social control, thinking about child abuse virtually demands it. Child abuse cases reveal suffering that is incontrovertible, unnecessary, and remediable. However severe the biases of the social workers attempting to "save" the children and reform their parents—and I will have more to say about this later—one could not advocate a policy of inaction in regard to children chained to beds, left in filthy diapers for days, turned out in the cold. Children, unlike women, lack even the potential for social and economic independence. A beneficial social policy could at least partly address the problem of wifebeating by empowering women to leave abusive situations, enabling them to live in comfort and dignity without men, and encouraging them to espouse high standards in their expectations of treatment by others. It is not clear how one could empower children in analogous ways. If children are to have "rights," then some adults must be appointed and accepted, by other adults, to define and defend them.

Women, who do most of the labor of childcare and have the strongest emotional bonds to children, fought for and largely won rights to child custody over the last 150 years. Yet women are often the abusers and neglecters of children. Indeed, child abuse becomes the more interesting and challenging to feminists because in it we meet women's rage and abuses of power. Furthermore, child abuse is a gendered phenomenon, related to the oppression of women, whether women or men are the culprits, because it reflects the sexual division of the labor of reproduction. Because men spend, on the whole, so much less time with children than do women, what is remarkable is not that women are violent toward children but that men are responsible for nearly half of the child abuse. But women are always implicated because even when men are the culprits, women are usually the primary caretakers who have been, by definition, unable to protect the children. When protective organizations remove children or undertake supervision of their caretakers, women often suffer greatly, for their maternal work, trying as it may be, is usually the most pleasurable part of their lives.

Yet in the last two decades of intense publicity and scholarship about child abuse, the feminist contribution has been negligible. This silence is the more striking in contrast to the legacy of the first wave of feminism, particularly in the period 1880 to 1930, in which the women's rights movement was tightly connected to child welfare reform campaigns. By contrast, the second wave of feminism, a movement heavily influenced by younger and childless women, has spent relatively little energy on children's issues. Feminist scholars have studied the social organization of mothering in theory but not the actual experiences of childraising, and the movement as a whole has not significantly influenced child welfare debates or policies. When such issues emerge publicly, feminists too often assume that women's and children's interests always coincide. The facts of child abuse and neglect challenge this assumption as does the necessity sometimes of severing maternal custody in order to protect children.

Protecting Children

Child abuse was "discovered" as a social problem in the 1870s. Surely many children had been ill-treated by parents before this, but new social conditions created an increased sensitivity to the treatment of children and, possibly, actually worsened children's lot. Conditions of labor and family life under industrial capitalism may have made poverty, stress, and parental anger bear more heavily on children. The child abuse alarm also reflected growing class and cultural differences in beliefs about how children *should* be raised. The anti-cruelty-to-children movement grew out of an anti-corporal-punishment campaign, and both reflected a uniquely professional-class view that children could be disciplined by reason and with mildness. The SPCCs also grew from widespread fears among more privileged people about violence and "depravity" among the urban poor; in the United States, these fears were exacerbated by the fact that these poor were largely immigrants and Catholics, threatening the WASP domination of city culture and government.

On one level, my study of the case records of Boston child-saving agencies corroborated the anti-social-control critique: the work of the agencies did represent oppressive intervention into working-class families. The MSPCC attempted to enforce culturally specific norms of proper parenting that were not only alien to the cultural legacy of their "clients" but also flew in the face of many of the economic necessities of the clients' lives. Thus, MSPCC agents prosecuted cases in which cruelty to children was caused, in their view, by children's labor: girls doing housework and childcare, often staying home from school because their parents required it; girls and boys working in shops, peddling on the streets; boys working for organ grinders and lying about their ages to enlist in the navy. Before World War I, the enemies of the truant officers were usually parents, not children. To immigrants from peasant backgrounds it seemed irrational and blasphemous that adult women should work while able-bodied children remained idle. Similarly, the MSPCC was opposed to the common immigrant practice of leaving children unattended and allowing them to play and wander in the streets. Both violated the MSPCC's norm of domesticity for women and children; proper middle-class children in those days did not—at least not in the cities—play outside on their own.

The child savers were attempting to impose a new, middle-class urban style of mothering and fathering. Mothers were supposed to be tender and gentle and, above all, to protect their children from immoral influences; the child savers considered yelling, rude language, or sexually explicit talk to be forms of cruelty to children. Fathers were to provide models of emotional containment, to be relatively uninvolved with children; their failure to provide adequate economic support was often interpreted as a character flaw, no matter what the evidence of widespread, structural unemployment. MSPCC agents in practice and in rhetoric expressed disdain for immigrant cultures. They hated the garlic and olive oil smells of Italian cooking and considered this food unhealthy (overstimulating, aphrodisiac). The agents were unable to distinguish alcoholics and heavy drinkers from moderate wine and beer drinkers, and they believed that women who took spirits were degenerate and unfit as mothers. They associated many of these forms of depravity with Catholicism. Agents were also convinced of the subnormal intelligence of most non-WASP and especially non-English-speaking clients; indeed, the agents' comments and expectations in this early period were similar to social workers' views of black clients in the mid-twentieth century. These child welfare specialists were particularly befuddled by and disapproving of non-nuclear childraising patterns: children raised by grandmothers, complex households composed of children from several different marriages (or, worse, out-of-wedlock relationships), children sent temporarily to other households.

The peasant backgrounds of so many of the "hyphenated" Americans created a situation in which ethnic bias could not easily be separated from class bias. Class misunderstanding, moreover, took a form specific to urban capitalism: a failure to grasp the actual economic and physical circumstances of this immigrant proletariat and subproletariat. Unemployment was not yet understood to be a structural characteristic of industrial capitalism. Disease, overcrowding, crime, and—above all—dependence were also not understood to be part of the system but, rather, were seen as personal failings.

This line of criticism, however, only partially uncovers the significance of child protection. Another dimension and a great deal more complexity are revealed by considering the feminist aspect of the movement. Much of the child welfare reform energy of the nineteenth century came from women and was organized by the "woman movement."[9] The campaign against corporal punishment, from which the anti-child-abuse movement grew, depended upon a critique of violence rooted in feminist thought and in women's reform activity. Women's reform influence, the "sentimentalizing" of the Calvinist traditions,[10] was largely responsible for the softening of childraising norms. The delegitimation of corporal punishment, noticeable among the prosperous classes by mid-century, was associated with exclusive female responsibility for childraising, with women's victories in child custody cases, even with women's criticisms of traditionally paternal discipline.[11]

Feminist thinking exerted an important influence on the agencies' original formulations of the problem of family violence. Most MSPCC spokesmen (and those who represented the agency in public were men) viewed men as aggressors and women and children, jointly, as blameless victims. However simplistic, this was a feminist attitude. It was also, of course, saturated with class and cultural elitism: these "brutal" and "depraved" men were of a different class and ethnicity than the MSPCC agents, and the language of victimization applied to women and children was also one of condescension. Nevertheless, despite the definition of the "crime" as cruelty to children, MSPCC agents soon included wifebeating in their agenda of reform.

Even more fundamentally, the very undertaking of child protection was a challenge to patriarchal relations. A pause to look at my definition of patriarchy is necessary here. In the 1970s a new definition of that term came into use, first proposed by Kate Millett but quickly adopted by the U.S. feminist movement: patriarchy became a synonym for male supremacy, for "sexism." I use the term in its earlier, historical, and more specific sense, referring to a family form in which fathers had control over all other family members—children, women, and servants. This concept of a patriarchal family is an abstraction, postulating common features among family forms that differed widely across geography and time. If there was a common material base supporting this patriarchal family norm (a question requiring a great deal more study before it can be answered decisively), it was an economic system in which the family was the unit of production. Most of the MSPCC's early clients came from peasant societies in which this kind of family economy prevailed. In these families, fathers maintained control not only over property and tools but also, above all, over the labor power of family members. Historical patriarchy defined a set of parent-child relations as much as it did relations between the sexes, for children rarely had opportunities for economic independence except by inheriting the family property, trade, or craft. In some ways mothers, too, benefited from patriarchal parent-child relations. Their authority over daughters and young sons was important when they lacked other kinds of authority and independence, and in old age they gained respect, help, and consideration from younger kinfolk.

The claim of an organization such as an SPCC to speak on behalf of children's rights, its claim to the license to intervene in parental treatment of children, was an attack on patriarchal power. At the same time, the new sensibility about children's rights and the concern about child abuse were symptoms of a weakening of patriarchal family expectations and realities that had already taken place, particularly during the eighteenth and early nineteenth centuries in the United States. In this weakening, father-child relations had changed more than husband-wife relations. Children had, for example, gained the power to arrange their own betrothals and marriages and to embark on wage work independent of their fathers' occupations (of course, children's options remained determined by class and cultural privileges or the lack of them, inherited from fathers). In contrast, however, wage labor and long-distance mobility often made women, on balance, more dependent on husbands for sustenance and less able to deploy kinfolk and neighbors to defend their interests against husbands.

Early child protection work did not, of course, envision a general liberation of children from arbitrary parental control or from the responsibility of filial obedience. On the contrary, the SPCCs aimed as much to reinforce a failing parental/paternal authority as to limit it. Indeed, the SPCC spokesmen often criticized excessive physical violence against children as a symptom of inadequate parental authority. Assaults on children were provoked by children's insubordination; in the interpretation of nineteenth-century child protectors, this showed that parental weakness, children's disobedience, and child abuse were mutually reinforcing. Furthermore, by the turn of the century, the SPCCs discovered that the majority of their cases concerned neglect, not assault, and neglect exemplified to them the problems created by the withdrawal, albeit not always conscious or deliberate, of parental supervision and authority (among the poor who formed the agency clientele there were many fathers who deserted and many more who were inadequate providers). Many neglect and abuse cases ended with *children* being punished, sent to reform schools on stubborn-child charges.

In sum, the SPCCs sought to reconstruct the family along lines that altered the old patriarchy, already economically unviable, and to replace it with a modern version of male supremacy. The SPCCs' rhetoric about children's rights did not extend to a parallel articulation of women's rights; their condemnation of wifebeating did not include endorsement of the kind of marriage later called "companionate," implying equality between wife and husband. Their new family and childraising norms included the conviction that children's respect for parents needed to be inculcated ideologically, moralistically, and psychologically because it no longer rested on an economic dependence lasting beyond childhood. Fathers, now as wage laborers rather than as slaves, artisans, peasants, or entrepreneurs, were to have single-handed responsibility for economic support of their families; women and children should not contribute to the family economy, at least not monetarily. Children instead should spend full-time in learning cognitive lessons from professional teachers, psychological and moral lessons from the full-time attention of a mother. In turn, women should devote themselves to mothering and domesticity.

Feminism, Mothering, and Industrial Capitalism

This childraising program points to a larger irony—that the "modernization" of male domination, its adaptation to new economic and social conditions, was partly a result of the influence of the first wave of feminism. These first "feminists" rarely advocated full equality between women and men and never promoted the abolition of traditional gender relations or the sexual division of labor. Allowing for differences of emphasis, the program just defined constituted a feminist as well as a liberal family-reform program in the 1870s. Indeed, organized feminism *was* in part such a liberal reform program, a program to adapt the family and the civil society to the new economic conditions of industrial capitalism, for consciously or not, feminists felt that these new conditions provided greater possibilities for the freedom and empowerment of women.

To recapitulate, child protection work was an integral part of the feminist as well as the bourgeois program for modernizing the family. Child saving had gender as well as class and ethnic content, but in none of these aspects did it simply or homogeneously represent the interests of a dominant group (or even of the composite group of WASP elite women, that hypothetical stratum on which it is fashionable to blame the limitations of feminist activity). The antipatriarchalism of the child protection agencies was an unstable product of several conflicting interests. Understanding this illuminates the influence of feminism on the development of a capitalist industrial culture even as feminists criticized the new privileges it bestowed on men and its degradation of women's traditional work. The relation of feminism to capitalism and industrialism is usually argued in dichotomous and reductionist fashion: either feminism is the expression of bourgeois woman's aspirations, an ultimate individualism that tears apart the remaining noninstrumental bonds in a capitalist society; or, feminism is inherently anticapitalist, deepening and extending the critique of domination to show its penetration even of personal life and the allegedly "natural." Although there is a little truth in both versions, at least one central aspect of feminism's significance for capitalism has been omitted in these formulations—its role in redefining family norms and particularly norms of mothering.

Changes in the conditions of motherhood in an industrializing society were an important part of the experiences that drew women to the postbellum feminist movement. For most women, and particularly for urban poor women, motherhood became more difficult in wage-labor conditions. Mothers were more isolated from support networks of kin, and mothering furthered that isolation, often requiring that women remain out of public space. The potential dangers from which children needed protection multiplied, and the increasing cultural demands for a "psychological parenting" increased the potential for maternal "failure."[12] These changes affected women of all classes, while, at the same time, motherhood remained the central identity for women of all classes. Childbirth and childraising, the most universal parts of female experience, were the common referents—the metaphoric base of political language—by which feminist ideas were communicated.

As industrial capitalism changed the conditions of motherhood, so women began to redefine motherhood in ways that would influence the entire culture. They "used" motherhood simultaneously to increase their own status, to promote greater social expenditure on children, and to loosen their dependence on men, just as capitalists "used" motherhood as a form of unpaid labor. The working-class and even sub-working-class women of the child abuse case records drew "feminist" conclusions— that is, they diagnosed their problems in terms of male supremacy—in their efforts to improve their own conditions of mothering. In their experiences, men's greater power (economic and social), in combination with men's lesser sense of responsibility toward children, kept them from being as good at mothering as they wanted. They responded by trying to rid themselves of those forms of male domination that impinged most directly on their identity and work as mothers and on children's needs as they interpreted those needs.

But if child protection work may have represented *all* mothers' demands, it made *some* mothers—poor urban mothers—extremely vulnerable by calling into question the quality of their mothering, already made more problematic by urban wage-labor living conditions, and by threatening them with the loss of their children. Poor women had less privacy and therefore less impunity in their deviance from the new childraising norms, but their poverty often led them to ask for help from relief agencies, therefore calling themselves to the attention of the child-saving networks. Yet poor women did not by any means figure only on the victim side, for they were also often enthusiastic about defending children's "rights" and correcting cruel or neglectful parents. Furthermore, they used an eclectic variety of arguments and devices to defend their control of their children. At times they mobilized liberal premises and rhetoric to escape from patriarchal households and to defend their custody rights; they were quick to learn the right language of the New World in which to criticize their husbands and relatives and to manipulate social workers to side with them against patriarchal controls of other family members. Yet at other times they called upon traditional relations when community and kinfolk could help them retain control or defend children. Poor women often denounced the "intervention" of outside social control agencies like the SPCCs but only when it suited them, and at other times they eagerly used and asked such agencies for help.

Let me offer another case history to illustrate this opportunistic and resourceful approach to social control agencies. An Italian immigrant family, which I will call the Amatos, were "clients" of the MSPCC from 1910 to 1916.[13] They had five young children from the current marriage and Mrs. Amato had three from a previous marriage, two of them still in Italy and one daughter in Boston. Mrs. Amato kept that daughter at home to do housework and look after the younger children while she earned money doing piece-rate sewing at home. This got the family in trouble with a truant officer, and they were also accused, in court, of lying to Associated Charities (a consortium of private relief agencies), saying that the father had deserted them when he was in fact living at home. Furthermore, once while left alone, probably in the charge of a sibling, one of the younger children fell out of a window and had to be hospitalized. This incident provoked agency suspicions that the mother was negligent.

Despite her awareness of these suspicions against her, Mrs. Amato sought help from many different organizations, starting with those of the Italian immigrant community and then reaching out to elite social work agencies, reporting that her husband was a drunkard, a gambler, a nonsupporter, and a wifebeater. The MSPCC agents at first doubted her claims because Mr. Amato impressed them as a "good and sober man," and they blamed the neglect of the children on his wife's incompetence in managing the wages he gave her. The MSPCC ultimately became convinced of Mrs. Amato's story because of her repeated appearance with severe bruises and the corroboration of the husband's father, who was intimately involved in the family troubles and took responsibility for attempting to control his son. Once the father came to the house and gave his son "a warning and a couple of slaps," after which he improved for a while. Another time the father extracted from him a pledge not to beat his wife for two years!

Mrs. Amato wanted none of this. She begged the MSPCC agent to help her get a divorce; later she claimed that she had not dared take this step because her husband's relatives threatened to beat her if she tried it. Then Mrs. Amato's daughter (from her previous marriage) took action, coming independently to the MSPCC to bring an agent to the house to help her mother. As a result of this complaint, Mr. Amato was convicted of assault once and sentenced to six months. During that time Mrs. Amato survived by "a little work and . . . Italian friends have helped her." Her husband returned, more violent than before: he went at her with an axe, beat the children so much on the head that their "eyes wabbled [*sic*]" permanently, and supported his family so poorly that the children went out begging. This case closed, like so many, without a resolution.

The Amatos' case will not support the usual anti-social-control interpretation of the relation between oppressed clients and social agencies. There was no unity among the client family and none among the professional intervenors. Furthermore, the intervenors were often dragged into the case and by individuals with conflicting points of view. Mrs. Amato and Mrs. Kashy were not atypical in their attempts to use "social control" agencies in their own interests. Clients frequently initiated agency intervention; even in family violence cases, where the stakes were high—losing one's children—the majority of complaints in this study came from parents or close relatives who believed that their own standards of childraising were being violated.[14]

In their sparring with social work agencies, clients did not usually or collectively win because the professionals had more resources. Usually no one decisively "won." Considering these cases collectively, professional social work overrode working-class or poor people's interests, but in specific cases the professionals did not always formulate definite goals, let alone achieve them. Indeed, the bewilderment of the social workers (something usually overlooked because most scholarship about social work is based on policy statements, not on actual case records) frequently enabled the clients to go some distance toward achieving their own goals.

The social control experience was not a simple two-sided trade-off in which the client sacrificed autonomy and control in return for some material help. Rather, the clients helped shape the nature of the social control itself. Formulating these criticisms about the inadequacy of simple anti-social-control explanations in some analytic order, I would make four general points.

First, the condemnation of agency intervention into the family, and the condemnation of social control itself as something automatically evil, usually assumes that there can be, and once was, an autonomous family. On the contrary, no family relations have been immune from social regulation.[15] Certainly the forms of social control I examine here are qualitatively and quantitatively different, based on regulation from "outside," by those without a legitimate claim to caring about local, individual values and traditions. Contrasting the experience of social control to a hypothetical era of autonomy, however, distorts both traditional and modern forms of social regulation.

The tendency to consider social control as unprecedented, invasive regulation is not only an academic mistake. It grew from nineteenth-century emotional and political responses to social change. Family autonomy became a symbol of patriarchy only in its era of decline (as in 1980s' New Right rhetoric). Family "autonomy" was an oppositional concept in the nineteenth century, expressing a liberal ideal of home as a private and caring space in contrast to the public realm of increasingly instrumental relations. This symbolic cluster surrounding the family contained both critical and legitimating responses to industrial capitalist society. But as urban society created more individual opportunities for women, the defense of family autonomy came to stand against women's autonomy in a conservative opposition to women's demands for individual freedoms. (The concept of family autonomy today, as it is manipulated in political discourse, mainly has the latter function, suggesting that women's individual rights to autonomous citizenship will make the family more vulnerable to outside intervention). The Amatos' pattern, a more patriarchal pattern, of turning to relatives, friends, and, when they could not help, Italian-American organizations (no doubt the closest analogue to a "community" in the New World), was not adequate to the urban problems they now encountered. Even the violent and defensive Mr. Amato did not question the right of his father, relatives, and friends to intervene forcibly, and Mrs. Amato did not appear shocked that her husband's relatives tried, perhaps successfully, to hold her forcibly in her marriage. Family autonomy was not an expectation of the Amatos.

Second, the social control explanation sees the flow of initiative going in only one direction: from top to bottom, from professionals to clients, from elite to subordinate. The power of this interpretation of social work comes from the large proportion of truth it holds and also from the influence of scholars of poor people's movements who have denounced elite attempts to blame "the victims." The case records show, however, that clients were not passive but, rather, active negotiators in a complex bargaining. Textbooks of casework recognize the intense interactions and relationships that develop between social worker and client. In the social work version of concern with countertransference, textbooks often attempt to accustom the social worker to examining her or his participation in that relationship.[16] This sense of mutuality, power struggle, and intersubjectivity, however, has not penetrated historical accounts of social work/social control encounters.

Third, critics of social control often fail to recognize the active role of agency clients because they conceive of the family as a homogeneous unit. There is an intellectual reification here which expresses itself in sentence structure, particularly in academic language: "The family is in decline," "threats to the family," "the family responds to industrialization." Shorthand expressions attributing behavior to an aggregate such as the family would be harmless except that they often express particular cultural norms about what "the family" is and does, and they mask intrafamily differences and conflicts of interest. Usually "the family" becomes a representation of the interests of the family head, if it is a man, carrying an assumption that all family members share his interests. (Families without a married male head, such as single-parent or grandparent-headed families, are in the common usage broken, deformed, or incomplete families, and thus do not qualify for these assumptions regarding family unity.) Among the clients in family violence cases, outrage over the intervention into the family was frequently anger over a territorial violation, a challenge to male authority; expressed differently, it was a reaction to the exposure to others of intrafamily conflict and of the family head's lack of control. Indeed, the interventions actually *were* more substantive, more invasive, when their purpose was to change the status quo than if they had been designed to reinforce it. The effect of social workers' involvement was often to change existing family power relations, usually in the interest of the weaker family members.

Social work interventions were often invited by family members; the inviters, however, were usually the weaker members of a family power structure, women and children. These invitations were made despite the fact, well known to clients, that women and children usually had the most to lose (despite fathers' frequent outrage at their loss of face) from MSPCC intervention because by far the most common outcome of agency action was not prosecution and jail sentences but the removal of children, an action fathers dreaded less than mothers. In the immigrant working-class neighborhoods of Boston the MSPCC became known as "the Cruelty," eloquently suggesting poor people's recognition and fear of its power. But these fears did not stop poor people from initiating contact with the organization. After the MSPCC had been in operation ten years, 60 percent of the complaints of known origin (excluding anonymous accusations) came from family members, the overwhelming majority of these from women, with children following second. These requests for help came not only from victims but also from mothers distressed that they were not able to raise their children according to their own standards of good parenting. Women also maneuvered to bring child welfare agencies into family struggles on their sides. There was no Society for the Prevention of Cruelty to Women, but in fact women like Mrs. Amato were trying to turn the SPCC into just that. A frequent tactic of beaten, deserted, or unsupported wives was to report their husbands as child abusers; even when investigations found no evidence of child abuse, social workers came into their homes offering, at best, help in getting other things women wanted—such as support payments, separation and maintenance agreements, relief—and, at least, moral support to the women and condemnation of the men.[17]

A fourth problem is that simple social control explanations often imply that the clients' problems are only figments of social workers' biases. One culture's neglect may be another culture's norm, and in such cultural clashes, one group usually has more power than the other. In many immigrant families, for example, five-year-olds were expected to care for babies and toddlers; to middle-class reformers, five-year-olds left alone were neglected, and their infant charges deserted. Social control critiques are right to call attention to the power of experts not only to "treat" social deviance but also to define problems in the first place. But the power of labeling, the representation of poor people's behavior by experts whose status is defined through their critique of the problematic behavior of others, coexists with real family oppressions. In one case an immigrant father, who sexually molested his thirteen-year-old daughter, told a social worker that that was the way it was done in the old country. He was not only lying but also trying to manipulate a social worker, perhaps one he had recognized as guilt-ridden over her privileged role, using his own fictitious cultural relativism. His daughter's victimization by incest was not the result of oppression by professionals.

Feminism and Liberalism

The overall problem with virtually all existing critiques of social control is that they remain liberal and have in particular neglected what feminists have shown to be the limits of liberalism. Liberalism is commonly conceived as a political and economic theory without social content. In fact, liberal political and economic theory rests on assumptions about the sexual division of labor and on notions of citizens as heads of families.[18] The currently dominant left-wing tradition of anti-social-control critique, that of the Frankfurt school, merely restates these assumptions, identifying the sphere of the "private" as somehow natural, productive of strong egos and inner direction, in contrast to the sphere of the public as invasive, productive of conformity and passivity. If we reject the social premises of liberalism (and of Marx), that gender and the sexual division of labor are natural, then we can hardly maintain the premise that familial forms of social control are inherently benign and public forms are malignant.

Certainly class relations and domination are involved in social control. Child protection work developed and still functions in class society, and the critique of bureaucracies and professionalism has shown the inevitable deformation of attempts to "help" in a society of inequality, where only a few have the power to define what social order should be. But this critique of certain kinds of domination often serves to mask other kinds, particularly those between women and men and between adults and children. And it has predominantly been a critique that emphasizes domination as opposed to conflict.

Social work and, more generally, aspects of the welfare state have a unique bearing on gender conflicts. Women's subordination in the family, and their struggle against it, not only affected the construction of the welfare state but also the operations of social control bureaucracies. In fact, social control agencies such as the MSPCC, and more often, individual social workers, did sometimes help poor and working-class people. They aided the weaker against the stronger and not merely by rendering clients passive. Social work interventions rarely changed assailants' behavior, but they had a greater impact on victims. Ironically, the MSPCC thereby contributed more to help battered women, defined as outside its jurisdiction, than it did abused children. Industrial capitalist society gave women some opportunity to leave abusive men because they could earn their own livings. In these circumstances, even a tiny bit of material help, a mere hint as to how to "work" the relief agencies, could turn these women's aspirations for autonomy into reality. Women could sometimes get this help despite class and ethnic prejudices against them. Italian-American women might reap this benefit even from social workers who held derogatory views of Italians; single mothers might be able to get help in establishing independent households despite charity workers' suspicions of the immorality of their intentions. Just as in diplomacy the enemy of one's enemy may be *ipso facto* a friend, in these domestic dramas the enemy of one's oppressor could be an ally.

These immigrant clients—victims of racism, sexism, and poverty, perhaps occasional beneficiaries of child welfare work—were also part of the creation of modern child welfare standards and institutions. The welfare state was not a bargain in which the poor got material help by giving up control. The control itself was invented and structured out of these interactions. Because many of the MSPCC's early "interventions" were in fact invitations by family members, the latter were in some ways teaching the agents what were appropriate and enforceable standards of childcare. A more institutional example is the mothers' pension legislation developed in most of the United States between 1910 and 1920. As I have argued elsewhere, the feminist reformers who campaigned for that reform were influenced by the unending demands of single mothers, abounding in the records of child neglect, for support in raising their children without the benefit of men's wages.[19]

The entire Progressive era's child welfare reform package, the social program of the women's rights movement, and the reforms that accumulated to form the "welfare state" need to be reconceived as not only a campaign spearheaded by elites. They resulted also from a powerful if unsteady pressure for economic and domestic power from poor and working-class women. For them, social work agencies were a resource in their struggle to change the terms of their continuing, traditional, social control, which included but was not limited to the familial. The issues involved in an anti-family-violence campaign were fundamental to poor women: the right to immunity from physical attack at home, the power to protect their children from abuse, the right to keep their children—not merely the legal right to custody but the actual power to support their children—and the power to provide a standard of care for those children that met their own standards and aspirations. That family violence became a social problem at all, that charities and professional agencies were drawn into attempts to control it, were as much a product of the demands of those at the bottom as of those at the top.

Still, if these family and child welfare agencies contributed to women's options, they had a constricting impact too. I do not wish to discard the cumulative insights offered by many critiques of social control. The discrimination and victim blaming women encountered from professionals was considerable, the more so because they were proffered by those defined as "helping." Loss of control was an experience articulated in many different ways by its victims, including those in these same case records. Often the main beneficiaries of professionals' intervention hated them most, because in wrestling with them one rarely gets what one really wants but rather another interpretation of one's needs. An accurate view of the meanings of this "outside" intervention into the family must maintain in its analysis, as the women clients did in their strategic decisions, awareness of a tension between various forms of social control and the variety of factors that might contribute to improvements in personal life. This is a contradiction that women particularly face, and there is no easy resolution of it. There is no returning to an old or newly romanticized "community control" when the remnants of community rest on a patriarchal power structure hostile to women's aspirations. A feminist critique of social control must contain and wrestle with, not seek to eradicate, this tension.

NOTES

1. E. A. Ross, *Social Control* (New York, 1901).

2. A few examples follow: Anthony M. Platt, *The Child Savers: The Invention of Delinquency* (Chicago: University of Chicago Press, 1969); Barbara Ehrenreich and Deirdre English, *For Her Own Good: One Hundred and Fifty Years of the Experts' Advice to Women* (Garden City, N.Y.: Anchor/Doubleday, 1978); Christopher Lasch, *Haven in a Heartless World: The Family Besieged* (New York: Basic Books, 1977); and his *The Culture of Narcissism: American Life in an Age of Diminishing Expectations* (New York: Norton, 1979); Jacques Donzelot, *The Policing of Families*, trans. Hurley (New York: Pantheon, 1979); Barbara M. Brenzel, *Daughters of the State: A Social Portrait of the First Reform School for Girls in North America, 1856–1905* (Cambridge: MIT Press, 1983); Stuart Ewen, *Captains of Consciousness: Advertising and the Social Roots of the Consumer Culture* (New York: McGraw-Hill, 1976); Daniel T. Rodgers, *The Work Ethic in Industrial America, 1850–1920* (Chicago: University of Chicago Press, 1974); and Nigel Parton, *The Politics of Child Abuse* (New York: St. Martin's Press, 1985).

3. Eileen Boris and Peter Bardaglio, "The Transformation of Patriarchy: The Historic Role of the State," in *Families, Politics, and Public Policy: A Feminist Dialogue on Women and the State,*

ed. Irene Diamond (New York: Longman, 1983), 70–93; Judith Areen, "Intervention between Parent and Child: A Reappraisal of the State's Role in Child Neglect and Abuse Cases," *Georgetown Law Journal* 63 (March 1975): 899–902; Mason P. Thomas, Jr., "Child Abuse and Neglect," pt. 1: "Historical Overview, Legal Matrix, and Social Perspectives," *North Carolina Law Review* 50 (February 1972): 299–303.

4. John H. Ehrenreich, *The Altruistic Imagination: A History of Social Work and Social Policy in the United States* (Ithaca: Cornell University Press, 1985).

5. Alice Kessler-Harris, *Out to Work: A History of Wage-Earning Women in the United States* (New York: Oxford University Press, 1982), esp. chap. 7; Gwendolyn Wright, *Moralism and the Modern Home: Domestic Architecture and Cultural Conflict in Chicago, 1873–1913* (Chicago: University of Chicago Press, 1980); Kathryn Sklar, "Hull House as a Community of Women in the 1890s," *Signs* 10 (Summer 1985); Susan Ware, *Beyond Suffrage: Women in the New Deal* (Cambridge: Harvard University Press, 1981).

6. Exceptions include Michael C. Grossberg, "Law and the Family in Nineteenth-Century America" (Ph.D. diss., Brandeis University, 1979); Boris and Bardaglio.

7. The agencies were the Boston Children's Service Association, the Massachusetts Society for the Prevention of Cruelty to Children, and the Judge Baker Guidance Center. A random sample of cases from every tenth year was coded and analyzed. A summary of the methodology and a sampling of findings can be found in my "Single Mothers and Child Neglect, 1880–1920," *American Quarterly* 37 (Summer 1985): 173–92.

8. Case code no. 2044.

9. In Boston the MSPCC was called into being largely by Kate Gannett Wells, a moral reformer, along with other members of the New England Women's Club and the Moral Education Association. These women were united as much by class as by gender unity. Wells, for example, was an antisuffragist, yet in her club work she cooperated with suffrage militants such as Lucy Stone and Harriet Robinson, for they considered themselves all members of a larger, loosely defined but nonetheless coherent community of prosperous, respectable women reformers. This unity of class and gender purpose was organized feminism at this time. See New England Women's Club Papers, Schlesinger Library; MSPCC Correspondence Files, University of Massachusetts/Boston Archives, folder 1; Arthur Mann, *Yankee Reformers in the Urban Age* (Cambridge: Harvard University Press, 1954), 208.

10. Ann Douglas, *The Feminization of American Culture* (New York: Knopf, 1977).

11. For examples of the growing anti-corporal-punishment campaign, see Lyman Cobb, *The Evil Tendencies of Corporal Punishment as a Means of Moral Discipline in Families and School* (New York, 1847); Mrs. C. A. Hopkinson, *Hints for the Nursery* (Boston, 1863); Mary Blake, *Twenty-Six Hours a Day* (Boston: D. Lothrop, 1883); Bolton Hall, "Education by Assault and Battery," *Arena* 39 (June 1908): 466–67. For historical commentary, see N. Ray Hiner, "Children's Rights, Corporal Punishment, and Child Abuse: Changing American Attitudes, 1870–1920," *Bulletin of the Menninger Clinic* 43, no. 3 (1979): 233–48; Carl F. Kaestle, "Social Change, Discipline, and the Common School in Early Nineteenth-Century America," *Journal of Interdisciplinary History* 9 (Summer 1978): 1–17; Myra C. Glenn, "The Naval Reform Campaign against Flogging: A Case Study in Changing Attitudes toward Corporal Punishment, 1830–1850," *American Quarterly* 35 (Fall 1983): 408–25; Robert Elno McGlone, "Suffer the Children: The Emergence of Modern Middle-Class Family Life in America, 1820–1870" (Ph.D. diss., University of California at Los Angeles, 1971).

12. Nancy Chodorow and Susan Contratto, "The Fantasy of the Perfect Mother," in *Rethinking the Family: Some Feminist Questions,* ed. Barrie Thorne and Marilyn Yalom (New York: Longman, 1982); Joseph Goldstein, Anna Freud, and Albert J. Solnit, *Beyond the Best Interests of*

the Child (New York: Free Press, 1973); and *Before the Best Interests of the Child* (New York: Free Press, 1979).

13. Case code no. 2042.

14. To this argument it could be responded that it is difficult to define what would be a parent's "own" standards of childraising. In heterogeneous urban situations, childraising patterns change rather quickly, and new patterns become normative. Certainly the child welfare agencies were part of a "modernization" (in the United States called Americanization) effort, attempting to present new family norms as objectively right. However, in the poor neighborhoods, poverty, crowding, and the structure of housing allowed very little privacy, and the largely immigrant clients resisted these attempts and retained autonomous family patterns, often for several generations. Moreover, my own clinical and research experience suggests that even "anomic" parents, or mothers, to be precise, tend to have extremely firm convictions about right and wrong childraising methods.

15. Nancy Cott, for example, has identified some of the processes of community involvement in family life in eighteenth-century Massachusetts, in her "Eighteenth-Century Family and Social Life Revealed in Massachusetts Divorce Records," *Journal of Social History* 10 (Fall 1976): 20–43; Ann Whitehead has described the informal regulation of marital relations that occurred in pub conversations in her "Sexual Antagonism in Herefordshire," in Diana Leonard Barker and Sheila Allen, *Dependence and Exploitation in Work and Marriage* (London: Longman, 1976), 169–203.

16. For example, see William Jordan, *The Social Worker in Family Situations* (London: Routledge and Kegan Paul, 1972); James W. Green, *Cultural Awareness in the Human Services* (Englewood Cliffs, N.J.: Prentice-Hall, 1982); Alfred Kadushin, *Child Welfare Services* (New York: Macmillan, 1980), chap. 13.

17. Indeed, so widespread were these attempts to enmesh social workers in intrafamily feuds that they were responsible for a high proportion of the many unfounded complaints the MSPCC always met. Rejected men, then as now, often fought for the custody of children they did not really want as a means of hurting their wives. One way of doing this was to bring complaints against their wives of cruel treatment of children, or the men charged wives with child neglect when their main desire was to force the women to live with them again. Embittered, deserted wives might arrange to have their husbands caught with other women.

18. Zillah Eisenstein, *The Radical Future of Liberal Feminism* (New York: Longman, 1981); Joan B. Landes, "Hegel's Conception of the Family," 125–44; and Mary Lyndon Shanley, "Marriage Contract and Social Contract in Seventeenth-Century English Political Thought," 80–95, both in Jean Bethke Elshtain, ed., *The Family in Political Thought* (Amherst: University of Massachusetts Press, 1982).

19. See my "Single Mothers and Child Neglect," *American Quarterly* 37 (Summer 1985): 173–92.

Chapter Twenty

Locating a Secret Problem
Sexual Violence in Elementary and Secondary Schools

Nan D. Stein

I. Introduction

This is a story of a hunch and a hunt that began after many decades of studying peer-to-peer sexual harassment in schools (Stein, 1981, 1992, 1995, 1999, 2005a, 2005b). Garden-variety sexual harassment seemed to have become more aggressive and violent, transforming itself into illegal sexual assault—by peers, during the school day, on school grounds, and occurring at younger and younger ages, no longer restricted to high school students. My hunch began when more lawyers than usual in a short period of time during the spring and summer of 2002 asked me to serve as an expert witness in Title IX lawsuits against school districts where sexual assaults by peers against their clients (usually girls but, in a few cases, some very young boys) had occurred on school grounds, during the school day.

To see if there was any foundation to my hunch, I turned to three sources of information: (1) a LexisNexis search of the fifty-three largest newspapers in the United States to locate news reports of sexual assault by peers in schools; (2) a search for lawsuits or administrative complaints to state or federal agencies initiated by students against the school district in state or federal civil courts; and (3) a review of federally sponsored surveys of (a) school administrators about crime at their school or (b) students inquiring about their victimization (Stein, 2005b).

This chapter posits that over the course of the past few decades, incidents of sexual harassment in K–12 schools have been occurring at younger and younger ages and have become noticeably more sexually violent. This chapter documents the paucity of survey data from elementary and middle-school students and the general difficulty of acquiring data on sexual violence in schools using ethnographic data, narratives acquired from lawsuits and complaints, media reports, and federal survey data.

Sexual violence in schools, which often gets named as something else in an effort to cast it as benign (e.g., the use of the term "bullying"), frequently is not reported to law-enforcement or school officials; when it is surveyed, it is not disaggregated from incidents of physical violence, so these incidents of sexual violence are often classified as "physical violence." Moreover, the well-documented rise of teen dating violence (sometimes called "intimate partner violence"), as revealed though the Youth Risk Behavior

Survey, may also lend evidence to an overall increase in teen violence, whether it is restricted to dating partners or not (Brown, Chesney-Lind, and Stein, 2004; Stein, 2005b).

In the midst of my quest, the survey questions for school administrators that the federal government had asked from 1998 to 2002 to determine sexual violence in schools changed in a way that rendered the problem of sexual violence invisible. All the questions related to gender/sexual violence in schools had been removed and merged with questions that asked about generic physical violence (see the postscript at the end of this chapter). Thus, the secret problem of sexual violence in schools had become even harder to locate than when I first initiated the review.

Despite the documented rise of sexual harassment and sexual violence in schools, the popular and more palatable term "bullying" is often used instead to describe these sexually violent incidents. Whether used innocently or as shorthand, when school officials call these sexual violent events "bullying," the violent and illegal (either under civil or criminal law) nature of these incidents is obscured and the school's responsibility and potential liability is deflected (Stein, 2003; Brown, Chesney-Lind, and Stein, 2004).

The final sections of this chapter cover possible reasons for the increase of sexual harassment and sexual violence in schools. My hypothesis is that the convergence of several developments has led to the erosion of attention to sexual harassment in schools. Finally, I conclude with a series of suggested measures to reduce sexual violence among youth in schools.

II. National Newspaper Reports of Sexual Assaults in Schools

Daily newspapers often include articles about incidents of sexual assaults that occur at schools during the course of the school day. My LexisNexis search for the years 2000–2004 produced eighty-four articles about incidents of sexual violence in middle schools and twenty-seven articles about incidents in elementary schools. The search was restricted to incidents that had happened during the school day, on the school grounds, and among children who were classmates. Two additional articles reported on three incidents among middle-school students that occurred on a school bus (Frazier, 2001, 2003). In the vast majority of cases, the victims of these attacks were girls and the assailants were their male classmates. There were only a few instances where boys were the targets, and in those cases, other boys were their attackers and the sexual attacks often took place in the bathroom (*Katz v. St. John the Baptist Parish School*; Chanen and Padilla, 2001; Pesznecker, 2005). As we will see when we review the results from juvenile crime surveys, the picture that emerges from the incidents covered in newspapers (a nonscientific sample) comport with crime surveys—girls are much more likely than boys to be the victims of sexual assaults. Of all juvenile sex offenses, girls are victims in 82 percent of the cases, whereas boys are victims in 18 percent of the cases (Finkelhor and Ormrod, 2000, pp. 2, 3).

Some national newspapers have conducted in-depth reporting on sexual assaults in their area schools. For example, over a two-year period in 2002–2004, eleven sexual batteries, 113 sexual offenses, and sixty-seven cases of sexual harassment were reported in Broward County public elementary schools. Many more incidents occurred at higher grade levels, for a total of forty sexual batteries (Malernee, 2004). On the other side of the country in the San Francisco School District, twenty-five sexual-assault incidents occurred in the first five months of the 2003—2004 school year. Two took place at elementary schools, seventeen at middle schools, and six at high schools (Knight, 2004). During the comparative period in the 2002—2003 school year, six incidents occurred across the district (Knight, 2004).

Although the preponderance of victims in sexual assaults are girls (in fact, three-fourths of victims of juvenile sexual assault are female), young boys are also targeted (McCurley and Snyder, 2004). In Louisiana, a lawsuit resulted from an attack on a five-year-old boy who went to the bathroom in the company of three other male kindergarten students (*Katz v. St. John the Baptist Parish School Board*). While in the restroom, the three boys sexually assaulted the one child by pulling down his pants, attempting anal intercourse with him, and forcing him to perform sexually explicit oral behavior with them. In another bathroom episode that occurred in the Minneapolis, Minnesota, public schools, a six-year-old boy was allegedly sexually assaulted by three boys between the ages of ten and twelve years old (Chanen and Padilla, 2001). In November 2004, in Anchorage, Alaska, a six-year-old boy was sexually assaulted by another six-year-old classmate while the two boys were left unattended in a school bathroom (Pesznecker, 2005). Clearly, bathrooms have emerged as dangerous places, even at age six (Brown, Chesney-Lind, and Stein, 2004, p. 14).

III. Limited Survey Information about Sexual Violence in Schools

Survey data on the prevalence of sexual violence in elementary and middle schools (children younger than twelve years old) is difficult to obtain and has not been consistently collected, disaggregated, or reported. Researchers lack a complete picture of the violence that children experience, including whether that violence is experienced at home, in the streets, in public spaces, or at school. The paucity and the inconsistency of the information collected on students in this age group is largely due to resistance from parents who forbid researchers from gathering data from children about childhood (sexual) victimization (Brown, Chesney-Lind, and Stein, 2004; Stein, 2005b).

Only recently has self-reported data from children younger than twelve years old been collected. Since its origin in 1929, neither the FBI's Uniform Crime Reporting (UCR) system nor the Bureau of Justice Statistics' National Crime Victimization Survey (NCVS) collected information about crimes committed against persons younger than twelve years old and, therefore, could not provide a comprehensive picture of juvenile crime victimization (Finkelhor and Ormrod, 2000). The new National Incident-Based Reporting System (NIBRS), which was designed to replace the UCR as the national database for crimes reported to law enforcement, now includes data about juvenile victims. However, participation by states and local jurisdictions is incremental and voluntary; at the current time, criminal incidents in large urban areas are particularly underrepresented (Finkelhor and Ormrod, 2000).

In the 2004 analysis containing data from seventeen states, family members constitute 27 percent, acquaintances constitute 66 percent, and strangers constitute 3 percent of the offenders (McCurley and Snyder, 2004). That such a large percentage of crimes are committed by acquaintances may indicate that some, or even a majority, of these incidents may be occurring at school. Unfortunately, information about the location of the crimes is not available from this report. Once again, yet another survey provides only partial, albeit new, information, in the quest to know the prevalence of sexual assaults that occur at school, during the school day, by students. The frustrating search to compose a full and accurate picture continues (Brown, Chesney-Lind, and Stein, 2004, p. 13).

Additional information on sexual violence can be found in a report of school crime and safety based on 2000 data (Miller and Chandler, 2003). These data were derived from a nationally representative sample of 2,270 public school principals who reported information about violent deaths, crime and violence frequency, school policies, disciplinary problems, and other information related to school crime. In a category titled "serious violent incidents," which includes rape, sexual battery, physical attack or fight with a weapon, threat of physical attack with a weapon, and robbery with or without a weapon, the authors reported that 20 percent of all schools experienced one or more serious violent incidents, with 14 percent of elementary schools, 29 percent of middle schools, and 29 percent of high schools reporting "serious violent incidents." The results for the category of "rape or attempted rape" revealed a total of 143 incidents in 126 middle schools, representing 1 percent of all schools. There were no reported rapes or attempted rapes in elementary schools. A total of 650 incidents of "sexual battery other than rape" occurred in 520 elementary schools, representing 1 percent of all schools. A total of 582 middle schools reported 1,141 incidents of "sexual battery other than rape," representing 4 percent of all schools (Miller and Chandler, 2003).

Clearly, a self-reporting mechanism by school principals has limitations. Principals can only provide information that has come to their attention; therefore, undercounting is an inevitable problem. In addition, the survey may ask for information that principals did not retain (Miller and Chandler, 2003). Moreover, some principals may withhold information from law enforcement for a variety of reasons, including preserving their school's reputation (Brown, Chesney-Lind, and Stein, 2004; Stein, 2005b).

IV. Naming the Real Problem as Gendered or Sexual Violence

Interpersonal violence seems to be a normative feature in the lives of many youth. The existence of peer-to-peer sexual harassment in K–12 schools has been well documented for decades (AAUW, 1993, 2001; Stein, 1981, 1995, 1999; Stein, Marshall, and Tropp, 1993; Strauss, 1988). Sexual harassment is now accepted as an unfortunate fact of life. Nearly thirty years after the passage of Title IX, a 2000–2001 survey found rampant evidence of sexual harassment in schools (AAUW, 1993, 2001). Students continue to report that school personnel behave in sexually harassing ways and/or that they do not intervene when sexual harassment occurs (Stein, 1995, 1999).

In the most recent scientific survey about sexual harassment in schools, the American Association of University Women (AAUW), along with the Harris polling firm (2001), found that among 2,064 students in grades eight to eleven, sexual harassment was widespread in schools, with 83 percent of girls and 79 percent of boys indicating that they had been sexually harassed, and 30 percent of the girls and 24 percent of the boys reporting that they were sexually harassed "often." Nearly half of all students who experienced sexual harassment felt "very" or "somewhat upset" afterward, pointing to the negative impact that sexual harassment has on the emotional and educational lives of students (AAUW, 2001). When compared to the 1993 AAUW survey on sexual harassment among eighth- to eleventh-graders, the results from 2001 show an increase in both awareness about, and incidents of, sexual harassment, yet students in 2001 had come to accept sexual harassment as a fact of life in schools (AAUW, 2001). The greatest change in the eight-year period was in students' awareness of their schools' policies and materials to address sexual harassment (AAUW, 2001).

Gay, lesbian, bisexual, and transgendered (GLBT) students report daily harassment, sometimes rising to the magnitude of criminal assault and/or grounds for federal civil rights lawsuits (Pogash, 2004; Quinn, 2002; Walsh, 2003). In a variety of surveys, including a 2005 online survey of 3,450 students ages thirteen to eighteen and 1,011 secondary-school teachers (Harris Interactive and GLSEN, 2005), as well as interviews of school staff and students and calls into hotlines (Human Rights Watch, 2001), the overwhelming portrait is of a school climate that includes verbal and physical harassment because of perceived or actual appearance, gender, sexual orientation, gender expressions, race/ethnicity, disability, or religion (Harris Interactive and GLSEN, 2005). One-third of teens report that students are harassed due to perceived or actual sexual orientation. Because of their sexual orientation, two-thirds of GLBT students have been verbally harassed, 16 percent have been physically harassed, and 8 percent have been physically assaulted (Harris Interactive and GLSEN, 2005, p. 4). Results from educators show that 73 percent of them felt they had an obligation to create a safe, supportive learning environment for GLBT students, and 53 percent of them acknowledged that bullying and harassment of students was a serious problem at their schools (Harris Interactive and GLSEN, 2005).

Educational personnel are also responsible for some of the sexual harassment, sometimes as perpetrators and other times as spectators. According to the 2001 AAUW survey, 38 percent of students report being sexually harassed by teachers and other school employees (AAUW, 2001). Moreover, school personnel can turn away or ignore incidents of sexual harassment when they happen in front of them or when reports are brought to their attention (Stein, 1995, 1999; Stein, Marshall, and Tropp, 1993).

The federal courts, including the Supreme Court (*Davis v. Monroe County Board of Education*), have ruled that school districts have liability if they knew about peer-to-peer sexual harassment and did nothing to prevent it. After decades of battling for recognition of the problem, the Supreme Court's decision in the *Davis* case clarified the requirements and standards under Title IX and established that peer-to-peer sexual harassment exists among our youth and that adults are liable for damages.

The omission or denial of gender from the dominant construction of school safety and violence contributes to the disproportionate focus on the most extreme, rare forms of violence while the more insidious threats to safety are largely ignored (Lesko, 2000;

Stein, 1995; 1999; Stein, Tolman, Porche, and Spencer, 2002). An example of this failure to factor in the saliency of gender in school violence is reflected in the many reports and analyses of the spate of school shootings—the form of school violence that has attracted the most national attention and incited the most panic (Kimmel, 2001). In general, the school shootings were widely reported in a gender-neutral way, when in fact, the majority of these tragedies were perpetrated by White middle-class boys who were upset about either a break-up or being rejected by a girl (e.g., Jonesboro, Arkansas; Pearl, Mississippi), or who did not meet traditional expectations and norms of masculinity (e.g., Columbine, Colorado), and were thus persecuted by their peers (Kimmel, 2001; National Research Council and Institute of Medicine, 2003; Perlstein, 1998; Vossekuil et al., 2002).

This failure to consider the role of gender is also endemic to much of the bullying research. Researchers of bullying, for the most part, have unfortunately failed to consider the ways in which adolescent boys (and adult men) unmercifully police one another with rigid and conventional notions of masculinity and the imposition of compulsive heterosexuality. Not to factor in, or even recognize, these potent elements is to deny a central operating feature in boy culture, namely, the maniacally driven, tireless efforts to define oneself as "not gay." Although researchers such as J. Pleck (1981), Connell (1987, 1995a), Kimmel (1987, 1996, 2000, 2001), and Messner (1990) have written about this phenomenon and its consequences for several decades, most bullying researchers have failed to draw on their findings (Brown, Chesney-Lind, and Stein, 2004; Stein, 2005a).

Interestingly, the effectiveness of bullying training has been challenged by results from a study on sexual coercion in Australia, which is part of a six-country study, which found that antibullying policies are not effective in reducing or eliminating sexual harassment (Ken Rigby, personal correspondence, September 4, 2004; Australian Broadcasting Online, 2004). In a study of approximately two hundred fourteen-year-old students who attended four schools in Adelaide, South Australia, all of which had antibullying policies, a substantial minority said they would ignore sexual harassment if they saw it happening, and a smaller minority (boys) thought they would support the boy aggressor (Rigby and Johnson, 2004). About 37 percent estimated that sexual harassment happened on a weekly basis at school with bystanders present, and somewhat higher estimates were obtained for some other countries that participated in the study (Rigby and Johnson, 2004; Rigby, personal correspondence). Among the Australian students, 14 percent indicated that they would report the harassment to a teacher (Rigby and Johnson, 2004). In the absence of similar studies in the United States, this sobering data from Australia points to the ineffectiveness of antibullying policies in changing or challenging the culture of sexual harassment in schools.

A. Mean Girls or Sexually Violent Hazing among Youth?

In the late spring through the early fall of 2003, a series of hazing episodes occurred among high school students. In Glenbrook, Illinois, the incident involved girl-on-girl violence as an initiation rite by the senior girls to younger girls; in both Mepham and Friendship, New York, boy-on-boy violence occurred within sports teams. These events offer some insight into the ways in which the problems are framed (and obscured) and point the way toward the need to understand these events as gendered and as violence (Stein, 2005b). Interestingly, at the time these hazing episodes were being reported in the national media, girls as a whole were categorically being demonized as "mean," and this meanness was made equivalent to the perpetration of sexual violence (Brown, Chesney-Lind, and Stein, 2004; Stein, 2005b).

The hazing instances that involved boys on the football team at Mepham High School on Long Island, New York, and on the soccer team in Friendship, New York, resulted in criminal charges of sexual assault, sexual abuse, or sodomy—not merely criminal hazing or the overused term "bullying" (Healy, 2003b, 2003c; Healy and Aktar, 2003; Kessler, 2003; Schuster, Molinet, and Morris, 2003; Staba, 2003). The accusations against the older girls who hazed the younger girls in the Glenbrook, Illinois, incident did not include some of the horrific charges that appeared in the incidents at Mepham High School, where the younger boys were bound with duct tape, stripped naked against their will, and sexually assaulted and sodomized by the older boys on the football team. Indeed, the girls from Glenbrook were charged with assault as they mimicked violent masculinity in front of the boys who were videotaping their abuse of the young girls, showing the boys that they could both outgross and outperform them (Fuller, 2003; Napolitano, 2003; Stein, 2005a).

Interestingly, the Mepham and Friendship cases did not produce a national outrage as did the incident with the girls from Glenbrook, Illinois (Paulson, 2003; S. Roberts, 2003). The Glenbrook incident generated a manufactured panic about the state of meanness among girls and the supposed rise in their violent conduct, yet there was never any mention of the increasing rates of rape and sexual assault of girls, particularly at the hands of boys and men they know (Stein, 2005a, 2005b). However, the hazing behaviors of the boys from Mepham and Friendship did not generate discussions about the type of normative masculinity that includes perpetrating sexual violence coupled with colluding silence and lack of intervention from the other observing teammates (Brown, Chesney-Lind, and Stein 2004).

B. Some Hypotheses about the Increase in Sexual Violence in Schools

I propose that the convergence of several developments has led to the rise in sexual violence in schools and the erosion of attention to sexual harassment. Briefly, my hypotheses are the following: (1) new legal mandates that are largely symbolic attempt to elevate the "bullying" prevention framework over the civil rights framework of sexual harassment as discrimination and therefore create a distraction from the more pressing problems of sexual harassment and sexual violence; (2) zero tolerance, which is the hegemonic and conventional mantra of school and government officials, emphasizes suspensions and expulsions of alleged perpetrators instead of education, counseling, and reform; and (3) high-stakes standardized tests that all students must pass to be promoted take teachers' time and attention away from attending to the safety of their students. In total, the confluence of these three factors has produced schools that are leaner, meaner, and may have helped to create an atmosphere that has allowed sexual harassment and sexual violence to flourish (Stein, 2005a, 2005b).

V. Action Steps

We need to acknowledge and confront the sexual violence problem in our country, whether it is enacted as sexual harassment, sexual assault, or sexually violent hazing. In addition, we need to implement immediate and vast corrective actions in order to curb and eliminate these injustices.

First, we must reconfigure the school violence prevention movement and discourse to acknowledge the presence of gendered violence in our schools among our youth. By using the momentum from the child-abuse scandal perpetrated by Catholic priests and hidden by the Church hierarchy, as well as sexual-assault scandals in the military and at other academic institutions, we need also to bring attention to the increasing incidence of sexual assault of girls that are occurring even among elementary and middle-school children, by their classmates, during the school day.

In addition, we need to add high-quality, age-appropriate, and successfully evaluated lessons about sexual violence, as it is experienced by both boys and girls, into the school curriculum, over the course of the whole year, throughout all grades. We can no longer rest on the original "stranger-danger" approach, which does not reflect the reality of sexual assault, rape, hazing, or child sexual abuse. Schools must adequately train staff to recognize these injustices and to intervene and teach about these troubling issues in the classroom—not just in the auditorium or the principal's office.

Furthermore, we need to equip witnesses and bystanders with strategies for intervention, ways to get help, and techniques to disrupt the assaults that are taking place in front of their eyes. The deleterious effects of being on the sidelines of these violent episodes or fearing that you might be next should not be minimized, though it cannot be compared to the terror experienced by those who have been sexually assaulted.

Equally important is to add quality mental-health services to our schools, including counseling groups for adolescents who find themselves in abusive relationships, either as abuser or victim. Professionally trained staff from sexual-assault and domestic-violence agencies, as well as a few gender-violence prevention groups composed of both men and women, are available to work in schools and lead counseling groups or classroom discussions in partnership with school staff. Finally, it is not enough to suspend the alleged perpetrators, ban them from graduation exercises or the prom, cancel the football or soccer season, or even to criminally charge the attackers. Rather, we must engage in deep and hard conversations both in school and in the larger community about the meanings of masculinity and the ways in which it is expressed: boys-on-boys, boys-on-girls, and even girls-on-girls, some of whom seem to yearn to be as tough as the guys.

At the national, state, and local levels, as a matter of policy, we must acquire data from elementary- and middle-school-aged children on their experiences, whether as witness/bystander, victim, or perpetrator of sexual harassment and sexual violence in schools. Gathering this data will take cooperation from parents and guardians to give researchers permission to ask questions of their young children about victimization, witnessing, and perpetration.

The problem of sexual violence among peers looms large in elementary and secondary schools. Sexual violence among youngsters is largely hidden—because of the ways the questions are asked and/or analyzed in federal surveys, because of the difficulty that researchers have in gaining access to children younger than twelve years old in order to learn about their experiences of victimization, witnessing, or perpetration, and finally because of the many other priorities (or one might also call them "distractions") that have put sexual violence and sexual harassment out of teachers' and administrators' minds, which are instead filled with national mandates for testing. However, we ignore sexual violence among youngsters at our peril; it will come back to haunt the whole society unless we work to expose it, teach about it, and eradicate it.

Postscript

In late January 2005, as I was reviewing a copy of the most recent school crime report, *Indicators of School Crime and Safety, 2004* (DeVoe, Peter, Kaufman, Miller, et al., 2004), published by the U.S. Departments of Education and Justice (NCES 2005–002/NCJ 205290), I was shocked to find out that it had omitted the information and the charts that disaggregated sexual-assault statistics.

The mapping of sexual violence in schools using information that had been available from 1998 through 2002 had become more difficult because data that had been available in prior reports had been removed. The Indicators of School Crime and Safety reports present a comprehensive measure of crimes occurring at the nation's schools using "indicators" considered significant (e.g., physical fights or threats with a weapon). From 1998 to 2002, one indicator that the report included was specific statistics on sexual battery and rape that happened in school and were reported to the police. But in the 2004 report, precise data on sexual violence had gone missing and was subsumed under broad categories of violence; all the sexual-violence data was aggregated under "serious violent" and "violent" crime. This new way of categorizing the sexual-violence statistics ensured that trends in sexual violence would be impossible to locate —sexual violence in schools had been rendered invisible to the public.

My Wellesley College research assistant, Hao Nguyen, and I began a correspondence in late February 2005 with the authors of the Indicators, a group of researchers employed at the Department of Justice, the Department of Education, and two of their subcontractors, the American Institutes for Research (AIR) and MPR Associates, informing them of our concerns about the difficulty of locating (or absence of) data on sexual violence in schools. Rape and sexual battery are inherently gendered crimes; the vast majority of the victims are females and the assailants are male. The gendered nature of these crimes sets them apart from the other crimes in the categories of "serious violent crime," "violent crime," and "theft." After a month of correspondence, we were delighted to learn that they accepted our arguments and agreed to report total incidence of rape and sexual assault. This significant change in the way data on sexual violence in schools is reported will help researchers and the public understand the context and role of this growing pandemic and will allow us to locate with more clarity this secret problem.

ACKNOWLEDGMENTS

The author thanks friend and Wellesley College colleague Sally Engle Merry for countless conversations, walks, and precision guidance with a title for this chapter. In addition, Wellesley College students Janet Megan Ditzer and Hao M. Nguyen provided valuable research assistance over several years.

Portions of this chapter have appeared in Lyn Mikel Brown, Meda Chesney-Lind, and Nan Stein, "Patriarchy Matters: Toward a Gendered Theory of Teen Violence and Victimization," Wellesley College Center for Research on Women, Working Paper No. 417, 2004; in Nan Stein, "Bullying and Harassment in a Post-Columbine World," in *Child Victimization,* ed. Kathy Kendall-Tackett and Sarah Giacomoni (Kingston, NJ: Civic Research Institute, 2005); and in Nan Stein, "A Rising Pandemic of Sexual Violence in Elementary and Secondary Schools: Locating a Secret Problem," *Duke Journal of Gender Law and Policy* 12 (spring 2005): 33–52.

Chapter Twenty-one

Men, Masculinity, and Child Sexual Abuse
A Sex and Gender Question

Annie Cossins

Introduction

Empirical evidence shows that child sexual abuse is overwhelmingly committed by men and male adolescents, irrespective of the sex of the children who are abused, indicating that, like all other crime categories, sex is the key predictor of involvement in this type of criminal activity (Collier 1998). The central question that has engaged many social scientists in relation to the sexual abuse of children is what motivates men to engage in sexual activities with children rather than with their adult peers. Implicit in this question is the belief that sex with adult peers is the norm, whereas sex with children is a deviation from that norm. Much of the psychological literature on the behavior of child sex offenders contains studies that emphasize the nonsexual motivations behind child sexual abuse, the abnormality of sexual desire for children, and the normality of sex with adult women (Cossins 2000). Because such studies *begin* with the value judgment that sexual behavior with children is abnormal, they have failed to consider its prevalence as a sexual practice, thus failing to distinguish between what is abnormal as opposed to what is socially unacceptable. As Liddle (1993: 105) has recognized, "even a brief perusal of the [psychological] literature suggests that 'masculine sexuality' is not widely regarded as having causal centrality in the genesis of child sexual abuse."

Given the prevalence of child sexual abuse reported in various studies,[1] arguably a distinction needs to be made between what is considered to be socially unacceptable sexual practices and sexual practices that may be relatively common within the general community. In other words, it cannot be assumed that because child sex offending is socially unacceptable behavior, it therefore occurs infrequently or is only committed by "deviant" men. Because of the prevalence and sex specificity of child sexual abuse, this chapter argues it is necessary to examine the role that sexual behavior with children plays in offenders' lives as *men*. In undertaking this task, however, this chapter is not intended to condone or justify child sexual abuse or to imply that child sex offending is something of which any man might be capable.

The approach in this chapter challenges the methodology of the disciplines of psychology and psychiatry, which have tended to reduce a historically widespread and tolerated cultural practice (sex with children) to the individual biological or psychological natures of the offender. A focus on the characteristics or "pathology" of an offender might tell us something about that man's individual "makeup" but nothing about the wider social context of which he is a part or about the fact that the majority of victims are female and the majority of offenders are male. In fact, such an approach obscures the historical background of child sexual abuse (see Cossins 2000), the structures of power in men's lives, the social context of an offender's life, his active engagement with that social context, and how we might understand child sexual abuse as part of that engagement.

The aim, then, is to propose an explanation that addresses the motivations of offenders from an entirely different perspective, one that considers the role that child sex offending plays as a particular gender practice. This will involve analyzing whether there is a link between an offender's sexual behavior with children, his social practices, and the effects of other men's social practices on him. I argue that child sex offending, rather than being a deviant sexual practice, is a practice that is related to normative masculine sexual practices. In doing so, it will be necessary to examine the role that masculine sexual practices play in men's lives, in order to understand how such practices construct relations of power between men. At the same time, I consider the social significance of sex, that is, the specific cultural values associated with the male body and how these values affect individual social and sexual practices; such an approach is not commonly used in attempting to understand the relationship between men and crime.

Sex, Gender, and Child Sexual Abuse

To begin this inquiry it is necessary to recognize that much of the discourse about men and crime in the social sciences has failed to make a conceptual distinction between sex and gender. These terms are often used interchangeably, and yet, in talking about sex, gender, and crime, it is necessary to be clear about the meanings of these terms. A number of feminist theorists have criticized the concept of gender on the grounds that it assumes that the body has no cultural or social significance and is an immutable, biological pre-given upon which gender inscriptions are made (see Collier 1998: 21–22; Davies 1997: 25–46; Gatens 1996: 3–20). In fact, the term *gender* has often been used to refer to sex in the social sciences, so that "the distinction between sex and gender turns out to be no distinction at all" (Butler 1990: 7). Similarly, the concept of gender has been criticized as being "an empty tautology" on the grounds that if everything men do is masculine, then "gender collapses into sex" (Hood-Williams 2001: 45). This means that attempting to understand men's various criminal and sexual practices needs to begin with making a distinction between the concepts of sex and gender and to recognize the meanings that different sexes carry at a cultural level. In particular, what meanings do men attach to their bodies, and how do these meanings influence sexual practices such as rape and child sexual abuse?

In this chapter, *sex* is used to describe the sexual and physical differences between the two categories of human referred to as male and female, whereas the term *sexed* refers to the cultural values associated with particular sexual characteristics. *Gender* describes the cultural differences that arise from performance (Hood-Williams 1996), that is, active social practices or recurring accomplishments to use the terminology of West and Zimmerman (1991), who coined the phrase "doing gender" to describe the active participation of individuals in the construction of social categories.

A number of feminist theorists (Butler 1990, 1993; Gatens 1996; Grosz 1990, 1994; Grosz and Probyn 1995) have analyzed the role of sexual difference in the construction of male and female subjectivities, with the term *sexing* meaning that male and female bodies acquire specific cultural meanings at both an individual and institutional level. The "sexed bodies approach" is concerned with discerning these cultural meanings and the individual experiences that derive from the cultural significance ascribed to sex.

Although gender is created through active social practices, individuals give very specific cultural meanings to their bodies through these practices so that sex and gender are not arbitrarily linked (Gatens 1996). The sexed bodies approach views the body as being "interwoven with and constitutive of systems of meaning, signification and representation" (Grosz 1990: 18), which means there can be no conception of the body that is independent of the cultural values ascribed to different sexual characteristics. Indeed, the many social practices that are described as masculine or feminine constitute shared expectations about male and female biologies (Gatens 1996) in that different cultural meanings are ascribed to different bodies even though they may exhibit the *same* practices, with these meanings being contingent on the *sex* of the body carrying out the practice. This is most clearly seen in relation to the different meanings ascribed to male and female bodies engaging in similar sexual behavior—it is implicit in the term *stud* that the body is sexed male, and it is implicit in the term *slut* that the body is sexed female.

Although it is important to recognize that the relationship between the body and gender is not arbitrary in terms of social/cultural expectations, the body does not *determine* the social—although the body is "inescapable" in the practice and construction of gender, "what is inescapable is not fixed" (Connell 1995a: 56). This is a mistake that sociobiologists frequently make when trying to explain different male and female sexual behaviors, such as rape and child sexual abuse. The view that men are "naturally" promiscuous and women are "naturally" sexually conservative relies on the belief that male and female traits are "hard-wired," unchangeable and unaffected by context.

Although the sexed bodies approach has not generally been used to explain the relationship between the body and crime, the theoretical premise of the approach illustrates that it is necessary to understand the meanings associated with different bodies —male, female, black, white—in order to understand crime as a social practice and the response of legal institutions to crime (Cossins 2003). The body matters, and what the body does matters. In this statement there are encapsulated two concepts: the social meanings that individuals ascribe to their female or male bodies (the sexed body) and the social meanings ascribed to what these specifically sexed bodies do (gender). Individuals and institutions construct "types" of men and "types" of women in social discourse so that bodies matter to those who commit crime (for example, male-on-male violence, men's sexual assault of women), to those who fear crime (the fear of crime is a fear of the sexed male body or a particular "raced" and sexed male body), and to those who seek to impose a rigid law-and-order agenda (for example, overpolicing of the adolescent, black, male body).

When it comes to the construction of male sexualities, the body matters in understanding the cultural differentiation that is made between heterosexual and gay men and the fact that gay bashings are a particular criminal phenomenon. This differentiation must mean that different cultural meanings are ascribed to same-sexed bodies because of the expectations associated with the sexed male body. Similarly, it can be said that the body matters in attempting to understand the meanings attached to the body of the child sex offender, such as "monster," "predator," "pervert," and "deviant," since it is implicit in such descriptions that the body is male. But what is the relationship between how men's bodies are sexed and their engagement in particular sexual practices such as the sexual abuse of children? In particular, how do we *become* sexed and gendered subjects?

In considering these questions, it is obvious that masculine "identities" are not fixed and unchanging, given the different characteristics of the male body from childhood to adolescence to middle age and finally old age and the cultural values associated with differently aged men. This means that individuals and institutions *produce more than one type* of sexed male subject: hooligan, stud, father, worker, sports hero, boss, gayboy are different masculine identities with specific cultural meanings that are as much about the male body as they are about what the sexed male body does. What then is the relationship between sex and gender? If "[m]asculinity and femininity as forms of sex-appropriate behaviors are manifestations of a historically based, culturally shared [f]antasy about male and female biologies, [then] sex and gender are not arbitrarily connected. . . . [Indeed,] masculine and feminine forms of behavior are not arbitrary inscriptions on an indifferent consciousness which is joined to an indifferent body" (Gatens 1996: 13–14).

In other words, whereas the sexed bodies approach recognizes the cultural significance of the way the body is constructed in social discourse and how that construction (sexed male or female) affects the formation of individual consciousness, this individual consciousness informs the active social practices in which *differently* sexed bodies engage. But what informs the different social practices of *same*-sexed bodies, particularly sexual practices?

Masculinities are specific social practices that are within themselves highly variable, although, as I have argued, they are not arbitrarily related to sex. The different cultural meanings that are ascribed to the sexed male body will, therefore, depend on the social practices of the man in question, which are influenced by other factors such as race, class, and ethnicity. This suggests that a conceptual distinction can be made between the cultural significance of sex and the cultural significance of the social practices that sexed bodies engage in. Such a distinction warrants the continued use of the term *gender* as a way of describing the lived experiences of same-sexed bodies in response to a variety of cultural and structural constraints.

The sexed bodies approach reveals that the male body is associated with very particular cultural meanings: strength, reliability, courage, aggression, and toughness, in fact, everything the sexed female body is *not*. However, different categories of men are constructed by reference to the male body's social practices—crying versus stoicism, fighting versus fleeing—creating "real" men and sissies. In fact, ideals of manhood are very much premised on the heterosexual/homophobic divide, with the conditions of potency and prowess being tied to the male body that practices heterosexuality. The concept of gender tells us that the different cultural meanings ascribed to same-sexed bodies are contingent not only on sex but also on the specific sexual and social practices of the sexed male body. *Gender* is a term that describes the relationships of power that exist between men on the basis of these distinctions; for example, although it is implicit in the construction of the "stud" that his body is sexed male, the gendered dimension of the construct is dependent on particular sexual and social practices. Thus, in the construction of male subjectivities, men engage in both sexing and gendering processes to create oppositional relationships between each other and to create relationships of power with their objects of desire. In this way, the concepts of sex and gender are simultaneous processes, leading to different social experiences for different men.

So why is *child* sexual abuse a particular social and sexual practice for some men? Cultural values associated with different sexual practices are central to the social construction of masculinities and relationships of power between men. More particularly, "Although personal conceptions of masculine identity . . . vary according to race, class, age and other social variables . . . , there remains a stable common core . . . called 'heterosexual masculinity' " (Herek 1987: 72). Homophobia is a social practice that creates relationships of power between men—a man becomes a "faggot" or a "poofter" in the eyes of other men by reference not to his sexual characteristics but to his social practices. A man does not actually have to have sex with other men to be the recipient of gay jibes since heterosexual men regularly differentiate between each other based on a range of social practices that the male body does or fails to do. Across cultures, men engage in homophobic practices to differentiate between themselves and construct relations of power, so that homophobia can be a particular social practice for the accrual of power for any man irrespective of his class or racial background: "The taunt *What are you, a fag?*' is used in many ways to encourage certain types of male behavior and to define the limits of 'acceptable' masculinity" (Lehne 1995: 332; emphasis in original).

The body is intrinsic to this differentiation between gay and straight men because of the dominance of the specific cultural values ascribed to the male body. For some men, gay bashings and other types of homophobia reaffirm their allegiance to a particular conception of the male body. Through homophobic practices, a man can prove or exaggerate his masculinity by constructing another man as a legitimate target for reaffirming his heterosexual status. The dominant forms of both homosexual and heterosexual masculinities are heterosexist in the sense that many men seek to define themselves as everything the female body is not. Thus, homophobia is a sexual practice that constructs relations of power between men, but it is always referable to a particular conception of the male body. In the practice of homophobia, the body matters.

This analysis raises the question of whether child sex offending is a particular social/sexual practice that involves the construction of relations of power and allows some men to express a type of sexuality characterized by dominance and control. In Western societies, the construction of masculine sexualities (as opposed to the ability to be sexual) involves the attribution of particular cultural values to the male body:

virile, potent, penetrating, initiating, aggressive, conquering, focused, piercing, incisive, strong, purposeful, erect, unemotional, tough, hard-hitting, as well as impotence, such that the male body is a site for both success and failure. Men's sexual practices involve not only actual sexual acts but also a variety of ways in which this masculine sexual ideal is affirmed or at least the illusion of potency is created. Sexist jokes, sexual innuendo, sexual gestures toward women, sexual put-downs, and masturbatory gestures are examples of sexual practices that may create relations of power between men, as well as between women and men. At the heart of these sexual practices, a particular conception of the sexed male body is paramount since it is from the body that some men clearly believe their power is derived. Adherence to the masculine ideal (the sexed male body) is likely to lead to experiences of social inadequacy since most men will fail to live up to the ideal given its idealised and illusory nature. The masculine sexual ideal, as a cultural construct, is not a biological reality but rather an ideology (see Kaufman, this volume) that is always contested by other men and has to be proved and reaffirmed, thus creating experiences of success and failure, of both power and powerlessness. For those men who compete for status with other men through sexual practices, the stakes are extremely high since they know that sexual performance goes to the core of their self-worth as a man (their "manliness") and influences their social power with other men. This, then, raises the question of whether the same analysis can be made of child sex offending so that for some men, the struggle for experiences of power and the association of the male body with potency and prowess takes place through sexual behavior with children.

The foregoing discussion has shown that sexuality (as opposed to the ability to be sexual) is socially constructed through the attachment of particular cultural values both to the sexed male body and to the way that body behaves. Sexual practices occur in a relational context, and different men will create different masculine sexualities as a function of their dynamic positions within the structural divisions created by class, ethnicity, and race (Connell 1995a). For some men, it can be argued that sexual practices with children allow them to experience power since correspondence with the masculine ideal and experiences of potency are more likely with those who are perceived to have less social power than the individual man in question.

As a sexual practice, child sex offending is similar to those normative sexual practices that conform to the masculine sexual ideal, given the fact that the relationship of adult to child is a relationship of power par excellence, if it is accepted that up until a certain age, children do not have the developmental and cognitive abilities to consent to sexual relations. Indeed, offenders' self-report studies (Cossins 2000) have shown that they typically choose a child who is emotionally vulnerable, suggesting that the choice of a relatively passive, nonthreatening, or vulnerable sexual partner (or image) is remarkably consonant with the masculine sexual ideal. A child has an inferior social status and represents no threat to an offender's sexual performance since a child's lack of adult sexual needs and sexual experience allows an offender to ignore any inadequacies he may have about his sexuality. Child sex offending also takes place in a cultural environment where the bodies of girls (who constitute the majority of victims) are inscribed with cultural meanings of desire in literature, the media, advertisements, film, and pornography. It is, therefore, arguable that child sex offending is consonant with normative masculine sexual practices in a cultural environment in which men's lives are characterized by a combination of experiences of powerlessness and power as a result of their complex relationships with other men.

What is meant by power and powerlessness? The power that men derive through interactions with other men is "inherently unstable" compared to power that men assert over women. Although men derive power from acting in concert together and from existing structures of power (Archer 1994; Connell 1995a), on an individual level, men's interpersonal power can be fragile, dynamic, and changing. Men's power is a competitive enterprise and involves contradictory experiences of power and powerlessness in a context of dynamic and changing gender relations between men, since "[s]ocial structures originate, are reproduced, and change through social practice" (Messerschmidt 1993: 62).

This chapter has shown that heterosexism, that is, the meanings given to the male body, is central to the reproduction of power through sexual practices. One of the ways that men can accrue experiences of power is through particular sexual practices with women, other men, or children. The sexual abuse of children can be seen as both an expression of an offender's public power (in the sense of being able to gain access to a child, gaining the trust of parents, and "grooming" a child) and an expression of his lack of personal power as a result of his relationships with other men. For some men, child sexual abuse may be a key experience through which power is derived, and chronic experiences of powerlessness may explain chronic practices of sex offending against children (Cossins 2000). Arguably, men engage in exploitative sexual practices in circumstances in which their power is in jeopardy and they have limited material and/or social resources for competing for status with other men. The choice of a child may be related to the lack of congruence with, or inability to conform to, some aspects of the masculine sexual ideal, so that engagement in "pedosexuality" may give an offender the illusion of achieving the standard prescribed by that ideal.

This hypothesis can explain the range of different men who engage in sex with children—from those with considerable public power (white, middle class) to those with little public power (black, unemployed)—since the degree of public power a man has does not necessarily equate with his experiences of power at a personal level. This means that some men may experience "powerlessness within power," a concept that recognizes "that men's personal inadequacies and self-brutalization are the flip side to their mastery of the public sphere in capitalist patriarchy" (Liddle 1993: 116). As Kimmel (1994) has recognized, there is not necessarily a symmetry between the *public* power that men as a group may have, particularly white, middle-class men, and the *private* experience of power with partners, male peers, and authority figures.

This analysis does not, however, allow us to predict when a man will engage in child sexual abuse as a way of experiencing power. Even though different social variables, such as race, class, ethnicity, religion, and disability, produce particular structures of power among men and different experiences of power/powerlessness, not all men sexually abuse children. Is child sex offending, therefore, an indication of the *degree* of powerlessness experienced by offenders? Such a proposition would predict that the *least* socially powerful men engage in exploitative sexual practices to experience power (however illusory) and that, in particular, men from lower socioeconomic groups would commit more rape and child sexual abuse than other groups of men. However, victim-report studies show that child sexual abuse does not have socioeconomic, ethnic, or racial boundaries (Cossins 2000), so that it is not confined to the most socially disenfranchised men. It is also too simplistic to argue that child sexual abuse is a "resource for 'doing gender'" and accomplishing masculinity (Messerschmidt 1993: 84), since if everything a man does accomplishes masculinity, then gender collapses into sex and we are faced with deterministic explanations as to why men commit this crime.

As discussed earlier, "there are different forms of structural power and powerlessness among men" (Kaufman 1994: 152), with that power always being relative and contested, even for the most privileged men in a given society. Men "on top" compete with other men on top or those who aspire to be on top; they rarely compete directly with men from lower socioeconomic groups unless they are involved, for example, in violence in a public place. Heterosexist sexual practices are, arguably, practised by those men who adhere or aspire to the masculine sexual ideal, irrespective of their racial, ethnic, or socioeconomic background, and these practices reinforce the fact that the sexed male body is associated with cultural values that are illusory and ultimately impossible to achieve.

It is hypothesised that a man's particular attachment to the masculine sexual ideal and the link he makes between sexual prowess and experiences of power will be a key indicator that determines how he does sex and whom he chooses as a sexual partner. Paradoxically, even though it is considered to be pathological behavior, sex with children affirms all the aspects of the masculine sexual ideal and the cultural values ascribed to the sexed male body. It enables a man to be dominant, predatory, phallocentric, sexually successful, detached, self-focused, in control, and to minimise sexual inadequacy. However, a man may choose adult sexual partners with whom to derive similar sexual experiences, so that factors such as access, opportunity, risk of being caught, or religious beliefs may all contribute to the choice to sexually abuse a child.

The argument that derivation of power through sexual practices is central to understanding child sex offending has specific practical and intellectual consequences. This analysis applies to both homosexual and heterosexual offenders because of the centrality of heterosexism (the masculine sexual ideal), the sexed male body, sexuality, and power to the reproduction of both homosexual and heterosexual masculinities. Children are likely to be "emotionally congruent objects for sexual desire" (Finkelhor 1984: 39) for those men whose lives are characterized by chronic experiences of powerlessness as a result of their relationships with other men and who seek to alleviate that powerlessness through sexual practices, both homosexual and heterosexual. Although such a view challenges the discourse of deviance evident in other disciplines, it is consonant with historical evidence that shows that sexual practices with children were socially and legally tolerated and, even when criminalized, difficult to prosecute (Cossins 2000).

This analysis means that preventive measures need to take account of the cultural environment in which child sex offenders live, work, and socialize. Not only could this knowledge assist in attempting to illuminate an offender's original motivations for targeting children as objects of desire, but it may also be crucial to an offender's choices postconviction. This would mean that preventive programs would need to focus on those aspects of an offender's life that lead to experiences of powerlessness and the sexual behaviours by which the offender seeks to alleviate those experiences.

1. For example, Fleming (1997) studied a random community sample of 710 Australian women and found that 33% had experienced noncontact or contact abuse before the age of sixteen, and 20% had experienced contact before the age of sixteen. In 2000, Dunne et al. (2003) conducted a survey of 1,784 Australian women and men aged eighteen to fifty-nine and found that 33.6% of women and 15.9% of men reported "nonpenetrative" sexual abuse before the age of sixteen, and 12.5% of women and 4% of men had experienced unwanted penetration or attempted penetration before the age of sixteen. Similar prevalence rates had previously been reported by Finkelhor, Hotaling, Lewis, and Smith (1990) and Anderson et al. (1993).

Chapter Twenty-two

Child Sexual Abuse and the Regulation of Women
Variations on a Theme

Carol-Ann Hooper

The current wave of recognition of child sexual abuse is not the first in the history of child-protection work. From the 1870s for roughly sixty years, intermittent anxieties emerged and attempts at legal reform were made, culminating in a specific campaign on sexual offences against children, initiated by feminists in the 1930s. At the end of this period, however, the criminal justice system was still hopelessly ineffective, the campaign fizzled out, and a public silence ensued (broken briefly during the 1950s) until the 1970s, when feminists again brought the issue to public attention. In both the earlier period and the present one, a number of interest groups have promoted and laid claims to the issue, offering competing definitions. Feminist definitions locating the problem in the social construction of masculinity have commonly been marginalised from the policy agenda.

Child sexual abuse is itself a site of informal social control by men over women. As girls who are victimised themselves, as partners of abusive men and as mothers and primary carers of sexually abused children, the sexual abuse of children operates to restrict women's autonomy and control of their own lives. The responses of voluntary and statutory agencies to child sexual abuse have also been centrally concerned with the regulation of women, much more so than with the control of men who abuse. In the earlier period, it was the behaviour of sexually abused girls themselves that was most subject to surveillance, although often in the name of their future as mothers. Today, it is the mothers of sexually abused children whose behaviour is the prime concern of child-protection agencies.

The shift from girls to their mothers is attributable to two main trends. First, increased attention through the present century first to children's physical needs and later to their psychological needs, within an ideological context which defines child welfare as women's private business, has generated redefinitions of motherhood which accord women increased responsibilities. Definitions of fatherhood have been much less implicated (if at all) by attention to child welfare, despite the evidence now available that men far outnumber women as sexual abusers of children and play a more or

From *Regulating Womanhood: Historical Essays on Marriage, Motherhood and Sexuality,* ed. C. Smart, Routledge, 1992, pp. 53–77. Reprinted by permission.

less equal role in physical abuse (Gordon 1988; Stark and Flitcraft 1988). Second, state intervention in the home to protect children has gained greater (although by no means uncontested) acceptability. The voluntary activities of philanthropists and charitable organisations in the late nineteenth century, to which contemporary child-protection work owes its roots (Behlmer 1982; Ferguson 1990), have been replaced by a child-abuse management system which attempts to coordinate the activities of a wide range of professionals and statutory agencies. The combined effect of these trends has been to legitimate greater surveillance of mothers, alongside a still-limited commitment of resources to public services to contribute to the work and costs of childcare.

This chapter considers both periods of anxiety about child sexual abuse to illustrate the variety of ways in which women have been constructed in regulatory discourses. In the first period, I focus on how the construction of the problem changed, influenced by changing social anxieties and the strengths and orientations of social movements. In the later period, I discuss the alternative constructions of motherhood involved in contemporary discourses on child sexual abuse, and their influence on and resistance by mothers and social workers, the prime actors in the protection of children. In this section I draw on my contemporary study of mothers of sexually abused children, which involved interviews with both mothers and social workers (Hooper 1990).

The analysis of both periods is necessarily selective and the focus on girls in the early period and their mothers in the contemporary period to some extent schematic. The greater emphasis on protecting children today is certainly not unproblematic for girls who are sexually abused, and the control of their sexuality is clearly still an issue in medical, child protection, and judicial discourse (see Kitzinger 1988; Mitra 1987). Moreover, from its nineteenth-century beginnings, child-protection work in England has sought where possible to enforce rather than replace parental responsibility for children and in doing so has reflected and perpetuated gendered definitions of proper parenting (Ferguson 1990). In child-protection practice, there has probably therefore been as much continuity as change. However, constructions of women are continually renegotiated in specific contexts, and this chapter seeks to identify some sources of variability.

There has been some speculation recently that the current anxiety about child sexual abuse is not simply a product of changed social anxieties and political movements but is a response to a new and growing problem (see Gledhill et al. 1989; O'Hagan 1989). Before discussing the historical shifts in visibility and definitions, therefore, it is worth reviewing briefly the available evidence on incidence.

On the Incidence of Child Sexual Abuse

It is difficult to unearth the history of a problem kept so invisible. The most reliable sources of evidence on historical trends are contemporary surveys of adults using age-stratified samples. These are limited in scope by the lifespan and age of those interviewed, and by problems of memory, but the evidence of two such surveys, both conducted in the USA, is instructive. Russell (1984) found that incestuous abuse, but not extrafamilial child sexual abuse, had increased over the years 1916 to 1961, although the peak occurred in 1956. It is possible, however, that memories of incestuous abuse were more deeply buried for older women, for whom the subject had been unspeakable for so much of their lives. Finkelhor et al.'s (1990) more recent survey found no consistent upward trend over time. Lower rates of abuse were reported by women aged over sixty, but those born 1955–67 reported no higher level of abuse than their immediate predecessors.

Both studies, however, suggest that the most significant fluctuations have coincided with war. Women born during the Second World War reported the highest levels of abuse in both surveys. Russell's analysis of period rates found that the incidence of incestuous abuse declined during both world wars, and increased immediately after. Extrafamilial child sexual abuse also declined during the Second World War and increased after, although in contrast it increased during the First World War. Although other fluctuations cannot be linked to war, these findings are illustrative of one of the many dilemmas child sexual abuse raises. Children tend to be safest from sexual abuse in the absence of men, but it is in part men's separation from children which makes them a threat when they return.

Since it is some years since any of those interviewed were children, these studies do not answer the question of whether child sexual abuse is currently increasing. It is highly likely, however, that the rapid increase during the 1980s in the number of cases of child sexual abuse on child-protection registers[1] held by local authorities reflects increased reporting by members of the public, increased awareness and detection by professionals, and/or increased use of the child-protection register in the management of cases.

Nor do these studies reach back into the nineteenth century. Gordon's (1988) study of child-protection records in Boston 1880–1960, however, found a consistent level of 10 percent of cases involving incest throughout the period, despite fluctuating levels of public awareness.

It seems safe to assume that whatever its exact incidence child sexual abuse is not a new problem. This should not be surprising, since the social conditions which support it have remained consistent—the construction of masculine sexuality as predatory and not requiring reciprocity, the eroticisation of dominance, and the lack of responsibility men have for childcare.

It is not in fact correct to say that child sexual abuse has been wholly invisible. Rather, it has at certain periods been partially visible, its definition as a problem mediated through other social anxieties about "the family," sexuality, and reproduction. It is often these other concerns—with the "health of the race" in the 1900s or with the "decline of the traditional family" in the 1980s, for example—that have shaped the dominant discourses.

1870s to 1930s: From Victims to Delinquents and Law to Medicine

Public awareness of what we would now call child sexual abuse arose in the 1870s in the context of concern about child prostitution. Shortly after, the National Society for the

Prevention of Cruelty to Children (NSPCC), formed by philanthropic reformers in 1889, drew attention also to sexual abuse in the home. Up until the end of the First World War, it referred regularly (if euphemistically) to these in its annual reports, indicating that they were far more common than would easily be believed.[2] Other nineteenth-century reformers, too, encountered incestuous abuse, most notably during the investigation of housing conditions (Wohl 1978). Campaigns were waged by the social-purity movement (primarily the National Vigilance Association [NVA]), by the NSPCC itself, and by feminist groups, focusing initially on legal reforms to facilitate an effective response from the criminal justice system both to incestuous and extrafamilial abuse.

Some successes were achieved in these campaigns, and two major pieces of legislation concerning sexual assault were passed during this period. Neither was unproblematic. The Criminal Law Amendment Act 1885, which raised the age of consent for sexual intercourse from thirteen to sixteen, was supported by a range of groups brought together in a short-lived coalition. This Act could be and was used to prosecute men, including fathers, for sexual abuse. However, by portraying young prostitutes as sexually innocent, passive victims of individual evil men, the reformers had also paved the way for the increased surveillance of working-class girls and diverted attention from the economic reasons why many engaged in prostitution (Gorham 1978). The potential for "protection" to become control of female sexuality is a recurring theme in responses to child sexual abuse. The Punishment of Incest Act 1908, again supported by a range of groups, made incest a criminal, as opposed to an ecclesiastical, offence for the first time (Bailey and Blackburn 1979). Calls for legislation specific to incest had been made from the 1890s, suggesting the inclusion of assaults by men in positions of authority, including employers, schoolmasters, and guardians under this label (*The Vigilance Record*, December 1895). The Act passed excluded even stepfathers, adopting consanguinity as the defining feature, after debates which were concerned far more with the regulation of sexuality than the protection of children. Further campaigns achieved amendments to the 1885 Act, including the raising of the age of consent for indecent assault from thirteen to sixteen (1922), the partial removal of "the defence of reasonable belief" (that the man had believed a girl was over the age of consent when she was not) (1922), and extending the time limit under which prosecutions could be brought, from three months (1885), to six months (1904), nine months (1922), and finally to twelve months in 1928.

However, when a government review was conducted in 1925, a number of further problems were noted with the law and its administration. The Report of the Departmental Committee on Sexual Offences against Young Persons (1925) noted that many cases were unreported, that many more, once reported, were sifted out before reaching court for lack of proof, and that for those that did reach court, the acquittal rate was unusually high. Its recommendations involved measures to ease the strain of the process on children (including the greater use of women as police, doctors, and magistrates in such cases, and the quicker and less formal conducting of court proceedings) and changes to the rules of evidence (since in effect a higher level of proof was required for sexual offences than in most others, making convictions almost impossible). A recommendation was also made that the age of consent be raised to seventeen, although four members of the Committee dissented, three wanting no change and one wanting it raised to eighteen.

The report did not concern itself only with the criminal law. It made a range of recommendations on prevention, and also on changes to the civil law to facilitate the removal of children from their homes. However, it was the role of the criminal law that was the spark for action, since groups hoping to see these recommendations incorporated in the forthcoming Children's Bill were disappointed when it was published in 1932.[3] Resolutions were passed at various organisations' annual conferences, and the feminist Association of Moral and Social Hygiene, then led by Alison Neilans, a former active suffragist, held a small specific conference in November 1932. From this a Joint Committee on Sexual Offences against Children was established, representing fourteen national organisations (including AMSH itself, the NVA, the National Council of Women, the British Social Hygiene Council, the National Council of Mental Hygiene, and the Howard League for Penal Reform, amongst others). Representatives of these groups met over the next three years, with the aim of agreeing a limited bill with a good chance of success around which to mobilise a campaign. They were not able to do so. They dissolved in 1935 having published a brief report and two leaflets,[4] and little further campaigning occurred on the problem of child sexual abuse.

I am not suggesting that had they achieved further legal reforms, this would have solved the problem of child sexual abuse. The law was and is one of the ways in which patriarchal power is maintained and has rarely provided protection for women or girls from male violence, as feminists have frequently pointed out. Furthermore, many of the recommendations of the 1925 report, on which the campaign focused, did not require legislation. It is probably more important that the degree of disagreement within the campaigns, in which the significance of the criminal law was a key issue, weakened the commitment to any further action. The result, however, was that the major legislation passed in the wake of the government review, the Children and Young Persons Act 1933, focused on the control of juvenile delinquency (defined for girls in relation to their sexuality) and on the removal of children "in moral danger" or "beyond parental control" from their parents (identifying parental, primarily maternal, neglect as the problem). How did this reconstruction of the problem come about? And how, then, did the issue disappear from public attention effectively until the 1970s? Viewing the period of sixty years or so very broadly, two major shifts seem significant. First, social anxieties about the "health of the race" from the turn of the century resulted in an increasing significance attached to motherhood in the latter part of the period. Changing concepts of childhood and adolescence at the same time made the problem of defining abuse, represented by debates on the age of consent, increasingly contentious. Second, popular support for the social-purity movement, whose main focus had been legal reform, had declined, the strength of the medical profession, which offered a new alliance of science and morality in the discourse of social hygiene, had increased, and the declining feminist movement increasingly sided with the latter rather than the former. The disputes that occurred in debates on child sexual abuse during the 1930s reflected these broader changes.

The growing influence of Freudian ideas in the interwar years no doubt also played its part. Freud's volte-face which led him to attribute his women patients' accounts of sexual abuse to incestuous fantasy has been well documented elsewhere (Masson 1985; Rush 1980). But the reluctance to believe children's accounts, which was displayed by some (though not all) members of the Joint Committee, and to name the abuse of paternal power, was neither new, nor is it passed today.

The Health of the Race and the Rise of Maternalism

Around the turn of the century, the health of the population became a major national concern. Anxieties about the falling birth rate, high infant mortality, the poverty uncovered by Booth and Rowntree, and the poor physical conditions of recruits to the Boer War combined in a rising fear that the nation's health was degenerating. This fear continued and increased during the war as deaths at the front increased, and the birth rate continued to fall. In response, childhood, motherhood, and sex were all accorded new meanings. Child-protection and child-welfare reforms were facilitated by these concerns, since children were the raw material to be safeguarded in the name of national efficiency. Motherhood became defined as crucial to child health. High infant mortality and physical deterioration were attributed not to poverty but to ignorant motherhood, the solution seen as the education of working-class mothers better to fulfil their national duty as "guardians of the race" (Bland 1982; Davin 1978). Sex became the key to the question of population, both in its effects on the health of the individual (particularly via VD) and on the future of the population (via the association of VD with sterility, and the higher infant mortality of unmarried mothers) (Weeks 1989). At the same time, the notion of adolescence as a distinct period of development, and one of particular significance for the channeling of sexuality towards responsible parenthood, emerged.

These shifts influenced the way sexual abuse was constructed in a number of ways. First, concern focused often not on the victimised girl herself but on her potential offspring as the true victim. In the Commons debate on the Incest Bill 1908, the main argument put forward by Herbert Samuel, Home Office Under-Secretary, for criminalising incest was that "it might entail consequences of a disastrous kind on the offspring which sometimes followed from such intercourse, and from that point of view society had a special interest that should lead to steps being taken to put a stop to it" (Hansard, 26 June 1908, col. 284).

Second, and linked to this, the response to the victimised girl increasingly reflected concerns about her potential performance as a mother. The Royal Commission on the Care and Control of the Feeble-Minded, which sat in 1908, heard evidence that "feeble-minded" girls were particularly vulnerable to sexual assault, that many had illegitimate children as a result, and that such children were likely to be "imbeciles, or degenerates, or criminals." Its response was to recommend the segregation of such girls in order to prevent them from reproducing themselves.[5]

The NVA, whose aim was to transform sexual behaviour towards a high standard of chastity in both men and women, increasingly adopted the new concern for the national stock in place of the moral language of vice and corruption it had previously used. Germany was criticised for allowing earlier marriage in order to counter the falling birth rate, since to "prematurely exploit young girlhood" would not pay off "from the racial point of view" (*The Vigilance Record*, October 1915: 79–80). In 1922 an article in the *Evening Standard* was cited approvingly, arguing against the use of the "reasonable cause to believe" defence as follows:

> (the law) should, in fact, regard adolescent women as at least as important as adolescent fish or breeding animals. It is an offence to shoot game in the close season, or to take fish below a certain size, and no "reasonable cause" can be pleaded. Why should there be a necessity for a big loophole regarding the age of consent? (*The Vigilance Record*, September 1922: 59)

Motherhood and promiscuity were constructed as separate routes by the social-hygiene movement during this period, and the concern of the newly developing sex education was primarily to divert girls from "promiscuity" towards responsible and healthy motherhood (Bland 1982). Hence this concern with motherhood facilitated the shift of concern from abuse itself to its consequences (perceived through the lens of women as reproducers), since the diversion of girls from "promiscuity," from the risk of VD, and from unmarried motherhood (all of which were for some girls the consequence of sexual abuse) became a high priority. It was considerably easier and less threatening to prevailing power structures to patrol and control girls in all these circumstances, sending them to homes for their reform, than effectively to counter the abuses of men in the home or on the street.

This concern to preserve girls for their future reproductive roles was one continued justification for those who sought the further raising of the age of consent. Debates on this issue were complex, however, and are not adequately represented as concerned solely with the repressive regulation of female sexuality sought by social purity or a feminist obsession with male vice. Feminists in the 1885 debates were sometimes drawn into an alliance with social purity in opposition to the attempts of upper-class men to preserve their unfettered access to working-class girls, losing sight temporarily of the risks of such legislation for the civil liberties of young women (Gorham 1978). Despite increasing recognition of the problems the age of consent brought, however, many continued to be ambivalent. While purity campaigners sought the protection of girls "from themselves," some feminists noted more their protection from exposure to the full rigours of the double standard (e.g., *The Vote*, 11 May 1912). The age of consent marked the dividing line around which the contradictions of women's responsibility for sexuality, both less and more responsible than men, polarised (Bland 1982). Below it, girls were perceived as without responsibility, justifying (sometimes oppressive) protection. But above it, they bore responsibility not only for themselves but also for men, as illustrated by the prosecution of women for soliciting.

Later, the arguments of some feminists for raising the age of consent to eighteen were allied to the cause of sexual equality by calling for the raising of the age of criminal responsibility also to eighteen. This was justified by the new medicalised concept of adolescence as an inherently unstable time when neither boys nor girls were fit to decide for themselves.[6] The NVA had by the 1930s also bowed to the new definition of adolescence, although they took a different, and in this instance less repressive, approach, laying strong emphasis on distinguishing between assaults on young children and what they referred to as "technical assaults" or "boy and girl cases" involving "foolish youths and precocious girls." The 1925 report was criticised for conflating the two quite different issues, and the NVA consistently attempted to exclude the latter from campaigns. Divisions on this issue continued to emerge in the 1930s, although the Joint Committee agreed from the beginning to exclude the age of consent from their remit as too contentious. The Home Office had already indicated that further legislation on the issue would get nowhere.

The third way in which concerns with motherhood influenced the construction of sexual abuse was by the new responsibilities and powers accorded women as mothers. Concern with child health and the role of mothers in securing it brought a shift towards greater emphasis on women as mothers and a lesser emphasis on women as wives. The extended length of childhood further exaggerated the role of women as mothers. As women were accorded greater powers to influence their children, attention to their own victimisation declined. Feminist groups continued in the suffrage campaigns to draw attention to the victimisation of women as well as children,[7] and to the inequity of the responsibilities accorded mothers for children when they had few legal rights and limited access to resources. But while the link between delinquency and parental neglect was not new,[8] it was firmly established in the 1933 Act. Family breakdown and working mothers became the key culprits, both seen as the result of economic deprivation (League of Nations 1934). Many feminists by then felt the new responsibilities of motherhood offered potential for enhancing women's status in the home and pursued welfare reforms with this aim, simultaneously moving away from the earlier critique of sexual exploitation by men. Thus, AMSH cited approvingly a reference to the causes of delinquency which commented, "a home without a mother is only half a home" (*The Shield,* November 1934), and in the debates on child sexual abuse of the 1930s, a National Council of Women conference observed that "a great many problem cases would never have arisen if children had been brought up in the right knowledge" (*Scotsman,* 21 November 1933). Parent education was advocated as a preventive measure, as was the speeding up of slum clearance. The former in effect accorded mothers the responsibility for preventing sexual abuse. The latter implied that incestuous abuse was the product of overcrowded housing and did nothing to tackle the power of men within households.

Social Purity, Social Hygiene, and Feminism

The weakening of the feminist critique of masculinity reflects another important shift, the relative decline of the social-purity movement and the rise of social hygiene, alongside changing attitudes amongst feminists both to sex and to the law. During the late nineteenth century, the social-purity movement had mobilised a major campaign for moral reform and the suppression of vice. Their stress on criminal legislation as a means of achieving this reflected a then new perception of the state's capacity to transform sexual and moral behaviour (Mort 1987). The NVA, for example, claimed that in Ireland, where incest was a criminal offence, it did not occur (*The Vigilance Record,* December 1895). In the suffrage campaigns many feminists shared this faith in the potential role of law, despite its current male bias. The Women's Freedom League made similarly wild claims for a legal system open to the beneficial influence of women (see, e.g., *The Vote*, 9 March 1912). Many (although not all) feminists had also shared social-purity concerns with male lust and the double standard, campaigning for women's right to say no to unwanted sex.[9] However, by the 1930s popular support for social purity, with its explicitly moral language of sin, vice, and degeneracy and adherence to criminal law as a deterrent, had declined. The social-hygiene movement, on the other hand, which had emerged in the 1900s offering new scientific knowledges to the population debates, was well established, speaking an apparently more progressive language. Many of the same moral judgements were in fact reworked into the medical discourse of science, but social hygiene promoted a more positive image of sex, with an emphasis on education and prevention as regulatory practices rather than suppression and punishment.

Many feminists by this time had moved to some degree away both from their earlier suspicion of the medical profession (derived from the involvement of the latter in the regulation of prostitution in the nineteenth century) and from their faith in the efficacy of legal reform, recognising that the latter often resulted in greater surveillance of women. Increasingly, they also focused on women's right to sexual pleasure rather than on protection from sexual exploitation (Bland 1982). Hence, they allied themselves with the seemingly more progressive forces of social hygiene. Alison Neilans was an enthusiastic representative of this trend, calling for legislation on sexual assault that would "take people out of the category of criminals and put them into the category of mental invalids" (*Scotsman*, 21 November 1933). AMSH, in its calls for new legislation, focused entirely on the medical examination and treatment of offenders against children under thirteen. The medicalisation of sexual offences against young children that took place in this period was part of a broader trend occurring, although not without conflict, towards psychological explanations for crime and delinquency (Weeks 1989). Its basis in moral criteria is illustrated by the label adopted of "moral perversion" and by the claim made for the role of the medical profession by Dr. W. D. Fairbairn: "I submit that, since a child does not constitute a natural object of overt sexual behaviour on the part of an adult, such behaviour in itself constitutes a perverse act" (Fairbairn 1935: 15). Such elaborate claims for a disease model were not apparently inhibited by the fact that neither the cause nor the cure had yet been found.

Neither earlier feminists nor social-purity campaigners had been hesitant in naming the construction of normal male sexuality as a problem. The medical profession, however, relied on the concept of abnormality for its claims both to seek and to treat pathology, and feminists who dissented from this were increasingly marginalised. The receptiveness of feminists to the medical model was increased both by sympathy for men's suffering in the war and by increasing interest in the problem of persistent offenders, since the case was made that treating one offender successfully would prevent a series of further assaults. Broader ideas of prevention were drawn from social hygiene's image of sex as a healthy instinct in need of channelling towards socially approved goals. The 1925 report recommended sex education and the provision of facilities for healthy indoor and outdoor recreation as preventive measures, and in some later debates allowing earlier marriage was suggested. Feminist proposals for prevention also included sex education, along with talks to parents and improved housing.

Representatives of the medical profession claimed their analysis did not affect the issue of criminal responsibility. Purity campaigners, however, saw it as a direct challenge to their ideas, and one not to be taken lying down. While some members of the NVA shifted towards a medical discourse, and officially it endorsed calls for medical examination and treatment, internally members were divided, and Frederick Sempkins, the current Secretary, waged a personal campaign against "throwing (the issue) over to the alienists." Medical treatment was to him both a soft option and of limited relevance, since it mattered little what was done with convicted offenders when the main problem was the impossibility of gaining convictions in the first place. The latter point (still pertinent today) seems to have fallen on deaf ears, in part because feminists (and others) were preoccupied with resisting his punitive emphasis on the law as a deterrent and occasional advocacy of flogging and in part because of the intransigence of the legal profession when faced with any proposal which addressed the problem.

While the general public had received the 1925 report well (with the exception of the proposal to raise the age of consent to seventeen), the legal profession had not. They objected strongly and consistently to proposals for changes in legal procedure. The report was attacked for being "founded on the popular misconception that every prosecution is necessarily well-founded and every defence inevitably a speculative subterfuge" (*Law Journal*, 6 March 1926: 215). The recommendation for the greater involvement of women police and doctors in sexual offences received almost equal hostility, on the grounds that this would bias the system further against men. This latter argument resonates ironically with the arguments of the suffrage campaign. The Women's Freedom League for instance had claimed, "it would be quite as intelligible to expect a Tory to legislate to a Liberal's satisfaction as to expect one sex to legislate fairly for another" (*The Vote*, 19 March 1910). Given the shared assumption of inevitable difference, and "sex antipathy" (*Law Journal*, 6 March 1926: 215), clearly the legal profession preferred the option of unfettered male bias. It was not uncommon for the intimidating nature of a court appearance for young girls to be deliberately increased by the exclusion of women magistrates and jury members from sexual assault cases (Report of the Departmental Committee on Sexual Offences against Young Persons 1925). While in the 1930s, Sempkins located one sympathetic judge, Judge Cecil Whiteley, willing to argue for changes in procedure, including relaxation of corroboration rules and a tribunal system of questioning,[10] even he appeared to give up on so controversial a subject, and the legal advisers to the Joint Committee dismissed proposals for any change to legal procedure out of hand.

The Joint Committee dissolved in 1935, having failed to resolve the conflicts between medical and legal definitions of child sexual abuse which were frequent during the 1920s and 1930s. Both the declining strength of feminism and the shifts in its orientation towards a focus on sexual pleasure more than danger, on economic rather than sexual exploitation, on education rather than legal reform, and on strengthening women's maternal role all contributed further to the loss of child sexual abuse as a public issue, as the medical profession took it over in its claims to a new scientific discourse on sex.

The 1970s On: Women as Cause, Protection, and Control

There can be few people who are not aware of the rediscovery of child sexual abuse in the present. Initiated by feminist campaigns against male violence in the 1970s, child sexual abuse became a high-profile public issue during the late 1980s and remains one today. Contemporary social anxieties about sex and the family have influenced this, and child sexual abuse has been attributed both to the "sexual permissiveness" of the 1960s (O'Hagan 1989) and to the "decline of the traditional family" (Gledhill et al. 1989). Concerns about demographic changes, the increased divorce rate and propor-tion of lone-parent families, underlie anxiety that the extent of child sexual abuse revealed by research will lead to a further escalation in "fragmented (i.e., fatherless) families" (Fawcett 1989). At the same time, the relative rights and powers of children, parents, and the different agencies and professional groups involved in child protection to define what constitutes abuse remain hotly contested. The ineffectiveness of the criminal justice system has continued, despite some changes facilitated by the existence of new technology as well as a considerably stronger child-protection lobby.[11] The context of response by other agencies, however, has changed.

The medical profession's dominance over the fields of both child abuse and sexuality is now well established, reflected in policy debates if not necessarily in practice. Postwar developments in childcare have attributed changed significance to family life, reflected in the acquisition of new duties by local authorities, first to return children from care to their families where possible (the Children Act 1948) and then to prevent their reception into care by helping families with children at home (the Children and Young Persons Act 1963). The idealised view of family life underlying these changes retracted a little after the battering to death of Maria Colwell by her stepfather in 1973 (after being returned home to her natural mother), and the Children Act 1975 made it easier to extricate children from their natural parents.[12] Further changes are enshrined in the Children Act 1989, implemented in 1991, which was influenced by a series of inquiries held during the 1980s, first involving three children who died at home at the hands of their fathers or stepfathers, for whom professionals were blamed for doing too little too late,[13] and later involving 121 children suspected of being sexually abused in Cleveland, for whom professionals were accused of doing too much too soon.[14] The Act attempts again to rework the balancing act, both increasing the grounds for state intervention to protect children and setting out a new framework for partnership with parents geared to the preservation and support of parental responsibilities. Despite these shifts, child-care work throughout has focused primarily on mothers, with child abuse defined as a problem of poor mothering but separation from mothers also defined as a key trau-matic event to be avoided for children. Child sexual abuse as a problem for statutory agencies landed in this context. Consequently, the surveillance of girls in the previous period has been to some extent replaced (and certainly supplemented) by the increased surveillance of women as mothers of sexually abused children.

Feminist criticisms of mother-blaming in relation to child sexual abuse have focused primarily on "family dysfunction theory," a medical discourse preoccupied with causality, which, having shifted its focus from the individual to the family as unit, sought it in any deviation from androcentrically defined and historically specific norms (see, e.g., MacLeod and Saraga 1988; Nelson 1987). In the dominant versions of this, sexuality as the core feature of marriage and a construction of motherhood defined in relation to children's psychological and emotional needs (both developments of the postwar period) were enshrined, as was a functionalist model of the family which defined the sexual division of labour as natural. The result was the implication of women in the cause of abuse, via sexual estrangement from their partners, the unmet needs of their children, and/or their absence from the home (e.g., CIBA Foundation 1984), a model which has been roundly condemned by feminists, to some effect. However, the influence this model exerted over the social practices of agencies involved in child protection was never obvious, since social workers generally pay more attention to pragmatic concerns than theoretical explanations (Corby 1987) and their resources for therapeutic work are limited. In this section I want to consider, first, what influence this discourse has had on social workers (the prime actors in the surveillance of women), and on mothers themselves (the prime actors in child protection), and second, to discuss the problems and potential of the child-protection discourse which I would argue is more central for both groups. Finally, I discuss the construction of motherhood in contemporary judicial discourse. While there is overlap between the constructions of women in different discourses, there are also significant differences.

Social Workers, Mothers, and Medical Discourse

Social workers draw on the available professional discourses alongside other sources of knowledge, from the wider community and their own experience, in their efforts to make sense of their work (Pithouse 1987). In my study, labels such as "a collusive wife" and "a dysfunctional family" were employed with little meaning in themselves as part of the process of distancing the worker from the client. Judgements such as "she knew" or "she disbelieved" were also made in relation to mothers of sexually abused children, despite evidence of far more complex processes involving doubt, uncertainty, and ambivalence, as shorthand for "not doing enough." "Enough," however, was often defined with the benefit of hindsight, and the label served the purpose primarily of attributing fault (Hooper 1990).

For social workers, "blaming" clients, by constructing them as a "particular sort of person" to whom it could be expected that awful things would happen, is one of the main ways in which they manage "occupational impotence" (Pithouse 1987). Where child sexual abuse is concerned, the sources of occupational impotence are numerous: the tightrope social workers must walk between criticism for unwarranted intervention in the family on the one hand and failure to protect children on the other, difficulties of gaining direct access to children and to evidence of abuse, uncertainty about both the definition of abuse and often about the best solution, an inadequate knowledge base to predict accurately the risk to children that leaving them in the care of a particular adult involves, the relatively low status of social workers in the professional networks involved in child protection compared with the medical profession and police, the inadequacy of the criminal justice system, the lack of resources both for alternative accommodation for children and therapeutic work with individuals and families, and the reluctance of some individuals and families to participate in what services are offered. The result is high levels of anxiety. As one social worker in my study put it, "My protectiveness to her is like an Aertex vest . . . total protection is a myth." Since mothers are the main alternative sources of child protection, it is they who bear the brunt of social workers' frustration in their talk of cases. Such talk does not translate in any direct way into practice. In order to gain access to the detailed personal information their work depends on, practitioners have to withhold judgement on the moral worth of their clients (Pithouse 1987). To blame them directly is counterproductive, and women confronted in the heat of a worker's anxiety with no consideration for their own feelings rarely confided in social workers again. In practice the expectations social workers set for mothers depended more on the alternatives they had available for children than on any theoretical model of child sexual abuse (Hooper 1990).

Mothers experienced the medical discourse in other ways than through their contact with agencies, however, through its influence on lay understandings of child sexual abuse, on which they also drew in order to make sense of their experience. Women who discover that their children have been sexually abused, especially by their own partner, face a situation of severe loss and confusion, in which many former assumptions about their worlds are overturned. In their search for meaning they are both vulnerable to and often resist available definitions of their roles.

Perhaps the most popular definition of mothers' roles in medical discourse is now the idea that there is a "cycle of abuse" between mothers and daughters. The thesis of "intergenerational transmission" is based on limited evidence but fits neatly within a family-systems perspective, legitimating professional intervention, and frequently making the abuser himself invisible. For mothers, "cycle of abuse" theories have a subjective appeal in the "why me? why her?" stage of coming to terms with loss, and one which carries strong risks, particularly where the guilt often felt in response to childhood sexual abuse is still unresolved. The following account illustrates this:

> I . . . thought to myself well maybe it was something that I did in my life, something bad, you know really bad that I'd done and she was being punished for it . . . all sorts of things went through my mind, I thought perhaps that it was because of when my father was abusing me, there were times when I actually enjoyed it.

While their own histories of abuse could cause extra distress, however, women also saw them positively as a resource, sometimes actively searching memory for experiences of their own that would help them understand those of their children.

Other components of the medical model also influenced women. The idea that abusers were "sick" diminished their responsibility, since illness is generally regarded as outside the individual's control, and not deserving of blame (see Cornwell 1984). It also implies the possibility of cure. To be an effective ally to a child requires attributing responsibility clearly to the offender, and those women who did so rejected such explanations, adopting an explicitly moral discourse involving conscious action ("He knew what he was doing") and personal responsibility ("old enough to know right from wrong"). Similarly, the idea that sexual problems in their own relationships might explain the abuser's actions both diminished his responsibility and could cause devastating guilt for mothers, unless it was accompanied by a clear sense of their own right to sexual autonomy.

Child-Protection Discourse

The medical discourse is not insignificant in its impact on either social workers or mothers. However, in their practice social work agencies draw more, I would argue, on a child-protection discourse which is preoccupied not with causality but with parental responsibility. A phrase reminiscent of the earliest and most misogynistic of advocates of family dysfunction, that mothers are crucial or central, recurs in child-protection discourse but for different reasons, that as primary carers, mothers are usually the key person in preventing further abuse and thus obviating the need to receive the child into care. The role and responsibility accorded mothers in this discourse raises more complex issues for feminists, at least if the need for some social control role on behalf of children is accepted (see Gordon 1988).

There are two main problems with the way in which parental responsibility is commonly attributed to women. First, the problem is that women are commonly accorded sole responsibility for the welfare of children (not that they bear any responsibility), and further, that they lack the resources to exercise it effectively. Motherhood is thus characterized by "powerless responsibility" (Rich 1977). The implicitly gendered assumptions that underlie discussion of parental responsibilities are illustrated by the argument of Bentovim and colleagues that "a parent who knows that the other parent is in a state of depression, anger or frustration and leaves that parent to care for the child . . . indicates a failure in sharing responsibility" (Bentovim, Elton, and Tranter 1987: 29). This clearly means mothers leaving depressed fathers. If fathers who left depressed mothers to care for children were cause for state intervention, social services departments (SSDs) would be swamped.

Second, parents are commonly presented as an indivisible unit with identical interests, obscuring the conflicts between them. The Department of Health, for example, suggests that showing remorse and taking responsibility for abuse are positive indicators in the assessment of parents (DOH 1988). For a nonabusing mother in cases of child sexual abuse, the opposite is more likely to be the case. Despite evidence that the battering of women frequently precedes both physical and sexual child abuse (see Hooper 1990; Stark and Flitcraft 1988; Truesdell, McNeil, and Deschner 1986), this rarely merits a mention in the mainstream child-abuse literature or policy debate. While both women and children often seek help from agencies to control the more powerful members of the household, official discussion of the social control role of social work constructs it as one way, between the state and the family as a unit, and in practice the burden commonly falls on women.

Consequently, women in my study who sought help when their children were sexually abused sometimes received little but surveillance of themselves in return. Where they had been victimised themselves, an approach to authority by social workers which failed to disaggregate parents was particularly counterproductive. Women used to resisting their partner's control and fighting to retain some of their own simply adopted similar strategies, focusing on "beating the system," when another authority stepped in to set rules for them. Children, too, already used to seeing their mothers powerless, are likely to have this perception reinforced in witnessing such encounters with professionals, increasing their own insecurity. The control role was not always unwelcome to mothers, but they wanted it used to back up their own efforts rather than turned against them. Their criticisms were of the failure of social workers to exercise authority at the appropriate time and with the appropriate person, and the tendency to accord them greater powers than they had to control abusive men themselves.

Despite these common problems, the discourse of child protection could be used to empower women, since local authorities and social workers have considerable discretion to negotiate their policies and practices within the broad framework set out by central government. Both mothers' and social workers' accounts of the child-protection register illustrated this. All local authorities are required to hold a register, listing children who are known to have been abused or are thought to be at risk of abuse. There has been much confusion about the exact purpose of registers, and decisions to place children's names on them are often inconsistent (Corby 1987). It is generally assumed that they are stigmatising to parents, and suggestions have been made that they be scrapped. However, registration has variable meanings, both to social workers and to mothers. Social workers did not perceive the decision simply as a bureaucratic one, but one made within the context of negotiating a complex set of relationships. Thus, decisions were sometimes influenced by the message that registration might give to the mother (the possibility of either damaging an existing relationship of cooperation or of motivating an improved one), to the child (showing a complaint had been taken seriously), or to a new authority when a family was moving (attempting to ensure the allocation of a social worker). Some mothers certainly did experience registration as unjust, especially where the child had no further contact with the abuser, saying, for example, that it was like a criminal conviction against them. Others, however, did not, seeing it positively as giving either entitlement to priority help, or backing to exclude an abusive partner from the house.

Judicial Discourse

Judicial discourse involves further constructions of women whose children are sexually abused, as sources of domestic stress (primarily through the breakdown of sexual relationships), the financial dependents of men, and agents of informal control, which are crucial to approaches to offenders. The Parole Board for 1968 advocated a welfare approach to incest offenders on the assumption that inadequate sexual relationships with their wives were at root (Bailey and McCabe 1979), implicitly endorsing men's right to sexual satisfaction within the family. Sentencing practice reinforces traditional family structures by its use both of sexual estrangement and a continuing marital relationship as mitigating factors. Thus, fathers are returned to the position of power in families, which is at the root of incestuous abuse (Mitra 1987). The case for noncustodial sentences with conditions of treatment is also based to a large extent on the effects of family breakup and the loss of a breadwinner on "the family" (Glaser and Spencer 1990).

In this debate women are presented as naturally, or at least happily, dependent and hence invariably resistant to the prosecution of their husbands. In my study, however, while fear of losing a breadwinner was an issue for some women, inhibiting reporting, for others fear that no effective legal action would be taken was the more important factor increasing their sense of isolation and powerlessness in the family. The possibility of prosecution had both negative and positive meanings, the most important of the latter being the clear message it gave about the individual responsibility of the abuser, and an opportunity to discover their own capacity for independence. In practice, the effectiveness of noncustodial alternatives for offenders rests on the informal controls operated by the family (i.e., women) as well as court orders on treatment and residence (Wolf, Conte, and Engel-Meinig 1988), although this role is often invisible in debates.

Concluding Remarks

I have aimed in this chapter to highlight some of the varying ways in which responsibilities have been attributed to women and girls in constructions of child sexual abuse, both at different periods of history and in competing discourses. Over the period considered, from the 1870s to the present, the greater recognition of children's needs alongside a recurring reluctance to consider collective or male responsibility for meeting them, has resulted in increased expectations of mothers. Women have gained rights as well as responsibilities over this period, of course, to political citizenship, greater access to education and paid employment, divorce, and a minimal level of welfare provision. While they are therefore somewhat less subject to the control of individual men in the household, their move into the public sphere has been accompanied by continued subordination within it (Walby 1990). Women's disadvantage in the labour market and responsibility for childcare (before and after divorce) mean divorce carries a high risk of poverty. Yet "reasonable parental care," as expressed in the Children Act 1989, is defined according to expectations of "the average or reasonable parent," abstracted from social context, who must, if unable to meet their child's needs themselves, seek help from others who can (DOH 1989b). If women are to meet these expectations when a partner abuses their child, then the economic dependence which inhibits them both from stopping such abuse themselves and from seeking help must be addressed, and when they do seek help, services which meet their own needs and their children's must be available.

In conclusion, I want to comment briefly on the impact of feminist definitions of child sexual abuse on current policy. There are increasing attempts to sever family-systems thinking from its preoccupation with causality and its reactionary sexual politics, and to integrate it with feminist analyses (see, e.g., Masson and O'Byrne 1990). The DOH no longer attributes incestuous abuse to "distorted family relationships" (DHSS 1988) but cautiously accepts the need for further explanatory frameworks (DOH 1989a). At the same time as the claims of family therapists are being modified, however, wider social anxieties about "family breakdown" encourage resort to its practices. The danger is that the use of such practices will be driven more by the New Right's attempt to buttress the traditional family than any evidence of their effectiveness in preventing abuse, and attention diverted from alternative strategies to reduce the social and economic disadvantages that family breakdown brings for women and children.

The DOH has also adopted the concept of nonabusing parents (usually mothers), who "may need help to adjust to the changes in their lives" (DOH 1989a: 29), and the recommendation that abusing men should be excluded from the home in preference to removing children into care. Here, there is a danger that in the current political context, the changes for which feminists have campaigned may have perverse effects. Where SSDs are starved of resources and collective responsibility for childcare is minimal, the designation of women as nonabusing parents may facilitate their definition simply as resources for their children rather than women with their own needs, and the exclusion of abusing men may increase women's responsibilities while depleting their resources. To turn such strategies to the empowerment of women and children demands their location within a broader programme of social change.

NOTES

1. The figures produced by the NSPCC, based on a sample of registers covering about 10 percent of the child population in England and Wales, show that the number of children on registers more than doubled from 1983 to 1987, and the proportion of these who had been sexually abused increased from 5 percent in 1983 to 28 percent in 1987 (S. J. Creighton and P. Noyes, *Child Abuse Trends in England and Wales 1983–1987*, London: NSPCC, 1989).

2. NSPCC, *Annual Reports*, 1893–94, 1906–7, 1907–8, 1908–9, 1910–11, 1912–13, 1913–14, 1914–15, and 1918–19.

3. The Home Office had issued a circular in 1926 backing some of the recommended changes in police and court practice, but allowing discretion for varying local circumstances.

4. See *Report of the Joint Committee on Sexual Offences*, December 1935; *Sexual Offences against Young Persons: Memorandum for Magistrates*, December 1935; *Memorandum on "The Need for a Medical-Mental Examination of Persistent Sexual Offenders"* by Dr. Gillespie, December 1935. These, the minutes of the Joint Committee and correspondence concerning it, on which this chapter draws, are located in the NVA archives, Fawcett Library, London.

5. See *Report of the Royal Commission on the Care and Control of the Feeble-Minded*, vol. VIII (London: HMSO, 1908), 120–21.

6. Miss E. H. Kelly, a member of the 1925 Committee and of the National Council of Women, made this case. AMSH also claimed to have suggested it in 1918 (*The Shield*, Feb.–Mar. 1926).

7. *The Vote*, for example, carried a column entitled variously "How Men Protect Women," "How Some Men Protect Women," and "The Protected Sex," which reported cases of violence against women and children and the paltry sentences which men commonly received for them.

8. Behlmer (1982) traces it back to 1816.

9. See Jeffreys (1985) for a review of these campaigns and Bland (1982) for variations amongst Victorian feminists in attitudes to sex.

10. See discussion on "The Problem of the Moral Pervert," reported in *Journal of the Institute of Hygiene*, April 1933: 236–38.

11. The Criminal Justice Act 1988 introduced an experimental scheme allowing children to give evidence in the Crown Court through a live, closed-circuit television link. Further changes have recently been proposed using video-recorded interviews, which would allow children to

give evidence before the trial, thus avoiding the distress caused by long delays (Pigot Committee, *Report of the Advisory Group on Video Evidence,* London: Home Office, 1989). The Children Act 1989 also enabled civil proceedings relating to children to admit hearsay evidence and the unsworn evidence of a child.

12. See MacLeod (1987) for a review of these changes and their implications.

13. See London Borough of Brent, *A Child in Trust: Report of the Panel of Inquiry Investigating the Circumstances Surrounding the Death of Jasmine Beckford,* 1985; London Borough of Greenwich, *A Child in Mind: Protection of Children in a Responsible Society, The Report of the Commission of Inquiry into the Circumstances Surrounding the Death of Kimberley Carlisle,* 1987; and London Borough of Lambeth, *Whose Child? A Report of the Public Inquiry into the Death of Tyra Henry,* 1987.

14. See Secretary of State for Social Services, *Report of the Inquiry into Child Abuse in Cleveland,* 1987 (London: HMSO, 1988).

Chapter Twenty-three

Who Stole Incest?

Louise Armstrong

In 1978, when people asked what I'd written about, I'd say "incest." And they would then most often ask, "Oh? Are you a feminist?"

Now, when I say (with some reticence) that I have written about incest, people ask, "Oh? Are you a psychologist?"

Incest, the sexualization of children cast in Procrustean form, has been transmogrified—hijacked. From a political issue framed by feminists as one of male violence against women and children—a sexual offense on the part of men, for which we demanded accountability, and censure—incest has, in these years, been coopted and reformulated by the therapeutic ideology, as an illness in women, to be treated. In children, it is a prediction of illness to be treated.

In 1971, we spoke of what caused child sexual abuse and its role in socializing women, and training them for sexual submission.

By now, you will hear few speak of what causes incest. Most speak only of what incest causes: sleeplessness, lack of trust, sexual acting-out, timidity, aggression, destiny itself. Children raped by fathers and stepfathers are said to be doomed—to become depressed, dissociated, drug-addicted, suicidal . . .

The issue of incest is now one of illness.

It is not social, but medical.

The response is not a call for change, but a call for "treatment."

It is not that we were wrong. Far from it. We identified incest as something fathers and stepfathers had done throughout history and continued to do, not in spite of the fact that they knew it was wrong, but because they believed it was their right: *justifiable.*

And this is what the offenders said as well. ("It's natural; it's perfectly normal.") By 1980, men were helping our understanding still more, as academics and other professionals spoke to us as the "pro-incest lobby" of "positive incest." They told us that "children have the right to express themselves sexually, even with members of their own family." They told us that, in any case, "the rate of incidence is so high as to make prohibition absurd." They told us that incest could be *beneficial.*

Well, we knew it could be, too. And we knew who benefitted.

We knew that incest was not only the grotesque absurdity of men turning the full

From *On the Issues* 3, no. 4 (fall 1994): 30–32. Reprinted by permission.

power of adult male sexuality against infants, toddlers, and pre-teens. It was also a form of violence against women. Our fathers had helped us out here as well. ("This would kill your mother if she found out." "She's not good for anything anyway, the bitch.")

During the 1980s, we had further corroboration that incest was not confined to the rape of children, but among the many male violences against women. Children, we learned, were now being abused by fathers in retaliation for divorce. And they were being abused with far less finesse.

Yet by then what we knew, what could be seen from the evidence, had already been overridden, suppressed by male-protective forces. From the moment of our first speaking out, newfound experts on the rape of children had risen full-blown from the sea, pronouncing with the authority of mental health professionals, knowledge. The oddest thing was that even they knew that the rape of daughters was also violence against women. They said so. In their own language, of course, their own sort of way.

The mothers of incest victims, they pronounced, simply did not put out enough, weren't attractive enough, weren't nice enough to their men, they were rejecting or frigid (or sexually rapacious). This, they said, is what drives men to the beds of their five-year-olds, this "incest mother."

Well, this was not exactly the way we would have put it. But it meant these new experts saw what we did: That when men sexually assault their children, it is often driven by rage at women.

There was a subtle but serious distinction between the "pro-incest" folks and the new experts. The "pro-incesters" wanted incest legalized, where the new experts wanted it "decriminalized." Legalized had the virtue of candor. But decriminalized won. That meant that as a matter of policy incest was subject to state intervention: civil, not criminal. An intervention that would target—not rapist fathers, but—"incest families." Civil statutes were now written that faulted the mother who "knew or should have known." Well, looked at generously, even that message was not so very different from ours: women should know that men feel at liberty to rape children.

One problem with their way of putting things was that in order to have "intrafamilial child sexual abuse" for which the woman was equally (or more) culpable, you absolutely had to have this "incest mother" hanging around, in the picture, choosing her husband over her child, denying what the kid said . . . You had to have her, alive or dead ("sometimes the incest mother is absent from the home, or terminally ill").

So women who, discovering the abuse, left and tried to protect the child were simply not playing their role in the drama as now scripted. For this outrageous failure to read their lines as written (in a script essential to defraying male accountability), the mothers had to be viciously punished. And so these women, "vindictive, hysterical," lost custody of their children—to the alleged abusers. They were that dangerous. They threatened to expose the whole conceptual fraud. War on children and their mothers had been declared.

Another problem with the new experts' way of putting things was that in practice a policy of decriminalization not only resulted in punishing women and children; it also diminished the import of adult survivors' testimony. It rendered individual survivors vulnerable to the newly emerging specialists in problem management—those in the therapeutic arena who, alone, assured survivors that what had happened to them mattered.

Alas, in this medicalized world, survivors' experience mattered in direct proportion to the degree of manifest illness. How sick you were proved how bad it was. Checklists offered expanding lists of expected symptoms, the display of which was said to be evidence of your past abuse.

Within this individualized universe, some individual survivors sought personal, rather than united political, action: they did battle against statutes of limitation and instigated lawsuits against alleged perpetrators. Making incest a pocketbook issue for offenders, of course, galvanized a spirited, quickly organized, political response. The oxymoronic False Memory Syndrome was born. War on adult survivors' credibility had been declared.

On both fronts of this war against children and mothers and against adult survivors —it was the other side that had the army and the medics. Individualization, medicalization had precluded political organization.

By now, friends-in-this-struggle would say, "Things are not going well."

To which I replied, "Things are going very well. Just not for us."

We have been re-silenced. Within the larger world. And within a world that is labeled feminist as well.

You cannot hear us anymore—those who spoke out early on and have spoken out since about incest as a licensed abuse of male power. Our voices have been drowned out by those who speak of incest as "gender neutral." Drowned out by those who speak of incest-as-illness—who would have us hear only that women survivors have been made fragile and helpless by the event in their childhood vaguely rendered by the word incest. Women are portrayed to us, in tones of great sympathy, as damaged, suffering from diminished capacity. And signs of damage in women, signs of diminished capacity—working backwards—are taken as "indicators" that they have been wounded by incest. Incest has become a metaphor for all the oppressions that feminism named.

What has happened in this brief fifteen years since feminists first spoke out on incest is the explicit exoneration of fathers, the implication of mothers—and the infantilization of women as survivors.

The personal is political. You may still hear the words, but you can no longer hear the meaning behind them. You cannot hear that the point of speaking out was to identify commonalities that, once identified, could lead to political action for change. We spoke out publicly to break a silence—when there was a silence to break. But speaking out was never meant to be all there was.

We endorsed help for individual women. But that was never meant to be all there was: the building of field hospitals to tend a predictably endless supply of wounded.

You cannot hear us anymore. Even though—in the tiniest tucky-holes of this country—you cannot any longer hear silence on the prevalence of incest, you cannot anywhere hear what all this talk of incest means. You can't hear that it is about a license that is historical. Or that, until recently, what silenced women was not reticence or shame, but intimidation. You can't hear that, as recently as 1978, the law in Texas, for instance, held the complaining child liable as an accomplice-witness, a "participant," an instigator. For all the loose talk of the "crime" of incest, you can't hear that this male abuse of power continues to be quasi-semi-more-or-less legal in this country. Or that where children and their protective mothers refuse to be silent—they will be silenced by the courts, and punished. And you cannot hear that these things are all connected, all part of the same weave. That the myth of the incest "triad," that the exclusive focus on victim pathology is all tailored to protect the male offender. You can't hear this even within most gatherings of feminists.

Even the incest stories you now hear are selective. The stories of children yanked into the child welfare system are unheard. The stories of those children placed under psychiatric surveillance, sometimes institutionalized, presumed according to mental health ideology to be at risk of emotional disturbance because their fathers raped them—are unheard. And yet we are everywhere told that we are, at last, *listening to the children.*

Nor do survivor's stories speak clearly of incest as male violence, nor of the deliberateness of that violence. Indeed, with the focus so heavily on illness, you can barely discern the fact of human agency: it is as though "incest" is on the order of a natural catastrophe—not rape by Daddy, who could just as easily have not done it.

What you can hear now is that we are, at last—fifteen years after women began publicly speaking out, ten years after the televising of the breakthrough documentary, "Something about Amelia," five years after every talk show in the nation has routinized the airing of incest stories—breaking the silence.

Women continue to speak out, but seldom in their own, authentic voices. Rather, their speech echoes that of therapists; they speak the language of mental health—of their disorders, and their path to healing. They speak of being in recovery—as though it were a geographical space. Their stories are absent context, without larger meaning.

In being framed as medical, incest has been rendered trivial.

Somehow, mental health ideology infiltrated and subverted feminist rationality. Once incest was reformulated by treaters and healers, speaking out itself was transformed. Its meaning was changed. The personal became public, but not political. It was not the abuse of male power, but individual women and their symptoms who needed to change.

What we are speaking of here is not therapy, the private event. It is the therapeutic ideology—a way of seeing the world that enlarges the personal, with no agenda for the political. It is a belief system, a way of seeing the world that subverts the goals of feminism: it promotes the personal to the paramount, sells belonging in suffering, offers consolation that what afflicts you is not politically engineered, but an individual fate. When the therapeutic ideology triumphs—feminism loses.

Alas, it has proved very seductive. The therapeutic ideology infiltrated feminism through the issue of incest. It hijacked the issue from under feminism's nose. It pretended to feminism by hijacking feminist language.

Combining that language with mental health credo, it offered to survivors something it called *empowerment.* All women needed was the *courage* to cede their power to experts. The language promised *liberation*; spoke of the *struggle.* By the early 1990s, you no longer distinguish what survivors were calling the survivor movement from what everyone else was calling the recovery movement. And all of this in the name of feminism.

Speaking out—lopped free from all political foundation—was bankrupt. No more than confession. It was now said to be a "stage" in healing.

But who would dare challenge such things? To speak out on this is to seem to be making rude noises on an intensive-care ward. Who among us is brutal enough to speak against healing?

We have been re-silenced.

Fathers and stepfathers continue to rape children. Children pay a high price for that. Their mothers pay a high price for that. The cost-benefit analysis of incest remains the same. The fact of incest, the incidence of incest—routine, banal, nonexotic incest—is the sexualization of children in everyday reality: the expression of rage at women by wounding their children, in everyday reality. Pictures in the media of children sexualized are signifiers of the licensed act. Images of women dressed as children, of children made up and photographed as little women, are signifiers, a warning of license.

As long as the act itself remains uncensured, and the aggressors remain publicly unchallenged as a collective force, by a collective force as long as feminist analysis and energy is submerged in and overridden by mental health doctrine, images of the sexualization of children are (to use the old incest cliché) the "tip of the iceberg."

The iceberg remains the socially tolerated act of child-rape by fathers.

Commodifying Bodies

Aisha Parveen was knocked unconscious and kidnapped on her way to school as a fourteen-year-old in northwest Pakistan. She woke up in the far southeastern region of her country in a brothel. For years, Parveen has been beaten, tortured, and raped by the man who captured her and his clients; yet she is considered guilty for her own misfortune by virtue of being a fallen woman. At age twenty, she was rescued by, and married for love, a man hired to do some work for the brothel owner who got to know her. Both Parveen and her husband took great risks; both of their families of origin are now disgraced and will not offer them safe shelter. Put on trial for adultery, for which she could have been put to death, the international outcry after the publication of her story led to her release and the subsequent arrest of the brothel owner who abused her. At this writing the Pakistani government has provided her with twenty-four-hour protection (Kristoff 2006a and 2006b). The story of Aisha Parveen is, unfortunately, a common story for poor women and children around the globe. The primary difference is that most of these stories never make the international news; thus, the endings are typically not so hopeful. Pawns in the increasingly burgeoning sex industry, they are not only the "products" in a lucrative trade but are also at the center of a bitter debate that involves the moral and legal dimensions of commodifying bodies.

As we have demonstrated throughout this book, controversy seems to lie at the heart of gender issues. There is now both legal and public acknowledgment that sexual harassment, rape, domestic violence, and child abuse are social problems, even as certain aspects of their definitions and the claims of victims continue to be debated. The controversy around the commodification of bodies in sex work and pornography is emblematic of a much deeper definitional schism that anchors most of the contested areas of sex and gender relations in society. There is still a deep theoretical division over what constitutes sexual oppression and sexual liberation. Seidman refers to such issues as "boundary disputes" and links the contestation over their meanings to competing understandings of marriage, family, work, and the private and public spheres (2003, 96). The complex moral and legal components involved are further complicated by the reality that these boundary disputes have fractured societies internally and created tensions internationally.

In this section, we conceptualize pornography, prostitution, and trafficking in persons as social problems. We problematize the commodification of bodies, given the extent to which the contemporary contexts of economic exchange are generally exploitative and situated within systems of gender inequality. We articulate the competing political frames of discourse about these issues, highlighting those that posit a relationship between these phenomena and gendered violence within and among various societies and cultures. It is interesting to note, however, that compared to other hot-button sexual issues in the United States such as gay marriage, date rape, and even pornography, there is a "striking absence of discussion about prostitution in public debate" (Stetson 2004, 245).

Pornography and Violence

Prior to the emergence of the "sexual revolution" of the 1960s, advocacy against pornography was primarily the preserve of a small contingent of religious conservatives, given that pornography was neither as mainstream nor available as it is today. Contemporary feminism emerged simultaneously with the sexual revolution, and some scholars suggest that the real revolution was in the changed sexual attitudes and practices of women, not men (Ehrenreich, Hess, and Jacobs 1986). Historians of the pornography debate note that activists in the contemporary feminist movement initially embraced the use of pornography as a tool for the sexual liberation of women. In the late 1970s, the dual threats of changing sexual mores and feminist politics were central themes in the crystallization of the New Religious Right in the United States, which made pornography a central issue in the quest for a return to traditional morality. Ironically, it is during the same period that pornography became the subject of radical feminist critique. Kappeler (1986) suggests that the sexual-liberation movement, particularly in the form of pornography, actually produced more mechanisms to oppress women than to liberate them. Much of the liberal feminist mainstream supported the rights of women and men to produce and consume pornography. The debate intensified throughout the 1980s and 1990s, particularly with the proliferation of materials and access to them via the Internet. Pornography is still a hotly contested issue in feminist discourse and in the "culture wars" over sexuality and violence in the mass media.

There is no definitive research that finds pornography to be a direct cause of gender violence. The imperfect methodologies and conflicting results of pornography research contribute to the lack of resolution of the debate. The only conclusion that one can make from reviewing the research is that neither propornography nor antipornography camps can stake legitimacy claims based on the findings of experts. Predictably, the debate has been rooted more deeply in ideological and theoretical discourse than in the empirical realm. The failure of social science to provide empirical proof of pornography's harm has also led to a general stagnation in the legal realm: prohibition of child pornography reflects a widespread cultural consensus and is legally upheld, while the lack of either cultural consensus or definitive evidence of harm maintains a situational and arbitrary system of dealing with pornographic depictions of adults. Linz and colleagues (1995) suggest, however, that there are frequent discrepancies between court interpretations and the empirical reality of public *values*, particularly in the case of violent materials. Their research in Tennessee suggests that although obscenity laws have historically been used to condemn sexual explicitness rather than sexual violence, it is the latter that a substantial constituency finds unacceptable.

Prostitution and Trafficking as Gendered Violence

Prostitution involves the sale of sex acts for money (Seidman 2003). Invariably touted as an ancient institution, its persistence is frequently used to justify its existence. The seemingly insatiable demand for commercial sex, fueled increasingly by globalization and facilitated by the ease of consumption through the Internet and tourism, has enabled feminist researchers and activists to build a strong case to situate prostitution within exploitative and violent contexts. That a significant amount of prostitution is contracted without the free consent of the women (and sometimes men) who provide sexual "service" contributes to the problematic nature of the industry.

Denise Brennan's observation about sex workers in the Dominican Republic tourism industry captures the complexity of the situation for most of them: they "are at once independent and dependent, resourceful and exploited. They are local agents caught in a web of global economic relations" (2002, 156). Women in sex work may be anchored to their local communities or become mobile in the global service economy —either by choice or by coercion and conscription. It is clear that demand for sexual services, although substantial, is not the only driver of the sex industry. Many women migrate to sex work in the face of extreme poverty and growing economic disparities in their countries of origin (Augustin 2002; Corrin 2005; Kligman and Limoncelli 2005). Given women's responsibility for the well-being of their families, the migration market is "a highly gendered affair" (Outshoorn 2005, 143).

Recent research on the experiences of prostitutes illustrates the precarious nature of the phenomenon and the risks they endure. Women continue to constitute the majority of prostitutes and sex workers. Whatever the conditions of their work, street prostitutes or brothel workers, legal or illegal, they are frequently the victims of a wide range of violent abuse. Prostitutes are also more likely than other women to be assaulted with weapons (Farley 2004). Most studies suggest that at least half, and probably more than three-quarters, of prostitutes are sexually assaulted by clients. Race, ethnicity, and class are factors that make sex workers even more vulnerable, although legalization advocates do not often address this problem. Length of time in prostitution and extreme poverty are predictors of even greater violence (Farley 2004, 1095).

Sanders (2004) finds that female street prostitutes face both public and private risks. The public risks include harassment and violence from clients and other predatory men, police, and the general public. In her research among street prostitutes in Birmingham, England, she also found that women were subject to harassment and violence from street protesters against prostitution in their neighborhoods. Sanders suggests that prostitutes experience a great deal of private trauma related to their stigmatization and marginalization as sex workers (2004, 1705). In the contemporary climate, street prostitutes face increasing danger as they are pushed into unfamiliar territories as a result of punitive policing and zoning ordinances. Prostitutes depend on geographical space to make money, and the spaces in which they work are all the more hazardous if they are unable to control them (Sanders 2004).

Farley's (2004) review of violence against prostitutes in areas where prostitution has been decriminalized or legalized suggests that women working in these localities have not been protected from harm. This is true despite the fact that protecting sex workers and their clients from violence and disease is the primary rhetorical logic for legalization. For example, sex workers in Germany and New Zealand, where prostitution is legal, did not feel any safer than a sample of prostitutes in Washington, D.C. The overwhelming majority of women in countries with legal prostitution regimes are still routinely victimized.

Male sex workers, although a minority, also experience violence and violation—especially those who are younger and more vulnerable. As with women, the greater hazards seem to be related to the type of work, although no men are immune from abuse. Male prostitutes, like their female counterparts, encounter rape and sexual assault, although the most common form of abuse for men appears to be homophobic and heterosexist verbal abuse (Scott et al. 2005). Leichtentritt and Arad suggest that a high percentage of male prostitutes come from dysfunctional homes and enter the work after being thrown out or running away (2005, 485). Their research among young male street prostitutes in Tel Aviv found that, for their informants, prostitution was perceived to be the only available work option, based on financial and housing needs, their experience of sexual abuse as children, and their subsequent ability to construct acceptable perspectives on sex work (Leichtentritt and Arad 2005, 496).

Perhaps the most attention, in both the political realm and the mass media over the past decade, has been focused on sex tourism and trafficking. It is estimated that the value of the market for trafficking of women and girls for sexual exploitation is over $7 billion per year (Corrin 2005). The concept of trafficking refers to

> recruitment, transportation, transfer, harbouring or receipt of persons, by means of the threat or use of force or other forms of coercion, of abduction, of fraud, of deception, of the abuse of power or of a position of vulnerability or of the giving or receiving of payments or benefits to achieve the consent of a person having control over another person, for the purpose of exploitation. Exploitation shall include, at a minimum, the exploitation of the prostitution of others or other forms of sexual exploitation, forced labour or services, slavery or practices similar to slavery, servitude or the removal of organs. (United Nations 2000)

Although many people consider trafficking in women to be a "subset of the broader category of prostitution" (Kligman and Limoncelli 2005, 120), it clearly involves other forms of forced labor and includes the abuse of men and boys.

Sex work, and indeed sex tourism, in many parts of the world was fueled and organized during the first wave of globalization in the late nineteenth and twentieth centuries (Kligman and Limoncelli 2005, 118), with a large demand-push from militarization. It has increased for the same structural reasons in the first years of the twenty-first century (Corrin 2005; Tambiah 2005). Initially, women were trafficked to service military men of their own ethnic and or national heritage; proscriptions against interethnic sex have declined in recent years (Kligman and Limoncelli 2005). In fact, both military and nonmilitary men, especially from the West, are courted by companies and governments marketing the lure of sex with "exotic" women. The socialization of military personnel for violence also raises the risk of abuse and death for sex workers in militarized environments (Tambiah 2005).

Erez and Laster (2000) document how the Internet is used to commodify and trade Filipino women as mail-order brides for Australian men. The marketing of male erotic fantasies on these websites deploys "exotic" stereotypes to construct a representation of perfect, and forever grateful, partners. The sixfold overrepresentation of these women as victims of homicides, however, suggests a less-than-idyllic reality for them once they are sold (Erez and Laster 2000, 6).

For the countries in which sex tourism is prominent, it is increasingly conceptualized as a form of economic development (Hearn and Parkin 2001). This is the case in many Asian countries, where the United Nations estimates that over one million children alone are held in conditions of slavery (Klain 1999; Kristof 2006a). Since the collapse of the Soviet Union, the poorest Eastern European countries have become supplier states of sex workers for the wealthier European countries. Prior to 1989, these countries had comparatively little income inequality and high rates of government spending on the social well-being of citizens. Since these countries have reorganized as market economies, the economic disparities within already gendered systems have become comparable to those in other developed countries and a devastating reality for women. The gap between the wealthy and poor there, as in the United States, has only increased in times of economic growth (Corrin 2005; Kligman and Limoncelli 2005). Since data show that 70 percent of the world's poor are women (Corrin 2005), it is no surprise that so many migrate or find themselves deceptively trafficked into the violent world of street tricks and brothels with promises of marriage or legitimate work.

Perspectives on Commodification

Arguments against pornography and prostitution originate from within two primary constituencies: religious conservatives and abolitionist feminists. There are distinct differences in definition and rationale, however, across these two groups. Equating pornography and prostitution with violence is not a core aspect of religious conservatives' analysis; the major problems articulated for this group are the construction of sex as recreational rather than procreational and the nonmarital and frequent nonheterosexual liaisons that are conducted or portrayed. For example, Cottle and colleagues (1989) found that religious conservatives view pornography as a threat to the moral development of children, traditional family values, and the moral fabric of society.

The antipornography feminist stance posits that pornography is a form of sexual discrimination and, as such, that it contributes to the violation of women's rights (Cottle et al. 1989). The major focus of this perspective is on the exploitative, degrading, and frequently racist nature of pornography, as differentiated from erotica—material that depicts consensual sex or explicit sexual imagery that does not objectify the subject, whether male or female. The distinction between pornography and erotica for these advocates is clear: depictions of dominant-submissive sex, coerced sex, or images that dehumanize subjects are pornographic.

A strong antipornography contingent has emerged among profeminist men who accept the major premises of the antipornography feminist critique but who expand the notions of harm and victimization to include men. Stoltenberg, for example, suggests through his use of the following analogy that aggressive pornography is a mechanism for maintaining systemic inequality: pornography is to male supremacy as segregation is to white supremacy (1989, 454). Pornography imprisons the sexual experience of men *and* women, a condition that is denied by those who would define pornography as a central manifestation of sexual liberation.

There are a variety of perspectives that advocate preserving the current cultural and legal norms that govern the production and use of pornography and legalizing, or at least decriminalizing, prostitution. Articulated through classic liberal prescriptions for freedom of self-expression and political autonomy, sexual libertarianism was initially framed by participants in social movements for sexual liberalization and liberation in the 1960s and 1970s. Sex, from this perspective, is defined as beneficial and joyous; moreover, sexual expression in a variety of forms is connected to personal health, self-fulfillment, and social progress, a legitimate and culturally acceptable form of sexual expression (Seidman 1992). Within the discourses of liberal and libertarian analysis, prostitution is conceptualized as "sex work," an occupational choice—and in some cases a viable option for poor women—that should be protected by laws and workers'-rights initiatives. Moreover, as active agents, women should have the capacity to determine how they will use their bodies.

Research suggests that many liberal feminists are personally opposed to pornography and prostitution but view the resurgence of sexual repression and the potential for widespread censorship to be potentially more problematic for society than the effects of pornography or sex work that is properly regulated to protect the rights and health of women. The liberal feminist stance would preserve the legal status quo, while attempting to subvert the power of pornography and the lure of prostitution and sex tourism through progressive gender socialization and the promotion of egalitarian sexual relationships among men and women in daily life.

By and large, the persistence of the legal definition of pornography as a form of speech, and the guarantee of free speech provided under the First Amendment to the U.S. Constitution, has set the stage for a legal stalemate between abolitionists and their opponents in the pornography debate. It seems that few U.S. citizens other than the most radical conservatives are prepared to challenge the slippery slope of free-speech guarantees, even those who express a personal distaste for pornography. In regard to prostitution, the demands for legalization of sex work are generally made with the good intentions of providing legal protection and workers' rights to those involved in commercial sex trades.

Independent of liberal political perspectives, some feminists argue that antipornography feminism has incorrectly portrayed pornography (and we extend this analysis to prostitution) as the cause of gender violence rather than a symptom of misogyny and institutionalized sexism (Segal 1990; Small 1985). By defining the commodification of women in pornography and prostitution as the cause of gender violence, these feminists mute critiques of the larger political and economic conditions that contribute to gender violence; moreover, the predominantly male perpetrators of gender violence are provided with a cultural scapegoat that diminishes their personal responsibility for their actions as producers and consumers of pornography and prostitution.

Levy (1993) believes the deep wedge that the pornography debate has driven into the feminist community is the manifestation of distinctly different stances toward justice articulated in abolitionist and libertarian perspectives. We might also extend this analysis to the debate over whether prostitution is just another form of work that deserves legal protection or is a particularly exploitative situation that is exacerbated by its links to overt physical and emotional violence. Using Gilligan's (1982) typology of adversarial and situational moralities, Levy suggests that the inability of feminists to reach consensus has less to do with attitudes toward censorship than with perceptions of justice. The liberal stance is consistent with the typically male moral-ethical system of determining justice through balancing the proposed regulation against the rights of individuals. In the case of pornography, the liberal opponents of pornography legislation see the issue as a "choice between absolute free speech and censorship" (Levy 1993, 17). For abolitionist feminists, these issues are not either/or propositions but are embedded in complex situations in which the potential for harm should outweigh the preservation of a decidedly sexist legal system in which purportedly neutral justice is often skewed toward protecting the privilege of men. The theoretical logic of the abolitionist stance is thus more consistent with the typically female "ethic of care" that Gilligan delineates in her work: "While an ethic of justice proceeds from the premise of equality—that everyone should be treated the same, an ethic of care rests on the premise of non-violence—that no one should be hurt" (1982, 174).

In either case, feminists do agree that despite the many legal gains of the past fifty years, the status of women in political and economic systems across the world is precarious at best. Women are still the majority of the world's poor, underrepresented demographically and substantively in legislative bodies and courts, and deprived of the rights to good health, literacy, and self-determination in so many corners of the world. Eradicating these conditions within which the commodification of women occurs requires a transnational sea change in the political will of men and women. If we situate the debates around pornography, prostitution, and trafficking within the global context that features the absence of substantive justice, connections to violence and violation become clear.

Contributions to This Section

The articles in this section's compendium reflect the various social constructions of pornography, prostitution, and trafficking. The authors explore the complexity of these issues in relation to race, gender, economic issues, and political ideologies in both historical and contemporary contexts.

In "Pornography, Civil Rights, and Speech," Catharine MacKinnon presents the primary theoretical argument of antipornography feminists. She makes the case for prohibition of pornography using the notion of harm and the symbolic use of pornography to silence women.

The pornographic treatment of African American women under slavery is theorized to be antecedent to the construction of contemporary pornographic images, according to Patricia Hill Collins in "Pornography and Black Women's Bodies." Beyond the historical use of Black women as sexual objects by white men, Collins suggests that the animalistic portrayal of Black women in much contemporary pornography is emblematic of the stratification among women in Western societies, and particularly of the subordinate status of African American women.

In "Pornography and the Alienation of Male Sexuality," Harry Brod argues that pornography has a detrimental effect on male sexuality. He asserts that although patriarchy clearly operates to the advantage of men over women, one of its contradictions as an oppressive system is that it also disadvantages the group it privileges. Brod frames his analysis using an approach that emphasizes the significance of men's applying a feminist analysis to their own experiences.

Anastasia M. Hudgins critiques current U.S. policy initiatives on trafficking in "Problematizing the Discourse: Sex Trafficking and Ethnography." Drawing on interviews conducted among female sex workers, she explicates the structural conditions that lead women to brothel work as a viable, if not desirable, form of labor.

Jane Anthony's essay "Prostitution as Choice" is a first-person narrative of someone who, through personal experience, came to problematize prostitution. She critiques the argument that most women who work as prostitutes can be understood as exercising choice.

SUGGESTIONS FOR FURTHER READING

Kathleen Barry, *The Prostitution of Sexuality* (New York: New York University Press, 1995).

Gail Dynes, Robert Jensen, and Ann Russo (eds.), *Pornography: The Production and Consumption of Inequality* (New York: Routledge, 1998).

Kemala Kempadoo (ed.), *Trafficking and Prostitution Reconsidered* (Boulder, CO: Paradigm, 2005).

Michael Kimmel (ed.), *Men Confront Pornography* (New York: Crown, 1990).

Eva J. Klain, *Prostitution of Children and Child-Sex Tourism: An Analysis of Domestic and International Responses* (Alexandria, VA: National Center for Missing and Exploited Children, 1999).

Joyce Outshoorn, *The Politics of Prostitution: Women's Movements, Democratic States and the Globalisation of Sex Commerce* (Cambridge: Cambridge University Press, 2004).

Steven Seidman, *The Social Construction of Sexuality* (New York: Norton, 2003).

Nadine Strossen, *Defending Pornography: Free Speech, Sex, and the Fight for Women's Rights* (New York: Scribner, 1995).

Philadelphia Story
September 1987

Kathleen O'Toole

Another set of bones in an attic, more
elaborate details of shackles and torture,
numbered female body parts, what
the neighbors saw and did not hear.

See the grainy photographs of victims.
Hear the shock in commentators' voices
repeating, one more time . . . The leering's in
the language, the lingering, live at 11:00.

Obligatory cries of outrage greet
each new scenario's atrocity revealed.
It's equal opportunity for mass murderers
this month, in one city. Yet the double digit

dead, these statistics, happen to be sisters.
My sisters the carrion here, as greedy vultures
Circle—newspapier mâché with camera eyes—
under blood red, white and blue skies. Odd

glory in the city of filia, the repository
of constitutional pride, where you'll hear
no cry to stake the heart of this vampire.
Not while publicists' dollars stack up

around women's bodies. Seeing our own
likeness distorted, traded like soiled currency,
we circle the ring, attraction and spectator
both, trapped in this cynical circus.

Chapter Twenty-four

Pornography, Civil Rights, and Speech

Catharine MacKinnon

There is a belief that this is a society in which women and men are basically equals. Room for marginal corrections is conceded, flaws are known to exist, attempts are made to correct what are conceived as occasional lapses from the basic condition of sex equality. Sex discrimination law has concentrated most of its focus on these occasional lapses. It is difficult to overestimate the extent to which this belief in equality is an article of faith for most people, including most women, who wish to live in self-respect in an internal universe, even (perhaps especially) if not in the world. It is also partly an expression of natural law thinking: if we are inalienably equal, we can't "really" be degraded.

This is a world in which it is worth trying. In this world of presumptive equality, people make money based on their training or abilities or diligence or qualifications. They are employed and advanced on the basis of merit. In this world of just deserts, if someone is abused, it is thought to violate the basic rules of the community. If it doesn't, victims are seen to have done something they could have chosen to do differently, by exercise of will or better judgment. Maybe such people have placed themselves in a situation of vulnerability to physical abuse. Maybe they have done something provocative. Or maybe they were just unusually unlucky. In such a world, if such a person has an experience, there are words for it. When they speak and say it, they are listened to. If they write about it, they will be published. If certain experiences are never spoken about, if certain people or issues are seldom heard from, it is supposed that silence has been chosen. The law, including much of the law of sex discrimination and the First Amendment, operates largely within the realm of these beliefs.

Feminism is the discovery that women do not live in this world, that the person occupying this realm is a man, so much more a man if he is white and wealthy. This world of potential credibility, authority, security, and just rewards, recognition of one's identity and capacity, is a world that some people do inhabit as a condition of birth, with variations among them. It is not a basic condition accorded humanity in this society, but a prerogative of status, a privilege, among other things, of gender.

I call this a discovery because it has not been an assumption. Feminism is the first theory, the first practice, the first movement, to take seriously the situation of all women

From *Harvard Civil Rights–Civil Liberties Law Review* 20, no. 1 (1985): 1-17. Reprinted by permission.

from the point of view of all women, both on our situation and on social life as a whole. The discovery has therefore been made that the implicit social content of humanism, as well as the standpoint from which legal method has been designed and injuries have been defined, has not been women's standpoint. Defining feminism in a way that connects epistemology with power as the politics of women's point of view, this discovery can be summed up by saying that women live in another world: specifically, a world of *not* equality, a world of inequality.

Looking at the world from this point of view, a whole shadow world of previously invisible silent abuse has been discerned. Rape, battery, sexual harassment, forced prostitution, and the sexual abuse of children emerge as common and systematic. We find that rape happens to women in all contexts, from the family, including rape of girls and babies, to students and women in the workplace, on the streets, at home, in their own bedrooms by men they do not know and by men they do know, by men they are married to, men they have had a social conversation with, and, least often, men they have never seen before. Overwhelmingly, rape is something that men do or attempt to do to women (44 percent of American women according to a recent study) at some point in our lives. Sexual harassment of women by men is common in workplaces and educational institutions. Based on reports in one study of the federal workforce, up to 85 percent of women will experience it, many in physical forms. Between a quarter and a third of women are battered in their homes by men. Thirty-eight percent of little girls are sexually molested inside or outside the family. Until women listened to women, this world of sexual abuse was *not spoken* of. It was the unspeakable. What I am saying is, if you are the tree falling in the epistemological forest, your demise doesn't make a sound if no one is listening. Women did not "report" these events, and overwhelmingly do not today, because no one is listening, because no one believes us. This silence does not mean nothing happened, and it does not mean consent. It is the silence of women of which Adrienne Rich has written, "Do not confuse it with any kind of absence."

Believing women who say we are sexually violated has been a radical departure, both methodologically and legally. The extent and nature of rape, marital rape, and sexual harassment itself, were discovered in this way. Domestic battery as a syndrome, almost a habit, was discovered through refusing to believe that when a woman is assaulted by a man to whom she is connected, that it is not an assault. The sexual abuse of children was uncovered, Freud notwithstanding, by believing that children were not making up all this sexual abuse. Now what is striking is that when each discovery is made, and somehow made real in the world, the response has been: it happens to men too. If women are hurt, men are hurt. If women are raped, men are raped. If women are sexually harassed, men are sexually harassed. If women are battered, men are battered. Symmetry must be reasserted. Neutrality must be reclaimed. Equality must be reestablished.

The only areas where the available evidence supports this, where anything like what happens to women also happens to men, involve children—little boys are sexually abused—and prison. The liberty of prisoners is restricted, their freedom restrained, their humanity systematically diminished, their bodies and emotions confined, defined, and regulated. If paid at all, they are paid starvation wages. They can be tortured at will, and it is passed off as discipline or as means to a just end. They become compliant. They can be raped at will, at any moment, and nothing will be done about it. When they scream, nobody hears. To be a prisoner means to be defined as a member of a group for whom the rules of what can be done to you, of what is seen as abuse of you, are reduced as part of the definition of your status. To be a woman is that kind of definition and has that kind of meaning.

Men *are* damaged by sexism. (By men I mean the status of masculinity that is accorded to males on the basis of their biology but is not itself biological.) But whatever the damage of sexism to men, the condition of being a man is not defined as subordinate to women by force. Looking at the facts of the abuses of women all at once, you see that a woman is socially defined as a person who, whether or not she is or has been, can be treated in these ways by men at any time, and little, if anything, will be done about it. This is what it means when feminists say that maleness is a form of power and femaleness is a form of powerlessness.

In this context, all of this "men too" stuff means that people don't really believe that the things I have just said are true, though there really is little question about their empirical accuracy. The data are extremely simple, like women's pay figure of fifty-nine cents on the dollar. People don't really seem to believe that either. Yet there is no question of its empirical validity. This is the workplace story: what women do is seen as not worth much, or what is not worth much is seen as something for women to do. *Women* are seen as not worth much, is the thing. Now why are these basic realities of the subordination of women to men, for example, that only 7.8 percent of women have never been sexually assaulted, not effectively believed, not perceived as real in the face of all this evidence? Why don't *women* believe our own experiences? In the face of all this evidence, especially of systematic sexual abuse—subjection to violence with impunity is one extreme expression, although not the only expression, of a degraded status—the view that basically the sexes are equal in this society remains unchallenged and unchanged. The day I got this was the day I understood its real message, its real coherence: *This is equality for us.*

I could describe this, but I couldn't explain it until I started studying a lot of pornography. In pornography, there it is, in one place, all of the abuses that women had to struggle so long even to begin to articulate, all the *unspeakable* abuse: the rape, the battery, the sexual harassment, the prostitution, and the sexual abuse of children. Only in the pornography it is called something else: sex, sex, sex, sex, and sex, respectively. Pornography sexualizes rape, battery, sexual harassment, prostitution, and child sexual abuse; it thereby celebrates, promotes, authorizes, and legitimizes them. More generally, it eroticizes the dominance and submission that is the dynamic common to them all. It makes hierarchy sexy and calls that "the truth about sex" or just a mirror of reality. Through this process pornography constructs what a woman is as what men want from sex. This is what the pornography means.

Pornography constructs what a woman is in terms of its view of what men want sexually, such that acts of rape, battery, sexual harassment, prostitution, and sexual abuse of children become acts of sexual equality. Pornography's world of equality is a harmonious and balanced place. Men and women are perfectly complementary and perfectly bipolar. Women's desire to be fucked by men is equal to men's desire to fuck women. All the ways men love to take and violate women, women love to be taken and violated. The women who most love this are most men's equals, the most liberated; the most participatory child is the most grown-up, the most equal to an adult. Their consent merely expresses or ratifies these preexisting facts.

The content of pornography is one thing. There, women substantively desire dispossession and cruelty. We desperately want to be bound, battered, tortured, humiliated, and killed. Or, to be fair to the soft core, merely taken and used. This is erotic to the male point of view. Subjection itself, with self-determination ecstatically relinquished, is the content of women's sexual desire and desirability. Women are there to be violated and possessed, men to violate and possess us, either on screen or by camera or pen on behalf of the consumer. On a simple descriptive level, the inequality of hierarchy, of which gender is the primary one, seems necessary for sexual arousal to work. Other added inequalities identify various pornographic genres or sub-themes, although they are always added through gender: age, disability, homosexuality, animals, objects, race (including anti-Semitism), and so on. Gender is never irrelevant.

What pornography *does* goes beyond its content: it eroticizes hierarchy, it sexualizes inequality. It makes dominance and submission into sex. Inequality is its central dynamic; the illusion of freedom coming together with the reality of force is central to its working. Perhaps because this is a bourgeois culture, the victim must look free, appear to be freely acting. Choice is how she got there. Willing is what she is when she is being equal. It seems equally important that then and there she actually be forced and that forcing be communicated on some level, even if only through still photos of her in postures of receptivity and access, available for penetration. Pornography in this view is a form of forced sex, a practice of sexual politics, an institution of gender inequality.

From this perspective, pornography is neither harmless fantasy nor a corrupt and confused misrepresentation of an otherwise natural and healthy sexual situation. It institutionalizes the sexuality of male supremacy, fusing the erotization of dominance and submission with the social construction of male and female. To the extent that gender is sexual, pornography is part of constituting the meaning of that sexuality. Men treat women as who they see women as being. Pornography constructs who that is. Men's power over women means that the way men see women defines who women can be. Pornography is that way. Pornography is not imagery in some relation to a reality elsewhere constructed. It is not a distortion, reflection, projection, expression, fantasy, representation, or symbol either. It is a sexual reality.

In Andrea Dworkin's definitive work, *Pornography: Men Possessing Women*, sexuality itself is a social construct gendered to the ground. Male dominance here is not an artificial overlay upon an underlying inalterable substratum of uncorrupted essential sexual being. Dworkin presents a sexual theory of gender inequality of which pornography is a constitutive practice. The way pornography produces its meaning constructs and defines men and women as such. Gender has no basis in anything other than the social reality its hegemony constructs. Gender is what gender means. The process that gives sexuality its male supremacist meaning is the same process through which gender inequality becomes socially real.

In this approach, the experience of the (overwhelmingly) male audiences who consume pornography is therefore not fantasy or simulation or catharsis but sexual reality, the level of reality on which sex itself largely operates. Understanding this dimension of the problem does not require noticing that pornography models are real women to whom, in most cases, something real is being done; nor does it even require inquiring into the systematic infliction of pornography and its sexuality upon women, although it helps. What matters is the way in which the pornography itself provides what those who consume it want. Pornography *participates* in its audience's eroticism through creating an accessible sexual object, the possession and consumption of which *is* male sexuality, as socially constructed; to be consumed and possessed as which, *is* female sexuality, as socially constructed; pornography is a process that constructs it that way.

The object world is constructed according to how it looks with respect to its possible uses. Pornography defines women by how we look according to how we can be sexually used. Pornography codes how to look at women, so you know what you can do with one when you see one. Gender is an assignment made visually, both originally and in everyday life. A sex object is defined on the basis of its looks, in terms of its usability for sexual pleasure, such that both the looking—the quality of the gaze, including its point of view—and the definition according to use become eroticized as part of the sex itself. This is what the feminist concept "sex object" means. In this sense, sex in life is no less mediated than it is in art. Men have sex with their image of a woman. It is not that life and art imitate each other; in this sexuality, they *are* each other.

To give a set of rough epistemological translations, to defend pornography as consistent with the equality of the sexes is to defend the subordination of women to men as sexual equality. What in the pornographic view is love and romance looks a great deal like hatred and torture to the feminist. Pleasure and eroticism become violation. Desire appears as lust for dominance and submission. The vulnerability of women's projected sexual availability, that acting we are allowed (that is, asking to be acted upon), is victimization. Play conforms to scripted roles. Fantasy expresses ideology, is not exempt from it. Admiration of natural physical beauty becomes objectification. Harmlessness becomes harm. Pornography is a harm of male supremacy made difficult to see because of its pervasiveness, potency, and principally, because of its success in making the world a pornographic place. Specifically, its harm cannot be discerned, and will not be addressed, if viewed and approached neutrally, because it *is* so much of "what is." In other words, to the extent pornography succeeds in constructing social reality, it becomes invisible as harm. If we live in a world that pornography creates through the power of men in a male-dominated situation, the issue is not what the harm of pornography is, but how that harm is to become visible.

Obscenity law provides a very different analysis and conception of the problem of pornography. In 1973 the legal definition of obscenity became that which the average person, applying contemporary community standards, would find that, taken as a whole, appeals to the prurient interest; that which depicts or describes in a patently offensive way—you feel like you're a cop reading someone's *Miranda* rights—sexual conduct specifically defined by the applicable state law; and that which, taken as a whole, lacks serious literary, artistic, political, or scientific value. Feminism doubts whether the average person gender-neutral exists; has more questions about the content and process of defining what community standards are than it does about deviations from them; wonders why prurience counts but powerlessness does not and why sensibilities are better protected from offense than women are from exploitation; defines sexuality, and thus its violation and expropriation, more broadly than does state law; and questions why a body of law that has not in practice been able to tell rape from intercourse should, without further guidance, be entrusted with telling pornography from anything less. Taking the work "as a whole" ignores that which the victims of pornography have long known: legitimate settings diminish the perception of injury done to those whose trivialization and objectification they contextualize. Besides, and this is a heavy one, if a woman is subjected, why should it matter that the work has other value? Maybe what redeems the work's value is what enhances its injury to women, not to mention that existing standards of literature, art, science, and politics, examined in a feminist light, are remarkably consonant with pornography's mode, meaning, and message. And finally—first and foremost, actually—although the subject of these materials is overwhelmingly women, their contents almost entirely made up of women's bodies, our invisibility has been such, our equation as a sex *with* sex has been such, that the law of obscenity has never even considered pornography a women's issue.

Obscenity, in this light, is a moral idea, an idea about judgments of good and bad. Pornography, by contrast, is a political practice, a practice of power and powerlessness. Obscenity is ideational and abstract; pornography is concrete and substantive. The two concepts represent two entirely different things. Nudity, excess of candor, arousal or excitement, prurient appeal, illegality of the acts depicted, and unnaturalness or perversion are all qualities that bother obscenity law when sex is depicted or portrayed. Sex forced on real women so that it can be sold at a profit and forced on other real women; women's bodies trussed and maimed and raped and made into things to be hurt and obtained and accessed, and this presented as the nature of women in a way that is acted on and acted out, over and over; the coercion that is visible and the coercion that has become invisible—this and more bothers feminists about pornography. Obscenity as such probably does little harm. Pornography is integral to attitudes and behaviors of violence and discrimination that define the treatment and status of half the population.

At the request of the city of Minneapolis, Andrea Dworkin and I conceived and designed a local human rights ordinance in accordance with our approach to the pornography issue. We define pornography as a practice of sex discrimination, a violation of women's civil rights, the opposite of sexual equality. Its point is to hold those who profit from and benefit from that injury accountable to those who are injured. It means that women's injury—our damage, our pain, our enforced inferiority—should outweigh their pleasure and their profits, or sex equality is meaningless.

We define pornography as the graphic sexually explicit subordination of women through pictures or words that also includes women dehumanized as sexual objects, things, or commodities; enjoying pain or humiliation or rape; being tied up, cut up, mutilated, bruised, or physically hurt; in postures of sexual submission or servility or display; reduced to body parts, penetrated by objects or animals, or presented in scenarios of degradation, injury, torture; shown as filthy or inferior; bleeding, bruised, or hurt in a context that makes these conditions sexual. Erotica, defined by distinction as not this, might be sexually explicit materials premised on equality. We also provide that the use of men, children, or transsexuals in the place of women is pornography. The definition is substantive in that it is sex-specific, but it covers everyone in a sex-specific way, so is gender neutral in overall design. . . .

This law aspires to guarantee women's rights consistent with the First Amendment by making visible a conflict of rights between the equality guaranteed to all women and what, in some legal sense, is now the freedom of the pornographers to make and sell, and their consumers to have access to, the materials this ordinance defines. Judicial resolution of this conflict, if the judges do for women what they have done for others, is likely to entail a balancing of the rights of women arguing that our lives and opportunities, including our freedom of speech and action, are constrained by—and in many cases flatly precluded by, in and through—pornography, against those who argue that the pornography is harmless, or harmful only in part but not in the whole of the definition; or that it is more important to preserve the pornography than it is to prevent or remedy whatever harm it does.

In predicting how a court would balance these interests, it is important to understand that this ordinance cannot now be said to be either conclusively legal or illegal under existing law or precedent, although I think the weight of authority is on our side. This ordinance enunciates a new form of the previously recognized governmental interest in sex equality. Many laws make sex equality a governmental interest. Our law is designed to further the equality of the sexes, to help make sex equality real. Pornography is a practice of discrimination on the basis of sex, on one level because of its role in creating and maintaining sex as a basis for discrimination. It harms many women one at a time and helps keep all women in an inferior status by defining our subordination as our sexuality and equating that with our gender. It is also sex discrimination because its victims, including men, are selected for victimization on the basis of their gender. But for their sex, they would not be so treated.

The harm of pornography, broadly speaking, is the harm of the civil inequality of the sexes made invisible as harm because it has become accepted as the sex difference. Consider this analogy with race: if you see Black people as different, there is no harm to segregation; it is merely a recognition of that difference. To neutral principles, separate but equal was equal. The injury of racial separation to Blacks arises "solely because [they] choose to put that construction upon it." Epistemologically translated: how you see it is not the way it is. Similarly, if you see women as just different, even or especially if you don't know that you do, subordination will not look like subordination at all, much less like harm. It will merely look like an appropriate recognition of the sex difference.

Pornography does treat the sexes differently, so the case for sex differentiation can be made here. But men as a group do not tend to be (although some individuals may be) treated the way women are treated in pornography. As a social group, men are not hurt by pornography the way women as a social group are. Their social status is not defined as *less* by it. So the major argument does not turn on mistaken differentiation, particularly since the treatment of women according to pornography's dictates makes it all too often accurate. The salient quality of a distinction between the top and the bottom in a hierarchy is not difference, although top is certainly different from bottom; it is power. So the major argument is: subordinate but equal is not equal.

Particularly since this is a new legal theory, a new law, and "new" facts, perhaps the situation of women it newly exposes deserves to be considered on its own terms. Why do the problems of 53 percent of the population have to look like somebody else's problems before they can be recognized as existing? Then, too, they can't be addressed if they do look like other people's problems, about which something might have to be done if something is done about these. This construction of the situation truly deserves inquiry. Limiting the justification for this law to the situation of the sexes would serve to limit the precedential value of a favorable ruling.

Its particularity to one side, the *approach* to the injury is supported by a whole array of prior decisions that have justified exceptions to First Amendment guarantees when something that matters is seen to be directly at stake. What unites many cases in which speech interests are raised and implicated but not, on balance, protected, is harm, harm that counts. In some existing exceptions, the definitions are much more open-ended than ours. In some the sanctions are more severe, or potentially more so. For instance, ours is a civil law; most others, although not all, are criminal. Almost no other exceptions show as many people directly affected. Evidence of harm in other cases tends to be vastly less concrete and more conjectural, which is not to say that there is necessarily less of it. None of the previous cases addresses a problem of this scope or magnitude —for instance, an eight-billion-dollar-a-year industry. Nor do other cases address an abuse that has such widespread legitimacy. Courts have seen harm in other cases. The question is, will they see it here, especially given that the pornographers got there first. I will confine myself here to arguing from cases on harm to people, on the supposition that, the pornographers notwithstanding, women are not flags. . . .

To reach the magnitude of this problem on the scale it exists, our law makes trafficking in pornography—production, sale, exhibition, or distribution—actionable. Under the obscenity rubric, much legal and psychological scholarship has centered on a search for the elusive link between harm and pornography defined as obscenity. Although they were not very clear on what obscenity was, it was its harm they truly could not find. They looked high and low—in the mind of the male consumer, in society or in its "moral fabric," in correlations between variations in levels of antisocial acts and liberalization of obscenity laws. The only harm they have found has been harm to "the social interest in order and morality." Until recently, no one looked very persistently for harm to women, particularly harm to women through men. The rather obvious fact that the sexes *relate* has been overlooked in the inquiry into the male consumer and his mind. The pornography doesn't just drop out of the sky, go into his head, and stop there. Specifically, men rape, batter, prostitute, molest, and sexually harass women. Under conditions of inequality, they also hire, fire, promote, and grade women, decide how much or whether we are worth paying and for what, define and approve and disapprove of women in ways that count, that determine our lives.

If women are not just born to be sexually used, the fact that we are seen and treated as though that is what we are born for becomes something in need of explanation. If we see that men relate to women in a pattern of who they see women as being, and that forms a pattern of inequality, it becomes important to ask where that view came from or, minimally, how it is perpetuated or escalated. Asking this requires asking different questions about pornography than the ones obscenity law made salient.

Now I'm going to talk about causality in its narrowest sense. Recent experimental research on pornography shows that the materials covered by our definition cause measurable harm to women through increasing men's attitudes and behaviors of discrimination in both violent and nonviolent forms. Exposure to some of the pornography in our definition increases the immediately subsequent willingness of normal men to aggress against women under laboratory conditions. It makes normal men more closely resemble convicted rapists attitudinally, although as a group they don't look all that different from them to start with. Exposure to pornography also significantly increases attitudinal measures known to correlate with rape and self-reports of aggressive acts, measures such as hostility toward women, propensity to rape, condoning rape, and predicting that one would rape or force sex on a woman if one knew one would not get caught. On this latter measure, by the way, about a third of all men predict that they would rape, and half would force sex on a woman.

As to that pornography covered by our definition in which normal research subjects seldom perceive violence, long-term exposure still makes them see women as more worthless, trivial, nonhuman, and objectlike, that is, the way those who are discriminated against are seen by those who discriminate against them. Crucially, all pornography by our definition acts dynamically over time to diminish the consumer's ability to distinguish sex from violence. The materials work behaviorally to diminish the capacity of men (but not women) to perceive that an account of a rape is an account of a rape. The so-called sex-only materials, those in which subjects perceive no force, also increase perceptions that a rape victim is worthless and decrease the perception that she was harmed. The overall direction of current research suggests that the more expressly violent materials accomplish with less exposure what the less overtly violent —that is, the so-called sex-only materials—accomplish over the longer term. Women are rendered fit for use and targeted for abuse. The only thing that the research cannot document is which individual women will be next on the list. (This cannot be documented experimentally because of ethics constraints on the researchers—constraints that do not operate in life.) Although the targeting is systematic on the basis of sex, for individuals it is random. They are selected on a roulette basis. Pornography can no longer be said to be just a mirror. It does not just reflect the world or some people's perceptions. It *moves* them. It increases attitudes that are lived out, circumscribing the status of half the population.

What the experimental data predict will happen actually does happen in women's real lives. You know, it's fairly frustrating that women have known for some time that these things do happen. As Ed Donnerstein, an experimental researcher in this area, often puts it, "We just quantify the obvious." It is women, primarily, to whom the research results have been the obvious, because we live them. But not until a laboratory study predicts that these things *will* happen do people begin to believe you when you say they *did* happen to you. There is no—*not any*—inconsistency between the patterns the laboratory studies predict and the data on what actually happens to real women.

Show me an abuse of women in society, I'll show it to you made sex in the pornography. If you want to know who is being hurt in this society, go see what is being done and to whom in pornography and then go look for them other places in the world. You will find them being hurt in just that way. We did in our hearings.

In our hearings women spoke, to my knowledge for the first time in history in public, about the damage pornography does to them. We learned that pornography is used to break women, to train women to sexual submission, to season women, to terrorize women, and to silence their dissent. It is this that has previously been termed "having no effect." The way men inflict on women the sex they experience through the pornography gives women no choice about seeing the pornography or doing the sex. Asked if anyone ever tried to inflict unwanted sex acts on them that they knew came from pornography, 10 percent of women in a recent random study said yes. Among married women, 24 percent said yes. That is a lot of women. A lot more don't know. Some of those who do testified in Minneapolis. One wife said of her ex-husband, "He would read from the pornography like a textbook, like a journal. In fact when he asked me to be bound, when he finally convinced me to do it, he read in the magazine how to tie the knots." Another woman said of her boyfriend, "[H]e went to this party, saw pornography, got an erection, got me . . . to inflict his erection on. . . . There is a direct causal relationship there." One woman, who said her husband had rape and bondage magazines all over the house, discovered two suitcases full of Barbie dolls with rope tied on their arms and legs and with tape across their mouths. Now think about the silence of women. She said, "He used to tie me up and he tried those things on me." A therapist in private practice reported:

> Presently or recently I have worked with clients who have been sodomized by broom handles, forced to have sex with over 20 dogs in the back seat of their car, tied up and then electrocuted on their genitals. These are children, [all] in the ages of 14 to 18, all of whom [have been directly affected by pornography,] [e]ither where the perpetrator has read the manuals and manuscripts at night and used these as recipe books by day or had the pornography present at the time of the sexual violence.[1]

One woman, testifying that all the women in a group of exprostitutes were brought into prostitution as children through pornography, characterized their collective experience: "[I]n my experience there was not one situation where a client was not using pornography while he was using me or that he had not just watched pornography or that it was verbally referred to and directed me to pornography." "Men," she continued, "witness the abuse of women in pornography constantly and if they can't engage in that behavior with their wives, girl friends or children, they force a whore to do it."

Men also testified about how pornography hurts them. One young gay man who had seen *Playboy* and *Penthouse* as a child said of such heterosexual pornography: "It was one of the places I learned about sex and it showed me that sex was violence. What I saw there was a specific relationship between men and women. . . . [T]he woman was to be used, objectified, humiliated and hurt; the man was in a superior position, a position to be violent. In pornography I learned that what it meant to be sexual with a man or to be loved by a man was to accept his violence." For this reason, when he was battered by his first lover, which he described as "one of the most profoundly destructive experiences of my life," he accepted it.

Pornography also hurts men's capacity to relate to women. One young man spoke about this in a way that connects pornography—not the prohibition on pornography—with fascism. He spoke of his struggle to repudiate the thrill of dominance, of his difficulty finding connection with a woman to whom he is close. He said: "My point is that if women in a society filled by pornography must be wary for their physical selves, a man, even a man of good intentions, must be wary for his mind. . . . I do not want to be a mechanical, goose-stepping follower of the Playboy bunny, because that is what I think it is. . . . [T]hese are the experiments a master race perpetuates on those slated for extinction." The woman he lives with is Jewish. There was a very brutal rape near their house. She was afraid; she tried to joke. It didn't work. "She was still afraid. And just as a well-meaning German was afraid in 1933, I am also very much afraid."

Pornography stimulates and reinforces, it does not cathect or mirror, the connection between one-sided freely available sexual access to women and masculine sexual excitement and sexual satisfaction. The catharsis hypothesis is fantasy. The fantasy theory is fantasy. Reality is: pornography conditions male orgasm to female subordination. It tells men what sex means, what a real woman is, and codes them together in a way that is behaviorally reinforcing. This is a real five-dollar sentence, but I'm going to say it anyway: pornography is a set of hermeneutical equivalences that work on the epistemological level. Substantively, pornography defines the meaning of what a woman is seen to be by connecting access to her sexuality with masculinity through orgasm. What pornography means *is* what it does.

So far, opposition to our ordinance centers on the trafficking provision. This means not only that it is difficult to comprehend a group injury in a liberal culture—that what it *means* to be a woman is defined by this and that it is an injury for all women, even if not for all women equally. It is not only that the pornography has got to be accessible, which is the bottom line of virtually every objection to this law. It is also that power, as I said, is when you say something, it is taken for reality. If you talk about rape, it will be agreed that rape is awful. But rape is a conclusion. If a victim describes the facts of a rape, maybe she was asking for it or enjoyed it or at least consented to it, or the man might have thought she did, or maybe she had had sex before. It is now agreed that there is something wrong with sexual harassment. But describe what happened to you, and it may be trivial or personal or paranoid, or maybe you should have worn a bra that day. People are against discrimination. But describe the situation of a real woman, and they are not so sure she wasn't just unqualified. In law, all these disjunctions between women's perspective on our injuries and the standards we have to meet go under dignified legal rubrics like burden of proof, credibility, defenses, elements of the crime, and so on. These standards all contain a definition of what a woman is in terms of what sex is and the low value placed on us through it. They reduce injuries done to us to authentic expressions of who we are. Our silence is written all over them. So is the pornography.

We have as yet encountered comparatively little objection to the coercion, force, or assault provisions of our ordinance. I think that's partly because the people who make and approve laws may not yet see what they do as that. They *know* they use the pornography as we have described it in this law, and our law defines that, the reality of pornography, as a harm to women. If they suspect that they might on occasion engage in or benefit from coercion or force or assault, they may think that the victims won't be able to prove it—and they're right. Women who charge men with sexual abuse are not believed. The pornographic view of them is: they want it; they all want it. When women bring charges of sexual assault, motives such as venality or sexual repression must be invented, because we cannot really have been hurt. Under the trafficking provision, women's lack of credibility cannot be relied upon to negate the harm. There's no woman's story to destroy, no credibility-based decision on what happened. The hearings establish the harm. The definition sets the standard. The grounds of reality definition are authoritatively shifted. Pornography is bigotry, *period*. We are now—the world pornography has decisively defined—having to meet the burden of proving, once and for all, for all of the rape and torture and battery, all of the sexual harassment, all of the child sexual abuse, all of the forced prostitution, all of it that the pornography is part of and that is part of the pornography, that the harm *does happen* and that when it happens it looks like this. Which may be why all this evidence never seems to be enough.

It is worth considering what evidence has been enough when other harms involving other purported speech interests have been allowed to be legislated against. By comparison to our trafficking provision, analytically similar restrictions have been allowed under the First Amendment, with a legislative basis far less massive, detailed, concrete, and conclusive. Our statutory language is more ordinary, objective, and precise and covers a harm far narrower than the legislative record substantiates. Under *Miller,* obscenity was allowed to be made criminal in the name of the "danger of offending the sensibilities of unwilling recipients or exposure to juveniles." Under our law, we have direct evidence of harm, not just a conjectural danger, that unwilling women in considerable numbers are not simply offended in their sensibilities, but are violated in their persons and restricted in their options. Obscenity law also suggests that the applicable standard for legal adequacy in measuring such connections may not be statistical certainty. The Supreme Court has said that it is not their job to resolve empirical uncertainties that underlie state obscenity legislation. Rather, it is for them to determine whether a legislature could reasonably have determined that a connection might exist between the prohibited material and harm of a kind in which the state has legitimate interest. Equality should be such an area. The Supreme Court recently recognized that prevention of sexual exploitation and abuse of children is, in their words, "a governmental objective of surpassing importance." This might also be the case for sexual exploitation and abuse of women, although I think a civil remedy is initially more appropriate to the goal of empowering adult women than a criminal prohibition would be.

Other rubrics provide further support for the argument that this law is narrowly tailored to further a legitimate governmental interest consistent with the goals underlying the First Amendment. Exceptions to the First Amendment—you may have gathered from this—exist. The reason they exist is that the harm done by some speech outweighs its expressive value, if any. In our law a legislature recognizes that pornography, as defined and made actionable, undermines sex equality. One can say—and I have—

that pornography is a causal factor in violations of women; one can also say that women will be violated so long as pornography exists; but one can also say simply that pornography violates women. Perhaps this is what the woman had in mind who testified at our hearings that for her the question is not just whether pornography causes violent acts to be perpetrated against some women. "Porn is already a violent act against women. It is our mothers, our daughters, our sisters, and our wives that are for sale for pocket change at the newsstands in this country." *Chaplinsky v. New Hampshire* recognized the ability to restrict as "fighting words" speech which, "by [its] very utterance inflicts injury." Perhaps the only reason that pornography has not been "fighting words"—in the sense of words that by their utterance tend to incite immediate breach of the peace—is that women have seldom fought back, yet.

Some concerns that are close to those of this ordinance underlie group libel laws, although the differences are equally important. In group libel law, as Justice Frankfurter's opinion in *Beauharnais* illustrates, it has been understood that an individual's treatment and alternatives in life may depend as much on the reputation of the group to which that person belongs as on their own merit. Not even a partial analogy can be made to group libel doctrine without examining the point made by Justice Brandeis and recently underlined by Larry Tribe: would more speech, rather than less, remedy the harm? In the end, the answer may be yes, but not under the abstract system of free speech, which only enhances the power of the pornographers while doing nothing substantively to guarantee the free speech of women, for which we need civil equality. The situation in which women presently find ourselves with respect to the pornography is one in which more *pornography* is inconsistent with rectifying or even counterbalancing its damage through speech, because so long as the pornography exists in the way it does there *will not be more speech by women.* Pornography strips and devastates women of credibility, from our accounts of sexual assault to our everyday reality of sexual subordination. We are stripped of authority and reduced and devalidated and silenced. Silenced here means that the purposes of the First Amendment, premised upon conditions presumed and promoted by protecting free speech, do not pertain to women because they are not our conditions. Consider them: individual self-fulfillment—how does pornography promote our individual self-fulfillment? How does sexual inequality even permit it? Even if she can form words, who listens to a woman with a penis in her mouth? Facilitating consensus—to the extent pornography does so, it does so one-sided by silencing protest over the injustice of sexual subordination. Participation in civic life—central to Professor Meiklejohn's theory—how does pornography enhance women's participation in civic life? Anyone who cannot walk down the street or even lie down in her own bed without keeping her eyes cast down and her body clenched against assault is unlikely to have much to say about the issues of the day, still less will she become Tolstoy. Facilitating change—*this law* facilitates the change that existing First Amendment theory had been used to throttle. Any system of freedom of expression that does not address a problem where the free speech of men silences the free speech of women, a real conflict between speech interests as well as between people, is not serious about securing freedom of expression in this country.

For those of you who still think pornography is only an idea, consider the possibility that obscenity law got one thing right. Pornography is more actlike than thought-

like. The fact that pornography, in a feminist view, furthers the idea of the sexual inferiority of women, which is a political idea, doesn't make the pornography itself into a
political idea. One can express the idea a practice embodies. That does not make the
practice into an idea. Segregation expresses the idea of the inferiority of one group to
another on the basis of race. That does not make segregation an idea. A sign that says
"Whites Only" is only words. Is it therefore protected by the First Amendment? Is it not
an act, a practice, of segregation because what it means is inseparable from what it
does? *Law* is only words.

The issue here is whether the fact that words and pictures are the central link in the
cycle of abuse will immunize that entire cycle, about which we cannot do anything
without doing something about the pornography. As Justice Stewart said in *Ginsburg*,
"When expression occurs in a setting where the capacity to make a choice is absent,
government regulation of that expression may coexist with and *even implement* First
Amendment guarantees." I would even go so far as to say that the pattern of evidence
we have closely approaches Justice Douglas's requirement that "freedom of expression
can be suppressed if, and to the extent that, it is so closely brigaded with illegal action
as to be an inseparable part of it." Those of you who have been trying to separate the
acts from the speech—that's an act, that's an act, there's a law against that act, regulate
that act, don't touch the speech—notice here that the illegality of the acts involved
doesn't mean that the speech that is "brigaded with" it *cannot* be regulated. This is when
it *can* be.

I take one of two penultimate points from Andrea Dworkin, who has often said that
pornography is not speech for women, it is the silence of women. Remember the mouth
taped, the woman gagged, "Smile, I can get a lot of money for that." The smile is not her
expression, it is her silence. It is not her expression not because it didn't happen, but
because it *did* happen. The screams of the women in pornography are silence, like the
screams of Kitty Genovese, whose plight was misinterpreted by some onlookers as a
lovers' quarrel. The flat expressionless voice of the woman in the New Bedford gang
rape, testifying, is silence. She was raped as men cheered and watched, as they do in and
with the pornography. When women resist and men say, "Like this, you stupid bitch,
here is how to do it" and shove their faces into the pornography, this "truth of sex" is the
silence of women. When they say, "If you love me, you'll try," the enjoyment we fake, the
enjoyment we learn is silence. Women who submit because there is more dignity in it
than in losing the fight over and over live in silence. Having to sleep with your publisher or director to get access to what men call speech is silence. Being humiliated on
the basis of your appearance, whether by approval or disapproval, because you have to
look a certain way for a certain job, whether you get the job or not, is silence. The
absence of a woman's voice, everywhere that it cannot be heard, is silence. And anyone
who thinks that what women say in pornography is women's speech—the "Fuck me,
do it to me, harder," all of that—has never heard the sound of a woman's voice.

The most basic assumption underlying First Amendment adjudication is that,
socially, speech is free. The First Amendment says Congress shall not abridge the
freedom of speech. Free speech, get it, *exists*. Those who wrote the First Amendment
had speech—they wrote the Constitution. *Their* problem was to keep it free from the
only power that realistically threatened it: the federal government. They designed the

First Amendment to prevent government from constraining that which, if unconstrained by government, was free, meaning *accessible to them*. At the same time, we can't tell much about the intent of the framers with regard to the question of women's speech, because I don't think we crossed their minds. It is consistent with this analysis that their posture toward freedom of speech tends to presuppose that whole segments of the population are not systematically silenced socially, prior to government action. If everyone's power were equal to theirs, if this were a nonhierarchical society, that might make sense. But the place of pornography in the inequality of the sexes makes the assumption of equal power untrue.

This is a hard question. It involves risks. Classically, opposition to censorship has involved keeping government off the backs of people. Our law is about getting some people off the backs of other people. The risks that it will be misused have to be measured against the risks of the status quo. Women will never have that dignity, security, compensation that is the promise of equality so long as the pornography exists as it does now. The situation of women suggests that the urgent issue of our freedom of speech is not primarily the avoidance of state intervention as such, but getting affirmative access to speech for those to whom it has been denied.

NOTE

1. *Public Hearings on Ordinances to Add Pornography as Discrimination against Women,* Committee on Governmental Operations, City Council, Minneapolis, MN, December 12–13, 1983.

Chapter Twenty-five

Pornography and Black Women's Bodies

Patricia Hill Collins

> *For centuries the black woman has served as the primary pornographic "outlet" for white men in Europe and America. We need only think of the black women used as breeders, raped for the pleasure and profit of their owners. We need only think of the license the "master" of the slave women enjoyed. But, most telling of all, we need only study the old slave societies of the South to note the sadistic treatment—at the hands of white "gentlemen"—of "beautiful young quadroons and octoroons" who became increasingly (and were deliberately bred to become) indistinguishable from white women, and were the more highly prized as slave mistresses because of this. (Walker 1981, 42)*

Alice Walker's description of the rape of enslaved African women for the "pleasure and profit of their owners" encapsulates several elements of contemporary pornography. First, Black women were used as sex objects for the pleasure of white men. This objectification of African-American women parallels the portrayal of women in pornography as sex objects whose sexuality is available for men (McNall 1983). Exploiting Black women as breeders objectified them as less than human because only animals can be bred against their will. In contemporary pornography women are objectified through being portrayed as pieces of meat, as sexual animals awaiting conquest. Second, African-American women were raped, a form of sexual violence. Violence is typically an implicit or explicit theme in pornography. Moreover, the rape of Black women linked sexuality and violence, another characteristic feature of pornography (Eisenstein 1983). Third, rape and other forms of sexual violence act to strip victims of their will to resist and make them passive and submissive to the will of the rapist. Female passivity, the fact that women have things done to them, is a theme repeated over and over in contemporary pornography (McNall 1983). Fourth, the profitability of Black women's sexual exploitation for white "gentlemen" parallels pornography's financially

From *Making Violence Sexy: Feminist Views on Pornography*, ed. D. E. H. Russell, Teacher's College Press, 1993, pp. 97–103. Reprinted by permission.

lucrative benefits for pornographers (Eisenstein 1983). Finally, the actual breeding of "quadroons and octoroons" not only reinforces the themes of Black women's passivity, objectification, and malleability to male control but reveals pornography's grounding in racism and sexism. The fates of both Black and white women were intertwined in this breeding process. The ideal African-American woman as a pornographic object was indistinguishable from white women and thus approximated the images of beauty, asexuality, and chastity forced on white women. But inside was a highly sexual whore, a "slave mistress" ready to cater to her owner's pleasure.[1]

Contemporary pornography consists of a series of icons or representations that focus the viewer's attention on the relationship between the portrayed individual and the general qualities ascribed to that class of individuals. Pornographic images are iconographic in that they represent realities in a manner determined by the historical position of the observers, their relationship to their own time, and to the history of the conventions which they employ (Gilman 1985). The treatment of Black women's bodies in nineteenth-century Europe and the United States may be the foundation upon which contemporary pornography as the representation of women's objectification, domination, and control is based. Icons about the sexuality of Black women's bodies emerged in these contexts. Moreover, as race/gender-specific representations, these icons have implications for the treatment of both African-American and white women in contemporary pornography.

I suggest that African-American women were not included in pornography as an afterthought, but instead, form a key pillar on which contemporary pornography itself rests. As Alice Walker points out, "the more ancient roots of modern pornography are to be found in the almost always pornographic treatment of black women who, from the moment they entered slavery . . . were subjected to rape as the 'logical' convergence of sex and violence. Conquest, in short" (1981, 42).

One key feature about the treatment of Black women in the nineteenth century was how their bodies were objects of display. In the antebellum American South white men did not have to look at pornographic pictures of women because they could become voyeurs of Black women on the auction block. A chilling example of this objectification of the Black female body is provided by the exhibition, in early nineteenth-century Europe, of Sarah Bartmann, the so-called Hottentot Venus. Her display formed one of the original icons for Black female sexuality. An African woman, Sarah Bartmann was often exhibited at fashionable parties in Paris, generally wearing little clothing, to provide entertainment. To her audience she represented deviant sexuality. At the time European audiences thought that Africans had deviant sexual practices and searched for physiological differences, such as enlarged penises and malformed female genitalia, as indications of this deviant sexuality. Sarah Bartmann's exhibition stimulated these racist and sexist beliefs. After her death in 1815, she was dissected. Her genitalia and buttocks remain on display in Paris (Gilman 1985).

Sander Gilman explains the impact that Sarah Bartmann's exhibition had on Victorian audiences:

> It is important to note that Sarah Bartmann was exhibited not to show her genitalia—but rather to present another anomaly which the European audience . . . found riveting. This

was the steatopygia, or protruding buttocks, the other physical characteristic of the Hottentot female which captured the eye of early European travelers. . . . The figure of Sarah Bartmann was reduced to her sexual parts. The audience which had paid to see her buttocks and had fantasized about the uniqueness of her genitalia when she was alive could, after death and dissection, examine both. (1985, 213)

In this passage Gilman unwittingly describes how Bartmann was used as a pornographic object similar to how women are represented in contemporary pornography. She was reduced to her sexual parts, and these parts came to represent a dominant icon applied to Black women throughout the nineteenth century. Moreover, the fact that Sarah Bartmann was both African and a woman underscores the importance of gender in maintaining notions of racial purity. In this case Bartmann symbolized Blacks as a "race." Thus the creation of the icon applied to Black women demonstrates that notions of gender, race, and sexuality were linked in overarching structures of political domination and economic exploitation.

The process illustrated by the pornographic treatment of the bodies of enslaved African women and of women like Sarah Bartmann has developed into a full-scale industry encompassing all women objectified differently by racial/ethnic category. Contemporary portrayals of Black women in pornography represent the continuation of the historical treatment of their actual bodies. African-American women are usually depicted in a situation of bondage and slavery, typically in a submissive posture, and often with two white men. As Bell observes, "this setting reminds us of all the trappings of slavery: chains, whips, neck braces, wrist clasps" (1987, 59). White women and women of color have different pornographic images applied to them. The image of Black women in pornography is almost consistently one featuring them breaking from chains. The image of Asian women in pornography is almost consistently one of being tortured (Bell 1987, 161).

The pornographic treatment of Black women's bodies challenges the prevailing feminist assumption that since pornography primarily affects white women, racism has been grafted onto pornography. African-American women's experiences suggest that Black women were not added into a preexisting pornography, but rather that pornography itself must be reconceptualized as an example of the interlocking nature of race, gender, and class oppression. At the heart of both racism and sexism are notions of biological determinism claiming that people of African descent and women possess immutable biological characteristics marking their inferiority to elite white women (Fausto-Sterling 1989; Gould 1981; Halpin 1989). In pornography these racist and sexist beliefs are sexualized. Moreover, for African-American women pornography has not been timeless and universal but was tied to Black women's experiences with the European colonization of Africa and with American slavery. Pornography emerged within a specific system of social class relationships.

This linking of views of the body, social constructions of race and gender, and conceptualizations of sexuality that inform Black women's treatment as pornographic objects promises to have significant implications for how we assess contemporary pornography. Moreover, examining how pornography has been central to the race, gender, and class oppression of African-American women offers new routes for understanding the dynamics of power as domination.

Investigating racial patterns in pornography offers one route for such an analysis. Black women have often claimed that images of white women's sexuality were intertwined with the controlling image of the sexually denigrated Black woman: "In the United States, the fear and fascination of female sexuality was projected onto black women; the passionless lady arose in symbiosis with the primitively sexual slave" (Hall 1983, 333). Comparable linkages exist in pornography (Gardner 1980). Alice Walker provides a fictional account of a Black man's growing awareness of the different ways that African-American and white women are objectified in pornography: "What he has refused to see—because to see it would reveal yet another area in which he is unable to protect or defend black women—is that where white women are depicted in pornography as 'objects,' black women are depicted as animals. Where white women are depicted as human bodies if not beings, black women are depicted as shit" (Walker 1981, 52). Walker's distinction between "objects" and "animals" is crucial in untangling gender, race, and class dynamics in pornography. Within the mind/body, culture/nature, male/female oppositional dichotomies in Western social thought, objects occupy an uncertain interim position. As objects white women become creations of culture—in this case, the mind of white men—using the materials of nature—in this case, uncontrolled female sexuality. In contrast, as animals Black women receive no such redeeming dose of culture and remain open to the type of exploitation visited on nature overall. Race becomes the distinguishing feature in determining the type of objectification women will encounter. Whiteness as symbolic of both civilization and culture is used to separate objects from animals.

The alleged superiority of men to women is not the only hierarchical relationship that has been linked to the putative superiority of the mind to the body. Certain "races" of people have been defined as being more bodylike, more animallike, and less godlike than others (Spelman 1982, 52). Race and gender oppression may both revolve around the same axis of disdain for the body; both portray the sexuality of subordinate groups as animalistic and therefore deviant. Biological notions of race and gender prevalent in the early nineteenth century which fostered the animalistic icon of Black female sexuality were joined by the appearance of a racist biology incorporating the concept of degeneracy (Foucault 1980). Africans and women were both perceived as embodied entities, and Blacks were seen as degenerate. Fear of and disdain for the body thus formed a key element in both sexist and racist thinking (Spelman 1982).

While the sexual and racial dimensions of being treated like an animal are important, the economic foundation underlying this treatment is critical. Animals can be economically exploited, worked, sold, killed, and consumed. As "mules," African-American women become susceptible to such treatment. The political economy of pornography also merits careful attention. Pornography is pivotal in mediating contradictions in changing societies (McNall 1983). It is no accident that racist biology, religious justifications for slavery and women's subordination, and other explanations for nineteenth-century racism and sexism arose during a period of profound political and economic change. Symbolic means of domination become particularly important in mediating contradictions in changing political economies. The exhibition of Sarah Bartmann and Black women on the auction block were not benign intellectual exercises—these practices defended real material and political interests. Current transformations in international capitalism require similar ideological justifications. Where does pornography fit in these current transformations? This question awaits a comprehensive Afrocentric feminist analysis.

Publicly exhibiting Black women may have been central to objectifying Black women as animals and to creating the icon of Black women as animals. Yi-Fu Tuan (1984) offers an innovative argument about similarities in efforts to control nature—especially plant life—the domestication of animals, and the domination of certain groups of humans. Tuan suggests that displaying humans alongside animals implies that such humans are more like monkeys and bears than they are like "normal" people. This same juxtaposition leads spectators to view the captive animals in a special way. Animals require definitions of being like humans, only more openly carnal and sexual, an aspect of animals that forms a major source of attraction for visitors to modern zoos. In discussing the popularity of monkeys in zoos, Tuan notes: "Some visitors are especially attracted by the easy sexual behavior of the monkeys. Voyeurism is forbidden except when applied to subhumans" (1984, 82). Tuan's analysis suggests that the public display of Sarah Bartmann and of the countless enslaved African women on the auction blocks of the antebellum American South—especially in proximity to animals—fostered their image as animalistic.

This linking of Black women and animals is evident in nineteenth-century scientific literature. The equation of women, Blacks, and animals is revealed in the following description of an African woman published in an 1878 anthropology text:

> She had a way of pouting her lips exactly like what we have observed in the orangutan. Her movements had something abrupt and fantastical about them, reminding one of those of the ape. Her ear was like that of many apes. . . . These are animal characters. I have never seen a human head more like an ape than that of this woman. (Halpin 1989, 287)

In a climate such as this, it is not surprising that one prominent European physician even stated that Black women's "animallike sexual appetite went so far as to lead black women to copulate with apes" (Gilman 1985, 212).

The treatment of all women in contemporary pornography has strong ties to the portrayal of Black women as animals. In pornography women become nonpeople and are often represented as the sum of their fragmented body parts. Scott McNall observes:

> This fragmentation of women relates to the predominance of rear-entry position photographs. . . . All of these kinds of photographs reduce the woman to her reproductive system, and, furthermore, make her open, willing, and available—not in control. . . . The other thing rear-entry position photographs tell us about women is that they are animals. They are animals because they are the same as dogs—bitches in heat who can't control themselves. (McNall 1983, 197–98)

This linking of animals and white women within pornography becomes feasible when grounded in the earlier denigration of Black women as animals.

Developing a comprehensive analysis of the race, gender, and class dynamics of pornography offers possibilities for change. Those Black feminist intellectuals investigating sexual politics imply that the situation is much more complicated than that advanced by some prominent white feminists (see, e.g., Dworkin 1981) in which "men oppress women" because they are men. Such approaches implicitly assume biologically deterministic views of sex, gender, and sexuality and offer few possibilities for change. In contrast, Afrocentric feminist analyses routinely provide for human agency and its corresponding empowerment and for the responsiveness of social structures to human action. In the short story "Coming Apart," Alice Walker describes one Black man's growing realization that his enjoyment of pornography, whether of white women as "objects" or Black women as "animals," degraded him:

> He begins to feel sick. For he realizes that he has bought some of the advertisements about women, black and white. And further, inevitably, he has bought the advertisements about himself. In pornography the black man is portrayed as being capable of fucking anything . . . even a piece of shit. He is defined solely by the size, readiness and unselectivity of his cock. (Walker 1981, 52)

Walker conceptualizes pornography as a race/gender system that entraps everyone. But by exploring an African-American man's struggle for a self-defined standpoint on pornography, Walker suggests that a changed consciousness is essential to social change. If a Black man can understand how pornography affects him, then other groups enmeshed in the same system are equally capable of similar shifts in consciousness and action.

NOTE

1. Offering a similar argument about the relationship between race and masculinity, Paul Hoch (1979) suggests that the ideal white man is a hero who upholds honor. But inside lurks a "Black beast" of violence and sexuality, traits that the white hero deflects onto men of color.

Chapter Twenty-six

Pornography and the Alienation of Male Sexuality

Harry Brod

This chapter is intended as a contribution to an ongoing discussion. It aims to augment, not refute or replace, what numerous commentators have said about pornography's role in the social construction of sexuality. I have several principal aims in this chapter. My primary focus is to examine pornography's model of male sexuality. Furthermore, in the discussion of pornography's role in the social construction of sexuality, I wish to place more emphasis than is common on the social construction of pornography. As I hope to show, these are related questions. One reason I focus on the image of male sexuality in pornography is that I believe this aspect of the topic has been relatively neglected. In making this my topic here, I do not mean to suggest that this is the most essential part of the picture. Indeed, I am clear it is not. It seems clear enough to me that the main focus of discussion about the effects of pornography is and should be the harmful effects of pornography on women, its principal victims. Yet, there is much of significance which needs to be said about pornography's representation, or perhaps I should more accurately say misrepresentation, of male sexuality. My focus shall be on what is usually conceived of as "normal" male sexuality, which for my purposes I take to be consensual, nonviolent heterosexuality, as these terms are conventionally understood. I am aware of analyses which argue that this statement assumes distinctions which are at least highly problematic, if not outright false, which argue that this "normal" sexuality is itself coercive, both as compulsory heterosexuality and as containing implicit or explicit coercion and violence. My purpose is not to take issue with these analyses, but simply to present an analysis of neglected aspects of the links between mainstream male sexuality and pornography. I would argue that the aspect of the relation between male sexuality and pornography usually discussed, pornography's incitement to greater extremes of violence against women, presupposes such a connection with the more accepted mainstream. Without such a link, pornography's messages would be rejected by, rather than assimilated into, male culture. My intention is to supply this usually missing link.

My analysis proceeds from both feminist and Marxist theory. These are often taken to be theories which speak from the point of view of the oppressed, in advocacy for their interests. That they indeed are, but they are also more than that. For each claims

From *Social Theory and Practice* 14, no. 3 (1988): 265–84. Reprinted by permission.

not simply to speak for the oppressed in a partisan way, but also to speak a truth about the social whole, a truth perhaps spoken in the name of the oppressed, but a truth objectively valid for the whole. That is to say, Marxism is a theory which analyzes the ruling class as well as the proletariat, and feminism is a theory which analyzes men as well as women. It is not simply that Marxism is concerned with class, and feminism with gender, both being united by common concerns having to do with power. Just as Marxism understands class as power, rather than simply understanding class differences as differences of income, lifestyle, or opportunities, so the distinctive contribution of feminism is its understanding of gender as power, rather than simply as sex role differentiation. Neither class nor gender should be reified into being understood as fixed entities, which then differentially distribute power and its rewards. Rather, they are categories continually constituted in ongoing contestations over power. The violence endemic to both systems cannot be understood as externalized manifestations of some natural inner biological or psychological drives existing prior to the social order, but must be seen as emerging in and from the relations of power which constitute social structures. Just as capitalist exploitation is caused not by capitalists' excess greed but rather by the structural imperatives under which capitalism functions, so men's violence is not the manifestation of some inner male essence, but rather evidence of the bitterness and depth of the struggles through which genders are forged.[1]

For my purposes here, to identify this as a socialist feminist analysis is not, in the first instance, to proclaim allegiance to any particular set of doctrinal propositions, though I am confident that those I subscribe to would be included in any roundup of the usual suspects, but rather to articulate a methodological commitment to make questions of power central to questions of gender, and to understand gendered power in relation to economic power, and as historically, materially structured.[2] If one can understand the most intimate aspects of the lives of the dominant group in these terms, areas which would usually be taken to be the farthest afield from where one might expect these categories to be applicable, then I believe one has gone a long way toward validating claims of the power of socialist feminist theory to comprehend the totality of our social world. This is my intention here. I consider the analysis of male sexuality I shall be presenting part of a wider socialist feminist analysis of patriarchal capitalist masculinity, an analysis I have begun to develop elsewhere.[3]

As shall be abundantly clear, I do not take a "sexual liberationist" perspective on pornography. I am aware that many individuals, particularly various sexual minorities, make this claim on pornography's behalf. I do not minimize or negate their personal experiences. In the context of our society's severe sexual repressiveness, pornography may indeed have a liberating function for certain individuals. But I do not believe an attitude of approval for pornography follows from this. Numerous drugs and devices which have greatly helped individual women have also been medical and social catastrophes—the one does not negate the other.

I shall be claiming that pornography has a negative impact on men's own sexuality. This is a claim that an aspect of an oppressive system, patriarchy, operates, at least in part, to the disadvantage of the group it privileges, men. This claim does not deny that the overall effect of the system is to operate in men's advantage, nor does it deny that the same aspect of the system under consideration, that is, male sexuality and pornography under patriarchy, might not also contribute to the expansion and maintenance of male power even as it also works to men's disadvantage. Indeed, I shall be arguing precisely for such complementarity. I am simply highlighting one of the "contradictions" in the system. My reasons for doing so are in the first instance simply analytic: to, as I said, bring to the fore relatively neglected aspects of the issue. Further, I also have political motivations for emphasizing this perspective. I view raising consciousness of the prices of male power as part of a strategy through which one could at least potentially mobilize men against pornography's destructive effects on both women and men.

It will aid the following discussion if I ask readers to call to mind a classic text in which it is argued that, among many other things, a system of domination also damages the dominant group, and prevents them from realizing their full humanity. The argument is that the dominant group is "alienated" in specific and identifiable ways. The text I have in mind is Marx's "Economic and Philosophic Manuscripts of 1844." Just as capitalists as well as workers are alienated under capitalism according to Marxist theory (in a certain restricted sense, even more so), so men, I shall argue, and in particular male modes of sexuality, are also alienated under patriarchy. In the interests of keeping this chapter a manageable length, I shall here assume rather than articulate a working familiarity with Marx's concept of alienation, the process whereby one becomes a stranger to oneself and one's own powers come to be powers over and against one. Since later in the chapter I make use of some of Marx's more economistic concepts, I should however simply note that I see more continuity than rupture between Marx's earlier, more philosophical writings and his later, more economic ones.[4] While much of this chapter presents an analysis of men's consciousness, I should make clear that while alienation may register in one's consciousness (as I argue it does), I follow Marx in viewing alienation not primarily as a psychological state dependent on the individual's sensibilities or consciousness but as a condition inevitably caused by living within a system of alienation. I should also note that I consider what follows an appropriation, not a systematic interpretation, of some of Marx's concepts.

Alienated pornographic male sexuality can be understood as having two dimensions, what I call the objectification of the body and the loss of subjectivity. I shall consider each in greater detail, describing various aspects of pornographic male sexuality under each heading in a way which I hope brings out how they may be conceptualized in Marx's terms. Rather than then redoing the analysis in Marx's terms, I shall then simply cite Marx briefly to indicate the contours of such a translation.

Objectification of the Body

In terms of both its manifest image of and its effects on male sexuality, that is, in both intrinsic and consequentialist terms, pornography restricts male sensuality in favor of a genital, performance-oriented male sexuality. Men become sexual acrobats endowed with oversized and overused organs which are, as the chapter title of a fine book on male sexuality describes, "The Fantasy Model of Sex: Two Feet Long, Hard as Steel, and Can Go All Night."[5] To speak noneuphemistically, using penile performance as an index of male strength and potency directly contradicts biological facts. There is no muscle tissue in the penis. Its erection when aroused results simply from increased blood flow to the area. All social mythology aside, the male erection is physiologically nothing more than localized high blood pressure. Yet this particular form of hypertension has attained mythic significance. Not only does this focusing of sexual attention on one organ increase male performance anxieties, but it also desensitizes other areas of the body from becoming what might otherwise be sources of pleasure. A colleague once told me that her favorite line in a lecture on male sexuality I used to give in a course I regularly taught was my declaration that the basic male sex organ is not the penis, but the skin.

The predominant image of women in pornography presents women as always sexually ready, willing, able, and eager. The necessary corollary to pornography's myth of female perpetual availability is its myth of male perpetual readiness. Just as the former fuels male misogyny when real-life women fail to perform to pornographic standards, so do men's failures to similarly perform fuel male insecurities. Furthermore, I would argue that this diminishes pleasure. Relating to one's body as a performance machine produces a split consciousness wherein part of one's attention is watching the machine, looking for flaws in its performance, even while one is supposedly immersed in the midst of sensual pleasure. This produces a self-distancing self-consciousness which mechanizes sex and reduces pleasure. (This is a problem perpetuated by numerous sexual self-help manuals, which treat sex as a matter of individual technique for fine-tuning the machine rather than as human interaction. I would add that men's sexual partners are also affected by this, as they can often intuit when they are being subjected to rote manipulation.)

Loss of Subjectivity

In the terms of discourse of what it understands to be "free" sex, pornographic sex comes "free" of the demands of emotional intimacy or commitment. It is commonly said as a generalization that women tend to connect sex with emotional intimacy more than men do. Without romantically blurring female sexuality into soft focus, if what is meant is how each gender consciously thinks or speaks of sex, I think this view is fair enough. But I find it takes what men say about sex, that it doesn't mean as much or the same thing to them, too much at face value. I would argue that men do feel similar needs for intimacy, but are trained to deny them, and are encouraged further to see physical affection and intimacy primarily if not exclusively in sexual terms. This leads to the familiar syndrome wherein, as one man put it:

> Although what most men want is physical affection, what they end up thinking they want is to be laid by a Playboy bunny.[6]

This puts a strain on male sexuality. Looking to sex to fulfill what are really nonsexual needs, men end up disappointed and frustrated. Sometimes they feel an unfilled void, and blame it on their or their partner's inadequate sexual performance. At other times they feel a discomfiting urgency or neediness to their sexuality, leading in some cases to what are increasingly recognized as sexual addiction disorders (therapists are here not talking about the traditional "perversions," but behaviors such as what is coming to be called a "Don Juan Syndrome," an obsessive pursuit of sexual "conquests"). A confession that sex is vastly overrated often lies beneath male sexual bravado. I would argue that sex seems overrated because men look to sex for the fulfillment of nonsexual emotional needs, a quest doomed to failure. Part of the reason for this failure is the priority of quantity over quality of sex which comes with sexuality's commodification. As human needs become subservient to market desires, the ground is laid for an increasing multiplication of desires to be exploited and filled by marketable commodities.[7]

For the most part the female in pornography is not one the man has yet to "conquer," but one already presented to him for the "taking." The female is primarily there as sex object, not sexual subject. Or, if she is not completely objectified, since men do want to be desired themselves, hers is at least a subjugated subjectivity. But one needs another independent subject, not an object or a captured subjectivity, if one either wants one's own prowess validated, or if one simply desires human interaction. Men functioning in the pornographic mode of male sexuality, in which men dominate women, are denied satisfaction of these human desires.[8] Denied recognition in the sexual interaction itself, they look to gain this recognition in wider social recognition of their "conquest."

To the pornographic mind, then, women become trophies awarded to the victor. For women to serve this purpose of achieving male social validation, a woman "conquered" by one must be a woman deemed desirable by others. Hence pornography both produces and reproduces uniform standards of female beauty. Male desires and tastes must be channeled into a single mode, with allowance for minor variations which obscure the fundamentally monolithic nature of the mold. Men's own subjectivity becomes masked to them, as historically and culturally specific and varying standards of beauty are made to appear natural and given. The ease with which men reach quick agreement on what makes a woman "attractive," evidenced in such things as the "1–10" rating scale of male banter and the reports of a computer program's success in predicting which of the contestants would be crowned "Miss America," demonstrates how deeply such standards have been internalized, and consequently the extent to which men are dominated by desires not authentically their own.

Lest anyone think that the analysis above is simply a philosopher's ruminations, too far removed from the actual experiences of most men, let me just offer one recent instantiation, from among many known to me, and even more, I am sure, I do not know. The following is from the *New York Times Magazine*'s "About Men" weekly column. In an article titled "Couch Dancing," the author describes his reactions to being taken to a place, a sort of cocktail bar, where women "clad only in the skimpiest of bikini underpants" would "dance" for a small group of men for a few minutes for about twenty-five or thirty dollars, men who "sat immobile, drinks in hand, glassy-eyed, tapping their feet to the disco music that throbbed through the room."

> Men are supposed to like this kind of thing, and there is a quite natural part of each of us that does. But there is another part of us—of me, at least—that is not grateful for the traditional male sexual programming, not proud of the results. By a certain age, most modern men have been so surfeited with images of unattainably beautiful women in preposterous contexts that we risk losing the capacity to respond to the ordinarily beautiful women we love in our bedrooms. There have been too many times when I have guiltily

resorted to impersonal fantasy because the genuine love I felt for a woman wasn't enough to convert feeling into performance. And in those sorry, secret moments, I have resented deeply my lifelong indoctrination into the esthetic of the centerfold.[9]

Alienation and Crisis

I believe that all of the above can be translated without great difficulty into a conceptual framework paralleling Marx's analysis of the alienation experienced by capitalists. The essential points are captured in two sentences from Marx's manuscripts:

1. *All* the physical and intellectual senses have been replaced by the simple alienation of *all* these senses; the sense of *having*.[10]
2. The wealthy man is at the same time one who *needs* a complex of human manifestations of life, and whose own self-realization exists as an inner necessity, a need.[11]

Both sentences speak to a loss of human interaction and self-realization. The first articulates how desires for conquest and control prevent input from the world. The second presents an alternative conception wherein wealth is measured by abilities for self-expression, rather than possession. Here Marx expresses his conceptualization of the state of alienation as a loss of sensuous fulfillment, poorly replaced by a pride of possession, and a lack of self-consciousness and hence actualization of one's own real desires and abilities. One could recast the preceding analysis of pornographic male sexuality through these categories. In Marx's own analysis, these are more properly conceived of as the results of alienation, rather than the process of alienation itself. This process is at its basis a process of inversion, a reversal of the subject-object relationship, in which one's active powers become estranged from one, and return to dominate one as an external force. It is this aspect which I believe is most useful in understanding the alienation of male sexuality of which pornography is part and parcel. How is it that men's power turns against them, so that pornography, in and by which men dominate women, comes to dominate men themselves?

To answer this question I shall find it useful to have recourse to two other concepts central to Marxism, the concept of "crisis" in the system and the concept of "imperialism."[12] Marx's conception of the economic crisis of capitalism is often misunderstood as a prophecy of a cataclysmic doomsday scenario for the death of capitalism. Under this interpretation, some look for a single event, perhaps like a stock market crash, to precipitate capitalism's demise. But such events are for Marx at most triggering events, particular crises, which can shake the system, if at all, only because of the far more important underlying structural general crisis of capitalism. This general crisis is increasingly capitalism's ordinary state, not an extraordinary occurrence. It is manifest in the ongoing fiscal crisis of the state as well as recurring crises of legitimacy, and results from basic contradictory tensions within capitalism. One way of expressing these tensions is to see them as a conflict between the classic laissez-faire capitalist market mode, wherein capitalists are free to run their own affairs as individuals, and the increasing inability of the capitalist class to run an increasingly complex system without centralized management. The result of this tension is that the state increasingly becomes a managerial committee for the capitalist class, and is increasingly called upon to perform functions previously left to individuals. As entrepreneurial and laissez-faire capitalism give way to corporate capitalism and the welfare state, the power of capitalism becomes increasingly depersonalized, increasingly reft from the hands of individual capitalists and collectivized, so that capitalists themselves come more and more under the domination of impersonal market forces no longer under their direct control.

To move now to the relevance of the above, there is currently a good deal of talk about a perceived crisis of masculinity, in which men are said to be confused by contradictory imperatives given them in the wake of the women's movement. Though the male ego feels uniquely beleaguered today, in fact such talk regularly surfaces in our culture—the 1890s in the United States, for example, was another period in which the air was full of a "crisis of masculinity" caused by the rise of the "New Woman" and other factors.[13] Now, I wish to put forward the hypothesis that these particular "crises" of masculinity are but surface manifestations of a much deeper and broader phenomenon which I call the "general crisis of patriarchy," paralleling Marx's general crisis of capitalism. Taking a very broad view, this crisis results from the increasing depersonalization of patriarchal power which occurs with the development of patriarchy from its precapitalist phase, where power really was often directly exercised by individual patriarchs, to its late capitalist phase where men collectively exercise power over women, but are themselves as individuals increasingly under the domination of those same patriarchal powers.[14] I would stress that the sense of there being a "crisis" of masculinity arises not from the decrease or increase in patriarchal power as such. Patriarchal imperatives for men to retain power over women remain in force throughout. But there is a shift in the mode of that power's exercise, and the sense of crisis results from the simultaneous promulgation throughout society of two conflicting modes of patriarchal power, the earlier more personal form and the later more institutional form. The crisis results from the incompatibility of the two conflicting ideals of masculinity embraced by the different forms of patriarchy, the increasing conflicts between behavioral and attitudinal norms in the political/economic and the personal/familial spheres.

From Patriarchy to Fratriarchy

To engage for a moment in even broader speculation than that which I have so far permitted myself, I believe that much of the culture, law, and philosophy of the nineteenth century in particular can be reinterpreted as marking a decisive turn in this transition. I believe the passing of personal patriarchal power and its transformation into institutional patriarchal power in this period of the interrelated consolidation of corporate capitalism is evidenced in such phenomena as the rise of what one scholar has termed "judicial patriarchy," the new social regulation of masculinity through the courts and social welfare agencies, which through new support laws, poor laws, desertion laws and other changes transformed what were previously personal obligations into legal duties, as well as in the "Death of God" phenomenon and its aftermath.[15] That is to say, I believe the loss of the personal exercise of patriarchal power and its diffusion through the institutions of society is strongly implicated in the death of God the Father and the secularization of culture in the nineteenth century, as well as the modern and post-modern problem of grounding authority and values.

I would like to tentatively and preliminarily propose a new concept to reflect this shift in the nature of patriarchy caused by the deindividualization and collectivization of male power. Rather than speak simply of advanced capitalist patriarchy, the rule of the *fathers,* I suggest we speak of fratriarchy, the rule of the *brothers.* For the moment, I propose this concept more as a metaphor than as a sharply defined analytical tool, much as the concept of patriarchy was used when first popularized. I believe this concept better captures what I would argue is one of the key issues in conceptualizing contemporary masculinities, the disjunction between the facts of public male power and the feelings of individual male powerlessness. As opposed to the patriarch, who embodied many levels and kinds of authority in his single person, the brothers stand in uneasy relationships with each other, engaged in sibling rivalry while trying to keep the power of the family of man as a whole intact. I note that one of the consequences of the shift from patriarchy to fratriarchy is that some people become nostalgic for the authority of the benevolent patriarch, who if he was doing his job right at least pre-vented one of the great dangers of fratriarchy, fratricide, the brothers' killing each other. Furthermore, fratriarchy is an intragenerational concept, whereas patriarchy is inter-generational. Patriarchy, as a father-to-son transmission of authority, more directly inculcates traditional historically grounded authority, whereas the dimension of tem-poral continuity is rendered more problematic in fratriarchy's brother-to-brother rela-tionships. I believe this helps capture the problematic nature of modern historical con-sciousness as it emerged from the nineteenth century, what I would argue is the most significant single philosophical theme of that century. If taken in Freudian directions, the concept of fratriarchy also speaks to the brothers' collusion to repress awareness of the violence which lies at the foundations of society.

To return to the present discussion, the debate over whether pornography reflects men's power or powerlessness, as taken up recently by Alan Soble in his book *Pornog-raphy: Marxism, Feminism, and the Future of Sexuality,* can be resolved if one makes a distinction such as I have proposed between personal and institutional male power. Soble cites men's use of pornographic fantasy as compensation for their powerlessness in the real world to argue that "pornography is therefore not so much an expression of male power as it is an expression of their lack of power."[16] In contrast, I would argue that by differentiating levels of power one should more accurately say that pornography is both an expression of men's public power and an expression of their lack of personal power. The argument of this chapter is that pornography's image of male sexuality works to the detriment of men personally even as its image of female sexuality enhances the powers of patriarchy. It expresses the power of alienated sexuality, or, as one could equally well say, the alienated power of sexuality.

With this understanding, one can reconcile the two dominant but otherwise irrec-oncilable images of the straight male consumer of pornography: on the one hand the powerful rapist, using pornography to consummate his sexual violence, and on the other hand the shy recluse, using it to consummate his masturbatory fantasies. Both images have their degree of validity, and I believe it is a distinctive virtue of the analysis presented here that one can understand not only the merits of each depiction, but their interconnection.

Embodiment and Erotica

In the more reductionist and determinist strains of Marxism, pornography as ideology would be relegated to the superstructure of capitalism. I would like to suggest another conceptualization: that pornography is not part of patriarchal capitalism's superstructure, but part of its infrastructure. Its commodification of the body and interpersonal relationships paves the way for the ever more penetrating ingression of capitalist market relations into the deepest reaches of the individual's psychological makeup. The feminist slogan that "The Personal Is Political" emerges at a particular historical moment, and should be understood not simply as an imperative declaration that what has previously been seen solely as personal should now be viewed politically, but also as a response to the real increasing politicization of personal life.

This aspect can be illuminated through the Marxist concept of imperialism. The classical Marxist analysis of imperialism argues that it is primarily motivated by two factors: exploitation of natural resources and extension of the market. In this vein, pornography should be understood as imperialism of the body. The greater public proliferation of pornography, from the "soft-core" pornography of much commercial advertising to the greater availability of "hard-core" pornography, proclaims the greater colonization of the body by the market.[17] The increasing use of the male body as a sex symbol in contemporary culture is evidence of advanced capitalism's increasing use of new styles of masculinity to promote images of men as consumers as well as producers.[18] Today's debates over the "real" meaning of masculinity can be understood in large part as a struggle between those espousing the "new man" style of masculinity more suited to advanced corporate, consumerist patriarchal capitalism and those who wish to return to an idealized version of "traditional" masculinity suited to a more production-oriented, entrepreneurial patriarchal capitalism.[19]

In a more theoretical context, one can see that part of the reason the pornography debate has been so divisive, placing on different sides of the question people who usually find themselves allies, is that discussions between civil libertarians and feminists have often been at cross purposes. Here one can begin to relate political theory not to political practice, but to metaphysical theory. The classical civil liberties perspective on the issue remains deeply embedded in a male theoretical discourse on the meaning of sexuality. The connection between the domination of nature and the domination of women has been argued from many Marxist and feminist points of view.[20] The pivot of this connection is the masculine overlay of the mind-body dualism onto the male-female dichotomy. Within this framework, morality par excellence consists in the masculinized mind restraining the feminized body, with sexual desires seen as the crucial test for these powers of restraint. From this point of view, the question of the morality of pornography is primarily the quantitative question of how much sexual display is allowed, with full civil libertarians opting to uphold the extreme end of this continuum, arguing that no sexual expression should be repressed. But the crucial question, for at least the very important strain of feminist theory which rejects these dualisms which frame the debate for the malestream mainstream, is not *how much* sexuality is displayed but rather *how* sexuality is displayed. These theories speak not of mind-body dualism, but of mind/body wholism, where the body is seen not as the limitation or barrier for the expression of the free moral self, but rather as the most immediate and intimate vehicle for the expression of that self. The question of sexual morality here is not that of restraining or releasing sexual desires as they are forced on the spiritual self by the temptations of the body, but that of constructing spirited and liberating sexual relationships with and through one's own and others' bodies. Here sexual freedom is not the classical liberal freedom *from* external restraint, but the more radical freedom *to* construct authentically expressive sexualities.

I have argued throughout this chapter that pornography is a vehicle for the imposition of socially constructed sexuality, not a means for the expression of autonomously self-determined sexuality. (I would add that in contrasting imposed and authentic sexualities I am not endorsing a sexual essentialism, but simply carving out a space for more personal freedom.) Pornography is inherently about commercialized sex, about the eroticization of power and the power of eroticization. One can look to the term's etymology for confirmation of this point. It comes from the classical Greek "*pornographos,* meaning 'writing (sketching) of harlots,' " sometimes women captured in war.[21] Any distinction between pornography and erotica remains problematic, and cannot be drawn with absolute precision. Yet I believe some such distinction can and must be made. I would place the two terms not in absolute opposition, but at two ends of a continuum, with gray areas of necessity remaining between them. The gradations along the continuum are marked not by the explicitness of the portrayal of sexuality or the body, nor by the assertiveness vs. passivity of persons, nor by any categorization of sexual acts or activities, but by the extent to which autonomous personhood is attributed to the person or persons portrayed. Erotica portrays sexual subjects, manifesting their personhood in and through their bodies. Pornography depicts sex objects, persons reduced to their bodies. While the erotic nude presents the more pristine sexual body before the social persona is adopted through donning one's clothing, the pornographic nude portrays a body whose clothing has been more or less forcibly removed, where the absence of that clothing remains the most forceful presence in the image. Society's objectification remains present, indeed emphasized, in pornography, in a way in which it does not in erotica. Erotica, as sexual art, expresses a self, whereas pornography, as sexual commodity, markets one. The latter "works" because the operation it performs on women's bodies resonates with the "pornographizing" the male gaze does to women in other areas of society.[22] These distinctions remain problematic, to say the least, in their application, and disagreement in particular cases will no doubt remain. Much more work needs to be done before one would with any reasonable confidence distinguish authentic from imposed, personal from commercial, sexuality. Yet I believe this is the crucial question, and I believe these concepts correctly indicate the proper categories of analysis. Assuming a full definition of freedom as including autonomy and self-determination, pornography is therefore incompatible with real freedom.

Conclusions

It has often been noted that while socialist feminism is currently a major component of the array of feminisms one finds in academic feminism and women's studies, it is far less influential on the playing fields of practical politics.[23] While an analysis of male sexuality may seem an unlikely source to further socialist feminism's practical political agenda, I hope this chapter's demonstration of the interconnections between intimate personal experiences and large-scale historical and social structures, especially in what may have initially seemed unlikely places, may serve as a useful methodological model for other investigations.

In one sense, this chapter hopes to further the development of socialist feminist theory via a return to Hegel, especially the Hegel of the *Phenomenology*. Not only is Hegel's master-servant dialectic the *sine qua non* for the use of the concept of alienation in this chapter, but the inspiration for a mode of analysis, which is true to the experimental consciousness of social actors while at the same time delimiting that consciousness by showing its partiality and placing it in a broader context, is rooted in Hegel's *Phenomenology*. It is not a coincidence that the major wave of socialist feminist theory and practice in the late 60s and early 70s coincided with a wave of Marxist interest in Hegel, and that current signs of a new feminist interest in Hegel coincide with signs of the resurgence of radical politics in the United States.[24] Analogous to the conception of socialist feminism I articulated in the introduction to this chapter, my conception of Hegelianism defines Hegelianism as method rather than doctrine.[25] In some sense, contemporary Marxism and feminism can already be said to be rooted in Hegel, in the case of Marxism through Marx himself, and in the case of feminism through Beauvoir's *The Second Sex*. A more explicitly Hegelian-influenced socialist feminism would embody a theory and practice emphasizing the following themes: the dialectic between individual consciousness and social structure; a thoroughly historical epistemology; a nondualistic metaphysics; an understanding of gender, class, and other differences as being constituted through interaction rather than consisting of isolated "roles"; the priority of political over moralistic or economistic theory; a probing of the relations between state power and cultural hegemony; a program for reaching unity through difference rather than through sameness; a tolerance of, if not preference for, ambiguity and contradiction; and an orientation toward process over end product.[26]

I would like to conclude with some remarks on the practical import of this analysis. First of all, if the analysis of the relationship between pornography and consumerism and the argument about pornography leading to violence are correct, then a different conceptualization of the debate over the ethics of the feminist antipornography movement emerges. If one accepts, as I do, the idea that this movement is not against sex, but against sexual abuse, then the campaign against pornography is essentially not a call for censorship but a consumer campaign for product safety. The proper context for the debate over its practices is then not issues of free speech or civil liberties, but issues of business ethics. Or rather, this is the conclusion I reach remaining focused on pornography and male sexuality. But we should remember the broader context I alluded to at the beginning of this chapter, the question of pornography's effects on women. In that context, women are not the consumers of pornography, but the consumed. Rather than invoking the consumer movement, perhaps we should then look to environmental protection as a model.[27] Following this line of reasoning, one could in principle then perhaps develop under the tort law of product liability an argument to accomplish much of the regulation of sexually explicit material some are now trying to achieve through legislative means, perhaps developing a new definition of "safe" sexual material.

Finally, for most of us, most of our daily practice as academics consists of teaching rather than writing or reading in our fields. If one accepts the analysis I have presented, a central if not primary concern for us should therefore be how to integrate this analysis into our classrooms. I close by suggesting that we use this analysis and others like it from the emerging field of men's studies to demonstrate to the men in our classes the direct relevance of feminist analysis to their own lives, at the most intimate and personal levels, and that we look for ways to demonstrate to men that feminism can be personally empowering and liberating for them without glossing over, and in fact emphasizing, the corresponding truth that this will also require the surrender of male privilege.[28]

NOTES

1. I am indebted for this formulation to Tim Carrigan, Bob Connell, and John Lee, "Toward a New Sociology of Masculinity," in Harry Brod, ed., *The Making of Masculinities: The New Men's Studies* (Boston: Allen & Unwin, 1987).

2. For the *locus classicus* of the redefinition of Marxism as method rather than doctrine, see Georg Lukacs, *History and Class Consciousness: Studies in Marxist Dialectics,* trans. Rodney Livingstone (Cambridge, MA: MIT Press, 1972).

3. See my introduction to Brod, *The Making of Masculinities.* For other recent books by men I consider to be engaged in essentially the same or a kindred project, see Jeff Hearn, *The Gender of Oppression: Men, Masculinity, and the Critique of Marxism* (New York: St. Martin's Press, 1987), and R. W. Connell, *Gender and Power* (Stanford, CA: Stanford University Press, 1987), particularly the concept of "hegemonic masculinity," also used in Carrigan, Connell, and Lee, "Toward A New Sociology of Masculinity." Needless to say, none of this work would be conceivable without the pioneering work of many women in women's studies.

4. For book-length treatments of Marx's concept of alienation, see Istvan Meszaros, *Marx's Theory of Alienation* (New York: Harper & Row, 1972), and Bertell Ollman, *Alienation: Marx's Conception of Man in Capitalist Society* (Cambridge: Cambridge University Press, 1971).

5. Bernie Zilbergeld, *Male Sexuality: A Guide to Sexual Fulfillment* (Boston: Little, Brown, 1978).

6. Michael Betzold, "How Pornography Shackles Men and Oppresses Women," in *For Men against Sexism: A Book of Readings,* ed. Jon Snodgrass (Albion, CA: Times Change Press, 1977), p. 46.

7. I am grateful to Lenore Langsdorf and Paula Rothenberg for independently suggesting to me how this point would fit into my analysis.

8. See Jessica Benjamin, "The Bonds of Love: Rational Violence and Erotic Domination," *Feminist Studies* 6 (1980): 144–74.

9. Keith McWalter, "Couch Dancing," *New York Times Magazine,* December 6, 1987, p. 138.

10. Karl Marx, "Economic and Philosophic Manuscripts: Third Manuscript," in *Early Writings,* ed. and trans. T. B. Bottomore (New York: McGraw-Hill, 1964), pp. 159–60.

11. Marx., pp. 164–65.

12. An earlier version of portions of the following argument appears in my article "Eros Thanatized: Pornography and Male Sexuality" with a "1988 Postscript," in *Men Confronting Pornography,* ed. Michael Kimmel (New York: Crown, 1989). The article originally appeared (without the postscript) in *Humanities in Society* 7 (1984): 47–63.

13. See the essays by myself and Michael Kimmel in Brod, *The Making of Masculinities.*

14. Compare Carol Brown on the shift from private to public patriarchy: "Mothers, Fathers, and Children: From Private to Public Patriarchy," in *Women and Revolution,* ed. Lydia Sargent (Boston: South End Press, 1981).

15. According to Martha May in her paper " 'An Obligation on Every Man': Masculine Breadwinning and the Law in Nineteenth-Century New York," presented at the American Historical Association, Chicago, Illinois, 1987, from which I learned of these changes, the term "judicial patriarchy" is taken from historian Michael Grossberg, *Governing the Hearth: Law and the Family in Nineteenth-Century America* (Chapel Hill: University of North Carolina Press, 1985), and "Crossing Boundaries: Nineteenth-Century Domestic Relations Law and the Merger of Family and Legal History," *American Bar Foundation Research Journal* (1985): 799–847.

16. Alan Soble, *Pornography: Marxism, Feminism, and the Future of Sexuality* (New Haven, CT: Yale University Press, 1986), p. 82. I agree with much of Soble's analysis of male sexuality in capitalism, and note the similarities between much of what he says about "dismemberment" and consumerism and my analysis here.

17. See John D'Emilio and Estelle B. Freedman, *Intimate Matters: A History of Sexuality in America* (New York: Harper & Row, 1988).

18. See Barbara Ehrenreich, *The Hearts of Men: American Dreams and the Flight from Commitment* (New York: Anchor-Doubleday, 1983); and Wolfgang Fritz Haug, *Critique of Commodity Aesthetics: Appearance, Sexuality, and Advertising in Capitalist Society,* trans. Robert Bock (Minneapolis: University of Minnesota Press, 1986).

19. See my "Work Clothes and Leisure Suits: The Class Basis and Bias of the Men's Movement," originally in *Changing Men* 11 (1983): 10–12 and 38–40, reprinted in *Men's Lives: Readings in the Sociology of Men and Masculinity,* ed. Michael Kimmel and Michael Messner (New York: Macmillan, 1989).

20. This features prominently in the work of the Frankfurt school as well as contemporary ecofeminist theorists.

21. Rosemarie Tong, "Feminism, Pornography and Censorship," *Social Theory and Practice* 8 (1982): 1–17.

22. I learned to use "pornographize" as a verb in this way from Timothy Beneke's introduction to his *Men on Rape* (New York: St. Martin's Press, 1982).

23. See the series of ten articles on "Socialist-Feminism Today" in *Socialist Review* 73–79 (1984–1985).

24. For the most recent feminist reexaminations of Hegel, see Heidi M. Raven, "Has Hegel Anything to Say to Feminists?" *Owl of Minerva* 19 (1988): 149–68; Patricia Jagentowicz Mills, *Women, Nature, and Psyche* (New Haven, CT: Yale University Press, 1987); and Susan M. Easton, "Hegel and Feminism," in *Hegel and Modern Philosophy,* ed. David Lamb (London: Croom Helm, 1987). Hegel enters contemporary radical legal thought primarily through the Critical Legal Studies movement. Especially relevant here is the work of Drucilla Cornell, for example, "Taking Hegel Seriously: Reflections on Beyond Objectivism and Relativism," *Cardozo Law*

Review 7 (1985): 139; "Convention and Critique," *Cardozo Law Review* 7 (1986): 679; "Two Lectures on the Normative Dimensions of Community in the Law," *Tennessee Law Review* 54 (1987): 327; "Toward a Modern/Postmodern Reconstruction of Ethics," *University of Pennsylvania Law Review* 133 (1985): 291. See also papers from the conference on "Hegel and Legal Theory," March 1988 at the Cardozo Law School of Yeshiva University, New York City, in the *Cardozo Law Review* 10 (1989). For signs of radical resurgence in the United States, I would cite such phenomena as the Jesse Jackson candidacy and the 1988 National Student Convention. Jefferson Morley writes: "The most fundamental idea shared by popular movements East and West is the principle of 'civil society.'" Jefferson Morley, "On 'Civil Society,'" *Nation,* May 7, 1988, p. 630.

25. I believe this is true to Hegel's own conception of Hegelianism, for Hegel put the Logic at the core of his system, and at the center of the Logic stands the transfiguration and transvaluation of form and content.

26. Much of the feminist critique of the philosophical mainstream echoes earlier critiques of the mainstream made in the name of "process thought." See *Feminism and Process Thought: The Harvard Divinity School/Claremont Center for Process Studies Symposium Papers,* ed. Sheila Greeve Davaney (Lewiston, NY: Edwin Mellen Press, 1981).

27. I am indebted to John Stoltenberg for this point.

28. I attempt to articulate this perspective principally in the following: *The Making of Masculinities,* introduction and "The Case for Men's Studies"; *A Mensch among Men: Explorations in Jewish Masculinity* (Freedom, CA: Crossing Press, 1988), especially the introduction; and "Why Is This 'Men's Studies' Different from All Other Men's Studies?'" *Journal of the National Association for Women Deans, Administrators, and Counselors* 48 (1986): 44–49. See also generally the small men's-movement magazines *Changing Men: Issues in Gender, Sex and Politics* (306 North Brooks St., Madison, WI 53715), *brother: The Newsletter of the National Organization for Changing Men* (1402 Greenfield Ave., #1, Los Angeles, CA 90025), and *Men's Studies Review* (Box 32, Harriman, TN 37748).

Chapter Twenty-seven

Problematizing the Discourse
Sex Trafficking Policy and Ethnography

Anastasia M. Hudgins

Trafficking for prostitution is currently a widely discussed yet narrowly framed phenomenon. It is easy to conflate concern and distaste about the violence of the commercial sex industry, and the harm it does to women and girls, with a simple description of prostitution and trafficking that says that "women are victimized by their 'johns' and by traffickers," and to just stop there. Many women are victimized by the commercial sex industry, and violence is rampant, but acknowledging that does not stop it. It is important to examine how women's bodies are not simply physically forced into prostitution (though many are), but that because gender inequality is so entrenched many women and their families find that sex work is the best choice of many bad choices.

By assuming that all migration for sex work is forced, and calling it "trafficking," women and girls in the commercial sex industry are doubly harmed: first by the harms associated with prostitution; second by policy makers ignoring the factors that cause women to make the decision to enter the commercial sex industry, thereby perpetuating the conditions that lead to trafficking. Most policies on trafficking, especially those influenced by or promulgated by the United States, assume that all trafficked women and children are bodily forced into sexual slavery (Haugen and Hunter 2005; Trafficking in Persons Report 2004). This is the reality for many, yet not all, as I realized during my fieldwork in a Cambodian brothel village where young Vietnamese debt-bonded women migrated to seek work in the commercial sex industry. The dominant stance wrongly simplifies a very complex phenomenon by reducing it to dichotomies such as "victim:victimizer," "innocence:depravity," "good:evil," and "supply:demand."

In this chapter, I discuss the discourse that guides much of the policy around trafficking, critically positioning it within a larger political field, and compare it to the words of some women in my research (Hudgins 2006). Of primary concern here is the Trafficking Victims Protection Act (TVPA), which was passed into law in the United States in October 2000, and the Global AIDS Act of 2003. I build on Ditmore's call for trafficking itself to be more thoroughly problematized, as trafficking and prostitution are conflated in the minds of policy makers and the public. Ditmore, a sociologist, writes that concerns about the morality of women are expressed in legislation such as the TVPA. The legislation does not liberate women; rather, it "contains" women by limiting their autonomy, and it reflects a political and ideological position held by those who would protect such things as "family values" (Ditmore 2002).

My analysis is based on textual research and ethnographic fieldwork in a brothel village outside Phnom Penh, where I analyzed the relationship between U.S. policy, the people in the village (brothel owners and sex workers), and nongovernmental organizations' efforts to serve the sex workers. At the time of my research (2000–2001) there were as many as twenty-five brothels in the small village and 325 brothel-based sex workers. These young women were largely debt-bonded, which means that they or their families borrowed sums of money against their future earnings in the commercial sex industry.

The TVPA requires the U.S. Department of State to issue an annual Trafficking in Persons Report (TIPR), in which countries around the world are ranked according to their efforts to eradicate or prevent human trafficking. Those countries deemed to make egregiously insufficient efforts are targeted for sanctions (TIPR 2004). In the report the United States categorizes countries around the world into first-, second-, and third-tier countries, according to how much human trafficking takes place within or across their borders, what steps they take to reduce it, and how effective they are in reducing it. Third-tier countries ostensibly have the most severe problems. Some third-tier countries are Sudan, Venezuela, North Korea, Bangladesh, Cuba, Burma, and Guyana. The placement of countries into these different tiers greatly affects them, as movement from second tier to third tier can come with financial penalties and sanctions. "The U.S. Government may withhold non-humanitarian, non-trade-related assistance" (TIPR 2004 31) and withhold assistance from international financial institutions like the International Monetary Fund (IMF) or the World Bank. This first came into effect in 2003.

Placement in the tiers, and penalties attached to a tier, is politicized in some cases. For example, Japan is a second-tier country, while Venezuela is categorized as third-tier. Japan is an economic and political ally, while Venezuela is veering sharply away from U.S. neoliberal policies. In 2003 Japan issued fifty-five thousand entertainer visas to women from the Philippines, many of whom "are suspected of having become trafficking victims" (TIPR 2004, 14), while Venezuela does not have a trafficking problem, according to a search on the Human Rights Watch website and sex-work listservs. This politicization casts doubt on other aspects of the policy.

The report describes the phenomenon of trafficking as one that can be analyzed and solved by employing analogies of supply and demand, meaning the supply of women and the demand for them. A focus on demand, not supply, requires an emphasis on techniques for stemming the demand, and the United States promotes a "law and order" approach to the sex industry. According to this discourse, there is a high occurrence of sex trafficking because people can make money from selling the women's bodies and because there are so many clients with unequal power over the women, especially economic power. But this is only part of the problem. This perspective denies the prevalence of voluntary sex work, thereby denying its relevance as an economic strategy that the sex workers and their families deploy. Consequently, policy makers do not figure structural issues key to resolving the sex-work problem and, in fact, deny that addressing poverty and gender equity is a solution that can effectively limit commercial sex work. In my research I found that current economic policies in Vietnam that liberalized the economy (Tep and Ek 2000; Tep, Ek, and Maas 2001; Tran Thi Van Anh 1999; Vu Tuan Anh et al. 2000) were a driving factor in the women's migration for work in the sex industry (Hudgins 2006).

The report says that the causes of the supply of "victims of trafficking" include poverty, the attraction of a perceived higher standard of living elsewhere, weak social and economic structures, a lack of employment opportunities, organized crime, violence against women and children, discrimination against women, government corruption, political instability, and armed conflict. Factors driving the demand for trafficking include the sex industry and the growing demand for exploitable labor. But then, counterintuitively, the report says that social causes and governments addressing them are not important enough to consider when categorizing countries into one of the three tiers. Only law enforcement and judicial actions are relevant in determining where a country falls in the hierarchy. A view of the women as victims determines the response to the sex-work problem. Such a perspective infers that women are brought into the sex industry, not that they choose the sex industry. This assumption shapes the questions that are asked and the solutions that are pursued. Quoting from the report:

> The report focuses on concrete actions governments have taken to fight trafficking, highlighting prosecutions, convictions, prison sentences for traffickers, victim protection and prevention efforts. . . . the report does not focus on other government efforts that contribute indirectly to reducing trafficking, such as education programs, support for economic development, or programs aimed at enhancing gender equality, although these are worthwhile endeavors. (TIPR 2004, 25–26)

In essence, the United States ignores the causes of trafficking, instead choosing to respond to the trafficking after the fact and requiring other countries to do so as well. The report goes on to say that factors that provide a supply of workers should be addressed, that traffickers should be pursued and prosecuted, that the demand for trafficked persons should be eliminated by identifying those who exploit trafficked persons, and that people should be withdrawn from "slave-like working situations and reintegrated into their families and communities" (TIPR 2004, 22). But as one woman in my research said, "What would I do? I still have to earn money."

Seidel and Vidal (1997) say that discourse can veer public thinking about a problem onto one path that re/misdirects thinking, money, and efforts toward "hegemonic discourses." They point out the danger of the dominant perspective in driving policy discourse and discursive activity: they can have disastrous outcomes because the only input they have is their own. The Global AIDS Act exemplifies this hegemonic misdirection.

The Global AIDS Act, officially named the U.S. Leadership against HIV/AIDS, Tuberculosis, and Malaria Act of 2003 and signed into law May 27, 2003, significantly increased U.S. allocation of monies for HIV/AIDS programs around the world ($15 billion over five years, from 2004 to 2008). Among other measures the act imposed, it requires any agency receiving funding from the State Department, the U.S. Agency for International Development (USAID, a branch of the State Department), the Department of Justice, or the Department of Commerce to renounce prostitution and sex trafficking (Saunders 2004). A movement by the Centers for Disease Control and

Prevention involved similar stipulations that broadened the scope to include any recipients of monies from the Global Fund to Fight AIDS, Tuberculosis, and Malaria (a multilateral agency officially conceived in 2001 by UN Secretary-General Kofi Annan), WHO, or any other UN agency, but this was later rescinded after much outcry (Boonstra 2003). The act stipulates that any organization that receives U.S. funding, and works with sex workers, must be actively working to remove women from brothels, even if they made the decision to be there. This means that any work to empower sex workers to help them reduce the risks they face, or to provide them with condoms, is disallowed under the act. Unfortunately, this approach ignores the pragmatics of life on the ground for women who work in brothels. The act codified the approach of prioritizing demand for women over the supply.

One of the solutions to the problem of trafficking, if the problem is defined as being caused primarily by demand for prostitution, is to arrest brothel owners and pimps, and to rescue young women from brothels.

Ping Pong, a sex worker affiliated with Empower Chiang Mai, a Thai sex-worker-run organization that advocates for sex workers, criticizes efforts to "rescue" "trafficked" women. She says raids have been conducted for the past twelve years in Thailand and points out that there has been increased international and national attention on trafficking recently.

> However, the focus on trafficking in persons has meant many groups with little or no experience on the issues of migration, labour, sex work or women's rights have been created to take advantage of the large sums of money available to support anti-trafficking activities. Their inexperience and lack of contact with our community has meant they are unable or unwilling to differentiate between women who have been trafficked and migrant workers. They also show a great deal of trouble differentiating between women and girls, often applying identical standards and solutions for both. It is obviously inappropriate to treat a girl as an adult and just as obviously inappropriate to treat an adult as a child. (Pong 2003, 9)

Although conducting raids is offered as a measure that protects human rights, and in some cases it may, raids and rescues constitute a violation of most sex workers' rights: "traffickers and many anti-trafficking groups employ very similar methods to achieve their goals. Both groups deceive women, transport them against their will, detain them, and put them in dangerous situations, i.e., forced repatriation" (Pong 2003, 9).

Surtees (2003), the training manager of the International Catholic Migration Commission's Counter-Trafficking Program in Indonesia, argues that raids have negative ramifications for women who are not rescued, and for service providers, and that raids do not end forced trafficking. Specifically, health services are curtailed as brothel owners limit the involvement of outside organizations and restrict the movement of the women.

Surtees says that most organizations that conduct raids do not differentiate between the involuntary and voluntary sex workers. "Raids fail to recognize and respect women's right to choose sex work as an occupation. . . . While we can debate the issue of 'choice' in the context of limited life options, we must acknowledge that women are decision-makers in their own lives, even where their choices are not acceptable in mainstream society" (Surtees 2003, 6).

Undeniably, many women and girls are completely unable to exercise significant control over their lives, and for those women and girls, rescues are arguably appropriate, if properly planned and executed. Yet, to shape macrogovernmental policy such as the Global AIDS Act and the Trafficking Victims Protection Act around that perspective, to see rescues as a panacea for exploitation in the sex industry, is problematic, and possibly ineffectual, if not harmful for the long-term well-being of the people in the commercial sex industry.

Defining the problem as caused by demand, policy makers fail to see other significant factors at play, factors subsumed under the "supply" category. Looking at the problem from a "supply" perspective, one can see how the women and their families might profit from the commercial sex industry, however bleakly. Most of the brothel-based women in my study come from impoverished situations, and sex work provides a source of income that is better paid, with fewer hurdles to leap (such as literacy, job skills, social networks) than work in the formal economy. In this realistic scenario, women's choices are shaped both by individual agency and structural conditions. An examination of "supply" would have to address these structural conditions. Women would have to be seen as rational actors, not simply victims of someone else's profit motive. Incorporating these factors would require a much more comprehensive response than simply arresting the brothel owners, pimps, clients, and traffickers, and rescuing women.

Many of the women I spoke with in Cambodia expressed a desire to earn money for their family members as a rationale for coming to the brothel village. Here I excerpt their words.

> My mother has no money. People told me about this place, recruited me. But it is my decision to come. When I'm sad, it's when I worry about my mother. That I have not made enough money for her, to help her.
>
>   —twenty-eight-year-old woman, in Cambodia for three years

> I don't have a mother or father. My life is very poor and difficult. I don't have any money. My sister is ill. Life is very difficult. We don't have enough food and water to survive on. I had to look for a way to make money to help my sister. I came here with a friend. She told me about the life here, but I decided to come here to help make money for my sister. I only have my older sister. I grew up without parents.
>
>   —twenty-four-year-old woman, in Cambodia for one year

> My family is very poor. If they were doing well, I would not be here. My parents are very old and I have to work to take care of the family.
>
>   —twenty-five-year-old woman, in Cambodia for two to three years

> My aunt brought me here. My mother doesn't even know about this. I came because we have a large family and I need to work.
>
>   —twenty-two-year-old woman, in Cambodia for one year

> I had a job outside of [the brothel village], but my boss returned to Vietnam. My mother didn't have any money and we had to pay off debts, so I came here to borrow money from

the brothel owner to give to my mother to pay back the debts. Because of our situation I had to come here to borrow money.

—twenty-year-old woman, in Cambodia for seven to eight months

I have a friend who has helped me, who told me that if I make enough money she'd help me get back home. But I don't want to go home. I want to stay here with my brothel owner.

—eighteen-year-old woman, in Cambodia for five months

Another woman, Diep, said that she wants to work in the brothel village and earn a lot of money for her future, when she gets old and sick. "But I cannot earn a lot of money because I'm not pretty, and I'm older than others in the brothel. It's depressing and sad." Instead, using the English she has learned, she works helping the brothel owner deal with the clients. She said,

At the moment my mother is sick, and the house is ramshackle and has a leaky roof. I'm thinking that if I go back to Vietnam, I need to have money to build my house and repair it, and pay off the debts she owes to people in Vietnam. I also need some funds to start a business when I go back home. But in this type of situation—I'm not pretty, I don't have many clients, how can I make money to go back home. That is why I had to stay longer, to earn more money.

—Diep, twenty-six-year-old debt-bonded sex worker

In the interviews I conducted with sex workers, all but one of the women said they wanted to leave. But in the same breath of saying they wanted to leave, they also said they needed the job because they wanted to earn money to help their families—building a house, financially supporting their family, or sending a sibling to school, for example. Policy makers have no concept of these factors yet push their agenda forward on the simplistic construction of commercial sex workers as victims, with no input from the women themselves. The proposed solution is premised on moralistic understandings of womanhood and childhood (Hecht 1998), and this moralizing gets in the way of solving real problems. The physical and mental violence women experience through prostitution is reinforced by the structural violence of these policies.

It is critical to clarify that I am not arguing that women should be seen as exercising free will simply for the sake of advancing an anthropological debate or to romanticize resistance (Best and Kellner 1991). This is important because the quality of women's lives, and their families', is at stake under the conditions that make sex work a viable employment choice. And given the high rate of HIV infection in sex-worker communities, their very lives are at stake.

In conclusion, the push for a "law and order" approach to sex work relies on a superficial understanding of sex work, of sex workers, of brothel owners, and of the context in which the commercial sex industry takes place. In the expression of this superficial understanding, the sex workers are cast as victims of fraud and force, victimized at the hands of evil perpetrators, not people making rational and difficult decisions.

The simplistic approach to sex work—arrest the bad guys and free the victims—is fundamentally flawed because it fails to recognize the structural conditions that caused the women and their families to seek this line of work; it fails to acknowledge the complexity of the context in which the inequality of the commercial sex industry takes place.

Chapter Twenty-eight

Prostitution as "Choice"

Jane Anthony

Prostitution remains today—as it has been for thousands of years—one of the most poorly understood, mythicized harms perpetrated against women. It is a cornerstone of patriarchy. The thirteenth-century philosopher Thomas Aquinas recognized this when he wrote that prostitution is like a sewer system—despicable *but necessary* (italics mine). Aquinas—along with many other "great thinkers," such as Augustine, the religious philosopher of the early Christian era, or Havelock Ellis, the twentieth-century sexologist—approached prostitution from this functional standpoint: as a victimless crime that helps preserve the institution of marriage by providing a readily available outlet for men's sexual desires.

Unfortunately, this viewpoint overlooks the casualties of such a system: one class of women is granted status as "wives" or "girlfriends" (each taking care of only one man), at the expense of another class, "whores" (who are reduced to sperm receptacles for numerous men).

Consequently, one might expect that feminism, which has dragged out of the closet such issues as rape, incest, and battering—all of which are frequently a part of the prostitution syndrome—would target commercial sex as the beginning and end of women's exploitation. But recent developments show that some individuals would like to see an "exclusive" place reserved in the feminist agenda for women in commercial sex. Some women who recognize rape and battering as violence (acts that could happen to them, regardless of their socioeconomic status) at the same time defend pornography and prostitution (acts that often involve rape and other violations, but are most likely not going to happen to them).

Nowhere is this pro-prostitution stance clearer than in certain recent literature, written by women, which attempts to portray prostitution as a "career choice." In general, those who most adamantly promote this view, organizing various "whores' conferences" and positioning themselves as prostitutes' spokespersons with the male-dominated media, do not choose prostitution for themselves: some have abandoned it; some never worked as prostitutes; some work as "madams," selling other women's bodies but not routinely marketing their own; a few actually work as prostitutes. The

From MS. (January / February 1992): 86–87.

numbers in the last group are much smaller than what the public is led to believe, especially given the millions of women worldwide who live as prostitutes in silence.

Pro-prostitution ideology, which has been linked to "sexual liberalism," is largely shaped by either/or dichotomies. It reflects a traditional masculinist mode of analysis, a dualism that easily lends itself to oversimplification. For example, in her introductory chapter in the anthology *A Vindication of the Rights of Whores*, editor Gail Pheterson contrasts nineteenth-century views of prostitutes as victims with current views of prostitutes as women who make active decisions to become "whores." Unfortunately, this distinction places in opposition things that are, in reality, not mutually exclusive. Even though prostitution may be a choice for women, *among limited choices*, this doesn't mean it isn't simultaneously the epitome of gender-based exploitation.

Only if one completely decontextualizes commercial sex from the cultural constructs burdening women's "choices"—job discrimination, gender inequality in the courts, and, in general, sexism so pervasive it is often invisible—can prostitution be seen as a "choice." But this is what pro-prostitution ideology does: it marches in tune with traditional definitions of abstractions like "freedom" and "choice," definitions historically centered around the needs of Anglo-Saxon men and dependent on a curiously selective ignorance. However, if a woman faces poverty, hunger, sexual abuse, homelessness, inaccessible education, unobtainable medical treatment, or inadequate funds for child care, her possibilities of establishing herself in mainstream culture, or merely surviving, are well beyond the traditional concept of "choice."

As feminist attorney Catharine MacKinnon pointed out in her essay "Liberalism and the Death of Feminism," feminists have generally recognized that women who stay with a battering husband for the sake of economic survival are not making a real choice, despite the so-called consent implicit in a marriage contract. Yet those who defend commercial sex seem to believe that women exploited and abused by not one but many men for the sake of economic survival are making a "real choice."

In decontextualizing women's choices, pro-prostitution ideology inadvertently trivializes prostitution. For example, in her introduction to the anthology *Sex Work,* coeditor Priscilla Alexander—who has never worked as a prostitute—compares her experiences as a coed at Bennington (a private college in Vermont) with prostitution. She notes that sometimes women in the dorms would wait for fraternity boys from nearby men's colleges to stop by and randomly pick up dates. Because of this, Alexander was, in her terms, "stigmatized" as a prostitute.

Indeed, a major premise of pro-prostitution thinking lies in the notion that the worst thing about prostitution is the stigmatization. Margo St. James, who organized COYOTE (Call Off Your Old Tired Ethics), a pro-prostitution group, has widely publicized this idea, noting that she herself was once "wildly promiscuous and was working as a prostitute." Thus pro-prostitution ideology stresses *secondary*, rather than *primary*, victimization: it views the name-calling as more harmful than the actual process of turning tricks, the very concrete risks of physical harm, and the psychic trauma that grows from having one's most private self routinely entered by one stranger after the next, day after day, week after week.

In general, those who view prostitution as a "career choice" see it as a form of empowerment, but this analysis is, again, shaped by decontextualization and logical inconsistency. For example, in *Sex Work,* Alexander notes a high incidence of previous sexual abuse (sometimes as high as 80 percent) among prostitutes. She also states that many prostitutes noted the first time they ever felt powerful was the first time they turned a trick; many even reported that prostitution was "a way of taking back control of a situation in which, as children, they had none." In spite of making this connection between abuse and "taking back control," Alexander does not acknowledge the empowerment as illusory or conditional. Instead she tells us that learning of this phenomenon began to change her ideas about the victimization of prostitutes.

Last, pro-prostitution ideology places itself in the tradition of "liberal reform." Its supporters generally see themselves as nonconformists working on behalf of their sisters in prostitution. They place themselves in opposition to "abolitionists," women who dare to envision the end of prostitution. Generally, they depict the abolitionists as conservative purists on moral crusades.

In reality, both liberal defenders of prostitution and abolitionists want prostitutes to be treated as "persons" under the law, that is, to have recognized civil rights so that they have legal recourse against crimes like rape or robbery. Abolitionists, however, see prostitution as a *crime against women* and therefore generally advocate the enforcement of laws against clients and pimps, as well as the eradication of laws punishing prostitutes. Reformers, on the other hand, would like to see prostitution decriminalized altogether. Abolitionists believe this would merely increase the number of women vulnerable to commercial sexual exploitation. It is the *abolitionists* who harbor the most radical stance insofar as they are challenging the patriarchal institution of commercial sex itself.

Perhaps the most disturbing aspect of the pro-prostitution movement is that while it parades as a forum for prostitutes' voices and claims to represent diversity among those voices, it may instead contribute to their silencing. For example, *Sex Work* appears to have been structured to reinforce the opinions of its nonprostitute editors. The first part, "In the Life," begins and ends with the pro-prostitution writings of a woman who works as a part-time hooker. Of the forty-five pieces in this section, her writing appears nine more times, composing nearly one-fourth of the selections.

Another example of questionable accuracy regarding claims of diverse representation can be seen in Amber Hollibaugh's review of *A Vindication.* Hollibaugh, whose work aligns her with the sexual liberal philosophy, states that this book represents the voices of "hundreds" of prostitutes. However, the book itself lists a total of fifty-seven contributors, including prostitutes and *nonprostitutes* alike.

No doubt it is easier to view prostitution as a "choice" than to address its implications. This institution has been with us for millennia, has no prospects of disappearing anytime soon, and is often, even as we approach the twenty-first century, a source of cruel and insensitive jokes about women's condition. It is no wonder that women would prefer not to ask themselves what this means about their own lives, their own relationships, and their own struggles for freedom. In "Confronting the Liberal Lies about Prostitution, Evenna Globbe of WHISPER (Women Hurt In Systems of Prostitution Engaged in Revolt), in Minneapolis, has noted, "Dismantling the institution of prostitution is the most formidable task facing contemporary feminism."

Feminist theory derives from concrete personal experience. So does the above analysis. My experience would fit the paradigm of "career choice" in pro-prostitution ideology: I made a decision *as an adult* to work as a prostitute and felt "empowered" when I turned my first trick. Shortly thereafter, I became aware of the disillusion. I lived as a full-time prostitute for a year and a half, and then continued prostitution on an occasional, part-time basis for three more years. Despite the relatively short period I was a prostitute, years later I find myself still, in my most vulnerable moments, living with the ghost of prostitution—the sense of being nonhuman.

It may be comforting for some women to see prostitution as a "career choice." But when they promote this message to an all-too-eager male-dominated media, they may be sentencing other women to years of dehumanization and numbness. Or, in some cases, death. *Real* death, unlike some "choices."

Part III

Creating Social Change

The last part of this book focuses on a very important aspect of contemporary discourse on gender violence—creating social change. We present a variety of perspectives on what can be done to bring about positive social change. We offer a roundtable of articles that explore routes toward nonviolence in gender relations from the perspectives of philosophy, linguistics, sociology, and feminist activism.

Changing Our Minds: Transforming Gender Relations

In previous sections, we explored the roots and context of gendered violence as it occurs throughout the world. In this closing section, we address the potential for change and suggest ways to create nonviolence in social relations.

Moving from Violence to Nonviolence

What will it take to diminish or end gender violence? Perhaps if we learn the lessons of the history of gender violence, and how such violence relates to political and social structures, we can choose to create alternative institutional and interpersonal patterns. Even then, we will need to understand how gendered social structures of inequality contribute to gendered expectations and social scripts, which in turn contain the blueprint for violence. First, we must work to make the invisible visible. As long as gender exists as a system of "omnipresent yet partly hidden plans" (Griffin 1992), which supports abuses and reproduces inequities, we will remain ignorant of its dangers.

We must inspect how masculinities and femininities are constructed and parse out the results of building rigidly defined systems of identity. The rituals that shape manhood from boyhood should come under scrutiny; the voices of men who have resisted or been excluded could serve as possible guides. Women's voices, which express the experience of patriarchy from the vantage point of its margins, must be placed at the center. We must understand how the binary nature of gendered identity places actual people in opposition to each other, how a discourse and practice of male/female disparity makes us unknowable, strange, and other as gendered beings, and how that otherness contributes to violence. At the same time we must continue to explore the specificity of maleness and femaleness, to understand how difference is practiced in the lives of men and women and learn how to move beyond conceptions of otherness fraught with hostility and fear.

We need to scrutinize socialization practices that force a dichotomization of the "male" and "female" qualities embodied by men and women, as well as analyze the role of our group identity as men and women. As we begin to understand the coerced nature of dichotomous gender systems, their effect on the individual's propensity for aggression and passivity will become clearer. Although it is imperative that we work to restructure systems that uphold and maintain gender violence, global solutions cannot take place without the action of individuals; and no individual can take responsibility for altering our entire system. Starting from the parameters of our own lives, we must identify each small change we can make that will contribute to the broader solutions.

Our relationship to violence must be acknowledged and understood. Violence is advocated in our culture as "the normal, appropriate and necessary behavior of power and control" (Ewing 1982, 7), and its practice is gendered. We have come to accept fear and anxiety as inevitable features of social life. Through the advocacy of violence as an effective form of behavior, men are permitted to abuse women, other men, and children. This is true whether they take advantage of that option or not.

Because changes in gender relations will take many forms and be precipitated by many causes, each of us must become familiar with how the interpersonal and the institutional connect. While we are no doubt endowed with human agency, we are at the same time influenced in our desires and our choices by the traditions of the past, the shape of contemporary institutions such as religion, education, and family, and the expectations attendant on our biological sex. Although change can develop in each of these areas, the most far-reaching and effective changes will combine both the personal and the institutional.

Signs of Change

It is heartening that politically influential organizations have issued official statements acknowledging that corporal punishment has negative consequences for children and that sexual assault and domestic violence imperil the physical and emotional well-being of Americans (American Academy of Pediatrics 1998; American Medical Association 1992, 1995). Indeed, using a public-health framework to conceptualize and respond to gendered violence has emerged as a promising approach to addressing this widespread, multifaceted problem (Novello, Rosenberg, Saltzman, and Shosky 1992).

We have also seen progress in the legal arena. In 2005, Congress reauthorized the Violence Against Women Act (VAWA), which was originally passed in 1994. As the first U.S. federal law to address gender-based crimes by providing funding for police, prosecution, and services for adult victims, the VAWA is significant for its recognition that violence against women is a gender-bias crime. That is, this legislation acknowledges that acts of violence against women discriminate against women as a social category. In what has been called "a giant step forward," Congress "extended the act's protections to teenage victims" when it reauthorized the VAWA in 2000 (Barnett, Miller-Perrin, and Perrin 2005, 246).

The international dialogue among women has become an important factor in forcing governments to pay attention to problems to which they have, both overtly and covertly, contributed. Gender violence occupied a significant position on the agenda at the 1995 Global Conference on Women in Beijing, China, where topics ranging from control of reproductive capacity to domestic violence to rape and sexual abuse within the context of war were addressed as urgent issues concerning women from every country. The conference resolutions compelled governments around the world to acknowledge and reform policies and practices that support gender violence. For example, following the conference, the United Nations Development Fund for Women (UNIFEM) launched an international campaign urging governments to devise national plans of action to eradicate violence against women. Another important development occurred during the summer of 1996, when the International Criminal Tribunal in The Hague, which is responsible for investigating Bosnian war crimes, announced several indictments for rape. More recently, the tribunal has prosecuted cases stemming from the genocidal conflict in Rwanda, representing tremendous progress in the development of international law regarding rape during armed conflict (Wood 2004). For the first time in history, sexual assaults are treated separately as war crimes; organized rape in time of war is now understood to be a crime against humanity (Simons 1996). International organizations that provide resources to advance women's rights are working to prevent a repeat of the horrors of Bosnia and Rwanda. Groups such as the Global Fund for Women recognize that in order to reach equality and create peace "cultures of violence both in the home and in conflict situations" must be transformed (Grossman and Smith 2004, inside front cover).

At the same time that these events inspire hope for the future, we should recognize that, due to increased public scrutiny, much sexual violence and exploitation has been forced underground. There is evidence that abuses that were once practiced openly and with impunity are now carried out subtly. The conditions that encourage and support gender violence are deeply entrenched, and efforts to alter them face tremendous resistance. Piecemeal solutions may correct—or appear to correct—specific problems, but they will not effectively change the social context that permits the abuses to flourish.

Like any book, this one has been limited by space constraints to what we see as the most virulent and established forms of gender violence. We would like to encourage the reader to use this book as a starting point. If we are to work toward ending gender violence, it is not enough simply to inform ourselves about the facts and occurrences of gender violence, or about the historical, philosophical, cultural, and interpersonal conditions that encourage and permit it. We must go on to learn about the conditions that make gender violence *impossible*.

Contributions to This Section

The chapters that follow comprise a few of the many voices that have offered visions and plans for a more peaceful future. The suggestions presented by the authors range from policy and program initiatives to altered forms of language and new patterns of consciousness. It is our intention that these voices not stand alone. We envision strands of a web that connect the disparate views, which, when woven together, provide a greater understanding of how we can eradicate gender violence.

In "Beyond the Masculine Mystique," Myriam Miedzian challenges us to utilize the knowledge and means at our disposal to end increasing male violence. The author identifies several key social conditions that encourage the development of a culture of violence expressed through a tough and unyielding masculinity.

William Gay argues that (hetero)sexist language contributes to gender violence by perpetuating multiple systems of oppression. In "Supplanting Linguistic Violence," Gay proposes specific methods through which nonsexist language can be created and deployed to transform gender relations.

Drawing on her own sociological research on rape-processing agencies, and that of other organizational and policy analysts, Patricia Yancey Martin discusses the ways in which victims of violence benefit from the integration of services. In "Coordinated Community Services for Victims of Violence," she outlines specific recommendations for program implementation and organizational transformation.

In "Queering Approaches to Intimate Partner Violence," Elizabeth Erbaugh theorizes the ways in which current responses to intimate partner violence are inadequate to address the issues faced by LGBTIQ (lesbian, gay, bisexual, trans, intersex, and queer) people. A first step is confronting heteronormativity; Erbaugh also addresses some very specific issues for antiviolence organizations wishing to serve more diverse populations.

We include Janice Raymond's testimony before the European Parliament to highlight the relationships among various forms of commodification in the sex industry and violence against women. As co-executive director of the Coalition Against Trafficking in Women, she represents one perspective on the sort of strategies that will empower and protect women in the global community against continued violation.

Jackson Katz's list of "10 Things Men Can Do to Prevent Gender Violence" is an excellent tool for everyone to use to interrogate their own thoughts and actions. It can also be the basis for organizing support groups of men to confront and transform gender relations on their campuses and in their communities.

Elizabeth Ward's poetic essay, "Action," suggests that imagination and creative action are the catalysts for creating a future free of gender violence. Ward's vision begins with the healing power and strength of women's shared identity.

These voices contribute to the search for an answer to the riddle of gender violence. It is likely that there are many answers, or at least many parts to the answer. It is too simplistic to imagine that there is only one possible resolution to such a multifaceted and complex problem. Indeed, it is the thesis of this book that we must understand the works of many people, across many disciplines, in order to comprehend the nature and scope of gender violence, as well as its resolutions.

SUGGESTIONS FOR FURTHER READING

Gregg Barak, *Violence and Nonviolence: Pathways to Understanding* (Thousand Oaks, CA: Sage, 2003).

Emilie Buchwald, Pamela R. Fletcher, and Martha Ross, *Transforming a Rape Culture* (Minneapolis: Milkweed Editions, 1993).

Rus Ervin Funk, *Stopping Rape: A Challenge for Men* (Philadelphia: New Society, 1993).

Charlotte Perkins Gilman, *Herland* (New York: Pantheon, 1979).

Susan Griffin, *A Chorus of Stones* (New York: Doubleday, 1992).

Susan Hawthorne, *Wild Politics: Feminism, Globalisation, and Bio/diversity* (Melbourne: Spinifex, 2002).

Jackson Katz, *The Macho Paradox: Why Some Men Hurt Women and How All Men Can Help* (Naperville, IL: Sourcebooks, 2006).

Marge Piercy, *Woman on the Edge of Time* (New York: Knopf, 1976).

Margaret Schuler (ed.), *Freedom from Violence: Women's Strategies from around the World* (New York: UNICEF, 1992).

Lynn Segal, *Slow Motion: Changing Masculinities, Changing Men* (New Brunswick, NJ: Rutgers University Press, 1990).

John Stoltenberg, *Refusing to Be a Man: Essays on Sex and Justice* (Portland, OR: Breitenbush Books, 1989).

Bessie Fenton
Redwing, 1888

Kathryn Howd Machan

for Carolyn Byerly

They laughed when I said I'd do it, eat
the worms. *Stupid girl, you wouldn't*
even touch one. Liar, liar!

But I showed them. I marched right to
the place where they'd been digging, black
dirt all damp and smelling of spring.

One, two, three—I swallowed,
thinking of little birds in nests,
hungry fish in a blue, blue stream.

Worm eater! Worm eater! Bessie is
a worm eater! Then they all ran off
still whooping like a pack of hounds.

I sat there, knowing only that
I couldn't cry. Now they'll tell
the others, make fun of me in school—

but I don't care. I challenged their
whole world of who is strong. They have
to run and try to change the rules.

Bessie Fenton is one of over one hundred voices in my fictional town of Redwing—one of the bravest.

From *Redwing: Voices from 1888* by Kathryn Howd Machan (FootHills Publishing, 2005).

Chapter Twenty-nine

Beyond the Masculine Mystique

Myriam Miedzian

Between 1960 and 1995 homicide rates have more than doubled in the United States. In recent years the violence has become increasingly haphazard, senseless, and committed by younger and younger perpetrators—between 1985 and 1995 there has been an increase of over 200 percent in the arrest of fifteen-year-old boys alone for murder. Between late July and mid-October 1990, eight children fourteen years old or younger were killed by random gunfire in New York City. "Your Sneakers or Your Life" is the title of the cover story on the May 13, 1990, issue of *Sports Illustrated.* The article describes how an increasing number of boys mug or murder their peers in order to get a pair of expensive sneakers or a coveted jacket bearing sports insignia. In Dallas, Texas, when ten current and former high school athletes were sentenced to prison for armed robbery, it turned out that their motives included "extra money for prom night" and "trips to an amusement park, food and athletic shoes."[1]

One would think that in light of this further escalation, every effort would be made to socialize boys so as to decrease violence. But this is not the case.

The atavistic values of the masculine mystique continue to be reinforced in most areas of entertainment, as well as in some sports.

Not only are fathers not being encouraged to play a major role in nurturant child-rearing, thus denying their sons nonviolent, caring masculine role models, but many boys are being deprived of adequate mothering. Most working mothers must conform to a marketplace designed for men with homemaker wives. This leaves millions of children unattended and emotionally deprived—a good breeding ground for anger and violence. Inadequate day care compounds the situation. Divorce leaves many women impoverished and makes child-rearing even more difficult for them. In the last forty years there has been a sixfold increase in the percentage of women giving birth who are unmarried. Very little is being done to change this or to encourage divorced or unmarried fathers to remain involved with and financially responsible for their children. With all due respect to *The Cosby Show* and a few other exceptions, the primary images of manhood projected by the media and reinforced by toy manufacturers have nothing to do with being a loving, nurturant father.

The increase in children deprived of fathering, the crisis in child care, and the

From Myriam Miedzian, "Boys Will Be Boys," in *Boys Will Be Boys: Breaking the Link between Masculinity and Violence,* 2nd ed., pp. 39–74 (New York: Lantern Books, 2002). Reprinted by permission.

creation of a culture of violence have gone hand in hand with a breakdown of moral values that emphasized personal and social responsibility, caring for and respecting others. While these values were seen as operating mainly in the personal realm— women guarded them and transmitted them to children while men went out into the "dog eat dog" world to earn a living—they did have some tempering effect on the world of men. Bribery and money scandals are nothing new, but they have reached new heights in recent years both on Wall Street and in government.

Prep school boys and high school football players who go on robbery sprees when they need some extra money are a recent phenomenon, as are high school boys who kill a classmate to see what it feels like.

Men who value money and power above all think nothing of hiring six-year-olds to help them sell drugs, or machine-gunning their rivals in drug wars that often take the lives of innocent bystanders as well.

The situation is aggravated by the ready availability of almost any weapon imaginable to boys and men who are raised to be violent. With two hundred million guns and seventy million gun owners in the United States, our current situation is analogous to making matches easily available to known pyromaniacs. This availability of weapons is facilitated by many men who seem to experience any form of gun control as emasculating.

Our government continues to misappropriate billions in taxpayers' money for military use. According to Robert Costello, the Pentagon's top procurement official in the late 1980s, 20 to 30 percent of defense expenditures for procurement of weapons and armed forces operations and purchasing "could be saved through the application of fundamental changes in procurement practices and . . . quality management principles."[2] In 1989, former Secretary of Defense Robert McNamara estimated that our annual military budget could be cut in half without any threat to our national security. At the same time, our national security is *genuinely* threatened by internal violence, drug use, and illiteracy. Programs geared toward helping children are regularly rejected for lack of funds, yet a small fraction of our close to three-hundred-billion-dollar annual military budget would help us begin to raise physically and mentally healthy, well-educated children who would genuinely be able to say no to drugs and to violence. This neglect goes hand in hand with the lack of recognition of the enormous importance of child-rearing as reflected in the $4.55 an hour earned by day-care-center employees in 1987. Child-care workers earn less than parking-lot attendants or animal caretakers.

Everywhere there is homophobia, the fear that if we don't raise boys who are tough and tearless, they will be gay or at the very least wimpish. There is an abysmal failure of the imagination here, as if our choice were between John Wayne and Mr. Milquetoast. It is as if we cannot imagine boys and men who are strong, courageous, curious, and adventurous without being violent and obsessed with domination and power.

Instead of moving beyond an outdated and dangerous concept of masculinity, our society has encouraged the escalation of the masculine mystique's violent content. We have come a long way from the 1950s, when the pressure to prove manhood tended to take the form of going to a hooker at age sixteen or seventeen, bragging about "scoring" with girls, making the football team, or "borrowing" mom or dad's car for a joy ride. In

Harlem, according to Claude Brown's autobiography, *Manchild in the Promised Land,* it often meant more, perhaps stealing and conning, but not the random, senseless assault or murder of the 1970s and '80s.

More than any other group, African-American males are negatively affected by the values of the masculine mystique. Men at the bottom of the social hierarchy, without other outlets for achieving dominance and power, are the most likely to prove manhood through violence. This tendency has been exacerbated in the last few decades by the enormous increase in African-American teenage girls having babies. Our inner cities are now filled with millions of fatherless boys who are extremely susceptible to "hypermasculinity" and the values of the masculine mystique. Since the mid- to late eighties, an increasing number of teenage girls and women in ghetto areas have become addicted to cheap and readily available drugs. Their sons, often born addicted and then emotionally and physically neglected or battered, are at an even greater risk for violence than the other boys. The mass media furnish them with endless images of violent males.

While poor, fatherless boys are especially likely to be affected, these images influence boys of all races and social classes who are entertained by sociopathic and sadistic role models such as slasher film "heroes" Freddy Krueger and Jason, as well as Rambo. Freddy Krueger even has a fan club; children proudly wear T-shirts portraying their favorite sadistic sociopath. Behavior that would have been unthinkably repugnant twenty-five years ago is now seen over and over again on the screen.

A teacher at a good junior high school in a middle- to upper-middle-class suburb recently told me how disturbed she was by her students' reaction to a social studies classroom discussion about alleged cannibalism in Jamestown, Virginia, in the early seventeenth century; a few students had seen a film on TV that depicted it as having taken place during a time of intense starvation. "They—especially the boys—weren't horrified or repelled at all; they were excited by it and wanted to get all the details. Were the people cooked or raw? How did they cut them up?"

I was not surprised by her story. It makes sense that boys who grow up surrounded by the gore of slasher films, the xenophobia of professional wrestling, the rapist lyrics of some heavy metal and rap groups, not to mention the endless violence on TV and in toys, will become so desensitized that nothing becomes unthinkable in terms of gore and violence.

Is there really something unmanly about a boy or young man who is repelled by luridly violent films, who does not enjoy breaking bones and rupturing muscles—his own or others'—whether it be in the school yard, on the street, or on the football field? Is there really something unmanly in choosing to seek adventure by biking cross-country, going white-water rafting, fighting forest fires, or volunteering for the Peace Corps in South America or Africa? We desperately need new heroes and new myths for our boys—heroes whose sense of adventure, courage, and strength are linked with caring, empathy, and altruism.

Women have much to gain from such a change. The present definition of masculinity leads many of them to admire and reinforce just those traits that are conducive to rape, wife abuse, child abuse, and murder.

There is the fear that if boys and girls are raised more alike, if boys are encouraged to play house and push baby carriages and make believe they are daddies, then we will obliterate all but the obvious physiological differences between men and women. Similar fears were expressed in the nineteenth century when women began to enter universities and wanted the vote. Today's women are not just like men, nor is there any reason to believe that if we cease raising boys by the values of the masculine mystique they will become just like girls. In fact, recent brain research suggests that there may well be differences in the male and female brain which will ensure some emotional, cognitive, and behavioral variance between males and females as a group, under any conditions.

As we approach the twenty-first century, we face a choice. We can begin to control violent behavior, both on a national and international level, or we can continue to let it control and perhaps ultimately destroy us. We have enough knowledge to be able to significantly decrease violence, which is not to say that our knowledge is definitive or that we don't have much to learn. Just as the work of research physicians ensures progress in the control of physical diseases, continued research in the social and biological sciences could ensure progress in the control of the social disease of violence.

As of now we can, with some assurance, make the following assertions:

1. *The traditional "either/or" debate between nature and nurture with respect to violence is simple-minded and obsolete.* Human behavior grows out of a complex interaction between a biologically given potential and environmental factors. If human beings had no biological potential for violence, it could never develop regardless of external conditions. On the other hand, the environment plays an all-important role in encouraging or discouraging this potential.

Equally simplistic is the notion that any *one* factor will *necessarily* cause an individual to act violently. Any serious study of violence—or of any other aspect of human conduct—is limited to researching and analyzing significant, *not universal*, correlations between behaviors.

2. *The behavior of human beings is extremely malleable.* Anthropological studies reveal the enormous variability of human behavior and values in different cultures. Studies in psychology and sociology show us how early childhood experiences, family, peer groups, and culture mold the individual. History reveals that radical changes have taken place within a given culture in a very short period of time: extremely violent groups have become peaceful, and vice versa.

We have the clearest example of the malleability of human beings within our own country. Boys raised in Hutterite communities start out just the same as other American boys. They have their conflicts and brawls. The community has its share of boys who suffer from attention deficit disorder and/or learning disabilities, and they are especially difficult to deal with. But Hutterite boys are raised to value community, charity, love, and nonviolence. Parents and teachers are intent on helping them resolve their quarrels nonviolently. Toy guns are not allowed. Play with make-believe guns is discouraged. Hutterite children's TV viewing is limited to carefully chosen videocassettes. Child-rearing is a focal point of community life. Fathers spend large amounts of time with their children.

Ian Winter, who is the principal at the Hutterian Brethren community school in Rifton, New York, tells me that physical fights do very rarely break out among thirteen- or fourteen-year-old boys. But by the time they are sixteen, the boys have learned to resolve their conflicts nonviolently. Domestic violence and criminal behavior are unheard of.

Benjamin Zablocki, professor of sociology at Rutgers and author of *The Joyful Community*, a study of the Hutterite Brethren, confirmed, in an interview, that violence is virtually unheard of among them.

3. Human beings, especially men, have a significant potential for violent behavior. A few of the twentieth-century manifestations of this potential have been two world wars that took tens of millions of lives, genocides of Armenians and Jews, the slaughter by their fellow countrymen of millions of Russian peasants and Cambodians. As I write, human beings all over the world are being beaten, tortured, and killed. This suggests that *if we are to significantly and lastingly decrease violence, it can only be done through an ongoing relentless effort. For short of widespread genetic mutations, the potential for violence, bigotry, and xenophobia will always be with us.*

We must acknowledge fully that many normal, otherwise decent people are capable of committing, either directly or indirectly, the most cruel and violent acts. Only if we do so will we be able to recognize and act on the enormous importance of encouraging empathy and discouraging xenophobia and bigotry in our children, and of teaching them the true courage and integrity of standing up for humane, altruistic, moral convictions and feelings regardless of external pressures or monetary rewards.

If we take these steps, if they become an integral part of early child-rearing, and a mandatory part of our educational system, then we may begin to move away from what political philosopher Hannah Arendt refers to as "the banality of evil." In her book *Eichmann in Jerusalem*, Arendt concluded that Nazi henchman Adolf Eichmann, who shared responsibility for the deaths of millions of Jews, was "normal." Again and again Eichmann explained to the Israeli court that put him on trial that he was only doing his duty. Arendt writes that Eichmann suffered from a "lack of imagination." He "*never realized what he was doing. . . .* It was sheer thoughtlessness . . . that predisposed him to become one of the greatest criminals of that period."[3] She comments that "such remoteness from reality and such thoughtlessness can wreak more havoc than all the evil instincts taken together."[4]

In a study of Greek military policemen who served as torturers during the period from 1967 to 1974, when Greece was ruled by a right-wing military regime, researchers found no evidence of any abusiveness, sadism, or authoritarianism in these men's previous histories. When interviewed, the men were all leading normal lives. The researchers are convinced that certain kinds of training can lead "decent people to commit acts, often over long periods of time, that otherwise would be unthinkable for them. Similar techniques can be found in military training all over the world."[5]

These findings and Arendt's analysis of Eichmann are borne out by Stanley Milgram's study on obedience. A majority of Milgram's subjects continued to give what they thought were increasingly high electric shocks to a "victim" even after the victim screamed in pain, and in spite of the fact that they were free to disobey the psychologist's orders. Many more subjects disobeyed when the victim was in the same room than when the victim could only be heard but not seen.

We do not need to look at laboratory studies, or at studies of torturers or people like Adolf Eichmann, to become aware of any of this.

John Floyd is a friend of mine, a perfectly decent, nice guy. Yet when he served in Vietnam, John enjoyed the excitement and feeling of power of dropping bombs on Vietnamese and Laotians whom he thought of as "Commie enemies" and could not see from the height of his plane. It was only after his trip to Hiroshima that he began to realize what he had done.

When I interviewed former Secretary of Defense Robert McNamara I found him to be a thoughtful, appealing man, deeply concerned about the danger of nuclear destruction, and about the plight of poor African-Americans. Several former friends of McNamara's have corroborated my positive impression. Some of them are still shocked at the thought that Robert McNamara shares major responsibility for the *unnecessary* deaths of over a million Americans and Vietnamese.

Neither Floyd nor McNamara seems to have thought of the people whose lives they took as anything but abstractions. As a result, they were devoid of empathy or, as Hannah Arendt put it, they suffered from a "lack of imagination."

The enormous human potential for emotional detachment, denial, and lack of empathy is increased further by modern technology. Millions can now be killed without any direct contact between perpetrators and victims. This makes it even easier for decent men raised on the values of the masculine mystique to commit horrendous acts of violence.

Boys suffering from attention deficit disorder with hyperactivity, learning disability, mental retardation, extra Y chromosome, and Asperger's syndrome will always require special attention and services, since many of them are even more prone than the rest of the population to engage in violent behavior. We must develop techniques for discouraging violence in them from the earliest age. The demise of the masculine mystique would ensure that the tendency on the part of some of them to reckless and violent behavior would in no way be admired and emulated by their peers. Instead it would be viewed as immature and problematic.

While many normal men can be recruited to participate in mass murder, it is nevertheless worth investigating whether inordinate numbers of men belonging to groups such as the Nazi brownshirts, the Haitian Tonton Macoute death squads, and the Ku Klux Klan suffered from some of these disabilities as children. More generally we need more research to determine the psychological profiles and backgrounds of the men who start and seek out these groups. Understanding will help us in taking the proper preventive measures.

4. Human beings, male and female, have a significant potential for empathy and altruism. According to recent studies, shortly after they have reached the age of one, virtually all children begin to have some level of understanding of other people's experiences and attempt to help or comfort the person who is in distress. From age one and a half to age two, there is a great increase in altruistic behavior. As children get older there is more variation in their behavior. Researchers have found that in older children the degree of empathy and altruism is linked to maternal and paternal behavior. Nurturant involvement in child-rearing on the part of fathers is linked to increased and enduring empathy in their children. Studies of mothers and children indicate that when mothers are themselves empathic, when they make their children aware emotionally of how hurtful behavior affects others, when they establish principled moral prohibitions against hurting others, then children will tend to be empathic and altruistic.[6]

Among adults, these empathic, altruistic tendencies manifest themselves in a variety of ways.

During World War II, in Le Chambon, a small French town near Switzerland, villagers, led by their Protestant minister and his wife, risked their lives to hide Jews from the Nazis. As a result, thousands of people were saved.

In the United States, Americans with low incomes, for whom the tax-deduction incentive is not a factor, give a larger percentage of their hard-earned incomes to charity than do wealthy Americans.

It is not at all unusual for human beings to spontaneously jump into a river or in front of a car to save the life of a complete stranger, often at great personal risk.

The upshot of all this is that we can, if we want to, decrease violence. Human beings are born with a vast array of often conflicting potential behaviors. The environment they grow up in determines which of these behaviors will become dominant in their lives. It is nothing short of tragic that while the results of research findings are used regularly to prevent physical illness, the findings of the social sciences are rarely used in preventive programs. Changes in hygiene, the creation of vaccines, and more recently recommendations for dietary changes play a major role in preventing illness and saving lives. But *there are analogous measures that could be taken to prevent the social disease of violence.*

American boys must be protected from a culture of violence that exploits their worst tendencies by reinforcing and amplifying the atavistic values of the masculine mystique. Our country was not created so that future generations could maximize profit at any cost. It was created with humanistic, egalitarian, and altruistic goals. We must put our enormous resources and talents to the task of creating a children's culture that is consistent with these goals.

NOTES

1. *New York Times,* September 24, 1989, 29.

2. Costello, interview with the author, 1990.

3. Hannah Arendt, *Eichmann in Jerusalem: A Report on the Banality of Evil* (New York: Penguin, 1977), 287–88.

4. Ibid., 288.

5. Janice T. Gibson and Mika Haritos-Fatouros, "The Education of a Torturer," *Psychology Today,* November 1986, 57.

6. See Carolyn Zahn-Waxler and Marian Radke-Yarrow, "The Development of Altruism:

Alternative Research Strategies," in *The Development of Prosocial Behavior,* edited by Nancy Eisenberg. In the same volume, see Martin L. Hoffman, "Development of Prosocial Behavior: Empathy and Guilt." See also Radke-Yarrow and Zahn-Waxler, "The Role of Familial Factors in the Development of Prosocial Behavior: Research Findings and Questions," in *Development of Antisocial and Prosocial Behavior,* edited by D. Olweus, J. Block, and M. Radke-Yarrow.

Chapter Thirty

Supplanting Linguistic Violence

William C. Gay

I. The Linguistic Violence of (Hetero)Sexist Language

Hannah Arendt says, "Violence is nothing more than the most flagrant manifestation of power" (1970, 35). Given this definition, as one might expect, violence is expressed in many forms. Numerous writers, in fact, have applied violence to more than direct bodily harm. Within philosophy, Newton Garver, for example, has developed a typology of violence that includes overt and covert forms, as well as personal and institutional forms (1968). In Garver's terms, what I call linguistic violence can be expressed as covert institutional violence or covert personal violence, since the harm is more psychological than physical. The covert harm is institutional when it is a consequence of the established lexicon and grammar of the sedimented sign system (*la langue*). The covert harm is personal when it results from an individual intentionally or unintentionally using in speaking (*la parole*) a negative term from a variety of signs when some of the alternatives are more neutral or even positive.

Throughout history, linguistic violence has occurred alongside physical violence, often preceding, facilitating, and rationalizing physical violence. Linguistic violence is so pervasive that every culture has suffered from it, and cross-culturally linguistic violence against women is especially common. But how does language do violence? How does language hurt or harm us? Rejecting the theory of etymological oppression, Stephanie Ross argues that "the ancient roots of ordinary English words cannot—by themselves—make those words oppressive" (1981, 195). Nevertheless, she contends, "Words can hurt, and one way they do is by conveying denigrating or demeaning attitudes" (1981, 195). To support her view, Ross utilizes Joel Feinberg's contention that hurt is a species of harm and that victims are necessarily aware of hurts. (For example, assault is an incidence of hurt, but undetected burglary is a case of harm.) Ross presents the distinction between offense and oppression as parallel to Feinberg's distinction between hurt and harm. As she puts it, "One can be oppressed unknowingly but offense requires (logically or conceptually) the awareness and acknowledgment of its victim" (1981, 197). Thus, we are conscious of the hurt inflicted by offensive language, though we may not be aware of the harm perpetuated by oppressive language.

The issue is whether linguistic violence is an unavoidable consequence of the institution of language and the speech acts of individuals or whether through conscious effort it can be eliminated from the system and its use. I am not going to argue for a primordial, monocausal root of linguistic violence, and I am not going to develop an extensive theory of linguistic violence. Instead, I will focus on efforts to identify and eliminate the violence of sexist language, although I recognize that linguistic violence occurs across a continuum that stretches from subtle forms such as children's jokes to grievous forms such as totalitarian and genocidal language (Gay 1999b). This continuum contains numerous abusive forms, such as racist, sexist, and heterosexist discourse. David Burgest, for example, notes how racist language serves to justify and rationalize the formation of groups for purposes of isolation (1973). Luce Irigaray goes further, observing that sexist language, along with racist language, pervades the history of discourse (1989). Another arena in which abusive language abounds is in the derogatory terminology used to describe gay and lesbian lifestyles. The long-standing and often physically violent reinforcement of the heterosexism of established discourse often makes an open discussion of sexual orientation quite difficult (McConnell-Ginet 2001; Murray 1979).

Feminist scholars, like Jean Bethke Elshtain, stress the violence of sexist language (1982). In this regard, Arthur Brittan and Mary Maynard contend, "Sexism is not defined by sexist language; it is sexism which gives sexist language its potency. The labeling . . . only has consequences if . . . supported by the possibility of force, violence, or other sanctions" (1984, 20). Furthermore, to explain the supposed inferiority and deficiency of women's language, they observe, "Women's language is inferior when compared to that of males, which is already assumed to be the important yardstick and the superior form" (1984, 164). As Deborah Cameron puts it, "Sexist language teaches us what those who use it and disseminate it think women's place ought to be: second-class citizens, neither seen nor heard, eternal sex-objects and personifications of evil" (1985, 91). These attitudes make clear several of the ways in which sexist language is violent. Cameron explicitly uses such a designation when she proceeds to refer "to violent speaking and writing and to violent-centric language" (1985, 4). Sexist language constitutes a large component of this violent language. Later, Cameron notes, "A whole vocabulary exists denigrating the talk of women who do not conform to male ideas of femininity: nag, bitch, strident. More terms trivialise interaction between women: girls' talk, gossip, chitchat, mothers' meeting" (1985, 155).

II. The Aim of Supplanting Linguistic Violence against Women

Feminism provides several models for those wishing to supplant linguistic violence against women and other linguistically abused groups in society. These models include both methods for empirical research and recommendations of political action. On the empirical level, feminism has exposed many practices of oppressive language. This exposure has been radical in the sense of going to the roots of our linguistic usage. On the political level, after uncovering the sexist roots of many forms of linguistic violence, feminism has attempted to supplant them. These suggestions for political action rely on an affirmation of linguistic voluntarism and facilitate a practice of linguistic nonviolence. A response to sexist language, however, should be distinguished from the general struggle against oppression. In *Oppression, Privilege, and Resistance*, editors Lisa Heldke and Peg O'Connor (2004) show very clearly the interconnections among racism, sexism, and heterosexism, though their focus, unlike mine here, is not on language per se. A response to sexist language is only a part of this much broader struggle.

In *Gender Voices*, David Graddol and Joan Swann provide one of several very helpful feminist models for supplanting linguistic violence. Going beyond the type of linguistic determinism reflected in the poststructuralist view that "discourse is the 'site of struggle' and a cause of oppression," they claim that "language both helps construct sexual inequality and reflects its existence in society" (1989, 164). Language does not so much determine thought as, for practical purposes, it makes some rows much easier to hoe and makes others require arduous and often unappreciated labor. However, such difficult linguistic labor is a key component in resistance by the oppressed.

In *Feminism and Linguistic Theory*, Deborah Cameron is particularly insightful, especially in refuting the type of determinist view to which Graddol and Swann refer. Cameron begins by noting how Mary Daly and Julia Kristeva have argued that since "language is part of patriarchy," we need a radical theory of language (1985, 1–3). In developing her argument that feminist linguistics should avoid linguistic determinism, Cameron contends that (1) "linguistic determinism is a myth," (2) "male control over meaning is an impossibility," and (3) "there is no reason in principle why language cannot express the experience of women to the same extent that it expresses the experience of men" (1985, 143–144). The aim is not to socialize women and other disenfranchised groups into the linguistic practices of the power elite. Instead, the aim is the transformation of language and of the social relations on which it rests.

III. Strategies for Supplanting Linguistic Violence against Women

Heldke and O'Connor have given attention to six different strategies of resistance to oppression, such as education, coalition, disobedience, and revolution (2004, 561–563). I applaud efforts to implement these strategies, but my focus here is much narrower. I will address four issues in developing strategies to supplant linguistic violence against women.

A. Resisting Oppression and the Language of Particularity

As children, we learn language. Most of us learn only one language. If we are lucky, this language, our native tongue, coincides with the language that currently provides the most linguistic capital in the society in which we live (Bourdieu 1982, 1991). Regardless, whether we know the official language or a dialect relegated to low social esteem, whether we know only one or many languages, in whatever language we speak and write, we are faced with its lexicon and grammatical structure, which have embedded within them a wide range of terms that express not only arbitrary designations of particularity but also actual relations of power.

Once one recognizes that we always speak and write in a language filled with arbitrary designations of particularity, dated by the power relations that are currently dominant, the quest for a discourse not structured by these biases seems quixotic. I want to suggest, on the contrary, that a discourse can be forged that places a priority on identification with humanity. Moreover, this discourse does not dismiss, though it does temper, expression of the particularities of our lives that are reflected in the terms and structure of the language of particularity.

Many writers, in fact, celebrate (and often appropriately so) such particularity, specifically that which a social group chooses for its own positive self-description. Lucius Outlaw has written about the importance of changing language in order to change consciousness and, as a result, to alter behavior. He argues that this linguistic transformation is one of the central features in the struggle for civil rights by African Americans (1974, 2005). An example from the historical period to which he refers is the expression "black is beautiful." Particular terms, with their respective histories, are being used in new ways. So, this changed discourse is still a language of particularity. Moreover, just as a language of particularity can be used to raise the self-esteem of one social group, it can be used just as easily to denigrate another social group. Typically, such linguistic denigration precedes and sustains physical violence—all the way from physical abuse to genocide. For example, the Nazis began referring to Jews as "bacillus" prior to the Holocaust, and in the years preceding the 1994 genocide in Rwanda the Tutsis were called *inyenzi,* a slang epithet meaning "cockroaches."

Many feminists have written extensively along lines similar to Outlaw. The effort to shift from the use of "Miss" or "Mrs." to use of "Ms." is one example. Just as "Mr." does not convey the marital status of a man, "Ms." does not convey the marital status of a woman. Use of "Mr." or "Ms." is neutral on marital status and even sexual orientation, but the particularity of designation of gender remains. Another example is an effort to give a negative term, like "bitch," a positive meaning. Such efforts face even greater challenges, and I will later address some of them.

In addressing feminist efforts to change language, Cameron argues a very critical point. In her feminist analysis of language, Cameron refuses to give language a privileged status in the construction of our "personalities." Language makes an important contribution to our sense of identity, but it is neither the only nor the greatest influence in shaping our self-understanding. In this regard, Cameron notes the equal or even greater influence of "socio-familial relations," "the division of labour and economic organisation that regulates societies," "the physical environment," and even "individual genetic make-up" (1985, 169–170). In her rejection of the view that language itself precipitates disadvantage and oppression, Cameron makes one additional point that needs to be stressed. If language itself were the culprit, then we could provide "compensatory" education to underprivileged children and assertiveness training to women; in other words, those with privilege need not give up anything, and society need not admit that its institutions "disadvantage the poor, the black and the female just because they are poor, or black, or female" (1985, 171).

Within virtually every community that includes classes, specific social groups are arbitrarily but systematically denied possibilities open to other, more privileged social groups. The social groups that face systematic discrimination and denial of a range of social opportunities are not unwilling to undertake these opportunities; they are not allowed to do so. We have clear examples of such discrimination in practices of colonialism, racism, sexism, and heterosexism. In part, liberation movements try to break the ideology that members of the oppressed group are dysfunctional and incapable in relation to the areas of opportunity denied to them. They are arguing that discrimination against them, opportunities denied to them, are unjustified because the differences between them and the dominant group are not functionally significant.

These points have been argued during each of the waves of feminism. In each, attention to language has been critical. Whether they have been exposing sexist language or crafting gender-neutral language, feminists have been breaking the silence. I turn now to the importance of speaking out.

B. Breaking the Violence of Silence

We need to recognize that often silence is violence; frequently, unless we break the silence, we are being complicitous to the violence of the situation, whether of physical or linguistic violence. The silence surrounding child abuse, partner abuse, social discrimination, and international injustice is all too pervasive. Cameron has observed, "Silence is a symbol of oppression, while liberation is speaking out, making contact" (1985, 5). However, in breaking the silence, our aim should be to avoid counterviolence, in its physical forms and in its verbal forms. I contend that genuine peace making and efforts to forge an understood language of inclusion occur between silence and violence (Gay 1994). We need to break the silence; the challenge is finding effective, nonviolent means of breaking the silence and giving voice to the interests of the oppressed.

As academic disciplines and public forums increasingly expect nonsexist speech and writing, a type of social tranquility can result. Open verbal battle against sexist language may well come to an end. Sexists learn when and how to curb their tongues, much like international adversaries learn to put weapons of war on hold following the signing of a peace accord. Although we lack a term for merely formal linguistic gender equity, we do have a term for a merely formal peace accord, namely, negative peace. I regard such "silence" or absence of sexist language as analogous to negative peace (Gay 1999a). So, the absence of linguistic violence against women can be beguiling and lull us into thinking sexism is now gone when it has merely shifted from the public to the private sphere.

Replacing sexist and other violent language with more neutral or positive forms of linguistic expression is part of a larger project of reducing cultural violence. In this regard and corroborating my point, Cameron has observed, "The first step is breaking our silence concerning the many forms of violence" (1985, 5). A very interesting case of silence as violence in which the violence has been broken by using the Internet is found in women's sports. Darcy Plymire and Pamela Forman review how women in sports are often assumed to be lesbians, and as a consequence, athletes, coaches, and administrators in women's sports avoid giving any appearance of or voice to lesbianism in sports (2000). Since the common prejudice is that fans and sponsors would abandon women's sports if lesbian athletes were to be visible and vocal as lesbians, the "code of silence" that has resulted has given these athletes few options for breaking the silence—until the Internet. Plymire and Forman document how newsgroups on the Internet offer fans a chance to challenge the "code of silence" and contribute to discussions among those who are supportive of lesbians in sport. For now, this outlet can thrive because it occurs outside the bright lights of mainstream media. Nevertheless, Plymire and Forman conclude that the embracing of "out" lesbian athletes as role models in these Internet sites could serve as a positive step for all women athletes (2000, 151).

C. The Limits of Reclamation

Lynne Tirrell observes that an analysis of derogatory terms helps show why individual speakers cannot easily escape the socially established meaning of their utterances (1999). She reviews the "Absolutist" position on derogatory terms, noting that "the Absolutist takes the assertional commitments of the derogatory term . . . to be *nondetachable*" (1999, 52). Then, she considers the opposing position of "Reclamation." This position connects reclaiming labels with regaining power. She notes, "Proponents of reclamation . . . say that sometimes when used by members of the in-group the term is a badge of pride that recognizes an important history of degradation without endorsing its continuation" (1999, 56). The Reclamation position contends that the oppressed group can give a new future to a word that has a sordid history. Tirrell illustrates this effort with the positive use of the term "dyke" by some activists. Nevertheless, Tirrell notes that the term "dyke" still has the same past, even when in the present and in the future significantly different use occurs. The problem is that the negative meaning is likely to serve as the default when clear markers are absent.

bell hooks is very aware of the dilemma posed by derogatory terms for those who seek to reclaim or replace these terms. In her chapter "Teaching New Worlds/New Words" in *Teaching to Transgress*, she cites the line "This is the oppressor's language yet I need it to talk to you" that is found in Adrienne Rich's poem "The Burning of Paper Instead of Children" (hooks 1994b). hooks stresses that Standard English is not the speech of exile; instead, it is the language of conquest and domination and masks the loss of the many tongues oppressed by it. She continues, "It is difficult not to hear in standard English always the sound of slaughter and conquest" (1994b, 169). Nevertheless, in relation to resistance, "Learning English, learning to speak the alien tongue, was one way enslaved Africans began to reclaim their personal power within a context of domination" (1994b, 170). This speech of resistance facilitates an alternative cultural production with different ways of thinking that are crucial for countering the hegemonic worldview that has been imposed on the oppressed.

The practice of forging such linguistic alternatives encounters formidable resistance from established prejudices. In many ways, the prejudices of heterosexism run even deeper than those of racism and sexism. For example, in anti-heterosexism training sessions, some heterosexuals suggest reverse discrimination occurs against heterosexuals, view non-heterosexuality as a deficit, and reject the diversity and difference between lesbians and gay men and heterosexuals (Peel 2001). Research on how educational institutions respond to people with disabilities provides a further demonstration of how deeply these prejudices are entrenched. This research confirms what we might expect, namely, that the situation is even more difficult for lesbian, gay, bisexual, and transgender (LGBT) students with disabilities. While colleges generally accommodate these students in relation to their disabilities, LGBT students with disabilities—multiple cultural minorities—are nevertheless simultaneously also marginalized because of their sexual orientation (Harley et al. 2002). So, whether the struggle is against heterosexism, sexism, racism, or any other oppression, the effort must go beyond transforming language to transforming the prejudices and biases at the cultural base.

D. The Prospects for Cultural Transformation

In order to begin to challenge the cultural base of a society and to forge alternatives, we need oppositional concepts. Since sexist language is an instance of linguistic violence, nonsexist language needs linguistic nonviolence as an oppositional concept or it will be in danger of only eliminating the violence of sexist language and not of avoiding other forms of linguistic violence. A clue to how to forge such nonsexist discourse can be found when one recognizes that linguistic nonviolence is the antonym to linguistic violence as peace is the antonym to war. Moreover, just as we distinguish negative peace (the mere absence of war) from positive peace (the presence of justice), we can distinguish a discourse that is merely politically correct (the mere absence of ethnocentric, racist, sexist, heterosexist, and classist discourse in the public sphere) from a discourse that arises from a culturally transformed base (the presence in society and language of the primacy of our common humanity and shared interests as members of the same species) (Gay 1997).

Nevertheless, changing language is like changing the law; it affects the form but not the substance; it may be necessary, but it is not sufficient. Along with linguistic transformation, cultural transformation is equally important. In other words, to expose and eliminate sexist language will not end linguistic violence against women. We also need the ideal of an understood language of inclusion that can be the fulcrum for the transformation of everyday speech in ways that are less linguistically alienating and less linguistically violent (Gay 1998).

When we realize the important connection between language and consciousness, we can also see how changing our language can lead to not only changed thought but also changed action. Thus, feminist critiques of linguistic violence, along with other emancipatory ones, are simultaneously contributions to the practice of linguistic nonviolence and to the quest for societies in which human emancipation, dignity, and respect are not restricted on the basis of irrelevant factors like ethnicity, race, gender, sexual orientation, or class. Nevertheless, vigilance is needed to guarantee that this linguistic nonviolence moves from being merely formal to becoming substantive. In relation to all forms of gender violence, achievement of gender equality at the cultural base is necessary for positive and substantial transformation of society.

Immanuel Kant observed long ago that peace is possible; for this reason, he argued that we have a moral duty to seek to advance peace (1923, 1983). Likewise, nonsexist discourse is possible. Linguistic violence against women, as well as other forms of physical and linguistic violence, can be overcome. We have a moral duty to seek to supplant linguistic violence and to forge an understood language of inclusion.

Chapter Thirty-one

Coordinated Community Services for Victims of Violence

Patricia Yancey Martin

If the police do their job, the hospital does its job, the rape crisis center or shelter functions properly, what do coordinated community services add to victims' well-being? The answer from scholars and policy makers alike is, "if done appropriately, a great deal." Coordinated services are better for victims of violence, according to Petersen, Gazmararian, and Clark (2001), Campbell (1998), Allen (2005), and Martin (2005). Furthermore, failing to coordinate can harm victims, sometimes fatally (Pence 1999). This chapter reviews research on such claims and, in the process, acknowledges that *community coordination* is not a singular practice or condition, nor is evidence of its effectiveness definitive (Gamache and Asmus 1999).

On the surface, the notion of coordinated community services seems straightforward. Common sense suggests that coordination trumps fragmentation. But is coordination a benefit and, either way, do we know what it entails? Campbell and Ahrens (1998:537) say that "coordinated programs reflect an understanding of the multiple contexts of service delivery and embody that knowledge in services that are consistent with victims' needs." For rape victims, Campbell (1998:371) asserts, "women who . . . lived in communities where there was more coordination of . . . services had relatively positive experiences across all three systems," meaning legal, medical, and mental health.[1] Her conception of coordination resembles my concept of network integration concerning organizations' interactions in order to do *rape work*.[2] My research indicates that coordinated services are positive signs about a community for victims of rape (Martin 2005). There is every reason to assume that a similar pattern holds for other violence victims as well.

What Are Coordinated Community Services?

The concept of coordinated community services generally means that staff in multiple organizations work together for the benefit of service recipients. Meeting face-to-face, planning, developing policies and protocols, cross-training of staff, appearing on educational panels, and communicating about victims are typical coordinating dynamics (Allen 2005; Campbell, Wasco, et al. 2001; Martin 2005). Police, prosecutors, health and mental health workers, victim advocates, rape crisis and shelter staff, and so forth, who meet face-to-face to plan, learn from each other, identify common goals, and develop practices to accommodate each other and maximize victims' welfare *are coordinating* (Martin 2005). An example is *Sexual Assault Response Teams* (SARTs) that bring law enforcement and rape advocates to the hospital to assist rape victims (Ahrens et al. 2000). Meeting face-to-face helps people get to know, trust, and learn from each other, and it helps victims receive services, have their sworn-statement interview conducted, and obtain support and information from crisis workers at a single site, among other benefits (Campbell 1998). Helping victims in this way can be empowering, depending on whether they are given choices and allowed to make decisions that affect their lives.

In contrast to this felicitous scenario, failing to coordinate can deprive victims of services and, in the extreme, place them at risk. A deadly outcome associated with one such failure is described by Pence (1999). A police department failed to provide full information to a judge about a violent husband's prior record, and the judge gave the batterer a light sentence. As a result, the batterer went free and subsequently killed his wife. Had the judge known all the facts about the batterer's record of violence, he would have incarcerated him; but the police failed to fully investigate and report. Although most instances of failed coordination are less dramatic, they may nevertheless deprive victims of needed services and support.

Community coordination takes varying forms. According to Allen (2006), following Gamache and Asmus (1999), three forms are typical: (a) a separate organization takes responsibility for coordinating, e.g., the Duluth Domestic Abuse Intervention Project (see Pence and Shepard 1999); (b) a staff member in each organization volunteers or is assigned to coordinate with staff in other organizations; and (c) a separate council, task force, or other similar group coordinates services and providers. The first and third structures often have personnel paid expressly to coordinate workers in multiple organizations by arranging meetings, sending memos, arranging staff training, developing protocols, and drafting policies.

Relative to rape services, Campbell says coordination entails cooperation by service providers in at least "two systems," for example, medical, mental health, legal, advocacy, and/or rape crisis (Campbell and Ahrens 1998; Campbell and Bybee 1997). "[W]hen a hospital has a standing relationship with a rape crisis center to have advocates come to the ER to provide support during the exam process, I count this as coordinated community services. . . . The earliest elements of coordination for rape victims entailed an alliance between rape crisis and hospital that expanded to include law enforcement" (Campbell, personal communication, 2006). According to Campbell and associates, "coordinated care comes from some type of planning effort on the part of service providers to work together" with a task force, individual, or other structure charged to keep the process going (Campbell, personal communication, 2006; Campbell, Sefl, et al. 1999; Campbell, Wasco, et al. 2001; Ahrens et al. 2000).

Allen (2005:53) says formal coordinating councils (concerned with domestic violence) require participation by at least two service sectors (e.g., criminal justice and domestic violence) and staff from three or more types of organizations (e.g., domestic violence shelter, courts/judge, and police). Coordinating councils have three aims: improve policies and practices in the institutional response to domestic violence, increase cooperation and communication across "systems" (criminal justice, human services), and increase public awareness and responsiveness (Allen 2005:51, citing Allen 2001). Although Allen makes no mention of empowering violence victims, the aim of increasing responsiveness implies that it may occur.

According to Gamache and Asmus (1999), "victim safety" *must be* the overarching goal of domestic violence coordinating councils (cf. Allen 2006). Rather than "the solution to coordination problems," coordinating councils are a means to an end. Bringing everyone to the table will help domestic violence victims only if "the cooperating agencies are willing to hold themselves accountable . . . to each other [and] ultimately to the victims in their communities" (Gamache and Asmus 1999:86–87).

Common Understandings, Goals, and Practices

Effective coordination requires common understanding, goals, and practices (Gamache and Asmus 1999). My research on organizations for two decades has shown that feelings of suspicion are common across organizational boundaries and that work overload, poor communication, and competing beliefs hamper coordination. I worked on a research team in the 1980s that evaluated a Florida law intended to improve coordination and reduce duplication, turf-guarding, and waste in social welfare services (Martin, Chackerian, et al. 1983). We found minimal agreement on the meaning or goals of coordination, much less the practices it entailed. Even the meaning of "referral" was not commonly understood. For instance, staff in division A thought referral meant sending a pink slip about a client to division B, while staff in division B thought it meant bringing a client to division A or making an appointment by telephone. Staff were unaware of how those in other divisions defined "referral" and many other practices, a condition that prompted misunderstanding, prevented coordination, and harmed clients.

Specially Designated Staff

Since coordination takes time, energy, and skill, workers given this duty on top of a "regular job" often resist. Expecting staff to take on the extra duty of coordinating is a mistake, according to Gamache and Asmus (1999:84), who advise hiring staff specifically to coordinate. (Alternatively, existing positions can be redefined so coordinating is an official obligation.) After the murder noted earlier occurred, the Duluth police department hired a coordinator to compile complete information and communicate with judges about alleged batterers' violent behavior, before their cases went forward.[3]

Effectiveness

Middle-level management and/or frontline workers must be "maximized in problem-solving discussions" (Gamache and Asmus 1999; Martin, DiNitto, et al. 1992) so council members will have access to victims' lives and experiences. A council needs members who work directly with victims—*not* police chiefs, hospital administrators, or elected prosecutors—and/or they need victims themselves. Certainly, councils need victim-advocate members (Gamache and Asmus 1999). Only if victims participate, or some members have regular contact with them, will their needs, concerns, and experiences be represented. If included, victims must be treated as full members, capable of reporting knowledgeably on their own lives.

Campbell and Ahrens (1998:567–569) say coordination helps rape victims in three ways. First, coordinated communities have better "understanding of the context of social service delivery from the perspective of the providers." Second, coordinated communities are better able to take the "perspective of the victim" into account, and rape workers are more aware of how rape affects victims' lives. Third, coordinated communities are better at representing the larger social context of rape as only one form of violence against women, educating the community about rape as violence, and linking rape to women's systematic oppression.

Allen's (2005) study of "community coordinating council" effectiveness (using data from 522 board members on forty-three domestic-violence community coordinating councils in Michigan) is helpful. She finds that "councils that fostered an inclusive climate (e.g., characterized by effective leadership, shared power in decision making, and shared mission) and active participation from a broad array of stakeholders were rated as more effective by members and leaders" (2005:49).[4] Different conditions were correlated with positive changes in the criminal justice system versus other arenas. For example, "Shared power in decision making was more strongly related to the degree to which they were accomplishing their goals to create changes within the criminal justice system, while having a shared mission was more related to the degree to which goals were accomplished in community sectors beyond the criminal justice system" (2005:62). "[S]trong leadership and a representative group of active members" were positively associated with (perceived) positive reforms in "the human service, social service, and community education arenas" (2005:58).

Evaluation

Gamache and Asmus (1999:80) say that coordinating councils can be effective only if they evaluate. Staff must be hired from the outset to collect, organize, interpret, report, and assess so the council can have feedback on its achievements. A willingness to expose internal organizational practices to other council members is required so that problems, in both process and practice, can be identified. Trust is necessary. How things are going must be available for "scrutiny of [the] partners," who must "participate fully in the discussion of how problems can be resolved" (Gamache and Asmus 1999:85). Gamache and Asmus (1999:85) say that "the coordination role is assumed by persons who possess exceptional negotiation skills and who are able to devote the time and resources necessary to adequately fulfill these responsibilities." An effective coordinator must be a good negotiator with problem-solving and interpersonal skills and a good community organizer who understands how things are done, how to work with people, and how to facilitate discussion and consensus.

Community Power Dynamics

To succeed, a coordinating body must take "account of the existing power dynamics in the justice system and community when developing decision-making procedures and strategies for resolving problems and conflicts" (Gamache and Asmus 1999:80). This requires attention to politics with a small *p* and a capital *P*. The capital *P* refers to elected officials who must be convinced to support coordination. Florida's sheriffs and prosecutors are elected, and any request for their staff to participate will require their approval. Concerned about their standing with the public, they will oppose any activity that places them at risk (Martin 2005). I saw this in Florida when a prosecutor opposed a Domestic Violence Task Force. He thought the task force was being critical of his office and encouraging someone to oppose him at the ballot box; thus, he refused to participate. When the election was over and his reelection was assured, he allowed his staff to join, although he never did, and progress was finally made.

Politics with a small *p* concern the delicacy of convincing *peer* organizations to coordinate. A case study in Florida showed how the president of a rape crisis center used "honey rather than vinegar" to convince processors in the community to form a "working task force" on rape and to view it as their "own" rather than the rape crisis center's project (Martin, DiNitto, et al. 1992). Additionally, conflicts must be handled in private, out of sight of the public, or else relationships may be harmed (Byington et al. 1991; Martin 2005; Martin, DiNitto, et al. 1992; Schmitt and Martin 1999). The director of a California rape crisis center said her organization pays a price for working with the establishment "behind the scenes" but that going public would deny them access to victims and to law-enforcement recruits, whom she wants to train (Schmitt and Martin 1999). Thus, her organization compromises for the greater good.

Are Some Organizations and Communities Better Than Others?

Yes, they are. Organizations and communities vary in terms of their *responsiveness* on rape (responsiveness is defined below). The better ones *own rape*, which means they place rape cases and victims on a par with other concerns such as efficiency, avoiding negative publicity, and doing things correctly (Martin 2005). They do not try to rid themselves of the pesky crime of rape and its victims by procrastinating, refusing to be trained, or downplaying its prevalence or importance.

Which organizations and communities *own rape*? Rape crisis centers most certainly do. Their specialization in rape and lack of a legal obligation for rape cases leaves them relatively free to focus on helping victims and pressuring other organizations to be more responsive. As products of second-wave feminism, they work to prevent rape, help victims, and improve the quality of the community's response to victims (Bevacqua 2000; Campbell 1998; Campbell and Martin 2001; Campbell, Sefl, et al. 1999; Ferree and Martin 1995; Martin 1990, 2005; Matthews 1994; Schmitt and Martin 1999, 2007). Police departments, prosecution offices, and the courts address rape as only one among many problems, and hospitals similarly prioritize "real patients"—physically ill or injured—over collecting physical evidence from rape victims' bodies.[5] As a result, many mainstream organizations see rape as an aggravation rather than an opportunity for doing good. And yet, despite the odds, some mainstream organizations do own rape. (I use the term "mainstream" for organizations funded by tax revenue that are legally or otherwise obligated [e.g., by local protocol] to process rape cases. See Martin and Powell [1994] and Martin [1997] on rape processing.)

Most mainstream organizations that own rape are located in responsive communities:

> Responsive communities [are those that] make victims' interests a high priority. . . . Organizations in responsive communities orient their staffs to place rape victims' interests on par with the organizations', express support, say they are sorry and avoid acting confrontational. They adopt multi-agency protocols to coordinate workers so everyone knows what to do and what others will do. They train each other's staffs and cooperate to educate the public and prevent rape. (Martin 2005:139–140)

So what fosters responsiveness? The short answer is owning rape, as indicated by *extensive interaction and coordination* among organizations in a community. Face-to-face interaction and coordination led by the rape crisis center, rape crisis center plus police, or elected prosecutor fostered responsiveness in Florida (Martin 2005).[6] Communities where most rape processors interacted face-to-face and coordinated efforts with each other also treated victims more responsively and undertook other activities to promote positive change.

Coordination of some form is required to process a rape victim.[7] At a minimum, law enforcement and hospital must interact when a victim reports, and often the rape crisis center becomes involved. The prosecutor participates if the case moves forward. Yet organizations coordinate around issues other than victims. In my study of 105 organizations in twenty-two Florida communities, four issues were identified: (a) processing victims, (b) training staff, (c) developing protocols and policies, and (d) educating outsiders (Martin 2005). Responsive communities were those where all organizations interacted extensively to train each other's staff, develop protocols, and prevent rapes. Furthermore, communities were more responsive when rape crisis centers or "rape crisis center plus police" coordinated victim-processing networks or prosecutors coordinated prevention networks. In contrast, communities where a hospital coordinated victim networks or the sheriff coordinated training networks were less responsive. This research suggests that hospitals may coordinate by default in communities that lack a rape crisis center, but it is unclear why training coordination led by a sheriff diminishes responsiveness. I hope future researchers will explore this and related questions.

Rape Crisis Centers, Feminism, and Victims

Early rape crisis centers, founded in accord with the antirape arm of second-wave feminism, favored political consciousness-raising to empower victims over ameliorative psychological treatment. They also favored avoidance of the mainstream to prevent cooptation (Bevacqua 2000; Schmitt and Martin 2007). Their early strategy of "standing outside and allocating blame" brought injustices to the public's attention and often stimulated positive changes, but it also provoked hostility and boycotts (Martin 2005). In the years since then, rape crisis centers promoted less radical versions of feminist ideology and practice and accepted that victims need support and counseling as well as political education. They found that refusing to work with the mainstream denied them access to victims and diminished the odds of producing community reforms (Campbell and Martin 2001; Matthews 1994; Schmitt and Martin 1999).

This review of coordinated community services prompts two conclusions. First, most scholars and policymakers agree that coordinated community services are a benefit to victims of violence. No research says coordinated communities are harmful, although some of my findings suggest that some forms of coordination are better than others (Martin 2005; cf. Glisson and Hemmelgarn 1997, who say that communities where one organization dominates relations among others provide less effective services to children). Second, we need more research to document how coordination is done and its effects on victims, organizations, and communities. When we know more about particular conditions and practices that produce coordination and that coordination produces, our ability to provide guidance to activists, policymakers, and professionals interested in helping violence victims in their communities will improve (Allen 2005, 2006; Byington et al. 1991; DiNitto et al. 1989; Konradi 2003; Martin 1993; O'Sullivan and Carlton 2001).

Although imperfect (Martin 1990; Scott 2005), rape crisis centers are vital—and rare—outposts of feminist activism. They promote feminist conceptions of rape, and they work for change, using an "occupy and indoctrinate" strategy (Bevacqua 2000; Campbell 1998; Lord and Rassel 2000; Martin 2005; Schmitt and Martin 1999). Instead of standing outside, most now work from within (Schmitt and Martin 1999). Does this strategy coopt them? To a degree, yes. And yet they do much more political work about, and promote more feminist understandings of, rape than their mainstream associates do (Martin 2005). Mainstream processors may also embrace feminist conceptions of rape more than previously, due to associating with rape crisis centers (Byington et al. 1991; Martin 2005). In any case, rape victims are treated more responsively than previously, and rape crisis centers are largely responsible for this result.

NOTES

1. Campbell (1998) found that 32 percent of victims had relatively positive experiences with all three aspects of the processing systems—legal, medical, and mental health—whereas about

39 percent had beneficial outcomes only with the medical system and a final group, 29 percent, had difficulty with all three. Campbell, Wasco, et al. (2001) compare rape crisis centers with medical, mental health, and religious organizations in terms of victims' "healing" versus "hurtful" experiences with them after a rape.

2. Rape work consists of

> helping victims, examining victims (their statements, accuracy, behavior), testing victims, collecting evidence (physical and verbal), . . . moving victims through a community's legal, health and social service systems . . . delving into the backgrounds of the accused rapist and, as a rule, the victim, . . . investigating and prosecuting rape crimes, presiding over legal proceedings, cooperating with other organizations, developing protocols, training staff, teaching outsiders about rape, and preventing rape. (Martin 2005:13)

3. Police departments can obtain funds from the federal Violence Against Women Act (VAWA) and/or Victims of Crime Act (VOCA) to hire a coordinator for such tasks.

4. Allen (2005) lacked data on "external" (community) outcomes, but she calls for attention to both "internal" and "external" effectiveness. Internal refers to the issues she studied—leadership, climate, composition—and external refers to material improvements in the community. I concur. Whether coordination is beneficial should be assessed relative to internal (council) conditions and dynamics and the impact of coordinating efforts on victims of violence (e.g., did internal conditions and external practices empower battered wives to leave their partners?).

5. These conditions prompted me to label hospitals as a "reluctant partner" in rape-processing work (Martin 2005).

6. *Direct interaction* refers to one-on-one transactions, such as meeting face-to-face or talking by telephone or writing letters; *indirect interaction* refers to connecting through a third (or higher) party. For example, when police interact with hospital and prosecutor, they create a direct linkage, but if the hospital and prosecutor do not interact with each other, they can still be indirectly linked through their relations with the police.

7. Coordination is *not* domination. Coordination is a linking function, whereas domination means all relations among organizations in a community run through a single organization, as spokes of a wheel must go through the hub to reach each other. Similar to my results on rape, Glisson and Hemmelgarn (1997) found that community services for children are less effective when one organization dominates relations among others. I explain how domination (or centralization) and coordination differ in my book *Rape Work* (Martin 2005).

Chapter Thirty-two

Queering Approaches to Intimate Partner Violence

Elizabeth B. Erbaugh

The problem of intimate partner violence cuts across multiple communities and relationship types, yet domestic violence theory and practice have focused mainly on men's violence against women in a limited range of contexts. Studies, edited volumes and other written accounts published over the past two decades make clear that violence occurs in lesbian and gay relationships (Island and Letellier 1991; Kaschak 2001; Leventhal and Lundy 1999; Lobel 1986; Renzetti 1992; Renzetti and Miley 1996; Ristock 2002), and that intimate partner violence affects trans[1] and intersex people[2] (Courvant 1997; Courvant and Cook-Daniels 1998). Although the data is scant and hard to gather, researchers estimate that intimate partner violence happens at about the same rates among LGBTIQ (lesbian, gay, bisexual, trans, intersex, and queer) people as among straight people (Renzetti 1992; Renzetti and Miley 1996; Ristock 2002). Although the prevailing feminist framework helps to explain men's violence against women (particularly in white, middle-class, and heterosexual contexts),[3] it does not adequately explain women's violence against women, men's violence against men, or violence involving people whose lives and identities do not neatly fit binary gender categories.

Examining intimate partner violence in LGBTIQ communities illuminates pitfalls in dominant theoretical and practical approaches to domestic violence. Responses to LGBTIQ intimate partner violence originate both from within LGBTIQ communities themselves and from organizations in the mainstream domestic violence movement. Investigating these responses provides opportunities to broaden approaches to intimate partner violence as it affects all communities.

Two types of assumptions that underlie dominant approaches to domestic violence have specific consequences for LGBTIQ communities: the structural factors thought to contribute to intimate partner violence, and the gendered construction of the categories of "victim" (or "survivor") and "perpetrator." In this chapter, based on my own research examining LGBTIQ experiences of intimate partner violence and related interventions, I suggest ways to reframe mainstream accounts of and responses to domestic violence so as to encompass a broader range of gender and sexual identities. I describe organizational attempts to improve the access of LGBTIQ populations to interventions and services for interrupting and healing from intimate partner violence, and I discuss implications of these efforts for expanding practical responses to intimate partner violence across a broad range of communities.

Structural Sources of Intimate Partner Violence

Dominant thinking about domestic violence has prioritized heteronormative gender dynamics, with results that are positive in many respects but limiting in others. Feminist movements against domestic violence and sexual assault have succeeded in making men's violence against women visible to the research, social service, and criminal justice sectors as a serious social problem with structural and cultural roots. Theories within the "violence against women" framework (as opposed to the "family violence" framework)[4] have historically focused on the rootedness of gender violence in patriarchal social systems and gender socialization. Feminist antiviolence activists have emphasized that most domestic violence is committed by men against women, and accordingly they have focused on gender as the main structural arrangement through which abusers exercise power and control over their partners. This analysis has marginalized other dimensions of power, domination, privilege, and oppression that contribute to violence (see Collins 2000; Crenshaw 1991b).

The dominant conceptual framework has distilled the numerous and complex structural origins of intimate partner violence into a simpler explanation—one that revolves around gender—for reasons that might best be understood as strategic. On the whole, it has not been the aim of domestic violence scholars and activists to exclude anyone experiencing violence from accessing resources and support. Rather, the urgent need to cultivate a widespread public commitment to reversing the social crises of male violence and female victimization has led to the development of educational campaigns and criminal justice and social service interventions that are based on a dichotomously gendered framework (Renzetti and Miley 1996). These campaigns and interventions have considerably heightened the visibility of men's violence against women, as well as resources for addressing the problem. But they are directed toward a limited segment of the population whose identities and experiences correspond to the heteronormative orientation of these efforts.

The gains of the feminist domestic violence movement can be extended by integrating conceptually the multiple social hierarchies that supplement the gender binary as structural factors in intimate partner violence. The experiences and perspectives of marginalized communities offer insights on these additional structural factors, as well as on the social and cultural mechanisms by which they fuel violence in intimate relationships. LGBTIQ people constitute a diverse community whose members are marginalized based on a number of social factors but who share in common the experience of marginalization based on hierarchies of gender and sexuality. Incorporating their experiences into the dominant domestic violence framework requires, at a minimum, revamping its underlying gender and sexual assumptions.

One step in developing a more complete analysis of the structural factors underlying intimate partner violence entails understanding the implications of homophobia, heterosexism, and heteronormativity for both LGBTIQ and straight relationships. Homophobia refers to outright anti-LGBTIQ hostility; heterosexism and heteronormativity refer to the more insidious, yet potentially more socially potent, centering of heterosexual identities and experiences, to the exclusion (or at least the marginalization) of non-heterosexual ones.

Homophobia is likely a factor in heterosexual intimate partner violence, but it certainly plays an important and specific contextual role in intimate partner violence involving LGBTIQ people. Intimate partner violence can be conceptualized as occurring within three concentric circles: the intimate relationship, its immediate social circle, and the larger society. For LGBTIQ people, the immediate social environment generally includes some acquaintances, family members, and co-workers who express homophobic attitudes or who can be expected to respond negatively to the revelation of a nonheterosexual orientation. A homophobic social environment, particularly in one's extended family or workplace, can limit access to social or economic support systems that might otherwise lessen likelihood of intimate partner violence or can offer support when such violence occurs or is threatened (Allen and Leventhal 1999; Balsam 2001).

In the larger society, which includes social service organizations, health care institutions and criminal justice systems, antigay or transphobic violence may be more socially accepted than other forms of violence (Lyons 2006). LGBTIQ life is characterized by constant encounters with homophobia and the persistent threat of homophobic violence. Antigay and transphobic violence has historically been practiced by police and otherwise officially sanctioned (Whitlock 2005). An episode of the popular sitcom *Will and Grace* that aired in January 2006 featured a running joke implying that for queer people, being hit in the head by a beverage container is an everyday occurrence barely worth noting (Burrows 2006). Everyday homophobia, including the constant threat and widespread social tolerance of homophobic and transphobic violence, constitutes an ever-present backdrop for LGBTIQ perspectives and experiences of intimate partner violence, as well as for the attitudes of individuals—both LGBTIQ and straight —who staff social service and criminal justice organizations.

Isolation, power, and control may take particular forms in LGBTIQ relationships; moreover, homophobia can be deployed strategically by abusers in either LGBTIQ or straight relationships (Allen and Leventhal 1999). Isolation is a central tactic of abuse, and abusers may emphasize or exploit the social isolation that their LGBTIQ partners experience as part of being closeted in work, family, or social circles, or they may threaten to out their partners at work or in social or institutional contexts. For example, an abuser may threaten to have a partner's children taken away by reporting to social services that she is lesbian or bisexual. Such threats are powerful, whether or not the partner actually claims a LGBTIQ identity. Abusers may also use homophobic or transphobic language as a psychological weapon to erode their partners' sense of self-worth. We need to improve our collective understanding of how cycles of violence develop in LGBTIQ relationships, how homophobic attitudes and stereotypes are exploited by abusers in both LGBTIQ and heterosexual relationships, and how homophobia prevents survivors from seeking or accessing competent services. Furthermore, we need to examine how heterosexism and heteronormativity shape the agendas of antiviolence institutions and the attitudes and practices of their personnel.

Structural dynamics beyond patriarchy contribute significantly to intimate partner violence across a range of communities, and identities beyond gender are central to individuals' perspectives and experiences of violence. Heterosexism and homophobia are building blocks in the construction of social hierarchies and are fundamental to LGBTIQ experiences of cultural and interpersonal violence, both within intimate relationships and in larger social contexts. Just as sexism and misogyny are now elemental to common understandings of domestic violence, homophobia and heterosexism—along with racism, classism, xenophobia, and other forms of oppression—must be fully incorporated into these understandings.

Gender, Sexuality, and the Victim-Perpetrator Binary

The victim-perpetrator binary is a pervasive conceptual element of dominant approaches to domestic violence. Antiviolence professionals serving both straight and LGBTIQ communities regularly channel clients toward services and criminal justice systems based on their assessment of which of these two roles the client most closely fits. Based on the dominant explanatory framework in which patriarchy is viewed as the core structural cause of domestic violence, the victim and perpetrator roles have traditionally been implemented in a gendered fashion, so that the victim or survivor role is generally associated with women or femininity, and the perpetrator role with men or masculinity. These gender associations permeate both commonly held stereotypes and professional approaches to intimate partner violence.

As with the patriarchal structural analysis of domestic violence, gendered assignment of the victim and perpetrator roles is functional for the majority of cases in which abuse occurs between a man and a woman, both of whom are exclusively heterosexual and neither of whom has a history of gender transition. However, when the gender identities of the individuals in a violent intimate relationship assume some nonnormative configuration, the patriarchal analysis of victim and perpetrator roles does not apply. Nor does it apply in every heterosexual relationship. Yet outside observers—whether encountering a violent relationship socially or professionally—may assume that the partner they read as more masculine is the perpetrator and that the partner they read as more feminine is the victim or survivor. This assessment is not necessarily accurate—victims and perpetrators are not so easily recognized, whether or not the individuals undergoing assessment fit binary gender categories (see Marrujo and Kreger 1996). It is impossible to know on sight, or based on how a voice sounds over the telephone, how an individual or her or his partner identifies with regard to gender. The gender identities of the participants in a given relationship may counter normative gender stereotypes, and first impressions based on gender-normative assumptions will not reliably reveal which partner has the upper hand in an abusive dynamic. Acknowledging and responding to intimate partner violence as a serious problem in LGBTIQ communities requires detachment of the victim and perpetrator categories from preconceived gender roles.

The domestic violence movement as a whole embodies the belief, borne out by empirical findings (Avakame 1998), that intimate partner violence has special characteristics and is especially dangerous, precisely because it occurs between intimates. If, however, only gender-normative, heterosexual man-woman pairings are seen as having the potential for violence, the intimate nature of violence in queer partnerships is rendered invisible. Based on the heteronormative domestic violence framework, outsiders to a violent nonheterosexual relationship may acknowledge the violence but deny that it is taking place between intimates and thereby downplay its seriousness. For example, police may dismiss intimate partner violence between two men as a "fight between roommates" or as otherwise less serious than violence between a heterosexual man and his woman partner. LGBTIQ people themselves might not take seriously the possibility that they are experiencing intimate partner violence, because they are unable to project themselves mentally into the gendered stereotypes commonly associated with the victim and perpetrator roles. Abusers may take advantage of this fact and of similar confusion on the part of fellow community members and domestic violence professionals (Allen and Leventhal 1999; Goddard and Hardy 1999). On the other hand, challenging the gendered assumptions associated with the victim and perpetrator roles increases the likelihood that intimate partner violence among LGBTIQ people will be recognized as both truly intimate and truly violent.

The victim and perpetrator categories are far from useless. On the contrary, the theoretical formulation and practical implementation of these categories has enabled the wide dissemination of an analysis of power and control in relationships. They constitute a clear conceptual framework based on which many survivors of violence are able to access the support of service agencies and criminal justice systems. Advocates with experience serving LGBTIQ communities are among those who support continued use of these categories and the provision of separate services for clients based on the specific nature of their participation in violent relationships (Goddard and Hardy 1999; Grant 1999).

However, the ways these roles are connected conceptually to gender identities, and the exclusion of nonnormative gender identities and other categories of identity from consideration in assessing individuals' participation in violence, merit serious review. Relying on unduly simplistic gendered binaries, in isolation from other dimensions of identity, restricts complete understanding of the contexts, causes, and correlates of intimate partner violence in both LGBTIQ and heterosexual relationships. Moreover, gendered applications of the victim-perpetrator binary reinforce the notion that patriarchy is the main contributing factor to domestic violence, while minimizing other hierarchical structural arrangements that contribute to violence.

The heteronormativity (centering of normative gender identities and heterosexual relationships) that characterizes dominant understandings of domestic violence reinscribes the othering that fuels homophobic violence against LGBTIQ people. To define the universe of domestic violence so that LGBTIQ people and their intimate relationships cannot intelligibly be located within it is to reinscribe society's eclipsing of LGBTIQ identities and experiences. Power and control must be conceptualized not only apart from gender stereotypes but also in ways that incorporate sources of personal identity beyond gender. More sophisticated understandings of individuals' identities and roles in intimate relationships will aid in assessing cases of intimate partner violence and in providing appropriate services to individuals with a wide range of gender and sexual identities.

Queering Responses to Intimate Partner Violence

Experienced domestic violence advocates who work with both straight and LGBTIQ communities know that several criteria must be met in order to interrupt intimate partner violence effectively. First, the survivor must acknowledge the violence and its destructive potential, hopefully with the aid of others in near social proximity. Then the survivor needs somewhere to go for help where the violence will readily be acknowledged as legitimate and dangerous by those in a position to offer helpful resources. The services offered there must be competent and well informed, both at the level of institutional policies and in the attitudes and behaviors of individual staff members and volunteers. Ideally these services must be based on a solid understanding of the social, cultural, and economic contexts of the survivor's relationship and of what is at stake in considering whether to leave it.

Feminist domestic violence activists have worked tirelessly to establish public awareness and competent social services so that straight women survivors of domestic violence are able to see their situations as legitimately dangerous, to seek appropriate services, and to reestablish safety and security for themselves and their children. The movement has prioritized the need not to revictimize heterosexual women survivors of violence once they enter criminal justice, medical, and social service systems seeking support and has made leaps forward in this regard. Commensurate changes on behalf of LGBTIQ survivors remain necessary. As the domestic violence movement has confronted patriarchy, so too must it confront heteronormativity.

Due to the same heterosexist and homophobic attitudes that contribute to antigay violence and, when internalized, LGBTIQ intimate partner violence, LGBTIQ survivors face the risk of revictimization by other community members, criminal justice systems, and social service agencies. In particular, victims who are read as masculine, or whose abusive partners are read as feminine, may face disbelief or dismissal of their fears or suffering, either in their communities or in service institutions. They may be told that violence against men or violence committed by women does not constitute domestic violence, that there are no services available for someone in their situation, or even that "a real man" or "a real butch" could "take it" (Allen and Leventhal 1999). Men or masculine people who report sexual violence face particular risk of having their claims minimized or even ridiculed (Pelka 1997). Gender stereotypes may be exploited to humiliate men or masculine people who are victimized or to demonize women or feminine people who use violence (Russo 2001a). On the other hand, violence committed against the more feminine-appearing partner in a relationship may be viewed as a socially acceptable expression of the masculine-appearing partner's gender role.

If, in the face of prevailing gender stereotypes, LGBTIQ people come to view their own situations as legitimate cases of intimate partner violence, they must be able to access competent professional resources where risks of revictimization are minimized. Provided that domestic violence agencies exist in the areas where they live, and that they are out enough about their gender and sexual identities to feel comfortable contacting those agencies in a crisis, LGBTIQ clients must be able to trust that the services offered will be suitable, respectful, and based on accurate information about their identities and specific needs.

In addition to redefining the structural contexts and personal identities associated with intimate partner violence, antiviolence institutions are developing responses and interventions that are sensitive to these expanded definitions. Responses to LGBTIQ intimate partner violence emerge primarily from two distinguishable but overlapping sources. LGBTIQ communities create new organizations tailored from the ground up to their own experiences and needs, and institutions previously established within the heterosexual battered women's movement alter their approaches to accommodate LGBTIQ communities. LGBTIQ-specific organizations may either use approaches based on the traditional heteronormative service model, or they may diverge from it and use LGBTIQ-community-driven models. Perhaps the best antiviolence programs blend what has been learned from heteronormative domestic violence practice with what has been excluded from it but has been recognized as significant by LGBTIQ communities.

Queer communities began establishing their own organizations to address violence in the late 1970s. Some LGBT organizations focus on both antigay hate violence and intimate partner violence. Like the feminist battered women's movement, the LGBT antiviolence movement got its start in community organizing and has become increasingly institutionalized. As a rule, LGBT antiviolence organizations combine services to address domestic violence, based at least in part on the "traditional" model, with community organizing approaches, which may or may not evolve into a more service-oriented approach. LGBTIQ-community organizing against violence continues to take place both within and outside established nonprofit organizations.

Institutionalized organizations within the LGBT antiviolence movement have grown in number to over twenty (NCAVP 2006) and continue to develop impressive levels of expertise in serving LGBTIQ communities. The majority of these organizations are located in urban centers of the United States and Canada with large queer populations, such as San Francisco, New York, Boston, and Seattle. Some LGBT intimate partner violence programs are linked to, or incorporated within, local LGBT community centers. To varying degrees, they draw on service approaches developed by the battered women's movement, adapting them as necessary for LGBTIQ clients.

The success of any antiviolence institution's attempt to address the local LGBTIQ community's needs depends on a number of factors. These include the representation of LGBTIQ people among the agency's staff and volunteers; the existence of meaningful partnerships with local LGBTIQ communities and organizations; effective means of addressing homophobia, transphobia, and heterosexism within the organization and its institutional network; the applicability of intake forms, procedures, counseling, and other services to the full range of human gender and sexual identities; and the ability to evaluate objectively and continually the agency's service model and to adapt it where necessary. Established LGBT antiviolence agencies constitute deep founts of expertise in these and other areas.

If a service agency initially based in the heteronormative framework can demonstrate to the local queer community that it is knowledgeable about and open to LGBTIQ identities and needs, the queer community will come to trust the agency and to access its services. If the agency partners effectively with existing LGBTIQ communities and organizations, hires openly LGBTIQ staff and volunteers, and consistently tailors its programming, forms, and procedures in accordance with a strong anti-heterosexist agenda, it will likely become known as a safe and helpful place for queer people to go for support when intimate partner violence occurs or is threatened.

Responding to LGBTIQ intimate partner violence requires the staff and volunteers of an antiviolence agency to develop appropriate knowledge, skills, and tools to meet the needs of LGBTIQ clients. Many of these needs resemble those of heterosexual and gender-normative clients, whereas others differ in important ways. For example, a crisis counselor should understand that a transsexual man or woman seeking shelter may need to retrieve specific clothing items, hormone supplements, shaving equipment, or makeup from home as a matter of daily survival or to preserve a sense of security and well-being. It is the responsibility of antiviolence agencies and their personnel to educate themselves (with the input of qualified and compensated LGBTIQ advisers) about daily realities of LGBTIQ life relevant to intimate partner violence and personal safety. At a more fundamental level, the organization and its personnel must acknowledge and address heterosexism and transphobia within the organization on an ongoing basis. Heterosexism, homophobia, and transphobia not only contribute to intimate partner violence but also shape institutional agendas and personal attitudes. In order to serve individuals and communities outside the heteronormative framework, antiviolence organizations must confront manifestations of heterosexism and other social hierarchies within domestic violence service provision itself, as well as within intimate relationships.

The feminist domestic violence movement has succeeded in articulating and disseminating an analysis of patriarchy as a root structural cause of gender violence generally and of intimate partner violence specifically. Queering dominant approaches to intimate partner violence requires accommodating the perspectives and experiences of queer-identified people, intersex people, transgender and transsexual people, bisexual people, lesbians, and gay men. These populations include people of color, immigrants (documented and undocumented), working-class people, young people, elders, people with disabilities, HIV-positive people, and members of drag, leather, poly,[5] and other subcultural communities. As many others have argued, in order to effectively interrupt and transform cycles of violence that harm multiple communities, the domestic violence movement must expand its analysis to confront the forms of violence associated with a number of intersecting social hierarchies beyond patriarchy. Confronting heteronormativity is an important step that will enable antiviolence movements to better understand and respond to intimate partner violence as it affects a wide range of communities.

NOTES

1. My use of the term *trans* encompasses transgender and transsexual identities.

2. See Chase (2002), Fausto-Sterling (2000) and ISNA (2006) for general discussions of *intersex*.

3. The recent anthology edited by Sokoloff and Pratt (2005) offers discussions of domestic violence in marginalized communities and directly addresses race, ethnicity, class, migration, and sexuality as factors in domestic violence.

4. See Kurz (1997) for a concise analysis of this debate.

5. "Poly" refers to polyamory. Poly communities support honest, respectful multipartner relationships. See Anderlini-D'Onofrio (2004) and Easton and Liszt (1998) for general discussions of polyamory.

Chapter Thirty-three

The Impact of the Sex Industry in the European Union

Janice G. Raymond

One of the most visible developments in the sex industry during the last thirty years has been its rapid expansion and massive diversification. Globalization of the economy means globalization of the sex industry, whether one is confronted with sex trafficking, prostitution, mail-order-bride marketers, lap dancing and other sex clubs, sex tourism, and/or pornography. There are few countries in which the sex industry is shrinking.

The sex industry thrives on renaming its sexual exploitation as "sex." Pornography is called "erotica" or "adult videos"; prostitution is renamed as "sex work" or "sexual services"; pimps are now called "third-party business managers" or "erotic entrepreneurs"; and lap dancing or sex clubs are called "gentlemen's entertainment."

The Internet has greatly enhanced the reach of the sex industry. The *World Sex Guide*, is an Internet-based trove of information informing men about what country, what brothel, and even what woman to exploit if the man prefers a certain ethnic group, a certain kind of sex, and a certain preference in women. In the UK, 33 percent of all Internet users access what is called hardcore pornography ("Men and Porn," 2003). The heaviest demand is for pornographic material featuring children, bondage, sado-masochism, and sex acts with various animals. The adult entertainment group called Private Media will soon beam pornography to UK mobile phones. In the United States, people (mostly men) spend more on pornography every year than they do on movie tickets and all the performing arts combined ("Men and Porn," 2003).

The Internet search engine Yahoo has clubs devoted to father-daughter incest, complete with pictures. There is an "Asphyxia and More Club" depicting naked women hung by the neck and other women who have been strangled. There are photos of emaciated concentration-camp victims lying naked in a mass grave, accompanied by a sexually suggestive caption (Nickson, 2003). The sex industry plays on the ever more transgressive nature of the pornographic content, mainstreaming what in former times would only have been found in seedy, marginal, pornographic emporiums.

What is most disturbing about all this information is that not only is the sex industry big business but that the selling of its "products"—pornography, prostitution, sex tourism, mail-order brides—all depending on the commodification of mostly women

This chapter is the text of testimony made before the European Parliament on January 19, 2004. Presented at Public Hearing of the Committee of Women's Rights and Equal Opportunities to the European Parliament. Reprinted by permission.

and children, has become much more acceptable, more normal, and even fashionable and "cool." And anyone who raises criticisms of the industry and its turning of sexual exploitation into "sex" is labeled out of touch, moralistic, and repressed. Ultimately, the sex industry has made sexual exploitation not only normal but respectable. As one woman explained, "It's like a joke among my close male friends. . . . I'll ask, 'What did you do last night?' and they say, 'I was up till five in the morning jerking off to the Internet'" (Amsdem, 2003). And many women have commented that many men seem incapable of having sexual relationships or, for that matter, genuine emotional relationships with women who don't act like women in pornography.

For many men, however, pornography is not enough. They want to enact the fantasies, the transgressions, and ultimately the degradation and violence of pornography with live women. And the place to do this is in prostitution. The sex industry expands to accommodate all tastes and all demands. For example, men buying women in prostitution don't just want the local women—they want exotic women from other countries who, according to their racial preferences, may be stereotyped as more pliable, more willing, or more sexy. An estimated five hundred thousand women and children, mainly from Eastern Europe, Africa, South America, and Southeast Asia are trafficked to EU countries for *sexual exploitation* every year, according to the European Institute for Crime Prevention and Control. The International Organization of Migration claims that this business generates US$8 billion per year and attributes the soaring rate of trafficking to the increasing demand for prostitution in the EU, the rise of organized crime in Eastern Europe especially, which capitalizes on the demand for prostitution in Western Europe, and the desperation of trafficked women from poorer countries.

The normalization of sexual exploitation has been greatly enhanced by the legalization/decriminalization of the sex industry in various countries in Europe. Legalization has been a gift to traffickers and pimps, who, overnight, become legitimate businessmen. Prostitution becomes a public good, and governments derive enormous revenues from its legal legitimation. Legalization, or what we call state-sponsored prostitution, has become so normalized in EU countries that brothels in Germany and elsewhere gain enormous acceptance by, for example, raising money for charity through throwing open their doors to the public and holding pornographic art exhibitions and displaying their wares ("Who Needs Charity," 2003).

But the impact of the sex industry's expansion doesn't stop with legal legitimation of prostitution through state approval. The state is also called upon to fund the training of prostitutes to service, for example, disabled men and to ensure that state-employed caretakers of these men take the men to brothels and help to physically facilitate their sex acts with women in prostitution where they are not able to engage in intercourse themselves. As one critic has written, "If sex is viewed as a human right needing state support, one could legitimately claim he belongs to an oppressed minority as an unattractive, desperate male. What about the lonely pensioner who can't find a companion, or can't afford Viagra? Should the state subsidize the fulfillment of his sexual appetite too?" (McGrail, 2003).

People ask what can be done. Government authorities and the press affirm that it's high time that something is done. But this "something" is usually to repeat the old and failed measures of legalizing, decriminalizing, or regulating prostitution—whether in tolerance zones where prostitution is restricted to certain parts of the city, mandatory health checks and registration of so-called sex workers, or decriminalizing pimps as third-party business agents or managers and/or brothels as "houses of protection" for women in prostitution. These are not "new" solutions to the problem. They are very old and very repressive measures.

As part of its mission, my organization, the Coalition Against Trafficking in Women (CATW), advocates against state-sponsored prostitution in many parts of the globe. We work with legislators to devise legal and programmatic remedies that do not involve decriminalizing the sex industry and abandoning women in prostitution to what has to be "the most demeaning job in the world." CATW supports the decriminalization of women in countries where women have been criminalized for prostitution, because we believe that no woman should be punished for her own sexual exploitation. But we do *not* support the decriminalization or legalization of the sex industry. Although forms of decriminalization or legalization of the industry may vary from country to country, or city to city, *we call all these forms state-sponsored prostitution because the common element is that the system of prostitution itself becomes accepted and legitimated by the state.*

Legalization of prostitution was promoted with the argument that legitimation of prostitution would control and curb the expansion of the sex industry and restrict the number of brothels, sex clubs, and entrepreneurs who could operate. But instead of restricting its expansion, legalization has increased the number of brothels and sex clubs and also increased trafficking. The goal of any industry, legitimate or not, is to expand. Advocates of legalization invoke a peculiar argument when they rationalize that legalization will bring the sex industry under control, restricting its reach and abuse.

Contrary to claims that legalization and decriminalization would control the expansion of the sex industry, prostitution now accounts for 5 percent of the Netherlands economy (Daley, 2001, p. 4). Over the last decade, as pimping was legalized, and brothels decriminalized in the year 2000, the sex industry increased by 25 percent in the Netherlands (Daley, 2001, p. 4).

Legalized or decriminalized prostitution industries are one of the root causes of sex trafficking. One argument for legalizing prostitution in the Netherlands was that legalization would help to end the exploitation of desperate immigrant women who had been trafficked there for prostitution. However, one report found that 80 percent of women in the brothels of the Netherlands were trafficked from other countries (Budapest Group, 1999). In 1994, the International Organization for Migration (IOM) stated that in the Netherlands alone, "nearly 70% of trafficked women were from CEEC [Central and Eastern European Countries]" (IOM, 1995, p. 4).

This expansion of the legal and illegal sex industry is not restricted to Europe. Legalization of prostitution in the State of Victoria, Australia, resulted in massive expansion of the sex industry.

Recommendations:

1. We must address the *growing trend to de-link prostitution and trafficking and reestablish the connections between prostitution and trafficking*. The trend to minimize prostitution, and now even trafficking for prostitution, has been growing for years. Particu-

larly in policy circles where antitrafficking legislation is being discussed and debated, legislators and NGOs are being told to concentrate only on trafficking and not on prostitution. Unfortunately, prostitution has been wiped off the policy agenda in many countries so that whenever antitrafficking legislation is discussed in interregional or international forums, countries are told not to discuss prostitution else it will jeopardize agreements against trafficking. Sadly, policy makers have caved in to this censoring of the linkages between trafficking and prostitution.

Are we going to maintain that trafficking in women is a horrendous violation of women's human rights when the same violence, exploitation, and health consequences happen to women who are in local prostitution, many of whom have been domestically trafficked from neighborhood to neighborhood, city to city, state to state, and province to province? Do we really want to ratify the notion that commercial sexual exploitation is only actionable when it happens to women who have been trafficked into a country and not within a country?

The Coalition Against Trafficking has interviewed almost two hundred victims of international and domestic trafficking in five countries: Thailand, Indonesia, the Philippines, Venezuela, and the United States. The information we have collected from victims of trafficking and prostitution, and from others involved in work against sexual exploitation—such as social services providers, human rights advocates, and law-enforcement authorities—clearly indicates that a significant number of *both* women who have been internationally trafficked, as well as those who are in local prostitution industries, endure similar kinds of violence and suffer similar and multiple health effects from the violence and sexual exploitation.

2. We must *combat the trend to legalize/regulate prostitution as work,* with all that legalization/regulation implies. We cannot redefine women in prostitution as "sex workers," without redefining the whole industry as work, unless we want to redefine men who buy women for the sex of prostitution as ordinary "customers," and pimps as "third-party business managers" for women who, it is alleged, have the right to contract with whomever they want to further their "profession." Many people think that they are dignifying women by referring to them as "sex workers." However, when we redefine women as sex workers, the whole industry becomes redefined as a legitimate economic sector.

Legalization/regulation of the sex industry doesn't address its primary consequence —that women in prostitution are *segregated* as a legal class whose occupation is to provide sexual services to men—albeit under regulated conditions but letting the male demand for commodification of women's bodies stand. In countries that tolerate prostitution, as one commentator noted, "there are more brothels than schools." Do we really want brothels everywhere? Is prostitution a career to which we want young girls to aspire?

3. We must *focus on the demand and combat the trend to make the buyers invisible.* The least discussed part of the prostitution and trafficking chain has been the men who buy women for sexual exploitation in prostitution, pornography, sex tourism, and mail-order-bride marketing.

We cannot shrug our shoulders and say "poor men," or "men are like this," or "prostitution has always been in existence," or "boys will be boys." Shall we tell women and girls in prostitution that they must continue to do what they do because prostitution is inevitable, or because that's the way men are?

Sweden's law against the buying of "sexual services" has been a model that should be emulated elsewhere. There is an urgent need for governments to put male buyers of women and children in prostitution on the policy and legislative agenda, taking seriously that the problem of global sex trafficking will not be dented unless those who create the demand for prostitution are addressed and punished. Sweden has clearly chosen to resist the legalization/regulation of prostitution and to address prostitution as a form of violence against women.

5. *We must not treat trafficked women as migration criminals*—i.e., as illegal migrants who should be deported from a country. Trafficking is not a migration crime. Many regard trafficked women as "undesirable and criminal aliens," crossing borders illegally to take advantage of greener pastures elsewhere. This perspective in reflected in national legislation in destination countries that makes immigration more restrictive, thus obstructing the flow of migrants seeking to enter countries legitimately and through applications for asylum.

Ironically, these restrictive immigration policies also tighten up border controls that often are used to harass vulnerable migrants but have little effect on the traffickers. As immigration becomes more restrictive and discriminatory, and ineffective border controls are utilized in receiving countries, traffickers become the major international players who facilitate international migration because the legitimate channels are so restrictive.

Antitrafficking policies and programs must address organized prostitution and domestic trafficking. Most trafficking is *for* prostitution and operates within the context of domestic sex industries. International women are trafficked into domestic sex industries, and both international and local women are trafficked within the country. In the face of a transnational sex industry that traffics women into all parts of the globe and that draws women into the industry at home and abroad, antitrafficking and antiprostitution legislation must be made as powerful as the sex industry.

Chapter Thirty-four

10 Things Men Can Do to Prevent Gender Violence

Jackson Katz

1. Approach gender violence as a MEN'S issue involving men of all ages and socio-economic, racial, and ethnic backgrounds. View men not only as perpetrators or possible offenders but also as empowered bystanders who can confront abusive peers.

2. If a brother, friend, classmate, or teammate is abusing his female partner—or is disrespectful or abusive to girls and women in general—don't look the other way. If you feel comfortable doing so, try to talk to him about it. Urge him to seek help. Or if you don't know what to do, consult a friend, a parent, a professor, or a counselor. DON'T REMAIN SILENT.

3. Have the courage to look inward. Question your own attitudes. Don't be defensive when something you do or say ends up hurting someone else. Try hard to understand how your own attitudes and actions might inadvertently perpetuate sexism and violence, and work toward changing them.

4. If you suspect that a woman close to you is being abused or has been sexually assaulted, gently ask if you can help.

5. If you are emotionally, psychologically, physically, or sexually abusive to women, or have been in the past, seek professional help NOW.

6. Be an ally to women who are working to end all forms of gender violence. Support the work of campus-based women's centers. Attend "Take Back the Night" rallies and other public events. Raise money for community-based rape crisis centers and battered women's shelters. If you belong to a team or fraternity, or another student group, organize a fundraiser.

7. Recognize and speak out against homophobia and gay-bashing. Discrimination and violence against lesbians and gays are wrong in and of themselves. This abuse also has direct links to sexism (e.g., the sexual orientation of men who speak out against sexism is often questioned, a conscious or unconscious strategy intended to silence them; this is a key reason few men do so).

8. Attend programs, take courses, watch films, and read articles and books about multicultural masculinities, gender inequality, and the root causes of gender

violence. Educate yourself and others about how larger social forces affect the conflicts between individual men and women.

9. Don't fund sexism. Refuse to purchase any magazine, rent any video, subscribe to any Web site, or buy any music that portrays girls or women in a sexually degrading or abusive manner. Protest sexism in the media.

10. Mentor and teach young boys about how to be men in ways that don't involve degrading or abusing girls and women. Volunteer to work with gender-violence prevention programs, including antisexist men's programs. Lead by example.

Chapter Thirty-five

Action

Elizabeth Ward

The stories of women's lives
do not appear in magazines
even when they seem to

The stories of women's lives
are etched in the shadow
of a young girl's brown eyes

The stories of women's lives
are seared in the muscle
at the corners of their mouths

The stories of women's lives
weep down from the moon
in huge silver drops

carrying the siren sounds of
the stories of women's lives.

i dream
  a world beyond rape

i dream
  a world where the very bodies
  that we live in
  do not incite violence against us

i dream
  a world where we can walk the streets
  or country roads, on the darkest nights,

lit only by the stars
and our own freedom to move

Dreaming is useful in envisaging where we want to go, because it helps us to get there. Such dreaming, however, grows out of an awareness of how we have been constructed and abused by patriarchy. The aim of this chapter is to help end the silence, lift the blinds, on the subject of Father–Daughter rape. As well as encouraging dreaming, I wish to emphasise the need for action. Action to change things in the world makes new dreaming possible.

The Speaking of Women

Women everywhere need to start talking about Father–Daughter rape. We need to talk with each other about our experiences of it, our fear of it, our confusions about it, our anger that is touched by it, and any other reactions that we have to it. We need to dredge our memories, the multiplicity of layers through which we know things, in search of our own experiences of growing up as a girl-child. We need to remember, see and understand that for girl-children there are constant messages being received about the power that men have over women. Girl-children are the receptors, as only children can be, of a multifarious network of visual, auditory, and vibrationary signals about the sexual role they are expected to play in order to please men/the Father/the seat of power. Like a clean wind blowing away fog, this process of women remembering and asking and talking and validating the truth about Father–Daughter rape is the only way in which the depths of silence and blindness that have crippled most victims are going to be lifted. As Adrienne Rich has written:

> One of the most powerful social and political catalysts of the past decade has been the speaking of women with other women, the telling of our secrets, the comparing of wounds and the sharing of words. This hearing and saying of women has been able to break many a silence and taboo; literally to transform forever the way we see.[1]

Transforming the way we see, seeing this patriarchal world and how it is structured, is both a painful and an exhilarating experience. It is painful because it means confronting the depths of the limitation, humiliation, and abuse that women and children suffer within patriarchy; it is exhilarating because new thoughts, new perceptions, visions of a truly humane society become possible.

Father–Daughter rape, Son–Mother rape, Brother–Sister rape: these are rape in its most intimate (family) form. Rape is about hatred. Male supremacist hatred of such proportions has been endured within the private sphere of the family by individual women for too long. As women begin to speak of these most intimate atrocities, the face, the very being of our society will change.

Mothers and Daughters

As the Daughters and Mothers emerge from the shades of silenced anger, they will find each other, form groups, speak, and share through the quietest night hours, and emerge into the light of day transformed by the knowledge that they each, in their aloneness, were victims, but that in their togetherness they can vision a new world into being: our world, beyond rape. Mothers will tell their Daughters, the Daughters will tell each other, on and on down the line, that some things are not to be borne.

The Daughter–Mother tie reveals a particularised form of the power that resides within the speaking of women with each other. We have seen that for the Mothers "the eyes not seeing what the heart cannot hold"[2] has locked them off from their Daughters behind a barrier of blindness and broken hearts. When the Daughters and Mothers break through this barrier, the scales of patriarchal vision fall from their eyes and their broken hearts are mended by the love that women share—a special kind of love which occurs as women begin to acknowledge their shared identity, in suffering and in change.

The particular poignancy of Mothers and Daughters re-finding each other as sisters derives from the patriarchal injunction which blames Mothers for everything and anything—thereby depreciating Motherhood, while at the same time insisting that it is Woman's highest vocation. Daughters learn of this depreciation of Mothers, much as they breathe air: it is integral to patriarchal social forms. Daughters, nearly always, do not want to be Mothers *in the same way*: every Daughter determines to do it differently from how her Mother did it, to do it better. But the fulcrum of patriarchal reproduction is that she has to do it: be a Mother or a Non-Mother, either way trapped in the linguistic and social imperative that a woman be defined in terms of her relationship to Mothering.

Thus Daughters reject their Mothers—and at the same time they long for them. They long for a Mother who will show them how to get out of the trap, how to be independent, whole, herself. We long for an acknowledgment of what could be possible between Mothers and Daughters.

> Mothers and daughters have always exchanged with each other—beyond the verbally transmitted lore of female survival—a knowledge that is subliminal, subversive, preverbal: the knowledge floating between two alike bodies, one of which has spent nine months inside the other.[3]

The knowledge floating between two alike bodies . . . While this knowledge can be felt between any two women, it is most strongly experienced between Mothers and Daughters: one woman has created another, one's body is the same as that of the being who created it. They have known each other most intimately, in what must surely be the most intimate form of knowing experienced within the human condition: one woman created by another.

This knowing is the area that is being touched, like butterfly wings caressing (beautiful and fragile), when Mothers and Daughters speak truly, each to each.

Protection, Care, and Change

As the Daughters and Mothers, supported by other women, identify what has been done to them, they will, hopefully, be involved in, even initiate, changes as to the type of protection and care which are needed. Ideally, after themselves being healed as far as is possible in the miasma of horror from which they are emerging, many of these girl-children and women will become involved in supportive networks and sheltered environments which they themselves will (help) establish and operate.

The social welfare model of care which is currently the only widely available form of institutional help needs to be publicly examined and contrasted with the self-help, grass-roots validation model being offered by rape crisis centres and women's refuges. The social welfare system must undergo an internal revolution in terms of knowledge and attitudes, if it is to be capable of even partially providing the kind of care needed by the victims of Father–Daughter rape. Instead of waiting rooms, medical examinations, welfare interviews, disconnected counselling sessions, and the stated or implicit moral imperatives which accompany such impersonal types of "care," we need intense and complex systems of involvement in the ongoing process each Daughter and Mother needs to navigate in order to (re-)find a sense of integrity and belief in herself. The welfare system needs, most of all, to change its primary focus from that of family "welder" (trying to get the family back together at all costs), to that of care and protection for the Daughter and understanding for the Mother.

Part of this process will include exposing the misuse of Freud's theory of infantile sexuality. It has been used as a blatant and outrageous form of invalidation of Father–Daughter rape. Quite apart from the vicious cruelty inflicted on individual victims by this myth, it has functioned to deepen the invisibility of Father–Daughter rape on a macro-social level. Functioning within the same cultural mode, the Fathers of the social sciences have diddled with the facts of Father–Daughter rape so as to further obscure reality. The academic interpreters of people's behaviour are just as guilty as the Fathers insofar as they purport to be "objective" when they are in fact operating from their own subjectivity. Eschewing passionless objectivity which is, by definition, rooted in the status quo, we need to direct our passionate attention to the validation of our own senses: to believe that the worst we see and feel really is happening; and to determine what we want to do about it. In this process we will find ways to name and reject the so-called objectivity of the social scientists who have manipulated our thoughts and feelings, misnaming the reality of Father–Daughter rape.

Mothers and Daughters will also have the most pertinent input into the immediately needed reforms of the law. In every state, territory, and nation, laws must be brought into existence which recognise the commonness of Father–Daughter rape, and address themselves primarily to protecting the Daughters from the now current processes of minute cross-examination and the need for evidence of corroboration, as well as the myriad effects of "normal" rape cases.

Laws nearly always follow, rather than lead, public opinion and mainstream values. Thus the multifaceted process of women talking, of naming, of mass publicity, of educating the silent majority, of convincing those who make and enforce laws, of involving those who deliver welfare systems and medical care, is still the first step, from which the rest will flow.

The Liberation of Women

The particular means by which women are kept dependent (on men) and oppressed as people must be eradicated so that Daughters no longer find themselves with Mothers who cannot see, who cannot say No.

For women to rise out of their subordinate status, they must have economic independence. This means that the struggles for nonsexist education, nonsexist job definitions, the right to work, the right to a decent income as workers or Mothers, and truly equal pay are part of the struggle to end Father–Daughter rape.

Women must also have control of their own bodies. This means that the struggles for truly safe contraception, the right to sterilisation, the right to abortion on demand, the right to full and truthful sex education, the right to sexual partners of their choice, the right to childbirth methods determined by the mother, and the right to full and honest information in medical matters are part of the struggle to end Father–Daughter rape.

Women must also be able to live their lives free of personal violence: the kind of personal violence which occurs because women are subordinate. This means that the struggles to eliminate wife-bashing, marital rape, street harassment, and sexual harassment on the job are part of the struggle to end Father–Daughter rape.

Ultimately, women will only be a liberated species when male supremacy ends. This means that any struggle which opposes the expression of male supremacy—expressions such as sexist advertising, pornography, the patriarchal nuclear family, rape in warfare, and the use of nuclear energy and armaments—are part of the struggle to end Father–Daughter rape.

Sex and Sexuality Information

We must expand the embryonic attempts to educate girl-children, and society generally, about female sexuality, and about rape. The repression of information about female sexuality is clearly linked to rape in that the traditional view of women as sexually passive feeds straight into the myths about rape. Girl-children will only begin to be able to protect themselves when they (a) value their own bodies, and (b) know that they may be sexually approached by a man they know and trust.

We must teach girl-children about their own sexuality, as a base from which they can love and value their own bodies. We must teach our Daughters to recognise the experience of pleasure for what it is: their own precious bodily reactions, rather than an emotional response implying consent. We must teach them that they can and must say No to anyone who touches them against their will. We must teach them to exert as much control over their own bodies as is possible; and we must teach it to them as early as possible, along with walking and talking.

This mode of social sex education, growing out of women talking together and thereby discovering what it is that girl-children need to know, is the first way in which girl-children are going to be empowered to say No. Social attitudes and availability of information which will allow them a sense of physical, emotional, and sexual integrity are the obverse of the current practice of conditioned passivity based on fear induced through purposely manipulated ignorance. The very least we can ask for girl-children is a fighting chance to protect themselves by giving them as much information as we can.

The Patriarchal Family

The Daughters should never be forced, or even encouraged, to live again with the Father who has been raping them. This is the crux, and the crunch, of the change that needs to be wrought immediately. As Judith Herman points out:

> Men cannot be expected to overcome their abusive tendencies or to develop their nurturant capacities overnight, and it makes no sense to expose children to the unsupervised care of men whose interest in them may be ambivalent at best, and perverse at worst. Women are going to have to be the teachers and the protectors for some time to come.[4]

Only an end to the patriarchal nuclear family, only a new kind of family based on complete sharing of matriarchal skills and values will bring about an end to Father–Daughter rape.

The value system of male supremacist society holds the family to be inviolable, except under the most extraordinary circumstances. It will be argued (and it is true) that there are no ideal places for the Daughters to be removed to on a long-term basis: too often, the family is all there is. Rather than shrugging in resigned acceptance at this truism and turning away in despair, we must set about creating crisis shelters specifically for Daughter-victims, and creating or finding other living arrangements where they can live on a long-term basis. If we face the fact that most raped Daughters do *not* want to live with the person that has raped them, and believe that they should not have to, then we will find alternatives.

Naming Blame

The best "alternative," of course, is the removal of the Fathers. They, after all, are the problem. The patriarchal power of the courts, of counsellors, of the police and the welfare system ensures that this solution is not widely possible yet. But there will come a day, not far off, when women make this utterly reasonable demand.

The Father-offenders must be named, isolated, punished. This would only be a reversal of what happens now in many instances, where the victims are the ones who feel, and are, punished. The Fathers must be named as rapists of girl-children. It must be made *socially impossible* for them to get away with it. Ostracism, public ignominy, and a complete ban on access to girl-children seems a small amount to ask in the face of the damage, suffering, and pain these men have inflicted. Therapy, "curing," counseling for individual Fathers are all very well for those who wish to deliver such services: the real problem is the social sanction of their behaviour. They must *not* be forgiven: what they have done is unforgivable.

The Power of Naming

In the development of the feminist movement, women have seized the power of naming. This is a revolutionary power because in naming (describing) what is being done to us (and inevitably to children and men as well), we are also naming what must change. The act of naming creates a new worldview. The power of naming resides in the fact that we name what we see from the basis of our own experience: within and outside patriarchal culture, simultaneously.

We are finding forms of expression which convey the reality of Father–Daughter rape; we are finding forms of expression which reject male supremacist language— that language which presumes to tell us what is happening to us and how we feel about it. Father–Daughter rape can no longer be called "interference," "molestation," "fooling around with," or "incest." The feelings and reactions of the Daughters must be named, described, accepted. The confusion and angst of the Mothers must be named, described, accepted. The totality of rape ideology and its integration into sex-role conditioning must be named, described, eradicated. This revolution of women naming is already under way and it is a revolution which will, one day, bring about an end to rape in all its manifestations.

We, the Mothers and Daughters, are seeing now through our own eyes. We do not forgive the Fathers. It will be said that we are uncaring; that we hate men; that we are creating a state of war. I say that the war has been declared and waged by men since the first act of rape. Whatever the reasons for men's hatred of women, we ourselves are changing the structure of the battle. We are resisting; we are strategically withdrawing; we are naming the hitherto unnameable. In doing these things *for our own sakes,* the corollary is that the Fathers have access to space in which to look at themselves: to hear what they have done, to see what they have done. The prognosis of changed behaviour on the far side of the battlefield is not promising: all types of rape statistics are rising at an alarming rate. But for us, the Mothers and Daughters, there is no going back.

> To dream a world into being
> is regarded by many as insanely
> impractical.
>
> *We know there is a world*
> *without rape and this world is*
> *in our minds.*
>
> As we struggle across the plains
> towards the mountains of freedom
> *we know*

what to take with us and
what to leave behind. Travelling
light

we know when to speak or be
dumb (eyes glazed with the matt
of our knowing)

we know when to run, or to lie
in the sun. We know when to run
from danger

and circle and weave and return
from behind, clearing the plains
of the canker.

And the plains will rise up,
the mountains sink down
when we dream

this world into being.

A day in the future dawns still and grey. Overcast and quiet. An unremarkable day.

A small grey woman, sleeping alone, wakes in her bedsitter. Remembering. Being eight years old, sleeping alone in the small room off the verandah at the back of the weatherboard house. Remembers how she taught herself to slip into the wall, from where she watched through a crack in the woodwork when her father came to her bed.

Watched the large red roughened hands lift up the little girl's nightgown, part her legs, touch her softest tissues. While the other large red roughened hand moved to the front of his own pants, grasped at the strange red thing which she knew was hot and sticky.

But this time, this remembering, she did not stay in the wall until it was all over, to creep out and slip inside the little girl when he went away. This time she came charging out of the wall, kicking, punching, and shouting, threw herself on the man, her father, with every cell in her body fighting.

The small grey woman watched this remembering with wonder. She felt a smile lifting her lips.

In the mountains, a fifteen-year-old girl-woman woke to the still grey day. A strand of her long black hair lay across her face. It reminded her of the night and the silent visitor who had come again to her bed. As he had been doing every week or so since she was eleven.

Her hand rose to move the hair; but it stayed, half raised to her face. The hair was speaking to her fingers: Today you will tell. Today you will speak. Today you can be strong. Today, you will stop being lonely.

A young married woman rose that day and did the things she normally did. She saw her husband off to work, dropped her daughter off at preschool, and set out to drive to work. As she turned the first corner, the memories came again, especially the one about the first time. She found she was no longer driving to work; she was going across town to her friend's place. I have to tell you something, she said, as she sat down at the kitchen table.

She found herself speaking, telling of how her grandfather used to stick his fingers up the leg of her pants and feel her.

It first happened when I was five. I'd loved him up till then: a lovely soft, cuddly old man who cradled me in his lap and told me stories.

But that day, after my father came into the room and it all stopped happening and I started to breathe again, my grandfather's eyes met mine. I hadn't seen those eyes of grandfather's before. That was when I knew that what had happened was really as awful as it felt. You will never speak of this, they said—and in the same movement, he slid his eyes blandly round to my father and chuckled about the idiosyncrasies of an elderly old man sitting in the dusk with his princess!

I remember I ran out to the kitchen and stood near the stove to get warm because my heart was thumping so loud. My mother didn't see my eyes, or hear my heart, even though I stood there and watched her make the whole meal and then serve it. In my mind I was screaming, telling her. And saying that I didn't want to be with grandpa any more. But I didn't say. I never have till now. But my mind has done that for years and years. Remembered. And screamed.

And as the twenty-four hours of that still, grey day rolled their gently inexorable way round the globe, all the women woke in turn, reliving their rememberings, and one by one they arose with a new new smile on their faces, and one by one they spoke. And the sound of their speakings drowned out all the other sounds in the world that day: the machines and the factories and the cars and newsreaders and doctors and priests and politicians and all the learned men were silent, because the noise of the women speaking filled up all the space. And any little places left in the silences that occurred amid the speakings and cryings and laughings of women were filled by the noise of children playing.

NOTES

1. A. Rich, *On Lies, Secrets and Silence*, Virago, London, 1979, pp. 259–60.
2. T. Morrison, *Sula*, Bantam, New York, 1975, p. 67.
3. A. Rich, *Of Woman Born*, Virago, London, 1977, p. 220.
4. J. Herman, *Father–Daughter Incest*, Harvard University Press, Cambridge, MA, 1982, p. 217.

Bibliography

Abrahamsen, D. 1960. *The Psychology of Crime.* New York: Columbia University Press.

Acker, Joan. 1990. "Hierarchies, Jobs, Bodies: A Theory of Gendered Organization." *Gender & Society* 4(2):139–58.

Acosta-Belen, Edna, and Christine E. Bose. 2001. "Gender and Development." In J. Lorber (ed.), *Gender Inequality: Feminist Theories and Politics.* Los Angeles: Roxbury.

Adam, A. 2001. "Cyberstalking: Gender and Computer Ethics." In E. Green and A. Adam (eds.), *Virtual Gender: Technology, Consumption and Identity.* London: Routledge.

———. 2002. "Cyberstalking and Internet Pornography: Gender and the Gaze." *Ethics and Information Technology* 4:133–42.

Adams, J. W., J. L. Kottke, and J. S. Padgitt. 1983. "Sexual Harassment of University Students." *Journal of College Student Personnel* 23:484–99.

Adkins, L. 1995. *Gendered Work: Sexuality, Family, and the Labour Market.* Buckingham, UK: Open University Press.

Ageton, S. S. 1983. *Sexual Assault among Adolescents.* Lexington, MA: D. C. Heath.

Ahluwalia, S. K., S. M. McGroder, M. J. Zaslow, and E. C. Hair. 2001. "Symptoms of Depression among Welfare Recipients: A Concern for Two Generations." Washington, DC: Child Trends.

Ahrens, Courtney A., Rebecca Campbell, Sharon M. Wasco, Gloria Aponte, Lori Grubstein, and William S. Davidson II. 2000. "Sexual Assault Nurse Examiner (SANE) Programs: Alternative Systems for Service Delivery for Sexual Assault Victims." *Journal of Interpersonal Violence* 15(9):921–43.

Alfaro, J. D. 1987. "Studying Child Maltreatment Fatalities: A Synthesis of Nine Projects." Unpublished manuscript.

Allen, Charlene, and Beth Leventhal. 1999. "History, Culture, and Identity: What Makes GLBT Battering Different." In B. Leventhal and S. E. Lundy (eds.), *Same-Sex Domestic Violence: Strategies for Change.* Thousand Oaks, CA: Sage.

Allen, Nicole E. 2001. "An Overview of Domestic Violence Coordinating Councils, Committees, and Task Forces in the State of Michigan." Unpublished manuscript, Department of Psychology, Michigan State University.

———. 2005. "A Multi-Level Analysis of Community Coordinating Councils." *American Journal of Community Psychology* 35(1–2):49–63.

———. 2006. "An Examination of the Effectiveness of Domestic Violence Coordinating Councils." *Violence against Women* 12(1):343–60.

Allison, A. 1994. *Nightwork: Sexuality, Pleasure and Corporate Masculinity in a Tokyo Hostess Club.* Chicago: University of Chicago Press.

Alvy, Lisa. 2004/2005. "Violence against Women of Darfur: A Devastating Weapon of War and Terror." *National NOW Times* (winter): 13.

American Academy of Pediatrics. 1998. "Guidance for Effective Discipline." *Pediatrics* 101(4):723–28.

American Association of University Women Foundation. 1993. *Hostile Hallways: The AAUW Survey on Sexual Harassment in America's Schools.* Washington, DC: AAUW.

American Association of University Women Foundation and Harris Interactive. 2001. *Hostile Hallways II: Bullying, Teasing and Sexual Harassment in School.* Washington, DC: Harris Interactive.

American Medical Association. 1992. *Diagnostic and Treatment Guidelines on Family Violence.* Chicago: American Medical Association.

———. 1995. *Strategies for the Treatment and Prevention of Sexual Assault.* Chicago: American Medical Association.

American Psychiatric Association. 1987. *The Diagnostic and Statistical Manual of Mental Disorders.* 4th ed. Washington, DC: American Psychiatric Association.

Amir, Menachem. 1971. *Patterns in Forcible Rape.* Chicago: University of Chicago Press.

Ammar, Nawal H. 2000. "In the Shadows of the Pyramids: Domestic Violence in Egypt." In E. Erez and K. Laster (eds.), *Domestic Violence: Global Responses.* Bicester, UK: A B Academic.

Amsdem, David. 2003. "Not Tonight Honey. I'm Logging On." *New York Magazine,* October 20, pp. 30–35.

Anderlini-D'Onofrio, Serena, ed. 2004. *Plural Loves: Designs for Bi and Poly Living.* Binghamton, NY: Harrington Park Press.

Andersen, Margaret L. 1993 [1988]. *Thinking about Women: Sociological Perspectives on Sex and Gender.* New York: Macmillan.

Anderson, J., J. Martin, P. Mullen, S. Romans, and P. Herbison. 1993. "Prevalence of Childhood Sexual Abuse Experiences in a Community Sample of Women." *Journal of American Academy of Child and Adolescent Psychiatry* 32:911–19.

Anderson, Kristin L., and Debra Umberson. 2001. "Gendering Violence: Masculinity and Power in Men's Accounts of Domestic Violence." *Gender & Society* 15(3):358–80.

Anonymous. 1991. "Sexual Harassment: A Female Counseling Student's Experience." *Journal of Counseling and Development* 69:502–6.

Antecol, Heather, and Deborah Cobb-Clark. 2003. "Does Sexual Harassment Training Change Attitudes? A View from the Federal Level." *Social Science Quarterly* 84(4):826–42.

Archer, John. 1994. "Power and Male Violence." In J. Archer (ed.), *Male Violence: The Territorial Imperative.* London: Routledge.

———. 2000. "Sex Differences in Aggression between Heterosexual Partners: A Meta-Analytic Review. *Psychological Bulletin* 126(5):651–80.

Ardrey, R. 1966. *The Territorial Imperative.* New York: Dell.

Arendt, Hannah. 1970. *On Violence.* New York: Harcourt, Brace and World.

Armstrong, Louise. 1978. *Kiss Daddy Goodnight.* New York: Hawthorne.

Arvey, R. D., and M. A. Cavanaugh. 1995. "Using Surveys to Assess the Prevalence of Sexual Harassment: Some Methodological Problems." *Journal of Social Issues* 51(1):39–52.

Association of American Colleges. 1978. *The Problem of Rape on Campus.* Washington, DC: Project on the Status and Education of Women.

Attorney General's Task Force on Family Violence. 1984. *Final Report.* Washington, DC: U.S. Department of Justice.

Augustin, Laura. 2002. "Challenging 'Place': Leaving Home for Sex Development." *Migration* 41(1):110–17.

Australian Broadcasting Online. 2004. "Anti-Bullying Policies Failing to Cut School Harassment." June 18. Available online at www.abc.net.au/pm/content/2004/s1135441.htm.

Avakame, Edem F. 1998. "How Different Is Violence in the Home? An Examination of Some Correlates of Stranger and Intimate Homicide." *Criminology* 36(3):601–32.

Avina, C., and W. O'Donohue. 2002. "Sexual Harassment and PTSD: Is Sexual Harassment Trauma?" *Journal of Traumatic Stress* 15:69–75.

Bachman, Ronet. 1992. *Death and Violence on the Reservation.* New York: Auburn House.

Back, L. 2002. "Aryans Reading Adorno: Cyber-Culture and Twenty-First Century Racism." *Ethnic and Racial Studies* 25:628–51.

Bailey, V., and S. Blackburn. 1979. "The Punishment of Incest Act 1908: A Case Study of Law Creation." *Criminal Law Review* (December): 749–64.

Bailey, V., and S. McCabe. 1979. "Reforming the Law of Incest." *Criminal Law Review* (December): 749–64.

Balsam, Kimberly F. 2001. "Nowhere to Hide: Lesbian Battering, Homophobia, and Minority Stress." In E. Kaschak (ed.), *Intimate Betrayal: Domestic Violence in Lesbian Relationships.* New York: Haworth.

Bancroft, Lundy, and Jay G. Silverman. 2002. "Assessing Risk to Children from Batterers." Available online at http://www.vawnet.org/DomesticViolence/ServicesAndProgramDev/Service-ProvAndProg/RisktoChildren.pdf (accessed June 14, 2006).

Bandy, N. 1989. "Relationships between Male and Female Employees at Southern Illinois University." Ph.D. diss., College of Education, Southern Illinois University, Carbondale, IL.

Barak, A. 1992. "Combating Sexual Harassment." *American Psychologist* 47:818–19.

———. 1994. "A Cognitive-Behavioral Educational Workshop to Combat Sexual Harassment in the Workplace." *Journal of Counseling and Development* 72:595–602.

———. 1997. "Cross-Cultural Perspectives on Sexual Harassment." In W. O'Donohue (ed.), *Sexual Harassment: Theory, Research and Treatment.* Boston: Allyn and Bacon.

———. 2004. "Internet Counseling." In C. D. Speilberger (ed.), *Encyclopedia of Applied Psychology.* San Diego, CA: Academic Press.

Barak, A., and W. A. Fisher. 2002. "The Future of Internet Sexuality." In A. Cooper (ed.), *Sex and the Internet: A Guidebook for Clinicians.* New York: Brunner-Routledge.

Barak, A., and N. Kaplan. 1996. "Relationships between Personal Characteristics and Sexual Harassment Behaviours in Male University Professors." In *NATCON Papers 1996.* Toronto: National Consultation on Career Development.

Barak, A., and S. A. King. 2000. "The Two Faces of the Internet: Introduction to the Special Issue on the Internet and Sexuality." *CyberPsychology and Behavior* 3:517–20.

Barak, A., Y. Pitterman, and R. Yitzhaki. 1995. "An Empirical Test of the Role of Power Differential in Originating Sexual Harassment." *Basic and Applied Social Psychology* 17:497–517.

Barak, Gregg. 2003. *Violence and Nonviolence: Pathways to Understanding.* Thousand Oaks, CA: Sage.

Baraka, Amina. 1983. "Soweto Song." In Amiri Baraka and Amina Baraka (eds.), *Confirmation.* New York: Quill.

Bargh, J. A., K. Y. A. McKenna, and G. M. Fitzsimmons. 2002. "Can You See the Real Me? Activation and Expression of the 'True Self' on the Internet." *Journal of Social Issues* 58:33–48.

Bargh, J. A., P. Raymond, J. B. Pryor, and F. Strack. 1995. "Attractiveness of the Underling: An Automatic Power? Sex Association and Its Consequences for Sexual Harassment and Aggression." *Journal of Personality and Social Psychology* 68:768–81.

Barnes, S. B. 2001. *Online Connections: Internet Interpersonal Relationships.* Cresskill, NJ: Hampton.

Barnett, Ola, Cindy L. Miller-Perrin, and Robin D. Perrin. 2005. *Family Violence across the Lifespan: An Introduction.* Thousand Oaks, CA: Sage.

Baron, L., and M. A. Straus. 1989. *Four Theories of Rape in American Society: A State-Level Analysis.* New Haven, CT: Yale University Press.

Baron, L., M. A. Straus, and D. Jaffe, 1988. "Legitimate Violence, Violent Attitudes, and Rape: A Test of the Cultural Spillover Theory." In R. A. Prentky and V. L. Quinsey (eds.), *Human Sexual Aggression: Current Perspectives*. New York: New York Academy of Sciences.

Barry, Kathleen. 1979. *Female Sexual Slavery*. New York: NYU Press.

Barry, Kathleen, Charlotte Bunch, and Shirley Castley (eds.). 1983. *International Feminism: Networking against Female Sexual Slavery*. New York: International Women's Tribune Center.

Bart, P. 1989. "Rape as a Paradigm of Sexism in Society: Victimization and Its Discontents." In D. L. Steinberg and R. D. Klein (eds.), *Radical Voices: A Decade of Feminist Resistance*. Oxford, UK: Pergamon.

Baynard, Victoria L., Linda M. Williams, Jane A. Siegel, and Carolyn M. West. 2002. "Childhood Sexual Abuse in the Lives of Black Women: Risk and Resilience in a Longitudinal Study." In Carolyn M. West (ed.), *Violence in the Lives of Black women: Battered, Black, and Blue*. New York: Hayworth.

Behlmer, G. K. 1982. *Child Abuse and Moral Reform in England 1870–1908*. Stanford, CA: Stanford University Press.

Belknap, Joanne, and Jennifer L. Hartman. 2000. "Police Responses to Woman Battering: Victim Advocates' Reports." In E. Erez and K. Laster (eds.), *Domestic Violence: Global Responses*. Bicester, UK: A B Academic.

Bell, H. 2003. "Cycles within Cycles: Domestic Violence, Welfare, and Low-Wage Work." *Violence against Women* 9(10):1245–62.

Bell, Laurie (ed.). 1987. *Good Girls/Bad Girls: Feminists and Sex Trade Workers Face to Face*. Toronto: Seal.

Bell, M. P., J. C. Quick, and C. S. Cycyota. 2002. "Assessment and Prevention of Sexual Harassment of Employees: An Applied Guide to Creating Healthy Organizations." *International Journal of Selection and Assessment* 10:160–67.

Benedict, Helen. 1992. *Virgin or Vamp: How the Press Covers Sex Crimes*. New York: Oxford University Press.

Beneke, Tim. 1982. *Men on Rape: What They Have to Say about Sexual Violence*. New York: St. Martin's Press.

Bennett, G. 1990. "Elder Abuse: Shifting Emphasis from Abused to Abuser." *Geriatric Medicine* 20(5):45–49.

Bennett, G., and P. Kingston. 1993. *Elder Abuse: Concepts, Theories and Interventions*. London: Chapman Hall.

Benson, D. J., and G. E. Thomson. 1982. "Sexual Harassment on a University Campus: The Confluence of Authority Relations, Sexual Interest, and Gender Stratification." *Social Problems* 29:236–51.

Bentovim, A., A. Elton, and M. Tranter. 1987. "Prognosis for Rehabilitation after Abuse." *Adoption and Fostering* 11(1):26–31.

Ben-Ze'ev, A. 2003. "Privacy, Emotional Closeness, and Openness in Cyberspace." *Computers in Human Behavior* 19:451–67.

———. 2004. *Love Online: Emotions on the Internet*. Cambridge: Cambridge University Press.

Berger, R. J., and P. Searles. 1985. "Victim-Offender Interaction in Rape: Victimological, Situational, and Feminist Perspectives." *Women's Studies Quarterly* 13:9–15.

Bernard, Cheryl, and Edit Schlaffer. 1983. "The Man in the Street: Why He Harasses." In Laurel Richardson and Verta Taylor (eds.), *Feminist Frontiers: Rethinking Sex, Gender and Society*. New York: Random House.

Berrill, K. 1990. "Anti-Gay Violence and Victimization in the United States." *Journal of Interpersonal Violence* 5(3):274–94.

Best, Steven, and Douglas Kellner. 1991. *Postmodern Theory: Critical Interrogations.* New York: Guilford.

Bevacqua, Maria. 2000. *Rape on the Public Agenda: Feminism and the Politics of Sexual Assault.* Boston: Northeastern University Press.

Biaggio, M. K., D. Watts, and A. Brownwell. 1990. "Addressing Sexual Harassment: Strategies for Prevention and Change." In Michele A. Paludi (ed.), *Ivory Power: Sexual Harassment on Campus.* Albany: State University of New York Press.

Biber, J. K., D. Doverspike, D. Baznik, A. Cober, and B. A. Ritter. 2002. "Sexual Harassment in Online Communications: Effects of Gender Discourse Medium." *CyberPsychology and Behavior* 5:33–42.

Bland, L. 1982. " 'Guardians of the Race' or 'Vampires upon the Nation's Health'? Female Sexuality and Its Regulation in Early Twentieth Century Britain." In E. Whitelegg, M. Arnot, E. Bartels, V. Beechey, L. Birke, S. Himmelweit, D. Leonard, S. Ruehl, and M. A. Speakman (eds.), *The Changing Experience of Women.* Oxford, UK: Blackwell.

Blanguernon, C. 1955. *Le Hogger (The Hogger).* Paris: B. Arthaud. (Translated from the French for the Human Relations Area Files by Thomas Turner.)

Bloch, Francis, and Vijayendra Rao. 2002. "Terror as a Bargaining Instrument: A Case Study of Dowry Violence in Rural India." *American Economic Review* 29(4):1029–43.

Bly, Robert. 1991. *Iron John.* Reading, MA: Addison Wesley.

Bohmer, C., and A. Parrot. 1993. *Sexual Assault on Campus: The Problem and the Solution.* New York: Lexington Books.

Boneva, B., and R. Kraut. 2002. "Email, Gender, and Personal Relationships." In B. Wellman and C. Haythornthwaite (eds.), *The Internet in Everyday Life.* Malden, MA: Blackwell.

Boonstra, Heather. 2003. "A Look at the U.S. Global AIDS Policy." *Guttmacher Report on Public Policy* (August). Available online at www.guttmacher.org (accessed March 28, 2006).

Bourdieu, Pierre. 1982. *Ce que parler veut dire: l'économie des échanges linguistiques.* Paris: Librairie Arthème Fayard.

———. 1991. *Language and Symbolic Power.* Ed. John B. Thompson. Trans. Gino Raymond and Matthew Adamson. Cambridge, MA: Harvard University Press.

Bourque, Linda Brookover. 1989. *Defining Rape.* Durham, NC: Duke University Press.

Bowker, Lee, with Michelle Arbitell and J. Richard McFerron. 1988. "On the Relationship between Wife Beating and Child Abuse." In Kersti Yllö and Michele Bograd (eds.), *Feminist Perspectives on Wife Abuse.* Newbury Park, CA: Sage.

Bowker, N., and K. Tuffin. 2002. "Disability Discourses for Online Identities." *Disability and Society* 17:327–44.

Bradley, Christine. 1994 [1990]. "Why Male Violence against Women Is a Development Issue: Reflections from Papua, New Guinea." UNIFEM Occasional Paper. New York: United Nations Fund for Women. Reprinted in M. Davies (ed.), *Women and Violence.* London: Zed Books.

Braithwaite, J., and K. Daly. 1994. "Masculinities, Violence and Communitarian Control." In T. Newburn and E. A. Stanko (eds.), *Just Boys Doing Business? Men, Masculinities, and Crime.* London: Routledge.

Brant, C., and Y. L. Too. 1994. "Introduction." In C. Brant, and Y. L. Too (eds.), *Rethinking Sexual Harassment.* London: Pluto.

Brennan, Denise. 2002. "Selling Sex for Visas: Sex Tourism as a Stepping Stone to International Migration." In B. Ehrenreich and A. R. Hochschild (eds.), *Global Woman: Nannies, Maids, and Sex Workers in the New Economy.* New York: Holt.

Brent, Linda. 1973 [1861]. *Incidents in the Life of a Slave Girl.* San Diego, CA: Harvest/Harcourt Brace Jovanovich.

Brittan, Arthur, and Mary Maynard. 1984. *Sexism, Racism and Oppression.* Oxford, UK: Blackwell.

Britton, D. M., and C. L. Williams. 1995. "Don't Ask, Don't Tell, Don't Pursue: Military Policy and the Construction of Hegemonic Masculinity." *Journal of Homosexuality* 30:1–21.

Broude, G. J., and S. J. Green. 1976. "Cross-Cultural Codes on Twenty Sexual Practices." *Ethnology* 15:409–29.

Brown, L. S. 1991. "Psychological Evaluation of Victims of Sexual Harassment." Paper presented at the National Conference to Promote Men and Women Working Together Productively, March, Bellevue, WA.

Brown, Lyn Mikel, Meda Chesney-Lind, and Nan Stein. 2004. "Patriarchy Matters: Toward a Gendered Theory of Teen Violence and Victimization." Working paper no. 417. Wellesley, MA: Wellesley College Center for Research on Women.

Browne, Angela. 1987. *When Battered Women Kill.* New York: Free Press.

Browne, Angela, and K. Williams. 1993. "Gender, Intimacy and Lethal Violence: Trends from 1976 through 1987." *Gender & Society* 7:78–98.

Brownmiller, Susan. 1975. *Against Our Will: Men, Women and Rape.* New York: Simon and Schuster.

Brush, Lisa D. 1990. "Violent Acts and Injurious Outcomes in Married Couples: Methodological Issues in the National Survey of Families and Households." *Gender & Society* 4:56–67.

———. 2003. "Effects of Work on Hitting and Hurting." *Violence against Women* 9(10):1213–30.

Brush, Lisa D., J. Raphael, and R. M. Tolman. 2003. "Guest Editors' Introduction." *Violence against Women* 9(10):1167–70.

Bucha, Sanna. 2005. "Twice Damned." Ansar Burney Welfare Trust Web site. Available online at http://www.ansarburney.org/news/n17.html (accessed January 31, 2006).

Buchanan, N., and A. Ormerod. 2002. "Racialized Sexual Harassment in the Lives of African American Women." *Women and Therapy* 25(3–4):105–21.

Budapest Group. 1999. "The Relationship between Organized Crime and Trafficking in Aliens." International Centre for Migration Policy Development, Austria.

Bureau of National Affairs. 1987. *Sexual Harassment: Employer Policies and Problems.* Washington, DC: U.S. Government Printing Office.

Burgess, Ann Wolbert, and Lynda L. Holmstrom. 1974. "The Rape Trauma Syndrome." *American Journal of Psychiatry* 131:981–86.

Burgest, David R. 1973. "The Racist Use of the English Language." *Black Scholar* (September): 37–45.

Burke, L. K., and D. R. Follingstad. 1999. "Violence in Lesbian and Gay Relationships: Theory, Prevalence, and Correlational Factors." *Clinical Psychology Review* 19:487–512.

Burns, S. E. 1995. "Issues in Workplace Sexual Harassment Law and Related Social Science Research." *Journal of Social Issues* 51:193–207.

Burrough, B., and J. Helyar. 1990. *Barbarians at the Gate: The Fall of RJR Nabisco.* New York: Harper Perennial.

Burrows, James. 2006. "Von Trapped." *Will and Grace.* KoMut Entertainment with Three Sisters Entertainment and NBC Studios.

Busch, R. 2002. "Domestic Violence and Restorative Justice Initiatives: Who Pays If We Get It Wrong?" In H. Strang and J. Braithwaite (eds.), *Restorative Justice and Family Violence.* Cambridge: Cambridge University Press.

Butler, Judith. 1990. *Gender Trouble: Feminism and the Subversion of Identity.* New York: Routledge.

———. 1993. *Bodies That Matter: On the Discursive Limits of Sex.* New York: Routledge.

Butterfield, Fox. 2003. "Rate of Serious Crime Held Largely Steady Last Year, Report by F.B.I. Says." *New York Times,* October 28, p. 5.

Buzawa, Eva S. 2003. *Domestic Violence: The Criminal Justice Response.* Thousand Oaks, CA: Sage.

Byington, Diane, Patricia Y. Martin, Diana DiNitto, and M. Sharon Maxwell. 1991. "Organizational Effectiveness and Affiliations of Rape Crisis Centers." *Administration in Social Work* 15:83–103.

Cahill, Ann J. 2001. *Rethinking Rape.* Ithaca, NY: Cornell University Press.

Calvert, S. L. 1999. *Children's Journeys through the Information Age.* New York: McGraw-Hill.

Cameron, Deborah. 1985. *Feminism and Linguistic Theory.* New York: St. Martin's Press.

Campbell, Jacquelyn C. 1989. "Women's Responses to Sexual Abuse in Intimate Relationships." *Health Care for Women International* 10(4):335–46.

Campbell, Jacquelyn C., Linda Rose, Joan Kub, and Daphne Nedd. 1998. "Voices of Strength and Resistance: A Contextual and Longitudinal Analysis of Women's Responses to Battering." *Journal of Interpersonal Violence* 13(6):743–62.

Campbell, Rebecca. 1998. "The Community Response to Rape: Victims' Experiences with the Legal, Medical, and Mental Health Systems." *American Journal of Community Psychology* 26(3):355–79.

Campbell, Rebecca, and Courtney E. Ahrens. 1998. "Innovative Community Services for Rape Victims: An Application of Multiple Case Study Methodology." *American Journal of Community Psychology* 26(4):537–71.

Campbell, Rebecca, and Deborah Bybee. 1997. "Emergency Medical Services for Rape Victims: Detecting the Cracks in Service Delivery." *Women's Health: Research on Gender, Behavior, and Policy* 3(2):75–101.

Campbell, Rebecca, and Patricia Yancey Martin. 2001. "Services for Sexual Assault Survivors: The Role of Rape Crisis Centers." In R. Bergen, C. Renzetti, and J. Edelson (eds.), *Sourcebook on Violence against Women.* Newbury Park, CA: Sage.

Campbell, Rebecca, Tracy Sefl, Holly E. Barnes, Courtney A. Ahrens, Sharon M. Wasco, and Yolanda Zaragoza-Diesfeld. 1999. "Community Services for Rape Survivors: Enhancing Psychological Well-Being or Increasing Trauma?" *Journal of Consulting and Clinical Psychology* 67(6):847–58.

Campbell, Rebecca, Sharon M. Wasco, Courtney E. Ahrens, Tracy Sefl, and Holly E. Barnes. 2001. "Preventing the 'Second Rape': Rape Survivors' Experiences with Community Service Providers." *Journal of Interpersonal Violence* 16 (December): 1239–59.

Cancian, Francesca M. 1988. "Love and the Rise of Capitalism." In B. J. Risman and P. Schwartz (eds.), *Gender in Intimate Relationships.* Belmont, CA: Wadsworth.

Caputi, Jane, and Diana E. H. Russell. 1990. "Femicide: Speaking the Unspeakable," *Ms.* 1(2):34–37.

Caputo, Richard. 1991. "Police Classification of Domestic-Violence Calls: An Assessment of Program Impact." In Dean Knudsen and JoAnn Miller (eds.), *Abused and Battered: Social and Legal Responses to Family Violence.* Hawthorne, NY: Aldine de Gruyter.

Carby, Hazel V. 1987. *Reconstructing Womanhood.* Oxford: Oxford University Press.

Carillo, Roxanna. 1992. *Battered Dreams: Violence against Women as an Obstacle to Development.* New York: UNIFEM.

Carlson, Bonnie E. 1984a. "Children's Observations of Interparental Violence." In A. R. Roberts (ed.), *Battered Women and Their Families.* New York: Springer.

———. 1984b. "Causes and Maintenance of Domestic Violence: An Ecological Analysis." *Social Service Review* 58:569—87.

Carnes, P. J. 2003. "The Anatomy of Arousal: Three Internet Portals." *Sexual and Relationship Therapy* 18:309–28.

Carothers, C., and P. Crull. 1984. "Contrasting Sexual Harassment in Female- and Male-Dominated Occupations." In K. Brodkin-Sachs and D. Remy (eds.), *My Troubles Are Going to Have Trouble with Me*. New Brunswick, NJ: Rutgers University Press.

Chanen, David, and Howie Padilla. 2001. "School Was Scene of Earlier Assaults: New Reports Surface at Banneker." *Minneapolis Star Tribune*, December 19, p. 1A.

Chase, Cheryl. 2002. "What Is the Agenda of the Intersex Patient Advocacy Movement?" Paper presented at First World Congress: Hormonal and Genetic Basis of Sexual Differentiation Disorders, May 17–18, Tempe, AZ.

Check, James V. P., Barbara Elias, and Susan A. Barton. 1988. "Hostility toward Men in Female Victims of Male Sexual Aggression." In Gordon W. Russell (ed.), *Violence in Intimate Relationships*. New York: PMA Publishing.

Check, James V. P., and N. M. Malamuth. 1983. "Sex Role Stereotyping and Reactions to Depictions of Stranger versus Acquaintance Rape." *Journal of Personality and Social Psychology* 45:344–56.

Chiles, Lawton. 1988. "Death before Life: The Tragedy of Infant Mortality." In *Report of the National Commission to Prevent Infant Mortality*. Washington, DC: U.S. Government Printing Office.

CIBA Foundation. 1984. *Child Sexual Abuse within the Family*. London: Tavistock.

Clark, K. A., A. K. Biddle, and S. L. Martin. 2002. "A Cost-Benefit Analysis of the Violence Against Women Act of 1984." *Violence against Women* 8(4):417–28.

Cobble, D. S. 1996. "The Prospects for Unionism in a Service Society." In C. L. MacDonald and C. Sirianni (eds.), *Working in the Service Society*. Philadelphia: Temple University Press.

Cockburn, C. 1991. *In the Way of Women*. Ithaca, NY: ILR Press.

Cody, Edward. 2005. "In China, Roots of Anger toward Japan Run Deep." *Washington Post*, April 20, p. A12.

Coles, F. S. 1986. "Forced to Quit: Sexual Harassment Complaints and Agency Response." *Sex Roles* 14:81–95.

Collier, Richard. 1998. *Masculinities, Crime and Criminology: Men Heterosexuality and the Criminal(ised) Other*. London: Sage.

Collins, E. G. C., and T. B. Blodgett. 1981. "Sexual Harassment: Some See It, Some Won't." *Harvard Business Review* 59 (March/April): 77–95.

Collins, Patricia Hill. 1986. "Learning from the Outsider Within: The Sociological Significance of Black Feminist Thought." *Social Problems* 33(6):S14–S32.

———. 1991. *Black Feminist Thought: Knowledge, Consciousness, and the Politics of Empowerment*. New York: Routledge.

———. 2000. *Black Feminist Thought: Knowledge, Consciousness, and the Politics of Empowerment*. Rev. ed. New York: Routledge.

Collinson, D. 1988. "Engineering Humour: Masculinity, Joking, and Conflict in Shop-Floor Relations." *Organization Studies* 9:181–99.

Collinson, D. L., and M. Collinson. 1989. "Sexuality in the Workplace: The Domination of Men's Sexuality." In J. Hearn, D. L. Sheppard, P. Tancred-Sheriff, and G. Burrell (eds.), *The Sexuality of Organization*. Newbury Park, CA: Sage.

———. 1991. "Live Fast and Die Young: The Construction of Masculinity among Young Working-Class Men on the Margin of the Labor Market." *Australian and New Zealand Journal of Sociology* 27(2):141–71.

Connell, R. W. 1987. *Gender and Power*. Stanford, CA: Stanford University Press.

———. 1995a. *Masculinities*. Berkeley: University of California Press.

———. 1995b. "Masculinity, Violence, and War." In Michael S. Kimmel and Michael A. Messner (eds.), *Men's Lives*. New York: Allyn and Bacon.

———. 2001. "Masculinities and Globalization." In Judith Lorber (ed.), *Gender Inequality: Feminist Theories and Politics*. Los Angeles: Roxbury.

Cooper, A., G. Golden, and J. Kent-Ferraro. 2002. "Online Sexual Behaviors in the Workplace: How Can Human Resource Departments and Employee Assistance Programs Respond Effectively?" *Sexual Addiction and Compulsivity* 9:149–65.

Cooper, A., I. P. McLoughlin, and K. M. Campbell. 2000. "Sexuality in Cyberspace: Update for the 21st Century." *CyberPsychology and Behavior* 3:521–36.

Cooper, A., I. McLoughlin, P. Reich, and J. Kent-Ferraro. 2002. "Virtual Sexuality in the Workplace: A Wake-Up Call for Clinicians, Employers and Employees." In A. Cooper (ed.), *Sex and the Internet: A Guidebook for Clinicians*. New York: Brunner-Routledge.

Cooper, A., C. R. Scherer, S. C. Boies, and B. L. Gordon. 1999. "Sexuality on the Internet: From Sexual Exploration to Pathological Expression." *Professional Psychology: Research and Practice* 30:154–64.

Cooper, A., and L. Sportolari. 1997. "Romance and Cyberspace: Understanding Online Attraction." *Journal of Sex Education and Therapy* 22:7–14.

Corby, B. 1987. *Working with Child Abuse: Social Work Practice and the Child Abuse System*. Milton Keynes, UK: Open University Press.

Cornwell, J. 1984. *Hard-Earned Lives: Accounts of Health and Illness from East London*. London: Tavistock.

Corrin, Chris. 2005. "Transitional Road for Traffic: Analysing Trafficking in Women from and Through Central and Eastern Europe." *Europe-East Asia Studies* 57(4):543–60.

Cortez, Jayne. 1983. "Rape." In Amiri Baraka and Amina Baraka (eds.), *Confirmation*. New York: Quill.

Cossins, Anne. 2000. *Masculinities, Sexualities and Child Sexual Abuse*. The Hague: Kluwer Law International.

———. 2003. "Saints, Sluts and Sexual Assault: Rethinking the Relationship between Sex, Race and Gender." *Social and Legal Studies* 12:77–103.

Cottle, Charles E., Patricia Searles, Ronald J. Berger, and Beth Ann Pierce. 1989. "Conflicting Ideologies and the Politics of Pornography." *Gender & Society* 3(3):303–33.

Courvant, Diana. 1997. *Domestic Violence and the Sex- or Gender-Variant Survivor*. Portland, OR: Survivor Project.

Courvant, Diana, and Loree Cook-Daniels. 1998. "Trans and Intersex Survivors of Domestic Violence: Defining Terms, Barriers, and Responsibilities." National Coalition of Domestic Violence. Available online at http://www.survivorproject.org/defbarresp.html (accessed August 25, 2005).

Crenshaw, Kimberlé. 1991a. "Demarginalizing the Intersection of Race and Sex: A Black Feminist Critique of Antidiscrimination Doctrine, Feminist Theory, and Antiracist Politics." In Katharine A. Bartlett and Rosanne Kennedy (eds.), *Feminist Legal Theory*. Boulder, CO: Westview.

———. 1991b. "Mapping the Margins: Intersectionality, Identity Politics, and Violence against Women of Color." *Stanford Law Review* 43:1241–99.

———. 1994. "Intersectionality and Identity Politics: Learning from Violence against Women of Color." In M. L. Shanley and U. Narayan (eds.), *Reconstructing Political Theory: Feminist Perspectives*. University Park: Pennsylvania State University Press.

Crites, Laura L. 1987. "Wife Abuse: The Judicial Record." In Laura L. Crites and Winifred L. Hepperle (eds.), *Women, the Courts and Equality*. Newbury Park, CA: Sage.

Crull, P. 1982. "Stress Effects of Sexual Harassment on the Job: Implications for Counseling." *American Journal of Orthopsychiatry* 52:539–44.

Culbertson, A. L., P. Rosenfeld, S. Booth-Kewley, and P. Magnusson. 1992. *Assessment of Sexual Harassment in the Navy: Results of the 1989 Navy-Wide Survey*. TR-92–11. San Diego, CA: Navy Personnel Research and Development Center.

Cunneen, C., and J. Stubbs. 2000. "Male Violence, Male Fantasy and the Commodification of Women through the Internet." *Interactive Review of Victimology* 7:5–28.

Cunningham, M., and F. Schumer. 1984. *Powerplay: What Really Happened at Bendix*. New York: Simon and Schuster.

Curry, T. J. 1991. "Fraternal Bonding in the Locker Room: A Profeminist Analysis of Talk about Competition and Women." *Sociology of Sport Journal* 8:119–35.

D'Alessandro, D. M., and N. P. Dosa. 2001. "Empowering Children and Families with Information Technology." *Archives of Pediatrics and Adolescent Medicine* 155:1131–36.

Daley, S. 2001. "New Rights for Dutch Prostitutes, but No Gain." *New York Times*, August 12, pp. Al and 4.

Danner, M. J. E. 1998. "Three Strikes and It's Women Who Are Out: The Hidden Consequences for Women of Criminal Justice Policy Reforms." In Susan L. Miller (ed.), *Crime Control and Women: Feminist Implications of Criminal Justice Policy*. Thousand Oaks, CA: Sage.

Dansky, B. S., and D. G. Kilpatrick. 1997. "Effects of Sexual Harassment." In W. O'Donohue (ed.), *Sexual Harassment: Theory, Research, and Treatment*. Needham Heights, MA: Allyn and Bacon.

Dasgupta, Shamita D. 2005. "Women's Realities: Defining Violence against Women by Immigration, Race, and Class." In N. J. Sokoloff (ed.), *Domestic Violence at the Margins*. New Brunswick, NJ: Rutgers University Press.

Davidson, T. 1978. *Conjugal Crime: Understanding and Changing the Wifebeating Pattern*. New York: Hawthorn.

Davies, Margaret. 1997. "Taking the Inside Out: Sex and Gender in the Legal Subject." In N. Naffine and R. J. Owens (eds.), *Sexing the Subject of Law*. London: Sweet and Maxwell.

Davies, Miranda. 1994. "Understanding the Problem." United Nations' resource manual, *Strategies for Confronting Domestic Violence*. Reprinted in M. Davies (ed.), *Women and Violence*. London: Zed Books.

Davin, A. 1978. "Imperialism and Motherhood." *History Workshop* 5:9–65.

Davis, Angela. 1971. "Reflections on the Black Woman's Role in the Community of Slaves." *Black Scholar* 3(4):3–15.

———— 1983. *Women, Race and Class*. New York: Vintage.

Davis, K. E., A. L. Coker, and M. Sanderson. 2002. "Physical and Mental Health Effects of Being Stalked for Men and Women." *Violence and Victims* 17:429–43.

Deadrick, D. L., S. W. Kezman, and R. B. McAfee. 1996. "Harassment by Nonemployees: How Should Employers Respond?" *HR Magazine* 41(12):108–12.

Decalmer, P., and F. Glendenning. 1993. *The Mistreatment of Elderly People*. London: Sage.

Defour, D. 1990. "The Interface of Racism and Sexism on College Campuses." In Michele A. Paludi (ed.), *Ivory Power: Sexual Harassment on Campus*. Albany: State University of New York Press.

Deirmenjian, J. M. 1999. "Stalking in Cyberspace." *Journal of American Academic Psychiatry Law* 27:407–13.

de la Luz Lima, Maria. 1992. "Reforms in the Criminal Justice System." In *Violence against Women: Addressing a Global Problem*. Transcript of the Ford Foundation Women's Program Forum. New York: Ford Foundation.

Delaware NOW. 2005. "Supreme Court Leaves Women More Vulnerable to Domestic Violence." Delaware NOW late summer newsletter.

Demby, Lela. 1990. "Investigating Complaints of Sexual Harassment." In Michele A. Paludi (ed.), *Ivory Power: Sexual Harassment on Campus.* Albany: State University of New York Press.

D'Emilio, John, and Estelle B. Freedman. 1988. *Intimate Matters: A History of Sexuality in America.* New York: Harper and Row.

Department of Health. 1988. *Protecting Children: A Guide for Social Workers Undertaking a Comprehensive Assessment.* London: HMSO.

———. 1989a. *Working with Child Sexual Abuse: A Guide for Training Social Services Staff.* Child Care Training Support Programme. London: HMSO.

———. 1989b. *An Introduction to the Children Act 1989.* London: HMSO.

Department of Health and Social Security. 1988. *Working Together: A Guide to Arrangements for Inter-Agency Co-operation for the Protection of Children from Abuse.* London: HMSO.

Department of Health Social Service Inspectorate. 1992. *Confronting Elder Abuse: An SSI London Region Survey.* London: HMSO.

De Vise, Daniel. 2005. "Defense Dept. Surveys Academy Sex Assaults." *Washington Post*, March 19, p. A1.

DeVoe, Jill, Katharin Peter, Phillip Kaufman, Amanda Miller, Margaret Noonan, Thomas Snyder, and Katrina Baum. 2004. *Indicators of School Crime and Safety: 2004.* NCES 2005-002/NCJ 205290. U.S. Departments of Education and Justice. Washington, DC: U.S. Government Printing Office.

DeVoe, Jill, Katharin Peter, Phillip Kaufman, Sally Ruddy, Amanda Miller, Mike Planty, Thomas Snyder, and Michael Rand. 2003. *Indicators of School Crime and Safety: 2003.* NCES 2004-004/NCJ 201257. U.S. Departments of Education and Justice. Washington, DC: U.S. Government Printing Office.

Dewan, Shaila. 2005. "After 24 Years in Prison, Man Has a Reason to Smile." *New York Times,* December 8, p. A21.

Dibbell, J. 1998. "A Rape in Cyberspace." Chapter 1 of Julian Dibbell, *My Tiny Life.* New York: Holt. Available at www.juliandibbell.com/texts/bungle.html (accessed September 15, 2004).

DiNitto, Diana, Patricia Y. Martin, M. Sharon Maxwell, and Diane Byington Norton. 1989. "Rape Treatment Programmes: Delivering Innovative Services to Survivors." *Medicine and Law* 8:21–30.

Ditmore, Melissa Hope. 2002. "Trafficking and Sex Work: A Problematic Conflation." Ph.D. diss., City University of New York.

DiTomaso, N. 1989. "Sexuality in the Workplace: Discrimination and Harassment." In J. Hearn, D. L. Sheppard, P. Tancred-Sheriff, and G. Burrell (eds.), *The Sexuality of Organization.* London: Sage.

Dobash, R. Emerson, and Russell P. Dobash. 1979. *Violence against Wives: A Case against the Patriarchy.* New York: Free Press.

———. 1987. "The Response of the British and American Women's Movements to Violence against Women." In Jalna Hanmer and Mary Maynard (eds.), *Women, Violence and Social Control.* Atlantic Highlands, NJ: Humanities Press.

———. 1992. *Women, Violence and Social Change.* London: Routledge.

Dobratz, Betty, and Stephanie Shanks Meile. 2001. *The White Separatist Movement in the United States.* Baltimore: Johns Hopkins University Press.

Dolan, Frances E. 2003. "Battered Women, Petty Traitors, and the Legacy of Coverture." *Feminist Studies* 29:249–78.

Dombrowski, S. C., J. W. LeMasney, C. E. Ahia, and S. A. Dickson. 2004. "Protecting Children from Online Sexual Predators: Technological, Psychoeducational, and Legal Considerations." *Professional Psychology: Research and Practice* 35:65–73.

Donnerstein, E., and D. Linz. 1986. "Mass Media Sexual Violence and Male Viewers: Current Theory and Research." *American Behavioral Scientist* 29(5):601–18.

Döring, N. 2000. "Feminist Views of Cybersex: Victimization, Liberation, and Empowerment." *CyberPsychology and Behavior* 3:863–64.

Dorsey, J. O. 1884. *Omaha Sociology*. Smithsonian Institution, Bureau of Ethnology, Third Annual Report, 1881–82, pp. 205–370. Washington, DC: U.S. Government Printing Office.

Douglas, K. M., and C. McGarty. 2001. "Identifiability and Self-Presentation: Computer-Mediated Communication and Intergroup Interaction." *British Journal of Social Psychology* 40:399–416.

———. 2002. "Internet Identifiability and Beyond: A Model of the Effects of Identifiability on Communicative Behavior." *Group Dynamics* 6:17–26.

Dunne, Michael P., David M. Purdie, Michelle D. Cook, Frances M. Boyle, and Jake M. Najman. 2003. "Is Child Sexual Abuse Declining? Evidence from a Population-Based Survey of Men and Women in Australia." *Child Abuse and Neglect* 27:141–52.

Dunwoody-Miller, V., and B. A. Gutek. 1985. *S.H.E. Project Report: Sexual Harassment in the State Workforce: Results of a Survey*. Sacramento: Sexual Harassment in Employment Project of the California Commission on the Status of Women.

Durkin, K. F. 1997. "Misuse of the Internet by Pedophiles: Implications for Law Enforcement and Probation Practice." *Federal Probation* 61(3):14–18.

Durkin, K. F., and C. D. Bryant. 1999. "Propagandizing Pederasty: A Thematic Analysis of the On-Line Exculpatory Accounts of Unrepentant Pedophiles." *Deviant Behavior* 20:103–27.

Dutton, D. G. 1988. *The Domestic Assault of Women: Psychological and Criminal Justice Perspectives*. Toronto: Allyn and Bacon.

Dworkin, Andrea. 1981. *Pornography: Men Possessing Women*. London: Women's Press.

———. 1993. "Take Back the Day: I Want a Twenty-Four-Hour Truce During Which There Is No Rape." In A. Dworkin, *Letters from a War Zone*. Brooklyn, NY: Lawrence Hill Books.

Dyer, Joel. 1997. *Harvest of Rage*. Boulder, CO: Westview.

Dziech, Billie Wright, and Linda Weiner. 1990. *The Lecherous Professor: Sexual Harassment on Campus*. Chicago: University of Illinois Press.

Eastman, M. 1984. *Old Age Abuse*. Mitcham, UK: Age Concern England.

Eastman, M., and M. Sutton. 1982. "Granny Battering." *Geriatric Medicine* (November): 11–15.

Easton, Dossie, and Catherine Liszt. 1998. *The Ethical Slut: A Guide to Infinite Sexual Possibilities*. Oakland, CA: Greenery Press.

Edleson, Jeffrey L. 1999. "Children's Witnessing of Adult Domestic Violence." *Journal of Interpersonal Violence* 14(8):839—70.

Edwards, Alison. n.d. "Rape, Racism, and the White Women's Movement: An Answer to Susan Brownmiller." Chicago: Sojourner Truth Organization.

Edwards, Susan. 1987. " 'Provoking Her Own Demise': From Common Assault to Homicide." In Jalna Hanmer and Mary Maynard (eds.), *Women, Violence and Social Control*. Atlantic Highlands, NJ: Humanities Press.

EEOC (U.S. Equal Employment Opportunity Commission). 2006. "Sexual Harassment." EEOC Web site. http://www.eeoc.gov/types/sexual_harassment.html.

Ehrenreich, Barbara. 1983. *The Hearts of Men*. New York: Doubleday.

———. 2001. "Veiled Threat." *Los Angeles Times*, November 4, p. M1.

Ehrenreich, Barbara, E. Hess, and G. Jacobs. 1986. *Re-Making Love: The Feminization of Sex*. New York: Doubleday.

Eisenstein, Hester. 1983. *Contemporary Feminist Thought.* Boston: G. K. Hall.

Eldridge, Larry D. 1997. "Nothing New under the Sun: Spouse Abuse in Colonial America." In L. L. O'Toole and J. Schiffman (eds.), *Gender Violence, Interdisciplinary Perspectives.* 1st ed. New York: NYU Press.

Elliott, Michael. 2001. "Hate Club." *Time,* November 12, pp. 58–62, 65–68, 70, 73–74, 77.

Elliott, P. 1996. "Shattering Illusions: Same-Sex Domestic Violence." In C. M. Renzetti and C. H. Miley (eds.), *Violence in Gay and Lesbian Domestic Partnerships.* Binghamton, NY: Harrington Park Press.

Ellis, Lee. 1989. *Theories of Rape: Inquiries into the Causes of Sexual Aggression.* New York: Hemisphere.

Ellis, S., A. Barak, and A. Pinto. 1991. "Moderating Effects of Personal Cognitions on Experienced and Perceived Sexual Harassment of Women at the Workplace." *Journal of Applied Social Psychology* 21:1320–37.

Elshtain, Jean Bethke. 1982. "Feminist Discourse and Its Discontents: Language, Power, and Meaning." *Signs: Journal of Women in Culture and Society* 7(3):603–21.

Elwin, V. 1947. *The Muria and Their Ghotul.* Bombay: Geoffrey Cumberlege/Oxford University Press.

Enloe, Cynthia. 1990. *Bananas, Beaches and Bases: Making Feminist Sense of International Politics.* Berkeley: University of California Press.

———. 1994. *The Morning After.* Berkeley: University of California Press.

———. 2000. *Maneuvers: The International Politics of Militarizing Women's Lives.* Berkeley: University of California Press.

Epstein, C. F. 1981. *Women in Law.* New York: Basic Books.

Erdland, P. A. 1914. *Die Marshall-insulaner* (*The Marshall Islanders*). Münster: Anthropos Bibliothek Ethnological Monographs, 2(1). (Translated by Richard Neuse for Human Relations Area Files.)

Erez, Edna, and Kathy Laster. 2000. "Introduction." In E. Erez and K. Laster (eds.), *Domestic Violence: Global Responses.* Bicester, UK: A B Academic.

Estrich, Susan. 1987. *Real Rape.* Cambridge, MA: Harvard University Press.

Evans-Pritchard, E. E. 1971. *The Azande.* Oxford: Oxford University Press.

Ewing, Wayne. 1982. "The Civic Advocacy of Violence." *M* (spring): 5–7, 22.

Fairbairn, W. R. D. 1935. "Medico-Psychological Aspects of the Problem of Child Assault." *Mental Hygiene* (April): 1–16.

Farley, L. 1978. *Sexual Shakedown: The Sexual Harassment of Women on the Job.* New York: McGraw-Hill.

Farley, Melissa. 2004. " 'Bad for the Body, Bad for the Heart': Prostitution Harms Women Even If Legalized or Decriminalized." *Violence against Women* 10(10):1087–1125.

Fausto-Sterling, Anne. 1989. "Life in the XO Corral." *Women's Studies International Forum* 12(3):319–31.

———. 2000. *Sexing the Body: Gender Politics and the Construction of Sexuality.* New York: Basic Books.

Fawcett, J. 1989. "Breaking the Habit: The Need for a Comprehensive Long Term Treatment for Sexually Abusing Families." In *The Treatment of Child Sexual Abuse.* NSPCC, Occasional Paper Series no. 7. London: NSPCC.

Feagin, J., A. Orum, and G. Sjoberg. 1991. *A Case for the Case Study.* Chapel Hill: University of North Carolina Press.

Federal Bureau of Investigation. 1993. *Uniform Crime Reports.* Washington, DC: U.S. Government Printing Office.

Feil, N. 1993. *The Validation Breakthrough.* Baltimore: Health Professions Press.

Felson, Richard. 2002. *Violence and Gender Reexamined*. Washington, DC: American Psychological Association.

Feltey, K. M., J. J. Ainslie, and A. Geib. 1991. "Sexual Coercion Attitudes among High School Students: The Influence of Gender and Rape Education." *Youth and Society* 23:229–50.

Ferguson, H. 1990. "Rethinking Child Protection Practices: A Case for History." In The Violence against Children Study Group (eds.), *Taking Child Abuse Seriously*. London: Unwin Hyman.

Fergusson, David M., L. John Horwood, and Elizabeth M. Ridder. 2005. "Partner Violence and Mental Health Outcomes in a New Zealand Birth Cohort." *Journal of Marriage and Family* 67(5):1103–19.

Ferree, Myra Marx. 1990. "Beyond Separate Spheres: Feminism and Family Research." *Journal of Marriage and the Family* 52(4):866–84.

Ferree, Myra Marx, Judith Lorber, and Beth B. Hess. 2000. "Introduction." In M. M. Ferree, J. Lorber, and B. B. Hess (eds.), *Revisioning Gender*. Walnut Creek, CA: Altamira.

Ferree, Myra Marx, and Patricia Yancey Martin. 1995. "Introduction." In M. M. Ferree and P. Y. Martin (eds.), *Feminist Organizations: Harvest of the New Women's Movement*. Philadelphia: Temple University Press.

Fine, G. A. 1986. "The Dirty Play of Little Boys," *Society* 24(1):63–67.

Finkelhor, David (ed.). 1984. *Child Sexual Abuse: New Theory and Research*. New York: Free Press.

———. 1986. *A Sourcebook on Child Sexual Abuse*. Beverly Hills, CA: Sage.

———. 1994. "Current Information on the Scope and Nature of Child Sexual Abuse." *Future of Children* 4(2):31—53.

Finkelhor, David, and J. Dziuba-Leatherman. 1994. "Victimization of Children." *American Psychologist* 49:173—83.

Finkelhor, David, G. Hotaling, I. A. Lewis, and C. Smith. 1990. "Sexual Abuse in a National Survey of Adult Men and Women: Prevalence, Characteristics, and Risk Factors." *Child Abuse and Neglect* 14:19–28.

Finkelhor, David, and Richard Ormrod. 2000. "Characteristics of Crimes against Juveniles." *Juvenile Justice Bulletin*, June. U.S. Department of Justice, Office of Justice Programs, Washington, DC.

Finkelhor, David, and K. A. Pillemer. 1988. "Elder Abuse: Its Relation to Other Forms of Domestic Violence." In G. T. Hotaling, D. Finkelhor, J. T. Kirkpatrick, and M. A. Strauss (eds.), *Family Abuse and Its Consequences: New Directions in Research*. Beverly Hills, CA: Sage.

Finkelhor, David, and Kersti Yllö. 1985. *License to Rape: Sexual Abuse of Wives*. New York: Free Press.

Finn, J., and M. Banach. 2000. "Victimization Online: The Downside of Seeking Human Services for Women on the Internet. *CyberPsychology and Behavior* 3:785–96.

Finn, P., and S. Colson. 1990. *Civil Protection Orders: Legislation, Current Court Practice, and Enforcement*. Issues and Practice Report. Washington, DC: National Institute of Justice.

Fisher, Bonnie S., Francis T. Cullen, and Michael G. Turner. 2000. "The Sexual Victimization of College Women." Washington, DC: National Institute of Justice and Bureau of Justice Statistics.

Fisher, Bonnie S., Leah E. Daigle, Francis T. Cullen, and Michael G. Turner. 2003. "Acknowledging Sexual Victimization as Rape: Results from a National-Level Study." *Justice Quarterly* 20(3):535–74.

Fiske, S. T., and P. Glick. 1995. "Ambivalence and Stereotypes Cause Sexual Harassment: A Theory with Implications for Organizational Change." *Journal of Social Issues* 51(1):97–115.

Fitzgerald, L. F. 1993. "Sexual Harassment: Violence against Women in the Workplace." *American Psychologist* 48(10):1070–76.

Fitzgerald, L. F., and K. F. Brock. 1992. "Women's Responses to Victimization: Validation of an Objective Inventory to Assess Strategies for Responding to Sexual Harassment." Unpublished manuscript, Department of Psychology, University of Illinois, Champaign.

Fitzgerald, L. F., F. Drasgow, and V. J. Magley. 1999. "Sexual Harassment in the Armed Forces: A Test of an Integrated Model." *Military Psychology* 11:329–43.

Fitzgerald, L. F., M. Gelfand, and F. Drasgow. 1995. "Measuring Sexual Harassment: Theoretical and Psychometric Advances." *Basic and Applied Social Psychology* 17:425–45.

Fitzgerald, L. F., V. J. Magley, F. Drasgow, and C. R. Waldo. 1999. "Measuring Sexual Harassment in the Military: The Sexual Experiences Questionnaire (SEQ-DoD)." *Military Psychology* 11:243–63.

Fitzgerald, L. F., and S. L. Shullman. 1993. "Sexual Harassment: A Research Analysis and Agenda for the 1990s." *Journal of Vocational Behavior* 42:5–27.

Fitzgerald, L. F., S. L. Shullman, N. Bailey, M. Richards, J. Swecker, Y. Gold, A. J. Ormerod, and L. Weitzman. 1988. "Incidence and Dimensions of Sexual Harassment in Academia and the Workplace." *Journal of Vocational Behavior* 32:152–75.

Fleming, Jillian M. 1997. "Prevalence of Childhood Sexual Abuse in a Community Sample of Australian Women." *Medical Journal of Australia* 166:65–68.

Foley, L. A. 1995. "Date Rape: Effects of Race of Assailant and Victim and Gender of Subjects on Perceptions." *Journal of Black Psychology* 21:6–18.

Folgero, I. S., and I. H. Fjeldstad. 1995. "On Duty—Off Guard: Cultural Norms and Sexual Harassment in Service Organizations." *Organization Studies* 16:299–313.

Foner, N. 1994. *The Caregiving Dilemma: Work in an American Nursing Home.* Berkeley: University of California Press.

Fontana-Rosa, J. 2001. "Legal Competency in a Case Study of Pedophilia: Advertising on the Internet." *International Journal of Offender Therapy and Comparative Criminology* 45:118–28.

Foucault, Michel. 1980. *Power/Knowledge: Selected Interviews and Other Writings, 1972–1977.* Ed. Colin Gordon. New York: Pantheon.

Frazier, Michael. 2001. "Students Face Felony Charges in Fondlings." *St. Petersburg Times,* October 27, p. 3B.

———. 2003. "Two Boys Charged with Rape in Assault on School Bus." *Arkansas Democrat-Gazette,* December 19, p. 17.

Frazier, P. A., C. C. Cochran, and A. M. Olson. 1995. "Social Science Research on Lay Definitions of Sexual Harassment." *Journal of Social Issues* 51(1):21–37.

Frederick, L., and K. C. Lizdas. 2003. "The Role of Restorative Justice in the Battered Women's Movement." Battered Women's Justice Project. Available online at http://www.bwjp.org/doc uments/finalrj.pdf.

Freeman, Jo. 1984. "The Women's Liberation Movement: Its Origins, Structure Activities, and Ideas." In J. Freeman (ed.), *Women: A Feminist Perspective.* Mountain View, CA: Mayfield Publishing Co.

Fulda, J. S. 2002. "Do Internet Stings Directed at Pedophiles Capture Offenders or Create Offenders? And Allied Questions." *Sexuality and Culture* 6(4):73–100.

Fuller, Janet. 2003. "Teen Guilty of Taking Two Kegs to Hazing." *Chicago Sun Times,* July 16, p. 6.

Fulmer, T., and T. A. O'Malley. 1987. *Inadequate Care of the Elderly.* New York: Springer.

Gallop, J. 1995. "The Lecherous Professor: A Reading." *Differences* 7:1–15.

Gamache, Denise, and Mary Asmus. 1999. "Enhancing Networking among Service Providers: Elements of Successful Coordination Strategies." In Melanie R. Shepard and Ellen L. Pence (eds.), *Coordinating Community Responses to Domestic Violence: Lessons from Duluth and Beyond.* Thousand Oaks, CA: Sage.

Game Over: Gender, Race, and Violence in Video Games. 2004. Media Education Foundation.

Gardner, Carol Brooks. 1995. *Passing By: Gender and Public Harassment.* Berkeley: University of California Press.

Gardner, T. A. 1980. "Racism in Pornography and the Women's Movement." In L. Lederer (ed.), *Take Back the Night: Women and Pornography*. New York: Morrow.

Garland A., and E. Zigler. 1993. "Adolescent Suicide Prevention: Current Research and Social Policy Implications." *American Psychologist* 48:169–82.

Garver, Newton. 1968. "What Violence Is." *Nation* 209 (June 24): 817–22.

Garvey, M. S. 1996. "Lecherous Clients May Be Costly for Companies." *National Law Journal* 18 (February 26): C2–C3.

Gatens, Moira. 1996. *Imaginary Bodies: Ethics, Power and Corporeality*. London: Routledge.

Gáti, Á., T. Tényi, F. Túry, and M. Wildmann. 2002. "Anorexia Nervosa Following Sexual Harassment on the Internet: A Case Report." *International Journal of Eating Disorders* 31:474–77.

Gay, William. 1994. "The Prospect for a Nonviolent Model of National Security." In William Gay and T. A. Alekseeva (eds.), *On the Eve of the 21st Century: Perspectives of Russian and American Philosophers*. Lanham, MD: Rowman and Littlefield.

———. 1997. "Nonsexist Public Discourse and Negative Peace: The Injustice of Merely Formal Transformation." *Acorn: Journal of the Gandhi-King Society* 9(1) (spring): 45–53.

———. 1998. "Exposing and Overcoming Linguistic Alienation and Linguistic Violence." *Philosophy and Social Criticism* 24(2–3):137–56.

———. 1999a. "The Language of War and Peace." In Lester Kurtz (ed.), *Encyclopedia of Violence, Peace, and Conflict*. San Diego, CA: Academic Press.

———. 1999b. "Linguistic Violence." In Deane Curtin and Bob Litke (eds.), *Institutional Violence*. Amsterdam: Rodopi Press.

Gelb, A. 1994. *Quincy Court Model Domestic Abuse Program Manual*. Swampscott, MA: Productions Specialties.

Gelles, Richard J. 1975. "Violence and Pregnancy: A Note on the Extent of the Problem and Needed Services." *Family Coordinator* 24:81–86.

Gelles, Richard J., and Murray Straus. 1988. *Intimate Violence*. New York: Simon and Schuster.

Gennetian, L. A. 2003. "Welfare Policies and Domestic Abuse among Single Mothers: Experimental Evidence from Minnesota." *Violence against Women* 9(10):1171–90.

Genovese, Eugene D. 1974. *Roll, Jordan, Roll: The World the Slaves Made*. New York: Pantheon.

Geraci, Linda. 1986. "Making Shelters Safe for Lesbians." In Kerry Lobel (ed.), *Naming the Violence: Speaking Out about Lesbian Battering*. Seattle: Seal.

Gherardi, S. 1995. *Gender, Symbolism, and Organizational Cultures*. London: Sage.

Gilligan, Carol. 1982. *In a Different Voice: Psychological Theory and Women's Development*. Cambridge, MA: Harvard University Press.

Gilligan, Leilah, and Tom Talbot. 2000. "Community Supervision of the Sex Offender: An Overview of Current and Promising Practices." Center for Sex Offender Management. Available online at http://www.nicic.org/Library/016075.

Gilman, Sander L. 1985. "Black Bodies, White Bodies: Toward an Iconography of Female Sexuality in Late Nineteenth-Century Art, Medicine, and Literature." *Critical Inquiry* 12(1):205–43.

Ginorio, Angela, and Jane Reno. 1986. "Violence in the Lives of Latina Women." In Maryviolet Burns (ed.), *The Speaking Profits Us: Violence in the Lives of Women of Color*. Seattle: Center for the Prevention of Sexual and Domestic Violence.

Giorgio, G. 2002. "Speaking Silence: Definitional Dialogues in Abusive Lesbian Relationships." *Violence against Women* 8(10):1233–59.

Giuffre, P. A., and C. L. Williams. 1994. "Boundary Lines: Labeling Sexual Harassment in Restaurants." *Gender & Society* 8(3):378–401.

Glaser, D., and J. R. Spencer. 1990. "Sentencing, Children's Evidence and Children's Trauma." *Criminal Law Review* (June): 371–82.

Gledhill, A., et al. 1989. *Who Cares? Children at Risk and Social Services.* London: Centre for Policy Studies.

Glendenning, C. 1987. "Impoverishing Women." In Alan Walker and Carol Walker (eds.), *The Growing Divide.* London: CPAG.

Glenn, E. N. 1992. "From Servitude to Service and Work: Historical Continuities in the Racial Division of Paid Reproductive Labor." *Signs* 18(1):1–43.

Glisson, Charles, and Anthony Hemmelgarn. 1997. "The Effects of Organizational Climate and Interorganizational Coordination on the Quality and Outcomes of Children's Service System." *Child Abuse and Neglect* 22(5):401–21.

Glomb, T. M., W. L. Richman, C. L. Hulin, F. Drasgow, K. T. Schneider, and L. F. Fitzgerald. 1997. "Ambient Sexual Harassment: An Integrated Model of Antecedents and Consequences." *Organizational Behavior and Human Decision Proce*sses 71:309–28.

Goddard, Alma Banda, and Tara Hardy. 1999. "Assessing the Lesbian Victim." In B. Leventhal and S. E. Lundy (eds.), *Same-Sex Domestic Violence: Strategies for Change.* Thousand Oaks, CA: Sage.

Godkin, M. A., R. S. Wolf, and K. A. Pillemer. 1989. "A Case-Comparison Analysis of Elder Abuse and Neglect." *International Journal of Aging and Human Development* 28(3): 207–25.

Goldberg-Ambrose, Carole. 1992. "Unfinished Business in Rape Law Reform." *Journal of Social Issues* 48(1):173–85.

Gondolf, Edward W. 1988. *Research on Men Who Batter: An Overview, Bibliography and Resource Guide.* Bradenton, FL: Human Services Institute.

Gonsiorek, J. C. 1993. "Threat, Success, and Adjustment: Mental Health and the Workplace for Gay and Lesbian Individuals." In L. Diamant (ed.), *Homosexual Issues in the Workplace.* Washington, DC: Taylor and Francis.

Goodman, Ellen. 1987. "My Equal Rights Winners." *Boston Globe*, August 25, p. 13.

Goodson, P., D. McCormick, and A. Evans. 2001. "Searching for Sexually Explicit Materials on the Internet: An Exploratory Study of College Students' Behavior and Attitudes." *Archives of Sexual Behavior*, 30:101–18.

Goolkasian, Gail A. 1986. *Confronting Domestic Violence: The Role of the Criminal Court Judges.* U.S. Department of Justice, National Institute of Justice. Washington, DC: U.S. Government Printing Office.

Gordon, L. 1988. *Heroes of Their Own Lives: The Politics and History of Family Violence.* New York: Viking.

Gordon, Margaret T., and Stephanie Riger. 1989. *The Female Fear.* New York: Free Press.

Gorham, D. 1978. "The 'Maiden Tribute of Modern Babylon' Reexamined: Child Prostitution and the Idea of Childhood in Late Victorian England." *Victorian Studies* 21(3):353–87.

Gossett, J. L., and L. Byrne. 2002. "'CLICK HERE': A content Analysis of Internet Rape Sites. *Gender & Society* 16:689–709.

Gould, Stephen Jay. 1981. *The Mismeasure of Man.* New York: Norton.

Graddol, David, and Joan Swann. 1989. *Gender Voices.* Cambridge, MA: Blackwell.

Graham-Kevan, Nicola, and John Archer. 2003a. "Intimate Terrorism and Common Couple Violence: A Test of Johnson's Predictions in Four British Samples." *Journal of Interpersonal Violence* 18(11):1247–70.

———. 2003b. "Physical Aggression and Control in Heterosexual Relationships: The Effect of Sampling. *Violence and Victims* 18(2):181–96.

Grant, Jennifer. 1999. An Argument for Separate Services." In B. Leventhal and S. E. Lundy (eds.), *Same-Sex Domestic Violence: Strategies for Change.* Thousand Oaks, CA: Sage.

Grauerholz, E. 1989. "Sexual Harassment of Women Professors by Students: Exploring the Dynamics of Power, Authority, and Gender in a University Setting." *Sex Roles* 21:789–801.

Gregory, J., and S. Lees. 1999. *Policing Sexual Assault.* London: Routledge.

Greif, Jeffrey, and Rebecca Hegar. 1993. *When Parents Kidnap.* New York: Free Press.

Griffin, Susan. 1971. "Rape: The All-American Crime." *Ramparts* 10:26–35.

———. 1992. *A Chorus of Stones.* New York: Doubleday.

Griffiths, A., G. Roberts, and J. Williams. 1992. *Sharpening the Instrument: The Law and Older People.* Stoke-on-Trent, UK: British Association of Service to the Elderly.

Griffiths, M. D. 1997. "Friendship and Social Development in Children and Adolescents: The Impact of Electronic Technology." *Educational and Child Psychology* 14(3):25–37.

———. 2000. "Excessive Internet Use: Implications for Sexual Behavior." *CyberPsychology and Behavior* 3:537–52.

Griffiths, M. D., M. E. Rogers, and P. Sparrow. 1998. "Crime and IT (Part II): 'Stalking the Net.' " *Probation Journal* 45:138–41.

Grose, C. 1995. "Same-Sex Sexual Harassment: Subverting the Heterosexist Paradigm of Title VII." *Yale Journal of Law and Feminism* 7(2):375–98.

Gross, J. 1993. "Where 'Boys Will Be Boys' and Adults are Befuddled." *New York Times,* March 29, p. A1.

Grossman, Leanne A., and Sande Smith. 2004. "Women Daring to Lead." The Global Fund for Women Report 2003–2004, San Francisco.

Grosz, Elizabeth. 1990. "A Note on Essentialism and Difference." In S. Unew (ed.), *Feminist Knowledge, Critique and Construct.* London: Routledge.

———. 1994. *Volatile Bodies: Toward a Corporeal Feminism.* Sydney: Allen and Unwin.

Grosz, Elizabeth, and Elspeth Probyn. 1995. *Sexy Bodies: Strange Carnalities of Feminism.* London: Routledge.

Groves, B. McAlister, and B. Zuckerman. 1997. "Interventions with Parents and Caregivers of Children Who Are Exposed to Violence." In J. D. Osofsky (ed.), *Children in a Violent Society.* New York: Guilford.

Groves, D. 1983. "Members and Survivors: Women and Retirement Pensions Legislation." In J. Lewis (ed.), *Women's Welfare, Women's Rights.* London: Croom Helm.

Groves, D., and J. Finch. 1983. "Natural Selection: Perspectives on Entitlement to the Invalid Care Allowance." In D. Groves and J. Finch (eds.), *A Labour of Love: Women, Work and Caring.* London: Routledge and Kegan Paul.

Gruber, J. E. 1997. "An Epidemiology of Sexual Harassment: Evidence from North America and Europe." In W. O'Donohue (ed.), *Sexual Harassment: Theory, Research, and Treatment.* Boston: Allyn and Bacon.

Gruber, J. E, and L. Bjorn. 1982. "Blue Collar Blues: The Sexual Harassment of Women Autoworkers." *Work and Occupations* 9(3):271–98.

———. 1986. "Women's Responses to Sexual Harassment: An Analysis of Sociocultural, Organizational, and Personal Resource Models." *Social Science Quarterly* 67(4):814–26.

Gunn Allen, Paula. 1986. "Violence and the American Indian Women." In Maryviolet Burns (ed.), *The Speaking Profits Us: Violence in the Lives of Women of Color.* Seattle: Center for the Prevention of Sexual and Domestic Violence.

Gutek, Barbara A. 1985. *Sex and the Workplace: Impact of Sexual Behavior and Harassment on Women, Men, and Organizations.* San Francisco: Jossey-Bass.

———. 1993a. "Responses to Sexual Harassment." In S. Oskamp and M. Costanzo (eds.), *Gender Issues in Social Psychology: The Claremont Symposium on Applied Social Psychology.* Newbury Park, CA: Sage.

Gutek, B. 1993b. "Sexual Harassment: Rights and Responsibilities." *Employee Responsibilities and Rights Journal* 6(4):325–40.

———. 1997. "Sexual Harassment Policy Initiatives." In W. O'Donohue (ed.), *Sexual Harassment: Theory, Research, and Treatment.* Boston: Allyn and Bacon.

Gutek, B. A., and R. S. Done. 2001. "Sexual Harassment." In R. K. Unger (ed.), *Handbook of the Psychology of Women and Gender.* New York: Wiley.

Gutek, B. A., and V. Dunwoody. 1988. "Understanding Sex and the Workplace." In A. H. Stromberg, L. Larwood, and B. A. Gutek (eds.), *Women and Work: An Annual Review.* Vol. 2. Newbury Park, CA: Sage.

Gutek, B., and M. Koss. 1993. "Changed Women and Changed Organizations: Consequences of and Coping with Sexual Harassment." *Journal of Vocational Behavior* 42:28–48.

Gutek, B. A., and B. Morasch. 1982. "Sex Ratios, Sex-Role Spillover, and Sexual Harassment of Women at Work." *Journal of Social Issues* 38, no. 4:55–74.

Gutek, B. A., C. Y. Nakamura, M. Gahart, I. Handschumacher, and D. Russell. 1980. "Sexuality in the Workplace." *Basic and Applied Social Psychology* 1:255–65.

Hagan, John, and Holly Foster. 2001. "Youth Violence and the End of Adolescence." *American Sociological Review* 66(6):874–99.

Hall, J. D. 1983. "The Mind That Burns in Each Body: Women, Rape, and Racial Violence." In A. Snitow, C. Stansell, and S. Thompson (eds.), *Powers of Desire: The Politics of Sexuality.* New York: Monthly Review Press.

Hall, M. 1989. "Private Experiences in the Public Domain: Lesbians in Organizations." In J. Hearn, D. L. Sheppard, P. Tancred-Sheriff, and G. Burrell (eds.), *The Sexuality of Organization.* London: Sage.

Hall, Ruth. 1985. *Ask Any Woman: A London Inquiry into Rape and Sexual Assault.* Bristol, UK: Falling Wall Press.

Hall, Ruth, Selma James, and Judith Kertesz. 1984. *The Rapist Who Pays the Rent.* Bristol, UK: Falling Wall Press.

Hallowell, A. I. 1955. *Culture and Experience.* Philadelphia: University of Pennsylvania Press.

Halpin, Zuleyma Tang. 1989. "Scientific Objectivity and the Concept of 'the Other.'" *Women's Studies International Forum* 12(3):285–94.

Hamberger, L. K., and C. E. Guse. 2002. "Men's and Women's Use of Intimate Partner Violence in Clinical Samples." *Violence against Women* 8(11):1301–31.

Hamilton, J. A., S. W. Alagna, L. S. King, and C. Lloyd. 1987. "The Emotional Consequences of Gender-Based Abuse in the Workplace: New Counseling Programs for Sex Discrimination." *Women and Therapy* 6:155–82.

Hamilton, J. A., and J. L. Dolkart. 1991. "Legal Reform in the Area of Sexual Harassment: Contributions from Social Sciences." Paper presented at the National Conference to Promote Men and Women Working Productively Together, March, Bellevue, WA.

Hamm, Mark. 2002. *In Bad Company: America's Terrorist Underground.* Boston: Northeastern University Press.

Harcourt, W. (ed.). 1999. *Women@Internet: Creating New Cultures in Cyberspace.* London: Zed Books.

———. 2000. "The Personal and the Political: Women Using the Internet." *CyberPsychology and Behavior* 3:693–97.

Harding, Sandra G. 1991. *Whose Science, Whose Knowledge? Thinking from Women's Lives.* Ithaca, NY: Cornell University Press.

Harley, Debra A., Theresa M. Nowak, Linda J. Gassaway, and Todd A. Savage. 2002. "Lesbian,

Gay, Bisexual, and Transgender College Students with Disabilities: A Look at Multiple Cultural Minorities." *Psychology in the Schools* 39(5):425–538.

Harlow, Carolyn Wolf. 1991. *Female Victims of Violent Crime.* Washington, DC: U.S. Department of Justice.

Harned, M. S., and L. F. Fitzgerald. 2002. "Understanding a Link between Sexual Harassment and Eating Disorder Symptoms: A Mediational Analysis." *Journal of Consulting and Clinical Psychology* 70:1170–81.

Harper, F. E. W. 1969. "Bury Me in a Free Land." In W. H. Robinson (ed.), *Early Black American Poets.* Dubuque, IA: W. C. Brown.

Harris, A. P. 1991. "Race and Essentialism in Feminist Legal Theory." In Katharine T. Bartlett and Rosanne Kennedy (eds.), *Feminist Legal Theory.* Boulder, CO: Westview.

Harris, M. 1977. *Cannibals and Kings.* New York: Vintage/Random House.

Harris Interactive and GLSEN. 2005. *From Teasing to Torment: School Climate in America: A Survey of Students and Teachers.* New York: GLSEN.

Hart, Timothy C., and Callie Rennison. 2003. "Reporting Crime to the Police, 1992–2000." Washington, DC: U.S. Department of Justice, Bureau of Justice Statistics.

Hass, Giselle A., Mary Ann Dutton, and Leslye E. Orloff. 2000. "Lifetime Prevalence of Violence against Latina Immigrants: Legal and Policy Implications." In E. Erez and K. Laster (eds.), *Domestic Violence: Global Responses.* Bicester, UK: A B Academic.

Hassan, Nasra. 2001. "An Arsenal of Believers." *New Yorker,* November 19, pp. 38–41.

Haugen, Gary, and Gregg Hunter. 2005. *Terrify No More.* Nashville, TN: W. Publishing Group.

Healy, Patrick. 2003a. "Coach on L.I. Says He Knew of No Hazing." *New York Times,* October 1, p. B1.

———. 2003b. "L.I. District Is Criticized in Hazing Case." *New York Times,* September 23, p. B1.

———. 2003c. "School District in Hazing Case Draws Anger from Parents." *New York Times,* September 19, p. B1.

Healy Patrick, and Faiza Akhtar. 2003. "Football Players on L.I. Face Abuse Accusations in Hazing." *New York Times,* September 12, p. B5.

Hearn, Jeff, and Wendy Parkin. 1987. *Sex at Work.* New York: St. Martin's Press.

———. 2001. *Gender, Sexuality, and Violence in Organizations.* London: Sage.

Hecht, Tobias. 1998. *At Home in the Street: Street Children of Northeast Brazil.* Cambridge: Cambridge University Press.

Hegar, R. L., S. J. Zuravin, and J. G. Orme. 1991. "Factors Predicting Severity of Child Abuse Injury: A Review of the Literature." Unpublished manuscript, School of Social Work, University of Maryland at Baltimore.

Heldke, Lisa, and Peg O'Connor (eds.). 2004. *Oppression, Privilege, and Resistance: Theoretical Perspectives on Racism, Sexism, and Heterosexism.* New York: McGraw-Hill.

Helliwell, Christine. 2000. " 'It's Only a Penis': Rape, Feminism, and Difference." *Signs* 25(3):789–816.

Hemming, H. 1985. "Women in a Man's World: Sexual Harassment." *Human Relations* 38:67–79.

Hennenberger, M., and M. Marriott. 1993. "For Some, Youthful Courting Has Become a Game of Abuse." *New York Times,* July 7, p. B1.

Herek, Gregory M. 1987. "On Heterosexual Masculinity: Some Psychical Consequences of the Social Construction of Gender and Sexuality." In Michael S. Kimmel (ed.), *Changing Men: New Directions in Research on Men and Masculinity.* Newbury Park, CA: Sage.

Herzberger, Sharon, and Noreen Channels. 1991. "Criminal Justice Processing of Violent and Nonviolent Offenders: The Effects of Familial Relationship to the Victim." In Dean Knudsen and JoAnn Miller (eds.), *Abused and Battered: Social and Legal Responses to Family Violence.* Hawthorne, NY: Aldine de Gruyter.

Hiller, J., and R. Cohen. 2002. *Internet Law and Policy.* Upper Saddle River, NJ: Prentice Hall.

Hindelang, M. J. 1981. "Variations in Sex-Race-Age Specific Incidence of Offending." *American Sociological Review* 46:461–74.

Hirst, E. 2003. "The Housing Crisis for Victims of Domestic Violence: Disparate Impact Claims and Other Housing Protection for Victims of Domestic Violence." *Georgetown Journal on Poverty, Law and Policy* 10(1):131–55.

Hoch, Paul. 1979. *White Hero, Black Beast: Racism, Sexism, and the Mask of Masculinity.* London: Pluto.

Hochschild, A. 1983. *The Managed Heart: Commercialization of Human Feeling.* Berkeley: University of California Press.

Hocking, E. D. 1989. "Miscare—A Form of Abuse in the Elderly." *Update,* May 15, pp. 2411–19.

Hoebel, E. A. 1960. *The Cheyennes.* New York: Holt, Rinehart and Winston.

Hoffman, Kristi L., K. Jill Kiecolt, and John N. Edwards. 2005. "Physical Violence between Siblings: A Theoretical and Empirical Analysis." *Journal of Family Issues* 26(8):1103–30.

Hoffman, R. 1986. "Rape and the College Athlete: Part One." *Philadelphia Daily News,* March 17, p. 23.

Hoffspiegel, L. 2002. "Abuse of Power: Sexual Misconduct in the Legal Workplace." *Sexual Addiction and Compulsivity* 9:113–26.

Högbacka, R., I. Kandolin, E. Haavio-Mannila, and K. Kauppinen-Toropainen. 1987. *Sexual Harassment in the Workplace: Result of a Survey of Finns.* Ministry of Social Affairs and Health, Equality Publications, Series E: Abstracts 1/1987. Helsinki: Valtion Painatuskeskus.

Hollway, W., and T. Jefferson. 1996. "PC or Not PC: Sexual Harassment and the Question of Ambivalence." *Human Relations* 49(3):373–93.

Holt, M. 1993. "Elder Sexual Abuse in Britain: Preliminary Findings." *Journal of Elder Abuse and Neglect* 5, no. 2.

Holtzworth-Munroe, Amy, Jeffrey C. Meehan, Katherine Herron, Uzma Rehman, and Gregory L. Stuart. 2000. "Testing the Holtzworth-Munroe and Stuart (1994) Batterer Typology." *Journal of Consulting and Clinical Psychology* 68:1000–1019.

Homer, A., and C. Gilleard. 1990. "Abuse of Elderly People by Their Carers." *British Medical Journal* 301:1359–62.

Hood-Williams, John. 1996. "Goodbye to Sex and Gender." *Sociological Review* 44:1–16.

———. 2001. "Gender, Masculinities and Crime: From Structures to Psyches." *Theoretical Criminology* 5:37–60.

hooks, bell. 1984. *From Margin to Center.* Boston: South End Press.

———. 1989. " 'Whose Pussy Is This': A Feminist Comment." In *Talking Back.* Boston: South End Press.

———. 1994a. "Sexism and Misogyny: Who Takes the Rap?" *Z Magazine* 7(2):26–29.

———. 1994b. *Teaching to Transgress: Education as the Practice of Freedom.* New York: Routledge.

Hooper, C. A. 1990. "A Study of Mothers' Responses to Child Sexual Abuse by Another Family Member." Ph.D. diss., University of London.

Hope, Akua Lezli. 1983. "Lament." In Amiri Baraka and Amina Baraka (eds.), *Confirmation.* New York: Quill.

Hopkins, P. 1978. *Contending Forces.* Carbondale: Southern Illinois University Press.

Hornstein, R., T. Kay, and D. Atkins. 2002. "One Strike for the Poor and How Many of the Rest of Us?" Law.com Web site, March 22. Available online at http://www.law.com (accessed November 2003).

Horrocks, P. 1988. "Elderly People: Abused and Forgotten." *Health Service Journal,* September 22. Available online at http://www.hsj.co.uk/healthservicejournal.

Howell, Signe, and Roy Willis (eds.). 1990. *Societies at Peace.* New York: Routledge.

Hudgins, Anastasia. 2006. "Policies and Competing Understandings of Risk: Nongovernmental Organizations' Discourses on Vietnamese Commercial Sex Workers in Cambodia." Ph.D. diss., Temple University, Department of Anthropology.

Human Rights Watch. 2001. "Hatred in the Hallways: Violence and Discrimination against Lesbian, Gay, Bisexual, and Transgender Students in US Schools." New York: Human Rights Watch.

Hume, David. 1999 [1748]. *An Enquiry Concerning Human Understanding.* New York: Oxford University Press.

Humphrey, Stephen E., and Arnold S. Kahn. 2000. "Fraternities, Athletic Teams, and Rape: Importance of Identification with a Risky Group." *Journal of Interpersonal Violence* 15(12):1313–22.

International Society for Human Rights. n.d. "Shari'ah Law, Adultery and Rape." ISHR Web site. http://www.steinigung.org/artikel/sharia_adultery_rape.htm (accessed January 31, 2006).

IOM (International Organization for Migration). 1995. "Trafficking and Prostitution: The Growing Exploitation of Migrant Women from Central and Eastern Europe." Budapest: IOM Migration Information Program.

Iovanni, L., and S. L. Miller. 2001. "Criminal Justice System Responses to Domestic Violence: Law Enforcement and the Courts." In C. M. Renzetti, J. L. Edleson, and R. K. Bergen (eds.), *Sourcebook on Violence against Women.* Thousand Oaks, CA: Sage.

Irigaray, Luce. 1989. "The Language of Man." Trans. Erin G. Carlston. *Cultural Critique* 13 (fall): 191–202.

Island, D., and P. Letellier. 1991. *Men Who Beat the Men Who Love Them.* New York: Harrington Park.

ISNA. 2006. Intersex Society of North America Web site. http://www.isna.org/.

Itano, Nicole. 2003. "S. Africa Finds 'Rape Courts' Work." *Christian Science Monitor,* January 29. Available online at http://www.christiansciencemonitor.com/2003/0129/p01s04-woaf.html (accessed January 31, 2006).

Jaffe, Peter, David Wolfe, and Susan Kaye Wilson. 1997. "Definition and Scope of the Problem." In L. L. O'Toole and J. R. Schiffman (eds.), *Gender Violence: Interdisciplinary perspectives.* 1st ed. New York: NYU Press.

Jeffreys, Sheila. 1985. *The Spinster and Her Enemies: Feminism and Sexuality, 1800–1930.* Boston: Pandora.

Jenkins, P. 2001. *Beyond Tolerance: Child Pornography on the Internet.* New York: NYU Press.

Jensen, I., and B. A. Gutek. 1982. "Attributions and Assignment of Responsibility for Sexual Harassment." *Journal of Social Issues* 38:121–36.

Jensvold, M. F. 1991. "Assessing the Psychological and Physical Harm to Sexual Harassment Victims." Paper presented at the National Conference to Promote Men and Women Working Productively Together, March, Bellevue, WA.

Johnson, Michael P. 1995. "Patriarchal Terrorism and Common Couple Violence: Two Forms of Violence against Women." *Journal of Marriage and the Family* 57(2):283–94.

———. 1999. "Two Types of Violence against Women in the American Family: Identifying Patriarchal Terrorism and Common Couple Violence." Paper presented at the National Council on Family Relations annual meeting, November, Irvine, CA.

———. 2001. "Conflict and Control: Symmetry and Asymmetry in Domestic Violence." In A. Booth, A. C. Crouter, and M. Clements (eds.), *Couples in Conflict.* Mahwah, NJ: Erlbaum.

———. 2005. "Domestic Violence: It's Not about Gender—Or Is It? *Journal of Marriage and Family* 67(5):1126–30.

———. 2006. "Gendered Communication and Intimate Partner Violence." In B. J. Dow and J. T. Wood (eds.), *The Sage Handbook of Gender and Communication.* Thousand Oaks, CA: Sage.

Johnson, T. F., J. G. O'Brien, and M. F. Hudson. 1985. *Elder Abuse: An Annotated Bibliography.* Westport, CT: Greenwood.

Joinson, A. N. 1998. "Causes and Implications of Disinhibited Behavior on the Internet." In J. Gackenbach (ed.), *Psychology and the Internet: Intrapersonal, Interpersonal, and Transpersonal Implications.* San Diego, CA: Academic Press.

———. 1999. "Social Desirability, Anonymity, and Internet-Based Questionnaires." *Behavior and Research Methods, Instruments, and Computers* 31:433–38.

———. 2001. "Self-Disclosure in Computer-Mediated Communication: The Role of Self-Awareness and Visual Anonymity." *European Journal of Social Psychology* 31:177–92.

———. 2003. *Understanding the Psychology of Internet Behaviour.* Basingstoke, UK: Palgrave Macmillan.

Jones, Gayle. 1975. *Corregidora.* Boston: Beacon.

Jordan, June. 1978. "Against the Wall." In *Civil Wars.* Boston: Beacon.

———. 1980a. "Rape Is Not a Poem." In *Passion: New Poems, 1977–1980.* Boston: Beacon.

———. 1980b. "The Rationale, or She Drove Me Crazy." In *Passion: New Poems, 1977–1980.* Boston: Beacon.

Kalof, L., K. K. Eby, J. L. Matheson, and K. Kroska. 2001. "The Influence of Race and Gender on Student Self-Reports of Sexual Harassment by College Professors." *Gender & Society* 15:282–302.

Kanin, Eugene J. 1967. "Reference Groups and Sex Conduct Norm Violations." *Sociological Quarterly* 8:495–504.

———. 1985. "Date Rapists: Differential Socialization and Relative Deprivation." *Archives of Sexual Behavior* 14:219–31.

Kanin, Eugene J., and Stanley J. Parcell. 1977. "Sexual Aggression: A Second Look at the Offended Female." *Archives of Sexual Behavior* 6:67–76.

Kant, Immanuel. 1923. *Zum ewigen Frieden, Kant's Werke, Band VIII, Abhandlungennach 1781.* Berlin: Forum-Verlag.

———. 1983. *Perpetual Peace and Other Essays.* Trans. Ted Humphrey. Indianapolis: Hackett.

Kanter, R. M. 1977. *Men and Women of the Corporation.* New York: Basic Books.

Kappeler, Susanne. 1986. *The Pornography of Representation.* Minneapolis: University of Minnesota Press.

Karsten, M. F. 1994. *Management and Gender: Issues and Attitudes.* Westport, CT: Praeger.

Kaschak, Ellyn (ed.). 2001. *Intimate Betrayal: Domestic Violence in Lesbian Relationships.* New York: Haworth.

Katz, J. 1995. "Strip Club's Debut on Nasdaq Reveals New Era of Legitimacy." *San Francisco Chronicle*, October 13, p. A16.

Katz, R. C., R. Hannon, and L. Whitten. 1996. "Effects of Gender and Situation on the Perception of Sexual Harassment." *Sex Roles* 34:35–42.

Kaufman, Michael. 1994. "Men, Feminism, and Men's Contradictory Experiences of Power." In Harry Brod and Michael Kaufman (eds.), *Theorizing Masculinities.* Thousand Oaks, CA: Sage.

———. 1995. "The Construction of Masculinity and the Triad of Men's Violence." In Michael S. Kimmel and Michael A. Messner (eds.), *Men's Lives.* Boston: Allyn and Bacon.

Kelly, E. E., and L. Warshafsky. 1987. "Partner Abuse in Gay Male and Lesbian Couples." Paper presented at the Third National Conference for Family Violence Researchers, Durham, NH.

Kelly, L. 1987. "The Continuum of Sexual Violence." In J. Hanmer and Mary Maynard (eds.), *Women, Violence and Social Control.* London: Macmillan.

———. 1988. *Surviving Sexual Violence.* Minneapolis: University of Minnesota Press.

Kendall, L. 2000. "'Oh No! I'm a Nerd!': Hegemonic Masculinity on an Online Forum. *Gender & Society* 14:256–74.

Kennedy, D. 1993. *Sexy Dressing, Etc.: Essays on the Power and Politics of Cultural Identity*. Cambridge, MA: Harvard University Press.

Kessler, Robert. 2003. "Two Teens Attacked Three Separate Times at Camp." *Newsday*, September 16, p. A2.

Kessler-Harris, A. 1990. *A Woman's Wage*. Lexington: University of Kentucky Press.

Kilpatrick, D. G. 1992. "Treatment and Counseling Needs of Women Veterans Who Were Raped, Otherwise Sexually Assaulted, or Sexually Harassed during Military Service." Testimony before U.S. Senate Committee on Veteran's Affairs, June 30.

Kimmel, Michael. 1987. *Changing Men: New Directions in Research on Men and Masculinity*. Newbury Park, CA: Sage.

——— (ed.). 1990. *Men Confront Pornography*. New York: Crown.

———. 1994. "Masculinity as Homophobia: Fear, Shame, and Silence in the Construction of Gender Identity." In Harry Brod and Michael Kaufman (eds.), *Theorizing masculinities*. Thousand Oaks, CA: Sage.

———. 1996. *Manhood in America: A Cultural History*. New York: Free Press.

——— (with Amy Aronson). 2000. *The Gendered Society Reader*. New York: Oxford University Press.

———. 2001. "Snips and Snails . . . and Violent Urges." *Newsday*, March 8, pp. A41, A44.

———. 2005. "Vatican's New Plan to Curb Abuse Is Based on Flawed Understanding of Human Sexuality." *Chronicle of Higher Education*, October 14.

Kirkwood, Catherine. 1993. *Leaving Abusive Partners: From the Scars of Survival to the Wisdom for Change*. Newbury Park, CA: Sage.

Kitzinger, C. 1994. "Anti-Lesbian Harassment." In C. Brant and Y. L. Too (eds.), *Rethinking Sexual Harassment*. London: Pluto.

Kitzinger, J. 1988. "Defending Innocence: Ideologies of Childhood." *Feminist Review* 28:77–87.

Klain, Eva J. 1999. *Prostitution of Children and Child-Sex Tourism: An Analysis of Domestic and International Responses*. Alexandria, VA: National Center for Missing and Exploited Children.

Klein, Renate C. A., and Robert M. Milardo. 2000. "The Social Context of Couple Conflict: Support and Criticism from Informal Third Parties." *Journal of Social and Personal Relationships* 17(4–5):618–37.

Kligman, Gail, and Stephanie Limoncelli. 2005. "Trafficking Women after Socialism: To, Through, and From Eastern Europe." *Social Politics* 12(1):118–40.

Knadler, Stephen. 2004. "Domestic Violence in the Harlem Renaissance: Remaking the Record in Nella Larsen's *Passing* and Toni Morrison's *Jazz*." *African American Review* 38:99–118.

Knight, Heather. 2004. "Schools Report More Sexual Assaults." *San Francisco Chronicle*, April 2. Available online at www.sfgate.com/cgibin/article/cgi?file=chronicle/archives/2004/04.02 BAGLV5VLUJ1.DTL.

Koehler, L. 1980. *A Search for Power: The "Weaker Sex" in Seventeenth-Century New England*. Urbana: University of Illinois Press.

Kolbert, Elizabeth. 1991. "Sexual Harassment at Work is Pervasive, Survey Suggests." *New York Times*, October 11, pp. 1, A17.

Konradi, Amanda. 2003. "A Strategy for Increasing Post-Rape Medical Care and Forensic Examination: Marketing Sexual Assault Nurse Examiners in the College Population." *Violence against Women* 9(8):955–88.

Koppel, M., S. Argamon, and A. R. Shimoni. 2002. "Automatically Categorizing Written Texts by Author Gender." *Literary and Linguistic Computing* 17:401–12.

Koss, M. P. 1990. "Changed Lives: The Psychological Impact of Sexual Harassment." In Michele A. Paludi (ed.), *Ivory Power: Sexual Harassment on Campus.* Albany: State University of New York Press.

Koss, M. P., C. A. Gidicz, and N. Wisniewski. 1987. "The Scope of Rape: Incidence and Prevalence of Sexual Aggression and Victimization in a National Sample of Higher Education Students." *Journal of Consulting and Clinical Psychology* 55:162–70.

Koss, M. P., and M. R. Harvey. 1991. *The Rape Victim: Clinical and Community Interventions.* 2nd ed. Newbury Park, CA: Sage.

Krakow, B., A. Artar, T. D. Warner, D. Melendrez, L. Johnston, M. Hollifield, et al. 2000. "Sleep Disorder, Depression and Suicidality in Female Sexual Assault Survivors." *Crisis* 21:163–70.

Kriesberg, Louis. 1989. "Defensive Revolutionaries: The Moral and Political Economy of Ethnic Nationalism in Industrial Nations." In L. Kriesberg (ed.), *Research on Social Movements, Conflict, and Change.* Vol. 11. Westport, CT: Greenwood.

Kristof, Nicholas. 2005. "The Rosa Parks for the 21st Century." *New York Times,* November 8, p. 27A.

———. 2006a. "A Woman without Importance." *New York Times,* March 26, sec. 4, p. 13.

———. 2006b. "Mother of a Nation." *New York Times,* April 2, sec. 4, p. 12.

Kurz, Demie. 1997. "Violence against Women or Family Violence? Current Debates and Future Directions." In L. L. O'Toole and J. R. Schiffman (eds.), *Gender Violence: Interdisciplinary Perspectives.* 1st ed. New York: NYU Press.

Kwolek-Folland, A. 1994. *Engendering Business: Men and Women in the Corporate Office, 1870–1930.* Baltimore: Johns Hopkins University Press.

Lacey, Marc. 2004. "In Congo War, Even Peacekeepers Add to Horror." *New York Times,* December 18, p. A8.

LaFree, Gary. 1989. *Rape and Criminal Justice: The Social Construction of Assault.* Belmont, CA: Wadsworth.

Lagae, C. R. 1926. *Les Azande ou Niam-Niam.* Bibleotheque-Congo 18. Brussels: Vromant. English translation published by Human Relations Area Files, New Haven, CT.

Lai, Tracy A. 1986. "Asian Women: Resisting the Violence." In Maryviolet Burns (ed.), *The Speaking Profits Us: Violence in the Lives of Women of Color.* Seattle: Center for the Prevention of Sexual and Domestic Violence.

Lambert, H. E. 1956. *Kikuyu Social and Political Institutions.* London: Oxford University Press.

Lane, T. 2003. "In Bangladesh, Women's Risk of Domestic Violence Is Linked to Their Status." *International Family Planning Perspectives* 29(3):147.

Langan, Patrick A., and Christopher Innes. 1986. "Preventing Domestic Violence against Women." Washington, DC: U.S. Department of Justice Bureau of Justice Statistics.

Langley, Roger, and Richard C. Levy. 1977. *Wife Beating: The Silent Crisis.* New York: E. P. Dutton.

Lawrence, Bonita. 1996. *Voix Feministes/Feminist Voices.* Ottawa: CRIAW/ICREF.

League of Nations. 1934. "Child Welfare Committee Enquiry into the Question of Children in Moral and Social Danger." Geneva.

Lee, John Y. 2001. "Placing Japanese War Criminals on the U.S. Justice Department's 'Watch List' of 3 December 1996." In Margaret Stetz and Bonnie B. C. Oh (eds.), *Legacies of the Comfort Women of World War II.* Armonk, NY: M. E. Sharpe.

Lefort, René. 2003. "Congo: A Hell on Earth for Women." *Le Nouvel Observateur,* September 11–18. Available online at http://www.worldpress.org/Africa/1561.cfm (accessed January 31, 2006).

Lehne, Gregory K. 1995. "Homophobia among Men: Supporting and Defining the Male Role." In Michael S. Kimmel and Michael A. Messner (eds.), *Men's Lives.* Boston: Allyn and Bacon.

Leiblum, S., and N. Döring. 2002. "Internet Sexuality: Known Risks and Fresh Chances for

Women." In A. Cooper (ed.), *Sex and the Internet: A Guidebook for Clinicians*. New York: Brunner-Routledge.

Leichtentritt, Ronit, and Bilha Davidson Arad. 2005. "Young Male Streetworkers: Life Histories and Current Experiences." *British Journal of Social Work* 35:483–509.

Lengnick-Hall, M. L. 1995. "Sexual Harassment Research: A Methodological Critique." *Personnel Psychology* 48:841–64.

Leonard, Elizabeth D. 2002. *Convicted Survivors: The Imprisonment of Battered Women Who Kill*. Albany: State University of New York Press.

Lerner, Gerda. 1986. *The Creation of Patriarchy*. New York: Oxford University Press.

Lesko, Nancy. 2000. *Masculinities at School*. Thousand Oaks, CA: Sage.

Lessig, L. 1999. *Code and Other Laws of Cyberspace*. New York: Basic Books.

Leventhal, Beth, and Sandra E. Lundy (eds.). 1999. *Same-Sex Domestic Violence: Strategies for Change*. Thousand Oaks, CA: Sage.

LeVine, R. A. 1959. "Gusii Sex Offenses: A Study in Social Control." *American Anthropologist* 61:965–90.

Levi-Strauss, Claude. 1969. *The Elementary Structures of Kinship*. Boston: Beacon.

Levy, Barrie. 1991. *Dating Violence: Young Women in Danger*. Seattle: Seal Press.

Levy, Ellen. 1993. "She Just Doesn't Understand: The Feminist Face-Off on Pornography Legislation." *On the Issues* (fall): 17–20.

Lewin, Tamar. 1991. "Law on Sex Harassment Is Recent and Evolving." *New York Times*, October 8, p. A22.

Lewis, Bernard. 2001. "The Revolt of Islam." *New Yorker*, November 19, pp. 57–59.

Lewis, M. 1989. *Liar's Poker: Rising through the Wreckage on Wall Street*. New York: Norton.

Liddle, A. M. 1993. "Gender, Desire and Child Sexual Abuse: Accounting for the Male Majority." *Theory, Culture and Society* 10:103–26.

Lincoln, Abbey (Aminata Moseka). 1983. "On Being High." In Amiri Baraka and Amina Baraka (eds.), *Confirmation*. New York: Quill.

Lindsey, K. 1977. "Sexual Harassment on the Job and How to Stop It." *Ms.* (November): 47–51, 74–78.

Linz, D., E. Donnerstein, B. J. Shafer, K. C. Land, P. L. McCall, and A. C. Graesser. 1995. "Discrepancies between the Legal Code and Community Standards for Sex and Violence: An Empirical Challenge to Traditional Assumptions in Obscenity Law." *Law and Society Review* 29:127–68.

Littel, Kristin, and Scott Matson (eds.). 2000. "Myths and Facts about Sex Offenders." Center for Sex Offender Management Web site. http://www.csom.org/pubs/mythsfacts.html (accessed November 29, 2005).

Lloyd, S., and N. Taluc. 1999. "The Effects of Male Violence on Female Employment." *Violence against Women* 5:370–92.

Lobel, Kerry. 1986. *Naming the Violence: Speaking Out about Lesbian Battering*. Seattle: Seal.

Lobel, S. A. 1993. "Sexuality at Work: Where Do We Go from Here?" *Journal of Vocational Behavior* 42:136–52.

Longino, H. E. 1980. "Pornography, Oppression and Freedom: A Closer Look." In L. Lederer (ed.), *Take Back the Night: Women on Pornography*. New York: Morrow.

Lord, Vivian B., and Gary Rassel. 2000. "Law Enforcement's Response to Sexual Assault: A Comparative Study of Nine Counties in North Carolina." *Women and Criminal Justice* 11(11):67–88.

Lorenz, K. 1966. *On Aggression*. London: Methuen.

Lott, B., M. E Reilly, and D. R. Howard. 1982. "Sexual Assault and Harassment: A Campus Community Case Study." *Signs: Journal of Women in Culture and Society* 8:296–319.

Loy, P. H., and L. P. Stewart. 1984. "The Extent and Effects of Sexual Harassment of Working Women." *Sociological Focus* 17:31–43.

Lynch, Colum. 2004. "U.N. Says Its Workers Abuse Women in Congo." *Washington Post*, November 27, p. A27.

Lyons, Christopher J. 2006. "Stigma or Sympathy: Attributions of Fault to Victims and Offenders of Bias Crime." *Social Psychology Quarterly* 69:39–51.

Maas, Peter. 2001. "Emroz Khan Is Having a Bad Day." *New York Times Magazine*, October 21, pp. 48–51.

MacDonald, B., and C. Rich. 1984. *Look Me in the Eye*. London: Women's Press.

MacKinnon, Catharine A. 1979. *Sexual Harassment of Working Women: A Case of Discrimination*. New Haven, CT: Yale University Press.

———. 1982. "Feminism, Marxism, Method and the State: An Agenda for Theory." *Signs* 7:515–44.

———. 1984. "Not a Moral Issue." *Yale Law and Policy Review* 2:321–45.

MacKinnon, M. 1995. "How Topless Bars Shut Me Out." *Sales and Marketing Management* (July): 52–53.

MacLeod, L. 1987. *Battered but Not Beaten: Preventing Wife Battering in Canada*. Ottawa, Ontario: Canadian Advisory Council on the Status of Women.

MacLeod, M., and E. Saraga. 1988. "Challenging the Orthodoxy: Towards a Feminist Theory and Practice." *Feminist Review* 28:16–55.

Madriz, Ester. 1997. *Nothing Bad Happens to Good Girls: Fear of Crime in Women's Lives*. Berkeley: University of California Press.

Maiskii, I. 1921. *Sovremennaia Mongolia (Contemporary Mongolia)*. Irkutsk: Gosudarstvennoe Izdatel'stvo, Irkutskoe Otedelenie. (Translated from the Russian for Human Relations Area Files by Mrs. Dayton and J. Kunitz.)

Malamuth, Neil M. 1989. "Sexually Violent Media, Thought Patterns, and Anti-Social Behavior." *Public Communication and Behavior* 2:159—204.

Malernee, Jamie. 2004. "Harassment Programs Scrutinized: School Must Do Better Job, Experts Say." *South Florida Sun-Sentinel*, February 8, p. 1B.

Malette, L., and M. Chalouh. 1991. *The Montreal Massacre*. Trans. M. Wildeman. Charlottetown, Prince Edward Island: Gynergy Books.

Malinowski, B. 1929. *The Sexual Life of Savages in North-Western Melanesia*. London: G. Routledge and Sons.

Mansfield, P. K., P. B. Koch, J. Henderson, J. R. Vicary, M. Cohn, and E. W. Young. 1991. "The Job Climate for Women in Traditionally Male Blue Collar Occupations." *Sex Roles* 25:63–79.

Mardorossian, Carine M. 2002. "Toward a New Feminist Theory of Rape." *Signs* 27(3):743–75.

Margolin, L., M. Miller, and P. B. Moran. 1989. "When a Kiss Is Not Just a Kiss: Relating Violations of Consent in Kissing to Rape Myth Acceptance." *Sex Roles* 20:231–43.

Marrujo, Becky, and Mary Kreger. 1996. "Definition of Roles in Abusive Lesbian Relationships." In C. M. Renzetti and C. H. Miley (eds.), *Violence in Gay and Lesbian Domestic Partnerships*. New York: Harrington Park.

Marsden, Peter. 2002. *The Taliban*. London: Zed Books.

Martin, Patricia Yancey. 1990. "Rethinking Feminist Organizations." *Gender & Society* 4:182–206.

———. 1993. "Feminist Practice in Organizations: Implications for Management." In E. Fagenson (ed.), *Women in Management: Issues, Trends, and Problems*. Newbury Park, CA: Sage.

———. 1997. "Rape Processing Work: Gender and Accounts." *Social Problems* 44:464–82.

———. 2002. "Sensations, Bodies, and 'the Spirit of a Place: Aesthetics in Residential Organizations for the Elderly." *Human Relations* 55(7):861–85.

Martin, Patricia Yancey. 2005. *Rape Work: Victims, Gender, and Emotions in Organizational and Community Context*. New York: Routledge.

Martin, Patricia Yancey, Richard Chackerian, Allen Imershein, and Michael Frumkin. 1983. "The Concept of 'Integrated' Services Reconsidered." *Social Science Quarterly* 64 (December): 747–63.

Martin, Patricia Yancey, Diana DiNitto, Diane Byington, and M. Sharon Maxwell. 1992. "Organizational and Community Transformation: A Case Study of a Rape Crisis Center." *Administration in Social Work* 16:123–45.

Martin, Patricia Yancey, and Robert A. Hummer. 1989. "Fraternities and Rape on Campus." *Gender & Society* 3:457–73.

Martin, Patricia Yancey, and R. Marlene Powell. 1994. "Accounting for the 'Second Assault': Legal Organizations' Framing of Rape Victims." *Law and Social Inquiry* 19:853–90.

Martin, Patricia Yancey, John R. Reynolds, and Shelley Keith. 2002. "Gender Bias and Feminist Consciousness among Judges and Attorneys: A Standpoint Theory Analysis." *Signs* 27(3):665–701.

Martin, S. 1978. "Sexual Politics in the Workplace: The Interactional World of Policewomen." *Symbolic Interaction* 1:55–60.

———. 1980. *Breaking and Entering: Policewomen on Patrol*. Berkeley: University of California Press.

Marx, Karl. 1978. "The German Ideology: Part I." In Robert C. Tucker (ed.), *The Marx-Engels Reader*. New York: Norton.

Masson, H., and P. O'Byrne. 1990. "The Family Systems Approach: A Help or a Hindrance?" In The Violence against Children Study Group (eds.), *Taking Child Abuse Seriously*. London: Unwin Hyman.

Masson, J. M. 1985. *The Assault on Truth: Freud's Suppression of the Seduction Theory*. Harmondsworth, UK: Penguin.

Matchen, J., and E. DeSouza. 2000. "The Sexual Harassment of Faculty Members by Students.: *Sex Roles* 41:295–306.

Matei, S., and S. J. Ball-Rokeach. 2002. "Belonging in Geographic, Ethnic, and Internet Spaces." In B. Wellman and C. Haythornthwaite (eds.), *The Internet in Everyday Life*. Malden, MA: Blackwell.

Matthews, Nancy. 1994. *Confronting Rape: The Feminist Anti-Rape Movement and the State*. London: Routledge.

Maybury-Lewis, D. 1967. *Akwe-Shavante Society*. Oxford, UK: Clarendon Press.

McConnell-Ginet, Sally. 2001. "'Queering' Semantics: Definitional Struggles." In Kathryn Campbell-Kibler, Robert J. Podesva, Sara J. Roberts, and Andrew Wong (eds.), *Language and Sexuality: Contesting Meaning in Theory and Practice*. Stanford, CA: CSLI.

McCormack, A. 1985. "The Sexual Harassment of Students by Teachers: The Case of Students in Science." *Sex Roles* 13:21–32.

McCormick, N., and J. Leonard. 1996. "Gender and Sexuality in the Cyberspace Frontier." *Women and Therapy* 19(4):109–19.

McCreadie, C. 1991. *Elder Abuse: An Exploratory Study*. London: Age Concern (Institute of Gerontology, King's College).

McCurley, Carl, and Howard Snyder. 2004. "Victims of Violent Juvenile Crime." *Juvenile Justice Bulletin*, July. U.S. Department of Justice, Office of Justice Programs, Washington, DC.

McFarlane, Judith, and Ann Malecha. 2005. "Sexual Assault among Intimates: Frequency, Consequences and Treatments." Research report. Available online at http://www.ncjrs.gov/pdf-files1/nij/grants/211678.pdf.

McGarth, M. G., and E. Casey. 2002. "Forensic Psychiatry and the Internet: Practical Perspectives on Sexual Predators and Obsessional Harassers in Cyberspace." *Journal of the American Academy of Psychiatry and the Law* 30:81–94.

McGrail, Amanda. 2003. "So Now We All Pay for Sexual Right." *New Zealand Herald.* Available online at http://nzherald.co.nz/storydisplay.cfm (accessed November 26, 2003).

McGrath, E., G. P. Keita, B. R. Strickland, and N. F. Russo. 1990. *Women and Depression: Risk Factors and Treatment Issues.* Washington, DC: American Psychological Association.

McGuire, B., and A. Wraith. 2000. "Legal and Psychological Aspects of Stalking: A Review." *Journal of Forensic Psychiatry* 11:316–27.

McIlwee, J. 1980. "Organization Theory and the Entry of Women into Non-Traditional Occupations." Paper presented at the Seventy-fifth Annual Meeting of the American Sociological Association, New York.

McKenna, K. Y. A., and G. Seidman. 2005. "You, Me, and We: Interpersonal Processes in Electronic Groups." In Y. Amichai-Hamburger (ed.), *The Social Net: Understanding Human Behavior in Cyberspace.* New York: Oxford University Press.

McMaster, L. E., J. Connolly, D. Pepler, and W. M. Craig. 2002. "Peer to Peer Sexual Harassment in Early Adolescence: A Developmental Perspective." *Development and Psychopathology* 14:91–105.

McMellon, C. A., and L. G. Schiffman. 2002. "Cybersenior Empowerment: How Some Older Individuals Are Taking Control of Their Lives." *Journal of Applied Gerontology* 21:157–75.

McNall, Scott G. 1983. "Pornography: The Structure of Domination and the Mode of Reproduction." In Scott McNall (ed.), *Current Perspectives in Social Theory.* Vol. 4. Greenwich, CT: JAI Press.

McNeal, Cosandra, and Paul R. Amato. 1998. "Parents' Marital Violence: Long-Term Consequences for Children. *Journal of Family Issues* 19(2):123–39.

McPherson, B. 1990. *Aging as a Social Process.* Toronto: Butterworths.

Mead, Margaret. 1932. *The Changing Culture of an Indian Tribe.* New York: Columbia University Press.

———. 1935. *Sex and Temperament in Three Primitive Societies.* New York: Morrow.

Mecca, S. J., and L. J. Rubin. 1999. "Definitional Research on African American Students and Sexual Harassment." *Psychology of Women Quarterly* 23(4):813–17.

"Men and Porn." 2003. *Guardian,* November 8. Available online at http://www.guardian.co.uk/weekend/story/O,3605,1079016,00.html (accessed November 13, 2003).

Messerschmidt, J. 1993. *Masculinities and Crime: Critique and Reconceptualization of Theory.* Lanham, MD: Rowman and Littlefield.

———. 1997. "Varieties of 'Real Men.' " In L. L. O'Toole and J. R. Schiffman (eds.), *Gender Violence: Interdisciplinary Perspectives.* 1st ed. New York: NYU Press.

Messner, Michael A. 1990. "Boyhood, Organized Sports and the Construction of Masculinities." *Journal of Contemporary Ethnography* 18(4):416—44.

Miceli, M. P., and J. P. Near. 1988. "Individual and Situational Correlates of Whistle-Blowing." *Personnel Psychology* 41:267–81.

Mill, J. S. 1988. "The Subjection of Women." In Donald Dutton (ed.), *The Domestic Assault of Women: Psychological and Criminal Justice Perspectives.* Newton, MA: Allyn and Bacon.

Miller, Amanda, and Kathryn Chandler. 2003. *Violence in U.S. Public Schools: 2000: School Survey on Crime and Safety.* Statistical analysis report, October. NCES 2004-314. U.S. Department of Education, National Center for Education Statistics, Washington, DC.

Miller, H., and J. Arnold. 2001. "Self in Web Home Pages: Gender, Identity and Power in Cyberspace." In G. Riva and C. Galimberti (eds.), *Towards Cyberpsychology: Mind, Cognition and Society in the Internet Age.* Amsterdam: IOS Press.

Miller, R. B., and R. A. Dodder. 1989. "The Abused-Abuser Dyad: Elder Abuse in the State of

Florida." In S. R. Ingman and R. Filinson (eds.), *Elder Abuse: Practice and Policy*. New York: Human Sciences Press.

Miller, Susan L. 1993. "Arrest Policies for Domestic Violence and Their Implications for Battered Women." In Roslyn Muraskin and Ted Alleman (eds.), *It's a Crime: Women and Justice*. Englewood Cliffs, NJ: Prentice Hall.

———. 2005. *Victims as Offenders: The Paradox of Women's Violence in Relationships*. New Brunswick, NJ: Rutgers University Press.

Miller, Susan L., Kay B. Forest, and Nancy C. Jurik. 2003. "Diversity in Blue: Lesbian and Gay Police Officers in a Masculine Occupation." *Men and Masculinities* 5(4):355–85.

Minneapolis City Council, Government Operations Committee. 1988. *Pornography and Sexual Violence: Evidence of the Links: The Complete Transcript of Public Hearings on Ordinances to Add Pornography as Discrimination against Women: Minneapolis City Council, Government Operations Committee, December 12 and 13, 1983*. London: Everywoman.

Mitchell, K. J., D. Finkelhor, and J. Wolak. 2001. "Risk Factors for and Impact of Online Sexual Solicitation of Youth." *Journal of the American Medical Association* 285:3011–14.

———. 2003. "The Exposure to Youth to Unwanted Sexual Material on the Internet: A National Survey of Risk, Impact, and Prevention." *Youth & Society* 34:330–58.

Mitra, C. 1987. "Judicial Disclosure in Father-Daughter Incest Appeal Cases." *International Journal of the Sociology of Law* 15(2):121–48.

Moe, A. M., and M. P. Bell. 2004. "Abject Economics: The Effects of Battering and Violence on Women's Work and Employability." *Violence against Women* 10(1):29–55.

Moffit, R. A. 2002. "From Welfare to Work: What the Evidence Shows: Welfare Reform and Beyond." Policy Brief No. 13. Washington, DC: Brookings Institution.

Mooney, L., David Knox, and Caroline Schacht. 2007. *Understanding Social Problems*. Belmont, CA: Wadsworth.

Moore, Barrington, Jr. 1966. *The Social Origins of Dictatorship and Democracy*. Boston: Beacon.

Moore, T., and V. Selkowe. 1999. *Domestic Violence Victims in Transition from Welfare to Work: Barriers to Self-Sufficiency and the W-2 Response*. Madison: Institute for Wisconsin's Future.

Morahan-Martin, J. 1998. "Males, Females, and the Internet." In J. Gackenbach (ed.), *Psychology and the Internet: Intrapersonal, Interpersonal, and Transpersonal Implications*. San Diego, CA: Academic Press.

———. 2000. "Women and the Internet: Promise and Perils." *CyberPsychology and Behavior* 3:683–91.

Morrison, Toni. 1970. *The Bluest Eye*. New York: Washington Square.

Morse, Barbara J. 1995. "Beyond the Conflict Tactics Scale: Assessing Gender Differences in Partner Violence.: *Violence and Victims* 10(4):251–72.

Mort, F. 1987. *Dangerous Sexualities: Medico-Moral Politics in England Since 1830*. London: Routledge and Kegan Paul.

Muehlenhard, C. L., and M. A. Linton. 1987. "Date Rape and Aggression in Dating Situations: Incidence and Risk Factors." *Journal of Counseling Psychology* 34:186–96.

Munson, L. J., C. Hulin, and F. Drasgow. 2000. "Longitudinal Analysis of Dispositional Influences and Sexual Harassment: Effects on Job and Psychological Outcomes. *Personnel Psychology* 53:21–46.

Murdock, G. P., and D. R. White. 1969. "Standard Cross-Cultural Sample." *Ethnology* 8:329–69.

Murphy, J. 1931. "Dependency in Old Age." *Annals of the American Academy of Political and Social Science* 154:38–41.

Murphy, Y., and R. Murphy. 1974. *Women of the Forest*. New York: Columbia University Press.

Murray, Stephen O. 1979. "The Art of Gay Insulting." *Anthropological Linguistics* 21(5):211–23.

Murrell, A. 1996. "Sexual Harassment and Women of Color: Issues, Challenges, and Future

Directions." In M. Stockdale (ed.), *Sexual Harassment in the Workplace: Perspectives, Frontiers, and Response Strategies.* Thousand Oaks, CA: Sage.

Mydans, S. 1993. "High School Gang Accused of Raping for Points." *New York Times,* March 20, p. 6.

Napolitano, Jo. 2003. "Girls' Game Turns Violent." *New York Times,* May 8, p. A30.

National Research Council and Institute of Medicine. 2003. *Deadly Lessons: Understanding Lethal School Violence.* Washington. DC: National Academy Press.

National Victim Center. 1992. *Rape in America: A Report to the Nation.* Prepared by the National Victim Center and the Crime Victims Research and Treatment Center, New York.

NCAVP. 2006. National Coalition of Anti-Violence Programs Web site. http://www.ncavp.org.

NCJRS (National Criminal Justice Reference Service). 2003. "Indicators of School Crime and Safety, 2003." Available online at http://www.ncjrs.gov.

Near, J. P., and M. P. Miceli. 1987. "Whistle-Blowers in Organizations: Dissidents or Reformers?" In L. L. Cummings and B. M. Staw (eds.), *Research in Organizational Behavior.* Vol. 9. Greenwich, CT: JAI Press.

Nelson, K. 1986. "Labor Demand, Labor Supply, and the Suburbanization of Low-Wage Office Work." In A. Scott and M. Stopper (eds.), *Production, Work, Territory.* Boston: Allen and Unwin.

Nelson, S. 1987. *Incest: Fact and Myth.* Edinburgh, UK: Stramullion.

Newberger, E. H., and R. Bourne. 1977. "The Medicalisation and Legislation of Child Abuse." In J. M. Eekelaar and S. N. Katz (eds.), *Family Violence: An International and Interdisciplinary Study.* London: Butterworths.

"News: Iraq: U.S. Soldiers Accused of Sex Assaults." 2005. *Off Our Backs* (May–June): 7–8.

Nickson, Elizabeth. 2003. "Is Porn Beginning to Beat a Retreat?" *National Post,* November 14. Available online at http://www.nationalpost.com/commentary/story.html (accessed November 16, 2003).

Nolen, Stephanie. 2005. "Not Women Anymore . . ." *Ms.* (spring): 56–58.

Novello, Antonia C., Mark Rosenberg, Linda Saltzman, and John Shosky. 1992. "From the Surgeon General, U.S. Public Health Service." *JAMA* 267:3132.

NOW Legal Defense and Education Fund. 2003. "Welfare and Poverty: Domestic and Sexual Violence." Available online at www.nowldef.org/html/issues/wel/violence.shtml. (accessed January 2005).

O'Donohue, W., K. Downs, and E. A. Yeater. 1998. "Sexual Harassment: A Review of the Literature." *Aggression and Violent Behavior* 3:111–28.

O'Farrell, B., and S. L. Harlan. 1982. "Craftworkers and Clerks: The Effects of Male Co-Worker Hostility on Women's Satisfaction with Non-Traditional Jobs." *Social Problems* 29:252–64.

Ogg, J., and G. Bennett. 1992. "Screening for Elder Abuse in the Community." *Geriatric Medicine* (February): 63–67.

Oh, Bonnie B. C. 2001. "The Japanese Imperial System and the Korean 'Comfort Women' of World War II." In Margaret Stetz and Bonnie B. C. Oh (eds.), *Legacies of the Comfort Women of World War II.* Armonk, NY: M. E. Sharpe.

O'Hagan, K. 1989. *Working with Child Sexual Abuse.* Milton Keynes, UK: Open University Press.

O'Hare, E. A., and W. O'Donohue. 1998. "Sexual Harassment: Identifying Risk Factors." *Archives of Sexual Behavior* 27:561–80.

O'Hare-Grundmann, E., W. O'Donohue, and S. H. Peterson. 1997. "The Prevention of Sexual Harassment." In W. O'Donohue (ed.), *Sexual Harassment: Theory, Research, and Treatment.* Needham Heights, MA: Allyn and Bacon.

Oravec, J. A. 2000. "Countering Violent and Hate-Related Materials on the Internet: Strategies for Classrooms and Communities." *Teacher Educator* 35(3):34–45.

O'Sullivan, Elizabethann, and Abigail Carlton. 2001. "Victim Services, Community Outreach, and Contemporary Rape Crisis Centers." *Journal of Interpersonal Violence* 16(4):343–60.

Outlaw, Lucius. 1974. "Language and Consciousness: Toward a Hermeneutic of Black Culture." *Cultural Hermeneutics* 1(4):403–13.

———. 2005. *In Search of Critical Social Theory in the Interests of Black Folk.* Lanham, MD: Rowman and Littlefield.

Outshoorn, Joyce (ed). 2004. *The Politics of Prostitution: Women's Movements, Democratic States and the Globalisation of Sex Commerce.* Cambridge: Cambridge University Press.

———. 2005. "The Political Debates on Prostitution and Trafficking of Women." *Social Politics* 12(1):141–51.

Padavic, Irene, and Barbara F. Reskin. 1990. "Men's Behavior and Women's Interest in Blue Collar Jobs." *Social Problems* 37:613–28.

Paludi, M., and R. B. Barickman. 1991. *Academic and Workplace Sexual Harassment.* Albany: State University of New York Press.

———. 1998. *Sexual Harassment, Work, and Education: A Resource Manual for Prevention.* 2nd ed. Albany: State University of New York Press.

Paludi, M., and C. Paludi. 2003. *Academic and Workplace Sexual Harassment: A Handbook of Social Science, Legal, Cultural, and Management Perspectives.* Westport, CT: Praeger.

Parker, Barbara, J. McFarlane, and K. Soeken. 1996. "Abuse during Pregnancy: Association with Maternal Health and Infant Birthweight." *Nursing Research* 45:32–37.

Parrot, Andrea, and Laurie Bechofer. 1991. *Acquaintance Rape: The Hidden Crime.* New York: Wiley.

Parton, N. 1985. *The Politics of Child Abuse.* London: Macmillan.

Pathe, M., and P. E. Mullen. 1997. "The Impact of Stalkers on Their Victims." *British Journal of Psychiatry* 170:12–17.

Paulson, Amanda. 2003. "Female Aggression: Brutal Hazing Ritual Renews Nation's Interest in Female Anger." *Christian Science Monitor*, May 13, p. 4.

Peel, Elizabeth. 2001. "Mundane Heterosexism: Understanding Incidents of the Everyday." *Women's Studies International Forum* 24(5):541–54.

Pelka, Fred. 1997. "Raped: A Male Survivor Breaks His Silence." In L. L. O'Toole and J. R. Schiffman (eds.), *Gender Violence: Interdisciplinary Perspectives.* 1st ed. New York: NYU Press.

Pence, Ellen L. 1999. "Some Thoughts on Philosophy." In Melanie R. Shepard and Ellen L. Pence (eds.), *Coordinating Community Responses to Domestic Violence: Lessons from Duluth and Beyond.* Thousand Oaks, CA: Sage.

Pence, Ellen L., and Michael Paymar. 1993. *Education Groups for Men Who Batter: The Duluth Model.* New York: Springer.

Pence, Ellen L., and Melanie F. Shepard. 1999. "An Introduction: Developing a Coordinated Community Response." In Melanie R. Shepard and Ellen L. Pence (eds.), *Coordinating Community Responses to Domestic Violence: Lessons from Duluth and Beyond.* Thousand Oaks, CA: Sage.

Penhale, B. 1993. "The Abuse of Elderly People: Considerations for Practice." *British Journal of Social Work* 23(2):95–112.

Perilla, J., K. Frndak, D. Lillard, and C. East. 2003. "A Working Analysis of Women's Use of Violence in the Context of Learning, Opportunity, and Choice." *Violence against Women* 9(1):10–46.

Perlstein, Daniel. 1998. "Saying the Unsaid: Girl Killing and the Curriculum." *Journal of Curriculum and Supervision* 14(1):88–104.

Pesznecker, Katie. 2005. "Parents Go After District for Rape." *Anchorage Daily News*, March 5, p. B1.

Peters, L. 1990. "A Student's Experience." *Initiatives* 52:17–21.

Petersen, R., J. Gazmararian, and K. A. Clark. 2001. "Partner Violence: Implications for Health and Community Settings." *Women's Health Issues* 11(2):116–25.

Peterson, David. 1992. "Wife Beating: An American Tradition." *Journal of Interdisciplinary History* 23(1):97–118.

Petrocelli, W., and B. K. Repa. 1998. *Sexual Harassment on the Job: What Is It and How to Stop It.* 4th ed. Berkeley, CA: Nolo.

Petry, Ann. 1946. *The Street.* Boston: Beacon.

Pew Internet Project. 2003. "America's Online Pursuits: The Changing Picture of Who's Online and What They Do." Report. Available online at www.pewinternet.org/reports/toc.asp?Report=106 (accessed September 15, 2004).

Phillips, L. R. 1986. "Theoretical Explanations of Elder Abuse." In K. A. Pillemer and R. S. Wolf (eds.), *Elder Abuse: Conflict in the Family.* Dover, MA: Auburn House.

Phillipson, C. 1993. "Abuse of Older People: Sociological Perspectives." In P. Decalmer and F. Glendenning (eds.), *The Mistreatment of Elderly People.* London: Sage.

Pillemer, K. A. 1986. "Risk Factors in Elder Abuse: Results from a Case-Control Study." In K. A. Pillemer and R. S. Wolf (eds.), *Elder Abuse: Conflict in the Family.* Dover, MA: Auburn House.

Pillemer, K. A., and D. Finkelhor. 1989. "Causes of Elder Abuse: Caregiver Stress versus Problem Relatives." *American Journal of Orthopsychiatry* 59(2):179–87.

Pillemer, K. A., and J. Suitor. 1988. "Elder Abuse." In V. Van Hasselt, R. Morrison, A. Belack, and M. Hensen (eds.), *Handbook of Family Violence.* New York: Plenum.

Pillemer, K. A., and R. S. Wolf (eds.). 1986. *Elder Abuse: Conflict in the Family.* Dover, MA: Auburn House.

Pithouse, A. 1987. *Social Work: The Social Organization of an Invisible Trade.* Aldershot, UK: Avebury.

Plaut, S. M. 1997. "Online Ethics: Social Contracts in the Virtual Community." *Journal of Sex Education and Therapy* 22:79–83.

Pleck, Elizabeth. 1987. *Domestic Tyranny.* New York: Oxford University Press.

———. 1989. "Criminal Approaches to Family Violence 1640–1980." In Lloyd Ohlin and Michael Tonry (eds.), *Family Violence.* Chicago: University of Chicago Press.

———. 1990. "Rape and the Politics of Race, 1865–1910." Working paper no. 213. Wellesley, MA: Wellesley College Center for Research on Women.

Pleck, Elizabeth H., and Joseph H. Pleck. 1980. *The American Male.* Englewood Cliffs, NJ: Prentice Hall.

Pleck, Joseph H. 1980. "Men's Power with Women, Other Men and Society: A Men's Movement Analysis." In Elizabeth H. Pleck and Joseph H. Pleck (eds.), *The American Male.* Englewood Cliffs, NJ: Prentice Hall.

———. 1981. *The Myth of Masculinity.* Cambridge, MA: MIT Press.

Plymire, Darcy C., and Pamela J. Forman. 2000. "Breaking the Silence: Lesbian Fans, the Internet, and the Sexual Politics of Women's Sport." *International Journal of Sexuality and Gender Studies* 5(2):141–53.

Pogash, Carol. 2004. "California School District Settles Harassment Suit by Gay Students. *New York Times*, January 7, p. A17.

Pong, Ping. 2003. " 'We Don't Want Rescue, We Want Our Rights!': Experiences on Anti-Trafficking Efforts in Thailand." *Research for Sex Work* 6:8–9.

Porter, Roy. 1986. "Rape—Does It Have a Historical Meaning?" In Sylvana Tomaselli and Roy Porter (eds.), *Rape.* New York: Blackwell.

Postmes, T., and R. Spears. 2002. "Behavior Online: Does Anonymous Computer Communication Reduce Gender Inequality?" *Personality and Social Psychology Bulletin* 28:1073–83.

Postmes, T., R. Spears, and M. Lea. 2002. "Intergroup Differentiation in Computer-Mediated Communication: Effects of Depersonalization." *Group Dynamics* 6:3–16.

Postmes, T., R. Spears, K. Sakhel, and D. DeGroot. 2001. "Social Influence in Computer-Mediated Communication: The Effects of Anonymity on Group Behavior." *Personality and Social Psychology Bulletin* 27:1243–54.

Presser, L., and E. Gaarder, E. 2004. "Can Restorative Justice Reduce Battering? In B. R. Price and N. J. Sokoloff (eds.), *The Criminal Justice System and Women*. 3rd ed. Boston: McGraw-Hill.

Preston, Julia. 2005. "For '73 Rape Victim, DNA Revives Horror, Too." *New York Times*, November 3, p. 1A.

Pringle, Rosemary. 1988. *Secretaries Talk: Sexuality, Power, and Work*. Sydney: Allen and Unwin.

———. 1989. "Bureaucracy, Rationality and Sexuality: The Case of Secretaries." In J. Hearn, D. L. Sheppard, P. Tancred-Sheriff, and G. Burell (eds.), *The Sexuality of Organization*. Newbury Park, CA: Sage.

Pritchard, J. 1992. *The Abuse of Elderly People: A Handbook for Professionals*. London: Jessica Kingsley.

Pryor, J. B., J. L. Giedd, and K. B. Williams. 1995. "A Social Psychological Model for Predicting Sexual Harassment." *Journal of Social Issues* 51:96–84.

Pryor, J. B., C. M. LaVite, and L. M. Stoller. 1993. "A Social Psychological Analysis of Sexual Harassment: The Person/Situation Interaction." *Journal of Vocational Behavior* 42:68–83.

Pryor, J. B., and L. M. Stoller. 1994. "Sexual Cognition Processes in Men High in the Likelihood to Sexually Harass." *Personality and Social Psychology Bulletin* 20:163–69.

Pryor, J. B., and N. J. Whalen. 1997. "A Typology of Sexual Harassment: Characteristics of Harassers and the Social Circumstances Under Which Sexual Harassment Occurs." In W. O'Donohue (ed.), *Sexual Harassment: Theory, Research, and Treatment*. Boston: Allyn and Bacon.

Ptacek, J. 1999. *Battered Women in the Courtroom: The Power of Judicial Responses*. Boston: Northeastern University Press.

Quayle, E., G. Holland, C. Linehan, and M. Taylor. 2000. "The Internet and Offending Behavior: A Case Study." *Journal of Sexual Aggression* 6:78–96.

Quayle, E., and M. Taylor. 2002. "Child Pornography and the Internet: Perpetuating a Cycle of Abuse." *Deviant Behavior* 23:331–62.

———. 2003. "Model of Problematic Internet Use in People with a Sexual Interest in Children." *CyberPsychology and Behavior* 6:93–106.

Quina, K. 1990. "The Victimizations of Women. In Michele A. Paludi (ed.), *Ivory Power: Sexual Harassment on Campus*. Albany: State University of New York Press.

Quina, K., and N. L. Carlson. 1989. *Rape, Incest, and Sexual Harassment: A Guide for Helping Survivors*. New York: Praeger.

Quinn, Andrew. 2002. "Nevada School District to Pay Student in Gay-Bashing Case." *Boston Globe*, August 29, p. A4.

Quinn, M. J., and S. K. Tomita. 1986. *Elder Abuse and Neglect: Causes, Diagnosis and Intervention Strategies*. New York: Springer.

Rabinowitz, V. C. 1990. "Coping with Sexual Harassment." In Michele A. Paludi (ed.), *Ivory Power: Sexual Harassment on Campus*. Albany: State University of New York Press.

Radford, Jill. 1987. "Policing Male Violence—Policing Women." In Jalna Hanmer and Mary Maynard (eds.), *Women, Violence and Social Control*. Atlantic Highlands, NJ: Humanities Press.

Rafaeli, S., and F. Sudweeks. 1997. "Networked Interactivity." *Journal of Computer-Mediated Communication* 2. Available online at www.ascusc.org/jcmc/vo12/issue4/rafaeli.sudweeks.html (accessed September 15, 2004).

Ragins, B. R., and T. A. Scandura. 1992. "Antecedents and Consequences of Sexual Harassment." Paper presented at the Society for Industrial/Organizational Psychology Conference, May, Montreal.

RAINN (Rape Abuse and Incest National Network). 2005. "FBI Crime Report." Press release. Available online at http://www.rainn.org/media-center/press-releases/fbi-crime-report (accessed November 29, 2005).

Raphael, J. 1996. "Domestic Violence and Welfare Receipt: Toward a New Feminist Theory of Welfare Dependency." *Harvard Women's Law Journal* 19:201–27.

———. 2000. *Saving Bernice: Battered Women, Welfare, and Poverty.* Boston: Northeastern University Press.

Raphael, J., and S. Haennicke. 1999. "Keeping Battered Women Safe through the Welfare-to-Work Journey: How Are We Doing?" Chicago: Taylor Institute.

Rattray, R. S. 1923. *Ashanti.* Oxford, UK: Clarendon.

———. 1927. *Religion and Art in Ashanti.* Oxford, UK: Clarendon.

Redfearn, A. A., and M. R. Laner. 2000. "The Effects of Sexual Assault on Sexual Attitudes." *Marriage and Family Review* 30:109–25.

Reicher, S. D. 1987. "Crowd Behaviour as Social Action." In J. C. Turner, M. A. Hogg, P. J. Oakes, S. D. Reicher, and M. S. Wetherell (eds.), *Rediscovering the Social Group: A Self-Categorization Theory.* Oxford, UK: Blackwell.

Remafedi G. (ed.). 1994. *Death by Denial: Studies of Suicide in Gay and Lesbian Teenagers.* Boston: Alyson.

Rennison, Callie Marie. 2003. "Intimate Partner Violence, 1993–2001." Washington, DC: U.S. Department of Justice, Bureau of Justice Statistics.

Renzetti, Claire M. 1992. *Violent Betrayal: Partner Abuse in Lesbian Relationships.* Newbury Park, CA: Sage.

———. 1999. "The Challenges to Feminism Posed by Women's Use of Violence in Intimate Relationships." In S. Lamb (ed.), *New Versions of Victims.* New York: NYU Press.

———. 2002. "Special Issue: Women's Use of Violence in Intimate Relationships, Part 2—Editor's Note." *Violence against Women* 8(12):1419.

Renzetti, Claire M., Jeffrey L. Edleson, and Raquel Kennedy Bergen (eds.). 2001. *Sourcebook on Violence against Women.* Thousand Oaks, CA: Sage.

Renzetti, Claire M., and C. H. Miley. 1996. *Violence in Gay and Lesbian Domestic Partnerships.* New York: Harrington Park.

Report of the Departmental Committee on Sexual Offenses against Young Persons. 1925. London: HMSO.

Reskin, B., and I. Padavic. 1994. *Women and Men at Work.* Thousand Oaks, CA: Pine Forge.

Rhode, Deborah L. 1989. *Justice and Gender: Sex Discrimination and the Law.* Cambridge, MA: Harvard University Press.

Rich, Adrienne. 1977. *Of Woman Born.* London: Virago.

———. 1993. "Compulsory Heterosexuality and Lesbian Existence." In Henry Abelove (ed.), *The Lesbian and Gay Studies Reader.* New York: Routledge.

Richie, Beth E. 2005. "A Black Feminist Reflection on the Antiviolence Movement." In N. J. Sokoloff (ed.), *Domestic Violence at the Margins.* New Brunswick, NJ: Rutgers University Press.

Richman, J. A., K. M. Rospenda, S. J. Nawyn, J. A. Flasherty, M. Fendrich, M. Drum, et al. 1999. "Sexual Harassment and Generalized Workplace Abuse among University Employees: Prevalence and Mental Health Correlates." *American Journal of Public Health* 89:358–63.

Ridgeway, Jim. 2001. "Osama's New Recruits." *Village Voice,* November 6, pp. 41–43.

Riemer, J., and Bridwell, L. 1982. "How Women Survive in Nontraditional Occupations." *Free Inquiry in Creative Sociology* 10(2):153–58.

Rigby, Ken, and Bruce Johnson. 2004. "Students as Bystanders to Sexual Coercion." *Youth Studies Australia* 23(2):11.

Riger, S. 1991. "Gender Dilemmas in Sexual Harassment Policies and Procedures." *American Psychologist* 46:497–505.

Riley, N. E. 1996. "China's 'Missing Girls': Prospects and Policy." *Population Today* 24(2):4.

Risman, Barbara. 2004. "Gender as a Social Structure: Theory Wrestling with Activism." *Gender & Society* 18(4):429–50.

Ristock, Janice L. 2002. *No More Secrets: Violence in Lesbian Relationships*. New York: Routledge.

Robb, L. A., and D. Doverspike. 2001. "Self-Reported Proclivity to Harass as a Moderator of the Effectiveness of Sexual Harassment-Prevention Training. *Psychological Reports* 88:85–88.

Roberts, Albert. 1984. "Police Intervention." In Albert Roberts (ed.), *Battered Women and Their Families: Intervention Strategies and Treatment Programs*. New York: Springer.

Roberts, Selena. 2003. "Code of Silence Corrupts the Young." *New York Times*, September 28, p. 8SP.

Robinson, Kerry H. 2005. "Reinforcing Hegemonic Masculinities through Sexual Harassment: Issues of Identity, Power, and Popularity in Secondary Schools." *Gender and Education* 17(1):19–37.

Rogers, L. C. 1984. "Sexual Victimization: Social and Psychological Effects on College Women." Ph.D. diss., Auburn University, Alabama.

Roiphe, Katie. 1994. *The Morning After: Sex, Fear, and Feminism on Campus*. Boston: Little, Brown.

Rollins, J. 1985. *Between Women: Domestics and Their Employers*. Philadelphia: Temple University Press.

Romero, D., W. Chavkin, Paul H. Wise, and L. A. Smith. 2003. "Low-Income Mothers' Experience with Poor Health, Hardship, Work, and Violence: Implications for Policy." *Violence against Women* 9(10):1231–44.

Rosenthal, Elizabeth. 2006. "Women Face Greatest Threat of Violence at Home, Study Finds." *New York Times*, October 6, p. A5.

Rospenda, K., J. Richman, and S. Nawyn. 1998. "Doing Power: The Confluence of Gender, Race and Class in Contrapower Sexual Harassment." *Gender & Society* 12(1):40–60.

Ross, Stephanie. 1981. "How Words Hurt: Attitude, Metaphor, and Oppression." In Mary Vetterling-Braggin (ed.), *Sexist Language: A Modern Philosophical Analysis*. Lanham, MD: Littlefield, Adams.

Rothstein, Edward. 2001. "Exploring the Flaws in the Notion of the 'Root Causes' of Terror." *New York Times*, November 17, p. B9.

Rotundo, M., D. H. Nguyen, and P. R. Sackett. 2001. "A Meta-Analytic Review of Gender Differences in Sexual Harassment." *Journal of Applied Psychology* 86:914–22.

Rowe, M. 1981. "Dealing with Sexual Harassment." *Harvard Business Review* 59 (May/June): 42–46.

Roy, D. F. 1960. " 'Banana Time': Job Satisfaction and Informal Interaction." *Human Organization* 18(4):158–68.

Rubin, Gayle. 1976. "The Traffic in Women: Notes on the Political Economy of Sex." In Rayna Rapp Reiter (ed.), *Toward an Anthropology of Women*. New York: Monthly Review Press.

Rubinstein, W. B. 1993. *Lesbians, Gay Men, and the Law*. New York: New Press.

Ruff-O'Herne, Jan. 1994. *50 Years of Silence*. Sydney: Editions Tom Thompson.

Rush, Florence. 1980. *The Best Kept Secret: Sexual Abuse of Children*. New York: McGraw-Hill.

Russell, Brenda L., and Kristin Y. Trigg. 2004. "Tolerance of Sexual Harassment: An Examination of Gender Differences, Ambivalent Sexism, Social Dominance and Gender Roles." *Sex Roles* 50(7–8):565–73.

Russell, D. E. H. 1982. *Rape in Marriage*. New York: Macmillan.

———. 1984. *Sexual Exploitation: Rape, Child Sexual Abuse, and Workplace Harassment*. Beverly Hills, CA: Sage.

———. 1986. *The Secret Trauma: Incest in the Lives of Girls and Women*. New York: Basic Books.

———. 1990. *Rape in Marriage*. 2nd ed. Bloomington: Indiana University Press.

Russo, Ann. 2001a. "Lesbians, Prostitutes, and Murder: Deconstructing Media Distortions." In Ann Russo (ed.), *Taking Back Our Lives: A Call to Action for the Feminist Movement*. New York: Routledge.

———. 2001b. *Taking Back Our Lives: A Call to Action for the Feminist Movement*. New York: Routledge.

Sadker, Myra, and David Sadker. 1994. *Failing at Fairness: How America's Schools Cheat Girls*. New York: Scribner's.

Safran, C. 1976. "What Men Do to Women on the Job: A Shocking Look at Sexual Harassment." *Redbook* 149 (November): 217–24.

Saguy, Abigail C. 2003. *What Is Sexual Harassment? From Capitol Hill to the Sorbonne*. Berkeley: University of California Press.

Salisbury, J., A. B. Ginorio, H. Remick, and D. M. Stringer. 1986. "Counseling Victims of Sexual Harassment." *Psychotherapy* 23:316–24.

Sanchez, Sonia. 1981. "Memorial." In Erlene Stetson (ed.), *Black Sister*. Bloomington: Indiana University Press.

Sanday, Peggy Reeves. 1981a. *Female Power and Male Dominance: On the Origins of Sexual Inequality*. New York: Cambridge University Press.

———. 1981b. "The Socio-Cultural Context of Rape: A Cross-Cultural Study." *Journal of Social Issues* 37:5–27.

———. 1990. *Fraternity Gang Rape: Sex, Brotherhood, and Privilege on Campus*. New York: NYU Press.

Sanders, Teela. 2004. "The Risks of Street Prostitution: Punters, Police, and Protesters." *Urban Studies* 41(9):1703–17.

Sassenberg, K., and S. Kreutz. 2002. "Online Research and Anonymity." In B. Batinic, U. D. Reips, and M. Bosnjak (eds.), *Online Social Sciences*. Seattle: Hogrefe and Huber.

Saum, Christine A., Nicole L. Mott, and Erik F. Dietz. 2001. "Rohypnol, GHB, and Ketamine: New Trends in Date-Rape Drugs." In J. A. Inciardi and K. McElraths (eds.), *The American Drug Scene*. 3rd ed. Los Angeles: Roxbury.

Saunders, B. E. 1992. "Sexual Harassment of Women in the Workplace: Results from the National Women's Study." Presentation of the Eighth Annual NC SC Labor Law Seminar, October 23, Asheville, NC.

Saunders, Penelope. 2004. "Prohibiting Sex Work Projects, Restricting Women's Rights: The International Impact of the 2003 U.S. Global AIDS Act." *Health and Human Rights* 7:179–90.

Savin-Williams, R. C. 2002. "Verbal and Physical Abuse as Stressors in the Lives of Lesbian, Gay Male, and Bisexual Youth. *American Journal of Public Health* 92(5):773–77.

Sbraga, T. P., and W. O'Donohue. 2000. "Sexual Harassment." *Annual Review of Sex Research* 11:258–85.

Scarborough, C. 1989. "Conceptualizing Black Women's Employment Experiences." *Yale Law Journal* 98(7):1457–78.

Scarville, J., S. B. Button, J. E. Edwards, A. R. Lancaster, and T. W. Elig. 1999. *Armed Forces Equal Opportunity Survey*. Report no. 97-027. Arlington, VA: Defense Manpower Data Center. DTIC/NTIS No. AD A366 037.

Schafran, Lynn H. 1987. "Documenting Gender Bias in the Courts: The Task Force Approach." *Judicature* 70:280, 283–84.

Schechter, Susan. 1982. *Women and Male Violence: The Visions and Struggles of the Battered Women's Movement.* Boston: South End Press.

Schemo, Diana Jean. 2003. "Rate of Rape at Academy Is Put at 12% in Survey." *New York Times,* August 29, p. A11.

Schmitt, Fredrika, and Patricia Yancey Martin. 1999. "Unobtrusive Mobilization by an Institutionalized Rape Crisis Center: 'All We Do Comes from Victims.'" *Gender & Society* 13 (June): 364–84.

———. 2007. "The History of the Anti-Rape and Rape Crisis Center Movements." In Claire Renzetti (ed.), *Encyclopedia of Violence against Women.* Thousand Oaks, CA: Sage.

Schneider, B. E. 1982. "Consciousness about Sexual Harassment among Heterosexual and Lesbian Women Workers." *Journal of Social Issues* 38(4):75–98.

———. 1993. "Peril and Promise: Lesbians' Workplace Participation." In L. Richardson and V. Taylor (eds.), *Feminist Frontiers III.* New York: McGraw-Hill.

Schneider, K. T., S. Swan, and L. F. Fitzgerald. 1997. "Job-Related and Psychological Effects of Sexual Harassment in the Workplace: Empirical Evidence from Two Organizations." *Journal of Applied Psychology* 82(3):401–15.

Schram, T. 2002. "Ruling on Housing Law a Blow to Battered Women." Women's E-news Web site, March 31. http://www.womensenews.org/article.cfm/dyn/aid/863/context/cover.

Schur, E. L. 1988. *The Americanization of Sex.* Philadelphia: Temple University Press.

Schuster, Karla, Jason Molinet, and Keiko Morris. 2003. "Trouble for Team: Mepham Football Players Accused of Sex Abuse at PA Camp." *Newsday,* September 11, p. A3.

Schweber, Claudine, and Clarice Feinman (eds.). 1985. *Criminal Justice Politics and Women: The Aftermath of Legally Mandated Change.* New York: Haworth.

Schwendinger, J. R., and H. Schwendinger. 1983. *Rape and Inequality.* Beverly Hills, CA: Sage.

Scott, A., L. Semmens, and L. Willoughby. 2001. "Women and the Internet: The Natural History of a Research Project." In E. Green and A. Adam (ed.), *Virtual Gender: Technology, Consumption and Identity.* London: Routledge.

Scott, E. K. 2005. "Beyond Tokenism: The Making of Racially Diverse Organizations." *Social Problems* 52(2):232–54.

Scott, E. K., A. S. London, and N. A. Myers. 2002. "Dangerous Dependencies: The Intersection of Welfare Reform and Domestic Violence." *Gender & Society* 16:878–97.

Scott, J., V. Minchiello, R. Marino, G. P. Harvey, M. Jamieson, and J. Brown. 2005. "Understanding the New Context of the Male Sex Work Economy." *Journal of Interpersonal Violence* 20(3):320–42.

Scully, Diana. 1990. *Understanding Sexual Violence: A Study of Convicted Rapists.* Boston: Unwin Hyman.

Scully, Diana, and Joseph Marolla. 1985. "Riding the Bull at Gilley's: Convicted Rapists Describe the Rewards of Rape." *Social Problems* 32:251–53.

Segal, Lynne. 1990. "Pornography and Violence: What the 'Experts' Really Say." *Feminist Review* 36:29–41.

Segura, D. A. 1992. "Chicanas in White-Collar Jobs: 'You Have to Prove Yourself More.'" *Sociological Perspectives* 35(1):163–82.

Seidel, Gill, and Laurent Vidal. 1997. "The Implications of 'Medical,' 'Gender in Development' and 'Culturalist' Discourses for HIV/AIDS Policy in Africa." In Chris Shore and Susan Wright (eds.), *Anthropology of Policy: Critical Perspectives on Governance and Power.* London: Routledge.

Seidman, Steven. 1992. *Embattled Eros: Sexual Politics and Ethics in Contemporary America.* New York: Routledge.

———. 2003. *The Social Construction of Sexuality.* New York: Norton.

Sengstock, M. C., and J. Liang. 1982. "Identifying and Characterising Elder Abuse." Unpublished manuscript, Wayne State University.

Shaheed, Farida. 1994. "The Experience in Pakistan." In Miranda Davies (ed.), *Women and Violence*. London: Zed Books.

Shalhoub-Kevorkian, Nadera. 2000. "The Efficacy of Israeli Law in Preventing Violence within Palestinian Families Living in Egypt." In E. Erez and K. Laster (eds.), *Domestic Violence: Global Responses*. Bicester, UK: A B Academic.

Shange, Ntozake. 1979. "Is Not So Good to Be Born a Girl." *Black Scholar* 10:28–30.

Sheffield, Carole. 1984. "Sexual Terrorism." In J. Freeman (ed.), *Woman: A Feminist Perspective*. 4th ed. Mountainview, CA: Mayfield.

———. 1987. "Sexual Terrorism: The Social Control of Women." In B. B. Hess and M. Marx Feree (eds.), *Analyzing Gender: A Handbook of Social Science Research*. Beverly Hills, CA: Sage.

———. 1989. "The Invisible Intruder: Women's Experiences of Obscene Phone Calls." *Gender & Society* 3(4):483–88.

Shepard, Melanie F., and Ellen L. Pence. 1999. "An Introduction: Developing a Coordinated Community Response." In M. F. Shepard and E. L. Pence (eds.), *Coordinating Community Responses to Domestic Violence: Lessons from Duluth and Beyond*. Thousand Oaks, CA: Sage.

Sheppard, D. 1989. "Organizations, Power, Sexuality: The Image and Self-Image of Women Managers." In J. Hearn, D. L. Sheppard, P. Tancred-Sheriff, and G. Burrell (eds.), *The Sexuality of Organization*. London: Sage.

Sheskin, R., and A. Barak. 1997. "Sexual Harassment Proclivities and Vocational Preferences." Paper presented at the annual conference of the Canadian Psychological Association, June, Toronto.

Silverman, D. 1976–77. "Sexual Harassment: Working Women's Dilemma." *Quest: A Feminist Quarterly* 3:15–24.

Simons, Marlise. 1996. "For the First Time, Court Defines Rape as War Crime." *New York Times*, June 28, pp. A1, A6.

Small, Fred. 1985. "Pornography and Censorship." In Michael S. Kimmel (ed.), *Men Confront Pornography*. New York: Crown.

Smith, Michael D., and Norman N. Morra. 1994. "Obscene and Threatening Telephone Calls to Women: Data from a Canadian National Survey." *Gender & Society* 8(4):584–96.

Soble, A. 1986. *Pornography: Marxism, Feminism, and the Future of Sexuality*. New Haven, CT: Yale University Press.

Sokoloff, Natalie J., with Christine Pratt (eds.). 2005. *Domestic Violence at the Margins: Readings on Race, Class, Gender and Culture*. New Brunswick, NJ: Rutgers University Press.

Soriano, C. G. 1994. "Hooters Girls Get Attention. *Washington Times*, April 16, p. B1.

Spears, R., T. Postmes, M. Lea, and A. Wolbert. 2002. "When Are Net Effects Gross Products? The Power of Influence and Influence of Power in Computer-Mediated Communication." *Journal of Social Issues* 58:91–107.

Spelman, Elizabeth V. 1982. "Theories of Race and Gender: The Erasure of Black Women." *Quest* 5(4):36–62.

Spencer, B., and F. J. Gillen. 1927. *The Arunta*. 2 vols. London: Macmillan.

Spitzberg, B. H., and G. Hoobler. 2002. "Cyberstalking and the Technologies of Interpersonal Terrorism." *New Media and Society* 4:71–92.

Staba, David. 2003. "High School Player Is Charged in Sexual Abuse." *New York Times*, October 14, p. B9.

Stanko, Elizabeth A. 1985. *Intimate Intrusions: Women's Experiences of Male Violence*. London: Routledge and Kegan Paul.

Stanko, Elizabeth A. 2000. "Unmasking What Should Be Seen: A Study of the Prevention of Domestic Violence in the London Borough of Hackney." In E. Erez and K. Laster (eds.), *Domestic Violence: Global Responses*. Bicester, UK: A B Academic.

Stark, Evan, and Anne Flitcraft. 1988. "Women and Children at Risk: A Feminist Perspective on Child Abuse." *International Journal of Health Services* 18(1):97–118.

Stearns, Carol, and Peter Stearns. 1986. *Anger: The Struggle for Emotional Control in America's History*. Chicago: University of Chicago Press.

Stearns, P. 1986. "Old Age Family Conflict: The Perspective of the Past." In K. A. Pillemer and R. S. Wolf (eds.), *Elder Abuse: Conflict in the Family*. Dover, MA: Auburn House.

Stein, M. B., and E. Barrett-Connor. 2000. "Sexual Assault and Physical Health: Findings from a Population-Based Study of Older Adults." *Psychosomatic Medicine* 63:838–43.

Stein, Nan. 1981. *Sexual Harassment of High School Students: Preliminary Research Results*. Unpublished manuscript. Boston: Massachusetts Department of Education.

———. 1992. *Secrets in Public: Sexual Harassment in Public (and Private) Schools*. Working paper no. 256. Wellesley, MA: Wellesley College Center for Research on Women.

———. 1995. "Sexual Harassment in K–12 Schools: The Public Performance of Gendered Violence." *Harvard Educational Review, Special Issue: Violence and Youth* 65(2):145—62.

———. 1999. *Classrooms and Courtrooms: Facing Sexual Harassment in K–12 Schools*. New York: Teacher's College Press.

———. 2003. "Bullying or Harassment? The Missing Discourse of Rights in an Era of Zero Tolerance." *Arizona Law Review* 45(3):783—99.

———. 2005a. "Bullying and Harassment in a Post-Columbine World." In Kathy Kendall-Tackett and Sarah Giacomoni (eds.), *Child Victimization*. Kingston, NJ: Civic Research Institute.

———. 2005b. "A Rising Pandemic of Sexual Violence in Elementary and Secondary Schools: Locating a Secret Problem." *Duke Journal of Gender Law and Policy* 12 (spring): 33—52.

Stein, Nan, Nancy Marshall, and Linda Tropp. 1993. "Secrets in Public: Sexual Harassment in Our Schools; A Report on the Results of a *Seventeen* Magazine Survey." Unpublished manuscript. Wellesley, MA: Wellesley College Center for Research on Women.

Stein, Nan, Deborah Tolman, Michele Porche, and Renee Spencer. 2002. "Gender Safety: A New Concept for Safer and More Equitable Schools." *Journal of School Safety* 1(2):35—50.

Steinglass, Matt. 2005. "The Question of Rescue." *New York Times*, July 24, sec. 6, p. 8.

Steinmetz, F. K. 1988. *Duty Bound: Elder Abuse and Family Care*. Beverly Hills, CA: Sage.

Steinmetz, Suzanne K. 1977–78. "The Battered Husband Syndrome." *Victimology* 2(3-sup-4):499–509.

Stephenson, W. 1953. *The Study of Behavior: Q-Technique and Its Methodology*. Chicago: University of Chicago Press.

Stetson, Dorothy McBride. 2004. "The Invisible Issue: Prostitution and Trafficking of Women and Girls in the United States." In Joyce Outshoorn (ed.), *The Politics of Prostitution: Women's Movements, Democratic States and the Globalisation of Sex Commerce*. Cambridge: Cambridge University Press.

Stetz, Margaret D. 2001. "Wartime Sexual Violence against Women: A Feminist Response." In Margaret Stetz and Bonnie B. C. Oh (eds.), *Legacies of the Comfort Women of World War II*. Armonk, NY: M. E. Sharpe.

———. 2002. "Representing 'Comfort Women': Activism through Law and Art." *Iris* 45:26–29, 83–84.

Stiehm, J. H. 1989. *Arms and the Enlisted Woman*. Philadelphia: Temple University Press.

Stoller, R. J. 1979. *Sexual Excitement*. New York: Pantheon Books.

Stoltenberg, John. 1989. "Pornography and Freedom." In Michael S. Kimmel and Michael A. Messner (eds.), *Men's Lives*. New York: Macmillan.

Stout, D. B. 1947. *San Blas Cura Acculturation*. New York: Viking Fund Publications in Anthropology.

Straus, Murray A. 1991. "Children as Witnesses to Marital Violence: A Risk Factor for Lifelong Problems among Nationally Representative Sample of American Men and Women." Paper presented at the Ross Roundtable on Children and Violence, Washington, DC.

———. 1994. *Beating the Devil Out of Them: Corporal Punishment in American Families*. Lexington, MA: Lexington Books.

———. 1999. "The Controversy over Domestic Violence by Women: A Methodological, Theoretical, and Sociology of Science Analysis." In X. B. Arriaga and S. Oskamp (eds.), *Violence in Intimate Relationships*. Thousand Oaks, CA: Sage.

Straus, Murray A., and Richard J. Gelles. 1992. *Physical Violence in American Families*. New Brunswick, NJ: Transaction.

Strauss, Susan. 1988. "Sexual Harassment in the School: Legal Implications for Principals." *Bulletin* 72(506):93—97. Reston, VA: National Association of Secondary School Principals.

Stubbs, Julie. 2002. "Domestic Violence and Women's Safety: Feminist Challenges to Restorative Justice." In Heather Strang and John Braithwaite (eds.), *Restorative Justice and Family Violence*. Cambridge: Cambridge University Press.

Sugarman, David B., and Susan L. Frankel. 1996. "Patriarchal Ideology and Wife-Assault: A Meta-Analytic Review." *Journal of Family Violence* 11(1):13–40.

Suler, J. R. 1999. "To Get What You Need: Healthy and Pathological Internet Use." *CyberPsychology and Behavior* 2:385–93.

———. 2004. "The Online Disinhibition Effect." *CyberPsychology and Behavior* 7:321–26.

Suler, J. R., and W. L. Phillips. 2000. "The Bad Boys of Cyberspace: Deviant Behavior in a Multimedia Chat Community." *CyberPsychology and Behavior* 1:275–94.

Sumrall, Amber Coverdale, and Dena Taylor. 1992. *Sexual Harassment: Women Speak Out*. Freedom, CA: Crossing Press.

Surtees, Rebecca. 2003. "Brothel Raids in Indonesia: Ideal Solution or Further Violation?" *Research for Sex Work* 6:3–4.

Sussman, N. M., and D. H. Tyson. 2000. "Sex and Power: Gender Differences in Computer-Mediated Interactions." *Computers in Human Behavior* 16:381–94.

Swan, Suzanne C., and David L. Snow. 2002. "A Typology of Women's Use of Violence in Intimate Relationships." *Violence against Women* 8(3):286–319.

Tambiah, Yasmin. 2005. "Turncoat Bodies: Sexuality and Sex Work under Militarization in Sri Lanka." *Gender & Society* 19(2):243–61.

Tamminen, J. M. 1994. *Sexual Harassment in the Workplace: Managing Corporate Policy*. New York: Wiley.

Tancred-Sheriff, Peta. 1989. "Gender, Sexuality and the Labour Process." In J. Hearn, D. L. Sheppard, P. Tancred-Sheriff, and G. Burrell (eds.), *The Sexuality of Organization*. London: Sage.

Tangri, S., M. Burt, and L. Johnson. 1982. "Sexual Harassment at Work: Three Explanatory Models." *Journal of Social Issues* 38:33–54.

Tavani, H. T., and F. S. Grodzinsky. 2002. "Cyberstalking, Personal Privacy, and Moral Responsibility." *Ethics and Information Technology* 4:123–32.

Taylor, N. (ed). 1986. *All in a Day's Work: A Report on Anti-Lesbian Discrimination in Employment and Unemployment in London*. London: Lesbian Employment Rights.

Taylor, R., and G. Ford. 1983. "Inequalities in Old Age." *Aging and Society* 3:183–208.

Teicher, J. 1999. "An Action Plan for Smart Internet Use." *Educational Leadership* 56:70–74.

Temkin, Jennifer. 1986. "Women, Rape and Law Reform." In Sylvana Tomaselli and Roy Porter (eds.), *Rape*. Oxford, UK: Blackwell.

Tep, Mony, and Salan Ek. 2000. "Crossing Borders, Crossing Realities: Vietnamese Sex Workers in Cambodia." CARAM (Coordination of Action Research on AIDS and Mobility) Cambodia.

Tep, Mony, Salan Ek, and Marjolein Maas. 2001. "Different Mindsets, Different Risks: Looking at Risk Factors Identified by Vietnamese Sex Workers in Cambodia." *Research for Sex Work* 4:4–6.

Terpstra, D. E., and D. D. Baker. 1988. "Outcomes of Sexual Harassment Charges." *Academy of Management Journal* 31:185–94.

———. 1989. "The Identification and Classification of Reactions to Sexual Harassment." *Journal of Organizational Behavior* 10:1–14.

———. 1992. "Outcomes of Federal Court Decisions on Sexual Harassment." *Academy of Management Journal* 35:181–90.

Thomas, D. A. 1989. "Mentoring and Irrationality: The Role of Racial Taboos." *Human Resource Management* 28(2):279–90.

Thomas, Dorothy. 1994. "In Search of Solutions: Women's Police Stations in Brazil." In M. Davies (ed.), *Women and Violence*. London: Zed Books.

Thomas, K. 1978. *Religion and the Decline of Magic*. Harmondsworth, UK: Penguin.

Thompson, F. 1973. "Testimony: The Memphis Riot 1865." In Gerda Lerner (ed.), *Black Women in White America*. New York: Vintage.

Thorne, Barrie. 1993. *Gender Play: Girls and Boys at School*. New Brunswick, NJ: Rutgers University Press.

Tiger, L. 1969. *Men in Groups*. New York: Random House.

Till, Frank J. 1980. *Sexual Harassment: A Report on the Sexual Harassment of Students*. Washington, DC: National Advisory Council on Women's Educational Programs.

Timmerman, G. 2003. "Sexual Harassment of Adolescents Perpetrated by Teachers and by Peers: An Exploration of the Dynamics of Power, Culture, and Gender in Secondary Schools." *Sex Roles* 48:231–44.

Tinsley, H. E. A., and M. S. Stockdale. 1993. "Sexual Harassment in the Workplace." *Journal of Vocational Behavior* 42:1–4.

Tirrell, Lynne. 1999. "Derogatory Terms: Racism, Sexism, and the Inferential Role Theory of Meaning." In Christina Hendricks and Kelly Oliver (eds.), *Language and Liberation: Feminism, Philosophy, and Language*. Albany: State University of New York Press.

Tjaden, Patricia, and Nancy Thoennes. 2000. "Prevalence and Consequences of Male-to-Female and Female-to-Male Intimate Partner Violence as Measured by the National Violence Against Women Survey. *Violence against Women* 6(2):142–61.

———. 2006. "Extent, Nature, and Consequences of Rape Victimization: Findings from the National Violence Against Women Survey." Washington, DC: U.S. Government Printing Office.

Tolman, R. M., and J. Raphael. 2000. "A Review of Research on Welfare and Domestic Violence." *Journal of Social Issues* 5:655–82.

Tomes, Nancy. 1978. "A 'Torrent of Abuse': Crimes of Violence between Working-Class Men and Women in London, 1840–1875." *Journal of Social History* 11:328–45.

Tomlin, S. 1989. *Abuse of Elderly People: An Unnecessary and Preventable Problem*. London: British Geriatrics Society.

Tong, R. 1984. *Women, Sex, and the Law*. Totowa, NJ: Rowman and Allanheld.

Trafficking in Persons Report. 2004. U.S. State Department, Washington, DC. Available online at http://www.state.gov/g/tip/rls/tiprpt/2004/ (accessed September 23, 2004).

Trafficking Victims Protection Act. 2001. "Implementation of the Trafficking Victims Protection

Act." Hearing before the Committee on International Relations, House of Representatives, 107th Congress, 1st session, November 29. Serial No. 107-63.

Tran Thi Van Anh. 1999. "Women and Rural Land in Vietnam." In Irene Tinker and Gale Summerfield (eds.), *Women's Rights to House and Land in China, Laos, and Vietnam*. Boulder: Lynne Rienner.

Traynor, J., and J. Hasnip. 1984. "Sometimes She Makes Me Want to Hit Her." *Community Care* (August): 22–24.

Truesdell, D. J., J. S. McNeil, and J. P. Deschner. 1986. "Incidence of Wife Abuse in Incestuous Families." *Social Work* (March–April): 138–40.

Tuan, Yi-Fu. 1984. *Dominance and Affection: The Making of Pets*. New Haven, CT: Yale University Press.

Turnbull, C. 1965. *Wayward Servants*. New York: Natural History Press.

Turrell, S. C. 2000. "A Descriptive Analysis of Same-Sex Relationship Violence for a Diverse Sample." *Journal of Family Violence* 15:281–93.

Tyson, Ann Scott. 2005. "Reported Cases of Sexual Assault in Military Increase." *Washington Post*, May 7, p. A3.

UCLA Center for Communication Policy. 2003. *The UCLA Internet Report: Surveying the Digital Future—Year Three*. Available online at http://ccp.ucla.edu/pdf/UCLA-Internet-Report-Year-Three.pdf (accessed September 15, 2004).

Umbreit, M. S. 2000. "The Restorative Justice and Mediation Collection: Executive Summary." Office for Victims of Crime Bulletin. Washington, DC: U.S. Department of Labor.

UN General Assembly. 2003. "Protocol to Prevent, Suppress and Punish Trafficking in Persons, Especially Women and Children." Annex 2, UN Convention against Transnational Organized Crime, Geneva.

UNIFEM. 2004. "In Africa, Rape Emerges as a Form of Genocide." Gender and HIV/AIDS Web site, August 13. http://www.genderandaids.org/modules.php?name=News&file=article&sid=412 (accessed January 31, 2006).

United Nations. 2000. *Convention against Transnational Organized Crime, Supplemental Protocol to Prevent, Suppress and Punish Trafficking in Persons, Especially Women and Children*. Available online at http://www.unodc.org/unodc/trafficking_convention.html.

United Nations Division for the Advancement of Women. 2005. "Good Practices in Combating and Eliminating Violence against Women." Available online at http://www.un.org/womenwatch/daw/egm/vaw-gp2005/docs/FINALREPORT.goodpractices.pdf.

United States Department of Justice. 1991. *Crime in the United States: Uniform Crime Reports, 1990*. Washington, DC: U.S. Government Printing Office.

———. 1992. *Criminal Victimization in the United States, 1990*. Washington, DC: U.S. Government Printing Office.

U.S. Conference of Mayors. 2003. "A Status Report on Hunger and Homelessness in America's Cities: A 25-City Survey." December.

U.S. Department of Health, Education and Welfare. 1975. "Title IX of Education Amendment of 1972," 20 U.S.C. sec. 1681 (P.L. 92-318). *Federal Register* 40, no. 108 (June 4, 1975): 24, 128.

U.S. Department of Health and Human Services, Administration on Children, Youth, and Families. 1988. *Study Findings: Study of National Incidence and Prevalence of Child Abuse and Neglect*. DHSS publication no. ADM 20-01099. Washington, DC: U.S. Government Printing Office.

———. 1996. *Child Maltreatment 1994: Reports from the States to the National Child Abuse and Neglect Data System*. Washington, DC: U.S. Government Printing Office.

U.S. Department of Health and Human Services, Administration on Children, Youth, and Families.. 2003. *Child Maltreatment 2001*. Washington, DC: U.S. Government Printing Office.

U.S. House of Representatives. 1980. *Hearings on Sexual Harassment in the Federal Government*.

Committee on the Post Office and Civil Service, Subcommittee on Investigations. Washington, DC: U.S. Government Printing Office.

U.S. Merit Systems Protection Board. 1981. *Sexual Harassment in the Federal Workplace: Is It a Problem?* Washington, DC: U.S. Government Printing Office.

———. 1987. *Sexual Harassment in the Federal Workplace: An Update.* Washington, DC: U.S. Government Printing Office.

U.S. Senate Committee on the Judiciary, Hearings on Women and Violence. 1990. "Ten Facts about Violence Against Women."

van Roosmalen, E., and S. A. McDaniel. 1998. "Sexual Harassment in Academia: A Hazard to Women's Health." *Women and Health,* 28(2): 33–54.

Vaught, C., and D. Smith. 1980. "Incorporation and Mechanical Solidarity in an Underground Coal Mine." *Sociology of Work and Occupations* 7:159–87.

Vaux, A. 1993. "Paradigmatic Assumptions in Sexual Harassment Research: Being Guided without Being Misled." *Journal of Vocational Behavior* 42:116–35.

Vázquez, Carmen. 1992. "Appearances." In W. J. Blumenthal (ed.), *Homophobia: How We All Pay the Price.* Boston: Beacon.

Victor, C. 1991. *Health and Health Care Later in Life.* Milton Keynes, UK: Open University Press.

Vinovskis, Maris A. 2001. "Historical Perspectives on Parent-Child Interactions." In Susan J. Ferguson (ed.), *Shifting the Center: Understanding Contemporary Families.* New York: McGraw-Hill.

Vossekuil, Bryan, Robert Fein, Marisa Reddy, Randy Borum, and William Modzeleski. 2002. *Final Report and Findings of the Safe School Initiative: Implications for the Prevention of School Attacks in the United States.* U.S. Department of Education, Office of Elementary and Secondary Education, Safe and Drug-Free Schools Program, and U.S. Secret Service, National Threat Assessment Center, Washington, DC.

Vu Tuan Anh, Tran Thi Van Anh, and Terry G. McGee. 2000. "Household Economy under Impacts of Economic Reforms in Viet Nam." In Peter Boothroyd and Pham Xuan Nam (eds.), *Socioeconomic Renovation in Viet Nam: The Origin, Evolution, and Impact of Doi Moi.* Ottawa: International Development Research Centre; Singapore: Institute of Southeast Asian Studies.

Walby, S. 1990. "From Private to Public Patriarchy: The Periodisation of British History." *Women's Studies International Forum* 13(1–2):91–104.

Walker, A. 1990. "Poverty and Inequality in Old Age." In J. Bond and P. Coleman (eds.), *Ageing and Society.* London: Sage.

Walker, Alice. 1981. "Coming Apart." In *You Can't Keep a Good Woman Down.* New York: Harcourt Brace Jovanovich.

———. 1982. *The Color Purple.* New York: Harcourt Brace Jovanovich.

———. 1989. "Trying to See My Sister." In *Living by the Word.* New York: Harcourt Brace Jovanovich.

Walker, Lenore E. 1989. *Terrifying Love.* New York: Harper and Row.

Walker, Margaret. 1967. *Jubilee.* New York: Bantam.

Walsh, Mark. 2003. "Administrators Not Immune in Suit over Alleged Taunts." *Education Week* 22(31):4.

Warshaw, Robin. 1988. *I Never Called It Rape: The Ms. Report on Recognizing, Fighting, and Surviving Date and Acquaintance Rape.* New York: Harper and Row.

Wasoff, F. 1982. "Legal Protection from Wifebeating: The Processing of Domestic Assaults by Scottish Prosecutors and Criminal Courts." *International Journal of the Sociology of Law* 10:187–204.

Wayne, J. H. 2000. "Disentangling the Power Bases of Sexual Harassment: Comparing Gender, Age, and Position Power." *Journal of Vocational Behavior* 57:301–25.

Weeks, Jeffrey. 1989. *Sex, Politics and Society.* 2nd ed. London: Longman.

Weis, Kurt, and Sandra S. Borges. 1973. "Victimology and Rape: The Case of the Legitimate Victim." *Issues in Criminology* 8:71–115.

Weis, Lois. 2001. "Race, Gender, and Critique: African-American Women, White Women, and Domestic Violence in the 1980s and 1990s." *Signs* 27(1):139–69.

Welsh, Sandy. 1999. "Gender and Sexual Harassment." *Annual Review of Sociology* 25:169–90.

West, Candace, and Sarah Fenstermaker. 1995. "Doing Difference." *Gender & Society* 9:8–37.

West, Candace, and Don H. Zimmerman. 1991. "Doing Gender." In Judith Lorber and Susan A. Farrell (eds.), *The Social Construction of Gender.* Newbury Park, CA: Sage.

West, Carolyn M. 2005. "Domestic Violence in Ethnically and Racially Diverse Families: The 'Political Gag Order' Has Been Lifted." In N. J. Sokoloff (ed.), *Domestic Violence at the Margins.* New Brunswick, NJ: Rutgers University Press.

West, Carolyn M., and S. Rose. 2000. "Dating Aggression among Low-Income African American Youth: An Examination of Gender Differences and Antagonistic Beliefs." *Violence against Women* 6(5):470–94.

West, D. 1982. *The Living Is Easy.* New York: Feminist Press.

Whaley, Rachel B. 2001. "The Paradoxical Relationship between Gender Inequality and Rape: Toward a Refined Theory." *Gender & Society* 15(4):531–55.

Whitlock, Kay. 2005. "Corrupting Justice: A Primer for LGBT Communities on Racism, Violence, Human Degradation and the Prison Industrial Complex." Philadelphia: American Friends Service Committee.

"Who Needs Charity." 2003. News24.com Web site, July 28. http://www.news24.com/ News24/Entertainment/Off_Beat/0,,2-1225-2107_1394032.htm (accessed July 28, 2003).

Wiehe, V. R. 1997. *Sibling Abuse: Hidden Physical, Emotional, and Sexual Trauma.* 2nd ed. Thousand Oaks, CA: Sage.

Williams, J. H., L. F. Fitzgerald, and F. Drasgow. 1999. "The Effects of Organizational Practices on Sexual Harassment and Individual Outcomes in the Military." *Military Psychology* 11:303–28.

Williams, Joyce E. 1984. "Secondary Victimization: Confronting Public Attitudes about Rape." *Victimology: An International Journal* 9:66–81.

Williams, K. B., and R. R. Cyr. 1992. "Escalating Commitment to a Relationship: The Sexual Harassment Trap." *Sex Roles* 27:47–72.

Winston, J. 1991. "Mirror, Mirror on the Wall: Title VII, Section 1981, and the Intersection of Race and Gender in the Civil Rights Act of 1990." *California Law Review* 79:775–805.

Wise, S., and S. Stanley. 1987. *Georgie Porgie: Sexual Harassment in Everyday Life.* London: Pandora.

Wohl, A. S. 1978. "Sex and the Single Room: Incest among the Victorian Working Classes." In A. S. Wohl (ed.), *The Victorian Family.* London: Croom Helm.

Wolf, R., and S. Bergman (eds.). 1989. *Stress, Conflict, and the Abuse of the Elderly.* Jerusalem: Brookdale Institute.

Wolf, S. C., J. R. Conte, and M. Engel-Meinig. 1988. "Assessment and Treatment of Sex Offenders in a Community Setting." In L. Walker (ed.), *Handbook on Sexual Abuse of Children.* New York: Springer.

Wolfgang, M. E., and F. Ferracuti. 1967. *The Subculture of Violence: Towards an Integrated Theory of Criminology.* London: Tavistock.

Wolshok, M. 1981. *Blue-Collar Women: Pioneers on the Male Frontier.* Garden City, NJ: Anchor Books.

Women's Legal Defense Fund. 1991. *Sexual Harassment in the Workplace.* Washington, DC: Women's Legal Defense Fund.

Wonderlich, S. A., R. D. Crosby, J. E. Mitchell, K. M. Thompson, J. Redlin, G. Demuth, et al. 2001.

"Eating Disturbance and Sexual Trauma in Childhood and Adulthood.: *International Journal of Eating Disorders* 30:401–12.

Wood, Stephanie K. 2004. "A Woman Scorned for the 'Least Condemned' War Crime: Precedent and Problems with Prosecuting Rape as a Serious War Crime in the International Criminal Tribunal for Rwanda." *Columbia Journal of Gender and Law* 13(2):274–327.

Woods, J. D., and J. H. Lucas. 1993. *The Corporate Closet: The Professional Lives of Gay Men in America*. New York: Free Press.

Worcester, N. 2002. "Women's Use of Force: Complexities and Challenges of Taking the Issue Seriously." *Violence against Women* 8(11):1390–1415.

Working Women's Institute. 1979. *The Impact of Sexual Harassment on the Job: A Profile of the Experiences of 92 Women*. New York: Working Women's Institute Research Series, Report no. 2.

Yardley, Jim. 2001. "A Portrait of the Terrorist." *New York Times*, October 10, p. B9.

————. 2005. "Fearing Future, China Starts to Give Girls Their Due." *New York Times*, January 31, p. B1.

Yllö, K., and M. Bograd (eds.). 1988. *Feminist Perspectives on Wife Abuse*. Newbury Park, CA: Sage.

Yoder, Janice D. 1991. "Rethinking Tokenism: Looking beyond Numbers." *Gender & Society* 5:178–92.

Yoder, Janice D., and Patricia Aniakudo. 1997. "Outside within the Firehouse: Subordination and Difference in the Social Interactions of African American Women Firefighters." *Gender & Society* 11(3):324–41.

Zalk, S. R. 1990. "Men in the Academy: A Psychological Profile of Harassment." In Michele A. Paludi (ed.), *Ivory Power: Sexual Harassment on Campus*. Albany: State University of New York Press.

Zeiger, R. 1995. "Sex, Sales, and Stereotypes." *Sales and Marketing Management* (July): 46–56.

Zimring, Franklin. 1989. "Toward a Jurisprudence of Family Violence." In Lloyd Ohlin and Michael Tonry (eds.), *Family Violence*. Chicago: University of Chicago Press.

Zinn, M. B., and B. T. Dill. 1996. "Theorizing Difference from Multiracial Feminism." *Feminist Studies* (22)2:321–31.

Zippel, Katherine S. 2006. *The Politics of Sexual Harassment: A Comparative Study of the United States, the European Union, and Germany*. Cambridge: Cambridge University Press.

Zorza, Joan. 1991. "Women Battering: A Major Cause of Homelessness." *Clearinghouse Review* 24(4) (Special Issue): 421–29.

Zurbriggen, E. L. 2000. "Social Motives and Cognitive Power-Sex Associations: Predictors of Aggressive Sexual Behavior. *Journal of Personality and Social Psychology* 78:559–81.

CASES

Carroll v. Village of Shelton, Nebraska, 4:CV95-3363 (1996).

Castle Rock v. Gonzales, N.04-278 U.S. (2005).

Chaplinsky v. New Hampshire, 315 U.S. 568 (1942).

Chatman v. Gentle Dental Center of Waltham, 95-12710-RCL (1997).

Davis v. Monroe County Board of Education, 526 U.S. 629 (1999).

Hernandez v. Patrick Wangen et al., Civil No. 95-1611 (1996).

HUD v. Rucker, 535 U.S. 125 (2002).

Katz v. St. John the Baptist Parish School Board, 860 /So, 2d 98 (La. App. 5 Cir. 2003).

Meritor Savings Bank v. Vinson, 477 U.S. 57 (1986).

Oncale v. Sundowner Offshore Services, Inc., 523 U.S. 75; 118 S. Ct. (1998).

Wanchik v. Great Lakes Health Plan Inc., 248 F.3d 1154 (2001).

Index